D1565202

Poetics
of the Holy

Poetics of the Holy

A Reading of *Paradise Lost*

by Michael Lieb

The University of North Carolina Press *Chapel Hill*

Both the initial
research and the publication
of this work were made possible in part
through grants from the National Endowment for
the Humanities, a federal agency whose mission is to
award grants to support education, scholarship, media
programming, libraries, and museums, in order to
bring the results of cultural activities to
a broad, general public.

Library of Congress Cataloging in Publication Data

Lieb, Michael, 1940–
Poetics of the holy.

Bibliography: p.
Includes index.
1. Milton, John, 1608–1674. Paradise lost.
2. Religion and poetry. I. Title.
PR3562.L52   821'.4   80-29159
ISBN 0-8078-1479-2

for Larry and Mark
Here behold so goodly grown
Two fair branches of my own.

Contents

Illustrations ix

Acknowledgments xi

Author's Note on the Citation of Sources xv

Introduction xvii

PART 1: The Holy

1. Preliminary Contexts 3

2. Renaissance and Miltonic Contexts 23

PART 2: "The Sacred Vein"

3. Sacral Poetics 43

4. Sacral Contexts 64

PART 3: *Res Sacrae*

5. Fruit 89

6. Place 119

7. Mount 140

8. Name 171

9. Light 185

10. Presence 212

11. War 246

12. Rest 313

Afterword 328
Notes 331
Bibliography 389
Index 425

Illustrations

1. Blake's Conception of Milton 44

2. Aaron, the High Priest 55

3. The Hieroglyphical Figure 82

4. The Temple Enclosure 123

5. The Tabernacle 124

6. Sinai Theophany 148

7. Horeb Theophany 150

8. Vision of the New Jerusalem 168

9. Luminous Theophany 211

10. "Let There Be Light" 225

11. "A Firmament in the Midst of the Waters" 226

12. Ark of the Covenant 227

13. Isaiah's Vision of God 229

14. Ezekiel's Vision of God 231

15. "The Likeness of Four Living Creatures" 232

16. Saint John the Divine's Vision of God 235

17. The Son of Man 238

18. The Laver 239

19. Marching Order of the Israelite Camps 284

20. The Israelite Encampment 288

21. Ezekiel's Vision of the Chariot 293

22. Wilderness Encampment 294

23. A Prospect of the Holy of Holies 315

Acknowledgments

A work that is over ten years in the making is bound to incur some debts. The guiding spirit of this book and, in fact, of all my work on Milton is my teacher John T. Shawcross, who first introduced me to the manifold complexities of the "higher Argument." In my attempt to illuminate that argument, I trust that I have justified his confidence in me. Of comparable importance to the shaping of my outlook is Albert Labriola, *animae dimidium meae*. His influence upon this work as a whole is to be felt everywhere. My book is a tribute both to his support and to his abiding faith. I also wish to express my personal gratitude for all the time and attention that Joseph A. Wittreich, Jr., devoted to my manuscript. His judicious eye compelled me to sharpen my own insights and to attend more closely to the minute particulars of my vision.

During the years that it was in the making, this work has also benefited from the counsel, scrutiny, and encouragement of a number of colleagues, whom I am honored to acknowledge here. William B. Hunter, Jr., Roland M. Frye, C. A. Patrides, John M. Steadman, Jason Rosenblatt, and Robert Fallon are scholars to whom my undertaking is especially indebted. They have nurtured its growth over the years and, in varying degrees, are responsible for whatever strengths it may claim as its own. Along with these colleagues, I would also like to thank Michael Masi, Jeffrey Kondritzer, Theodore Tracy, and Donald Register for their assistance. I am likewise grateful to those students with whom I have had the privilege of discussing many of the points analyzed here. A personal note of thanks goes to my undergraduate assistant, Betty Barkas, and my graduate research assistant, Jack L. Ritter, Jr., for all the time that they devoted to bibliographical matters. Finally, I wish to express my gratitude to Sandra Eisdorfer and David Perry of the University of North Carolina Press. Along with all those who helped me to see the book through the press, they were patient and encouraging from the very beginning.

Portions of the study have been presented to several groups and organizations. "'Holy Place': A Reading of *Paradise Lost*" was delivered as a paper on two occasions, once at the English Club of the College of William and Mary and later at the Tercentenary Celebration of Milton at Marquette University. *"Paradise Lost* and the Myth of Prohibition" (an earlier version of chapter 5) was presented to the English Symposium of the University of Illinois at Chicago Circle, and versions of " 'Holy War': A Reading of *Paradise Lost*" were delivered before the Renaissance Seminar of the University of Chicago and the Modern Language Association meeting in New York. Suggestions and comments from each of the groups and organizations addressed helped me to refine my perceptions.

I also owe debts to several institutions that have aided me in my study. I wish to acknowledge first the Research Board of the University of Illinois at Chicago Circle for the continuing support that has facilitated the research and writing of my book during the past decade. In addition to the aid offered by my university, financial assistance has come from other sources as well. A long-term fellowship from the National Endowment for the Humanities enabled me to spend a year in residence at the University of Chicago Divinity School. There, I benefited from the seminars, colloquia, and conversations that I had with Mircea Eliade, the late Norman Perrin, Nathan A. Scott, Jr., Joseph Kitagawa, Jonathan Z. Smith, and especially my good friend and colleague Anthony C. Yu. This book is very much a product of the intellectual climate that prevails at the divinity school. External financial support has also come from the Folger Shakespeare Library and the Henry E. Huntington Library. To the directors, librarians, and staff of those remarkable institutions, I extend my heartfelt thanks. I should like as well to express my gratitude for the many courtesies bestowed upon me by the staffs of the University of Illinois Library, the Regenstein Library of the University of Chicago, the Spertus College of Judaica Library, the McCormick Theological Seminary Library, and, most importantly, the Newberry Library.

Portions of this book represent substantial revisions of previously published work. Chapter 5 ("Fruit") draws upon an earlier essay, *"Paradise Lost* and the Myth of Prohibition," in *"Eyes Fast Fixt": Current Perspectives in Milton Methodology*, edited by Albert Labriola and Michael Lieb, *Milton Studies* series, vol. 7 (Pittsburgh: University of Pittsburgh Press, 1975). Chapter 6 ("Place") is a much-revised version of " 'Holy Place': A Reading of *Paradise Lost*," *Studies in English Literature* 17 (1977): 129–47 (copyright 1977 by the William Marsh Rice University). Chapter 8 ("Name") is a revision of " 'Holy Name': A Reading of *Paradise Lost*," *Harvard Theological Review* 67 (1974): 321–39 (copyright 1974 by the President and Fellows of Harvard College). Finally, chapter 12 ("Rest") draws upon an earlier essay, " 'Holy Rest': A Reading of

Paradise Lost," *Journal of English Literary History* 30 (1972): 238–53 (copyright 1972 by The Johns Hopkins University Press). Permission to use the foregoing material in its revised form as part of the present study is gratefully acknowledged.

For my family, I have reserved this concluding expression of gratitude and affection. I am grateful, as always, to my parents for their support and devotion. (A special note of thanks goes to my father for making an unexpected trip to the Huntington Library on my behalf.) To her who is my "individual solace dear," my wife Roslyn, I extend my love and thanks, the full expression of which would finally be unbefitting the decorum of this occasion. Finally, to my sons, Mark and Larry, I dedicate this book itself. Their stake in the whole affair is best summed up in an *Ad Patrem* that my son Mark addressed to me when he was eight years old: "There is a Father in a place writing till his work is done, writing, writing day and night. A hundred pages is his goal and then another hundred and comes spring the work is done. Now he has a goal to face. His favorite one is here, which is being with his family." I take this occasion to respond formally to both my sons: "The work is indeed done."

Michael Lieb
University of Illinois
Chicago, Illinois
June 27, 1980

Author's Note
on the Citation of Sources

All citations from Milton's poetry given parenthetically within the text
are from *The Complete Poetry of John Milton*, ed. John T. Shawcross,
2nd ed. rev. (Garden City, N.Y.: Doubleday, 1971). All citations from
Milton's prose given parenthetically within the text are from *The Works
of John Milton*, ed. Frank Allen Patterson, 18 vols. in 21 (New York:
Columbia University Press, 1931–38), hereafter referred to as *CM*. Ab-
breviations of Milton's poetry and prose are keyed to the table of ab-
breviations in the index volumes of the *CM*. Unless otherwise noted,
quotations from the Bible are from the King James Version. Hebrew and
Greek interpolations are from the Biblia Hebraica Stuttgartensia and the
Novum Testamentum Graece, respectively. References to the Hastings
Encyclopaedia of Religion and Ethics in the notes are abbreviated as
ERE. Additional information concerning the foregoing works is provided
in the bibliography.

Introduction

In his recent discussion of "the religious use and abuse of literature," Giles Gunn states that although the so-called field of religion and literature includes a number of scholars who have quite consciously associated themselves with that field, it also encompasses an even greater number of scholars who have professed no overt allegiances to the field at all.[1] By virtue of my announced concern with the holy, I suppose that I should be numbered among the former. Although my allegiances extend well beyond the confines of a particular field, that of religion and literature is certainly one to which I feel this study belongs. It is, in fact, a study that might well be placed among a growing number of books focusing upon the holy as a distinct and classifiable experience of profound importance to particular works of literature. I have in mind such books as August E. Hohler's *Das Heilige in der Dichtung* (1954), Vincent Buckley's *Poetry and the Sacred* (1968), Nathan A. Scott, Jr.'s *The Wild Prayer of Longing* (1971), René Girard's *La Violence et le sacré* (1972), and Eugene Webb's *The Dark Dove* (1975).[2] Extending backward to the origins of Greek tragedy and forward to modern American poets, these books concern themselves with a full range of writers and cultures. Doing so, they suggest the historical and literary continuity of the holy through writers as diverse as Sophocles, Sir Thomas Wyatt, Klopstock, and Theodore Roethke.

This is just as it should be: the kind of ecumenicalism that permeates these studies and that might be considered the hallmark of the writings of Rudolf Otto and Mircea Eliade, to whom the holy as an experience owes its formulation,[3] suggests the need to transcend partisan concerns and dispense with parochialism in the face of larger, more fundamental considerations. I am not, however, suggesting a frame of reference that divorces itself from the historical forces that shape a poet's thinking and make his vision distinctly his own. This study, in fact, is deeply rooted in the historical point of view. What I am arguing for here and throughout the study is a sensitivity to the universality of certain religious phenomena that might be said to unite all poets responsive to the dynamics

of those phenomena, whatever the particular "doctrinal" persuasions of
those poets.

In his discussion of the poetic assimilation of the holy, Octavio Paz
articulates the situation nicely. Arguing for "the anteriority of the sacred"
(that quality which makes it "ahistorical" or at least "prehistorical"), he
maintains that "the sacred is the original feeling from which the sublime
and poetic stem."[4] As such, "the poetic experience, like the religious one,
is a mortal leap" by which "our being suddenly remembers its lost identity; and then that 'other' that we are appears, emerges." In this sense,
"poetry and religion," he says, "are a revelation."[5] As "revelation," the
poetic and the religious "have a common origin" grounded in "our constitutive 'otherness.' " Whereas "religion interprets, channels, and system-
atizes inspiration within a theology," however, "poetry is the revelation
of our condition." In "a single instant of incandescence," it "opens up to
us the possibility of being that is intrinsic in every birth; it re-creates man
and makes him assume his true condition."[6]

These are large, if not grandiose, claims, but it is precisely in the tradition of the poet as the discloser of "the other" that I wish to place Milton.
The poetics that constitutes this tradition runs counter to the parochializ-
ing tendencies of all who would "tame" Milton by subjecting him to that
tyranny of paradigm that has dominated Milton criticism over the years
and that has domesticated him with such labels of convenience as "humanist," "puritan," and "rationalist."[7] At its most reductionist, this para-
digmatic point of view has superimposed the systematizing impulse of
religion upon "the anteriority of the sacred" to such an extent that
Milton's original poetic vision is relegated to the demands of the dog-
matic. This, I believe, is what happens in Malcolm M. Ross's *Poetry and
Dogma*, which maintains that the so-called Protestantism of Milton's art
desacramentalizes it in a process that moves it toward "the purely secular." That secularization, in turn, causes "the Christian symbols in Milton's poetry" to become "externalized" (in the sense of being external to,
rather than arising from, what Ross would consider genuine religious
feeling). "At the very point of externalization," these symbols, he argues,
"cease to be ritualistic."[8] It is not a particularly far cry from the kind of
schematizing that Ross engages in to that which, more recently, Mary
Ann Radzinowicz employs in her book *Toward "Samson Agonistes."*
Although her book is far more persuasively argued and sensitive to the
complex forces that shaped Milton's emerging outlook, Radzinowicz
adopts a stance in keeping with Dennis Burden's emphasis upon Milton's
purported rationalism. In so doing, she argues for a point of view by
which Milton is said to have "demythologized the role of the poet."[9] It is

precisely in opposition to the sort of attitude embraced by Ross, in his own way, and Radzinowicz, in hers, that the present study is offered. Given the currency of the secularizing and demythologizing points of view, I feel a certain urgency in demonstrating the extent to which Milton's religiosity not only aligns him with an outlook that is fundamentally sacral but causes him to become, in Paz's terms, the poet of "the other" par excellence. As such, Milton is a poet whose principal mode is that of providing us with a renewed sense of "our constitutive 'otherness.' "

I am not alone in this enterprise. A renewed understanding of Protestant aesthetics in general and Milton's poetics in particular has focused the matter nicely. Accordingly, Barbara K. Lewalski has called our attention to the intensely religious underpinnings of a Protestant poetics that has its wellspring in the biblical model of the Psalmist "with his anguished cries of *de profundis*, and his soaring *te deums* of praise." This biblical mode, Lewalski finds, has its counterpart in "the biblical prophetic mode" so essential to the poetry of Spenser, Milton, and a number of the Romantics. Their "great biblical models are the Old Testament prophets (Isaiah, Daniel, Ezekiel), and especially the Book of Revelation, which is said to subsume them all."[10] As Lewalski points out, the poetics of this biblical mode has received ample treatment in the works of Angus Fletcher, Joseph A. Wittreich, Jr., and William Kerrigan, among others.[11]

In Milton criticism, especially, that treatment has notably benefited from the insights of Kerrigan and Wittreich. Tracing the whole prophetic lineage back to its beginnings, Kerrigan provides a learned overview of the vatic tradition against which Milton's prose and poetry are to be placed. If I have any quarrel with Kerrigan's position at all, it is that he overemphasizes the rationalist elements in prophetic discourse and Milton's commitment to them. Nonetheless, his work is important in illuminating an aspect of the Miltonic sensibility that is crucial to a complete understanding of the vatic dimensions of Milton's works. In the field to which Lewalski has assigned the biblical prophetic mode, however, the one Miltonist who has made the greatest contribution is Wittreich. Through a series of studies (the most recent being *Visionary Poetics*) that places Milton in "the line of vision," Wittreich has taught us fully what constitutes the revelatory experience from the Miltonic point of view and how that experience represents, in Paz's terms, "the revelation of our condition."

If Kerrigan and Wittreich have established the visionary poetics of the prophetic Milton, my study, in turn, will address itself to a corresponding aspect of the Miltonic outlook, that of the sacerdotal.[12] As I shall discuss, the vatic finds its appropriate counterpart in the hierophantic. The dynamics of the visionary are given impetus as much by sacral concerns as by prophetic ones. At its core, the biblical prophetic mode is very much a priestly affair. When Ezekiel establishes his credentials at the very outset of his prophecy, he is at pains to proclaim that "the word of the Lord came expressly unto Ezekiel the priest [הכהן]" (Ezek. 1:3). It is as a priest that Ezekiel receives and proclaims the "visions of God" (מראות אלהים) (Ezek. 1:1). In turn, Saint John the Divine views himself not only as a witness of the "prophecy" (προφητείας) that he recounts but as one among the "priests unto God" (ίερεῖς τῷ θεῷ) (Rev. 1:3–6). It is likewise as a priest that Milton proclaims his own מראות אלהים and his own account of the προφητείας throughout his poetry and prose. In that role, he is at once הכהן and one among the ίερεῖς τῷ θεῷ. From the perspective that the entire body of his writings offers us, this study, then, will focus upon *Paradise Lost* as a sacral document, one that gives rise to a hierophantic outlook that complements and reinforces the vatic point of view. In so doing, the study will attempt to demonstrate the extent to which Milton fulfills the major criterion that Paz establishes for the religious poet, that his poetry provide the means by which we might have access to "the other" in that profound "instant of incandescence."

In its analysis of the holy, this study is divided into three parts: the first establishes some basic contexts by which the holy may be understood; the second investigates aesthetic dimensions of the concept; and the third explores fundamental aspects of sacral phenomena in *Paradise Lost*. Providing an overview of sacral contexts, the first part contains two chapters. Whereas chapter 1 treats both the Greco-Roman and Judeo-Christian sacral traditions that Milton inherited, chapter 2 considers Renaissance contexts and Milton's place in them. Focusing upon epic theory and poetic practice, the second part likewise contains two chapters. Chapter 3 explores the concept of the poet as hierophant in classical, medieval, and Renaissance aesthetics and the Miltonic bearing of that concept; chapter 4 represents a preliminary study of the holy in Milton's poetry, including the Latin poems, the sonnets, *Comus, Lycidas, Paradise Regained*, and *Samson Agonistes*. The purpose of the fourth chapter, then, is to provide a context for the analysis of *Paradise Lost* as sacral document. That analysis is carried out in the various chapters that constitute the third part. Accordingly, chapter 5 focuses upon the interdicted fruit as an expression of those "things" that are prohibited from common use by God. Chapter 6 considers the nature of consecrated areas with their respective "centers" and what the penetration of those areas signifies. Beginning with a treatment of the cosmic mount in mythic thought, chapter 7 investigates the movement from Sinai to Zion as a reflection of the transition from cultic to spiritual renderings of the holy in the Christian tradition. Chapter 8 focuses upon the Tetragrammaton and its traditions as an expression of "existence" and "creation" in Milton's epic. Whereas chapter 9 considers the traditions underlying the concept that "God *is* light" and the bearing that those traditions have upon the blind poet of *Paradise Lost*, chapter 10 explores the traditions underlying the concept that "God *dwells* in light" and the bearing that those traditions have upon the *visio Dei* as Milton conceives it. Chapter 11 investigates war as sacral event. Beginning with the Old Testament and New Testament wars of Jahweh and the impact of that warfare upon seventeenth-century and Miltonic conceptions of holy war, it then examines the sacral nature of celestial and spiritual combat in *Paradise Lost*. Concluding the treatment of Milton's epic as sacral document, chapter 12 discusses the way in which God's sabbatical rest is at once reflected in the universe of *Paradise Lost* and realized in the experience of the Christocentric vision that Milton's epic embraces.

Part 1
The Holy

1
Preliminary Contexts

As the *Encyclopaedia of Religion and Ethics* maintains, the idea of the holy is absolutely central to an understanding of the religious experience; in fact, the notion of the holy is "even more essential than the notion of God."[1] Whether or not this is the case, the holy as a distinct category of *Religionswissenschaft* has received detailed phenomenological and historical treatment for a number of years.[2] Nonetheless, the need for additional investigation, particularly within the context of the traditions that Milton inherited, continues to be felt. This study is, in part, an attempt to meet that need. To establish a frame of reference by which the holy may be understood in its own right and in its connection with Milton, it is necessary first to undertake a rather extensive analysis of the holy as it is commonly viewed and as it has manifested itself in various cultures.

No investigation of the holy can afford to overlook the seminal works of Rudolf Otto and Mircea Eliade. Coining the term *das Heilige* in *The Idea of the Holy*, Otto explores what he calls "the non-rational factors in the idea of the divine and its relation to the rational."[3] Otto's inquiry, then, is psychologically oriented: it purports to examine the effect that the holy has upon the human mind. As an experience that is both irrational and terrifying, the holy manifests itself in the "religious dread" to which the "*mysterium tremendum*," the awe-inspiring mystery, gives rise. Overwhelmed by the "power" and "majesty" (*majestas*) of the *mysterium*, one is concurrently repelled and fascinated by it. In their totality, these experiences are perfectly in accord with the "numinous" in all its splendor. That numinosity impresses upon one the fact of his own nothingness as he finds himself in the presence of that which is "wholly other" (*ganz andere*).[4]

Employing another approach in his book *The Sacred and the Profane*, Eliade concerns himself not with the relationship between "the rational and nonrational elements of religion" but with "the *sacred in its entirety*," that is, with that which is "the opposite of the profane."[5] The opposition between sacred and profane is discernible whenever and wherever the holy manifests itself. That manifestation is designated a *hierophany*, a term which "expresses no more than is implicit in its etymological content, i.e., that *something sacred shows itself to us*."[6] As "manifestations of sacred realities," hierophanies range from the most elementary embodiments *(kratophanies)*—for example, in an ordinary object, such as a stone or a tree—to the most sophisticated embodiments *(theophanies* or *epiphanies)*—for example, in "the supreme mystery of the Incarnation." "In each case," states Eliade, "we are confronted by the same mysterious act—the manifestation of something of a wholly different order, a reality that does not belong to our world, in objects that are an integral part of our natural 'profane' world."[7]

These objects, or *"Dinge,"* as Gerardus van der Leeuw calls them, contain "power" *(Macht)*,[8] which in its most elementary form at once vivifies and sanctifies the object. Such power, as Emile Durkheim maintains, is not merely "metaphorical"; it is represented by "forces" which "engender physical effects." Should an individual come into contact with these forces without having taken proper precautions, he receives a shock that is comparable to "the effect of an electric discharge."[9] Imbued with these impersonal forces, then, objects become dangerous and threatening; they are held in awe. In Melanesian terms, they contain *mana*, that potency which attaches itself to things and causes them to become *taboo*.[10] If mana is the source of power, taboo is "the expressly authenticated condition of being replete with power."[11]

The universality of the idea has long been recognized. All-pervasive, it strikes at the very heart of religious thought. What Otto calls the ganz andere and Eliade the hierophany to describe the numinous has a decidedly cross-cultural basis, with its source in the most primitive of religions. The *joia* of the Australian aborigines, the *brahman* of the Indians, the *tendi* of the Bataks, the *sumangat* and the *pemali* of the Malays, the *hasina* of the Malagasy, the *nlongo* of the Congolese, the *orunda* of the Mpongwe, the *eki* of the Fans, the *dzo* of the Ewe, the *oudah* of the Pygmies, the *wakanda* of the Siouan Indians, the *orenda* of the Iroquoian Indians, the *hamingja* of the Norsemen, and the *makt* of the Swedes—all serve to express an awareness of the holy as an experience that permeates religious thought.[12] In doing so, the holy undergoes a process of development that is at the center of the religious life.

The process referred to here has already received detailed treatment by Otto, who maintains that in the course of religious history the holy develops from an irrational, impersonal, nonmoral force to a rational, personal, moral imperative. Beginning simply as a "feeling-reflex" to an unknown and uncomprehended force, the experience of the holy then takes the form of "daemonic dread," after which it emerges as "fear of the gods," and then "fear of God." The δαιμόνιον as daemonic power progresses to θεῖον as divine power: dread evolves as worship. "Out of a confusion of inchoate emotions and bewildered palpitations of feeling grows 'religio,' and out of a 'shudder' a holy awe." Corresponding to this development in the idea of God, the holy is elevated and ennobled. Charged with ethical content, "holy" becomes "good," and "good" as a result becomes "holy," "sacrosanct." What results thereafter is an "indissoluble synthesis of the two elements," a synthesis that gives rise to a "fuller, more complex sense of 'holy,' in which it is at once *good* and *sacrosanct.*" "This development," Otto maintains, "constitutes the first central fact of religious study, and it is the task of religious history and psychology to trace its course."[13]

However one judges the particulars of Otto's thesis, his view of a development in the religious consciousness from nonmoral to moral has been upheld by such historians as James Henry Breasted. Treating what he calls the "process" or "evolution" of Egyptian religion over three thousand years, Breasted notes that in its primitive stages, religion had nothing to do with morals. Instead, it involved the awareness of "powers" inherent in objects worshiped through propitiatory offerings. Moral discernment, as a religious phenomenon, evolved at a later stage. The earliest known expression of that discernment in man's history is embodied in a Memphite drama that originated in the middle of the fourth millenium B.C. But even in that drama, the product of "a priestly body of temple thinkers," the sense of moral discernment is rudimentary. Conduct emerges as "a purely external matter," decreed by the Pharaoh. Moral discernment as we know it was not to appear for many centuries. When it did, it took the form of *Maat*, the Egyptian for "righteousness," "justice," or "truth." The concept of Maat "endured for a thousand years from the Thirty-fifth to the Twenty-fifth Century B.C. and made a profound impression on the human mind."[14] The significance of Breasted's findings lies in the historical verification that it gives to the attempt to trace the evolution of the holy from its earliest stages. As shown above, that evolution is essentially one involving the emergence of the ethical idea out of the nonethical. From the religious point of view, it is an evolution that accords with the movement from ritual practice to ethical conduct.[15]

The appropriateness of such an idea is confirmed by Edward Westermarck, who, in *The Origin and Development of the Moral Ideas*, points out the distinctions to which ἔθος-ἦθος (habit-character), on the one hand, and *mos-moralis* (custom-moral in nature), on the other, give rise.[16] Morality has its source in custom, which in the religious sphere is embodied in ritual. For the phenomenologist of the holy, this fact accords with the distinctions that Bernhard Häring draws between *"Kultus"* and *"Ethos."* Whereas Kultus depends upon the external manifestation of the numinous in acts of religious worship, Ethos depends upon the internal manifestation of the numinous in acts of moral conduct.[17] As such, Kultus commemorates the presence of that "power" (*einer unpersonlichen Macht*) inherent in "things" (*Dinge*). Ethos is an expression of the "moral imperative" (*Sittlichkeit*) inherent in the idea of "obligation" (*Verpflichtungscharacter*). Associated with the "body" (*Leib*), the one is decidedly *physical* (or, in Breasted's words, *material*) in its bearing. Associated with the "soul" (*Seele*), the other is decidedly *spiritual* in character.[18]

Developing the idea further, the transition from a holiness of Kultus to a holiness of Ethos is correspondingly a transition from spirit as the product of an impersonal force to spirit as the product of a higher moral presence. From the first point of view, spirit possesses those animistic qualities discernible in the beliefs of primitive cultures, as traced by Edward Tylor in his monumental work, which establishes the entirely nonmoral basis of lower animism.[19] In its earliest stages, spirit is devoid of an ethical dimension: it is simply a material or physical potency. As such, it is "power in manifestation, or energy."[20] The holy as *kratophany* is none other than the product of such a power. Evidence of its workings may be seen in the preexilic writings (ninth–eighth century B.C.) of the Old Testament. Although there it is produced by a divine agency, it retains its primitive characteristics. As material embodiment, it becomes the source of miraculous power bestowed by God (יהוה רוח) upon Elijah (1 Kings 18:12)[21] and transferred from Elijah to Elisha through the wonder-working mantle containing the spirit (2 Kings 2:8–16). With the great prophets of the eighth–sixth century B.C., however, the concept of spirit undergoes a change. According to this point of view, spirit, as the product of "the sole ethical Lord of Israel and the world," is responsible for "the inner life of man, and especially the moral renewal of the individual and the nation."[22] In this form, it achieves its highest expression in the New Testament as the Holy Spirit (τὸ πνεῦμα ἅγιον), which is the very basis of the Christian's ethical life (Gal. 5:9–23). It becomes, in Häring's terminology, *"das sakrale Ethos."* When that Ethos, in turn, is ritualized or sacramentalized (as it is, for example, in the liturgy of the Church), it assumes the form of what Häring calls *"das sanktionierte Ethos."* Combining moral and cultic, this outlook reflects a highly developed stage of the holy. It is true *Pietismus*.[23]

The foregoing observations should suggest something of the outlook that characterizes contemporary religious attitudes toward the holy. Now it is necessary to establish a historical perspective to bolster the phenomenological outlook provided above. Any discussion of the historical perspective should, of course, take into account the traditions that Milton inherited. For that reason, this study will explore the holy first in its Greco-Roman contexts and then in its Judeo-Christian contexts. Although these contexts overlap, they will be separated here for the sake of discussion.

To trace the history of the holy in its Greco-Roman contexts is to witness the emergence of holiness both as a cultic and as a moral phenomenon. Primitive Greek religion (pre-Hellenistic) conceived of the holy in physical terms. Holiness was seen as a physical quality inherent in divine things or persons.[24] As late as the eighth century B.C., something of the idea still resides in Hesiod, who, in the *Works and Days*, counsels an elaborate etiquette that reveres the power of the holy:

> Never omit to wash your hands before
> You pour to Zeus and to the other gods
> The morning offering of sparkling wine. . . .
> . . . Do not
> Expose your body, for the night belongs
> To the blessed gods. A man who's reverent
> And knows much wisdom sits or goes beside
> A courtyard wall, where he will not be seen. . . .
> Never pass through, on foot, a lovely brook
> Of ever-flowing water, till you pray
> And look into the beauty of the stream,
> And in her clean, sweet water, wash your hands.
> For if you cross a river with your hands
> And crimes uncleansed, the gods will punish you,
> And bring you countless pain in future times.

Never cut your nails at the feast of the gods, continues Hesiod, and "Never, when drinking, leave the ladle in / The mixing-bowl; that brings a fatal jinx. . . . / A pot unblessed by sacrifice brings harm; / Don't ever eat or wash from such a pot." Finally, do not let a child "sit on a tomb or other sacred thing," and "never scoff at things unknown; / This too enrages god."[25]

If these strictures spring from a poet whose moral sense is highly developed, they still indicate the extent of his indebtedness to inchoate and primitive forms. Even in Hesiod, who is "thoroughly orthodox" and whose "theology is emphatically and even noisily Olympian," one can behold "the flotsam and jetsam of earlier ages." If his Zeus is the anthropomorphic father of gods and men, his deities are impelled by a power and force replete with archaic meaning. His verse, as Jane Harrison has made clear, "is full of reminiscences, resurgences of early pre-anthropomorphic faith; he is haunted by the spirits of ghostly *mana* and *orenda* and Wa-kon'-da and *bráhman*."[26] These render all that is associated with Zeus holy; they, in turn, give rise to the etiquette so minutely elaborated in *Works and Days*.

When Herodotus, the first true historian of religion, considered the idea of the holy in the fifth century B.C., that is how he articulated it. Pointing up the similarities between Egyptian and Greek religions, he gives this account of the Egyptians: "They are beyond measure religious, more than any other nation; and these are among their customs:—They drink from cups of bronze, which they cleanse out daily; this is done not by some but by all. They are especially careful ever to wear newly-washed linen raiment. They practise circumcision for cleanliness' sake; for they set cleanliness above seemliness. Their priests shave the whole body every other day. . . . Twice a day and twice every night they wash in cold water. Their religious observances are, one may say, innumerable."[27]

The comparison is important, for through it, Herodotus suggests the way in which Egyptian religious observances underlie the practices of the ancient Greeks. By means of those practices, the Greeks, borrowing from the Egyptians, cultivate an adherence to that which is holy, τὸ ἅγιον. Doing so, they cultivate the cultic implications of a term found in the archaic ritual verb root ἁγ, characteristic of the ancient Minoan-Mycenaean texts. There, ἁγ suggests the idea of purification and the removal of guilt. Surviving in its root form in the participle ἁγνός, it also underlies the adjective ἅγιος.[28] Ἅγιος, in turn, implies two meanings, both that which is sacred and that which is accursed. In the latter sense, it is so used by Cratinus, the fifth-century B.C. poet.[29] With these connotations, ἅγιος takes on meanings similar to those of ἄγος, which suggests the ideas of pollution and guilt.[30] Ἄγος is used in this way, for example, by Aristotle in *The Athenian Constitution* (328–25 B.C.), which speaks of driving out a "curse" (ἄγος) and of "being under a curse" (ἐναγεῖς, from ἐναγής).[31] In this sense, ἁγνός as sacred and ἄγος as polluted are distinguished.[32] Both, in turn, are implicit in ἅγιος, as it, like ἁγνός, derives from the ancient root ἁγ. At its source, then, the Greek concept of τὸ ἅγιον originally had a double meaning: holy was not only pure but likewise polluted.[33] Thus, the verb ἀρᾶσθαι means both "to pray" and "to curse," and Homer uses ἀρητήρ to denote "priest." What these ideas have in common is that both the sacred and the accursed are prohibited from common use.[34]

Either as sacred or accursed, that which was holy in primitive Greek thought had at its root an undeniable and categorical physicality that characterized it as archaic. That sense is clearly evident in the later rationalist response of Hippocrates to the primitive outlook. In his discourse *On the Sacred Disease*, Hippocrates argues that epilepsy is no more sacred than any other disease, and if there is any sacredness in it, those who have it should be considered as having been purified by it, not as having been tainted by it. In using purifications and charms, those who would cure the disease treat the divine, Hippocrates maintains, in a manner that is most irreligious and godless, "for they purify the victims of this disease with blood and other such things, just as if they were tainted with some impurity, or under a curse, or bewitched, or had done some impious deed; whereas they ought, on the contrary, to offer sacrifice and prayer and take them to the temples to supplicate the gods. But, instead of doing that, they purify them. The objects used in the rite they either bury, or cast into the sea, or carry away to the mountains where no one shall touch or tread on them. They ought to take them to the temples and duly offer them to the god, if a god is really the cause." From his own rationalist point of view, he feels that no person's body is "tainted" by divinity, which purifies and cleanses rather than defiles. When it comes to acts of propitiation, we "sprinkle lustral water, not as if we were receiving a taint, but rather cleansing ourselves of an impurity we might have."[35] Hippocrates' observation is significant for a number of reasons. It attests not only to the prevailing belief in the physicality of the sacred but to the fusion of antithetical views (the holy as pure and the holy as impure) in the constitution of the sacred. By calling into question the latter view (the holy as impure) as not consonant with pious deeds, Hippocrates' observation suggests, moreover, the way in which the sacred evolved in Greek thought. Ceremonies of purification are to be experienced in order to rid ourselves of both cultic impurity and moral impurity.

Such is precisely the view underlying Orphism, a movement that greatly influenced Greek religion from the sixth century onward. Combining the ideas of ritual and moral consecration (ὁσιότης), Orphism emphasized absolute purity resulting in divinity.[36] This is nowhere more evident than in the Orphic grave tablets found in southern Italy and Crete. Containing extracts from a poem of Orphic origin that dates, at the latest, from fifth century B.C., these grave tablets provide instructions to the soul of the dead for its guidance in the other world. Among the formularies represented in the extracts, one finds such statements as, "Out of the Pure I come, Pure Queen of Them Below. . . . / I have paid the penalty for deeds unrighteous . . . / And now I come a suppliant to holy Persephoneia / That of her grace she receive me to the seats of the Hallowed."[37] This fusion of the cultic and the moral is followed, in turn, by a separation that reflects a higher ethical sensitivity to holy and unclean, represented by such writers as Diogenes Laertius ("Cleansing water cannot take away a moral fault any more than a grammatical blunder") and Heraclitus ("They purify themselves vainly by defiling themselves with blood, as if a man who had stepped into mud should wash his feet with mud").[38] These remarks move one ever more compellingly toward an understanding of the holy as a moral phenomenon. Plato undoubtedly had the entire process in mind in his discourse on the holy in the *Euthyphro*. There, he presents a question that lies at the very heart of what the Greeks understood as the holy: Is that which is holy "beloved by the gods because it is holy," or is it holy "because it is beloved of the gods?" (*Euthyphro* 10).[39] The first definition underlies the cultic point of view; the second, the moral point of view. Plato's understanding would appear to embody both points of view. For him, ὁσιότης signifies not only ceremonial purity but virtuous behavior.[40] Something of this distinction no doubt resides in Aristotle's definition of virtue (ἀρετή) in the *Nichomachean Ethics*. As a moral imperative (ἠθική), virtue is "the product of habit [ἔθος]." In this way, it is cultivated through proper action: the moral person thereby forms good "habits." He becomes "habituated" to virtuous behavior. Habit (ἔθος) gives rise to character (ἦθος), *mos* to *moralis*, as discussed earlier.[41]

The emergence of the holy traced here in Greek religious thought is no less discernible in Roman religious thought. There, the holy likewise has its roots in the cultic. Those roots may be found in "the most primitive conditions of life in ancient Italy, when man lived in the forest where spirits lurked, where charms and spells were potent, where every rock, tree, stream, and hill was sacred."[42] Thus, one finds magical formulae inscribed in the bronze tablets from Gubbia, ancient Iguvium, in Umbria. The formulae are invoked for the purpose of expiation. As such, they involve the performance of sacred acts, the carrying of the sacred staff, and the laying of the sacrificial hearth, accompanied by incantations: "O holy one, to thee I pray with supplications, O Jupiter Grabovius, trusting in the sacred . . . rite, I pray to thee with supplications, O Jupiter Grabovius." Among the most important of the sacred acts referred to on the bronze tablets is the consecration of the boundary stone:

> When they have got beyond Acedonia and have come to the exit, they shall make a halt at the boundary stone. The one who carries the sacred staff shall [then] pronounce the ban. Thus shall he banish: "Whoever belongs to the town of Tadina, to the tribe of Tadina, to

the Tadine, Etruscan, Naharcian, or Japudian names, let him depart from this people." . . . Three times shall he pronounce the ban. Then, accompanied by [two] escorts he shall make the circuit with the fat sacrifices. When they have gone all the way around, and have come back to the boundary stone, he shall pray beside the boundary stone, accompanied by his escorts: "O Cerfe Martius, Praestita Cerfia of Cerfe Martius . . . [these] shall you terrify, frighten, destroy, scatter, deafen, smite."[43]

Implicit in the bronze tablets, the cultus of the boundary stone represents only one of the many manifestations of an outlook based upon the physicality of the sacred.

The influence of that outlook upon the Romans may be seen in works ranging from Siculus Flaccus's *De Agrorum Conditionibus et Constitutionibus Limitum*, which discourses upon the sacrifices and ceremonies employed to consecrate the boundary stone, to Ovid's *Fasti*, which discourses upon the festival of the terminalia. Ovid even goes so far as fancifully to invoke the "holy Terminus" as a location for the sacred force (*numen*) inherent in the object used to set off boundaries: "O Terminus, whether thou art a stone or a post sunk in the ground thou too hast been held divine [*numen habes*] from days of old."[44] Ovid's use of numen is precisely to the point. For the Romans, numen (compare the Greeks' δύναμις) represented that peculiar force which causes the object of consecration to assume its sacred quality. As such, it is similar in meaning to the Melanesian mana, which " 'attaches itself to persons and things and is manifested by results which can only be ascribed to its operation.' "[45] Numen, which appears to signify a movement, specifically a nod of the head (*nuere* means "to nod"), developed a sense of that which is the product of a force or power. Thus, "Varro, explaining *numen* by the famous Homeric passage in which Zeus, by a mere nod of assent, makes the holy mountain Olympos shake, says it belongs to him whose authority is greatest, in other words to a supernatural being; and Cicero again, speaking of the Stoic Supreme Being, says that all things obey his *numen*."[46] Of course, numen need not be confined to the gods. In fact, its roots are in the primitive consecrations that are typified by the boundary stone. Examples of such consecrations abound. One thinks of the dining table, a thing in itself holy, imbued with numen, as Plutarch confirms in his *Roman Questions*. Since those who sit at it must be clean, Juvenal becomes angry at the thought of people of filthy life coming near it. According to Roman custom, food was set apart for the gods during meals, after which it was cast into the fire of the family altar as a sign of propitiation. In addition to the dining table, other objects were said to be laden with numen, such as the doorway, the very parts of which (like the door-posts) assumed a numen of their own.[47]

It is precisely this sense of numen that one discerns throughout the *Aeneid* as a representation of Vergil's attempt to recreate the aura of ancient Roman religion. Thus, in Book 8, for example, one is particularly struck by the numinosity of the Palatine, "the hill which was in the time of Vergil, and for many centuries before and after, the very heart of Rome, the sacred citadel of gods and kings, and was now, once more, under Augustus, the center of Roman religion."[48] Referring to the time when "the Tarpeian house and the Capitol, golden now," were "once covered with forest thickets," Vergil says that "even then the dread sanctity [*religio*] of the place held the terrified rustics in awe; even then they shuddered before the wood and the rock." "This grove," cries the figure of Evander, "this hill with its leafy crown is the dwelling of a god; our Arcadians believe that here they have looked upon Jove himself, when often he shook out the darkening aegis in his hand and gathered the storm clouds."[49]

As the very embodiment of the "piety" that such an aura would evoke, Aeneas is a hero whose actions demonstrate in every way the proper regard for the holy. That regard may be seen, for example, in Aeneas's burial of Misenus, whose corpse is "defiling all the fleet with death," and in his securing of the golden bough from within the sacred wood. These acts are preparatory to the journey through the "sacred portal" to the underworld, which is at once "sacred" (*sacra*) and "accursed" (*sceleratum*).[50] As sacred, it may be traversed only by those who have "sanctified" and "purified" themselves with proper observances. As accursed, it contains an area that may not be traversed by a "pure soul."[51] Thus, coming to a "place where the road divides," the Sibyl informs Aeneas, "There to the right [*dextera*] . . . is our pathway to Elysium; but the way to the left [*laeva*] wreaks vengeance on the wicked and sends them to unrelenting Tartarus." The way to the left (the "sinister" side) is specifically described as that which leads to the "accursed threshold" over which "no pure soul is permitted to cross." Beyond the threshold lies, in effect, an impure realm within the sacred confines of the underworld. Yet even this realm is guarded by sacred gates, "grating upon their jarring hinges," and before these gates, Aeneas "sprinkles his body with fresh water, and lays the bough on the opposite threshold" as if in obeisance to that which is holy.[52]

In this portrayal, Vergil combines two conceptions of the underworld, one cultic and the other moral. The cultic conception is founded upon an underlying tendency in Roman thought: that which is sacred (*sacrum*) suggests "the condition of being given over entirely to the underworld."[53] To recall the words of the Orphic grave tablets, Proserpine herself is "holy," "Pure Queen of Them Below." The Roman conflation of sacred and accursed carries through and in fact intensifies the Greek view of ἄγος as that which "connects with the underworld" in such a way that "two apparently opposite domains, that of purity and that of death, are in contact."[54] With this idea in mind, Cicero maintains that "*sanctitas*" refers to the *Manes*—the ghosts of the departed.[55] The idea returns us to the paradoxical concept implicit in the holy: pure and impure, sacred and accursed, are opposite sides of the same coin. Their roots are part of a cultic tradition that manifests itself in an elaborate code of conduct befitting the holy as a physical phenomenon. What evolves out of that phenomenon is an all-pervasive sense of the moral. This sense leads us to the second conception that characterizes Vergil's underworld as a place that is holy and pure, on the one hand, and accursed and impure, on the other.

From the moral point of view, Vergil distinguishes between those who dwell in the accursed region and those who dwell in the blessed region. The first group comprises rebels against Jove, murderers, frauds, misers, adulterers, and perpetrators of monstrous crimes.[56] The second comprises "chaste priests," "devout poets," and faithful warriors.[57] The members of the first suffer the wrath of Jove in the depths of Tartarus; those of the second enjoy the rewards of happiness in the fields of Elysium. But even this second group must be purified through suffering before entering Elysium. As Anchises says, "Some are hung stretched out to the empty winds; some have their taint of guilt [*infectum . . . scelus*] washed away in the seething tides, or burned out with fire."[58] Cultic impurity assumes the form of moral impurity, which must be properly purged before true moral holiness may be attained.

The idea finds its counterpart in Vergil's messianic eclogue, which looks forward to the purification of our "ancient sin" and "guilt" in the coming of the "golden race."[59] Horace's odes attest to the belief that such purification is necessary to the health of the state: "Your fathers' sins, O Roman, you, though not guiltless of them, must expiate, until you restore the temples and ruined shrines of the gods and their statues blackened with smoke."[60] It is precisely this restoration of temples and shrines that characterized the official revival of religious sentiment during the Augustan era. In fact, one of the reforms initiated by Augustus was the resuscitation of the old priestly college of the Arval Brothers, whose practice was to go in solemn procession every spring about the fields (*arva*) in order to supplicate for the protection of the seed from harm.[61]

The moral counterpart of these proceedings is provided by Horace's *Carmen Saeculare*, which celebrates the "holy season, at which the Sibylline verses command chosen maidens and unsullied youths to chant a hymn to the gods" and which asks the gods to "grant that our youth may be teachable and learn the ways of virtue."[62] For Horace, the model of that devotion and virtue is none other than "holy Aeneas,"[63] whose "piety," we recall, is represented by a veneration for the holy as both a cultic and a moral phenomenon. In his speech "On the Diviner's Reply," Cicero himself attests to the religiosity embodied in that outlook: "We ... excel all peoples in religiosity and in that unique wisdom (*pietate ac religione atque hac una sapientia*) that has brought us to the realization that everything is subordinate to the rule and direction of the gods (*deorum numine omnia regi gubernarique*)."[64] Excelling all peoples in "religiosity," the later Romans combined the cultic and moral impulses that we have seen as fundamental to the evolution of the holy.

Apparent in Greco-Roman thought, the course of that evolution is likewise discernible in the Judeo-Christian tradition. In his classic work *Lectures on the Religion of the Semites*, W. Robertson Smith brings to bear upon the Judaic tradition the basic distinctions already discerned here in the Greco-Roman tradition. For the Semites, as for the Greeks and Romans, holiness was founded squarely upon the movement from cultic to moral.[65] In the period that preceded Amos, 760 B.C., holiness was "not a moral but a physical quality."[66] It was not concerned with morality and purity of life. People were considered holy not because of their character but as the result of their race, function, or mere material sanctity.[67] For ancient Semitic religion, then, the physicality of the holy was of primary importance. Primitive Judaism attended to the holiness of "things": places (such as the sanctuary and the mount), natural objects (such as a spring or a tree), the apparatus of worship (such as altar-bowls, cups, and other vessels), animals (such as the camel, ox, cow, horse, pig, and mouse), certain portions of time (such as the Sabbath and the Jubilee Year), certain operations or processes (such as the sacrifice and the vow), certain events (such as war), the names of God (such as the Tetragrammaton), certain persons (such as the priest and the king).[68] These "things" were, for the Hebrews, "charged with divine energy and ready at any moment to discharge [themselves] to the destruction of the man who presumes to approach [them] unduly."[69]

Thus, Sinai cannot be touched without peril to one's life (Exod. 19:12–13), and the ark may not be looked into or touched without risking death (Num. 18:3–6; 1 Sam. 6:19; 2 Sam. 6:6–7). For the primitive Hebrew, the terror of the holy was among its most distinguishing characteristics.

What Otto terms the *mysterium tremendum* is nowhere more dramatically portrayed than in Numbers 16:1–50. Having been challenged by Korah to determine who is holy and who is not, Moses says, "Even to morrow the Lord will shew who *are* his, and who *is* holy" (Num. 16:5). God does so by separating Moses and his followers, who "separate" themselves "from among this congregation" (Num. 16:21), and by destroying Korah and his followers, who are "swallowed up" by the earth (Num. 16:32; cf. Lev. 10:1–3). God thereby separates sacred and profane with a terrifying finality.

If sacred and profane are not always so dramatically distinguished, the separation of the two underlies primitive Hebraic thought. That which is "holy" is קדש—that is, "separated, cut off"—whereas that which is "profane" is הל—that is, "open for common use." In this sense, the Israelites as God's chosen people are holy, others profane: "And ye shall be holy unto me," God says to Moses, "for I the Lord *am* holy, and have severed you from *other* people, that ye should be mine" (Lev. 20:26). In cultic terms, the distinctions also prevail. The "sin offering" is "most holy" and must be eaten only by the priest "in the court of the tabernacle"; "whatsoever shall touch the flesh thereof shall be holy" (Lev. 6:25–27). In that manner, the holy shares characteristics with the unclean: "If a soul touch any unclean thing . . . he also shall be unclean" (Lev. 5:2). Opposed to both these holy and unclean things are those which are "profane" or common: "These shall ye eat of all that *are* in the waters: whatsoever hath fins and scales in the waters, in the seas, and in the rivers, them shall ye eat" (Lev. 11:19). Thus, we find that the purpose of the Book of Leviticus is to "put difference between holy and unholy, and between unclean and clean" (Lev. 10:10). Ezekiel himself later invokes the same correspondence when he purports to reveal *"the difference* between the holy and profane," that is, "between the unclean and the clean" (Ezek. 44:23; cf. 22:26). On the one side, then, we have "holy" (קדש) and "unclean" (טמא); on the other, "profane" (הל) and "clean" (טהר). In keeping with this idea, the name of "holy" at the Canaanite shrines "was specially appropriated to a class of wretches whose life, apart from its connection with the sanctuary, would have been disgraceful even from the standpoint of heathenism," for these "wretches" were none other than the sodomite priest attendants and the priestess-prostitutes "who infested the Canaanite-Hebrew sanctuaries."[70] Although the pig was unclean among the Jews, the Greeks, observes Plutarch, "did not know whether the Jews abhorred it or worshipped it."[71] Correspondingly, in the Old Testament, "there are still cases where it cannot be decided whether the tabu-interdict implies holiness or impurity."[72] As late as the *Mishnah* itself, according to the teaching of the schools of both Hillel and Shammai, "the canonical Holy Scriptures defile the hands."[73]

This conflation of holy and unclean in primitive Hebraic thought demonstrates once again the fundamental religious distinctions implicit in Leviticus and enunciated later by Ezekiel—holy : profane :: unclean : clean.[74] Even in Leviticus, however, these distinctions are already being modified to the point of reversal. Holy comes to be associated with that which is clean and pure, profane with that which is impure. The first point of view is contained in God's statement: "For I *am* the Lord your God: ye shall therefore sanctify yourselves, and ye shall be holy; for I *am* holy: neither shall ye defile yourselves with any manner of creeping thing that creepeth upon the earth" (Lev. 11:44). Earlier, the passage states that "creeping things" are not only "unclean" but an "abomination" (Lev. 11:31, 41). Obviously, holy and unclean in this context stand in direct opposition: to be sanctified is to purify oneself in avoidance of that which is unclean. The second point of view may be found in God's statement that whoever has a blemish "shall not go in unto the vail" that "he profane not my sanctuaries: for I the Lord do sanctify them" (Lev. 21:23). To be blemished, of course, is to be unclean, a state that here is associated with the idea of profanation.[75] That which is profane, therefore, has a tendency to approach that which is unclean. The idea is implicit in the evolution of the words for "profane." The verb חלל, "to give out for use," comes to assume the sense of "to profane," "to unhallow," and approaches the meaning "to defile" (cf. Ezek. 43:7, 23:38).[76] As unclean is brought into opposition with holy, then, profane is brought into opposition with clean.[77] We are thereby returned to a conception of the holy which embodies a fundamental paradox. Like ἄγος and *sacer*, קדש gives rise to the opposed ideas of impure and pure. With its most primitive roots in the former, it undergoes a development that associates it with the latter. It is particularly this development that one must recognize in the evolution of the holy both as a cultic and as a moral phenomenon in postexilic Judaism.

Whereas the cultic manifests itself in the emphasis upon external sanctity by the Sadducean priesthood, "the ancient Ḥasidim, and their successors, the Pharisees and Essenes [made] inner holiness . . . the aim of life."[78] As indicated, the first point of view is implicit in the writings of Ezekiel, the prophet-priest who returned to the cult of Levitical legislation in order to revive its practices, to separate, as it were, holy from profane, unclean from clean. Ezekiel teaches a renewed reverence for God's "holy things" (Ezek. 44:8).[79] Concurrent with this outlook, however, a view of the holy emerges that is distinctly moral in its bearing. Thus, Ezekiel himself speaks at once of circumcision of the "heart" and circumcision of the "flesh" (Ezek. 44:7–9).[80] Discernible in the Ḥasidim and later in the Pharisees and Essenes, the emergence of the holy as a moral phenomenon is of first importance to Hebraic thought. With its foundation in the moral law of Moses (Exod. 20:1–17), this view of the holy may be seen in the prophets of the Assyrian period, including Amos, Hosea, Micah, Zephaniah, and Jeremiah. For these prophets, holy assumes a decidedly moral significance.[81] In this sense, Isaiah proclaims, "Holy, holy, holy, *is* the Lord of hosts: the whole earth *is* full of his glory" (Isa. 6:3) and "the Lord of hosts shall be exalted in judgment, and God that is holy shall be sanctified in righteousness" (Isa. 5:16). Habakkuk celebrates the "Holy One" by addressing him in this manner: "*Thou art* of purer eyes than to behold evil, and canst not look on iniquity" (Hab. 1:12–13). Similarly, for Isaiah, "holiness" is the removal of "iniquity," the purging of "sin" (Isa. 6:7). It is the state of spiritual "cleanness." As Jeremiah maintains, "Though thou wash thee with nitre, and take thee much soap, *yet* thine iniquity is marked before . . . the Lord God" (Jer. 2:22).[82]

In this context, "holy" as קדוש assumes the moral significance of "godly" as חסיד, the form that is found in Psalm 4: "Hear me when I call, O God of my righteousness: . . . know that the Lord hath set apart him that is godly for himself." One is now "set apart" as the result not of a cultic but of a moral distinction (cf. Pss. 12:1, 86:2, 145:17, among others). From that perspective, one enters into a more nearly refined atmosphere infused with the life of postexilic Judaism. In this era, the emphasis that the prophets place on God's righteousness and his ethical requirements (Amos 5:6–11, 21–27; Isa. 1:10–17, 21–23, 5:8–23) shifts the religious focus from matters of worship to those of conduct. Sanctions of ceremony and forms of sacrifice assume less significance. In the teachings of Jeremiah, the externalities of Israel's official religion give way to the new covenant that God establishes with his people. Devotion becomes internal, spiritual, and personal: "I will put my law within them, and in their heart will I write it" (Jer. 31:31–33). The results are profound indeed: what emerges is an "*Umwertung aller Werte*," a transmutation of all values that changes the conception of holiness and all related to it.[83] Its effects are particularly discernible in the form that the holy assumes in the Christian tradition.

The nature of New Testament holiness is best summed up by Otto: "In the Gospel of Jesus we see the consummation of that process tending to rationalize, moralize, and humanize the idea of God, which began with the earliest period of the old Hebrew tradition and became specially prominent as a living factor in the Prophets and the Psalms."[84] Accordingly, the New Dispensation embodies an outlook whose focal point is moral and ultimately spiritual rather than cultic. When asked by the Pharisees why his disciples "wash not their hands when they eat bread," Jesus replies, "Not that which goeth into the mouth defileth a man; but that which cometh out of the mouth, this defileth a man . . . [for] whatsoever entereth in at the mouth goeth into the belly, and is cast out into the draught. . . . But those things which proceed out of the mouth come forth from the heart; and they defile the man. For out of the heart proceed evil thoughts, murders, adulteries, fornications, thefts, false witness, blasphemies: These are *the things* which defile a man: but to eat with unwashen hands defileth not a man" (Matt. 15:1–20). The idea is reinforced in the Epistle to Titus: "Unto the pure all things *are* pure; but unto them that are defiled and unbelieving *is* nothing pure; but even their mind and conscience is defiled" (1:15).

In keeping with the spirit of postexilic Judaism, New Testament holiness is likewise based upon an Umwertung aller Werte. The things which defile have lost their physicality: they are things of the heart. Such is no less true of the things which purify: "For he is not a Jew, which is one outwardly; neither is *that* circumcision, which is outward in the flesh: But he *is* a Jew, which is one inwardly; and circumcision *is that* of the heart, in the spirit, *and* not in the letter; whose praise *is* not of men, but of God" (Rom. 2:28–29; cf. Deut. 10:16, 30:6). The movement from outward disposition to inward disposition, the letter to the spirit, the law to the faith, the old covenant to the new, is the hallmark of New Testament holiness. Sanctity no longer resides in things: it is brought *to* things by those who possess it. "For the unbelieving husband is sanctified by the wife, and the unbelieving wife is sanctified by the husband: else were your children unclean; but now they are holy" (1 Cor. 7:14). Recalling the old Platonic dichotomy, one might say that that which is holy is so not because it is loved by the gods but is loved by the gods because it is holy. In New Testament terms, it is holy as a result of its moral efficacy, as that efficacy approximates the holiness of God, whose prime epithet is the "holy, holy, holy" of Isaiah (6:3 [קָדוֹשׁ קָדוֹשׁ קָדוֹשׁ]) and Saint John the Divine (Rev. 4:8 [ἅγιος, ἅγιος, ἅγιος]).

The very use of ἅγιος here by the Septuagint to render the קָדוֹשׁ of the original trisagion reinforces the point. Causing ἅγιος to become "above all things a qualitative and ethical term," the New Testament "lifted it into accord with the highest ethical conceptions and gave it the idea of separateness from the sinful world, harmony with God, the absolutely good Being, moral perfection."[85] In this sense, ἅγιος, through its New Testament application, expresses something more and higher than its counterparts "ἱερός, *sacred, outwardly associated with God*"; "ὅσιος, *reverent, pious*"; "σεμνός, *worthy, honourable*"; "ἁγνός, *pure, free from defilement*." Ἅγιος is "more positive, more comprehensive, more elevated, more purely ethical and spiritual. It is characteristically Godlikeness."[86]

Under these circumstances, man's holiness is a reflection of his moral likeness to God. For that reason, the New Testament applies the same term to both God and man and exhorts us to be "holy as he is holy." As "the absolute moral Reality of the world, separate from all evil and infinite in every excellence," God is holy because "He is pledged by His own nature to secure a perfect and loving righteousness everywhere, even at the cost of redemption." Correspondingly, "man is holy when he is brought by grace into that relationship to God by which the Divine righteousness may be honoured and conserved." In this manner, "God is the 'Holy Father,' a Being who freely loves and saves His guilty children, not only without any sacrifice of His Divine sanctity, but even by its supreme exercise." As sons of the Divine Father, we are chastened "that *we* might be partakers in his holiness" (Heb. 12:10). Man's holiness is accordingly the product of "a perfect moral sonship, the consecration of all his powers and opportunities to the worship of God." Jesus Christ himself is, of course, the embodiment of that perfect holiness.[87]

In spite of this moral imperative, however, the numinous remains as central to the New Testament and the traditions that spring from it as it is to the Old Testament and its traditions. If the New Testament contains "the consummation of that process tending to rationalize, moralize, and humanize the idea of God," it also contains the ganz andere as "awe-compelling yet all-attracting," radiant in an atmosphere of genuine religious awe. "All is made into a 'mystery,'" says Otto; "all, that is, becomes 'numinous.'"[88] By means of that numinosity, one experiences what Teilhard de Chardin calls a "diaphany": one participates in the "incandescence" of *le milieu divin*.[89] In New Testament terms, one witnesses events ranging from Christ's baptism (Matt. 3:16–17) to his transfiguration (Matt. 17:1–9). When Christ is baptized, the heavens open and the Spirit of God descends like a dove, an event resonant with the sound of God's voice. When Christ is transfigured, his face shines like the sun and his clothing is as white as the light. Those who experience the effects of such occurrences participate in the numinosity of New Testament holiness.

Their baptism is that of the Holy Ghost and of fire (Matt. 3:1), their transfiguration that of Pentacostal flame and other tongues (Acts 2:1–4).

From the Christocentric point of view, these theophanies are nowhere more compelling than in the cultic formulations that they later assume.[90] All that is associated with Christ becomes a "mystery" (μυστήριον, sacramentum). "Take, eat; this is my body," and "Drink, . . . this is my blood" (Matt. 26:26–28), says Christ, who, in his incarnate form, becomes the veritable thank-offering, the veritable sacrifice whose source is in the Jewish meal (Exod. 12:7, 24:5; Lev. 17:11, 14). In that statement, Christ projects himself as one who is made sacred through the sacrifice of himself: he becomes a *sacrificium*.[91] He also becomes the embodiment of an outlook that has as great a reverence for holy things as is to be found anywhere in the traditions explored here. In keeping with this sense of the numinous, Christ himself admonishes his followers not to profane that which is holy: "Give not that which is holy unto the dogs" (Matt. 7:6), and "stand in the holy place" when "the abomination of desolation, spoken of by Daniel the prophet" occurs (Matt. 24:15). The New Testament warns us not to "speak blasphemous words" against the "holy place" (Acts 6:13) and not to "defile the temple of God," which is "holy" (1 Cor. 3:17). "Do ye not know," Paul asks, "that they which minister about holy things [τὰ ἱερά] live *of the things* of the temple? and they which wait at the altar are partakers with the altar?" (1 Cor. 9:13). The point of view implicit in these passages, in turn, gives rise to a tradition of Christian worship characterized by an extreme cultic veneration of the physical.[92]

The reconciliation of this cultic outlook with the decidedly moral and spiritual basis of New Testament teachings lies in the figure of Christ himself. He is the embodiment of the cultus and provides the justification for the cultic outlook. Both sacrificer and sacrifice, priest and offering, he stands at the center of all cultic observance. To deal in holy things is to deal in him, and to do so is to reconstruct in cultic terms the moral and spiritual imperatives underlying New Testament teachings. Assuming a decidedly Christocentric bearing, the cultic underpinnings of the Old Testament are thereby manifested in New Testament terms. That is the unique character given the Umwertung aller Werte represented by the New Testament. To follow Christ's career, to understand his mission, to examine the language that describes his actions is to see precisely how the New Testament appropriates for its own purpose the cultic use of the holy embodied in the original Old Testament outlook.

Thus, offering himself without blemish (ἄμωμος) to God (Heb. 9:14), the Son is sent into the world as Christ (Χριστός) the anointed (Acts 10:38; 2 Cor. 1:21), divinely born and preeminently holy. In fact, according to Luke, Gabriel announces to Mary the miracle of Christ's birth in the following terms: "The Holy Ghost shall come upon thee, and the power of the Highest shall overshadow thee: therefore also *that holy thing* [ἅγιον] which shall be born of thee shall be called the Son of God" (1:35). As one who is "holy, harmless, undefiled, separate from sinners, and made higher than the heavens," he becomes both "high priest" and ultimate sacrifice, "consecrated for evermore" (Heb. 7:25–28). Purging us of our sins through his blood upon the cross, he fulfills and abolishes the whole sacrificial system (Heb. 1:3, 9:28, 10:26). He becomes for man thereby a "sanctification" (1 Cor. 1:30), "the objective ground or warrant of the believer's new standing of holiness before God."⁹³ By sacrificing himself, he perfects for ever "them that are sanctified" (ἁγιαζομένους); that is, he effects in principle "the complete sanctification of his followers in the eternal future, rendering them independent of every other sacrifice (Heb. 10:14)." "Being separated unto God in baptism, believers find themselves washed, sanctified, justified in the name of the Lord Jesus (1 Cor. 6:11), and, entering into all the privileges of the old covenant on a new plane, they know themselves to be 'an elect race, a royal priesthood, a holy nation, a people for God's own possession' (1 Pet. 2:9)." Having Christ as ὁ ἁγιασμός (sanctification), they become ἅγιοι, "earmarked, destined, and set apart from everything profane, as belonging to God and His kingdom."⁹⁴

As such, they reflect a "positive notion of holiness," not that which separates them for the sake of separation ("Wherefore remember, that ye *being* in time past Gentiles in the flesh, who are called Uncircumcision by that which is called the Circumcision in the flesh made by hands" [Eph. 2:11]) but which unites them in love: "But now in Christ Jesus ye who sometimes were far off are made nigh by the blood of Christ. For he is our peace, who hath made both one, and hath broken down the middle wall of partition *between us*" (Eph. 2:13–14); in that way, we "are no more strangers and foreigners, but fellow citizens with the saints and of the household of God" (Eph. 2:19). Here we have, then, not the holiness of cult but the holiness of spirit, specifically the Divine Spirit (τὸ πνεῦμα ἅγιον), who fuses love into the believer's heart in the gradual process of sanctification or hallowing (ὁ ἁγιασμός).⁹⁵ The believer becomes a saint in Christ, "in whom all the building fitly framed together groweth unto a holy temple in the Lord; In whom ye also are builded together for an habitation of God through the Spirit" (Eph. 2:21–22).

Through this perspective, then, the New Testament appropriation of the cultic underlies the entire Christian tradition.[96] In the history of the phenomenon known as the holy, the New Testament provides its own unique way to "minister about holy things" and *"live of the things* of the temple." From that perspective, the holy flourishes as gloriously as it ever had.

2
Renaissance and Miltonic Contexts

Concern with the holy as a fundamental concept was of crucial importance to the Renaissance frame of mind. Particularly in the seventeenth century, whole treatises were devoted to the subject, treatises that form the basis of the modern historical and phenomenological approach to the holy. Included in this context are discourses ranging from Isaac Casaubon's *De Rebus Sacris* (1614) to John Owen's *ΠΝΕΥΜΑΤΟΛΟΓΙΑ* (1674). Undoubtedly, the most comprehensive and enlightening discourse on the subject is that of Joseph Mede, putatively the "old *Damaetas*" (36) of *Lycidas* and fellow of Christ's College when Milton attended Cambridge. In *Diatribae* (1648), Mede explores the phenomenon of the holy as an aspect of his treatise "The Sanctification of God's Name." Mede's insights in this treatise are remarkable in the extent to which they anticipate those of Otto, van der Leeuw, and Eliade.

What is so striking about the treatise is not only its comprehensiveness but its concern to delineate the holy as a phenomenon as unique and profound in its implications as baptism, say, or the Lord's Supper. The treatise, in effect, legitimates the holy as a distinct subject for religious discourse. In so doing, it attempts to universalize the phenomenon by associating it with various forms of human behavior. From that point of view, the following passage will indicate Mede's insistence upon the all-pervasiveness of the holy:

> Now as the Divine Majesty it self is separate and holy, so know, it is a part of that honour we owe unto his most Sacred Name, that the things whereby, and wherewith he is served, should not be promiscuous and common, but appropriate and set apart to that sacred end. It is an honour which in some degree of resemblance we afford unto Kings, Princes, and other persons of dignity . . . to interdict the use of that to others, which they are wont to use; sometimes the

whole kinde, sometimes the individuall onely. As we know in former times, to wear purple, to subscribe with the Ink called *Encaustum*, of a purple colour, and other the like, which the diligent may finde, were appropriate to the use of Kings and Emperours onely. In the Book of *Kings*, we reade of the *Kings Mule*, so appropriate to his use, as to ride upon him was to be made King. . . . In the Book of *Esther* . . . of the *Horse* that King *Ahasuerus* used to ride upon, put in the same rank with the *Crown* and royall apparell, which none but the King might weare. And of individuall Utensils thus appropriated, and as it were dedicated to the alone use of persons of eminency, our own times want not examples. . . . [Correspondingly,] all the Utensils of the Tabernacle and Temple were *sacred* and set apart to that use; and not the Utensils of the Altar onely, but even the instruments of musick, which *David* ordained to praise the Lord with in the Temple, were not common, but consecrated unto God for that end, whence they are called . . . *Instrumenta musica Dei. The musicall instruments of God*; that is, sacred ones. . . . Agreeably whereunto those who sung the fore-alleged song of victory over the Beast, are said to have had in their hands . . . *The harps of God*, that is, not prophane or common, but sacred Harps, the Harps of the Temple, for there they sung this their Antheme, standing upon the great Laver or Sea of glass, which was therein. (p. 32)

Discoursing upon the holy as a phenomenon of unique significance to religious thought, Mede suggests, then, that the characteristics of this phenomenon are so far-reaching that they may be found in fundamental modes of behavior, biblical and nonbiblical alike. For Mede, such behavior is based upon the consecration of particular things (clothing, animals, utensils, musical instruments) that are set aside or are otherwise interdicted for special uses. They constitute a class of things whose holiness may be designated "relative," as opposed to "essential." Thus, in a statement that reflects the views of a number of Renaissance exegetes, Mede says, "We are to take notice of a twofold *Holinesse*; One originall, absolute and essentiall in God; the other derived or relative in the things which are *His*, properly . . . called *Sacra, Sacred things*."[1] "The first originall or absolute *Holinesse* is nothing else, but the incommunicable eminency of the divine Majesty, exalted above all, and divided from all other ἀξιώματα, or Eminences whatsoever" (p. 23). The other, "relative" holiness is characterized by those "things" that are "his" (that is, God's) "not as other things are" but "as they are no longer *ours*, such as . . . are said, *to be called by his Name*, or *to have his Name called upon them*." "These," says Mede, "are things *sacred*" (p. 31).

Within that framework, Mede recalls the Old Testament view of the holy as that which implies separation: "Mark here, that to *separate* is to make *Holy*, and that to be *Holy* is to be *separated* from others of the same rank" (p. 18). Thus, says Mede, the Septuagint renders "יקדשׁו, which is *Sanctificerunt*, . . . διέσειλαν, *separarunt*, or *discreverunt*" (p. 19).[2] It is precisely this outlook that Mede sees as central to the New Testament view of the holy, so much so, in fact, that he argues that the New Testament even intensified the view. Accordingly, he interprets Christ's driving the money changers from the temple in these terms: "Nay, our blessed Saviour, *Mark* 11. would not suffer a profane or common vessell to be so much as carried through his Fathers House accounting it as great a profanation, as to buy and sell there. And yet was not this abuse (which is a thing well to be marked) within those steps of the Temple, which the Jews accounted sacred, but in the outmost Court called *Atrium gentium & immundorum*, the place in which together with such as were unclean, the Gentiles, and uncircumcised were admitted to pray. . . . This Court therefore the Jews made no other account of, then as of a prophane place, but our Saviour proved by Scripture, that this Gentiles Oratory was also part of his Fathers house, and accordingly not to be profaned with common use" (p. 33).

The attitude implicit here is no less discernible in other tracts. As one who oversees the holy things of his Father's house, Christ provides the example to his priests, who are likewise curators of the holy. As Stephen Penton says, "כהן, which we translate Priest, signifies one that Ministers about Holy things, and therefore the *Greek* word ἱερεύς and the *Latin sacerdos* do more truly express the meaning of that word, than our English Priest; for we should rather render it a Holy Minister, or a Minister about Holy Things; or one that attends about holy service."[3] For Renaissance exegetes, Christ himself is a "holy thing." As James Ussher maintains in *Immanuel* (1638), "Therefore our Saviour assuming the substance of our nature, but not by the ordinary way of natural generation, is thereby freed from all the touch and taint of corruption of our flesh. . . . Whereupon, hee being made *of* man but not *by* man, and so becoming the immediate fruit of the *womb*, and not of the *loyns*, must of necessity be acknowledged to be that HOLY THING, which so was born of so blessed a Mother" (p. 5). So imbued is Archbishop Ussher with the idea of Christ as holy thing, in fact, that he resorts to the experience of the Old Testament theophanies to suggest the nature of Christ's holiness.

To be aware of Christ's holiness, says Ussher, is to stand with Moses before "the bush burning with fire" (p. 6). Only in this way can we begin to possess what Ussher himself calls the "knowledge of the holy" (pp. 2–3). That knowledge is expressed for Ussher in decidedly theophanic terms: "as the glory of God filled the *Tabernacle* . . . with such a kinde of fulnesse, that *Moses* himself was not able to approach unto it; . . . and filled the Temple of *Solomon* . . . in such sort that the Priests could not enter therein: so *in him all the fullnesse of the Godhead should dwell bodily*" (p. 2).

Renaissance exegetes, then, did not hesitate to incorporate into their view of the holy a language indebted to the Old Testament theophanies. Such was true whether those exegetes were discoursing upon the figure of Christ or upon the nature of consecration in general. Thus, in reference to consecrated places, the seventeenth-century exegete John Turner observes that any consecration implies "that peculiar manifestation of the Divine Favour and Presence, which God was pleased at that time to afford."[4] As a result of this "manifestation," the consecrated thing has about it the aura of what Turner calls "the *Supreme Numen*."[5] With the exegetes of their time, Ussher and Turner consistently insist upon that same fundamental numinosity that flourished in Greco-Roman and Judeo-Christian thought, a numinosity that transcends sectarian and denominational differences and that lies at the heart of the religious sentiment.

That sentiment is precisely what Joseph Hall seeks to instill in a remarkable work entitled *The Remedy of Prophaneness* (1637).[6] In this work, "the first people of God" are seen as the true exemplars of those most fully imbued with "an awfull regard" for "the Holy." "What worlds of nice caution have the masters of the Synagogue prescribed to their disciples, for their demeanour towards the book of the Law, of their God?" says Hall. "No man might touch it, but with the right hand, and without a kisse of reverence; No man might sit in the presence of it. . . . No man might offer to read it, but in a cleane place. . . . And is the word of the everlasting God of lesse worth and authority, now, than it hath beene? Or is there lesse cause of our reverence of those divine Oracles, than theirs?" (pp. 120–22). Desiring to encourage "a meet veneration" of the house of God, whose "presence" gives "an holinesse to what place soever he is pleased to shew himselfe in," Hall quips: "I have read of some sects of men so curiously scrupulous, that their Priests were not allowed to breathe in their Temple, but were commanded . . . to hold their winde (like those that dive for sponges at *Samos*) to the utmost length of time; and when they would vent their suppressed aire, and change it for new, to go forth of the doores, and return with a fresh supply" (pp. 129–34). That, of course, is carrying matters a bit too far, Hall implies; nonetheless, it reflects a veneration that he feels his own times lack. Accordingly, he would instill what he calls a "holy Feare" or "an holy awe" before the presence of God, so that, upon experiencing "that all-glorious presence," we become "affected with a trembling kind of awfulnesse," "wholly possessed with a devout shivering, and religious astonishment" (pp. 47, 88–90).

In a similar vein, a writer so diverse as Richard Baxter, in *The Divine Life* (1644), counsels "a *holy awe*" before the "*Dreadfulness* or *Terribleness*" of God embodied in his theophanies (p. 148). As Baxter says,

> The *Holiness of God* must cause us to walk continually in his *Fear*, and to take heed to all the affections of our souls, and even to the manner of our behaviour, when we come near to him in his Holy Worship. What suffered the Bethshemites for unreverent looking into the Holy Ark, 1 *Sam.* 6. 19. and *Uzzah* but for touching it? And what a dreadful example is that of the two Sons of *Aaron*, that were slain by a devouring fire from the Lord, for offering strange fire which he commanded not, *Lev.* 10. 1, 2. And *Aaron* was awed into silence by this account from God. [*I will be sanctified in them that come nigh mee, and before all the people I will be glorified*] v. 3. Take heed lest unreverence, or deadness . . . should be brought before a *Holy God.* (pp. 137–38)

Underlying Renaissance religious thought, then, one finds a reverence for the holy as theophanic experience and a willingness to reinforce that experience with Old Testament analogues. Despite obvious doctrinal differences between writers like Hall and Baxter, that reverence supersedes local concerns of dogma and belief. It is a reverence whose universality recalls Cicero's celebration of *religione* in response to the numen resident in all theophanies. Such an observation is not meant, of course, to slight the very real distinctions to which the beliefs of a Hall and a Baxter gave rise. The differences between Anglican and Puritan are so commonplace that there is no need to recount them here. They are important here only in the bearing those differences might have upon Anglican and Puritan responses to the holy. Although those responses share a fundamental reverence for the numinous, they diverge, as one might expect, in the way that reverence is manifested in matters of religious observance.

Thus, in *A Sermon Preach't . . . at the Consecration of a new Buriall-place* (1637), Hall insists upon "the decent formes of the administration of Gods publique services, and the appendances thereof, in the fashion of buildings, of habits, of solemne musicke, and this of meet consecration of those things which are to be devoted to any holy use" (pp. 43–45). With that outlook in mind, Mede in *Diatribae* criticizes the Puritans' distrust of physical things as embodiments of the holy: "Yes, there are some in our age so far carried away into a contrary extreeme . . . that they hold that no oblation or consecration of things unto God . . . ought to be esteemed lawfull; but that all distinction between sacred and prophane in externall things . . . is flat superstition" (p. 33). On the other side, in what is obviously a reaction to the Anglicans' so-called cultivation of set forms of worship, Baxter cautions against too great a dependence upon externals in religious observance of the holy: "Take heed lest unreverence, or deadness, or customary heartless wordy services, should be brought before a *holy* God. Take heed of hypocritical carnal worship. The Holy God will not be mocked with compliments and shews." Rather, God inclines toward the soul that is "wholly" devoted to him "both in *Justice*, because we are *his own*, and in *Love*, because he is *most Holy* and perfectly *Good*" (pp. 134, 137–38).

The importance of such criticisms lies in what may be termed the Anglican insistence upon the holy as a physical phenomenon, on the one hand, and the Puritan insistence upon the holy as a nonphysical phenomenon, on the other. Whereas Hall emphasizes the "meet consecration" of "things" devoted to "holy use," Baxter opts for the virtues of "Justice" and "Love" as expressions of the devotion to a God who is both "Holy" and "Good." At the risk of oversimplification, it can be said that these distinctions recall those already traced in Greco-Roman and Judeo-Christian thought. That is, they suggest the cultic-moral distinctions that characterize evolving attitudes toward the holy at various stages of the religious experience. Because of the manifold complexities attendant upon the Anglican-Puritan points of view, one should not wish to push this point too far. To say that Anglicanism embodies the cultic to the exclusion of the moral and Puritanism the moral to the exclusion of the cultic would be a gross misrepresentation. Given the professed differences in temperament between Anglican and Puritan, however, it is reasonable to note the cultic-moral distinctions that they themselves raised in response to each other's view of the holy.

At the same time, the universality of those distinctions throughout the Renaissance and their presence in Anglican and Puritan alike can also be argued. That point is attested to by none other than John Buxtorf, who makes a point in his lexicons of distinguishing between the holy as a cultic phenomenon and as a moral phenomenon. According to both the

Lexicon Chaldaicum (1640) and the *Lexicon Hebraicum* (1646), that which embodies the holy as cultic phenomenon is קֹדֶשׁ; that which embodies the holy as moral phenomenon is חָסִיד. The holy as קֹדֶשׁ is "Sanctitas, Sanctum, Res sancta, & sacris usibus consecrata: . . . inter sanctum sanctorum, id est, sacratissimum locum," as in Exodus 26:33, 28:36, and Leviticus 19:24 (*Lexicon Chaldaicum*, p. 1980; see *Lexicon Hebraicum*, p. 631). The holy as חָסִיד, on the other hand, is "Benignus, Beneficus, Misericors: Item, Sanctus, qui piè et sancté vivit," as in Psalms 4:3, 145:17, and Jeremiah 3:12 (*Lexicon Hebraicum*, p. 283; see *Lexicon Chaldaicum*, p. 640).

Both points of view are basic to the Renaissance frame of mind. The cultic outlook expressed by such writers as Mede, Ussher, and Hall has already been explored.[7] The moral counterpart is argued with corresponding urgency by writers ranging from Robert Abbot and Stephen Penton to Jeremy Taylor and Richard Allestree.[8] In *The Divine Life*, Baxter speaks of "holiness" as that which is derived from "the Transcendentally Moral Goodness of God" (p. 134). That "transcendent moral goodness" characterizes God as the epitome of all that is "holy" and "the *Fountain of all Moral Good.*" As such, God is "*Transcendentally above* and *separated from all the Creatures*, in comparison of whom the *Heavens* are not *clean*; and from whom all things stand at an *Infinite distance.*" In us, God's "*Holiness* . . . is called *The Divine Nature* . . . and therefore is radically a *right inclination and disposition* of the soul; which hath its rise from a Transcendent Holiness in God" (pp. 133–38). From the moral point of view, that "*right inclination and disposition* of the soul" is called "godliness."

As Richard Sibbes maintains, in *Light from Heaven* (1638), "Godlinesse, is either the Principles of Christian Religion, or the inward disposition of the soule towards them, the inward holie affection of the soule; the word implyeth both: for *Godlinesse* is not onely the naked Principles of Religion, but likewise the Christian affection, the inward bent of the soule, suitable to Divine Principles; there must be a godly disposition, carrying us to godly Truths" (p. 4). According to Henry Ainsworth, in *The Communion of the Saincts* (1628), this movement toward godliness, which he calls "righteousness," is effected through the process of sanctification. Sanctification, in turn, finds its counterpart in the Old Testament idea of separating holy persons from "profaneness and pollution" and dedicating them to "divine use or service of God" (pp. 54–56).[9] Drawing upon the cultic basis of the idea, Ainsworth places sanctification in a spiritual context. We experience, he says, a twofold sanctification in

Christ: first as the result of Christ's offering of himself as a sacrifice and second as the result of Christ's gracious work in us, "baptising us with the holy spirit into his death, buriall, and resurrection." Both these "waies of our sanctification," Ainsworth says, "were shadowed out unto Israel" by "blood," sprinkled "in the inmost place of the Sanctuary," and by "oyle," used to "hallow and sanctifie the Tabernacle and all therein." "When the priests were consecrate," Ainsworth continues, "the blood of their sacrifice was put upon their right eares, thumbs, and toes, and sprinckled upon their bodies and garments, that so they might be *sanctified*: The Holy Ghost thereby signifying, how by the blood of Christ much more, our consciences should be purged; and therefore calleth it, the *blood of the testament wherewith we are sanctified*" (pp. 57–63).[10]

From his definition of a twofold sanctification, one can see that Ainsworth places great emphasis on the internal operations of the Spirit of God. Such is particularly true of John Owen, who argues that the Spirit is *"the immediate peculiar sanctifier* of all believers, and the author of all holiness in them."[11] That emphasis upon the significance of the Spirit in the process of sanctification leads Owen to distinguish between what he calls true "evangelical holiness" and mere "philosophical morality": "There is hence sufficiently evidenced a comprehensive difference between a *spiritual life* unto God by *evangelical holiness*, and a *life of moral virtue*, though pretended unto God also. Unto the first the original and continual purification of our nature and persons by the Spirit of God and blood of Christ is indispensably required. Where this work is not, there neither is nor can be any thing of that holiness which the gospel prescribes, and which we inquire after." Unto the second, "we understand the powers, faculties, or abilities of our souls, exercised with respect and obedience unto the commands of God, as excited, persuaded, and guided by outward motives, rules, arguments, and consideration."[12] Whereas evangelical holiness is a "spiritual habit" of mind, philosophical morality is an "intellectual or moral habit of mind."[13] Whereas the first is the only true foundation of sanctification, the second, although praiseworthy, has nothing in itself to do with actual sanctification.[14]

Through its dismissal of the moral outlook as the basis of holiness, Owen's point of view represents the extreme to which renderings of the holy can take us. In this respect, the evangelical becomes as radical in its outlook as the cultic. Whereas a categorical physicality underlies the one, a categorical spirituality underlies the other. The one is external in its bearing, the other internal. Both, in turn, exclude the criteria of ethical behavior as necessary determinants in the process of consecration. Paradoxically, both converge in a relationship that draws upon the cultic characteristics of the one in order to suggest the spiritual characteristics of the other. Owen expresses that relationship in the following terms:

> To what end were so many meats and drinks, so many diseases and natural distempers, so many external fortuitous accidents, as touching the dead, and the like, made religiously unclean by the law? It was no other but to teach us the nature of the spiritual defilement of sin. And to the same end, together with a demonstration of the relief and remedy thereof, were the ordinances of purification instituted; which, as they were outward and carnal, purged those uncleannesses as they also were outward and carnal, made so by the law. But internal and spiritual things were taught and prefigured hereby, yea, wrought and effected, by virtue of their typical relation to Christ, as the apostle teacheth: Heb. ix. 13, 14, "If the blood of bulls and of goats, and the ashes of an heifer sprinkling the unclean, sanctifieth to the purifying of the flesh: how much more shall the blood of Christ purge your conscience from dead works to serve the living God?" And hence the whole work of sanctification is expressed by opening a fountain for sin and for uncleanness, that is, the purging of them away, Zech. xiii. 1.[15]

The foregoing makes clear once again what has already been shown to be true of the New Testament frame of mind inherited by the Christian tradition: the spiritual has its own *cultus*, prefigured in Old Testament views of the holy and fulfilled in the person of Christ as New Testament ἅγιος. If Owen sees that fulfillment completely in spiritual terms as the basis of evangelical holiness, Milton adopts a more nearly normative position by integrating the idea of ethical behavior into his overall scheme. In so doing, he is in the mainstream of those Renaissance theoreticians already examined.

Like those theoreticians, Milton is admirably adept at discoursing upon holiness in its various forms. In fact, the experience of the holy, as traced throughout the traditions that Milton inherited, is central to his religious outlook. The validity of this observation is discernible, among other places, in Milton's *Christian Doctrine*, which displays a fully developed exposition of the holy as cultic, moral, and finally as spiritual phenomenon.

The cultic point of view is well illustrated in the chapter entitled "De Ecclesia Visibili" in the first book of *Christian Doctrine*. In that chapter, Milton maintains that the practices of "the visible church," whose "tokens" are "not dissimilar [*non absimiles*]" from "the Jewish church [*ecclesiae Iudaicae*] enumerated by St. Paul," include "the proper external worship of God [*verus Dei cultus externus*]" (*CM*, 16:22). The idea is elaborated in the second book of *Christian Doctrine*, appropriately entitled "De Dei cultu." As this book indicates, Milton was as sensitive as any of his contemporaries to the cultic dimension of the holy, particularly as that dimension assumed the form of genuine religious worship. Referred to in Scripture as "*λατρεία*" or "service" (Matt. 4:10) and "*δουλεία*" or "obedience" (Matt. 6:24), this worship, Milton maintains, is the very foundation of "true religion." For Milton, "Vera religio est qua Deus ritu et ratione ab ipso praescripta sincere colitur" (*CM*, 17:75). The cultic mode of that *ritu et ratione* falls under the heading of "*adoratio*" or the "adoration of God" and "*sanctificatio*" or the "sanctification of the divine Name" (*CM*, 17:81). Adoration manifests itself in the proper, indeed "reverent," observance of "verus Dei cultus externus."

The sacraments of baptism and the Lord's Supper represent a case in point. Although "not absolutely indispensable," these, Milton says, should at least be celebrated in "a proper place and season" as "*obsignatione foederis gratiae externa*" (*CM*, 16:164, 201, 211). They are, in fact, "ordained by God" who uses his sacraments to "set his seal on believers in token of his saving grace, or of the satisfaction of Christ," and by means of the sacraments "we . . . testify our obedience to God" (*CM*, 16:165). Accordingly, as an expression of "external sealing," the sacraments of baptism and the Lord's Supper retain for Milton a cultic legitimacy. Although not in themselves sacred, they become "religious emblems, or symbols of things sacred [*res sacras significent*]" (*CM*, 6:215–17).

In the case of the Lord's Supper, for example, the elements of the sacrament become seals of that which is sacred, namely, the body of Christ (*Sanctum Christi corpus*) (*CM*, 16:212). As such, they become emblems of that theophany by which the Son of God assumed incarnate form in order to sacrifice himself for man. They become insignias of what for Milton was one of the deepest religious mysteries, the Incarnation itself (*CM*, 15:263–65). If they are not to be worshiped, they are to be seen as visible and legitimate manifestations of the sacred things that *are* to be worshiped. In the cultus externus, they are the means by which we are to become "priests" in Christ (*CM*, 16:209). So conceived, they serve their appropriate purpose. When, however, they are worshiped for their own sake as things in themselves sacred or as possessing the efficacy of that which is sacred, they lead to sacrilege, which Milton defines as "the appropriation to private uses of things dedicated to God [*res Deo devotas*]" (*CM*, 17:117). Milton supports his view with the following significant proof texts: "[ye offer polluted bread upon mine altar; and ye say, Wherein have we polluted thee? . . .] And if ye offer the blind for sacrifice, *is it* not evil?" (Mal. 1:[7]–8), and "It is a snare to the man who devoureth that which is holy" (Prov. 20:25).

The second citation recalls Milton's view of the Roman Mass. There, "the sacred body of Christ . . . is broken and crushed, and bruised by the teeth not only of men but of brutes; till, having passed through the whole process of digestion, it is cast out at length into the draught, a profanation too horrible to be alluded to without shuddering" (*CM*, 16:213). Such a statement reflects Milton's professed adoration of that which is truly sacred and the horror that he feels when the holy undergoes a profanation of any kind. Milton is uncompromising in his expression of disgust toward anything that profanes the holy. In the Mass, this profanation occurs, Milton maintains, because the Papists insist upon attributing to the elements of the sacrament inherent sanctity, that is, the real presence of Christ himself. Seeing in the elements Christ's sacred body rather than the symbols of his body, they have "converted the Supper of the Lord into a banquet of cannibals" (*CM*, 16:197).

Considering the grimness of that statement, one might say that Milton's views regarding the exact province of res Deo devotas observe a scrupulousness, even a literalness, that is reverential or "religious" in the highest degree. In this instance, his reverence provides for the legitimacy of "things" as long as they remain "symbols of things sacred" and not "sacred things" in themselves, to be worshiped for their own sake. The holy has its place and things that manifest the holy theirs. When the two are confused, when the things that should serve as the transmission of the holy are looked upon themselves as inherently holy, sacrilege results, "the appropriation to private uses of things dedicated to God." That is why, Milton says, "the brazen serpent, the type of Christ, was commanded to be demolished, as soon as it became the object of religious worship, 2 Kings XVIII. 4" (*CM*, 17:141).

This statement suggests, in brief, the basis of Milton's iconoclasm, of his unwillingness to tolerate "false worship" in any form. Accordingly, he decries in *Paradise Lost*, as shall be explored in greater detail, the sacrilege that results when the "Devils," adored "for Deities," "durst" place "thir Altars" by God's "Altar," "thir Shrines" within "his Sanctuary," "and with cursed things / His holy Rites, and solemn Feasts profan'd" (1.373–90). Such an outlook underlies the rationale of *ΕΙΚΟΝΟΚΛΑΣΤΗΣ*. Because he cannot tolerate the worshiping of an *Εἰκὼν Βασιλική*, Milton explains that he chose the title "*Iconoclastes*, the famous Surname of

Many Greek Emperors, who in their zeal to the command of God, after long tradition of Idolatry in the Church, took courage, and broke all superstitious Images to peeces" (*CM*, 5:68).

That iconoclastic outlook, however, should not be taken to indicate that Milton is calling into question either the impulse to venerate the holy or the embodiment of the holy in res Deo devotas. When such things are properly used, they have a definite place in the verus Dei cultus externus. The cherubic images over the ark are a case in point. Milton defends their presence against the charge of idolatry, since they are not themselves "objects of worship" but representations of "the ministering spirits of Jehovah" who ordered them made by a "special commandment" (*CM*, 17:141). As such, they embody God's spirit as the manifestation of his "force and power" (*virtute et potentia*) (*CM*, 15:362–63). They accordingly have about them the aura of the "divine potency" (*virtutes divinae*) that Milton did not hesitate to ascribe to the Holy Spirit in its most archaic form (*CM*, 15:366, 367). In this way, they become vehicles of the theophany, "symbols of things sacred" that are fundamental to the notion of adoratio. If this is the case, they are likewise fundamental to the corresponding notion of sanctificatio.

For Milton, sanctificatio involves the "hallowing" or "consecration" of God's name as that which encompasses all other res Deo devotas. We should sanctify this name through "zeal," which is "an ardent desire" to consecrate or hallow "in word as well as in deed." "To hallow it in word is never to name it but with a religious purpose" and, at the risk of "blasphemy" (*Βλασφημία*), never to subject it to "irreverence" or "jest" (*CM*, 17:153–55). Through the process of sanctificatio, we are "separated" to a "particular form of worship [*ad cultum externum*]" (*CM*, 15:374–75). Far from impugning the consecratory impulse, then, Milton insists upon its primacy in the adoration and sanctification of the holy. His sense of religious observance, his sensitivity to the demands of the holy as a cultic phenomenon, is as genuine as the most religious of his contemporaries. For him, the cultic view of the holy retains its original force, even though the Mosaic law, and with it the holiness code, is abrogated by the New Dispensation.

Milton's attitude on this is clear: "On the introduction of the gospel, or new covenant through faith in Christ, the whole of the preceding covenant, in other words, the entire Mosaic law, was abolished" (*CM*, 16:125). Despite such a statement, however, Milton does not hesitate to attest to the legitimacy of the religious sentiment underlying ceremonial law. "Consecrated to God from the beginning of the world [*ab initio quidem mundi a Deo consecratus*]," the Sabbath, for example, was commanded to be observed by the Israelites "for a variety of reasons," says Milton; if we do not currently observe the Sabbath, as the Israelites did, that does not negate the appropriateness of its original institution. It was instituted, first, "as a memorial of God's having completed the work of creation on the seventh day," second, as a way of "distinguishing" or "separat[ing] the Israelites from other nations," third, as a means by which "slaves and cattle might enjoy a respite from labor," fourth, as a "remembrance of their [the Israelites'] liberation from Egypt," and fifth, "as a shadow or type of things to come" (CM, 17:169–75). Although "the Israelites alone are enjoined to observe it [the Sabbath]," the reasons for such observance apply "equally," or universally, to all other nations (CM, 17:171). The same, Milton maintains, is true of other aspects of the ceremonial law, such as "the command to abstain from creeping things, Lev. xi. 44. 'Ye shall therefore sanctify yourselves, and ye shall be holy, for I am holy; neither shall ye defile yourselves with any manner of creeping thing that creepeth upon the earth.'" Although this and similar precepts are themselves "no longer obligatory" and appear in fact "unreasonable" in light of gospel law, Milton still maintains that "the reasons on which these precepts are founded apply equally to believers in general, and to all ages [*rationes enim istae ad omnes etiam nunc fideles aeque pertinent, ad quos praecepta ipsa non pertinent*] (CM, 17:171–73, 6:36).

Judging by such statements, then, Milton's attitude toward the holy is as universal or comprehensive as that of a Mede or a Hall. Like them, he adopts a decidedly ecumenical outlook concerning the fundamental principle of the holy that governs even outmoded cultic practices. Such is true in his views on divorce, among other places. In *Christian Doctrine*, for example, he returns us to the spirit of Mosaic law to justify divorce when it is "positively commanded for the most sacred religious reasons [*religionis rationes sanctissimas severe praescribunt*]." In these cases, "marriage . . . gives place to religion," embodied in the "natural aversion with which we turn from whatever is unclean." In this sense, Christ "permitted divorce for the cause of fornication," which signifies "not adultery only but . . . what is called 'any unclean thing' [*res turpis aliqua dicitur*]," as may be seen in Deuteronomy 24:1, among other passages (CM, 15:167–71; T, CM, 4:113–14).

Accordingly, divorce becomes a separation of holy and profane, clean and unclean. For Milton, uncleanness comes to have a decidedly moral, if not spiritual, significance (T, CM, 4:198), but even here, the residue of the archaic concept of holiness—as קדש—continues to linger with not a little of its original force. Milton is quite able and quite willing to marshal that force when it suits his purpose. For the rationale underlying the holy as cultic entity still prevails in his thinking despite its abrogation by the New Dispensation. It may even be assimilated, if done so properly, in the verus Dei cultus externus, the "holy Rites" of God that constitute the practices "*de ecclesia visibili*." I have made this point at some length because the transformation of the Miltonic perspective from cultic to moral and finally to spiritual may tempt one to slight the prevailing cultic basis of Milton's outlook.

That dimension of his outlook that pertains to the holy as a moral category may be seen once again in the discourse on cultus in *Christian Doctrine*. There, Milton associates true cultus with moral perfection. Cultus becomes a decidedly moral act. As Milton says, "The true worship of God consists chiefly in the exercise of good works [*verus Dei cultus in studio bonorum operum praecipue positus est*]." "GOOD WORKS ARE THOSE WHICH WE PERFORM BY THE SPIRIT OF GOD WORKING IN US THROUGH TRUE FAITH, TO THE GLORY OF GOD, THE ASSURED HOPE OF OUR OWN SALVATION, AND THE EDIFICATION OF OUR NEIGHBOR" (*CM*, 17:2–5). Although Milton makes use of a number of proof texts to reinforce his point of view, his citation of Philippians 4:8–9 is particularly relevant: "Whatsoever things are true, whatsoever things *are* honest, whatsoever things *are* just, whatsoever things *are* pure, whatsoever things *are* lovely, whatsoever things *are* of good report, if *there be* any virtue, and if *there be* any praise, think on these things: those things which ye have both learned, and received, and heard, and seen in me, do; and the God of peace shall be with you" (*CM*, 17:2–5). The importance of this citation is that it draws upon the familiar idea of the holy as a category of things in order to suggest that which is "value oriented," rather than "thing oriented." Within this context, sacred things are deprived of their physicality: they occupy a moral sphere characterized by such virtues as truth, honesty, justice, ethical purity, loveliness, and goodness. These characteristics represent the moral dimension of Milton's res Deo devotas.

Involving the "cultivation of devout affections" ("LOVE, TRUST, HOPE, GRATITUDE, HUMILITY, PATIENCE, OBEDIENCE"), such characteristics constitute "internal worship," which must be united "in practice" with "external worship"; "nor are they ever separated, except by the impiety of sinners" (*CM*, 17:51, 73–75). "Internal worship, or worship of the heart," however, "is accepted of God even where external forms are not in all respects duly observed." Proof texts here include 2 Chronicles 30:18–20: "A multitude of the people . . . had not cleansed themselves, yet did they eat the passover . . . but Hezekiah prayed for them, saying, The good Jehovah pardon every one that prepareth his heart to seek

God, Jehovah God of his fathers, though he be not cleansed according to the purification of the sanctuary: and Jehovah hearkened to Hezekiah, and healed the people" (CM, 17:79–80). Such a view accounts for Milton's belief in the "superfluousness of set forms of worship," particularly in praying by rote, "in an unknown tongue," in a prescribed "posture" and "deportment" of the body, and in a fixed place or time (CM, 17:85–95). Too great an emphasis on these externalities for their own sake violates the true nature of cultus, which corresponds to the essentially moral holiness of God.

As the source of all holiness, God embodies "moral perfection." In him, holiness and moral perfection are synonymous (T, CM, 4:112). Accordingly, Milton describes God in *Christian Doctrine* as "INFINITELY PURE AND HOLY." He is "glorious in holiness" (Exod. 15:11). Only the trisagion, "*sanctus, sanctus, sanctus*," of Isaiah 6:3, befits him. In his holiness, he is "of purer eyes than to behold evil" (Hab. 1:13); "the heavens are not clean in his sight" (Job 15:15) (CM, 14:57). He inspires godliness, "that which is our beginning, regeneration, and happiest end, likenes to *God*" (R, CM, 3:37). In that likeness, we "love him" and "imitate him, as we may the neerest by possessing our souls of true virtue, which being united to the heavenly grace of faith makes up the highest perfection" (E, CM, 4:277).

Possessing godliness, man is aware of his own worth through a "pious and just honouring" of himself: "He that holds himself in reverence and due esteem, both for the dignity of Gods image upon him, and for the price of his redemption . . . accounts himselfe both a fit person to do the noblest and godliest deeds, and much better worth then to deject and defile, with such a debasement and such a pollution as sin is, himself so highly ransom'd and enobl'd to a new friendship and filiall relation with God" (CG, CM, 3:260–61). Having reached "this hill top of sanctity and goodness," he is given a new perspective. "As he is call'd by the high calling of God to be holy and pure, so is he by the same appointment or-dain'd, and by the Churches call admitted to such offices of discipline in the Church to which his own spirituall gifts by the example of Apostolick institution have autoriz'd him" (CG, CM, 3:261).

This new perspective allows him to reevaluate his standing with respect to the holy. Emancipated from the restrictions of "dead judaisms," he is no longer "to have an unworthy and abject opinion" of himself, "to approach to holy duties with a slavish fear," to think of himself as "unconsecrated," "unhallow'd," and "unclean," to feel himself separated by "a wide and terrible distance" between himself and "religious things," such as "Temples," "carpets," "table-clothes," and "flagon pot[s]." Rendered "more sacred then any dedicated altar or element," he is able to "open his eyes to a wise and true evaluation of himselfe," to show himself "worthy the honourable and grave imployment wherewith God and the Church hath dignifi'd him: not fearing lest he should meet with some outward holy thing in religion which his lay touch or presence might profane, but lest something unholy from within his own heart should dishonour and profane in himselfe that Priestly unction and Clergy-right whereto Christ hath entitl'd him. Then would the congregation of the Lord soone recover the true likeness and visage of what she is indeed, a holy generation, a royall Priesthood, a Saintly communion, the houshold and City of God" (CG, CM, 3:261–62).

Such a statement should indicate the major reorientation that the holy undergoes in Milton's thought. Holiness is not without but within, not an attribute of things but of self, meant not to denigrate but to ennoble, meant not to separate but to unite. Within the framework of this reorientation, man is both a royal priest and saint. Precisely how he achieves this stature may be seen in Milton's emphasis upon the holy not only as a moral category but as a spiritual category as well. What results is a distinction between man's "approved good life in the eye and testimony of the Church" and man's "place of spirituall government" within the Church (CG, CM, 3:262).

Corresponding to the latter perspective, Milton viewed the Church as an invisible entity. Drawing upon Ephesians 4:13–16 and 1 Corinthians 12:12–31, among other passages, Milton states in *Christian Doctrine* that the "*ecclesia invisibilis*" or "*corpus mysticum*" is the product of the "union and fellowship of the regenerate with the Father and Christ, and of the members of Christ's body among themselves" (CM, 16:61–63). These members, "composed of individuals of widely separated countries, and of all ages from the foundation of the world," are drawn together by a "mystical" fellowship in order to accord with the body of Christ, which is "mystically one" (CM, 16:63). Milton's proof text is Ephesians 2:19–22: "Now therefore ye are no more strangers and foreigners, but fellow citizens with the saints, and of the household of God; and are built upon the foundation of the apostles and prophets, Jesus Christ himself being the chief corner-stone; in whom all the building fitly framed together, groweth unto a holy temple in the Lord: in whom ye also are builded together for an habitation of God through the Spirit" (CM, 16:63–65).

The ecclesia invisibilis is held together, in turn, through "the love of Christ" (*Amor Christi*) (CM, 16:63–65). This love is essential to the spiritual rendering of the holy. Accordingly, Amor Christi finds its counterpart in "*caritas*," which results "from a consciousness and lively sense of the love wherewith [God in Christ] has loved us, and which in theology is reckoned the third after faith and hope" (*CM*, 16:11). For Milton, such caritas is synonymous with none other than cultus (*CM*, 17:2–3). As Milton describes it, caritas "ARIS[ES] FROM A SENSE OF THE DIVINE LOVE SHED ABROAD IN THE HEARTS OF THE REGENERATE BY THE SPIRIT, WHEREBY THOSE WHO ARE INGRAFTED IN CHRIST BEING INFLUENCED, BECOME DEAD TO SIN, AND ALIVE AGAIN UNTO GOD, AND BRING FORTH GOOD WORKS SPONTANEOUSLY AND FREELY. This is also called HOLINESS [*sanctitas*]. Eph. i. 4: 'that we should be holy and without blame before him in love'" (*CM*, 16:8–9). "In consequence of this love or sanctity all believers are called SAINTS [*sancti*]" (*CM*, 16:14–15). They become *sancti* in a twofold manner: through ingrafting and through regeneration. "Of this ingrafting, combined with regeneration, the effects are NEWNESS OF LIFE and INCREASE." From the first point of view, "the primary functions of the new life are comprehension of spiritual things, and love of holiness [*intelligentia rerum spiritualium, et caritas sive sanctitas vitae*]" (*CM*, 16:4–5).

For the purposes of this study, such a statement is of immense importance because it indicates the way in which Milton's view of the holy is all encompassing. That view is one which comprehends not only the nature of sacred things but the nature of spiritual things as well. Elaborating upon the spiritual dimension, Milton says that "THE COMPREHENSION OF SPIRITUAL THINGS IS A HABIT OR CONDITION OF THE MIND PRODUCED BY GOD, WHEREBY THE NATURAL IGNORANCE OF THOSE WHO BELIEVE AND ARE ENGRAFTED IN CHRIST IS REMOVED, AND THEIR UNDERSTANDING ENLIGHTENED FOR THE PERCEPTION OF HEAVENLY THINGS, SO THAT, BY THE TEACHING OF GOD, THEY KNOW ALL THAT IS NECESSARY FOR ETERNAL SALVATION AND THE TRUE HAPPINESS OF LIFE" (*CM*, 16:7). The effect of regeneration is a "spiritual increase" (*spiritualis auctio*) (*CM*, 16:16–19) that is implicit in the following definition: "REGENERATION IS THAT CHANGE OPERATED BY THE WORD AND THE SPIRIT, WHEREBY THE OLD MAN BEING DESTROYED, THE INWARD MAN IS REGENERATED BY GOD AFTER HIS OWN IMAGE, IN ALL THE FACULTIES OF HIS MIND, INSOMUCH THAT HE BECOMES AS IT WERE A NEW CREATURE, AND THE WHOLE MAN IS SANCTIFIED BOTH IN BODY AND SOUL, FOR THE SERVICE OF GOD, AND THE PERFORMANCE OF GOOD WORKS" (*CM*, 16:367). The whole process is depicted through the idea of cleansing, reinforced by such proof texts as Ephesians 5:26 ("that he might sanctify and cleanse it with the washing of water by the Word") and Titus 3:5 ("by the washing of regeneration and renewing of the Holy Ghost") (*CM*, 15:369). In that way do we undergo regeneration or sanctification in the gradual process leading to purification (*CM*, 15:377).

Milton traces the course of that process in the step-by-step account of "renovation" (including "repentance," "faith," "justification," "adoption," and "glorification") that *Christian Doctrine* provides. Repentance and faith initiate the process. Whereas repentance (μετάνοια) involves a humble "TURNING TO GOD" and an effort "TO FOLLOW RIGHTEOUSNESS," "faith" is that "FULL PERSUASION" "WHEREBY WE BELIEVE . . . THAT WHATSOEVER THINGS HE [God] HAS PROMISED IN CHRIST ARE OURS, AND ESPECIALLY THE GRACE OF ETERNAL LIFE" (*CM*, 15:379, 393). Thereafter follows justification, "WHEREBY THOSE WHO ARE REGENERATE AND INGRAFTED IN CHRIST ARE ABSOLVED FROM SIN AND DEATH THROUGH HIS MOST PERFECT SATISFACTION, AND ACCOUNTED JUST IN THE SIGHT OF GOD" (*CM*, 16:25). So justified, the regenerate undergo adoption as the children of God (*CM*, 16:51). In that way, they become part of the Invisible Church and experience a twofold glorification: the first ("imperfect") "is that state wherein, being JUSTIFIED AND ADOPTED BY GOD THE FATHER, WE ARE FILLED WITH A CONSCIOUSNESS OF PRESENT GRACE AND EXCELLENCY, AS WELL AS WITH AN EXPECTATION OF FUTURE GLORY, INSOMUCH THAT OUR BLESSEDNESS IS IN A MANNER ALREADY BEGUN"; the second ("perfect") is that whereby the regenerate "WILL AT LENGTH MOST CERTAINLY ATTAIN TO EVERLASTING LIFE AND THE CONSUMMATION OF GLORY" (*CM*, 16:65, 71). The first is effected in this life, the second in the next (*CM*, 16:337). Typified by the translation of Enoch (Gen. 5:24), "perfect glorification" involves the ultimate apotheosis, the "*visio Dei*" (*CM*, 16:337, 374–75). That vision will be experienced by those to whom salvation has been assured. "This assurance," says Milton, "produces a joy unspeakable" (*CM*, 16:75).

The full realization of the holy in spiritual terms leads to the ultimate point of perfect glorification in the experience of salvation. Holiness in its various forms (cultic, moral, and spiritual) is consummated here. But this, after all, is none other than the Christian paradigm, recapitulated in the doctrinal language of Milton's theological treatise. Whatever departures from orthodoxy that treatise may embody, it expresses a universality of sentiment toward a phenomenon that is basic to religious thought. With its sources in the Greco-Roman and Judeo-Christian cultures, that thought gave rise to a view of the holy that found its way into the Renaissance and manifested itself in a complexity of renderings.

Part 2
"The Sacred Vein"

3
Sacral Poetics

If one were to envision pictorially Milton's view of the poet, he could ask for no truer representations than those that accompany Blake's *Milton*. From the numinous perspective, one thinks particularly of the figure emerging from a luminous background, his head surrounded by the rays of the fiery nimbus that enhances the numinosity of his "lineaments divine" (see figure 1). Albeit ungirded, the figure in that illustration is entirely in keeping with Milton's conception of the poet as an embodiment of the holy. In Milton's self-depiction in *Mansus* as a poet-hierophant, he is "far-removed" to the "secret world" (*secreti mundi*) of the gods, where, in an apotheosis, he is "suffused with brilliant light [*suffundar lumine*] on . . . [his] serene face" (94–99).

The hierophantic vision is characteristically Miltonic. At least as early as *Elegia sexta* (1629) to Charles Diodati, he writes of the poet as a priest who, "shining with sacred vestment and lustral waters," goes before "the hostile gods" (65–66). "For truly," Milton says, "the poet is sacred to the gods and priest of the gods, / and his hidden heart and lips breathe Jove" (*Diis etenim sacer est vates, divûmque sacerdos, / Spirat et occultum pectus, et ora Jovem*) (77–78). He is one "who records wars and heavens under mature Jove, / And pious heroes and half-divine leaders, . . . who sings the sacred counsels of the supreme gods" and "the infernal realms bayed by the fierce dog" (55–58). A drinker of "nonintoxicating potions from the pure spring," he combines both moral and cultic purity, a nature void of "stain" (61–64). As such, he lives like the ascetic Pythagoras, has the prophetic powers of a Tiresias, and the magic of an Orpheus (60, 67–70). His songs are comparable to "the one poor of feast," Homer, "drinker of water" (71). The allusions anticipate those that are to gain genuine poignancy in *Paradise Lost*, in which, as models for his "sacred Song," he invokes "Blind *Thamyris* and blind *Maeonides*, / And *Tiresias* and *Phineus* Prophets old" (3.35–36). With them, he creates oracular poetry, the product of a "sacred rage" that transports him, as he sings in *Elegia quinta* (1629), to the "secret temples of the gods" (17–22). "Made delirious" and "agitate[d] . . . from within," he

FIGURE 1. Blake's Conception of Milton.
Reproduced from plate 16, in William Blake, *Milton* (1804),
by permission of the Library of Congress, Rosenwald Collection,
Washington, D.C.

becomes an oracle of Apollo (11–12). Inspired by Apollo's "sacred and ethereal fire," Milton wrote to Alexander Gill in 1628, the poet is one whose life is "the whole breath" of Phoebus (FE, CM, 12:7–9).

The concept receives even further elaboration in *Ad Patrem* (1638?), in which Milton compares the poet to "the priestesses of Apollo" who "disclose the mysteries of the distant future" (24–25) and to "the sacrificial priest" who "composes songs at altars, / both when he strews about the altar pieces of the bull which shakes its golden horns / and when, sagacious, he consults hidden destinies / in the streaming entrails" (26–29). As Milton says in *Ad Salsillum* (1638), the poet should be heeded, for "this man is your priest" (*hic tuus sacerdos est*) (26). Accordingly, Milton states in *The Reason of Church-Government* that the office of the poet corresponds to that of the pulpit. By means of his "glorious and lofty Hymns," the poet in his priestly role "celebrate[s] . . . the throne and equipage of Gods Almightinesse" and inspires a proper regard for "Gods true worship" (CM, 3:238).

To use Christ's words in *Paradise Regained*, the poems of the poet as hierophant are "*Sion*'s songs" that celebrate "the Holiest of Holies, and his Saints" (4. 347–49). In that capacity, the poet concerns himself with "whatsoever in religion is holy and sublime." His work is the direct result of offering "devout prayer to that eternall Spirit who can enrich with all utterance and knowledge, and sends out his Seraphim with the hallow'd fire of his Altar to touch and purify the lips of whom he pleases" (CG, CM, 3:238–41). Singing in what the *Nativity Ode* calls the "sacred vein" (15), the poet as priest derives his inspiration from God's "secret Altar toucht with hallow'd fire" (28). (Compare Isaiah 6:6–7: "Then flew one of the seraphims unto me, having a live coal in his hand, *which* he had taken with the tongs from off the altar: And he laid *it* upon my mouth, and said, Lo, this hath touched thy lips.") As priest, in turn, the poet is to be distinguished from all profane poets, those "libidinous and ignorant Poetasters," "vulgar Amorist[s]," and "riming parasite[s]" for whom Milton has nothing but contempt (CG, CM, 3:239–41).

The foregoing statements should indicate what might be called Milton's hierophantic poetics, in which the poet emerges not only as *sacer vates* but as *sacerdos*, not only as prophet but as priest. Although Milton's view of the poet as prophet has received ample consideration, the peculiar nature of the poet as priest has not received the consideration it merits.[1] Considering the long tradition that established the poet's priestly role and Milton's emphasis upon the poet as priest in his works, such a fact is surprising. To rectify this oversight, then, it might be advisable to say something about the tradition of the poet as sacerdos and Milton's understanding of that tradition before discussing the way in which the sacerdotal role is incorporated into his poetry.

At the outset, one matter should be made clear. For Milton, as for the traditions that he inherited, the roles of sacerdos and vates were largely interchangeable. In his poetry, the two are mentioned together with almost a formulaic quality. Thus, in the *Nativity Ode*, he says, "No nightly trance, or breathed spell, / Inspires the pale-ey'd Priest from the prophetic cell" (179–80). In the prose, that formulaic quality persists. Appropriately, *Christian Doctrine* speaks of the law of Moses "committed to the trust and guardianship of the priest and prophets [*custodes sacerdotes, prophetae aliique divinitus*]" (CM, 16:276–77). Throughout his works, Milton makes a point of underplaying specific doctrinal distinctions between the two. In fact, the priestly and prophetic roles are ones that may be shared by everybody. Each man, Milton maintains, should be his own priest, as much as he should be his own prophet. In a way, Milton would have "all the Lords people" become both priests and prophets (cf. AR, CM, 4:342–43; Num. 11:27–29). To be a priest, one need only be "inspir'd from God" with an "extraordinary calling"; to be a prophet, one need only be "endowed with extraordinary piety and wisdom" (A, CM, 3:155; CD, CM, 16:245). In neither case is there required a laying on of hands for ordination; rather, "it is the inward calling of God" that makes a man both priest and prophet, both sacerdos and vates (A, CM, 3:156).

Collapsing the distinctions between priest and prophet, Milton points out that both before and after the law of Moses priests and prophets shared similar responsibilities having to do with the promulgation of God's word through "teaching and exhortation [*docet et exhortatur*]." In this sense, "Aaron and his posterity, the whole tribe of Levi, and lastly the prophets" performed comparable functions. "In like manner," Milton argues, "anyone appearing to be in other respects qualified, was allowed to teach openly in the synagogue, though he were neither priest nor Levite; a permission which was granted to Christ, and subsequently to Paul at Antioch" (CD, CM, 16:238–41). From the Miltonic point of view, then, to concern oneself with the role of sacerdos is concurrently to concern oneself with the role of vates, a fact which is likewise accounted for by the mentioning of the two almost as synonyms in the traditions that Milton inherited.

At the same time, however, Milton is careful to make some important discriminations that should be understood before considering the traditions. Discussing Christ as mediator in *Christian Doctrine*, Milton considers his "threefold functions as PROPHET, PRIEST, and KING, and his manner of administering the same." The first two functions only are important to this discussion. Fulfilled in Christ, the function of the "prophet" (*propheticum*)[2] is "to instruct" (*erudire*) in "heavenly truth" (*coelesti veritate*) and to "declare" (*edocere*) the "will" (*voluntatem*) of God. Through him, truth is promulgated and understanding illuminated. In that capacity, the prophet may "preach" and "build temples," as well as "counsel" and "bear witness" (Isa. 61:1; Zech. 6:12, 13; Isa. 9:6; Rev. 1:5). Fulfilled in Christ, the function of the "priest" (*sacerdotale*), on the other hand, is to offer "sacrifice for sinners" (*pro peccatoribus hostiam*) and to "make intercession for us" (*proque nobis . . . intercesset*). Through him, the practices of the temple are manifested. In that capacity, the priest concerns himself with "sacred offerings," acts of "propitiation," and appearances before the "presence of God" in the sanctuary (Ephes. 5:12; 1 John 4:10; Heb. 9:24). He patterns himself after "the order of Melchizedek," the "high priest" (*summus sacerdos*) of God (Heb. 5:10; CM, 15:286–97).

Accordingly, one might say that if Milton distinguishes between prophet and priest, he does so by conceiving the prophetic role fundamentally in exhortative terms and the priestly role fundamentally in cultic terms. As discussed, both roles represent opposite sides of the same coin, and perhaps this is a matter of degrees of emphasis rather than of distinctions of kind. Nevertheless, I shall distinguish the two as a way of complementing the "prophetic" or "visionary" Milton with what I shall call the "priestly Milton."[3] This is the sacerdos, sacred to the gods, attired in holy vestments, purified by lustral waters, inspired with oracular knowledge, touched with holy fire, discloser of mysteries, performer of sacrifices, composer of hymns before the altar.

The traditions that conceive the poet as priest are not only Greco-Roman but Judeo-Christian. Thus, both in the *Ion* and in the *Phaedrus*, Plato associates the poet in his frenzy with the priests and prophets of Apollo. If Apollo inspires his seers with divine madness, the Muses inspire their poets with a similar kind of madness.[4] Through "inspired Prophecy," the poet, like "the prophetess at Delphi and the priestesses at Dodona," has "conferred great benefit on Hellas, both in public and private life."[5] As such, the poet is "holy," a prophet whose works are divine.[6] Such ideas are so well known that they hardly need to be repeated; yet they do constitute one major tradition within which Milton was working. Plato's attitude, of course, shifts from dialogue to dialogue, as, for example, his view of poets in *The Republic* (8.568) indicates. Even the *Ion* (533–34) is not without irony in its references to the poets. Nonetheless, the hierophantic-vatic outlook is as firmly entrenched in

Plato as anywhere. The cultic, the oracular, and, by implication, the pure as aspects of the holy are no less characteristic of the poet in Plato than they are in Milton.

So pervasive are these ideas in Greek thought that they emerge centuries later in Plutarch, who does not hesitate to associate the poet with this hierophantic-vatic outlook. In his discourse on the Pythian priestess, for example, Plutarch singles out, among other poets, Simonides, with whom he associates "a temple dedicated to the Muses, close by the source of the rivulet, whence . . . [was drawn] water for the sacrifices." Performing such sacrifices was in accord with the dictates of Simonides.[7] These sacrifices, in turn, are comparable to those performed by the priestesses of Apollo, to whom are offered victims and for whom the holy wine is poured. Like the poets mentioned by Plato, the hierophants are set apart as divine and deliver their oracles in a state of divine possession.[8] As part of their separation, these hierophants are obliged to "virginity and chastity" all their days. Thus, Plutarch says of the Pythian priestess, she must "keep her body pure and clean from the company of men, there being no stranger permitted to converse with her. And before she goes to the oracle, they are used by certain marks to examine whether she be fit or no, believing that the God certainly knows when her body is disposed and fit to receive . . . this enthusiastical inspiration."[9] As with Plato, it may be questioned how committed Plutarch is to the entire oracular atmosphere that he invokes. After all, Plutarch argues that he is "the best prophet" and "the wisest man" who "takes reason" for his "guide."[10] Nonetheless, this view does not discount the oracular-sacerdotal concept of the poet so basic to Greek thought. If anything, the view reinforces the concept as one that Plutarch felt called upon to confront in his works. As Michael Murrin indicates, it flourished in the Orphic religion and had a profound impact on the Renaissance.[11] If for Milton "the Oracles are dumm" (N, 173), the oracular is very much alive.

It was very much alive for the Romans too. Both Cicero and Horace defend poets as holy men and prophets, and Ovid refers to the poet as "the unstained priest of Phoebus and the Muses [*Musarum purus Phoebique sacerdos*]." "Yes," Ovid maintains, "we bards are called sacred, and the care of the gods; there are those who even think we have the god within [*at sacri vates et divum cura vocamur; sunt etiam qui nos numen habere putent*]."[12] One of the most enlightening of such views is that of Propertius, who conceives the poet in distinctly hierophantic terms in his elegies: "Shade of Callimachus and sacred rites of Philetus, suffer me, I pray, to enter your grove. I am the first with priestly service from an unsullied spring to carry Italian mysteries among the dances of Greece.

Tell me, in what grotto did ye weave your songs together? With what step did ye enter? What sacred fountain did ye drink? [*Callimachi Manes et Coi sacra Philetae, in vestrum, quaesa me sinite ire nemus primus ego ingredior puro de fonte sacerdos Itala per Graios orgia ferre choros. Dicite, quo pariter carmen tenuastis in anto? quove pede ingressi? Quomve bibistis aquam?*]."[13]

For Milton, however, the figure whose example would be most compelling is that of Vergil. Invoking Orpheus and Linus to establish his own oracular credentials in *Eclogue* 4, Vergil associates himself through Aeneas with the Sibylline priestess of Book 6 of the *Aeneid*. As he prays before the shrine of the Sybil, Aeneas placates the "holy seer" (*sanctissima vates*) of Phoebus with prayer. His mode of worship, Vergil implies, finds its counterpart in that of Orpheus with his "Thracian lyre." In his own way, Vergil too becomes a sacerdos of Phoebus and the Muses.[14] Although it would be possible to invoke additional analogues, the foregoing should suggest something of the Greco-Roman milieu out of which emerged Milton's view of the poet as priest. As indicated, the view is no less important to the Judeo-Christian worlds.

In ancient Israel, prophet (נביא) and priest (כהן) shared similar functions: both gave "oracular direction" and engaged in the cult of the temple. As such, their roles were not dissimilar to those of the hierophants that were responsible for the Oracle at Delphi. Like the hierophants of the cultus of the Tyrian Baal, for example, they were both seers and specialists in the rituals of sacrifice. More than that, however, their roles converged in what might be called the "poetic," for the cultic hierophants "appear to form the personnel of the Temple choirs." The verbal form נבא, in fact, means "to prophesy" and "is used to denote the specific function of the Temple singers."[15] That these are not associations that would be lost on Milton may be seen first by his references, already noted, in *Christian Doctrine* (CM, 16:238–41) to the ancient biblical conflation of priest and prophet and to his celebration, once again in *Christian Doctrine* (CM, 15:140–41), of "the holy prophets in their inspired hymns [*sanctissimi prophetae in suis divinis carminibus*]."

In the Judaic tradition, these ideas reach their fulfillment in the works of Philo. Reflecting his Hellenistic background, Philo does not hesitate to conflate the roles of prophet, priest, and poet: all such roles are embodied in the figure of Moses. Thus, in his works *On the Life of Moses* and *On the Creation of the World*, Philo suggests that Moses is to be seen not only as a king and lawgiver, his usual roles, but as one "instructed by the sacred oracles of God in everything that related to the sacred offices and ministrations" of "the high priesthood." In that capacity, Moses is the supreme rhetorician and relater of divine events, that is, a veritable "poet" who "recorded" the world's "creation, giving a very venerable account of God."[16] Professing an admiration both for Philo and for his views on Moses, Milton ascribed wholeheartedly to these associations (cf. 1 D, CM, 7:79). For Milton, Moses becomes both high priest and prophet, in short, God's "Mediator" (PL, 12.235–60; CD, CM, 15:287). In this hierophantic role, Moses is likewise conceived of as primal poet, who recounts the processes of creation. As such, he appears in the Trinity Manuscript's third draft of a drama on the Fall (CM, 18:229): "Moses προλογίζει" (speaks a prologue) within the "pure" confines of God's "mount." With a similar idea in mind, Milton refers in *Paradise Lost* to "that Shepherd, who, . . . on the secret top / Of *Oreb*, or of *Sinai*, . . . first taught the chosen Seed, / In the Beginning how the Heav'n and Earth / Rose out of *Chaos*" (1.6–10).[17]

For both Philo and Milton, then, the roles of prophet-priest-poet find consummate expression in the figure of Moses.[18] Appropriately, Philo conceives Moses' life in cultic terms reminiscent of Milton's view of the poet as one who is pure in nature, an undefiled ascetic. "Before assuming . . . [the priestly] office," Philo says of Moses, "it was necessary for him to purify not only his soul but also his body, so that it should be connected with and defiled by no passion, but should be pure from everything which is of a mortal nature, from all meat and drink, and from all connection with women." Abstaining from "all meat and drink for forty days together," he was in the mountain "initiated in the sacred will of God, being instructed in all the most important matters which relate to his priesthood" and to his office as prophet.[19] In similar fashion, Milton extols Moses' abstinence both in *Christian Doctrine* (CM, 17:331) and in *Paradise Regained* (1.350–52). In *Paradise Regained*, Moses, along with Elijah, becomes the type of Jesus who in his prolonged wilderness fast is also "initiated in the sacred will of God," to use Philo's language. There, he learns his priesthood and the nature of his prophetic role.[20]

As it relates to the poet as hierophant, this fusion of the cultic and the oracular, typified by Moses in the Judaic tradition, is no less central to the Christian tradition. There, the fusion of poet-prophet-priest is a commonplace. Clement of Alexandria has set forth the most eloquent and elaborate expression of the idea. In both the *Exhortation to the Heathen* and the *Miscellanies*, Clement makes his position quite clear. In the *Exhortation to the Heathen*, for example, he singles out "the Thracian Orpheus, the son of Oeagrus," as one who was a "hierophant and poet at once."[21] Elaborating upon the reference to Orpheus, Clement maintains in his *Miscellanies* that Orpheus, Linus, Musaeus, Homer, and Hesiod are poets who, taught in theology, "philosophize much by way of hidden sense." Poetry for them is a veil. It is similar, in this sense, to prophecy and oracle, which "are spoken in enigmas" and "not exhibited incontinently to all and sundry, but only after certain purifications and previous instructions." Thus, Callimachus relates "in iambics" how Branchus the seer "purif[ied] the Milesians from plague" by "sprinkling the multitude with branches of laurel" and by singing hymns. Likewise, Thespis the tragic poet offered libations and placed offerings on "sacred altars" as a priest. These pagan figures, in turn, are complemented by Moses, whose ritual activities are an integral part of his prophetic acts. According to Clement, the conflation of ritual and prophecy has its source in the Egyptians and the Hebrews: "Wherefore, in accordance with the method of concealment, the truly sacred Word, truly divine and most necessary for us, deposited in the shrine of truth, was by the Egyptians indicated by what were called among them *adyta*, and by the Hebrews the veil. Only the consecrated . . . were allowed access to them. For Plato also thought it not lawful for the 'impure to touch the pure.'" Accordingly, the Egyptians, who placed sphinxes before their temples to demonstrate that the doctrine respecting God is enigmatical and obscure, did not entrust the mysteries they possessed to everyone and did not divulge the knowledge of divine things to the profane; only those of the hierophants who were judged the worthiest could receive that knowledge.[22]

The pervasiveness of this view as characterizing the nature of the poet has already been traced in detail by Courtland Baker and Murrin, among others.[23] Henry Reynolds's *Mythomystes* (1633?) is representative.[24] In that work, Reynolds maintains that poets are like the "*Aegyptian* Priests," who, searching "the Misteries of Nature," created "*Hieroglyphicks* or sacred grauings" and delivered their writings in "Enigma's and mysticall riddles" in order to keep their knowledge "inuiolate from the prophane Multitude." Correspondingly, the "Mysteries and abstrusities of most high divinity" reveal "holy things" to the uninitiated. Hierophants of that persuasion, such poets as Orpheus, Homer, Plato, Ovid, and Vergil, hid their mysterious doctrines in poems that embodied "all the most important Secrets of Nature." In that way, they created a "*Theologia Philosophica*," of which they were the priests. Reynolds singles out an Orphic hymn as an example. Celebrating "the high Author of this Vniuerse," the hymn banishes all that are "prophane," so that only the initiate can see Him "face to face" and behold how "His sacred right hand graspes the Ocean, and, / Touch'd with it, [makes] the proud mountaines trembling stand, / Eu'n from the deep rootes to their utmost height." This is "He who aboue the heau'n doth dwell, yet guides / And gouernes all that under heau'n abides. / O're all, through all, doth his uast power extend; / Of th'Vniuerse beginning, midde & end."[25]

From the Christian perspective, the oracular character of such pronouncements culminates in the figure of Christ, who not only fulfills all oracles but is himself the ultimate source of oracular expression. Thus, Clement of Alexandria maintains that Christ's presence, "concealed in the enigma of prophecy," "loosed the latchet of the oracles of the [old] economy, by unveiling the meaning of the symbols."[26] One thinks of Jesus in *Paradise Regained*: ascribing all past oracles to the influence of Satan, Jesus silences the false pagan oracles by taking upon himself the role of God's "living Oracle," sent by God "into the World, to teach his final will" (1.455–61). In Milton's *Theologia Philosophica*, the Orphic gives way to the Christocentric. Through Christ as oracle, there will be no fear of suffering the fate encountered by "the *Thracian* Bard," whose source of inspiration is, in any case, "an empty dream" (PL, 7.34–39). "Mount[ing] high / Through the dear might of him that walkt the waves" (L, 172–73), the hierophant of Christ is in possession of all that true oracular knowledge can bestow. He possesses an "inward Oracle," the "Spirit of Truth," sent to "dwell / In pious Hearts" (PR, 1.462–63). In that sense, he has achieved an ultimate priesthood and become, as poet, a true sacer vates and sacerdos. Doing so, he finds himself in accord not only with ancient tradition but with modern tradition as well.

The hierophantic view of the poet that one encounters in the Middle Ages and the Renaissance reinforces the predisposition not only to conflate cultic and oracular but to embody that conflation in Christocentric form. So pervasive was the hierophantic view of the poet in the Middle Ages that it found its way into such works as Isidore of Seville's *Etymologiarum*, which looks upon the poet not only as vates, inspired by a "*furor divinus*," but as sacerdos, engaged in "consecration" and "sanctification." Under "*De Clericis*," Isidore states quite clearly that the offices of priest, prophet, and poet are one.[27] In another context, Giovanni Boccaccio, in his *Life of Dante*, emphasizes the sacerdotal role of the poet, who, as a priest (*sacerdos*), offers "sacred adulation" in a poetry of worship that complements the "divine services" of the "sacred and sequestered" "*sacerdoti*". At the same time, says Boccaccio, poets are comparable to the prophets, among them, Daniel, Isaiah, Ezekiel, and Saint John the Divine. In both cases, poets are "the first theologians," patterning their poetry after that of God, who is the supreme poet.[28]

Discernible in the Middle Ages, such an outlook is no less apparent in the Renaissance. One thinks of a multitude of writers ranging from Marco Vida to John Buchler. As early as Vida's *De Arte Poetica* (1527), the poet is cast in the roles of vates and sacerdos. In both instances, Vida maintains, the poet traces his origin to the oracles:

> First, the great father of the gods above
> Sang in Dodona and the Libyan grove;
> Next, to the inquiring nations Themis gave
> Her sacred answers from the Phocian cave;
> Then Phoebus warned them from the Delphic dome
> Of future time and ages yet to come. . . .
> Next, at their feasts, the people sang their lays
> (The same their prophets sang in former days).[29]

Such ideas became so commonplace that they found their way into the thesauri of the period. As late as Buchler's *Thesaurus Phrasium Poëticarum* (1665), the oracular association of the poet as concurrently sacer vates and sacerdos of Apollo is taken for granted (p. 195). During the English Renaissance, Sir Philip Sidney's comments upon the poet as vates in *The Defence of Poesy* (1595) are so well known that elaboration is hardly called for. Through the "heart-ravishing knowledge" provided by the vatic poet, Sidney maintains, we are inspired by the "divine force" of the Delphic and Sibylline oracles, on the one hand, and by the "heavenly poesy" of the Davidic psalms, on the other. As vates, David allows us to "see God coming in his majesty."[30] Almost sixty years later, Thomas Hobbes was to echo the same exalted view in his "Answer to D'avenant's Preface Before *Gondibert*" (1650). For Hobbes, the source of poetry is "the Holy stile" of "the Oracles," expressed "in their holy songs called Hymnes." The "Composers" of these "Hymnes," says Hobbes, "were called Prophets and Priests before the name of Poet was known. When afterwards the majesty of that style was observed, the poets chose it as best becoming their high invention."[31]

One of the most eloquent spokesmen for this hierophantic view is George Puttenham, whose treatise on *The Arte of English Poesie* (1589) asserts that poets were the first priests, prophets, legislators, politicians, philosophers, astronomers, historiographers, orators, and musicians of the world. Under the categories of priest and prophet, Puttenham conflates cultic and oracular in a way that precisely underscores the point made here:

Foreasmuch as they [poets] were the first that entended to the obseruation of nature and her works, and specially of the Celestiall courses, by reason of the continued motion of the heauens, searching after the first mouer, and from thence by degrees comming to know and consider the substances separate and abstract, which we call the divine intelligences or good Angels (*Demones*), they were the first that instituted sacrifices of placation, with inuocations and worship to them, as to Gods: and inuented and stablished all the rest of the obseruances and ceremonies of religion, and so were the first Priests and ministers of the holy misteries. And because for the better execution of that high charge and function, it behoued them to live chast, and in all holiness of life, and in continuall studie and contemplation: they came by instinct diuine, and by deepe meditation, and much abstinence (the same assubtiling and refining their spirits) to be made apt to receaue uisions, both waking and sleeping, which made them vtter prophesies, and foretell things to come. So they were the first Prophetes or seears, *Uidentes*, for so the Scripture tearmeth them in Latine after the Hebrve word, and all the oracles and answers of the gods were given in meeter or uerse, and published to the people by their direction.[32]

With its cultic-oracular emphasis, such a statement exactly defines Milton's attitude regarding the poet and his craft. The only element lacking is the Christocentric bearing of that attitude. One need not look far to find it.

The poems of George Herbert should be sufficient indication of its importance to the Renaissance. In "Aaron," Herbert depicts the "dressing" of Aaron the high priest (see figure 2) in a manner that causes the Old Testament account (Exodus 28) to prefigure the New: Aaron becomes a type of Christ, the true high priest (cf. Hebrews 7).[33] For the purposes of this study, the poem is important because in it Herbert discovers how to move from profaneness to holiness both as priest and poet. To do so, he need only recognize that the "noise of passions" undermining his priesthood and his poetry (in effect, "ringing" him "for dead") is to be reconciled only through "another musick, making live not dead." That music, of course, is produced by none other than Christ, by whom Herbert's "doctrine" (priestly and poetic) will now be "tun'd." Like Aaron, Herbert will be dressing himself in the accoutrements of his priesthood, but unlike Aaron, his attire will reflect the dress of the New Dispensation: "That to the old man . . . [he] may rest, / And be in him new drest." Precisely in what respect the priest dresses himself the poem makes clear: his attire includes "Holinesse on the head," that is, the "plate of pure gold" engraved with "HOLINESS TO THE LORD," to be worn upon the forehead; "Light and perfections on the breast," that is, the "breastplate of judgment," containing the ornaments and stones,

ORNATVS SVMMI SACERDOTIS.

A Superhumerale seu ephod.
B C Duæ oræ superhumeralis.
D Textura, siue artificium superhumeralis. La bordure.
E Lapides onychini duo, quibus insculpta erãt nomina duodecim filiorum Israel.
F Palæ aureæ, pro quibus interpres vertit vncinos.
G Catenulæ.
H Pectorale iudicij, pro quo interpres vertit rationale iudicij: in quo duodecim lapides in quibus incisa nomina duodecim filiorum Israel.
I Vncini in palis aureis.
K Annuli quatuor in extremitatibus pectoralis iudicij.
L Annuli in lateribus superhumeralis. Vitta hyacinthina.
N Tunica quæ superhumerali supponebatur, in cuius superiori parte erat capitium siue foramẽ, per quod caput traijciebat sacerdos.
O Tintinnabula aurea.
P Mala punica.
Q Lamina, quæ vitta hyacinthina religabatur tiaræ.
R Tunica byssina.
S Tiara.
T Balteũ, siue cingulũ.

FIGURE 2. Aaron, the High Priest.
Reproduced from a rendering of Exodus 28, in Biblia sacra (1566), by permission of the Newberry Library, Chicago, Illinois.

among them, the Urim and the Thummim; "Harmonious bells below," that is, the "bells of gold" upon the hem of the robe of the ephod, to serve Aaron "when he goeth in unto the holy *place* before the Lord, and when he cometh out, that he die not" (Exod. 28:2–38). In his new dress as priest and poet of Christ, Herbert is reanimated, struck "dead" with Christ's "musick," only to be reborn, "new drest." That dress reflects his new priesthood: holiness not *on* the head but *in* the head, light and perfections not *on* the breast but *in* the breast. Dress is internalized as the poem moves into the Christocentric perspective. Within that perspective, Aaron's accoutrements receive a new significance. One thinks of the Urim and Thummim on the breastplate. Literally signifying "lights and perfections," these stones assume something of an oracular importance in the Old Testament, a meaning implicit in Herbert's reference in "Aaron" to "Light and perfections on the breast." According to the Old Testament, they became for the high priest not only a sign of his right to appear before the Lord (Exod. 28:30) but a source of "counsel" (Num. 27:21). For the Renaissance, Urim and Thummim involved decidedly oracular overtones.

Thus, in *Diatribae*, Mede describes in detail the oracular knowledge bestowed by Urim and Thummim. Whereas Urim was the means by which God answered those who inquired "in hard and doubtful cases," Thummim was the means "whereby the High Priest knew whether God did accept the Sacrifice or no." Both Urim and Thummim, in turn, prefigured Christ, whose "rest is full of *Urim*, full of Light and Understanding," a "light which shone in darknesse," and whose "heart is . . . endowed with *Thummim*, with all kinds of Perfections," particularly those arising out of the fullness of sacrifice. When Christ "inspired his Apostles with knowledge of heavenly mysteries, he sent a new *Urim* from above, even fiery tongues, tongues of *Urim* from heaven." At the same time, Christ provided "ministers of the Gospel . . . another *Thummim*, like unto that which was proper to the High Priest; namely the power of binding and loosing, which is as it were a power of Oracle to declare unto the people the remission of their sins, by the acceptance of Christs sacrifice" (pp. 366–78).[34]

In Milton, both the oracular and prefigurative dimensions of Urim and Thummim are present. From the oracular point of view, Milton refers in *The Reason of Church-Government* to the practice of consulting "the Oracle of Urim" upon the "oraculous Ephod," a privilege granted in the Gospels to God's ministers (CM, 3:204). From the prefigurative point of view, Milton has Satan in *Paradise Regained* tempt Jesus to become what ironically he is already, one whose "Counsel would be as the Oracle /

Urim and *Thummim,* those oraculous gems / On *Aaron's* breast" (3.13–15). Jesus is the veritable embodiment of that oracle. No one has more right to attire himself in those oraculous gems than he. Accordingly, in *Paradise Lost* the Son of God appears "all armd" "in Celestial Panoplie" "of radiant *Urim,* work divinely wrought" (6.760–61), as he sets out to overcome the rebel angels, an event that will later be discussed in much greater detail. In Christ, then, cultic and oracular assume their most compelling form. Herbert's "Aaron" attests to what underlies the Miltonic outlook: the most perfect music is that "tun'd by Christ." For the Renaissance, the conception of the poet as hierophant, as one who combines the cultic and the oracular, finds consummate expression in the Christocentric vision. That is where the sacred vein achieves fulfillment.

To explore further the bearing of the hierophantic view on Milton's poetics, it might be advisable to consider separately Milton's view of the poet, his view of the poem, and his view of the audience. A discussion of these three categories should suggest the extent to which Milton's hierophantic poetics permeates his outlook.

This discussion of the nature of the cultic and the oracular has already commented at some length upon Milton's view of the poet as hierophant. Such poems as *Elegia quinta, Elegia sexta, Ad Patrem,* and *Ad Salsillum,* not to mention the prose works, establish quite conclusively the hierophantic character of the poet as he appears in Milton's works. Oracle and priest, the poet goes about purifying his clothing and himself, lives like an ascetic, penetrates sacred enclosures, sings of things divine and discloses mysteries in a state of agitation ("in holy vision, . . . pensive trance, and anguish, and ecstatick fit" [42–43], as Milton says in *The Passion*), and performs rites at altars. Milton's view, in line with tradition, is thoroughly cultic and thoroughly oracular. One way of underscoring this would be to single out one or two of the many figures that Milton invokes to support such high claims for the poet. In this effort, the Mosaic parallel, already discussed above, yields additional insights.

With its source in Jewish Hellenism, the tradition that sees Moses as hierophantic poet culminates in *Paradise Lost.* There, the poet, like Moses, sings on the "secret" tops of mountains. More than that, however, he fulfills the role of mediator, one who appears before the mysterium tremendum in order to communicate the experience of the holy to those incapable of confronting it directly. The import, as shall be seen later, is clear. Causing "the Mount of *Sinai*" to "tremble" with "Thunder, Lightning and loud Trumpets sound," "the voice of God / To mortal ear is dreadful"; accordingly, the Israelites "beseech / That *Moses* might report to them his [God's] will, / And terror cease; he grants what

they besaught / Instructed that to God is no access / Without Mediator"
(12.227–40). In that capacity, Moses receives God's "Laws; part such as
appertain / To civil Justice, part religious Rites / Of sacrifice" (12.230–
31), all of which are contained in God's "Tabernacle": "By his [God's]
precept a Sanctuary is fram'd / Of Cedar, overlaid with Gold, therein /
An Ark, and in the Ark his testimony, / The Records of his Cov'nant"
(12.247–52). Into this tabernacle, established by Moses in his mediatorial role, enters the high priest to supplicate before God's presence. In
like manner, the poet as hierophant causes his poem to become a vehicle
of the mediatorial role, the expression of God's laws in poetic form, a
temple to be entered for the purposes of supplication and worship. With
its Christocentric vision, however, *Paradise Lost* is the temple not of the
Old Law but of the New, the handiwork not of Moses as mediator but of
Christ, "whose high Office now / *Moses* in figure beares" (12.240–41).
Through Christ, the true "Oracle of God," the poet is inspired by the
"Spirit, that dost prefer / Before all Temples th'upright heart and pure"
(1.12, 17–18). In his poetics of the holy, he fashions not tabernacles of
"Cedar, overlaid with Gold," but the temple of Christ with its truly
"spiritual architecture."

Complementing the figure of Moses, in turn, is the figure of Pythagoras. The choice of Pythagoras in this context is not arbitrary. Recalling
his treatment of Moses, Milton points in *Elegia sexta* to "the Samian
teacher" as the prime example for the poet to follow in living "frugally"
(58–59). That view receives additional elaboration in *Prolusion 2*. There,
Pythagoras, principal exponent of the Music of the Spheres, is seen to
embody the outlook of "the poets, or what is almost the same thing, the
divine oracles, by whom no secret or hidden mystery is exhibited in
public, unless clad in some covering or garment." Pythagoras, in short,
becomes the discloser of mysteries, in this case, the nature of "Harmony,"
"secretly introduced in poetic fashion." Having heard the Music of the
Spheres, the song of the "Muses dancing day and night around the altar
of Jove," Pythagoras "instruct[s] the minds of men with holy knowledge." He is able to do this because of having lived as an ascetic (*CM*,
12:149–57).

The associations that Milton draws upon to characterize the Pythagorean hierophant are, of course, commonplace.[35] They could be gotten,
for example, from Iamblichus's *Life of Pythagoras*. According to Iamblichus, Pythagoras, whose "soul was sent to mankind from the empire
of Apollo" and whose coming was foretold by the Delphic prophet of
Apollo, lived the purest of lives. "Initiated in all the mysteries of Byblus
and Tyre, and in the sacred operations which are performed in many

parts of Syria," he learned his craft from the Egyptian priests and Phoenician hierophants. Like them, he immersed himself in the "arcana" of the gods, "separated [himself] from all society," and "abstained from wine and animal food."[36] His conditioning is thereby perfectly in accord with what Porphyry in *Abstinence from Animal Food* looks upon as requisite to the creation of holiness in the individual. In that sense, he is the opposite of the profane man, who "submits to the assumption of [every kind of] food, and voluntarily betakes himself to [alluring] spectacles, to conversation with the multitude," laughter, and the drinking of wine.[37]

The contrast is reminiscent of that invoked by Milton in *Elegia sexta* between those poets satisfied with "great banquets" and "soft with old wine" as opposed to those perfected by abstinence and purified by water (51–61). In spite of the rather jovial tone that Milton adopts toward Diodati in effecting the contrast, the purport is highly serious. It amounts to a declaration of the distinction between the profane and the sacred poet. For Milton, the sacred poet is one to whom the very act of writing is a religious experience. One does not engage in that act at will. Indeed, from it, one "keeps off with a sacred reverence, & religious advisement how best to undergoe," that is, sustain, its demands until he is fully (religiously) prepared to do so (EC, CM, 12:324). When he is thus prepared, he does so in a way that is entirely in keeping with his vocation. Judging by Milton's references to Pythagoras in *Elegia sexta* and *Prolusion 2*, that vocation is one in which the poet purifies himself through a process of abstinence and separation in order to impart secret knowledge derived from the gods.

It is in this role that Milton depicts himself as early as *Prolusion 7* (ca. 1632): "Separated from the world," set off by his knowledge of "the secrets of the goddesses," enjoying "the highest favor of the Muses," he is given prophetic power in seclusion "amid fields and remote woodlands" (CM, 12:249–51). From that perspective, he imparts oracular knowledge. He is able to do so because of those qualities that make him unique, qualities that would make him, as a poet, "a true Poem, that is, a composition, and patterne of the best and honourablest things" (AP, CM, 3:303). This he does, at his "own peril and cost," through a process of self-denial, diligent preparation, and the cultivation of those "talents" that marked him as select (CG, CM, 3:241). It is particularly this last characteristic that underlies the decidedly religious and ultimately oracular nature of his poetic outlook.

Constantly aware of the "terrible seasing of him that hid the talent" (EC, CM, 12:324), an awareness implicit in Sonnets 7 and 19, among other poems, Milton writes, in *The Reason of Church-Government*, "that

God even to a strictnesse requires the improvement of those his entrusted gifts." Accordingly, there is for the poet no "sorer burden of mind," no greater "toil or waight" than "how and in what manner he shall dispose and employ those summes of knowledge and illumination, which God hath sent him into this world to trade with." In this, the poet is like the prophet, whose vocation of dispensing truth is a divine but heavy burden. "Yea," Milton says, "that mysterious book of Revelation which the great Evangelist was bid to eat, as it had been some eye-brightening electuary of knowledge, and foresight, though it were sweet in his mouth, and in the learning, it was bitter in his belly; bitter in the denouncing. Nor was this hid from the wise Poet *Sophocles*, who in that place of his *Tragedy* where Tiresias is call'd to resolve *K. Edipus* in a matter which he knew to be grievous, brings him in bemoaning his lot, that he knew more than other men" (*CM*, 3:229–31). The oracular carries with it its liabilities as well as its benefits. In either case, the sacred poet fulfills the Pythagorean role of separateness that characterizes the hierophant. Such an idea gained particular significance after Milton became blind.

Thus, in the *Defensio secunda*, Milton says of the blind: "The divine law, the divine favour, has made us . . . sacred [*sacros*] . . . ; nor would seem to have brought this darkness upon us so much by inducing a dimness of the eyes, as by the overshadowing of heavenly wings; and not infrequently is wont to illumine it again, when produced, by an inward and far surpassing light" (*CM*, 8:72–73). To bolster this outlook, Milton enumerates those hierophants who have been set apart by their blindness and made sacred, including Tiresias, Phineus, Timoleen of Corinth, Appius Claudius, and Caecilius Metellus, "the high-priest, who lost his eyes, in saving from the flames not the city only, but the Palladium, on which hung the destiny of the city, as also the most sacred of the religious mysteries" (*CM*, 8:63–65). The list recalls that provided in *Elegia sexta* as an anticipation of that offered in *Paradise Lost*.

Both before and after his blindness, Milton did not hesitate to associate himself with those that he thought possessed an oracular power that separated them from the rest of mankind and made them sacred. His own blindness confirmed that association. He became "Blind *Thamyris* and blind *Maeonides*, / And *Tiresias* and *Phineus* prophets old" (*PL*, 3.35–36) in a way that he could not have earlier anticipated. But faced with that fact, he did not hesitate to conceive of himself in ways that were decidedly oracular. He even views himself in the *Defensio secunda* as one whose destiny, sealed "by a certain fatality in . . . [his] birth," was on a plane with that which had been prophetically derived through consultations with "the oracle at Delphi" in the *Iliad* (*CM*, 8:69).

It is this hierophantic view of himself and of his own mission that Milton was not averse to projecting into his poetry, embodied either in the figure of the poet, as in *Paradise Lost*, or in the form of characters that are sacred in their own right, Samson and Jesus, for example. Though fallen, Samson in his blindness retains that quality of separateness bequeathed him at his birth when "th'Angel" "Ordain'd . . . [his] nurture holy . . . / Select, and Sacred" (SA, 361–63). As son of "th'Eternal King" and virgin-born (PR, 1.234–54), Jesus, of course, is the very fulfillment of all that is sacred. Separating himself in order to undergo through abstinence trial in the wilderness, he thereby proves himself God's true Oracle. This he does in a poem whose stated function is the oracular rendering of "deeds" "in secret done" (PR, 1.14–15). Such a fact should provide insight not only into Milton's hierophantic conception of the poet and the characters that he portrays but into his hierophantic conception of the function of poetry.

That latter conception is supported by Milton's view of Pythagoras, whom he conceives as disclosing "secret and hidden mystery" in poetic form (PO, CM, 12:151). In his vision of Moses, like that of Enoch and Elijah, the prophet discloses mysteries within the pure confines of the mount (TM, CM, 18:229), a vision rearticulated in *Paradise Lost*, which invokes the "Heav'nly Muse, that on the secret top / Of *Oreb*, or of *Sinai*, didst inspire" Moses to sing of the creation, and that can just as well inspire the poet to sing of "*Sion* Hill" and "*Siloa*'s Brook that flow'd / Fast by the Oracle of God" (1.6–12). In this manner, Moses typifies the poet as mediator, a role fulfilled in Christ, who appears before God's oracular presence in the sanctuary, constructed not of "Cedar overlaid with Gold" but of things of the spirit, representing not the Mosaic but the Christocentric vision. In either case, Milton's conception of the poem is oracular. He would not be opposed to the views expressed by Clement of Alexandria, among others, that poetry embodies prophecy, that there is that about it which is enigmatic (or what Milton in the *Art of Logic* calls "cryptic" [CM, 11:297–99])[38] and which must "not be exhibited incontinently to all and sundry, but only after certain purifications and previous instructions." It is in this sense that Milton in *An Apology* praises "those celestiall songs to others inapprehensible, but not to those who were not defil'd with women" (CM, 3:306; cf. Rev. 14:4). It is likewise in this sense that Milton in *The Reason of Church-Government* praises "the Apocalyps of Saint *John*," whose work is both a "shutting up" (a *concealing* in the very act of *apocalypsis*) and an "intermingling" of "solemn Scenes and Acts with a sevenfold *Chorus* of halleluja's and harping symphonies" (CM, 3:238).

Such for Milton is the sacred vein with its source in God's "secret Altar touch with hallow'd fire." In celebrating God, its "harmony," that term which Pythagoras "secretly introduced in poetic fashion" (PO, CM, 12:151), is expressed in "mazes intricate, / Eccentric, intervolv'd, yet regular / Then most, when most irregular they seem" (PL, 5.622–24). It delights in the "mystical," to use Milton's term, in order to solemnize the sacred (PL, 5.618–20).[39] It concerns itself with what Milton in *Christian Doctrine* fittingly calls *"rerum occultarum,"* the "hidden things" of God (CM, 17:32–33). Emulating the oracular, it is the very Urim and Thummim of the hierophant's art.

If such is the case, one must account for Milton's pronouncement in *Of Education* that poetry should be "simple, sensuous and passionate" (CM, 4:286). At issue is the word *simple*, upon which Milton implicitly elaborates when, comparing poetry to logic, he says that poetry is "less suttle and fine" (CM, 4:286). Although Milton's comparison does not speak directly to the immediate concerns of this discussion, his emphasis upon the inherent simplicity of poetry needs considering. The problem is to reconcile that simplicity with the enigmatic, mystical, secretive, and, finally, oracular dimension in Milton's view of the poem as the expression of the hierophant.

In part, the key to that reconciliation may be found in what Milton says about Scripture, that holiest of poems, composed, as Jesus comments in *Paradise Regained*, of *"Sion's* songs" (4.347). Scripture, Milton categorically maintains in *Christian Doctrine*, is "plain" and "perspicuous": it is founded upon "simplicity" (CM, 16:259). Yet we recall from *Areopagitica*, that "it answers dubiously and darkly to the common reader" (CM, 4:312). The apparent contradiction is reconciled in the person of the reader, for whom Scripture is dark or clear, depending upon his ability to understand its truths. Thus, Milton says in *Of Reformation*, "The very essence of Truth is plainnesse, and brightnes; the darknes and crookednesse is our own. The *wisdome* of God created *understanding*, fit and proportionable to Truth the object, and end of it, as the eye to the thing visible. If our *understanding* have a film of *ignorance* over it . . . what is that to Truth? If we will but purge with sovrain eyesalve that intellectual ray which *God* hath planted in us, then we would beleeve the Scriptures protesting their own plainnes, and perspicuity." We would hold Scripture "ever in [our] faces like a mirror of Diamond, till it dazle, and pierce [our] misty ey balls . . . maintaining it the honour of its absolute sufficiency, and supremacy inviolable" (CM, 3:33, 35). It is in this sense that the blind poet of *Paradise Lost* asks for that illumination which will "Shine inward, and the mind through all her powers / Irradiate, there plant eyes, all mist from thence / Purge and disperse" (3.52–54).[40] So purged, he will be able to create a work "inapprehensible" and "dark" to "the common reader" but "plain" and "perspicuous" to his "fit audience," "though few" (PL, 7.31), whose eyes have likewise been "purge[d] with sovrain eyesalve" and who are prepared to hold his work, like "a mirror of Diamond," before their faces as it "dazle[s]" and "pierces" with an "absolute sufficiency, and supremacy inviolable." Such language (with its contrasts between sacred and profane, sight and blindness, brightness and darkness) should suggest the fundamentally hierophantic-oracular basis of Milton's poetics.

If his poetics characterizes poet and poem, it is no less applicable to audience. The concept of "fit audience" is directly in line with the idea of poems written in the sacred vein. Accommodating the Horatian dictum ("neque te ut miretur turba labores, / contentus paucis lectoribus") to his own sacral perspective,[41] Milton establishes the appropriate context for his audience. Only the initiated are equipped to hear "deeds in secret done," events related from the "secret tops" and pure confines of sacred mountains. Only those who are not "defil'd" can understand the "inapprehensible." Only those whose eyes have been "purged" can behold, through the hierophant's art, "the Holiest of holies." These are not the "miscellaneous rabble, who extol / Things vulgar" (PR, 3.50–51), the "*populo inerti*" who see only with "*oculos profanos*" (ADP, 103–4), but those who have proven themselves worthy to be admitted into the adytum to participate in the sacred vein. Derived from well-established traditions and incorporated into an outlook at once unique and universal, this, then, forms the basis of Milton's poetics of the holy, a poetics that distinguishes Milton's hierophantic-oracular view of poet, poem, and audience.

4
Sacral Contexts

The foregoing observations concerning hierophantic poetics establish Milton in a distinctly sacral environment. That environment at once transcends (but does not obliterate) doctrinal considerations and embraces an essential religiosity that has its roots in Greco-Roman and Judeo-Christian thought. Such religiosity gives rise to a consecratory impulse which in Milton represents the very foundation of his outlook as a poet. The entire thrust of my argument is that this impulse characterizes the fundamental sacrality of Milton's work and assumes its most compelling form in *Paradise Lost*. To establish my point, I shall consider some of the sacral contexts of Milton's poetry.

The early elegies on Lancelot Andrewes, bishop of Winchester, and Nicholas Felton, bishop of Ely, represent a fitting point of departure. In both elegies, the poet has a numinous vision of the other world where everything "shines" in translucent splendor (EL 3, 40; PE, 61–62). In the elegy on Winchester, the poet experiences a veritable hierophany:

> While I myself was marvelling at the dense shades
>   beneath the clustering vines
> and the shining regions everywhere,
>   behold, Winchester's bishop suddenly stood before me,
> the splendor of stars shone in his bright face;
> a dazzling white robe flowed down to his golden ankles,
> a white fillet encircled his divine head.
>
>   (51–56)

In hierophantic form, he suddenly manifests himself to the poet in all his numinous glory, an appearance that suggests Christ's transfiguration: "And his face did shine as the sun, and his raiment was white as the light" (Matt. 17:2). In one form or another, Milton's poetry is replete with such hierophanies.

They occur regularly in the elegies, where Milton delights in offering for adulation, if not for worship, the "hallow'd reliques," to borrow a phrase from the elegy *On Shakespear*, of the *sanctus*, that person who has been rendered holy. Anne Phillips, in the *Fair Infant* elegy, has about her a numinous quality "that shew'd [she] wast divine" (34–35); Jane Paulet, in the *Epitaph on the Marchioness of Winchester*, is enshrined as a "Saint" "far within the bosom bright / Of blazing Majesty and Light" (69–71); Edward King, in *Lycidas*, is bathed "with nectar pure" and "entertain[ed]" by "all the Saints above" (175–78); Charles Diodati, in *Epitaphium Damonis*, experiences a similar fate: living in "the pure air," this "Diodati," literally "god-given," is consecrated "with a shining crown" "encircled around [his] glorious head" (203–15). Milton's elegies are, in effect, hagiographies: they celebrate the life of the sanctus.

An elegy in its own right, Sonnet 23 provides a case in point. "Rescu'd" from the impurities of the "grave" and "washt from the spot of child-bed taint," the "late-espoused saint" appears "vested all in white, pure as her mind." As such, her sanctity combines both cultic and spiritual purification: on the one hand, a cleansing like that undergone by Alcestis after her release from Death[1] and by those bound to the rites of "th'old law" (Lev. 12:5) and, on the other, a cleansing like that undergone by those "made . . . white in the blood of the lamb" (Rev. 7:13–14). Moving from the cultic to the spiritual, this sancta radiates "love, sweetness, goodness." Yet her face is still "vail'd": she will not be seen face to face in a final hierophany until the proper time ("For now we see through a glass, darkly; but then face to face: now I know in part; but then shall I know even as also I am known" [1 Cor. 13:12]).

Visions of such holy figures are by no means confined to the elegiac poems, however. They find their way into the other poems, as well. The figure of Melancholy in *Il Penseroso*, for example, embodies what might be called a reverse hierophany or the depiction of the numinous in *via negativa* terms. Drawing once again upon the image of the veil, Milton invokes Melancholy in this manner:

> But hail thou Goddes, sage and holy,
> Hail divinest Melancholy,
> Whose Saintly visage is too bright
> To hit the Sense of human sight;
> And therfore to our weaker view,
> O're laid with black staid Wisdoms hue.
>
> (11–16)

Once again, we are presented with the "saint," the sanctus, invoked appropriately with the "hail," described by Milton as "the holy salutation" (PL, 5.386; cf. Luke 1:28). This sancta is so dazzling that she must overlay her visage with a veil. In this context, one thinks of Moses: having been in the presence of God (and even then unable to behold God's face on pain of death), Moses himself must put a veil on his face when he addresses the children of Israel because his face shines so (Exod. 33:20–23, 34:32–35). On a smaller scale, a similar hierophantic milieu emerges in Milton's treatment of Melancholy.

It is no less compelling in the other poems. There, the process of making sacred is likewise accompanied by a hierophany, that sudden "flam[ing] in the forehead of the morning sky," which surrounds the deified figure with resplendent numinosity. One recalls the Countess Dowager of Derby in *Arcades*. Appearing in a "sudden blaze of majesty . . . / Too divine to be mistook" (2–4), she is the very embodiment of the hierophany:

> Mark what radiant state she spreds
> In circle round her shining throne,
> Shooting her beams like silver threds.
> This this is she alone,
> Sitting like a Goddes bright
> In the center of her light.
>
> (14–19)

Situated on "hallow'd ground" (515), she receives those worthy to "approach, and kiss her sacred vestures hemm" (83). She is, in effect, Milton's conception of what it means to be holy: she radiates numen. Doing so, she is essentially passive, iconic, adored by others.

Assimilated into narrative form and assuming an active role, she finds her counterpart in the Lady of *Comus*. A "holy one" in her own right, the Lady has about her a numinosity that, in keeping with the holy, at once attracts and repells. For Milton, that numinosity resides in the virtue of chastity. As a substitute for the *caritas* of 1 Corinthians 13:13, chastity shares the moral characteristics of the virtues that make up Saint Paul's trilogy of faith, hope, and charity. Accordingly, the Lady calls upon the first two to help sustain her (213–15) and embodies the third in her concern for "every just man that now pines with want" (768) and finally in her association with the divine love of Cupid and Psyche (1003–11; cf. AP, CM, 3:305). That aspect of her personality, coupled with the "inchanting" nature of her physical presence, underlies her attractiveness. It causes Comus himself to exclaim, upon hearing her song, "But such a sacred and homefelt delight, / Such sober certainty of waking bliss / I never heard till now" (262–64). One is reminded of Satan's reaction to Eve's attractiveness in *Paradise Lost*: he becomes "stupidly good" (9.465). The Lady's attractiveness, like Eve's, is disarming. It sets her apart. As the Elder Brother maintains in *Comus*:

So dear to Heav'n is saintly chastity,
That when a soul is found sincerely so,
A thousand liveried angels lackey her,
Driving far off each thing of sin and guilt,
And in cleer dream, and solemn vision
Tell her of things that no gross ear can hear,
Till oft convers with heav'nly habitants
Begin to cast a beam on th'outward shape,
The unpolluted temple of the mind,
And turns it by degrees to the souls essence,
Till all be made immortal.

(452–63)

The effects of saintly chastity are such that they cause the body to assume a numinosity, "a beam of th'outward shape," until it is fully spiritualized. This is part of what makes the sanctus so attractive. At the same time, the effects of saintly chastity are such that they "driv[e] far off each thing of sin and guilt." This is part of what makes the sanctus so repellent (in the Latinate sense of that term).

From the second point of view, the sanctus participates in what has already been described as the ganz andere. The sanctus is associated with that which causes dread. In this sense, the Lady is not at all "attractive." Endowed with "a hidden strength" (414), a Macht, to use Gerardus van der Leeuw's term,[2] she is protected by "the sacred rayes of chastity" (425). She is "clad" like an armed warrior "in compleat steel" (421). She possesses, like "the huntress *Dian*," a "dred bow" that inspires "fear" in "gods and men" (441–46). More dreadful than that, she is able, through her "rigid looks of chast austerity" to "freez[e] her foes to congeal'd stone," like the "unconquer'd Virgin" Minerva with her "snaky-headed *Gorgon* sheild." All that behold her are "dash't" "with sudden adoration, and blank aw" (447–53). Such is precisely the effect that she has on Comus, who admits: "I feel that I do fear / Her words set off by som superior power; / And though not mortal, yet a cold shuddering dew / Dips me all o're" (800–803). What Comus is reacting to, of course, is the Lady's claim to possess the power of a "sacred vehemence" in defending, against the "profane tongue," not only "the Sun-clad power of Chastity" but "the sublime notion, and high mystery / That must be utter'd to unfold the sage / And serious doctrine of Virginity" (780–99). The relationship between chastity and virginity has already been traced by A. S. P. Woodhouse, among others.[3] This relationship serves to enhance further the hierophantic basis of Milton's description of the Lady in *Comus*.

As chastity moves toward virginity, it takes on those distinctly *religious* qualities that characterize it as uniquely "undefiled" and endow it with remarkable, if not magical, power. Thus, Milton speaks in his *Apology* of "having had the doctrine of holy Scripture unfolding those chaste and high mysteries with timeliest care infus'd, that *the body is for the Lord and the Lord for the body* [1 Cor. 6:13]" (*CM*, 3:306). With the religious cultivation of the body, God's "temple" (1 Cor. 6:19), Milton looks forward to "accompanying the Lamb" with those who are similarly "undefil'd" (Rev. 14:1–5). That is, he looks forward to being "present[ed] . . . as a chaste virgin to Christ" (2 Cor. 11:2). In this sense, "chastity" (*castitas*) becomes, as Milton maintains in *Christian Doctrine*, "*sanctimonia*," that is "sacredness" (*CM*, 17:216). In *Comus*, the type of such sacredness is Sabrina, "virgin pure" (826). This "goddess of the river" (842), worshiped by "the shepherds at their festivals" (848), is endowed with the power to "unlock / The clasping charm, and thaw the numming spell" of other virgins "in hard besetting need" (852–57). Thus, "invok't" through the Spirit's incantatory verse (859–89), she appears "to help insnared chastity" with her "powerful hand" (903–9), first by sprinkling "pure" liquid upon the Lady and then by "touch[ing]" the "venom'd seat" "with chast palms" (911–18). Considering the religious nature of the chastity involved, the ritualistic and thaumaturgical environment that Milton creates is only appropriate. That environment is precisely in keeping with the manifold traditions that shaped what John Main calls "religious chastity" and gave rise to the belief in chastity as a magical virtue worthy of adoration.[4] Within this context, one could trace customs ranging from those surrounding the Vestal Virgins to those commemorating the Virgin Mary, to whom Milton himself ascribed a "*divinâ virtute*" (MAR, *CM*, 18:342).[5] Implicit in all these customs is the hierophantic character of religious chastity: at its source, *castitas* participates in the cultic milieu of the holy. With that idea in mind, Milton subjects that which is sacred to that which is profane: the Lady as *sancta* encounters (and overcomes) the profane world of Comus. Finally liberated through the power of Sabrina, she attains true *sanctimonia*. The language that Milton uses to describe this idea is quite explicit in its consecratory overtones: "Com Lady," the Spirit says, "while Heav'n lends us grace, / Let us fly this *cursed place* . . . / Till we come to *holier* ground" (938–43; italics added). Having arrived at that holier ground, she and her brothers celebrate "in victorious dance" their "triumph" "o're sensual folly, and intemperance" (974–75). The process of making sacred is complete.

Portrayed through the vehicle of the masque in *Comus*, this process assumes epic form in *Paradise Regained*. There, the movement from profane to sacred is heightened because the object of that movement is ὁ ἅγιος, the holy one, himself, the antitype of all other holy personages that Milton celebrates throughout his poetry. More than that, he is the culmination of the Christological perspectives established in the other poems. His past is that of the Son, "Divine Similitude, / In whose conspicuous count'nance, without cloud / Made visible, th'Almighty Father shines" (PL, 3.384–86). His present is that of the anointed "Priest" whose "Tabernacle" is not "the Courts of everlasting Day" but the "darksom House" of flesh (PA, 15–17; N, 13–14). His future is that prefigured in his circumcision: he "bleeds to give us ease" (CI, 11). He becomes, that is, the primal sacrifice, what we have already seen in our discussion of the Christian tradition as the means by which all is made sacred (*sacrificare*).

As Michael prophesies to Adam in *Paradise Lost*, the Son shall come "in the Flesh / To a reproachful life and cursed death": "He shall live hated, be blasphem'd / Seis'd on by force, judg'd, and to death condemnd, / A shameful and accurst, naild to the Cross" (12.405–13). He shall willingly subject "that glorious Form, that Light unsufferable, / And that far-beaming blaze of Majesty" (N, 8–9) to all that is "darksom," "accurst," blasphemous, and profane, in order to render "holy," that is, to redeem. This fundamental Christological idea assumes a centrality in Milton that cannot be overestimated. In *Paradise Regained*, it is embodied in the passage of the "glorious Eremite / Into the Desert, his Victorious Field," there to encounter "the Spiritual Foe" (1.8–10). In that encounter, one finds the willing subjection of the sacred to the profane. Subjected to Satan's "wiles" in the "wast Wilderness" (1.6–7), Jesus not only establishes his own divinity but prepares the way for the consummate act of redemption on the cross. As God maintains, "But first I mean / To exercise him in the Wilderness; / There he shall first lay down the rudiments / Of his great warfare, ere I send him forth / To conquer Sin, and Death the two grand foes, / By Humiliation and strong Sufferance" (1.155–60).

In accord with Milton's hierophantic poetics, the prelude to this event is the baptism: preparatory to the encounter with "the Spiritual Foe," ὁ ἅγιος undergoes immersion and lustration. The reasons for this preparatory occasion are manifold. Narratively, of course, it accords with the biblical precedent set forth in Matthew and Luke, in which the wilderness sojourn (Matt. 4:1–11; Luke 4:1–13) is anticipated by the Baptist's preparing "the way of the Lord" (Matt. 3:3). Symbolically, it represents the death, burial, and resurrection of Christ: "Know ye not, that so many of us as were baptized into Jesus Christ were baptized into his death? Therefore we are buried with him by baptism into death: that like as Christ was raised up from the dead by the glory of the Father, even so we also should walk in newness of life" (Rom. 6:3–4). In accordance with this interpretation, Milton likewise views the rite of baptism as a symbol of the events surrounding the crucifixion (CD, *CM*, 16:169). As Michael says to Adam in *Paradise Lost*, baptism prepares us for "death, like that which the redeemer dy'd" (12.442–45).

The importance of this idea for *Paradise Regained* may be seen in Jesus' own account. First, he learns from the Law and Prophets that for the Messiah, the "way must lie / Through many a hard assay ev'n to the death": as sacrifice, he must bear the "full weight" of mankind's sins (1.260–67). Discovering that, he encounters the Baptist. His own baptism, as well as that of his faithful, Milton maintains, is thereby "intended to represent figuratively the painful life of Christ, his death and burial, in which he was immersed, as it were, for a season" (CD, *CM*, 16:185). In this sense, it is seen as "a kind of initiatory measure [*initiatio*]" to anticipate what lies ahead (CD, *CM*, 16:188–89). As such, it is commonly associated with the rite of circumcision as a prefiguration of the crucifixion (Col. 2:11–12). At the same time, it represents that process of purification attendant upon sanctification, "the signe," Milton says, "of washing . . . from guilt of sin to Life / Pure" (PL, 12.442–45). If such is the case, in what sense is Christ, who is already holy, baptized? As John the Baptist says, "I have need to be baptized of thee, and comest thou to me?" Jesus answers prefiguratively: "Suffer *it to be so* now: for thus it becometh us to fulfill all righteousness" (Matt. 3:14–15). Fulfilling that righteousness, Jesus fulfills the Baptist's prophecy: "I indeed baptize you with water unto repentance: but he that cometh after me is mightier than I . . . : he shall baptize you with the Holy Ghost, and *with* fire" (Matt. 3:11). In so doing, he shall enact the final purification of which the sacrament of baptism is the type, the initiatio. In part, *Paradise Regained* is an account of how that enactment will be brought to pass. We experience with Christ a baptism "into death" as a way of "walking in newness of life." Such is the process of sanctification embodied in the action of Milton's brief epic. The bearing of that process upon the encounter between ὁ ἅγιος and the Spiritual Foe will become clear in the ensuing discussion. For the present, it is necessary to explore some additional ramifications to which the baptism gives rise.

Drawing upon the Gospels, Milton uses the baptism as the occasion for a theophany. Thus, Matthew 3:16–17 states: "And Jesus, when he was baptized, went up straightway out of the water: and, lo, the heavens were opened unto him, and he saw the Spirit of God descending like a dove, and lighting upon him: And lo a voice from heaven, saying, This is my beloved Son, in whom I am well pleased." The importance of this theophany for *Paradise Regained* may be seen in that it is thrice repeated, first from the perspective of the narrator, second from the perspective of Satan, third from the perspective of Jesus. Although each perspective is distinct, all three emphasize the awesomeness of the theophany, in Otto's terms, its "majestas": it becomes the occasion for the manifestation of the mysterium tremendum that gives rise to religious fear.[6] Thus, Milton speaks of the "awful" effects of "the great Proclaimer['s]" voice ("More awful then the sound of Trumpet") and of the "aw" inspired in those who participate in the baptism (1.18–22). Satan, "nigh Thunder-struck" "with the voice divine" that he hears from "Heav'n," relates, "I saw / The Prophet do him reverence, on him rising / Out of the water, Heav'n above the Clouds / Unfold her Crystal Dores, thence on his head / A perfect Dove descend . . . / And out of Heav'n the Sov'raign voice I heard, / This is my Son belov'd, in him am pleas'd" (1.35–36, 79–85). Jesus' account is equally taken up with what Otto calls the "*mysterium fascinans*" of the theophany. Having been "proclaim'd" divine by John the Baptist, Jesus relates how that proclamation is confirmed, first by the dovelike descent of the Spirit and then by heavenly testimony: "And last the sum of all, my Father's voice, / Audibly heard from Heav'n, pronounc'd me his, / Me his beloved Son, in whom alone / He was well pleas'd" (1.281–86). In *Christian Doctrine*, Milton provides the following interpretation of the theophany: it represents the "ineffable affection of the Father for the Son, communicated by the Holy Spirit under the appropriate image of a dove, and accompanied by a voice from heaven declaratory of that affection" (CM, 14:367). Signaling the beginning of Christ's mission, the theophany legitimates the action that is to follow. By that theophany, Jesus realizes "the time / Now full, that . . . [he] no more should live obscure, / But openly begin, as best becomes / Th'Authority which . . . [he] deriv'd from Heav'n" (1.286–89). That beginning "openly," that showing of the self, is in direct accord with the theophanic nature of the baptism.

Accordingly, the combat with the Spiritual Foe in the wilderness is the first instance of the revelation. Done in secret, it is nonetheless performed before our eyes as an anticipation of what will be performed before the eyes of others. We witness the fulfillment, in narrative form, of the theophanic proclamation from Heaven. As we might expect, the action itself will be theophanic. At the same time, it will bring to the fore the purificatory process, the baptism "into death," that was a fundamental dimension of Christ's baptism. Both dimensions, the purificatory and the theophanic, converge in the sojourn of ὁ ἅγιος in the wilderness. What form that convergence assumes may be seen by exploring briefly the action of *Paradise Regained*. That exploration should establish even further the hierophantic basis of Milton's poetics.

From the purificatory point of view, Jesus enters the wilderness, "not thence to be more pure" (1.76) but, as he says of the baptism, "to fulfil all righteousness," to prepare himself, as it were, for the *sacrificium*, represented in the travails of his existence and culminating in his crucifixion. That period of preparation, that *initiatio* embodied in the baptism, is rendered in the narrative that follows. The nature of this narrative, with its manifold trials and temptations, is made explicit in the language that describes how Christ, led by "the Spirit," "enter'd . . . the bordering Desert wild": "Fed" "with holiest Meditations," "thought following thought, and step by step led on," he "into himself descended," "the better to converse / With solitude" (1.189–93, 2.110–11). He confronts in that "descent," in that immersion, the human dimension of his personality in order to emerge from it. The experience becomes for him a baptism "into death" as a way of "walking in newness of life." Immersed in "holiest Meditations," he arises out of the "laving stream" (1.280), indeed, the "Consecrated stream" (1.72), of his sojourn in a reaffirmation of his own godhead. Doing so, he proves his ability to adhere to the world of the spirit against the temptations of the Spiritual Foe, who would have him succumb to the world of the material, whether in the form of food, wealth, temporal glory, or kingship.

Resisting the lures of these temptations, among others, Jesus is prepared for the ascent to the Tower (4.541–49), there to confirm the full bearing of his sacrificial office. With the Tower as the occasion for the enactment of the mediatorial role as priest, Christ is symbolically crucified in a scene that epitomizes his passion, death, and, finally, his ascension.[7] Correspondingly, he experiences there the full awareness of his godhead in what amounts to a theophanic rearticulation of the final temptation, that of "stand[ing] upright," by "shew[ing]" his "Progeny." He does so by miraculously maintaining his balance in the face of Satan's disbelief. The theophany results symbolically in the revelation of his divinity and in the downfall of Satan, who, "smitten with amazement," falls, while "a fiery Globe of angels" bears up the revealed Christ (4.544–82). The event results in what amounts to a theophanic celebration of Jesus as holy and a denunciation of Satan as profane. Thus, Jesus is "true image of the Father whether thron'd / In the bosom of bliss, and light of light / Conceiving, or remote from Heav'n, enshrin'd / In fleshly Tabernacle, and human form" (4.596–99), whereas Satan, with his legions, is to be "chase[d]" by the "terror" of the Son's "voice" from his "Demoniac holds, possession foul," and is to "beg" to be hidden "in a herd of Swine" (4.627–30). From the theophanic point of view, *Paradise Regained* ends, then, not only in a celebration of ὁ ἅγιος in his revealed splendor but in a contrast between two categories essential to the poem's meaning, sacred and profane.

Fundamental to Milton's poetry, these categories are of particular importance to *Samson Agonistes*. Indeed, Milton's closet drama is founded upon sacred-profane distinctions. Samson himself is a "Select, and Sacred" character, whose "breeding" was "order'd and prescrib'd / As of a person separate to God" and whose "nurture" was "ordain'd" by "th'Angel" to be "holy" (30–31, 361–63). The events surrounding that ordination are of particular importance to this discussion of the holy. Samson's birth is announced through a theophany: an angel of the Lord appears twice, the second time departing in an altar flame that Manoah has prepared to "offer a burnt offering" to God (Judg. 13:2–20). The event is graphically recounted by Samson himself in Milton's drama: "In sight / Of both my Parents," an "Angel," Samson says, "all in flames ascended / From off the Altar, where an Off'ring burn'd, / As in a fiery column charioting / His Godlike presence" (24–28). According to the biblical account, Manoah and his wife respond by falling "on their faces to the ground" (Judg. 13:30). Biblically, the awesomeness of the event is further enhanced by the refusal of the angel to reveal his name, "seeing it is secret" (Judg. 13:18).

That sense of secrecy is significant both for the biblical story and for *Samson Agonistes*. Characterizing the separateness implicit in the holy, it accords with the attitude toward Samson fostered by the Bible and dramatized by Milton. In part, this attitude is reflected in the injunctions that the angel communicates to Manoah's wife: she should, the angel says, "drink no wine nor strong drink, neither eat any unclean *thing*"; of Samson, the angel says, "no razor shall come on his head: for the child shall be a Nazarite unto God from the womb" (Judg. 13:2–24). The emphasis upon Samson as "Nazarite" (literally, one *separated*), not for a circumscribed period, as was customary, but for life, pervades the entire story. (In fact, only two other such life-long Nazarites are mentioned in the Scriptures: Samuel and John the Baptist.)

The obligations of the Nazarite are enumerated in Numbers 6:1–21. As the text indicates, those obligations are wholly cultic:

> When either man or woman shall separate *themselves* to vow a vow of a Nazarite, to separate *themselves* unto the Lord: He shall separate *himself* from wine and strong drink, and shall drink no vinegar of wine, or vinegar of strong drink, neither shall he drink any liquor

of grapes, nor eat moist grapes or dried. . . . All the days of the vow of his separation there shall no razor come upon his head: until the days be fulfilled, in the which he separateth *himself* unto the Lord, he shall be holy, *and* shall let the locks of the hair of his head grow. All the days that he separateth *himself* unto the Lord he shall come at no dead body. He shall not make himself unclean for his father, or for his mother, for his brother, or for his sister, when they die: because the consecration of his God *is* upon his head. All the days of his separation he *is* holy unto the Lord. (Num. 6:2–8)

When the "days of his separation are fulfilled," the Nazarite, in addition to other sacrificial acts, "should shave the head of his separation *at* the door of the tabernacle of the congregation, and shall take the hair of the head of his separation, and put *it* in the fire which *is* under the sacrifice of the peace offerings" (Num. 6:13, 18). As a result of his separation, the Nazarite, then, is truly a holy man, consecrated to God through strict observances of the cult. In his own way, he becomes a hierophant whose consecration does, in fact, resemble that of none other than the high priest (Lev. 21:10–12). Such, then, is the Nazaritic milieu out of which Milton's own Samson emerges. As Milton himself never forgot, to write about Samson is to concern oneself with a figure of decidedly cultic origins, origins that mark him as holy in the most archaic sense.

Samson Agonistes is the account not only of a fallen deliverer but of one who has violated his obligations as Nazarite. In short, it is the account of the violation of the sacred. The Bible provides the rationale for this point of view because it ties the Nazaritic prohibition against cutting the hair, as a symbol of holiness ("separation"), to the implicit narrative prohibition against revealing the secret of one's strength, which (in the Samson story) resides in the hair. Thus, when Samson finally tells Delilah "all his heart," the revelation of the secret is wholly in Nazaritic terms: "There hath not come a razor upon mine head: for I *have been* a Nazarite unto God from my mother's womb: if I be shaven, then my strength will go from me, and I shall become weak, and be like any *other* man" (Judg. 16:17). He shall, in short, be no longer separate, no longer holy: he shall, in fact, suffer the fate of those who have committed a profanation. Milton's Samson interprets his act of disobedience precisely in these terms.

Charged with a "hallow pledge" not to "violate the sacred trust of silence," Samson laments that, in divulging God's "holy secret," he has "profan'd / The mystery of God" and "betray'd it to a woman, / A Canaanite, . . . [his] faithless enemy" (377–80, 428, 497, 535). Nor is this the first time that he has done so: "This well I know," Samson admits, "nor was at all surpris'd, / But warn'd by oft experience: did not she / Of *Timna* first betray me, and reveal / The secret wrested from me in her highth / Of Nuptial Love profest [?]" (381–85). The reference, of course, is to Samson's riddle of the honey and the lion (Judg. 14:12–18). Although the secrecy surrounding that riddle shares none of the sacredness implicit in the secrecy involving Samson's source of might, the betrayal of the secret in each instance, Milton suggests, represents a profanation. Moreover, the vehicle of that profanation in each instance is a woman whose very association with Samson possibly represents ceremonial uncleanness[8] and, more important, whose betrayal of Samson certainly represents a moral impurity.

Accordingly, the violation of the sacred in *Samson Agonistes* is both complex and multifaceted. That violation accounts for Samson's fall and provides the modus operandi for the enactment of the drama. In that enactment, Samson is confronted with what amounts to the task of restoring his sacrality, of reinstating himself as Nazarite before God. In cultic terms, that is done through a series of sacrifices: if the Nazarite "hath defiled the head of his consecration . . . he shall shave his head in the day of his cleansing," offer "a sin offering" and "a burnt offering" for the sake of "atonement" and in order to "hallow his head"; "And he shall consecrate unto the Lord the days of his separation, and shall bring a lamb of the first year for a trespass offering: but the days that were before shall be lost, because his separation was defiled" (Num. 6:9–12). Although one cannot argue that *Samson Agonistes* is the dramatic counterpart of this cultic process, it is possible to see in Milton's drama elements of a process by which the Nazarite who has defiled his separation cleanses himself and atones through self-sacrifice as a way of "hallow-[ing] his head," as it were. In this sacrificial drama of atonement, Samson himself, finally, becomes the true *sacrificium*. How this "rendering sacred" occurs becomes discernible in the movements of the drama.

At the outset, it is not only a deliverer who has fallen but a sacred person who has undergone a defilement. That defilement is reflected both in his external environment and in his internal makeup. Externally, he is subjected to the "debas't" "labour" and "servile toyl" of "the common Prison," where "the vilest" "excel" him (5–6, 37, 74). In that environment, he recalls "what once . . . [he] was" in contrast to "what . . . [he is] now." His past was one of holiness and separation, foretold in the theophany (22–30). Had he not been "effeminatly vanquish't" (562), he would have remained true to the Nazaritic code. Both the Chorus and Samson attest to that: "Desire of wine and all delicious drinks," the

Chorus says, "thou couldst repress"; and Samson responds, "Where ever fountain or fresh current flow'd / Against the Eastern ray, translucent, pure, / . . . I drank" (540–49). Eschewing all "forbid'n" drinks, God's "mighty Champion," according to the vow of Nazarite, drank "only from the liquid brook" (556–57). Why, then, he laments, did he violate that vow through an intemperate act, that of "lay[ing] . . . [his] head and hallow'd pledge / Of all . . . [his] strength in the lascivious lap / Of a deceitful Concubine who shore . . . [him] / . . . Then turn'd . . . [him] out ridiculous, despoil'd, / Shav'n, and disarm'd among [his] enemies"? (535–40).

The consequences of this act may be seen in Samson's internal makeup, characterized by "Sores," "tumors," and "wounds" that have "fester'd" (184–86). As Samson complains, "My griefs not only pain me / As a lingring disease, / But finding no redress, ferment and rage, / Nor less then wounds immedicable / Ranckle, and fester, and gangrene, / To black mortification. / Thoughts my Tormentors . . . / Exasperate, exulcerate, and raise / Dire inflammation" (617–26). Drawing upon the language of disease, then, Milton associates Samson's state of mind with bodily defilement. In biblical terms, he becomes "unclean": "When any man hath a running issue out of his flesh, *because of* his issue he *is* unclean. And this shall be his uncleanness in his issue: whether his flesh run with his issue, or his flesh be stopped from his issue, it *is* his uncleanness" (Lev. 15:2–3). Complementing this state of psychological uncleanness in Samson is his blindness, which places him, he believes, beneath the "vilest" things that "creep" (74–75).

Blindness becomes the means by which one who was separate *to* God is now separate *from* God. Accordingly, Samson complains, "O dark, dark, dark, amid the blaze of noon, / Irrecoverably dark, total Eclipse / Without all hope of day" (79–82). He becomes in effect "the Dungeon of . . . [him]self," whereby his "Soul" is "imprison'd" in the "real darkness of the body" (153–59). "Buried" in that way, he feels that he has become "a living death," a "moving Grave" (100–103). His blindness causes his bodily state to accord with his mental state. If he is defiled by the latter, he is likewise defiled by the former: "Blind or broken or maimed, or having a wen, or scurvy, or scabbed, ye shall not offer these unto the Lord, nor make an offering by fire of them upon the altar unto the Lord" (Lev. 22:22). As suggested, to purge himself of this defilement, Samson must undergo a process of cleansing. He must "atone": "Let me here," he says to his father, "pay on my punishment; / And expiate, if possible, my crime" (489–90).

Precisely what is involved in atonement and expiation Milton describes in detail in *Christian Doctrine* (CM, 15:302–92) and dramatizes in *Samson Agonistes*. Although there is not space enough to explore the expiatory process in detail, suffice it to say that it accords with the cathartic experience that Milton associates in his headnote with all genuine tragedy, an experience that leaves us finally with a "calm of mind all passion spent" (1777). We arrive homeopathically at that state of mind as Samson purifies himself by withstanding the temptations that confront him throughout the drama in the form of Manoa, Dalila, and Harapha. In the agon by which he overcomes their assaults upon the true faith in God's ways, he undergoes what has been seen in the discussion of Milton's view of spiritual holiness as the "gradual process" of "sanctification." Through that process, one is "cleansed" as with water (Ephes. 5:26, Tit. 3:5) in order to be "purified" and "separated."

So purified and separated, Samson undergoes a spiritual awakening and enlightenment that prepares him for an unexpected theophany: "Be of good courage," he admonishes, "I begin to feel / Some rouzing motions in me which dispose / To something extraordinary my thoughts" (1381–83). With that anagnorisis, there follows the peripeteia: "I with this Messenger will go along, / Nothing to do, be sure, that may dishonour / Our Law, or stain my vow of *Nazarite*" (1384–86). Given the Nazaritic contexts explored here, that turn of events is, to use Samson's word, "remarkable" (1388), since Samson has just finished arguing that he will not perform in the feast to Dagon, because, as "an *Ebrew*," he is forbidden by "Law" to be present at the "Religious Rites" of the heathen (1319–21). As he says to the Chorus:

> Shall I abuse this Consecrated gift
> Of strength, again returning with my hair
> After my great transgression, so requite
> Favour renew'd, and add a greater sin
> By prostituting holy things to Idols;
> A *Nazarite* in place abominable
> Vaunting my strength in honour to thir *Dagon*?
> Besides, how vile, contemptible, ridiculous,
> What act more execrably unclean, prophane?
>   (1354–62)

This outlook undergoes a reversal with the sudden anagnorisis that Samson experiences, as a further exploration of the sacral implications of the drama will indicate. For Milton, the "rouzing motions" that Samson experiences as the result of his sanctification are what is called in *Christian Doctrine* a divine "impulse" (*vim*) that is truly "extraordinary" (*extraordinariam*). As it does God's "servant Caleb," it inspires with "another Spirit" (*spiritum etiam*) to follow God "fully" (Num. 14:24). As it does Jesus, it "anoints" (*unxerit*) with "power" (*potentia*) (Acts 10:38). In the case of Samson, it causes him to stand in potential violation of legal obligations in order to fulfill divine obligations. Milton found the rationale for that reversal of outlook in Judges 14:1–4, whereby Samson, to the dismay of his parents, "take[s] a wife of the uncircumcised Philistines" as the result of God's promptings: "But his father and his mother knew not that it *was* of the Lord, that he sought an occasion against the Philistines: for at that time the Philistines had dominion over Israel." As Milton's Samson says of his "Parents," "they knew not / That what I motion'd was of God; I knew / From intimate impulse, and therefore urg'd / The Marriage on; that by occasion hence / I might begin *Israel's* Deliverance, / The work to which I was divinely call'd" (221–26). Although it is questionable under the circumstances whether the "intimate impulse" that Samson feels here has the same legitimacy and significance for Milton as do the "rouzing motions" that Samson feels later,[9] the rationale offered for the marriage to the woman of Timnath is relevant to an understanding of the peripeteia.

What Milton does is to appropriate the cultic overtones of the marriage in his rendering of the events surrounding Samson's sudden decision to participate in the feast of Dagon and in his destruction of the "Temple" (1370). Samson commits what might potentially be a defilement in order to obey a higher law. There is, of course, no sense of this appropriation in the original story: Samson is called for, he goes, he makes the Philistines "sport," and he destroys the house of Dagon, first, "that . . . [h]e may be at once avenged of the Philistines for . . . [his] two eyes" and, second, that he may himself die in the process (Judg. 16:25, 28, 30). In Milton, the sacral implications are at the forefront. Having just maintained that he will not defile himself before Dagon, he reverses himself completely, disclaiming that in appearing at the feast, he will not "stain" his "vow of *Nazarite*." He does so because, with the "rouzing motions," he knows that God, to use the Chorus's justification for Samson's marriage, "hath full right t'exempt / Whom so it pleases him by choice / From National obstriction, without taint / Of sin or legal debt; / For with his own Laws he can best dispence" (310–14). Otherwise, God "would not else . . . / Have prompted this Heroic *Nazarite*, / Against his vow of strictest purity" (315–19) to be "present in Temples at Idolatrous Rites / For some important cause" (1378–79).

That cause, of course, is to act as an ἐικονοκλάστης, as one who in his "zeal to the command of God . . . took courage, and broke all superstitious Images to peeces." In so doing, Samson becomes a sacrificium to God's higher purpose, the destruction of those who have desecrated the holy. It is here, of course, that the drama rises to the theomachic level as, in its own way, an embodiment of the "holy war" between God and Dagon (462), a theme that will receive additional elaboration in chapter 11. Anticipated in Samson's challenge to Harapha to decide in combat "whose God is strongest" (1145–55), it is fulfilled in the undermining of the profane, represented ironically by the solemnity held to hallow Dagon in his temple on what is for the Philistines a decidedly holy day (1421). The sacrality of the event is summed up by the Semichorus: while the Philistines were "drunk with Idolatry," "chaunting thir Idol," they were, through Samson, overwhelmed by "our living Dread who dwells / In *Silo* his bright Sanctuary" (1670–74). In that battle between deities embodied in their sanctuaries, Samson emerges victorious (1663): "Dying," he has "fulfill'd / The work for which . . . [he] wast foretold / To *Israel*" (1661–63). Returning "unexpectedly" and bearing "witness gloriously" to "his faithful Champion" (1750–52), God provides the means by which Samson yet once more becomes a warrior-deliverer. Held by the Philistines an "irreligious / Dishonourer of *Dagon*" (860–61), he proves himself religious once again before God by destroying Dagon and causing "confusion [to] blank his Worshippers" (471).

Samson's victory is depicted as a glorious theophany, first through the images of the "Assailant" "Dragon" and "Eagle," emissaries of "wrath divine," and then through the image of the "Phoenix," symbol of rebirth. In each case, an "inward" illumination accompanies the rousing of "fierie vertue." "Lay[ing] e're while a Holocaust," Samson suddenly "teem[s]" "from out . . . [the] ashie womb," "revives, reflourishes, then vigorous most / When most unactive deem'd" (1683, 1687–07). Having "trick[ed] his beams," like Lycidas, he suddenly "flames in the forehead of the morning sky" (L, 170–71). In theophanic terms, his fiery rebirth, with all its iconoclastic implications, fulfills the announcement of his birth by means of the angel who "ascended" in "flames" "from off the Altar, where an Off'ring burn'd." From the cultic point of view, he is readmitted as a "suppliant" (1173).

More than that, he becomes a saint in his own right (1288). Having achieved this stature through the cleansing of sanctification and the consequent sacrifice of death, he receives the oblations due the sanctus: "Let us," says Manoa, "go find the body where it lies / Soak't in his enemies blood, and from the stream / With lavers pure and cleansing herbs wash off the clotted gore." Thus purified, the body will be borne solemnly, "with silent obsequie and funeral train," home to the "sacred house" of God. "There," continues Manoa, "will I build him / A Monument," "enroll'd" as with saints' legends; at the monument the votaries, whether "valiant youth" or "Virgins," will "resort" at appropriate times to do him honor (518, 1725–42). Thus has the Nazarite, "brought unto the door of the tabernacle of the congregation," made "his offering unto the Lord for his separation" (Num. 6:13, 21). Thus has Milton, in keeping with the sacred vein, portrayed the reclamation of the holy in a drama that depicts the destruction of the profane by God's ἐικονοκλάστης. Doing so, he once again performs his function as hierophant, as one who deals in holy things.

If such is true of *Samson Agonistes*, as well as the other poetry already discussed, it is no less true of *Paradise Lost*, the consummate expression of Milton's hierophantic disposition. To assess the nature of that disposition even further, it might be instructive to compare *Paradise Lost* as sacral document with works that have a similar focus. *The Faerie Queene* represents a case in point. The stated purpose of Book 1, of course, is to depict "Holiness" through the legend of Saint George, Knight of the Red Cross. Transfused with the kind of sentiment reflected in the four *Hymns* (particularly the last two), its vision of holiness recreates the Christian paradigm. It does so, as is well-known, by portraying allegorically man's fall and his redemption through Christ. The soteriological element, including Christ's sacrifice, is constantly present in the working out of the allegory. It culminates in the defeat of the dragon, the freeing of Una's parents, and the divine marriage in the last two cantos. Types of the Book of Revelation are everywhere. In this respect, the allegory is fundamentally revelatory: it offers one theophany after another, culminating in that of the numinous countenance of Una, whose "blazing brightnesse" and "glorious light" overwhelm the poet's ability to portray the divine.[10] Underlying this whole revelatory framework is the stated social purpose of the epic, as Spenser states in his letter to Ralegh: "The generall end therefore of all the booke is to fashion a gentleman or noble person in virtuous and gentle discipline."[11] Within this context, holiness, like the other moral virtues supposedly derived from the *Nicomachean Ethics* for depiction in *The Faerie Queene* takes on a decidedly ethocentric bearing.

In contrast, *Paradise Lost* is in conception theocentric and finally Christocentric: its vision of holiness places the theocentric in the most prominent position; all else radiates from that. The experience is comparable to that portrayed by Dante, who beholds in ecstatic vision the *"luce etterna"* which enfolds its divinity within itself.[12] Milton likewise celebrates this experience through "sacred song," as he joins the angelic choir:

> Thee Author of all being,
> Fountain of Light, thy self invisible
> Amidst the glorious brightness where thou sit'st
> Thron'd inaccessible, but when thou shad'st
> The full blaze of thy beams, and through a cloud
> Drawn round about thee like a radiant Shrine,
> Dark with excessive bright thy skirts appear,
> Yet dazle Heav'n, that brightest Seraphim
> Approach not, but with both wings veil their eyes.
>
> (3.373–82)

It is this vision, this theophany of theophanies, that permeates Milton's epic, that gives it focus and meaning, that establishes its rendering of the holy.

If the matter can be envisioned in iconic terms, it might best be done through the frontispiece accompanying the 1661 edition of the *Mundorum Explicatio* (see figure 3), a poem Watson Kirkconnell has seen fit to excerpt in *The Celestial Cycle*.[13] Attributed to Samuel Pordage, the poem, as the subtitle indicates, represents an explanation of the hieroglyphical figure that accompanies it. Depicted in the figure is the theophany of the "Deus inscrutabilis," the "Ens increatum," radiating the blinding light of its divinity from a central fixed point, encircled above the other images. To use the language of the poem: "As several Circles one within another / Drawn, some are farther, some more near than th'other / Unto the Centre . . . / The Centre of them all / We highest . . . call."[14] Below this depiction are all the figures involved in the Christian paradigm, including the crucified Christ, likewise encircled, mediating between the "Arbor Mortis" and the "Mundus tenebrosus" (encircled) to the left and the "Arbor Vitae" and the "Mundus Luminosus" (encircled) to the right. Reclining at the bottom of the picture is the "Adamus Lapsus." Responding to the hieroglyph, the poet says that his purpose is to sing of "the Sacred."[15] The *Mundorum Explicatio* and its accompanying hieroglyph is singled out here not because it is in any sense comparable to *Paradise Lost* in quality but simply because it suggests in visual terms that sense of the holy that Milton is working with in *Paradise Lost*.

In his dedicatory poem to *Paradise Lost*, Andrew Marvell revealed his awareness of precisely this dimension: "That Majesty which through thy work doth Reign / Draws the Devout, deterring the Profane. / And things divine thou treat'st of in such state / As them preserves, and thee, inviolate" (31–34). The idea of drawing the "Devout" and deterring the "Profane" in treating "things divine" strikes at the very heart of the sa-

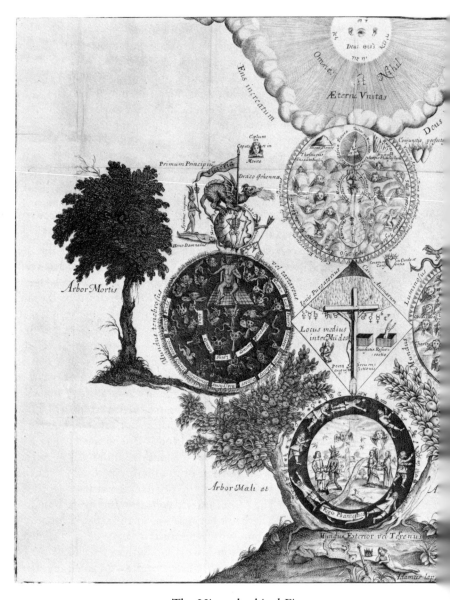

FIGURE 3. The Hieroglyphical Figure.
Reproduced from the frontispiece of [Samuel Pordage],
Mundorum Explicatio (1661), by permission of the Huntington Library,
San Marino, California.

crality that underlies Milton's epic: "*Messiah* Crown'd, God's Reconcil'd Decree, / Rebelling Angels, the Forbidden Tree, / Heav'n, Hell, Earth, Chaos, All," to use Marvell's language again (3–5),[16] represent the holy matter of Milton's poem. Milton treats such things divine, as Marvell observes, in a way that "preserves" them and their poet "inviolate." He treats them, that is, as a priest treats the things of the temple, and as William Riggs observes, it is precisely the image of the temple, inspired by Milton's own view of *Paradise Lost* as a temple, that Marvell has in mind.[17]

This view, of course, places *Paradise Lost* in that body of devotional poetry that deliberately conceived of itself as a verbal representation of the sanctuary. Herbert's *The Temple*, Harvey's *The Synagogue*, and Crashaw's *Steps to the Temple* come immediately to mind. Although *Paradise Lost* and the foregoing works are the products of entirely different traditions, not to mention temperaments, they share that sense of the poem as the vehicle of worship that underlies all poetry written in the sacred vein. In its own way, *Paradise Lost* is the epic embodiment of the engraved frontispieces that grace the 1648 and 1670 editions of *Steps to the Temple*: the first depicting the inside of the temple with steps leading into its recesses; the second the outside of the temple with steps leading up to its opened door.[18] At the threshold of that opening, Herbert's temple invites those who have been "sprinkled and taught" to "approach, and taste / The churches mysticall repast" but warns those who bear "Profanenesse" to withdraw, since "nothing but holy, pure, and cleare, / Or that which groneth to be so, / May at his perill further go."[19] The price of entrance into the interior is high, but the rewards are great.

One enters *Paradise Lost* with the same feeling of what Milton in *Christian Doctrine* defined as "adoratio" and "sanctificatio" (*CM*, 17:81). One enters with a knowledge that here is worship ("cultus," to use Milton's term) of the highest sort, where the poem itself becomes sacrament, the symbol of things sacred, and where one becomes a participant "in an extraordinary act" of "liturgical service" that is "ceremonially sacramental."[20] That fact is apparent from the outset. As one moves from the secret tops of sacred mountains to consecrated temples and finally to the "upright" and "pure" heart, he participates with the poet in an act of supreme worship, in prayer for illumination, before proceeding into the recesses that assume the form of epic narrative. Instructed through the examples of Moses and Christ, he is "sprinkled," cleansed in "*Siloa*'s Brook that flow'd / Fast by the Oracle of God" (PL, 1.11–12). Thus baptized, he beholds the Anointed offering himself as "first fruit" (the collocation of "First" and "Fruit" in the opening of *Paradise Lost* is, of course, meaningful here) in order to "re-store" those who suffer the consequences of the "mortal tast" (1.1–5; cf. 1 Cor. 15:20–23). He beholds, that is, the poem as a vehicle for the expression of that ultimate sacrificium, that ultimate "repast," to use Herbert's term, through which man may be reunited in communion with God. If Herbert thought of his *Temple* as his "first fruits,"[21] Milton thought of his "temple" in no less sacramental fashion. Although the nature of *Paradise Lost* as sacrament, as thing sacred, is far different from that of *The Temple*, one encounters in the sacramental experience offered by Milton's epic a vision of the holy in full resplendency.

Part 3
Res Sacrae

5
Fruit

Perhaps the most productive point of departure in this analysis of the sacral elements in *Paradise Lost* would be a consideration of what Adam calls "the sacred Fruit forbidd'n" (9.904). With its ties to the traditions of the holy, this fruit assumes momentous importance in any consideration of Milton's epic. At once "sacred" and "forbidd'n," it brings to the fore overtones that the modifiers that surround it accentuate stylistically, setting it apart as a thing select and separate, not to be "violate[d]," as Adam says, by common touch (9.902). Such, of course, is traditionally true of the fruit of God. Its source, as F. R. Tennant observes, is in the myth of the sacred tree. Found in Babylonian religion, among other places, this tree assumes the form of "a famous oracle-tree," a sacred palm "with a root of bright lapis." The tree is part of "a grove 'into which no man hath entered'" and which constitutes "a sanctuary of the gods, 'the centre of the earth.'"[1] An ancient Akkadian hymn describes the tree growing in the garden of Edin or Eden, situated, according to Babylonian tradition, near Eridu, a city that flourished at the mouth of the Euphrates between 3000 and 4000 B.C.: "In Eridu a stalk grew overshadowing; in a holy place did it become green; / Its roots were of white crystal, which stretched towards the deep . . . / Into the heart of its holy house, which spread its shade like a forest, hath no man entered."[2]

If this suggests something of the sacral milieu surrounding "the sacred Fruit forbidd'n," the underlying ambivalence that the fruit embodies should not be overlooked. For while it is sacred, it is also accursed: it is the fruit, after all, of "the Tree / Of prohibition, root of all our woe" (9.644–45). As such, it combines that primal view of the holy as both sacred and accursed in sacral thought. Implicit in קדש, ἅγιος, and sacrum, it is that quality of the holy which attaches itself to the underworld and associates it with the most primitive of conceptions. Precisely how this set of circumstances comes about with respect to the fruit will be seen in an exploration of the traditions underlying "the strict forbiddance" (9.903) and its bearing upon Milton's thought.

Since the source of "the strict forbiddance" is, of course, Genesis 2:16–

17, it is there that this discussion must begin: "And the Lord commanded [ויצו] the man, saying, Of every tree of the garden thou mayest freely eat: But of the tree of the knowledge of good and evil [הדעת טוב ורע ומעץ], thou shalt not eat of it: for in the day that thou eatest thereof thou shalt surely die." That command (צו) forms the basis of the Jahwistic (J) document of the Genesis account. Extending from Genesis 2:5 to 3:2, the J document is remarkably distinct from the Priestly (P) document that precedes it. Whereas the P document, extending from Genesis 1:1 to 2:4, is nothing more than a straightforward chronicle of the work of the six days, the J document is a complex narrative whose very origins are mythical "not only in the strictly anthropological sense of the term, but also in the vaguer poetic sense."[3] Indeed, as John M. Evans states, J is "a full-blooded myth" with legendary and cultic elements that were "probably old even at the time the Jahwist was writing." Derived from an "ancient religious tradition," these elements exhibit an "incomplete assimilation into the structure of a monotheistic and ethical theology which makes some of J's features so puzzling."[4]

Not the least of these puzzling elements is the command not to eat of the interdicted tree. In the J account, that command appears all the more puzzling when compared with its notable absence in the P account: "And God said, Behold, I have given you every herb bearing seed, which is upon the face of all the earth, and *every tree* [ראת–כל–העץ], in the which is the fruit of a tree yielding seed; to you it shall be for meat" (Gen. 1:29; italics added). Unlike the restrictions placed upon man in the J document, these dispensations are all-inclusive and all-embracing: they restrict nothing. They exhort man to follow his own natural inclinations ("Be fruitful, and multiply, and replenish the earth, and subdue it" [Gen. 1:28].) In the J account, those inclinations are contravened by a perplexing prohibition that runs directly counter to both the letter and the spirit of the P account.

Even considered on its own terms, the prohibition raises questions. From the point of view of the Jahwist, what, after all, is the nature of the knowledge prohibited? What precisely does the Jahwist mean by "the knowledge of good and evil"? Why prohibit the knowledge of good, as well as the knowledge of evil? Why does the knowledge of these bring death? What is the relationship of the "benefits" bestowed by the interdicted tree to those bestowed by the tree of life? Possessing the benefits of the interdicted tree, in what respect has man become like God (Gen. 3:22)? How are we to understand God's statement to that effect?[5] These, and similar questions, have prompted historians of religion to investigate the sources of those ancient traditions that gave rise to the Jahwistic account.

Theories abound. The tree of the knowledge of good and evil, maintains Theodor Gaster, was originally "a tree of death, not of knowledge," in contrast to "the tree of life," which, in the earlier version of this story, probably played a much more active role than it does in the Genesis account. In the earlier version, suggests Gaster, man was given a choice of eating the fruit of one (death) or of the other (life) and, misled by the serpent, ate the fruit of the tree of death.[6] Something of these elements may, in fact, be found in the Babylonian Adapa legend (ca. 1300 B.C.) with which the Jahwistic account is often compared. In that legend, Adapa is offered the food and water of life by the gods. Rejecting that offer on the advice of Ea, Adapa, and therefore all mankind ("Adapa" suggests "man"), remains mortal.[7] Even if this is not the *Ur*-version of the story, however, the tree of the knowledge of good and evil, maintains Samuel Hooke, bestowed not originally "moral knowledge," as is suggested in the Jahwistic rendering, but cultic knowledge, "the knowledge of friendly and hostile forces" and "of powerful incantations by which these forces might be controlled."[8] Misappropriation of this knowledge through a violation (conscious or inadvertent) of the strictures surrounding the tree might lead to disease or even death. In this context, one of the most ancient of paradise stories—that of the Sumerian Enki and Ninhursag (ca. 2000 B.C.)—comes immediately to mind. Desiring to "know" the "heart" of eight sacred plants within the paradise of Dilmun (196–217), Enki is cursed for unwittingly violating the prohibition against eating them (250–68).[9] A Sumerian prayer (ca. 2000 B.C.) that antedates the higher monotheism of Genesis suggests the liturgical context of the violation: "The transgression [I have committed]—I know not. . . . Food [of my god (?)—unwittingly I have ea]ten. . . . What was forbidden by my god—unw[ittingly] I have eaten. . . . The forbidden thing I have eaten—I (know) not. . . . God, known [or unknown, turn to me]. . . . How long, god known or unknown until thy hostile heart returns to its place? Mankind is dumb and knows nothing. . . . Whether one does wrong or does right one knows not. . . . The sin I have sinned—turn thou to good" (11–56).[10]

By the time the Jahwist came to assimilate these elements into his own monotheistic version of the biblical account, the ethical dimension was thrust to the forefront: the interdicted food came to assume a decidedly moral bearing. The interdict placed upon the tree made off limits not simply a tree of death or a tree of the knowledge of uncanny forces but a "tree of the knowledge of good and evil." A violation of the interdict upon that tree accounted for the travails of the fallen world: the interdict became part of an etiological myth. As stated, however, the myth was not self-sufficient: the nagging questions surrounding the interdict upon which it is based continued to persist. Those encountering the interdict were put to the expense of attempting to provide an explanation for it.

Appropriately, the rationale for what has been defined here as the J command became the subject of discourse from the time of the Church Fathers to the biblical exegetes of the Renaissance. Determined to make sense of the command, they almost universally appropriated it into a covenant theology founded upon natural law, on the one hand, and moral law, on the other. The first point of view is supported by Henry Vane, who, in *The Retired Mans Meditations* (1655), maintains that "when we speak of this Covenant in reference to the state of innocency, it is to be understood for the same thing with the law of nature, under which *Adam* was created" (pp. 60–61). The second point of view is ascribed to by Andrew Willet, who, in *Hexapla in Genesin* (1605), maintains that "this precept . . . containeth the very foundation of all precepts, and of the whole morall law" (p. 33). Willet has in mind here Tertullian's assertion in *An Answer to the Jews* that God's divine command contains "in embryo [*condita*] all the precepts which afterwards sprouted forth when given through Moses; that is, Thou shalt love the Lord thy God from thy whole heart and out of thy whole soul; Thou shalt love thy neighbour as thyself; Thou shalt not kill; Thou shalt not commit adultery; Thou shalt not steal; False witness thou shalt not utter; Honour thy father and mother; and, That which is another's shalt thou not covet. For the primordial law was given to Adam and Eve in paradise, as the womb of all the precepts of God."[11]

In *A Treatise of the Divine Promises* (1633), Edward Leigh sums up both points of view when he says that God's first prohibition constituted both a "*Foedus Naturale*, the *Covenant* of nature, because it was made by God with man at his first Creation, and because it is contained in the Law which is known to men by nature; and [a] *Foedus Legale*, the *Covenant* of workes, because workes were the condition of it" (p. 63). It was customary to combine the two laws, because they were both universally seen as having been founded upon the same principle. In his discussion of the written and unwritten laws in *Christian Doctrine*, Milton himself reflects that outlook when he says that "the law of nature has the same obligatory force, and is intended to serve the same purposes as the law of Moses" (*CM*, 16:109; Rom. 3:19). It is an outlook that is given full expression by Robert Rollock in *A Treatise of Gods Effectual Calling* (1603): "The couenant of workes, which may also be called a legall or natural couenant, is founded in nature, which by creation was pure and holy, and in the law of God, which in the first creation was ingrauen in mans hart" (p. 66). Both laws, in turn, are tied by the bond of reason. If Milton sees in the law of nature the expression of "right reason" (CD, CM, 15:117), he sees in the moral law the expression of "morall reason" (D, CM, 3:410). As he says in *Brief Notes*, "That which is grounded on the light of nature or right reason [is] commonly call'd *moral law*" (CM, 4:158). From that point of view, he maintains in *The Doctrine and Discipline of Divorce* that "what is against nature is against Law . . . ; by this reckning *Moses* should bee most unmosaick, that is, most illegal, not to say most unnaturall" (CM, 3:458).

But this is precisely Milton's attitude in *Christian Doctrine* toward what is implied by God's issuing of the divine command. Taking into account both natural and moral law in his consideration of that command, Milton adopts a position that runs counter to the prevailing outlook. Of natural law, he says: "Seeing, however, that man was made in the image of God, and had the whole law of nature so implanted and innate in him, that he needed no precept to enforce its observance, it follows, that if he received any additional commands . . . these commands formed no part of the law of nature, which is sufficient of itself to teach whatever is agreeable to right reason, that is to say, whatever is intrinsically good" (CM, 15:115–17). Of moral law, he maintains that although the divine command "is sometimes called 'the covenant of works,' . . . it does not appear from any passage of Scripture to have been either a covenant, or of works. No works whatever were required of Adam; a particular act only was forbidden" (CM, 15:113). Milton's treatment of the divine command, then, categorically dismisses both laws and, in so doing, dismisses the principles upon which those laws are based. As such, the command becomes for Milton "an act in its own nature indifferent [*neque bonum in se esset, neque malum*]": "For since it was the disposition of man to do what was right, as a being naturally good and holy, it was not neccessary that he should be bound by the obligation of a covenant to perform that to which he was of himself inclined; nor would he have given any proof of obedience by the performance of works to which he was led by a natural impulse, independently of the divine command" (CM, 15:113–15).

At the same time, however, Milton refers elsewhere in *Christian Doctrine* to the divine command as that which may be classifiable with what he calls "contingent decrees" founded upon "implied conditions": "If thou stand, thou shalt abide in Paradise; if thou fall, thou shalt be cast out; if thou eat not the forbidden fruit, thou shalt live; if thou eat, thou shalt die" (CM, 14:69, 81). It is within this context that the fallen Adam complains of God's justice in *Paradise Lost*:

> inexplicable
> Thy Justice seems; yet to say truth, too late,
> I thus contest; then should have been refus'd
> Those terms whatever, when they were propos'd:
> Thou didst accept them; wilt thou enjoy the good,
> Then cavil the conditions?
>
> (10.755–59)

Despite Milton's declaration that the divine command is not a covenant but "an exercise of jurisdiction," since "no command . . . can properly be called a covenant, even where rewards and punishments are attached to it" (CD, *CM*, 15:115), that command embodies even for him something that resembles a covenant psychology. Indeed, he actually refers to the command as a "covenant" (*"in foedere, sive mandata accipiendo"*) whose violation involves none other than "a transgression of the whole law" "written by Moses . . . long subsequent" to "the special command which proceeded out of the mouth of God" (*CM*, 15:179–83).

Thus, Milton dismisses a covenant theology based upon moral and natural law, as those laws are bound by the principle of reason, and accepts something associated with a covenant theology founded upon the "implied conditions" of "contingent decrees": that is, a command at once "unmosaick," "illegal," and "unnaturall," and at the same time indebted to the conditional terms of the Mosaic outlook. The result is a point of view that emphasizes the extralegal nature of the command while maintaining its dispensational ties. Any consideration of such a divine command must take into account a point of view that is decidedly complex. The way in which that view functions in Milton's thought will become clear through a further exploration of the divine command.

As a command that is "unmosaick," "illegal," and "unnaturall," the prohibition against eating the fruit has absolutely no basis for Milton in anything that governs rational behavior as that behavior is determined by natural or moral law. Having categorically dismissed natural and moral laws as the underlying principle of the first prohibition, Milton postulates a situation in which a command is issued in order to impose upon man a deliberately arbitrary injunction that *by its very nature* runs counter to the dictates of human reason. Milton is unequivocal on this point. The arbitrariness of the command, its irrationality, is attested to by the fact that for Milton the idea of not eating of the tree of the knowledge of good and evil "would not have been obligatory on any one, had there been no law to enjoin or prohibit it" (CD, *CM*, 17:117). Only the prohibition itself, imposed quite arbitrarily from without, makes the tree off limits. As Milton states in *Tetrachordon*, "For albeit our first parent had lordship over sea, and land, and aire, yet there was a law without him, as a guard set over him" (*CM*, 4:74).

Were it not for this prohibition, man might very well have eaten of the tree, as he ate of the others, and suffered no punishment as a consequence. But because of the prohibition, the tree becomes forbidden, a circumstance that causes to attach to it the experience of the fallen world, what God calls in *Paradise Lost* the "knowledge of Good lost, and Evil got" (11.87). And, after such knowledge, what forgiveness? "Be lowlie wise," Raphael admonishes Adam. "Think onely what concerns thee and thy being" (8.173–74). What the fruit of the tree appears to offer does not concern Adam and his being. Man's reason concerns other matters. The reason underlying the prohibition is not for man to know: that reason is God's, not man's. As Richard Hooker states in *Of the Lawes of Ecclesiastical Politie*: "To find out *supernatural laws*, there is no natural way, because they have not their foundation or ground in the course of nature. Such was the law before Adam's fall, which required abstinence from the tree of knowledge touching good and evil. For by his reason, he could not have found out this law, inasmuch as the only commandment of God did make it necessary and not the necessity thereof procure it to be commanded."[12] Although she slights God's prohibition by calling it "sole Daughter of his voice" (*PL*, 9.653), even Eve is aware of the fundamental distinction between "supernatural" and "natural" law. Distinguishing between what Milton earlier calls that "one restraint" and the fact that she and Adam are otherwise "Lords of the World besides" (1.32), she says, "The rest, we live / Law to our selves, our Reason is our Law" (9.653–54). God's reason, Eve thereby implies, is his own law, to be obeyed because God is God.

From that point of view, the prohibition functions as a means of establishing or testing man's ability to obey even that which is arbitrarily imposed and to believe in the justness of that imposition (CD, *CM*, 15:115).[13] As God says to Adam, the interdicted tree becomes "the Pledge of thy Obedience and thy Faith" (*PL*, 8.325). Since the "seat of faith," Milton states in *Christian Doctrine*, "is not in the understanding, but in the will" (*CM*, 15:407), to obey the command becomes an act of the will, not of the understanding. However, in refusing to compromise one's faith, Milton would maintain, one paradoxically demonstrates not only his freedom to choose but his ability to understand. As God states in *Paradise Lost*:

> Freely they stood who stood, and fell who fell.
> Not free, what proof could they have given sincere
> Of true allegiance, constant Faith or Love,
> Where onely what they needs must do, appear'd,
> Not what they would? what praise could they receive?
> What pleasure I from such obedience paid,
> When Will and Reason (Reason also is choice)
> Useless and vain, of freedom both despoild,
> Made passive both, had serv'd necessitie,
> Not mee.
>
> (3. 101–11)

Ironically, Satan leads man precisely to the point of relinquishing his freedom, his power of choice, and thus his ability to reason by tempting man to question the rational basis of what is deliberately without reason. He leads man, that is, to assume his own posture toward the divine command, a posture that he assumes early in the epic after he has overheard Adam and Eve speak of the injunction:

> All is not theirs it seems:
> One fatal Tree there stands of Knowledge call'd,
> Forbidden them to taste: Knowledge forbidd'n?
> Suspicious, reasonless. Why should thir Lord
> Envie them that? can it be sin to know,
> Can it be death? and do they onely stand
> By Ignorance, is that thir happie state,
> The proof of thir obedience and thir faith?
>
> (4.513–20)

Although Satan obviously misinterprets the motives behind the issuing of the command, his reaction is perfectly in keeping with the nature of the command as that which is deliberately "reasonless," even upon initial scrutiny "suspicious." It is precisely this reasonlessness, this suspiciousness, that Satan capitalizes upon in order to destroy man: "O fair foundation laid whereon to build / Thir ruin!" (4.521–22). He establishes that foundation, of course, by attributing to God those very motives that characterize his own personality—envy and jealousy. "Why then was this forbid?" asks the Tempter of Eve. "Why but to awe, / Why but to keep ye low and ignorant, / His worshippers" (9.703–5). In this sense, God becomes the "Threatner" (9.687), the "great Forbidder, safe with all his Spies" (9.815).

If this response to God runs directly counter to the doctrinal view that

Milton establishes in *Paradise Lost*, it, like Satan's response to the divine command, has an ironic appropriateness. For it recalls none other than the Jahwistic deity of the J document, as opposed to the Elohistic deity of the P document. Whereas the Elohistic deity is fundamentally an idea, the conceptualized expression of an elevated and sophisticated theology, the Jahwistic deity is a "person," portrayed vividly and pictorially.[14] As such, the Jahwistic deity betrays a personality whose "shortcomings" seem to be "more human than divine." "Appear[ing] to be jealous in denying his creatures knowledge," he is "envious and fearful in His desire to prevent them from . . . becoming like Him."[15]

Although the deity of *Paradise Lost* is far removed in this respect from the Jahwistic deity of the J document, he shares, when appropriate, the same decidedly anthropomorphic characteristics that distinguish Jahweh from Elohim. Nowhere is this fact more dramatically apparent than in God's issuing of the divine command in *Paradise Lost*. As Adam recalls of God:

> Sternly he pronounc'd
> The rigid interdiction, which resounds
> Yet dreadful in mine ear, though in my choice
> Not to incur; but soon his clear aspect
> Return'd and gracious purpose thus renew'd.
>
> (8.333–37)

Here, as elsewhere in *Paradise Lost*, the anthropomorphisms of the J document are dramatically apparent. Indebted to the anthropomorphic presence of God implicit in the Old Testament, this vision of the Deity is, of course, perfectly in keeping with Milton's view of God as expressed in *Christian Doctrine*: "Our safest way is to form in our minds such a conception of God, as shall correspond with his own delineation and representation of himself in the sacred writings" (*CM*, 14:31). "If God habitually assign to himself the members and form of man, why," asks Milton, "should we be afraid of attributing to him what he attributes to himself?" (*CM*, 14:35). In that sense, "let us believe that it is not beneath the dignity of God to grieve in that for which he is grieved, or to be refreshed in that which refresheth him, or to fear in that he feareth. For however we may attempt to soften down such expressions by a latitude of interpretation, when applied to the Deity, it comes in the end to precisely the same" (*CM*, 14:35). As such, the "majestas" of one who is the "invisible" and "inaccessible" "Fountain of Light" (PL, 3.373–82), referred to earlier, manifests itself, when occasion demands it, as a distinctly "personal" deity. As the remainder of this book will attempt to demonstrate, Milton's God mediates between the two conceptions: He is at once "infinite," "omnipresent," and "incomprehensible," to use the language of *Christian Doctrine* (CM, 14:41–61), and, as just stated, accessible "through the members and form of man." In either case, he is perfectly in accord with the numinous bearing that Otto sees as essential to the deity of both the Old Testament and the New.[16]

From the anthropomorphic point of view, his presence resonates with the overpowering quality of the *ganz andere*. Particularly in the issuing of the prohibition, those resonances in *Paradise Lost* are intensified rather than "soften[ed] down." Specifically, Milton assimilates into the prohibition the strictures not only against eating of the interdicted tree but against *touching* the fruit of that tree. Biblical precedent for that point of view may be found, of course, in Eve's statement to the serpent in Genesis 3:3: "But of the fruit of the tree which *is* in the midst of the garden, God hath said, Ye shall not eat of it, neither shall ye touch it [ולא תגעו בו], lest ye die." From the very beginning, exegetes never tired of pointing out that the "touching" of the fruit had nothing at all to do with God's original prohibition to Adam in Genesis 2:16–17. Either Adam himself communicated that aspect of the interdiction to Eve or Eve made it up at the time of the temptation. In either case, the addition of this further restriction was both unprecedented and unnecessary. Thus, according to the *Aboth of Rabbi Nathan*, the addition of that restriction was like making "a fence higher than the object which it is to guard," with the result that "the fence fell and crushed the plants":[17] that is, by adding to the prohibition, man helped pave the way for his own undoing.[18]

For Milton, however, the restriction against touching becomes a natural extension of the divine command, one that deliberately intensifies the rigor of its bearing. Although we never directly witness the pronouncement of that restriction to man by God or his messengers, Milton implies clearly enough that it is the office of the "affable Arch-Angel" to make certain that man is "charg'd not to touch the interdicted Tree" (7.41–46). Touching and tasting, in a sense, become interchangeable, two acts derived from the same root, one *tangere* that implies them both. Thus, when Eve is tempted by Satan, she invokes the two acts as if they embodied one forbidden act: "But of this Tree we may not taste nor touch" (9.651) and "God hath said, Ye shall not eat / Thereof, nor shall ye touch it, least ye die" (9.662–63). Adam's initial response to Eve's transgression, in turn, not only reflects but elaborates upon that point of view: "Much more to taste it under bann to touch" (9.925). But Adam does not stop there: he carries the interdiction still further by suggesting that even looking upon or "coveting to Eye" the fruit represents a daring and perilous affront (9.921–23). From that point of view, the inherent reasonlessness of the command is additionally reinforced to the extent that the interdiction against tasting comes to involve both touching and seeing as well.

If such is the case, then the threatened punishment of violating the interdiction is perfectly in accord with what becomes, after all, most "unmosaick," "illegal," and "unnaturall." Within this context, God warns Adam that "the day thou eat'st thereof, my sole command / Transgrest, inevitably thou shalt dye" (8.329–30). Even though God qualifies the warning by explaining that to "dye" means to be both "mortal" and "expell'd from hence into a World / Of woe and sorrow" (8.331–33), Adam does not know in any absolute sense the meaning of death. Under the circumstances, his response to the threatened punishment is quite appropriate: "What ere Death is, / Som dreadful thing no doubt" (4.425–26). Thus not only is Adam given an arbitrary prohibition not to eat (and, by implication, touch and even look upon) that which would be acceptable under any other circumstances but he is warned that if he disobeys the prohibition, he will suffer a punishment the true signification of which he has absolutely no idea.

To understand the full impact of what God has imposed upon Adam, one might render the situation in the following terms: "Do not touch the tip of your left ear with your right forefinger, or else you will *squibbledydib*." One's response, like Adam's, would appropriately be, "What ere *squibbledydib* is, / Som dreadful thing no doubt." The situation is projected in these terms not to make fun of it but to indicate the true nature of its reasonlessness. At its very source, *Paradise Lost* embodies a logic of illogic, a sense of nonsense. In that way, it recreates with deadly earnestness the irrationality of the Jahwistic account from which it is drawn.

Such a view is hardly alien to seventeenth-century thought. In his *Archaeologiae Philosophicae* (1692), Thomas Burnet questions the rationality of God's caveat that disobedience of the prohibition will result in death: "*Mori!* Quid hoc rei est, inquit ignara virgo, quae nihil unquam mortuum viderat, ne florem quidem" (p. 29).[19] In a work appropriately entitled *The Oracles of Reason* (1693), Charles Blount translates Burnet's observation as follows: "Die! what does that mean, says the poor ignorant Virgin, who as yet had not seen any thing dead, no not so much as a flower" (p. 41). Although Burnet substitutes Eve (the *ignara virgo* or "poor ignorant Virgin") for Adam, the significance of the correspondence still holds. As C. S. Lewis states, the prohibition and the manner in which it is cast are quite simply "inexplicable," if not irrational,[20] but not for that any the less "dreadful."

Accordingly, Death becomes a "thing" whose "dreadfulness" is truly nightmarish: a "Goblin," "black . . . as Night / Fierce as ten Furies, terrible as Hell," a "Monster" shaking its "dreadful Dart" (PL, 2.670–72, 688). Milton surrounds the disobedience of the prohibition with terror. Eden itself is enveloped in nightmare: once expelled, Adam and Eve look back to behold "thir happie seat, / Wav'd over by that flaming Brand, the Gate / With dreadful Faces throng'd and fierie Armes" (12.641–44; cf. Gen. 3:24). Such are the consequences of disobeying the "rigid interdiction," the mere pronouncement of which by a stern-faced Deity resounds dreadfully in Adam's ear and still unnerves him long after it has been pronounced.

Its effects are quite in accord with the language that describes it. The word *rigid* itself tells the tale. One thinks of *Comus*:

> What was that snaky-headed *Gorgon* sheild
> That wise *Minerva* wore, unconquer'd virgin,
> Wherewith she freez'd her foes to congeal'd stone?
> But rigid looks of chast austerity,
> And noble grace that dash't brute violence
> With sudden adoration and blank aw.
>
> (447–52)

The figure of Death in *Paradise Lost* appears with his "Mace petrific" and his "look" which binds "with *Gorgonian* rigor not to move" (10.294–97). One is not certain whether he would rather be confronted by Minerva's shield with its "snaky-headed *Gorgon*" or with the "Goblin" Death with his "Mace petrific" and "*Gorgonian*" "look." In either case, the specter of violating a terrifying rigidity is not something that one would willingly contemplate. In the case of the rigid interdiction, the only way of overcoming the effects of that violation is through fulfilling the momentous demands of an equally "rigid satisfaction." As God pronounces sternly in the heavenly council of Book 3 of *Paradise Lost*: "Man with his whole posteritie must die, / Die hee or Justice must; unless for him / Som other able, and as willing, pay / The rigid satisfaction, death for death" (3.209–12).

As so many have recognized before, the fundamental terms upon which *Paradise Lost* is predicated are essentially archaic. Despite the complex logical superstructure of doctrinal explanation and rational discourse that characterizes Milton's epic, *Paradise Lost* retains, and even intensifies, that subimperative sense of myth that pervades the Jahwistic account of Genesis. In this respect, the logic that underlies the prohibition against the fruit in *Paradise Lost* has about it the nonlogic of mythic or prediscursive thought. That thought, maintains Lucien Lévy-Bruhl, is what characterizes "*la mentalité primitive*," which is essentially nonanalytic. Rather, it is "synthetic": "The syntheses which compose it do not imply previous analyses of which the result has been registered in definite concepts, as is the case with those in which logical thought operates. In other words, the connecting links of the representations are given, as a rule, with the representations themselves. In it, too, the syntheses appear to be primitive and . . . they are nearly always both undecomposed and undecomposable." As a result, primitive thought is "always bound up with preperceptions, preconceptions, preconnections, and . . . with prejudgments; and thus it is that primitive mentality . . . is also prelogical."[21] "Causal connection," as the logical mind conceives it, does not exist for the primitive.[22] Among primitives, such is the basis of mythic reasoning, characterized, as Ernst Cassirer maintains, not by the establishment of "an unequivocal relation between *specific* 'causes' and *specific* 'effects'" but by that which "has a free selection of causes at its disposal. Anything can *come from* anything."[23]

Embodying this mentality, *Paradise Lost* has elements that run counter to any view that would label it as Milton's "logical epic."[24] Rather, as Isabel MacCaffrey, among others, has demonstrated, it is essentially "mythic."[25] At its source, says Wayne Shumaker, *Paradise Lost* is "an enormous 'tell-me-why story,' infinitely more complex than those told by children and savages but similar in basic nature."[26] Shumaker is referring to the many *pour quoi* legends of a fall, "found everywhere in mythology," that is "regularly the effect of some transgression. For instance, among the Andaman Islanders, a Negrito people isolated for centuries in the Bay of Bengal, it resulted from the breaking of a taboo against the making of noise while the cicadas are singing. . . . As a result of the violation, say the Andamanese, 'a great storm came and killed many people, who were turned into fishes and birds.' The human survivors were dispersed, each pair being provided with a different dialect. Although reported versions of the myth vary slightly, we seem to have here an amalgam of three separate incidents in the Christian story—the fall, the deluge, and the building of Babel."[27]

If invoking such a parallel seems at first glance a spurious way of underlining the so-called mythic elements in *Paradise Lost*, one would do well to remember that the attempt to bolster biblical truth through the discovery of cultural parallels was by no means new to either Milton or the Renaissance. Milton's expressed attitude toward the Fall in *Christian Doctrine* is that of a cultural anthropologist. His treatment of the "principle" governing original sin and its effects upon the human race is typical. For Milton, the truth of that principle is not only attested to by the "divine proceedings" of established doctrine but is "recognized by all nations and under all religions from the earliest period" (CD, CM, 15:185). Drawing at once upon the testimonies of the Bible, the *History of the Peloponnesian War*, and the *Aeneid*, Milton points to the customs of the Hebrews and the Egyptians, on the one hand, and to those of the Greeks and the Romans, on the other, to establish that the sins of the fathers are visited upon their offspring from one generation to the next as the result of divine enmity, which in turn can only be appeased through rituals of expiation (CD, CM, 15:184–91). "Hence," Milton states, "the penitent are enjoined to confess not only their own sins, but those of their fathers. . . . Thus also entire families become obnoxious to punishment for the guilt of their head" (CD, CM, 15:189).

Viewing the Genesis narrative in this way, Milton thereby attempts to establish the cross-cultural basis of what he sees as religious truth. In doing so, he places himself within the tradition established by tracts ranging from John Owen's Θεολογουμενα Παντοδαπα (1661) to Johannes Bompart's *Parallela sacra et profana* (1689).[28] Infused with the outlook of comparative religion, these tracts are the works of exegetes who sought to discover the universality of their own beliefs in the beliefs of other cultures. With them, Milton derives from the narrative of the Fall what Owen calls a "Theologia *Adamica*" giving rise to the "*cultum institutum*" of all races.[29] It is precisely this cultural framework that helps establish even further the precise nature of what Milton understood as God's prohibition not to eat of the interdicted tree. For if, according to Milton, the principle governing original sin and its consequences finds expression in all cultures, the principle governing that command whose violation resulted in original sin might likewise be said to find expression in "all nations and under all religions from the earliest period." Although Milton never explicitly makes this point, his view of the command as the expression of a law totally removed from what underlies the rational dictates of natural and moral law invites a response that has its basis in cultural anthropology.

Milton hints at that approach when he suggests that God's ways in the issuing of such a command are reflected in the customs of men. Springing from what Milton calls God's "positive right," his absolute prerogative to do as he wishes, the injunction not to eat of the fruit has its counterpart for Milton in those injunctions issued when "any one invested with lawful power, commands or forbids what is in itself neither good nor bad" (CD, CM, 15:117). Milton does not elaborate further upon the association here, but exegetes concerned specifically with what Owen calls the "cultum institutum" do.[30] One thinks in particular of biblical commentators like Edward Stillingfleet. In his *Origenes Sacrae* (1666), Stillingfleet defends the reasonlessness of the divine command by asking:

> Hath not then a *Legislator* power to require any*thing*, but what he *satisfies* every one of his *reason* in commanding it? if so, what becomes of *obedience* and *subjection*? It will be impossible to make any *probative precepts* on this account; and the *Legislator* must be charged with the *disobedience* of his *subjects*, where he doth not give a particular *account* of every thing which he requires. [This is] contrary to all *Laws* of *Policy*, and the general sense of the world. This *Plutarch* gives a good account of when he discourseth so *rationally* of the *sobriety* which men ought to use in their inquiries into the *grounds* and *reasons* of *Gods actions*; *for*, saith he, *Physitians will give prescriptions without giving the patient a particular reason of every circumstance in them. . . . Neither have humane Laws alwayes apparent reason for them, nay, some of them are to appearance ridiculous*; for which he instanceth in that *Law* of the *Lacedemonian Ephori* . . . , to which no other reason was annexed but this . . . : *they commanded every Magistrate at the entrance of his office to shave himself, and gave this reason for it, that they might learn to obey Laws themselves.* He further instanceth, in the *Roman* custom of *manumission*, their *Laws* about *testaments*, *Solons Law* against *neutrality* in seditions, and concludes thence. . . . *Any one would easily find many absurdities in Laws, who doth not consider the intention of the Legislator, or the ground of what he requires. . . .* What wonder is it, if we are so puzled to give an account of the actions of men, that we *should be to seek as to those of the Deity*? This cannot be then any ground on the account of mere reason, to lay the *charge* of *mans disobedience upon God*, because he required from him the observance of that *positive command* of not eating of the *forbidden fruit.* (pp. 480–81)

Simply stated, Stillingfleet's approach to the divine command is that of an anthropologist who provides a rationale for the reasonlessness of the command by pointing to certain customs that seem to have no basis in rational behavior, such as the apparently "ridiculous" custom fostered by the "Lacedemonian Ephori" that "every Magistrate" must "shave himself" "at the entrance of his office." What Stillingfleet is addressing himself to, of course, is the taboo, a phenomenon that was to become the particular concern of ethnologists in the centuries following the publication of *Origines Sacrae*. First recorded by Captain James Cook in his

1777 voyage to the Pacific Islands, the taboo received extensive treatment in the nineteenth century by Robert Henry Codrington and others.[31] In its earliest definition, the taboo is spoken of by Captain Cook as that which "signifies that a thing is forbidden," a signification that has no basis in rational explanation.[32] Since Captain Cook's definition, the basic understanding of the taboo still prevails: it represents, as discussed earlier, a "prohibition for which to the civilized mind, there is no obvious meaning."[33] "In proportion as a taboo becomes a custom and its sanctions fall into the background and are forgotten, its obligations thus transformed are one source of the categorical imperative, the distinguishing feature of which is that it is non-rational and instinctive."[34] In his own writings, Milton delighted in recounting such prohibitions. Thus, in the *History of Muscovia*, he is careful to note that one "*Antony Jenkinson*," having voyaged to "*Mosco*," "arriv'd while the Emperour was celebrating his marriage with a *Circassian* Lady; during which time the City Gates for three daies were kept shut; and all men whatsoever strictly commanded to keep within their Houses; except some of his Houshold; the cause whereof is not known" (*CM*, 10:372).

As the foregoing discussion has made clear, it is precisely this kind of prohibition that Renaissance exegetes who viewed the Genesis account anthropologically would apply to the divine command itself. To be sure, there are obvious differences between the prohibition that Milton cites in his *History* and the divine command of Genesis 2:16–17. The command certainly does not give rise to a "custom" whose "sanctions fall into the background and are forgotten." As Milton's treatment of the command in *Christian Doctrine* makes clear, there is even a sense in which the "cause" of the command is "known." To use the language of Milton's *Art of Logic*, God himself is the "efficient cause" and man's ability to sustain the "test" occasioned by the command, the "final cause." Nonetheless, this discussion of Milton's understanding of the command has also shown an equally compelling reason for maintaining that the command is one about which one could assuredly say, "The cause [t]hereof is not known." That "reason," to continue in the language of Milton's *Logic*, is the "form" the command assumes in the world of "matter":[35] that is, the context created by placing an interdiction against eating upon the fruit of a particular tree. The rationale underlying the context out of which these "causes" (both "formal" and "material") arise, according to Milton's point of view, is decidedly unknown: why does this particular interdiction fall upon this particular tree? Whatever the reason, the situation is distinctly classifiable in anthropological terms. Specifically, it is a situation growing out of what Emile Durkheim calls a "negative cult," by which certain objects are forbidden or "withdrawn from common use" as the result of interdictions or taboos placed upon them.[36]

In Milton's other writings, the most graphic example of such interdictions can be found in the association of the Nazaritic prohibition against cutting the hair with Samson's pledge not to reveal the source of his strength. Having "profan'd / The mystery of God" (377–78) by "violat[ing] the sacred trust of silence" (428) and betraying the secret of his strength, Samson suffers, among other indignities, that of having the "hallow'd pledge / Of all . . . [his] strength" "shav'n" (535–40). He thereby loses that power, that Macht, which makes him the "Select, and Sacred" Nazarite (363). Subjected to "servile toyl" in "the common Prison" (5–6), he can only call into question the logic of God's ways: "God, when he gave me strength, to shew withal / How slight the gift was, hung it in my Hair" (58–59). Samson is, of course, finally reclaimed in his resignation to "the will / Of highest dispensation" (60–61). Nonetheless, the issue of the precise nature of the logic that underlies the workings of that will still remains. It is no accident that in recounting the Fall of Adam and Eve Milton thought of that "*Danite* strong / *Herculean Samson*" "shorn of his strength" (PL, 9.1059–62).

Something of the magical quality that adheres to the sacral milieu surrounding the Nazaritic prohibition in the Samson account likewise adheres to the special trees of the Genesis account. The one taboo before the Fall, the other taboo after it, these trees may be associated with the animism that Northcote Whitridge Thomas, in his classic essay on the taboo, suggests is an essential constituent of at least certain kinds of tabooed objects.[37] How closely such an outlook accords with Milton's handling of the special trees may, of course, be open to question. Indeed, judging by what he says in *Christian Doctrine*, that outlook would appear to run directly counter to his point of view. The tree of knowledge, for example, derives its name not from anything inherent in the tree itself but from the "event" ("Dicta est autem scientiae boni et mali ab eventu" [It was called the tree of the knowledge of good and evil from the event], *CM*, 14:114–15). Here, Milton's outlook seems to reflect that of Saint Augustine, who says in his treatise *On Merits and Forgiveness of Sins* that whatever evil Adam and Eve brought upon themselves, the interdicted tree "did not produce it to their detriment from any noxious or pernicious quality in its fruit, but entirely from the fact of their violated disobedience."[38]

From this perspective, Milton classifies the tree of knowledge as nothing more than "a pledge, as it were, and memorial of obedience" (*CM*, 15:114, 115). In the same way, the tree of life is "a symbol of eternal life" (*CM*, 15:114, 115). Such is precisely the language of *Paradise Lost*, where the trees become nothing more than the "Pledge" of "Obedience" and "Faith," on the one hand, and of "immortality," on the other (8.325, 4.200–201). It is none other than this attitude which prompts scholars such as Joseph Duncan to label the special trees of *Paradise Lost* as "chiefly physical realities."[39] Despite this outlook, the trees still become assimilated into the cultum institutum that forms the basis of the mythic point of view. They do so through the "mythical" affinities of the first prohibition itself: that which is prohibited shares the mythos of the prohibition. Milton suggests something of that mythos when, discoursing upon the customs of the Britons in *The History of Britain*, he says that "thir Religion was governd by a sort of Priests or Magicians call'd *Druides* from the Greek name of an *Oke*, which Tree they had in great reverence, and the *Missleto* especially grown thereon" (*CM*, 10:49–51).

The aura is mythologized in *Paradise Lost* through reference to the Hesperian myth. It is in the "groves" of Eden, after all, that the "*Hesperian* Fables" prove to be "true," that the trees actually do hang "with Golden Rind" (*PL*, 4.249–50), and that, in particular, "all amid them" stands "the Tree of Life, / High eminent, blooming Ambrosial Fruit / Of vegetable Gold" (4.218–20). This tree may not be precisely the one on which "the scaly harnest dragon ever keeps / His unenchanted eye," but it is close enough to the "golden tree" of myth to suggest similar associations.[40] Shakespeare's rendering of the idea in *Pericles* is particularly apt: "Before thee stands this fair Hesperides, / With golden fruit, but dangerous to be touch'd; / For death, like dragons, here affrights the hoard" (1.1.27–29).[41] If there are no dragons surrounding the tree of life, there are those frightening angels assigned to "guard all passage" to that tree (*PL*, 11.120–22, 12.641–44; Gen. 3:24) once Adam and Eve have fallen. They certainly will not be able to steal any "golden apples" or, as Milton says, be "delude[d]" with "stol'n Fruit" (11.125).

If the golden apples characterize the tree of life, they likewise have about them qualities that come to be associated with the other tree. In *The Faerie Queene*, Spenser makes the association explicit in his depiction of the "*Gardin of Proserpina*," in which "did grow a goodly tree, / With braunches broad dispred and body great, / Clothèd with leaues, that none the wood mote see, / And loaden all with fruit as thicke as it might bee" (2.7.53). The fruits of this tree "were golden apples glistring bright," the likes of which may be found, among other places, in the garden of Hesperides (2.7.54).[42] By placing the tree in the "*Gardin of Proserpina*," Spenser no doubt has in mind Pluto's promise to Proserpine of a tree consecrated to her, as recounted by Claudian in the *Rape of*

Proserpine. From this tree, Proserpine "took the apple which, when she ate it, condemned her to spend a part of each year in Hades. Proserpine's fate is a type of the fall of Eve."[43] The significance of this entire context would not have been lost on Milton. Having invoked the "fruit burnisht with Golden Rind" of the "*Hesperian* Fables" (PL, 4.249–50) to characterize the fruit of paradise, Milton makes the following comparison a few lines later: "Not that fair field / Of *Enna,* where *Proserpin* gathring flowrs / Her self a fairer Flowr by gloomie *Dis* / Was gatherd, which cost *Ceres* all that pain / To seek her through the world . . . / . . . might with this Paradise / Of *Eden* strive" (4.273–75). The allusion is proleptic: it places the image of paradise, with its golden apples, in a context that looks forward to the fallen world. In mythic terms, "next to Life / Our Death the Tree of Knowledge grew fast by" (4.220–21). The alternatives not only exist side-by-side but share the same mythic aura.

If such is true of the tree of life in its association with the tree of knowledge, it is particularly true of the latter tree. That tree assumes an undeniably mythical centrality in *Paradise Lost* because it is the object at which the divine command is first directed. That command bestows upon the tree an aura that characterizes primitive thought. In particular, it causes the tree to embody the archaic predisposition to reverence the tabooed object for the powers that are latent within it. The tree thereby assumes a magical cast by virtue of its supposedly indwelling powers. Animating and thereby sanctifying the tree, those powers, in their most archaic form, are demonic, giving rise to the idea that associates certain kinds of *jinn* or demons with trees in primitive thought. "In Hadramant," states W. Robertson Smith, "it is still dangerous to touch the Mimosa, because the spirit that resides in the plant will avenge the injury."[44] "A demonic plant of the northern Semites is the Baaras, described by Josephus . . . , which flees from those who try to grasp it, and whose touch is death."[45]

Such is true of the interdicted tree, as Genesis introduces and *Paradise Lost* elaborates upon the relationship between touching and dying. Eve's repeated admonitions not to touch the tree in *Paradise Lost* are perfectly in accord with the primitive associations to which the magical trees of the Genesis account give rise. The *Pirkê de Rabbi Eliezer* dramatizes the situation in distinctly animistic terms: "The serpent went and touched the tree, which commenced to cry out, saying: 'Wicked One! do not touch me!' . . . The serpent went and said to the woman: 'Behold, I touched it, but I did not die; thou also mayest touch it, and thou wilt not die.' The woman went and touched the tree, and saw the angel of death coming towards her."[46] Accordingly, when Eve eats of the fruit in

Paradise Lost, Milton depicts that event through a language that draws upon the animistic idea: Eve, says Milton, "knew not eating Death" (PL, 9.792), as if the goblin resided in the fruit itself. As such, Eve implicitly becomes for Milton a kind of Pandora who, having disobeyed the command not to open the magic container, inadvertently allows its demonic contents to escape (4.714–19).

That event, in turn, brings the animistic figure of "Death into the World, and all our woe" (1.3), as Sin and Death, "there in power before, / Once actual, now in body" (10.586–87), fly up from the gates of Hell in order to perpetuate "the Race of *Satan*" (10.385–86) on earth. Adam and Eve, commanded to "encrease and multiply" (10.730), are their vehicles. Indeed, Eve, "deflourd" (9.901) by her fall, becomes Death's "consort" (9.954), through whom all that she and Adam "eat or drink, or shall beget, / Is propogated curse" (10.728–29). In animistic terms, the consequences of the transgression are cosmic indeed: "Earth felt the wound, and Nature from her seat / Sighing through all her Works gave signs of woe, / That all was lost" (9.782–84), while the "Skie lowr'd, and muttering Thunder, som sad drops / Wept at compleating of the mortal Sin / Original" (9.1002–4).

Ironically, Eve's immediate response to her transgression fosters, in a perverse way, this animistic sense. First, she apostrophizes the tree: "O Sovran, vertuous, precious of all Trees / In Paradise, of operation blest / To Sapience"; next she bows in "low Reverence . . . as to the power / That dwelt within" (9.795–97, 835–36). Both gestures suggest Eve's willingness to worship the tree as the receptacle of a power that animates it. Replacing God as the rightful recipient of worship, the tree becomes for Eve the object of adoration. As its votary, she promises to "cultivate" the tree by "caring" for it, "tending" it with "Song" and "praise" "each Morning," and "easing" it of its "fertil burden" until she becomes god-like in the special knowledge that the tree is supposed to bestow upon her (9.799–804). In so doing, she would become a priestess of the tree about which she would create her own particular kind of fetish, one which would look upon the tree as magic, its fruit "infus'd" with "sciential sap, deriv'd / From Nectar, drink of Gods" (9.834–38).

The application of the term *fetish* in this instance is not arbitrary. Renaissance ethnologists were already quite familiar with the fetish and its cultic manifestations. In treatises ranging from Samuel Purchas's *Pilgrimage* (1613) to John Ovington's *Voyage to Suratt* (1696), the fetish had received ample elaboration. In his discourse on Africa, for example, Purchas speaks of "strawen Rings, called *Fetissos*, or *Gods*," attended by their priests or "*Fetisseros*." To those who worship them, the fetissos are "sacred things," animated by a spirit of one kind or another.[47] Purchas's observation about the relationship of fetish worship and trees is particularly significant here:

> When the King will sacrifice to *Fetisso*, he commaunds the *Fetissero* to enquire of a Tree, whereto he ascribeth Diuinitie, which he will demaund. He, with his wives, comes to the Tree, and in a heape of ashes, there prouided, prikes in a braunch plucked off the Tree, and drinking water out of a Bason, spouts it out on the braunch, and then daubeth his face with the ashes: which done, he declareth the Kings question, and the Deuill out of the Tree makes answere. The Nobles also adore certaine Trees, and esteeme them Oracles: and the Deuill sometimes appeareth vnto them in the same in forme of a blacke Dogge, and otherwhiles answereth without any uisible apparition.[48]

The magical quality ascribed to the trees by the fetisseros is not lacking in the effects that the "fallacious Fruit" (10.1046) has upon Adam and Eve in *Paradise Lost*. First, it "intoxicates" with a deceptive sense of godlike transcendence (cf. Eve's dream [5.28–92]) and then "enflames" with a carnal "Lust" (9.1008–15) that results finally in humiliation, as Adam and Eve are "naked left / To guiltie shame" (9.1057–58). In that state, they rush into "the thickest Wood" and cover themselves with the leaves of the fig tree (9.1100–1101), itself traditionally associated with the tree of the knowledge of good and evil.[49] Thus covered, they are reminiscent, Milton implies, of those American savages that "*Columbus* found" "so girt / With featherd Cincture, naked else and wild / Among the Trees on Iles and woodie Shores" (9.1115–18).

Before that humiliation occurs, however, Adam's response to the transgression is no less desperate than Eve's, as he slights the prohibition by saying, "If such pleasures be / In things to us forbidden, it might be wish'd, / For this one Tree had been forbidden ten" (9.1024–26). (Freudian psychology would see here the characteristic overreaction to having disobeyed the taboo, which, as a "primaeval prohibition . . . imposed [by some authority] from outside," is "directed against the most powerful longings to which human beings are subject," longings that give rise to an incessant desire to "violate" the taboo.)[50] From the cultic point of view, Adam, like Eve, desires to engage in a fetish, one that would create many forbidden trees to be violated time and again.

The absurdity of both Adam and Eve's responses to their disobedience is made dramatically apparent in Book 10. There, Milton mythologizes the entire situation by recounting what becomes purportedly the "annual humbling" (10.577) of Satan and his accomplices. Forcibly transformed into serpentine form, they are drawn to a "grove . . . laden with fair Fruit, like that / Which grew in Paradise, the bait of *Eve* / Us'd by the Tempter" (10.548–54). "Imagining / For one forbidden Tree a multitude / Now ris'n," the snakes "greedily" "pluck'd / The Fruitage fair to sight" (10.553–61). Unable to "abstain" even though the fruit is filled with "soot and cinders," the snakes "oft . . . assayd," only to be repulsed with "bitter Ashes" at every turn (10.558–70).

Emphasized through local allusion and contextual pattern, the cultic implications of the scene are manifold. Locally, the sight of the trees with their "fair Fruitage" that contain nothing but "bitter Ashes" recalls the delusive Dead Sea apples with their ashes and smoke, mentioned by commentators extending from Josephus to John Mandeville.[51] These apples, implies Milton, are like those "which grew / Neer that bituminous Lake where *Sodom* flam'd" (10.561–62; Gen. 18–19). With this allusion, Milton appropriately places his tree of the knowledge of good and evil within the context of the cultum institutum. His tree thereby comes to inhabit the same mythos as the rigid interdiction, a mythos that Milton even further enhances by associating his vision of the serpents' "climbing" "up the Trees" with the "snakie locks / That curld *Megaera*" (PL, 10.558–60). Confronted with that Fury, we are returned implicitly to the Gorgonian rigidity of the interdiction itself. We are face to face with Death, a singularly appropriate circumstance considering the way in which Milton makes clear that the tree of knowledge is no less than the tree of "Death" (4.220–21).

Contextually, the circumstances surrounding the serpents' devouring the fruit recalls the fetishism of Adam and Eve's response to their own transgression. If Adam desires not one but many trees to violate, they are present here, violated time and again by the serpents. If Eve desires to worship what she has just violated, here she may do so in the form of serpents that are unwitting and unwilling votaries, drawn to the trees by an irresistible force. But when they "ease" the trees of their "fertil burden," they do not sing "praises" to the trees. Rather, their songs are those of spewing and "spattering," as they spit out the "soot and cinders" "with hatefullest disrelish" (10.567–70). Such "worship" they are "yearly enjoynd" (10.575) in an unwelcome process of self-humbling that parodies, like a perverse cult, the whole idea of the fetish as the Renaissance understood it. Creating his own "Theologia *Adamica*," based upon cultic parallels, then, Milton causes his tree of the knowledge of good and evil to reflect a point of view that associates the tree with that which is magical and demonic and about which perverse cults arise.

Milton's attitude toward the tree of knowledge is decidedly ambivalent. For while that tree accrues to itself demonic associations as a result of the interdiction, it also enjoys the stature of that which is divine. In doing so, it subscribes to that pattern of religious thought which conflates demonic and divine. In its most primitive form, the tabooed object "diverges in two contrary directions": it embodies, on the one hand, that which is dangerous and forbidden and, on the other, that which is consecrated and sacred.[52] But such is precisely true of the Semitic attitude toward the sacred tree. With its roots in the demonic, the tree of the Semite evolves into a sacred object of worship. As Smith states, "No Canaanite high place was complete without its sacred tree standing beside the altar." In fact, in the local sanctuaries of the Hebrews, altar-sanctuaries "were habitually set up 'under green trees' " or situated beside the *ashera*, a living tree or treelike post. "The *ashera* undoubtedly was an object of worship; for the prophets put it on the same line with other sacred symbols" (cf. Isa. 17:8 and Mic. 5:12 ff.).[53]

Accordingly, Milton suggests in *Christian Doctrine* that to have disobeyed the first prohibition was to have engaged in a "sacrilege" (*sacrilegus*) involving "the violation of things sacred (and such was the tree of knowledge of good and evil)" (*rem sacram violasset [sacra autem erat arbor ista]*) (CM, 15:184–85). Such an outlook is reflected in Adam's response to Eve's disobedience in *Paradise Lost*: "How hast thou yeelded to transgress / The strict forbiddance, how to violate / The sacred Fruit forbidd'n" (9.902–4). Thereafter, Adam attempts to appease them both with this telling rationalization: "Perhaps," he says to Eve, "thou shalt not Die, perhaps the Fact / Is not so hainous now, foretasted Fruit, / Profan'd first by the Serpent, by him first / Made common and unhallowd ere our taste" (9.928–31).

The doctrinal answer to Adam's rationalization is to be found in *Christian Doctrine*. There, Milton maintains that as an embodiment of God's "hidden things" (*rerum occultarum*), the tree of knowledge must remain inviolate at all costs. In that way, it resembles God's holy name (Gen. 19:26, 22:19), his holy mount (Exod. 19:23), and his ark (1 Sam. 6:19). Around these things, he has "set bounds," Milton suggests, so that they might not be profaned (CD, *CM*, 17:32–35). Milton is not alone in assuming such a posture. His outlook is part of a prevailing tradition, most notably expressed by Martin Luther in his *Lectures on Genesis*: whereas today we have altars and pulpits in our churches, for Adam "this tree of the knowledge of good and evil was Adam's church, altar, and pulpit," and if Adam had not fallen, "this tree would have been like a common temple and basilica to which people would have streamed."[54]

Such a statement springs from the common Renaissance predilection to view both the tree of knowledge and the tree of life in ecclesiastical terms. Precisely how far Milton would have been willing to accept these terms might, however, be open to some question. One is inclined to feel that his outlook is more nearly mythic than ecclesiastical when it comes to the place of the interdicted tree in his understanding of the Genesis narrative. This distinction is made here because those who embraced the ecclesiastical view did not hesitate to place their interpretation within a ceremonial context. In short, they sacramentalized not only the tree of knowledge but the tree of life. In so doing, they envisioned the special trees as sacramental prefigurations of God's will. Thus, John Salkeld observes in *A Treatise of Paradise* (1617) that while the tree of knowledge foreshadows "the tree of the crosse," the tree of life foreshadows "the sacred communion, and bread of life" (p. 51). Underlying such an observation is a point of view that Milton, in one instance, has been shown to reject in *Christian Doctrine*. That view is one which relates the divine command with the covenant of works. Expressing precisely that point of view in his *Compendium Theologiae Christianae*, Johannes Wollebius maintains that the covenant of works was "confirmed" by the "twofold sacraments" embodied in the trees.[55] So consistent was that view with reformed dogmatics that it was incorporated into the Westminster Confession.[56] Milton, of course, dismisses the view outright. Both the tree of knowledge and the tree of life, states Milton, are "not a sacrament, as [they] are generally called; for a sacrament is a thing to be used, not abstained from" (CD, *CM*, 15:114–15). Taken at face value, such a statement would seem to suggest that Milton divorces his trees entirely from all but the most literal of considerations.

As demonstrated, however, such is hardly the case. Because of the mythos implicit in the first prohibition, the special trees are a great deal more than the "chiefly physical realities" that Duncan and others have seen in them. Reflecting the *cultum institutum* engendered by Milton's handling of the first prohibition, they veritably inhabit the world of myth. Anthropologically, they share the aura of the sacred so integral to primitive thought. Because of the first prohibition, they become taboo. It has already been shown how alive that concept was for the Renaissance and how readily it was applied to the first prohibition. The question that now presents itself is what specific connection the concept of the taboo might have with the traditions of religious thought that Milton inherited from the Bible and what particular bearing that thought might have on Milton's understanding of the Genesis account. The answer lies paradoxically in that very ceremonial law that Milton would appear to reject in his dismissal of the sacramental basis of the special trees.

The aptness of that assertion becomes discernible in Milton's treatment of the sacraments in general. The meaning of the term *sacrament*, Milton maintains in *Christian Doctrine*, need not be confined to the strict interpretation that has been imposed upon it by the churches throughout the ages. Since the word "nowhere occurs in Scripture," "it is unnecessary to be very scrupulous" about its doctrinal significance (*CM*, 16:215–17). The term finally may be understood as that which is expressed by "religious emblems, or symbols of things sacred" (*res sacras significent*) (*CM*, 16:214–17). It is in this sense that the special trees are to be understood. If the tree of the knowledge of good and evil is not a sacrament in the sense of that which is "to be used," it is sacred in the sacramental sense, as that which is to be "abstained from" (*CM*, 15:115). "Sacred to abstinence," Adam calls it in *Paradise Lost* (9.924).

The ceremonial basis of that point of view may be found in the חֻקִּת that underlie the Levitical code.[57] It is there that exegetes were most inclined to discover the cultic basis of the first prohibition. From the Judaic point of view, the *Midrash Rabbah* maintains that the interdicted fruit takes on the character of "a limb torn from a living animal" (Lev. 22:18: "That which dieth of itself, or is torn *with beasts*, he shall not eat to defile himself therewith: I *am* the Lord").[58] The *Aboth of Rabbi Nathan* contains the following statement: "R. Simeon b. Elazar said: Adam can be likened to an Israelite who married a proselyte woman, and he constantly sought to impress upon her mind the following regulations: 'My daughter, eat not bread when thy hands are unclean, eat not of fruits which were not tithed, do not violate the Sabbath, do not get into the habit of making vows, and walk not with another man. If thou shouldst violate any of the commands, thou wilt die!'"[59] This outlook is carried through to the Christian tradition in writers extending from the time of the Church Fathers to the Renaissance. Whereas Novatian, in his discourse *On the Jewish Meats*,[60] implies a relationship between the interdicted fruit and the interdicted food of Levitical law, such writers as Gervase Babington and Joseph Mede make that relationship overt. Thus, in *Comfortable Notes Vpon the bookes of Exodvs and Leuiticvs* (1604), Babington suggests that although the interdicted fruit is not in itself unclean, it becomes so by virtue of the prohibition. In that way, the fruit assumes the character of unclean meat (p. 93). In *Diatribae*, Mede maintains that the interdicted fruit, as that which is cursed, is similar to those foods in Levitical law that are cursed (p. 400).

Milton undoubtedly had something of this idea in mind in *Paradise Regained* when he has Satan defend the "purity" of the feast that is set before Jesus by maintaining that "no interdict / Defends the touching of these viands pure" (2.369–70): here, Jesus will find neither "Meats by the law unclean" (2.328) nor "Fruits forbidd'n" (2.369).[61] (Compare Leviticus 19:23–25: "And when ye shall come into the land, and shall have planted all manner of trees for food, then shall ye count the fruit thereof as uncircumcised: three years shall it be as uncircumcised unto you: it shall not be eaten of. But in the fourth year all the fruit thereof shall be holy to praise the Lord *withal*. And in the fifth year shall ye eat of the fruit thereof, that it may yield unto you the increase thereof: I *am* the Lord your God.")

Appropriately, in *Paradise Lost*, when Adam and Eve do violate God's command, they contract the uncleanness of the fruit itself, thereafter to be reproached as both "unclean" (9.1097) and "impure" (10.735). (Compare Leviticus 5:2: "If a soul touch any unclean thing, whether *it be* a carcase of unclean beast, or a carcase of unclean cattle, or the carcase of unclean creeping things . . . he also shall be unclean, and guilty.") As Sebastian Franck says in *The forbidden fruit: or a treatise of the tree of knowledge* (1640), the Fall was an "offense" to God, causing man to become "unclean": we shall become clean again only when we "doe vomitt up the Fruit of the Tree of Knowledge of Good and Evill" (pp. 14–16). In the meantime, Adam and Eve must be expelled from paradise. As God declares in *Paradise Lost*:

> But longer in that Paradise to dwell,
> The Law I gave to Nature him forbids:
> Those pure immortal Elements that know
> No gross, no unharmoneous mixture foul,
> Eject him tainted now, and purge him off
> As a distemper, gross to air as gross.
>
> (11.48–53)

The idea recalls the original concept of the taboo and its effects upon the tabooed object. Those effects are such that the tabooed object becomes divine: it contains mana, the power to destroy upon contact. As such, it is distinct from that which is *noa* or common. That which is noa must never come in contact with that which is taboo. The noa must obey "a complicated etiquette" that surrounds the tabooed object.[62] To violate that etiquette is to suffer the wrath of the god who has made the object taboo. Durkheim describes the situation in these terms:

Owing to the contagiousness inherent in all that is sacred, a profane being cannot violate an interdict without having the religious force, to which he has unduly approached, extend itself over him and establish its empire over him. But as there is an antagonism between them, he becomes dependent upon a hostile power, whose hostility cannot fail to manifest itself in the form of violent reactions which tend to destroy him. This is why sickness or death is considered the natural consequence of every transgression of this sort; and they are consequences which are believed to come by themselves, with a sort of physical necessity. The guilty man feels himself attacked by a force which dominates him and against which he is powerless. Has he eaten the [tabooed] animal? Then he feels it penetrating him and gnawing at his vitals; he lies down on the ground and awaits death. Every profanation implies a consecration, but one which is dreadful, both for the subject consecrated and for those who approach him. It is the consequences of this consecration which sanction, in part, the interdict.[63]

Those consequences involve the subjecting of that which is profane to what Durkheim calls "the contagiousness of the sacred."[64] Thus, Eve in *Paradise Lost* finds herself not only "defac't" and "deflowrd" but "to Death devote" because she has "violate[d] / The sacred Fruit forbidd'n" (9.901–4), having become, as God says, "to destruction sacred and devote" (3.208; Lev. 27:28–29: "Every devoted thing *is* most holy unto the Lord. None devoted . . . shall be redeemed; *but* shall surely be put to death").

The foregoing should provide ample indication of what was already shown to be true of the sacred tree: the ambivalence of the sacred is fundamental to the tabooed object. As Wilhelm Wundt states, "Two opposing ideas are combined in the conception of the taboo: the idea of the sacred as something to be avoided because of its sanctity, and that of the impure or loathsome, which must be avoided because of its repulsive or harmful nature."[65] Thus, "there are two sorts of sacredness, the propitious and the unpropitious, and not only is there no break of continuity between these two opposed forms, but also one object may pass from the one to the other without changing its nature. The pure is made out of the impure, and reciprocally. It is in the possibility of these transmutations that the ambiguity of the sacred exists."[66] That this idea was familiar to Renaissance thought may be seen in Edward Leigh's discourse on ἅγιος in *Critica Sacra* (1639): "ἅγιος" or "*sanctus*," says Leigh, signifies not only "*purus*" but "*pollutus*," both that which is "*sacra*" and that which is "*scelus*" (p. 7). This recalls W. Robertson Smith's statement: "At the Canaanite shrines the name of 'holy' was specifically appropriated to a class of wretches, whose life, apart from its connection with the sanctuary, would have been disgraceful even from the standpoint of heathenism."[67] These wretches became "holy" because they were set apart from common use.

Such is precisely the character that tabooed objects take on as the result of the Levitical injunctions. "Alongside of taboos that exactly correspond to rules of holiness, protecting the inviolability of idols and sanctuaries, priests and chiefs, and generally of all persons and things pertaining to the gods and their worship, we find another kind of taboo which in the Semitic field has its parallel in rules of uncleanness. Women after childbirth, men who have touched a dead body and so forth, are . . . taboo and separated from human society, just as the same persons are unclean in Semitic religion."[68] In accord with the laws of clean and unclean, certainly the most fundamental and pervasive taboo is that which concerns the eating of the interdicted object.[69] In *Taboo and Perils of the Soul*, Sir James Frazer has an entire section devoted to the matter. He proceeds to offer one example after the next: "The Flamen Dialis was forbidden to eat or even name several plants and animals, and . . . the flesh diet of Egyptian kings was restricted to veal and goose. In antiquity many priests and many kings of barbarous peoples abstained wholly from a flesh diet. The *Gangas* or fetish priest of the Loango Coast are forbidden to eat or even see a variety of animals and fish, in consequence of which their flesh diet is extremely limited; often they live only on herbs and roots."[70] The list of examples goes on for pages.

That the nature of the taboos provided by these examples was hardly foreign to Milton is made evident once again in his treatment of the Britons in *The History of Britain*. Their religion, Milton observes, may be characterized by their custom of "abstaining from a Hen, a Hare, and a Goose, from Fish also" (*CM*, 10:50–51). Taboo for the Britons, these foods are interdict, Milton would maintain, because of the unwritten laws regulating custom, whose force is as strong as that of a written law. As Milton says in *Tetrachordon*, "All who understand Law will consent, that a tolerated custom hath the force of a Law, and is indeed no other but an unwritt'n Law . . . and is as prevalent as any writt'n statute" (*CM*, 4:111). Their most compelling characteristic is their irrationality, a characteristic that underlies the Levitical laws themselves. The "irrationality" of these laws is "so manifest that they must necessarily be looked on as having survived from an earlier form of faith and of society" and thus must be classed as "savage taboos."[71]

From the doctrinal point of view, of course, the Levitical laws represent the ceremonial counterpart of the moral law that forms the basis of the covenant of works.[72] As such, they form part of the Old Dispensation communicated by God himself to Moses on Sinai. This, of course, is how Milton understood them (CD, CM, 16:98–111). Nevertheless, their apparent irrationality proved perplexing right from the very beginning, so much so, in fact, that exegetes like Moses Maimonides felt compelled to set the record straight, to make sense of these laws, much in the manner that other exegetes felt called upon to make sense of the first prohibition. Thus, in *Guide of the Perplexed*, Maimonides states:

> No question concerning the end need be asked with regard to . . . [moral] *commandments*. For no one was ever so perplexed for a day as to ask why we were commanded by the Law that God is one, or why we were forbidden to kill and steal, or why we were forbidden to exercise vengeance and retaliation, or why we were ordered to love each other. The matters about which people are perplexed and opinions disagree—so that some say there is no utility in them at all except the fact of mere command, whereas others say there is a utility in them that is hidden from us—are the *commandments* from whose external meaning it does not appear that they are useful [that is, rational]. Such, for instance, are the prohibitions of the *mingled stuff*, of the *mingling* [of diverse species], and of *meat in milk*, and the commandment *concerning the covering of blood*, the *heifer whose neck was broken*, and the *firstling of an ass*, and others of the same kind. However, you will hear my explanation for all of them and my exposition of the correct and demonstrated causes of them all.[73]

He then presumes to show the truly rational basis of such injunctions and, in so doing, merely shows how irrational they are.

It is this irrationality that Milton, in keeping with his attitude toward the first prohibition, attributes to ceremonial law in general and to dietary law in particular. Emphasizing the "unreasonable" nature of ceremonial law in *A Treatise of Civil Power* (CM, 6:36),[74] he refers in *Christian Doctrine* to dietary law in the following terms: "Thus the eating of fat was forbidden by the law, . . . yet no one infers from hence that the use of fat is unlawful, this prohibition applying only to the sacrificial times" (CM, 16:161). That is, it represents a provisional or conditional prohibition. This idea recalls the initial discussion here of Milton's view of the first prohibition as not only that which is extralegal but that which is dispensational. For Milton's outlook regarding ceremonial law is perfectly in keeping with his outlook regarding the first prohibition. That outlook views both laws as conditional, on the one hand, and irrational, on the other. Although one should not push the analogy too far, associating the first prohibition with dietary law does serve finally to suggest the way in which Milton's extralegal and dispensational views complement each other.[75] If one is to make the analogy, however, it is to be done not in the doctrinal sense but in the cultic sense. The distinction is one that has already been seen to operate in Milton's treatment of the Fall in *Christian Doctrine* and in his unwillingness to subscribe in any doctrinal way to the theory of the sacraments.

What results from this point of view is a perspective that can only be termed mythic, a perspective that enhances its doctrinal viewpoints with nondoctrinal or perhaps extradoctrinal considerations. This approach is particularly true of Milton's attitude toward the first prohibition. That prohibition is at once extralegal and dispensational, a combination that associates it not doctrinally but culturally with ceremonial law. While it has no basis in reason (the foundation of moral and natural law), it is at the same time essential to the covenant of works.

If Milton dismisses the covenant of works in his consideration of the first prohibition, he also imposes upon that prohibition a dispensational framework, one that has affinities with none other than that ceremonial dimension that he would presume to reject in his consideration of the first prohibition. If he rejects it doctrinally, he accepts it in terms that must be called "cultic," a view which Milton himself defines in his treatment of the Fall as that which characterizes "all nations and . . . all religions from the earliest period" (CD, *CM*, 15:185). From this perspective, the ceremonial dimension forms part of the larger anthropological viewpoint that associates the first prohibition with the taboo. In doing so, it underlies the *cultum institutum* that the Renaissance was so fond of associating with the Genesis story. That is, it inhabits the world of myth —a world, after all, that has its very roots in the Jahwistic account out of which the narrative of the Fall emerged in the first place.

6
Place

If the ambivalence implicit in "the sacred Fruit forbidd'n" provides insight into that aspect of the holy which is at once pure and polluted, there are additional aspects of res sacrae that must be considered in order to appreciate the holy in its full resplendency. Only then can one, like Milton, "minister about holy things" and "live *of the things* of the temple." In his discussion of rerum occultarum in *Christian Doctrine*, Milton enumerates some of these "holy things," including God's name, his mount, and his ark (*CM*, 17:32–35). All these things provide for God a local habitation and a name: they provide for him what in sacral thought is designated המקום ("the place"), a designation that is significantly one of the names of God.[1] Before considering specific aspects of המקום, such as those that Milton himself enumerates in *Christian Doctrine*, it would be advisable to explore the significance of "holy place" as a general concept in *Paradise Lost* in order to establish a context for the chapters that are to follow. This chapter, then, will suggest some of the insights that will be explored in much greater depth in succeeding chapters.

In its concern with המקום, the *Zohar* speaks of "a place" that is "concealed and hidden, eluding all inquiry, a place which is the height of heights, the most high Temple, withdrawn from all cognition."[2] There, God's presence dwells in utmost sanctity. Similarly, in *Christian Doctrine*, Milton refers to "the invisible and highest heaven" as "the supreme citadel and habitation of God" (*Coelum enim supremum veluti summa arx et habitaculum Dei*) (*CM*, 15:28–30). As envisioned in *Paradise Lost*, that habitation is one in which God and the Son, "amidst as from a flaming Mount, whose top / Brightness had made invisible," are enclosed "Orb within Orb" of "circuit inexpressible" (5.594–599). For Milton, the concept of a Divine Presence enclosed within sanctified boundaries was very much alive. At the same time, however, he wrote in *Paradise Lost* that "God attributes to place / No sanctitie" per se (11.836–37): "Surmise not then / His presence to these narrow bounds confin'd / Of Paradise or *Eden*" (11.339–41), admonishes Michael. In his tracts against the prelates, of course, Milton speaks with disdain of what he calls "the railing in of a repugnant and contradictive Mount Sinai" in the form of a "woodden table" with a "perimeter of holy ground about it" (CG, *CM*, 3:261–62). Yet, in the *Logic*, he acknowledges that "place" may be considered an attribute of "divine beings" (*divinis entibus*) (*CM*, 11:80, 81). Clearly, a discussion of holy place in Milton's thought must take into account a frame of reference that is exceedingly complex.

According to Eliade, the concept of a holy place is fundamental to religious thought as a manifestation of the archaic "need to remain in direct communion with a 'centre' producing the sacred."[3] "Every microcosm, every inhabited region," says Eliade, "has what may be called a 'centre'; that is to say, a place that is sacred above all. It is there, in that centre, that the sacred manifests itself in its totality."[4] These "centres" assume so many forms in Western thought that one need only recall Plato's vision in *Critias* (116–17) of the "sacred island" of Atlantis to recognize their pervasiveness. Surrounded by "zones" that encircle the inmost center, Atlantis is an island enclosed from its outermost zone to its innermost. Having carefully detailed the dimensions of each zone, Plato states: "The entire circuit of the wall, which went round the outermost zone, they covered with a coating of brass, and the circuit of the next wall they coated with tin, and the third, which encompassed the citadel, flashed with the red light of orichalcum. The palaces in the interior of the citadel were constructed in this wise: in the center was a holy temple, dedicated to Cleito and Poseidon, which remained inaccessible, and was surrounded by an enclosure of gold."[5] This example should suggest something of the nature of what Eliade felicitously calls a "sacred, mythic geography."[6]

Among the essential characteristics of this geography, one finds an enclosure that separates profane space from sacred space within which a divinity dwells and communicates with those who have been able to penetrate the consecrated area. "The sacred," states Eliade, "is always dangerous to anyone who comes in contact with it unprepared, without having gone through the 'gestures of approach' that every religious act demands. 'Draw not nigh hither,' said the Lord to Moses, 'put off thy shoes from off thy feet, for the place [הַמָּקוֹם] whereon thou standest is holy ground [אַדְמַת-קֹדֶשׁ]' (Exod. 3:5)."[7] This holy ground in the Tantric schools takes the form of a *mandala* or "circle." As a series of circles inscribed in a square, the mandala contains images of the various Tantric divinities. As such, the mandala is both an *imago mundi* and a symbolic pantheon. "The initiation consists in the neophyte's penetration into the various zones or stages of the *mandala*. The rite may be looked on with equal justice as the equivalent of the *pradaksina*, the well-known ceremonial of going round a temple or sacred monument (*stūpa*), or an initia-

tion by way of ritual entry into a labyrinth."⁸ "These," says Carl Gustav
Jung, "are among the oldest religious symbols of humanity" and are
"distributed all over the world."⁹

Their exact bearing on Milton may be seen from two points of view,
the cultural and the biblical. The relationship between the two is striking
enough that the first will provide background for the second. From the
first point of view, Milton describes with obvious fascination and pains-
taking detail accounts of ceremonial entry into the walled cities of Mos-
cow and Cathay. "*Cathaia* the imperial City," Milton states, is "built of
White-stone four-square, in circuit four daies going, corner'd with four
White owers, very high and great, and others very fair along the Wall,
white intermingl'd with blew, and Loop-holes furnisht with Ordnance.
In midst of this White City stands a Castle built of Magnet, where the
King dwels, in a sumptuous Palace, the top whereof is overlaid with
Gold" (*CM*, 10:347–48). This description from the *History of Muscovia*
is one of many taken up with the nature of enclosed areas accompanied
by movements through "Presence-dore[s]" from outer courts to inner
courts (*CM*, 10:374–75). It is significant because the so-called archetypal
patterns of enclosure that Eliade and Jung find in so many cultures were
hardly foreign to Milton. In fact, they engaged him as a historian, and he
delighted in recounting them.

Exploring the biblical renderings that gave rise to and thereby legiti-
mated these concepts, we can see how Milton assimilated them into his
outlook as a poet. Certainly, the most comprehensive and detailed rendering may be found in Ezekiel, chapters 40–48. There, the Old Testament view of the divine sanctuary, expounded in Exodus, Leviticus, and
1 Kings, among other places,¹⁰ culminates in a vision of monumental proportions. Ezekiel is transported "in the visions of God" to Israel, where
he is guided through the divine sanctuary by a man "whose appearance
was like the appearance of brass, with a line of flax in his hand, and a
measuring reed" (Ezek. 40:1–3; cf. Rev. 11:1). Although the details
of the vision are too elaborate to describe here, its main characteristics
bear summarizing.

First, the sanctuary itself is represented by a series of enclosed squares
through which Ezekiel is led, beginning with the "outer court" and ending with the "inner court." Assigned to the laity, on the one hand, and to
the priests, on the other, each court is enclosed in order to admit only
those who rightfully belong there. In some respects, Ezekiel's vision is, of
course, a detailed elaboration of the Solomonic Temple, with its enclosed
דביר or "oracle," described as a cube: "And the oracle he prepared in the
house within, to set there the ark of the covenant of the Lord. And the

oracle in the forepart *was* twenty cubits in length, and twenty cubits in
breadth, and twenty cubits in the height thereof" (1 Kings 6:19–20).
Saint John the Divine appropriates the same idea in his depiction of
the New Jerusalem: "And the city lieth foursquare, and the length is as
large as the breadth. . . . The length and the breadth and the height of it
are equal" (Rev. 21:16). Within this perfect enclosure, other enclosures
separate that which is holy from that which is most holy. In his *Clavis
Apocalypticae*, Joseph Mede provides a visual rendering of the whole,
moving from the "Atrium exterius" through the "Atrium interius" to the
"Sanctum" and finally to the "Sanctum Sanctorum" (see figure 4).

   The idea goes back to God's directions to Moses for constructing the
tabernacle to house the "Holy of Holies" (קדש הקדשים) (Exod. 25–27).
The "ark of the testimony" is to be enclosed with a "veil," which "shall
divide unto you between the holy place and the most holy" (הקדשים
והבדילה . . . בין הקדש ובין קדש) (Exod. 26:33–34). "For there was
a tabernacle made; the first, wherein *was* the golden pot that had manna,
and Aaron's rod that budded, and the tables of the covenant; and over it
the cherubims of glory shadowing the mercyseat" (Heb. 9:1–5). Into the
first tabernacle, the lower order of priests was allowed to go, but "into
the second *went* the high priest alone once every year" to offer sacrifice
(Heb. 9:7). The construction of the entire tabernacle was such that there
were actually two veils, the first separating the holy place from the outside world and the second separating the most holy place from the holy
place (Exod. 26:30–37; see figure 5).

   Similarly, in Ezekiel the purpose of enclosing the temple from the
outside world (Ezek. 40:5) and the outer court from the inner court is "to
make a separation between the sanctuary and the profane place" (Ezek.
42:20). Emphasizing that separation, in the "holy chambers," the "priests
that approach unto the Lord shall eat the most holy things: there shall
they lay the most holy things, and the meat offering, and the sin offering,
and the trespass offering; for the place *is* holy [כי המקום קדש]. When
the priests enter therein, then shall they not go out of the holy *place* into
the utter court, but there shall they lay their garments wherein they
minister; for they *are* holy; and shall put on other garments, and shall
approach to *those things* which *are* for the temple" (Ezek. 42:13–14).

   The distinction that Ezekiel makes between sacred and profane through
the separation of enclosed spaces represents a fundamental propensity in
religious thought. In his *Antiquities of the Jews*, Flavius Josephus comments upon the partitioning of the tabernacle by suggesting that the
whole matter "correspond[s] to the nature of the universe": in com-

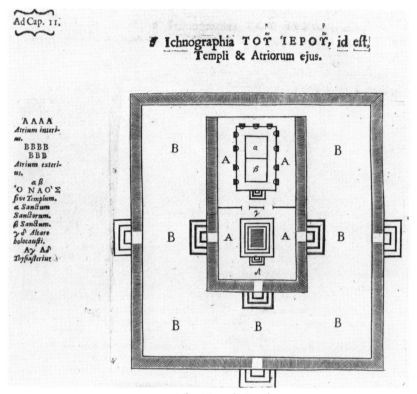

FIGURE 4. The Temple Enclosure.
Reproduced from Joseph Mede, *In Sancti Ioannis Apocalyps, The Works*
(1672), p. 480, by permission of the Joseph Regenstein Library of the
University of Chicago, Chicago, Illinois.

parison with the "Most Holy Place," which is, "as it were, heaven, set
apart to God," the space outside the inmost enclosure is, "as it were, sea
and land." The one is "inaccessible," the other "accessible and common."[11] The seventeenth-century expositor Matthew Poole recapitulates
the Talmudic commonplace: "We must remember here, that the *Jewes*
accounted the whole Earth profane, i.e., common or unclean, compar'd
with *Canaan*, and *Canaan* common, or less holy then *Jerusalem*, and
every part nearer the Temple, the more Holy, and so here the outward
Court was inclosed to distinguish it by its comparative Holiness, 'twas
more holy then all without it."[12] In its turn, the inward court is enclosed

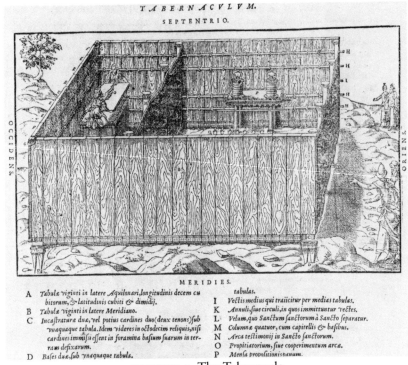

FIGURE 5. The Tabernacle.
Reproduced from a rendering of Exodus 26, in Biblia sacra (1566),
by permission of the Newberry Library, Chicago, Illinois.

from the outward, and within the inward court are still further enclosures (Ezek. 44:2). What results is a whole series of enclosures, each enclosure holier than and insulated from that which surrounds it.[13]

Within this divine topography, Ezekiel's movement is essentially *inward*, a traversing of one "threshold" after the next until the "most holy place" (קדש הקדשים) (Ezek. 41:4), the "secret place of the most High" (Ps. 91:1), is attained.[14] In that "secret place," Ezekiel experiences the glory of God: "And, behold, the glory of the God of Israel came from the way of the east [הקדים]: and his voice *was* like a noise of many waters: and the earth shined with his glory . . . and I fell upon my face," but "the spirit took me up, and brought me into the inner court, and, behold, the glory of the Lord filled the house" (Ezek. 43:2–6). There, Ezekiel is shown the "place" (מקום) of God's "throne" (כסאי), where He "will

dwell in the midst [בתוך] of the children of Israel for ever" (Ezek. 43:7).
A priest in his own right, Ezekiel is overwhelmed by God's presence
dwelling upon the restored ark, placed as it had been in the first Temple
(and earlier) directly in the center (בתוך) of the Holy of Holies as it
looked eastward (קדם) into the presence chambers (1 Kings 6:27, 8:6;
cf. Num. 2:17, 3:38 and 1 Chron. 16:1). In this confrontation, one is
given full cognizance of what it means to have penetrated to the center of
the holy. The experience is that of having appeared in the presence of
God (cf. Heb. 9:24) in order to know that "יהוה שמה," "The Lord *is*
there" (Ezek. 48:35).

Whether conceived as a sanctuary with outer and inner courts, divided
by encompassing walls, or as a tabernacle with a holy place and a most
holy place, divided by veils, the residence of the holy draws one further
and further into itself, threshold after threshold to a sanctified center
outside of which all becomes profane. That is why in his movement
inward Ezekiel learns to distinguish between inner and outer, "holy" and
"profane" (Ezek. 44:23). That is why Saint John the Divine, patterning
his own vision after that of Ezekiel (see esp. Rev. 21:12–27),[15] is commanded in Revelation: "Rise, and measure the temple of God, and the
altar, and them that worship therein. But the court which is without
the temple leave out, and measure it not; for it is given unto the Gentiles: and the holy city they shall tread under foot forty and two months
(Rev. 11:1–2).

The bearing of this tendency in *Paradise Lost* will become clear when
it is understood that both Ezekiel and Saint John the Divine are careful to
associate their visions of a holy place with the idea of a paradise itself.
Thus, Ezekiel syncretizes his temple vision with a paradisal vision by
which waters issuing from the temple create a veritable paradise. Measuring that paradise with the same care with which he had measured the
temple, Ezekiel's guide points out the "many trees" that line "the bank of
the river" bordering a paradise that shall endure: "And by the river upon
the bank thereof, on this side and on that side, shall grow all trees for
meat, whose leaf shall not fade, neither shall the fruit thereof be consumed: it shall bring forth new fruit according to his months, because
their waters they issued out of the sanctuary" (Ezek. 47:6–12). Similarly,
Saint John the Divine is shown "a pure river of water of life, clear as
crystal proceeding out of the throne of God and the Lamb. In the midst
of the street of it, and on either side of the river, *was there* the tree of life"
(Rev. 22:1–2). As Walter Eichrodt states in his commentary upon Ezekiel, "The river of paradise and the marvellous effect wrought by it
signify the transformation of this world into the garden of paradise."[16]

Biblically, temple and paradise become different forms of the same concept. Their topography is fused in one harmonious vision. That is precisely the way that centuries of exegetes saw the association. As early as the intertestamental period, the author of the pseudepigraphal Book of Jubilees makes this telling observation: "The Garden of Eden is the holy of holies, and the dwelling of the Lord." Its counterparts are "Mount Sinai the centre of the desert, and Mount Zion—the centre of the navel of the earth: these three were created as holy places facing each other" (8:19).[17] Later rabbinical commentary follows suit: Adam, states the *Pirkê de Rabbi Eliezer*, was created in "a pure locality, in the place of the Temple," thereafter to be transported to God's "palace."[18] The Christian tradition, of course, appropriated this milieu to conform to its typological association of paradise and church.[19]

Given this point of view, one may better understand the way in which Milton draws upon the biblical associations explored here. Recalling the spatial relationships envisioned by Ezekiel and, later, by Saint John the Divine, one thinks of Milton's spatial strategies, both in a holy and in a profane context.

In the context of the holy, one has the enclosures of Heaven and Eden, each surrounded in its outer limits and partitioned in its interior regions. Thus, Milton's Heaven, a מקום in its own right, is depicted as a divine enclosure, surrounded in its outer limits by "living dores" (7.566), partitioned in its interior regions by blissful "Courts" that lead to the "Temple" of God, located precisely in "mid Heav'n" (6.889–90), where God as "Center" (9.108) looks eastward toward "Heav'n Gate" (3.541).[20] As an "enclosure green" (4.133), Eden is surrounded in its outer limits by a "verdurous wall" (4.133) and an eastern "Gate" (4.178), partitioned in its interior regions by that "narrow room," "Paradise" itself, a "Heav'n on Earth," "planted" by God "in th'East / Of *Eden*" (4.207–10; cf. Gen. 3:24). Likewise a מקום, the earthly paradise recapitulates the heavenly: both accord with the New Jerusalem, the first as a type of the second, a "Heav'n on Earth." Directly in the center of the paradisal "Garden," as G. Stanley Koehler has shown, is Adam and Eve's sacred "inmost bowr" of "connubial Love," "fenc'd up" from the outside by a "verdant wall" (4.689–738).[21] As such, Milton's Heaven and Eden reenact the Renaissance understanding of the word *paradise* itself—*pairidaëza*, formed on *pairi* ("around") and *diz* ("to mold," "to form")—not only as a "park" or "pleasure ground" but also, significantly, as an "enclosure" or a "place walled in."[22]

If this fact brings to mind the tradition of the *hortus conclusus*, it should also recall the intimate association that Stanley Stewart, in his analysis of that tradition, establishes between the enclosed garden and the enclosed temple, an association that is made abundantly clear in works so diverse as Herbert's *The Temple*, which conflates the enclosures of "temple" and "paradise," and Henry Hawkins's *Partheneia Sacra*, which celebrates "the *Temple* of GOD, the *holie House*, where al glorie hath entred in, as to a chast Bower."[23] From the point of view of the Ezekiel account, Martin Luther places the entire situation in its appropriate perspective. According to Luther, "Moses implies that Paradise had a road or a gate toward the east through which there was an access to this garden [Gen. 3:24]. Likewise, in connection with the temple structure in Ezekiel (40:6), mention is made of the gate of the sanctuary which faced toward the east, obviously to have us realize that the temple was a figure of Paradise; for if nature had remained perfect, Paradise would have been the temple of the entire world. And so, on the road toward the east, which alone led to Paradise, cherubim or angels were placed, to guard the way so that neither Adam nor any of his descendants could enter Paradise."[24]

From this perspective, Milton's Heaven and Eden take on the characteristics of a hierophany. "Avoid, Profanenesse," admonishes Herbert at the entrance to his temple; "come not here: / Nothing but holy, pure and cleare / Or that which groneth to be so, / May at his perill further go."[25] In that sense, Milton is careful to refer to the celestial and terrestrial paradises in such a way that one cannot mistake their hierophantic significance. Responding to the biblical prototypes that have been discussed here, he associates Heaven and Eden with the idea of a sanctuary. If God's residence in the heavenly enclosure becomes, in fact, a "Sanctuarie" (6.762), man's residence in the earthly enclosure becomes not only the "pleasant place" that its name suggests (cf. 4.246–47) but, as "Earths great Altar" (9.195), a "hallowd ground" (11.106), whose "inmost bowr" is nothing less than a place of worship, a "holiest place" (4.759) befitting "adoration pure" (4.737). There, as in Heaven, the faithful residents properly engage in the purest form of "worship," destined, it is hoped, to breed one day "a Race of Worshippers" (5.194, 7.515, 630). Both instances contain that combination of *locus amoenus* and *locus sanctus* summed up in Tertullian's description of paradise as a "*locum divinae amoenitatis.*"[26]

In the context of the profane, Milton presents a parody of the true hierophany. In its own blasphemous way, Hell, whose very etymology means to "hide" or "conceal,"[27] reenacts the patterns explored here. Hardly exclusive, the enclosure of Hell (1.60–61) is surrounded in its outer limits by "gates of burning Adamant / Barr'd over" to "prohibit all egress" (2.436–37), partitioned in its interior regions by that profane "center," Pandaemonium (1.713), the "high Capitol" where "Satan and his Peers" (1.755–56) meet "in close recess and secret conclave" (1.795). As such, Hell is also an enclosure that contains within its confines further enclosures. Significantly, Pandaemonium, as an inmost enclosure, is likened to a "Temple" (1.713), where Satan's followers worship their own "Holy of Holies," while he sits enthroned in their midst (2.1–5). Both from a holy and from a profane point of view, then, Milton presents a spatial reenactment of fundamental religious ideas conceived as early as Ezekiel and as late as Saint John the Divine.

Reinforcing those ideas is the opposition represented by the enthroned figures of God and Satan.[28] This concept is closely related to that of the "divine center" in religious thought. According to Georges Poulet, the divine center has its roots in a "pseudo-hermetic manuscript of the twelfth century," the *Liber XXIV Philosophorium*, which states, as one of its definitions of God, that "Deus est sphaera cujus centrum est ubique, cujus peripheria nusquam."[29] In *A Treatise of the Divine Essence and Attributes* (1628), Thomas Jackson provides the following explanation:

God is a sphere, whose Center is everywhere, whose circumference is no where. Not the least particle of this universall Globe or sphere, but is supported by the indivisible unity of his Essence, as by an internall Center. And yet neither the utmost circumference of this visible world, nor any circumference conceivable, can so circumscribe or comprehend his essentiall presence, that it might be said, thus farre it reacheth and no further. For albeit hee would crowne the convexity of these Heavens with others, so much higher and more spacious, then these Heavens, as these are than the Earth, and continue this course unto the worlds end: yet all should be comprehended in his Essence; it could not be comprehended in any. Their circumference should still be some where, whereas his Essence, though still inlarging . . . the bounds of its actuall coexistence with these new creatures, is in it selfe altogether boundlesse. Omnipotencie it selfe, cannot pitch a circumference to it, because nothing can be, but it must be in it, which onely *truly* is, and cannot be contained in anything imaginable. In that all things are contained in him, he is rightly resembled by a sphere, which is of all figures the most capacious. In that all things cannot comprehend him, He is rightly resembled by a sphere whose circumference is no where! (p. 37)[30]

As Poulet shows, the idea was so pervasive throughout the Middle Ages and the Renaissance that it found expression in poets ranging from Dante to Crashaw. "The poetry of the Renaissance," states Poulet, "is not only a poetry of the center, it is also a poetry of the revolutions which operate around the center."[31] Milton's poetry represents a prime example of this point of view. His God becomes a "Center" (PL, 9.107–8), as he resides in his "holy Mount" (5.712), "amidst the glorious brightness where [he] sit'st / Thron'd inaccessible" (3.376–77). Milton, of course, long delighted in recounting such enthroned figures. The Countess Dowager of Derby comes to mind once again: "Mark what radiant state she spreds / In circle round her shining throne, / . . . This this is she alone, / Sitting like a Goddes bright / In the center of her light" (ARC, 14–18). Milton firmly believed that "he that has light within his own cleer brest / May sit i'th center, and enjoy bright day" (CO, 381–82). The center, then, becomes the source of all which revolves about it, the source of its own circumference. Indeed, in *Paradise Lost* even the "Terrestrial Heav'n" as "Center" both "extends to all" and is, in turn, "danc't round by other Heav'ns" "concentring" in it "all thir beams / Of sacred influence" (9.103–9). Correspondingly, within the "Heav'n of Heav'ns," God's "brightest Seraphim," "Day without Night, / Circle his Throne rejoycing" (5.162–63). Enthroned "Orb within Orb" of those angels that enclose him, God, in turn, is sanctified by their circular motion.[32]

Spenser would have understood. One thinks of Calidore's experience in Book 6 of *The Faerie Queene*. Happening upon a hill enclosed "round about" with "a wood / Of matchelesse hight" (6.10.6), Calidore beholds the Graces, themselves enclosed by "an hundred naked maidens lilly white, / All raunged in a ring, and dancing in delight" (6.10.11):

> All they without were raunged in a ring,
>   And daunced round; but in the midst of them
>   Three other Ladies did both daunce and sing,
>   The whilest the rest of them round about did hemme,
>   And like a girlond did in compasse stemme:
>   And in the middest of those same three, was placed
>   Another Damzell, as a precious gemme,
>   Amidst a ring most richly well enchaced,
> That with her goodly presence all the rest much graced.
>
> (6.10.12)

Once again, the center becomes the source of all that revolves about it, the source of its own circumference, deified through a process of *cir-*

cumambulatio.[33] In iconic terms, one need only consult the frontispiece of the *Mundorum Explicatio* (see figure 3) and its accompanying gloss of the "Centre" with its "Circles," referred to in Chapter 4, in order to appreciate the theocentric significance of that idea for the Renaissance.

From this perspective, the sacral ramifications become especially compelling when one realizes how readily the Renaissance conflated the pseudo-Hermetic concept of the *"Deus est sphaera"* with the Judaic concept of the הַמָּקוֹם. Thus, in his discourse on Isaiah 57:15 ("I shall dwell in the high and holy place"), the seventeenth-century expositor John Gregory maintains: "All things are full of God. He is therefore called in the Holy Tongue, הַמָּקוֹם *Hammakom, the Place.* Or that Fulnesse which filleth *All* in *All.* God (as the great *Hermes*) is a Circle, the Center whereof is every where, and the Circumference no where. *If I climbe up into Heaven thou art there, if I goe downe to Hell thou art there also."*[34] Gregory makes this observation to support an argument concerning the nature of the Shekinah, or "Divine Presence," a concept which will later occupy an entire chapter. For the time being, it is enough to note briefly the impulse in Judaic thought to conceive the presence in terms that correspond to the sanctification of the center implicit in pseudo-Hermetic thought. Doing so will suggest why expositors like Gregory so readily conflated the two points of view.

The *Zohar* may be taken as an example. It glosses the Song of Solomon 3:7 ("Behold his bed, which *is* Solomon's; threescore valiant men *are* about it, of the valiant of Israel") in the following manner: "Six luminaries form a circle surrounding a seventh luminosity in the centre. The six on the circumference sustain the sixty valiant angels surrounding the 'couch of Solomon.' The 'couch' is an allusion to the Shekinah, and 'Solomon' refers to the 'King to whom peace (*shalom*) belongs': 'threescore mighty men are about it'—these are the sixty myriads of exalted angels, part of the army of the Shekinah which accompanied Jacob into Egypt."[35] In the Christian tradition, the encircled Shekinah assumes a specifically Christocentric bearing. Although the Christocentric rendering of the הַמָּקוֹם will be discussed later in this chapter, it might be appropriate to point out here that Christ himself appropriately becomes the new "center" sanctified by its own unique circumference. So the Renaissance would have viewed the matter. In his discourse *Semper Idem*, Thomas Adams glosses Hebrews 13:8 ("Jesus Christ the same yesterday and to day, and for ever") in this manner: "The immovable *Center* is *Jesus Christ.* The *Circumference* that runnes round about him here, is *Eternitie: Yesterday, to day, and for ever.* The *Mediate line* referring to them is ὁ αὐτός, *The same. Jesus Christ the same yesterday, and to day, and for ever.*" Such is the immutable centeredness of "the *Father of lights,*" who "hath no *turning*" (James 1:17) and whose immutability is enhanced by those "lower lights" that do.[36] This again recalls the correspondences of *Paradise Lost.* Just as the "Terrestrial Heav'n" as "Center" both "extends to all" and is, in turn, "danc't round by other Heav'ns" (9.103–9), God as "Center" within the "Heav'n of Heav'ns" is surrounded by his "brightest Seraphim" that "circle his Throne rejoycing" (5.162–63).

If such is true of the "divine center," the profane counterpart of that concept is appropriately discernible in the figure of Satan. "Affecting all equality with God," Satan not only enthrones himself in his own "Mount" (see 1.670, 2.1–10, 5.756–71) but has himself "inclos'd" "Round" by "a Globe of fierie Seraphim" "with bright imblazonrie, and horrent Arms" (2.511–13; cf. 1.615–18).[37] In that posture, he anticipates those pagan deities that "durst" rival God's "Seat" with their own by placing "thir Shrines" within God's own "Sanctuary," a process of "Abominations" that would result in the profanation of God's "holy Rites" (1.382–89). Already alluded to, the process is one that will be discussed at much greater length in future chapters. For the time being, it is sufficient to recall God's statement in Ezekiel 43:7–8 that the house of Israel shall "no more defile" his "holy name" by placing "their threshold by [his] thresholds, and their posts by [his] posts," thereby committing "abominations," "wherefore [God] has consumed them in [his] anger." By doing so, he has separated the sacred from the profane.

In *Paradise Lost,* this separation occurs first in Heaven and then on earth. In Heaven, God separates the "pure," represented by the faithful angels, from the "impure," represented by Satan and his followers (6.742–43). On earth, he separates the purity of Eden from the "grossness" of man (11.50–53) by "driv[ing] out the sinful Pair, / From hallowd ground th'unholie" (11.105–6). In both instances, the divine enclosure cannot admit within its confines that which will defile it. Heaven's "Chrystal wall" opens "wide" (6.860–61) to disburden itself of Satan and his followers, thereafter repairing its "mural breach, returning whence it rowl'd" (6.878–79). Eden's "eastern Gate" opens to eject man, who, once outside, can only behold "th'Eastern side" of "Paradise" "wav'd over by that flaming Brand, the Gate / With dreadful Faces throng'd and fierie Armes" (12.638–44).

If that pattern suggests the exclusive nature of the divine enclosure as derived from biblical sources, the inclusive nature of the divine enclosure will become clear in a further examination of the action of *Paradise Lost.* From the latter perspective, one should recall the idea of penetration represented by Ezekiel: the traversing of a threshold into an enclosed area in order to attain the center of the holy. In *Paradise Lost*, such an idea assumes complex associations.

From the divine point of view, one thinks of the Son, who, as agent of the Father, departs from his Father's presence and returns to it after the completion of various acts. Having expelled the rebel angels from the confines of Heaven, the Son victoriously rides "through mid Heav'n, into the Courts / And Temple of his mightie Father," who receives him "into Glorie" "where now he sits at the right hand of bliss" (6.887–92). That movement is repeated in the Son's return to the Father after having created the world (7.565–88), after having pronounced God's sentence on fallen man (10.224–25), and after having risen as Christ to the heights of exaltation (12.451–58). In the first two instances, the Filial Power, passing through the wide opening of Heaven's "blazing Portals," moves inward toward "Gods Eternal house," where he reassumes his place within his Father's "blissful bosom." In the third instance, the Messiah "ascend[s]" to "the Heav'n of Heav'ns," where he "enter[s] into glory" in order to "resume / His Seat at Gods right hand." Such an entrance Milton associates in *Christian Doctrine* with the penetration of a divine enclosure (*CM*, 15:336–37).

From the human point of view, the pattern is equally as compelling. One may use as a point of reference the traversing of a threshold that Adam experiences after he has been created. Finding himself outside the threshold of Eden, Adam is guided by God to "the Garden of Bliss":

> . . . by the hand he took me rais'd,
> And over Fields and Waters, as in Air
> Smooth sliding without step, last led me up
> A woodie Mountain, whose high top was plain,
> A Circuit wide, enclos'd, with goodliest Trees
> Planted, with Walks, and Bowers, that what I saw
> Of Earth before scarse pleasant seemd.
>
> (8.295–306)

Through God, Adam moves from the world outside the enclosure to the world inside (cf. Gen. 2:8, 15). If, in this context, Milton associates such a movement with the locus amoenus by distinguishing between less "pleasant" (outside) and more "pleasant" (inside), he does not hesitate, in another context (4.153), to associate that movement with the locus sanctus by distinguishing between less "pure" (outside) and more "pure" (inside).[38] This recalls once again the distinction that Ezekiel draws, in his traversing of thresholds, between the outer court and the inner court. In Adam's movement toward the center, one is likewise asked to distinguish between the virtues of what lies within as opposed to what lies without.

But paradise, even with its "inmost bowr," is not the ultimate enclosure. The traversing of thresholds into a sanctified center has still further repercussions, if one considers God's statement that man, "by degrees of merit rais'd," may "open to [himself] at length the way / Up hither, under long obedience tri'd" (7.157–59). In the heavenly paradise, he may enter permanently into the presence of God. In the words of the *Mundorum Explicatio*, that will be the "time" when man will be "admitted" into "the *Sanctum Sanctorum*," "the *holyest* now of *holyest*," "the secret sacred *Place*," where "the *Deity*" "dwels" in "*Light*" immortal." Having entered through "th'Aeternal *Gate* of Blisse," he will behold God "without Vails" "face to face" (pp. 327–30).

As fallen man, the poet of *Paradise Lost* enjoys something of that experience when, "up led" by the Muse, he is permitted "into the Heav'n of Heav'ns" there, as an "Earthlie Guest," to breathe the "Empyreal Air" (7.12–14). "Look[ing] up" at "Heav'ns dore," he is able to traverse thresholds into the most sacrosanct of areas, where he sees "each blissful Deitie / How he before the thunderous throne doth lie" (V, 34–35). This experience accounts for Milton's vision of the poet as priest (sacerdos), who, "shining with sacred vestment and lustral waters," penetrates the "secret temples of the gods" (*et mihi fana patent interiorum Deum*) (EL 6, 65; EL 5, 18). Entering into their presence, he approaches them with due reverence while he extols their glory. As shall be discussed in a separate chapter, such is the posture that characterizes the apostrophe to "Light" opening Book 3 (3.1 ff.) of *Paradise Lost*, as well as the apostrophe to God as a "Fountain of Light" "thron'd inaccessible" "amidst [his] glorious brightness" somewhat later in the same Book (3.375–80). Both apostrophes reflect a concern with how one goes about approaching the unapproachable. In response to God's radiance, the "brightest Seraphim / Approach not, but with both wings veil thir eyes" (3.380–81). This recalls Moses, who must "put off . . . [his] shoes from off . . . [his] feet" before God's presence, the radiance of which is unbearable (cf. Exod. 19:21, 20:19), or Ezekiel, who, having penetrated to the center of the holy, falls upon his face before an overwhelming radiance that "fill[s] the house" (Ezek. 43:2–6). Such behavior upon finding oneself in the presence of the Divine is a distinct characteristic of what Eliade calls the "gestures of approach."

The precise bearing of those gestures upon Milton becomes discernible by recalling Ezekiel's emphasis upon due reverence in his vision of how the priests are to behave upon entering the sanctuary: those who "approach unto the Lord" shall eat only the most holy things, handle only the most holy things, dress only in the most holy garments (Ezek. 42:13–14). Although nothing in Milton justifies such elaborate procedures, one does find a similar emphasis upon how one must go about approaching a divine figure.[39] For that purpose, it is useful to consider briefly *Arcades*, a poem devoted in part to the gestures of approach. Those who desire to approach the enthroned Countess Dowager of Derby are instructed by the Genius of the Wood: "As we go . . . / I will assay, her worth to celebrate, / And so attend ye toward her glittering state; / Where ye may all that are of noble stemm / Approach, and kiss her sacred vestures hemm" (78–83).

In *Paradise Lost*, Adam approaches Raphael with a reverence that is both natural and stately: walking forth, "without more train / Accompani'd then with his own compleat / Perfections" but "with submiss approach and reverence meek," Adam "bow[s] low" (5.350–60; cf. 11.249–50). This is what Milton, in another context, calls "adoration pure / Which God likes best" (4.737–38).[40] Adam's response to finding himself for the first time in God's presence, however, is entirely different: he falls "in adoration at his [God's] feet . . . / Submiss" (8.314–16).[41] The perverted form of that behavior is aptly found in Satan. For example, in Satan's plea in *Paradise Regained* to gain "access" into the presence of Jesus, the language is replete with these associations. Even "Thy Father," says Satan, "suffers the Hypocrite or Atheous Priest / To tread his Sacred Courts, and minister / About his Altar, handling holy things, / Praying or vowing. . . . / [D]isdain not such access to me" (1.486–92). Satan's true posture, on the other hand, appears in *Paradise Lost* as that which disdains to "bow and sue for grace / With suppliant knee, and deify his [God's] power" (1.111–12). This defiance generates in Satan not only a disregard for the gestures of approach but an all-consuming need to penetrate, and thereby defile, enclosed, sacrosanct areas.

Thus, having escaped the confines of Hell, Satan traverses Chaos until he alights upon "the firm opacious Globe / Of this round World, whose first convex divides / The luminous inferior Orbs, enclos'd / From *Chaos* and th'inroad of Darkness old" (3.418–21). Within this "expos'd" area (3.425), he walks "up and down alone bent on his prey" (3.441), only to be mocked by the "Stairs" leading to "*the Gate of Heav'n*" (3.515). Reminded of "his sad exclusion from the dores of Bliss" (3.525), he turns to an "op'ning" "from beneath, / Just o're the blissful seat of Paradise, / A passage down to th'Earth, a passage wide" (3.526–39). "Without longer pause," he penetrates that enclosure, "throw[ing] / His flight precipitant" "down right into the Worlds first Region" (3.561–63), and in order to compensate for his inability to reenter Heaven, he enters the world of man. Disdaining proper entrance through Eden's gate once he has reached the borders of the earthly paradise, he is contemptuous of enclosing walls: "At one slight bound," he overleaps "all bound" and "sheer within / Lights on his feet" (4.180–83). Thereafter, from the prospect of "the Tree of Life" (4.194), he comments upon how poorly "fenc't" Adam and Eve's enclosure is "to keep out such a foe / As now is enterd" and promises ironically that "Hell shall unfold, / To entertain you two, her widest Gates" (4.372, 381–82). In line with this pattern, he goes still further to penetrate Adam and Eve's "inmost bowr," where he is found "squat like a Toad, close at the ear of *Eve*" (4.800). Through a series of penetrations that lead ultimately to the inmost enclosure, Satan disregards the proper form of reverence due a divine enclosure: "And there shall in no wise enter into it anything that defileth, neither *whatsoever* worketh abomination, or *maketh* a lie" (Rev. 21:7). It is precisely these things that Satan does, with the result that Eden is penetrated, its interior "exposed" (4.206), and its sanctity vitiated. The forced penetration of Eden makes possible the Temptation and Fall of man.

Accordingly, Eve is duped by the argument "Shall that be shut to Man, which to the Beast / Is open?" (9.691–92). The thrust of this argument is that because Eve is entitled to the kind of "knowledge" shared by the "Gods" (9.686), the "Trespass" of eating the "Fruit" will be "petty" (9.693). As previously indicated, such a trespass is to be viewed as a blasphemy, an outright "violation of things sacred" (*rem sacram violasset*) (CD, CM, 15:182–84). This violation is none other than the penetration of a divine enclosure, a "trespass" or *transgressus* in the true sense of the word. For, having fallen, Eve ironically praises "Experience" as a "guide" that "op'nst Wisdoms way, / And giv'st access, though secret she retire" (9.807–10). Milton depicts Wisdom as one who, along with the Muse her "Sister," is privileged to "play / In presence of th'Almighty Father" (7.9–10; see Prov. 8:30). By opening "Wisdoms way," then, Eve would presume to have gained access to the presence of God, a "way" she feels that has heretofore been closed to her because of her "Ignorance." She need only remember, however, that had she remained "lowly wise" (8.173) entrance into the Divine Presence would have been assured. Already manifested in Eden, it was to have been experienced ultimately in Heaven, as man opened to himself the way into transcendent bliss (7.158–59). In effect, then, by transgressing God's command, Eve attempts unwittingly to "open" that which has been open to her all the time. In so doing, she commits a transgression indeed, one which becomes an infringement of the profane upon the holy, a perversion of the true act of penetration.

For man, that perversion involves his unwillingness to remain content within the confines of his natural enclosure. Dissatisfied with prescribed boundaries (man's "just circumference" [7.231]), Adam and Eve violate God's act of "circumscribing" the universe and "all created things" (7.226–27).[42] In their desire to become "uncircumscrib'd" like God (7.170), they become like Satan, presumably restrained by "no bounds / Prescrib'd" (3.81–82) but, in fact, trapped by a threatening enclosure that "opens wide" only to reveal more horrible enclosures within (4.75–77). Thus, after Satan falls, "Hell at last / Yawning receav'd . . . [him] whole, and on . . . [him] clos'd" (7.874–75). Within Hell's enclosure, Satan must abandon all hope: "Lasciate ogni speranza, voi ch'entrate."

Unlike Satan, Adam and Eve are provided with the possibility of reopening to themselves the way into God's presence. ("Enter ye in at the strait gate: for wide is the gate, and broad *is* the way, that leadeth to destruction, and many there be which go in thereat: Because strait *is* the gate and narrow *is* the way, which leadeth unto life, and few there be that find it" [Matt. 7:13–14].) The "way, which leadeth unto life" is, of course, manifested in the Son of God, through whom Death becomes "the Gate of Life" (12.571). (Compare John 14:6: "I am the way, the truth, and the life: no man cometh unto the Father, but by me"; and John 10:9: "I am the door: by me if any man enter in, he shall be saved, and shall go in and out.") Ultimately, as God promises in *Paradise Lost*,

> . . . at one fling
> Of thy victorious Arm, well-pleasing Son,
> Both *Sin*, and *Death*, and yawning *Grave* at last
> Through *Chaos* hurld, obstruct the mouth of Hell
> For ever, and seal up his ravenous Jaws.
> Then Heav'n and Earth renewd shall be made pure
> To sanctitie that shall receive no stain.
>
> (10.633–39)

Before that time, however, Adam and Eve must be expelled from paradise and the Son must sacrifice himself to atone for man's sins, fulfilling "the rigid satisfaction, death for death" (3.212).

It is the promise of this sacrifice that causes Eden as a divine enclosure to lose its importance. If Adam and Eve's fall necessitates their expulsion from Eden, it also necessitates a reconsideration of what holy place means. For the ultimate fate of Eden is well-known: removed from its "place" by the Flood, it takes root on "an Iland salt and bare, / The haunt of Seals and Orces, and Sea-mews clang" (11.829–35). As an external entity, place itself is deprived of its sanctity (11.836–37). Interiorized, it takes the form of a "Paradise within" man, far happier than the one without (12.587). Anticipating such a reorientation, Milton, at the very outset of his epic, invokes the aid of that spirit which "dost prefer / Before all Temples th'upright heart and pure" (1.18). This preference, of course, is one that Milton expressed as early as *Comus*; there, the Elder Brother extols the "unpolluted temple of the mind" (461). Concerning the divine enclosure, Saint John the Divine's statement about the heavenly city in Revelation 21:21 is instructive: "And I saw no temple therein: for the Lord God Almighty and the Lamb are the temple of it" (cf. Ps. 15:1–2 and 1 Cor. 3:16).

In accord with that idea, it is not surprising to find Milton in *The Reason of Church-Government* commenting upon Ezekiel's vision of the temple in this manner: "God by his Prophet seeking to weane the hearts of the Jewes from their old law to expect a new and more perfect reformation under Christ, sets out before their eyes the stately fabrick & constitution of his Church, with al the ecclesiasticall functions appertaining; indeed the description is as sorted best to the apprehension of those times, typicall and shadowie, but in such manner as never yet came to passe, nor never must literally, unlesse we mean to annihilat the Gospel" (*CM*, 3:190). Through the "Gospel," God "cast[s] his line and levell upon the soule of man which is his rationall temple, and by the divine square and compasse thereof forme[s] and regenerate[s] in us the lovely shapes of vertues and graces, the sooner to edifie and accomplish that immortall stature of Christs body which is his Church in all her glorious lineaments and proportions" (*CM*, 3:191). Such a statement clearly indicates how the pattern explored here assumes a decidedly Christocentric bearing in Milton's thought.

The relocation of the holy place is accompanied by a corresponding emphasis upon the importance of the Savior to the overall scheme. His importance in this respect may best be appreciated by referring to Milton's discourse in *Christian Doctrine* on the offices of Christ. The immediate concern is "CHRIST'S SACERDOTAL FUNCTION": "that whereby HE ONCE OFFERED HIMSELF TO GOD THE FATHER AS A SACRIFICE [*hostiam*] FOR SINNERS, AND HAS ALWAYS MADE, AND STILL CONTINUES TO MAKE INTERCESSION [*intercessit*] FOR US" (*CM*, 15:291). A basic tenet of Christianity, Milton's definition of the sacerdotal office significantly relates

Christ as "sacrifice" and Christ as "intercessor." In the New Testament, the two functions are combined to offer a Christocentric interpretation of what it means to enter a divine enclosure.

The author of Hebrews provides the fullest account of this interpretation. Distinguishing between the Old Dispensation and the New, the author of Hebrews says that whereas under the "first *covenant*" the high priest sacrificed yearly in a man-made tabernacle, under the "better covenant" the tabernacle is "pitched" by God and the high priest is Christ himself (Heb. 8 and 9). "But Christ being come an high priest of good things to come, by a greater and more perfect tabernacle, not made with hands, that is to say, not of this building; Neither by the blood of goats and calves, but by his own blood he entered once into the holy place, having obtained eternal redemption *for us*" (Heb. 9:11–12). "For Christ is not entered into the holy places made with hands, *which are* the figures of the true; but into heaven itself, now to appear in the presence of God for us" (Heb. 9:24). Accordingly, Milton states in *The Reason of Church-Government* that the act of "entring yearly into the Holy of holies . . . rested upon the High Priest only as more immediately personating our Saviour" (*CM*, 3:205).

Given this perspective, one can better understand the prefigurative significance of entering a divine enclosure in *Paradise Lost*. Thus, Milton invokes Moses, whose mediatorial office to appear before God in the sanctuary causes him to become a "figure" "to introduce / One greater, of whose day he shall foretell" (12.239–57). The Son, too, anticipates his sacerdotal office by entering God's sanctuary as high priest to offer up the prayers of a repentant Adam and Eve. The language describing the Son's act is replete with these same associations. After Adam and Eve's prayers have "pass'd / Dimentionless through Heav'nly dores," the Son presents them "clad / With incense, where the Gold Altar fum'd" (11.16–18). In so doing, he becomes the "great Intercessor" who supplicates for man before the Divine Presence of "the Fathers Throne" (11.19–21): "See Father, what first fruits on Earth are sprung / From thy implanted Grace in Man, these Sighs / And Prayers, which in this Golden Censer, mixt / With Incense, I thy Priest before thee bring" (11.22–25). His "sacrifice" is not "by the blood of goats and calves" but by the promise of "his own blood" (cf. PL, 12.291–99): "All his works on mee / Good or not good ingraft, my Merit those / Shall perfet, and for these my Death shall pay" (11.33–35).

The Son's willingness to die for man brings to mind the statement in Hebrews 9:24 that because of his sacrifice, Christ has "entered" not into man-made "holy places" "but into heaven itself," where, as high priest, he is "set on the right hand of the throne of the Majesty" (Heb. 8:1). Moreover, the act of entering once only, rather than many times, into the Holy of Holies suggests the fundamental importance of this particular entrance: "Nor yet that he should offer himself often, as the high priest entereth into the holy place with blood of others . . . but now once in the end of the world hath he appeared to put away sin by the sacrifice of himself" (Heb. 9:25–26). Under those circumstances, all other acts of entering a divine enclosure prefigure this ultimate act. That is why Milton in *Paradise Lost* does not hesitate to celebrate in apocalyptic terms the triumphant effect of Christ's sacrifice: "With the multitude of . . . [his] redeemd / . . . [he] shall enter Heav'n long absent, and return" to see God's face (3.260–61). As the result of such an event, the "Paradise within" that has sustained man in spirit throughout history will finally be realized in fact throughout eternity.

With this Christocentric emphasis, *Paradise Lost* becomes a work in which the penetration of a divine enclosure may be viewed from a number of perspectives. As demonstrated, Milton's spatial strategies accord with the patterns established by Ezekiel and reinterpreted by Saint John the Divine. Both these biblical sources provide graphic representations of the exclusive and inclusive natures of the divine enclosure. Drawing upon those representations, Milton envisions holy place within both a divine and a profane context. As exclusive entity, the divine enclosure becomes a fitting means of portraying the sanctity of Heaven and Eden, on the one hand, and the blasphemy of Hell, on the other. As inclusive entity, the divine enclosure becomes a fitting means of portraying the proper form of penetration, on the one hand, and the perverted form, on the other.

But the matter does not rest there. Holy place is ultimately interiorized, as Milton stresses the importance of understanding the Son's role in *Paradise Lost*. From this point of view, the penetration of a divine enclosure in Milton's epic assumes a prefigurative significance. Subscribing to the doctrine made evident in Hebrews, Milton suggests how the role of the Son in *Paradise Lost* anticipates Christ's sacerdotal role, one which involves the view of the Savior both as sacrifice and as intercessor. In that way, Milton successfully accommodates Old and New Testament renderings of holy place to the Christocentric vision that permeates his epic.

7
Mount

Given the special significance that "place" holds in Milton's thought, the phenomenon of the "holy mount" provides a specific topography for המקום. The sacrality of the mountain is attested to repeatedly in world culture. "Everywhere in the world," says van der Leeuw, "there are sacred mountains." "Japan has its sacred Fujiyama, Greece its Olympus, or rather several of them, and every region has its own holy peak."[1] The sacred mountains of Taoism, the Kwan-lun range, have been the source of many legends. Mount Mandara in Bihār is the Hindu equivalent of Olympus. It became the means by which the gods churned the ocean for ambrosia. Correspondingly, Himavat (Himālaya) is looked upon as the sacred mountain chain, the divine mountain, dear to the gods. Albūrz or Hara Berezaiti in ancient Persia was regarded as especially sacred, the first of mountains. The sun and stars were said to revolve around it; light issued from it and returned to it; it was free of night or darkness, cold, wind, and sickness; on it the Amesha Spentas built a dwelling for Mithra, who looks upon all the world from it. All mountains are said to have grown from its roots.[2]

This example of the cosmic mountain suggests the association of the sacred and the cosmic in religious thought: the holy mountain is also the world mountain. As such, mountains, Eliade observes, are often looked upon as "the place where sky and earth meet." A "central point" through which the *axis mundi* goes, they become a region infused with the sacred, "a spot where one can pass from one cosmic zone to another." In Mesopotamian legend, "the Mountain of the Lands" accordingly unites earth and heaven, and in Indian myth, Mount Meru is to be found in the center of the world, while above it the Pole Star issues forth its light.[3] Daniel envisioned "a great mountain" that "filled the whole earth" (Dan. 2:35). Similar associations may be found among the Uralo-Altaic peoples, whose central mountain is Sumbur (also Sumur or Semeru). The very name of Himingbjorg in the Edda suggests its meaning: the "celestial mountain," where rainbow (Bifrost) touches the dome of heaven.[4] Given its cosmic centrality, the holy mountain is seen as the *omphalos*: etymologically, Tabor, the name of the mountain in Palestine, may well trace its origin to *tabbur*, "navel," *omphalos*; and Mount Gerizim was reputed to be "the navel of the earth."[5]

Around the cosmic mountain grew the universal mountain cults. Thus, Pausanius describes the worship of Zeus on Mount Lycaon. The cult involved a mound of heaped-up earth for an altar accompanied by two pillars that faced the rising sun. On both Mount Lycaon and Mount Tmolus, the priests saw to the production of rain through appropriate ceremonies. On the tops of mounts Ida and Berecyntus in Anatolia, Cybele was celebrated with festivals that honored her presence. Where she resided, the trees were sacred and never cut down.[6] As cult centers among the Semites, hills or high places are frequently referred to in the Old Testament in association both with pagan tribes and with Israel itself. Traditionally worshiped on high places, Jahweh was supposed to dwell there. Occasionally, even Israel offered sacrifice and incense on high places to the local gods, the Beālim of hills.[7] Thus, Hosea makes reference to the older forms of religious worship involving "sacrifice upon the tops of the mountains [עַל־רָאשֵׁי הֶהָרִים]" and the burning of incense "upon the hills [הַגְּבָעוֹת]" (Hos. 4:13). Numbers contains the following passage: "Balak took Balaam, and brought him up into the high places of Baal [בָּמוֹת בַּעַל]," where seven altars were constructed for the sake of worship and sacrifice (Num. 22:41–23:14).

With Yahweh worship, of course, the older forms of high-place worship became sacrilegious. "Ye shall utterly destroy all the places, wherein the nations which ye shall possess served their gods, upon the high mountains, and upon the hills" (Deut. 12:2). But, as indicated, Yahweh himself was worshiped in high places, his ark placed "in the hill [בַּגִּבְעָה]" (1 Sam. 7:1). Thus, David worships Yahweh appropriately "in the mount," in this case, Mount Olivet (2 Sam. 15:30–32). Distinguishing between true and false forms of high-place worship, Elijah challenges the prophets of Baal to participate in an altar contest upon Mount Carmel. Whereas Elijah's sacrifice is consumed, that of the Baal prophets is not. Yahweh thereby proves himself the true high God, to whom the altar is raised (1 Kings 18:19–40). As such, the altar itself becomes a fitting representation of the high place around which the cult emerges. Thus, in the Sinai theophany, God commands Moses to build him an "altar of earth" to attest that he has "talked" with Moses "from heaven" (Exod. 20:22–24).[8] To support this outlook, "archaeological research has discovered remains of many 'high places,' often on hills, and even now remains of temples and sacred groves are to be seen on Hermon and other mountains. On some mountains worship and sacrifice still take place, and circular enclosures of stone crown the summits."[9]

From the cultic point of view, mountain worship finds its most graphic expression in the *ziggurat,* an Akkadian word meaning "pinnacle" or "mountaintop." A "huge mass of brickwork, with its inward leaning faces relieved by wide buttresses, its irregular upper terraces (perhaps planted with trees to resemble a mountain), and three stairways converging to a monumental gateway at the level of the lowest terrace," the ziggurat was "the outstanding feature of a whole temple complex."[10] As an expression of man's attempt to construct artificial mountains that could correspondingly function as divine dwelling-places, it represented a transitional stage between the worship of real mountains as sacred realms and the constructing of man-made temples.[11] At the same time, it assumed cosmic significance, as it reflected both the sacral and the cosmic dimensions of the holy mountain. Viewed as a microcosm of the universe, the stages of the ziggurat symbolized its appropriate divisions: underworld, water, earth, heaven. Through a related concept, the ziggurat was seen as the link between the terrestrial and the celestial. Communication with the celestial and its inhabitants was effected through a holy spot on the summit of the ziggurat believed to be connected through its axis with the upper regions.[12] The universality of the ziggurat in the ancient world may be seen by the presence of a ziggurat in every Mesopotamian city. The most familiar one was built about 2070 B.C. at Ur.[13] The great temple of Marduk in Babylon (cf. the Tower of Babel) was also an example of this kind of stage-tower construction and suggests the influence of the earlier Sumerians, with their artificial mounts, upon the Babylonian culture.[14]

Of course, the ziggurat is not the only artificial construct by which the mountain is embodied in material form. The Babylonian temple-tower finds its counterpart in the Egyptian pyramid, which extends back to about 2700 B.C. Artificial mountains in their own right, pyramids belonged to temple complexes by which the pharaohs were both sanctified and preserved.[15] Even the Mexicans had their "*teocalli,* where no hills were available for worship." Of great size, these mounds were the seats of sacred buildings or were themselves occasionally erected on high mountains.[16]

From the perspective of the holy mount, then, the cultic and the cosmic are related forms of the same idea. Such is particularly true of the correspondence between mountain and temple in Hebraic thought. Because of its association with the Jerusalem Temple, itself the "navel of the earth"

(טבור הארץ),[17] Zion conflates temple and mount: it becomes in effect the Temple Mount. "For the Lord hath chosen Zion; he hath desired *it* for his habitation. This is my rest for ever: here will I dwell; for I have desired it" (Ps. 132:13–14). Thus, Isaiah memorializes Zion as "the mountain of the Lord's house [הר בית-יהוה]," "the mountain of the Lord [הר-יהוה]," that is, the "house [בית] of the God of Jacob" (Isa. 2:2–3). At this "new cult-centre of Israel," the Sinai theophany was ritualized through the annual celebration of the Feast of Tabernacles, a symbol of the movement of the ark from its Sinaic to its Zionic seat. Correspondingly, this major new year festival "combined a recollection of the founding of the covenant on Mount Sinai with a declaration of Yahweh's primal triumph in the creation of the world."[18] That mythic outlook, in turn, accords with the view of Zion as cosmic mountain. In this respect, it is associated with Zaphon (Isa. 14:12–15), the cosmic mountain of Canaanite mythology and the holy dwelling-place of Baal.[19] "Established in the top of the mountains" and "exalted above the hills" as a center to which "all nations shall flow" (Isa. 2:2–3), Zion, then, assumes decidedly cosmic proportions.

Those proportions are further reinforced by the Jerusalem Temple itself. In the Solomonic Temple, the furnishings were replete with cosmic symbolism, a reflection of the symbolism that permeated the Temple as a whole. "The very conception of such a building was founded on the belief that a correspondence existed between the earthly and the heavenly worlds. Yahweh's house in Jerusalem was intended to be a copy, or symbol, of the cosmic 'house' where He had His abode."[20] Not only Temple decorations like the palm trees and cherubim but the ornamental pomegranates on the masonry represented the fertility of the earth generally and the paradisal abode of Yahweh more specifically.[21] The traditions incorporating these cultic-cosmic perspectives, as suggested in the previous chapter, are manifold. One recalls the association of Eden as "holy of holies and the dwelling of the Lord" with "Mount Sinai the centre of the desert and Mount Zion—the centre of the navel of the earth" in the Book of Jubilees.[22] This outlook assumes a sort of apocalyptic cast in the Book of Enoch, where the prophet is shown "a mountain range of fire which burnt day and night." Going beyond it, Enoch sees "seven magnificent mountains," one of which is in the midst of the others and excels them "in height, resembling the seat of a throne," surrounded by "fragrant trees." The middle mountain, containing the Tree of Life, is, of course, none other than God's throne and temple.[23] Correspondingly, the Shepherd of Hermas envisions twelve mountains, in the midst of which is "a huge white rock, which rose out of the plain."

Higher than those mountains, the rock "seemed capable of supporting the whole world."[24]

The outlook prevails. In his *Praeparatio Evangelica*, Eusebius recounts a vision by which Moses saw "on Sinai a great Throne reaching to heaven." From there, God "beckoned to Moses to come and take his place on the throne." "From this seat the entire cosmos was opened to Moses' view, the circle of earth, the regions under the earth, and the heavens above. The stars came in a great host to do obeissance at his knees."[25] Thus, also the *Pirkê de Rabbi Eliezer*: "Rabbi Joshua ben Korach said: The feet of Moses stood on the mount, and all (his body) was in the midst of the heaven . . . beholding and seeing everything that is in the heavens."[26] The cultic counterpart is noted in the *Zohar*, where "everyone who comes to this region called 'Mountain' becomes a participant" in the divine "mystery" of the temple.[27] This, as the *Midrash* tells us, is the Temple Mount: "Those who . . . pray outside . . . Israel turn their faces to . . . Israel. . . . Those who pray in . . . Israel turn towards Jerusalem. . . . Those who pray in Jerusalem turn towards the Temple. . . . Those who stand on the Temple Mount turn towards the Holy of Holies."[28] Here is the absolute center of holiness, which is God.[29] From him, says Clement of Rome, emanate the six infinities—height, depth, right, left, front, back—of which he is the cosmic center and in whom the six infinities end.[30] Both for the Jewish and the Christian traditions, then, holy mount, in both its cosmic and cultic contexts, is of central importance.

These contexts were no less important to the Middle Ages and the Renaissance. Dante's Mount of Purgatory is so well known as to preclude the need for additional discussion. Placed within a decidedly meditative framework, the Mount Carmel of Saint John of the Cross assumes the characteristics of the Mons Dei, with its "incomprehensible" riches.[31] Likewise during the Renaissance, one finds discourses ranging from Anthony de Guevera's *The Mount of Calvarie* (1595) and William Symonds's *Pisgah Evangelica* (1606) to *Partheneia Sacra* (1633; attributed to Henry Hawkins), cited in the previous chapter, and the anonymous *Mount of Spirits* (1691). Even William Prynne has a poeticized discourse on *Mount-Orgueil* (1641). At once Sinai, upon which the "mighty man of God" "[d]welt fortie days"; Olivet, "that sacred hill" frequented "oft" by the "deare Lord"; and Parnassus, "that pleasaunt Mount" "renownd" as the seat of "the thrise three learned Ladies," Spenser's "highest Mount" in Book 1 of *The Faerie Queene*, conflates Jewish, Christian, and pagan mountains to suggest its own cosmic importance (1.10.53–57). From it, after all, the Redcrosse Knight views the New Jerusalem. Bunyan's own

Delectable Mountains, not to mention Milton's Hill of Speculation and Donne's Hill of Truth, also fall under this rubric.

From the sacral point of view, however, perhaps the most enlightening perspective is that provided by Sampson Price, whose *The Beauty of Holiness: Or the Consecration of a House of Prayer* (1618) speaks directly to the centrality of holy mount for the Renaissance. Because of its importance, the passage is offered in full:

In the foure hundredth and fourescore yeere after the children of *Israel* were come out of the land of Egypt, *hee* (Solomon) begann to build the house of the *Lord* at Ierusalem in Mount Moriah; where the *Lord* appeared unto *David* his Father, a place so called (saith *Aquila*) of shining because there was the Oracle of *God*: or of the aboundance of *myrrhe*, which was there as *Oleaster* deriveth it: or more fitly it was so called of *seeing*, because there the *Lord* was seene of *Abraham*, when the Ramme was offered by him in stead of his Son, *Gen.* 22. 13; and *the Lord foresaw that there his Temple should be built*. Upon a Mountaine *Paradise* was situated: the *Arke* rested upon the mountains of *Ararat*, *Gen.* 8. Lot was commanded to escape to the mountaine lest he should be consumed, *Gen.* 10. Upon a Mount the *Law* was given, *Exod.* 19. Christ is described by the Church to come, leaping upon the *mountaines*. . . . *He was tempted* upon a mountaine, *Mat.* 4. *Preached* upon a mountaine, *Mat.* 15. 29. Ordained the *twelve* upon a mountaine, *Mat.* 3. 13, 14. *Departed* to a mountaine, when by force they would have made him a King, *John* 6. 15. *Conferde* with a woman on a mountaine, Joh. 4. 20. *Prayed* on a mountaine all night, *Luc.* 6. 12. Celebrated his last *Supper* in a large upper roome, *Luc.* 22. 12, which *Ambrose* placeth on a mountaine. Was *crucified* on mount Calvarie, *Luc.* 23. 33. *Appeared* to his Disciples after his resurrection upon a Mount, *Matth.* 28. 16. *Ascended* into heaven from a mount, *Acts* 1. 9. 12. and therefore appointed his *Temple* to be built upon a mount. His *Foundation* is in the holy mountaines, *Psal.* 87. 1: The first ground of his Temple. Hee will bee *worshipped* at his holy hill, *Psal.* 99. 9. A hill which hee desireth to dwell in, yea the Lord will dwell in it for ever, *Psalm* 68; which *Salomon* truely acknowledged at the feast of the dedication of the Temple where were the Elders of *Israel*, and all the heads of the Tribes, the chiefs of the Fathers of the children of *Israel*, and all the Congregation, sacrificing sheepe and oxen, that could not be numbered, & the glory of the Lord filled the house in a cloud. (pp. 1–3)

This conflation of Old and New Testament mountains to support a cultic and consecratory outlook demonstrates amply enough the Renaissance understanding of holy mount and its manifold implications. For the Renaissance, this mount is quite simply the *mons sanctus*,[32] to which adhere all the cultic and cosmic associations ascribed to it in mythopoeic thought. It is the "high place," the "temple" of the "high God" (cf. 2 Chron. 1:3 and Mic. 6:6). So Renaissance ethnologists, such as Samuel Purchas, alluding to the consecrated high places and temple mounts of the Jews, were disposed to view it.[33] The bearing of this outlook is no less discernible in Milton, for whom holy mount is as significant as it is for the traditions that gave rise to it.

For Milton, the mount accrues to itself a decided sacrality: it becomes a theophanic center. In *Lycidas*, it is the seat of the vision of the archangel Michael (161); in *Ad Patrem* (16) and *Elegia quarta* (30), it contains the "sacred wood" that inspires "divine poetry"; in *Arcades*, it is the "hallow'd ground" guarded by the Genius (55); in the *Epitaphium Damonis*, it is the embodiment of divine ecstasis (219), as it is in *Mansus* (100), *In obitum Praesulis Eliensis* (62–63), and *Elegia quinta* (17–18), among other poems; in *Of Reformation*, it emanates "saving light" (*CM*, 3:5); in the *Nativity Ode*, it is the source of awesome proclamation (157–59), the recipient, as Milton says in *The Doctrine and Discipline of Divorce*, of God's "glory," which at once covers and sanctifies it (*CM*, 3:437), until it becomes a veritable "hilltop of sanctity" (*CG*, *CM*, 3:261).

Around it, Milton says in *Christian Doctrine*, God has "set bounds" (*terminum pone huic monte*) (*CM*, 17:33–35). The allusion is to Exodus 19:12: "And thou shalt set bounds [וְהִגְבַּלְתָּ] unto the people round about, saying, Take heed to yourselves, *that ye go not* up into the mount [בּוֹ] or touch the border of it: who soever toucheth the mount shall be surely put to death." Once again God's words to Moses on Horeb become significant: "Draw not nigh hither: put thy shoes from off thy feet, for the place [הַמָּקוֹם] whereon thou standest *is* holy ground [אַדְמַת־קֹדֶשׁ]" (Exod. 3:5). Visual representations of both mountain theophanies abound in Renaissance biblical illustration, the first assuming a terrifying aspect that causes all who surround it to be overwhelmed by its numinosity (see figure 6), the second assuming an otherworldly aspect that prompts the initiate admitted into its confines to kneel before its brightness (see figure 7). As portrayed, both theophanies underscore the Miltonic veneration of the holy, particularly in its Mosaic rendering.

The idea, as indicated, assumes embryonic form in Milton's early Trinity Manuscript jottings. Because Moses is "with god in the mount," he remains inviolate: the theophany purifies him (*CM*, 18:229): "And the children of Israel saw the face of Moses, that the skin of Moses' face shone: and Moses put the vail upon his face" (Exod. 34:35). Such a view reaches fruition in *Paradise Lost*, which, in one sense, is the product of "that Shepherd" inspired, "on the secret top / Of *Oreb*, or of *Sinai*," to teach "the chosen Seed" how "in the Beginning" "the Heav'ns and Earth / Rose out of *Chaos*" (1.6–10). As such, *Paradise Lost*, like the Torah, is the embodiment of a mountain theophany, the product of a high-place revelation, disseminated to the chosen. "We have been taught," says the *Zohar*, "that when the Holy One revealed Himself on Mount Sinai all the Israelites saw the Divine manifestation as one sees a light streaming through the glass of a lamp." Approaching "this region called 'Mountain,'" they thereby became "participant[s] in this mystery."[34] If we become participants through *Paradise Lost* as the embodiment of a Horeb or Sinai theophany, we likewise become participants through Milton's epic as the embodiment of a Zion theophany (1.10), a point that shall be explored later in more detail.

For the time being, it is sufficient to note Milton's fondness for high-place revelations. He is forever leading us to hillsides, as in *Of Education* (CM, 4:280), or to tops of speculation, as in *Paradise Lost* (11.367, 377, 381, 12.606; cf. the "specular Mount" in PR, 3.252–53, 265, 4.26, 236), and sanctity, as in *The Reason of Church-Government* (CM, 3:261). To a greater or lesser extent, these represent none other than what Milton calls "the Visions of God" (PL, 11.377).[35] From the theophanic point of view, these visions in *Paradise Lost* find apt expression in Milton's allusions to the experiences of Jacob in Mahanaim (Gen. 31:54–32:2) and Elisha in Dothan (2 Kings 6:13–17). Whereas Jacob, having sacrificed upon the mount, encounters "the field Pavilion'd with . . . Guardians bright" (11.214–15), Elisha, "on the flaming Mount," beholds an angelic "Camp of Fire" (11.216–17). Such allusions characterize the revelatory nature of Michael's "heav'nly Bands," which appear as a "blazing Cloud that veils the Hill" in Eden (11.208–10, 228) before Adam and Eve are exiled from paradise. (They make their appearance, Adam suspects, to "impose / New Laws" [11.227–28], an observation that suggests the Sinaic and Zionic dimensions to be discussed later.)

Theophanies of this kind repeatedly underscore Milton's sensitivity to the sacrality of the mount as a distinct manifestation of the holy. That is especially true of his handling of the Mount of God. Milton's translation of Psalm 87 is a good point of departure. There, the mons sanctus, with its essential cultic accoutrements, appears in all its splendor. Working with the "בהררי-קדש" of the original, Milton elaborates upon the phrase "holy Mountains" with his own adjective "*high*" and with

ינתן תורתו על ההר סני׃ יהוה   Exod: XX: 1-21   DOMINUS LE(

The promulgation of the Law in Mount Sinai.   *Le Seigneur don*

Der Herr giebt sein Gesetz auf dem Berge Sinai.   De plechtelyke

FIGURE 6. Sinai Theophany.
Reproduced from an engraving by Gerrit Adriaensz
(early seventeenth century) in the Kitto Bible, 13:2062, by permission
of the Huntington Library, San Marino, California.

RT, IN MONTE SINAÏ.
le mont Sinaï.
es Heeren op den Berg Sinaï.

C. vander Gucht sculp.

FIGURE 7. Horeb Theophany.
Reproduced from an engraving of Exodus 3 by Matthaeus Meriam
in [Veteris et Noui Testamenti] (1627), by permission of
the Newberry Library, Chicago, Illinois.

his own verses, *"There seated in his Sanctuary, / His Temple there is plac't"* (lines 1–4, verse 1). The divine abode of what Milton calls the "High God" (line 20, verse 5) thereby becomes not only Yahweh's "holy mount," "Sion," but his "high place," his *"Sanctuary"* and *"Temple."* Such is what Milton, like Saint Augustine, understood to be the "City of God" (line 9, verse 3), to be celebrated with "dance" and *"sacred Songs"* (lines 25–26, verse 7).

   This outlook is fully developed in *Paradise Lost*, in which Milton, with one bold stroke, conflates what his God calls "this our high place, our Sanctuarie, our Hill" (5.732). "Amidst as from a flaming Mount, whose top / Brightness had made invisible" (5.598–99), Milton's God resides in what is at once his "holy Mount," his "inaccessible high strength," and his "Temple," hidden by "incense Clouds / Fuming from Golden Censers" (6.743, 7.142, 148, 599–600). That Temple Mount, surrounded by its own holy courts (7.889–90), is where God is fittingly "shrin'd in his Sanctuarie of Heav'n secure" (6.671–72). It is, to use the language of

Christian Doctrine once again, his *"summa arx et habitaculum,"* his supreme height and habitation, his "high and holy place" (*CM,* 15:28–29). In that setting, he is worshiped "with Ministries due and solemn Rites" (7.150). "Circling" his "holy Mount" in "mystical dance," his "Saints" "bow" "lowly reverent" toward his and his Son's thrones "and to the ground / With solemn adoration down they cast / Thir Crowns" (6.743, 5.620, 3.349–52). Their worship, as indicated, is reflected in the solemnities of Adam and Eve, who, also bowing "lowly" in adoration, engage in evening and morning "Orisons," the "vocal Worship" of "holy rapture" (4.721–35, 5.144–208, 9.198, 5.147). As if in deference to God's "holy Mount," even the Mount of Eden, with its "humid Flowrs, that breath'd / Thir morning incense," becomes what we have seen as "Earths great Altar" that "send[s] up silent praise" as "a sign of Worship" (9.193–96, 5.194). For the Deity in his high place, the entire universe engages in a divine *adoratio,* thereby establishing Milton's epic as among the most supreme of *"Sion's* songs" as it celebrates "the Holiest of Holies" (*PR,* 4.347–49) in his mount.

The cultic dimension suggested in the foregoing discussion finds its counterpart in the cosmic dimension, which is also integral to the concept of holy mount. In the passages cited, something of the cosmic has already appeared. "Invisible" in its "brightness," God's "flaming Mount" is inaccessibly "high"; it is, after all, a *summa arx,* "th' Impereal Throne" of "heav'ns high-seated top" (7.584–85). There, in his "high abode," God sits "High Thron'd above all highth" (7.552, 3.57). From that vantage point, he becomes part of the cosmic milieu established through the image of his mount. Height, of course, is not the only attribute of such an image. The mount is also imbued with animism. From amidst the clouds that it exhales, God's voice issues (5.642, 6.27–28). When God becomes angry, "clouds beg[in] / To darken all the Hill, and smoak to rowl / In duskie wreaths, reluctant flames" (6.56–59). (Compare Exodus 19:18: "And mount Sinai was altogether on a smoke, because the Lord descended upon it in fire: and the smoke thereof ascended as the smoke of a furnace, and the whole mount quaked greatly.") Milton's fondness for such animistic accounts may be seen in the *Nativity Ode* with its reference to the clanging, smoldering, and flaming of Sinai (157–59) and, in a lighter vein, in both Milton's English and Greek paraphrases of Psalm 114, with their rushing and skipping, boundless "huge-bellied Mountains" (lines 10 and 8, respectively). From the Sinaic perspective, that animism has a long tradition. In the *Midrash Rabbah,* when God "came to reveal the Torah on Sinai, the mountains ran about and contended with each other, each claiming: 'The Torah shall be revealed on me.'"[36]

The animism implicit in Milton's vision of God's holy mount, in turn, is even further enhanced by the references to the fact that from it "spring" both "light and shade" (5.643–44):

> There is a Cave
> Within the Mount of God, fast by his Throne
> Where light and darkness in perpetual round
> Lodge and dislodge by turns. . . .
> Light issues forth, and at the other dore
> Obsequious darkness enters.
>
> (6.4–10)

As various editors have noted, the idea recalls Hesiod's *Theogony*.[37] There, Day and Night "draw near and greet one another" as they pass through the bronze threshold of heaven, which rests upon the head and hands of Atlas. While either Day or Night "is about to go down into the house, the other comes out at the door" (736–57).[38] Appropriating this idea, Milton makes it an attribute of God's holy mount, thereby reinforcing the mount's cosmic character. As already suggested, such a perspective accords well with the traditional cosmic mountain. Light issues from and returns to the ancient Persian Albūrz, the archetypal sacred mountain from which Mithra views the world. Correspondingly, the mountain of Milton's God is a source of generation in its own right. As a cosmic "Center," it becomes an omphalos (cf. *Comus*, 520), from which "issue" "light" and "darkness," at once the symbols of "grateful vicissitude" in "Heav'n" (5.8) and the emblems of God's essentially generative nature.[39]

If such cosmic symbolism is applicable to God's holy mount, it is no less applicable to the Edenic mount, a terrestrial replication of its celestial counterpart. A "rural mound," the "Mountain" of paradise is characterized by its great height: it is a "steep savage Hill," a "high rais'd" "Garden mould" that denies "access" to trespassers (4.134–37, 172, 226–27). Approaching this "steep wilderness," one beholds the "insuperable highth of loftiest shade," "ascend[ing]" "shade above shade" to the top, "crown'd" with an "enclosure green," "higher then" the "tops" of the trees that lead up to "the verdurous wall of Paradise up sprung," and still "higher then that Wall a circling row / Of goodliest Trees" (4.135–47, 8.304).[40] Accordingly, one moves from one height to the next, only to be confronted by still greater heights. Even when one gains access, he beholds "a Rock / Of Alabaster, pil'd up to the Clouds, / Conspicuous farr" (4.543–45). In its height, then, the Edenic mount assumes the essential cosmic attributes of the heavenly mount. Like the heavenly mount too, it is animistic: its "sides" are "hairie," it "thirsts," it contains those fruits imbued with potentially magical properties ("life-giving," as well as "life-destroying") (4.135, 199, 200–228). As the full embodiment of the natural world, it shares earth's properties: its feminine gender, its reactions to Adam and Eve's disobedience (earth's sighing, groaning, and trembling from her "entrails," as if in "pangs," accompanied by the weeping of the sky) (9.782–83, 1000–1004). It is a place of myth, where, in happier times, "Universal *Pan* / Knit with the *Graces* and the *Hours* in dance / Led on th'Eternal Spring" (4.266–68). It is no less than paradise itself: a *Zauberberg* crowned by its Edenic residence.

As such, it becomes a veritable axis mundi, the cosmic intersection of the divine and the human, where one can pass from one cosmic zone to another. Nowhere is this more graphically (and ironically) portrayed than in Satan's voyage from Hell to earth. Alighting upon an area since called "the Paradise of Fools" (3.496), he "descries," on the one hand, "a Structure high," "ascending by degrees magnificent / Up to the wall of Heav'n," "at top whereof, but farr more rich appeard / The work as of a Kingly Palace Gate"; leading up to the "Structure," "the Stairs were such as whereon *Jacob* saw / Angels ascending and descending . . . / Dreaming by night under the open Skie, / And waking cri'd, *This is the Gate of Heav'n*" (3.501–15). On the other hand, he beholds, "direct against" this towering structure with its "dores of Bliss," another opening "from beneath, / Just o're the blissful seat of Paradise, / A passage down to th' Earth, a passage wide, / Wider by farr then that of after-times / Over Mount *Sion*, and, though that were large, / Over the *Promis'd Land* . . . / So wide the op'ning seemd, where bounds were set / To darkness, such as bound the Ocean wave" (3.525–39). Both cosmic zones (the celestial and the terrestrial) provide insight into the nature of holy mount.

From the celestial perspective, the high structure ascending up to the walls of Heaven becomes the type of the New Jerusalem, God's mountain abode (Rev. 21:10–12). So the Redcrosse Knight witnessed the New Jerusalem, with "the blessed Angels" ascending to and descending from its heights (*Faerie Queene*, 1.10.56–57). In both Spenser and Milton, the suggestion of Jacob's vision is to the point. Witnessing "the angels of God ascending and descending" upon "a ladder" that "reached to heaven," Jacob commemorates his vision of "the gate of heaven" by setting up "a pillar" to represent "the house of God." He accordingly calls the place "Beth-el" or "house of God" as it is represented by the pillar: "And this stone, which I have set *for* a pillar, shall be God's house" (Gen. 28:11–22). His response is one of creating a high place as a memorial of the true high place he has seen. Thus, the rabbis associate the vision of the ladder, as it is reflected in the building of the high place, with the ascent of a sacred mountain to see God.[41] Thus, Milton, alluding to Jacob's vision of the ladder, speaks of man's attempts to recreate "on earth" a "Model" of God's "inimitable" high place (3.509).

From the terrestrial perspective, that high place finds its counterpart in the Jerusalemic high place with which it intersects in the "passage" that leads down to the "seat of Paradise." That seat, in turn, Milton associates both locally with "Mount *Sion*" and more expansively with all "the *Promis'd Land*." In the first case, the Zionic parallel speaks for itself. The terrestrial mount of paradise, as cosmic phenomenon, is none other than Zion, the Temple Mount of Jerusalem. (Compare Isaiah's suggestion of the parallel in 51:3.) In the second instance, the reference to the "*Promis'd Land*" suggests an additional dimension. For in the lines that follow, Milton proceeds to do nothing less than to survey from border to border the entire "*Holy Land*" (3.535–37). The act recalls at once Ezekiel's high mount vision of the Temple as a symbol of paradise, measured from border to border (Ezek. 40–48), and Saint John the Divine's vision of the New Jerusalem, similarly measured (Rev. 11:1–4).[42]

In each respect, then, Milton reinforces the basic pattern with which this discussion has been working all along. Both from the celestial and the terrestrial points of view, one beholds the intersection of two high places in a momentous vision of the axis mundi. This is what Satan, like "a Scout" who "obtains the brow of some high-climbing Hill" (3.546), beholds in his voyage from Hell to earth. Debarred from the heavenly high place, he turns his attention to the earthly, there to choose his place of destruction. Passing from one cosmic zone to the other, he leaves "the lower stair / That scal'd by steps of Gold to Heav'n Gate" and "throws / His flight precipitant" "down right into the Worlds first Region" (3.540–41, 562–63). With this event, the intersection of the cosmic zones represents not only a conceptual axis for the convergence of high places but a dramatic axis for the continuation of the narrative.

In the working out of the narrative, Satan's motives are precisely in keeping with the concept of holy mount explored here. The validity of such an assertion is already suggested in the foregoing references to the heavenly stairs. Commenting upon those stairs, the narrator observes that they "were then let down" possibly "to dare / The Fiend by easie ascent or aggravate / His sad exclusion from the dores of Bliss" (3.523–25). Whatever the precise reason for their immediate presence, the stairs symbolize in part, then, Satan's inability to reascend to God's high-place abode, an inability that accounts for the mountain drama that opens the fourth book of Milton's epic. In an event that parodies both Christ's transfiguration and his passion, Satan is "disfigur'd" upon "th'*Assyrian* mount" Niphates (3.742, 4.8–130). Cursing the light, much as Milton had blessed it in the previous book, Satan betrays both his motives and his true form, while he surveys Eden from his own "top / Of Speculation" (4.27, 12.588–89). Niphates thereby becomes the first terrestrial seat for what might be called "the Visions of Satan" (compare 11.377). Those visions reveal not the transfigured lineaments of one whose "face shone as the sun" and whose "garments became white as light" (Matt. 17:2; cf. Mark 9:2–8 and Luke 9:28–36) but the "disfigur'd" lineaments of one whose appearance is "dimm'd" and "marrd" (4.114–16). His sufferings are those conducive not to a *Christus patiens* (compare TM, CM, 18:240) but to a kind of *Satanus impatiens*. If what is revealed on Niphates does not escape the watchful eye of Uriel (4.125), it does indicate the extent to which Satan envies God, despite Satan's having been "lifted up so high" that he "sdeind subjection, and thought one step higher / Would set . . . [him] highest" (4.49–51). That motive, of course, bears directly upon the idea of the mount, since the attempt to ascend or reascend in *Paradise Lost* as a way of challenging divine authority inevitably results in the creation of mountains or mountainlike structures. Thus, the desire to "dispossess" God of his "inaccessible high strength, the seat / Of Deitie supream" (7.142–43) is embodied perversely in a Satanic "high strength," situated in Heaven's northern regions: there, one finds Satan's "Royal seat / High on a Hill, far blazing, as a Mount / Rais'd on a Mount, with Pyramids and Towrs . . . / The Palace of great *Lucifer*" (5.755–60). It is through this mount that Satan "affect[s] all equality with God" (5.762; cf. 5.725). An affront to God's mount, the Satanic mount, in one form or another, appears everywhere in *Paradise Lost*.

Aside from Satan's mount in Heaven, the most notable example is Pandaemonium in Hell. There, the Satanic crew erects a structure, a perverse ziggurat in its own right, that is at once a tower and a temple mount, created from "a Hill . . . whose griesly top / Belch'd fire and rowling smoak" (1.670–71). As a tower, it rivals "*Babel*" and the Egyptian pyramids, "the works of *Memphian* Kings" (1.694); as a temple mount (1.713), it rivals all such constructs: "Not *Babilon*, / Nor great *Alcairo* such magnificence / Equal'd in all thir glories, to inshrine / *Belus* or *Serapis* thir Gods, or seat / Thir Kings" (1.717–21).[43] If Belus and Serapis are enshrined in these high places, Satan is enshrined in Pandaemonium, where he sits exalted "high on a Throne of Royal State": "Thus high uplifted beyond hope," he "aspires / Beyond thus high" (2.1–8). There, as discussed earlier, he is adored (4.89–90; cf. 6.99–103). As the seat of adoration, the "ascending pile" (1.722) shares not only the cultic but the cosmic aspects of the high place. "Built like a Temple," it is fashioned within to reflect the cosmos: "From the arched roof / Pendant by suttle Magic many a row / Of starry Lamps and blazing Cressets ... / ... yeilded light / As from a sky" (1.713, 726–30). The "magic" of such illumination pervades the entire structure: the "Fabrick huge" rises "like an Exhalation" "out of the earth" (1.710–12). But, of course, the magic of this Zauberberg is illusory. Entrance into "the Hall / Of that infernal Court" evokes allusions to "Dwarfs," pygmies ("that Pigmean Race / Beyond the *Indian* Mount"), and "Faerie Elves" beheld in dream (1.777–84). The throne itself becomes the seat of false theophanies: not God's manifesting his deity from amidst the clouds that surround the high place but Satan's pulling off a magician's trick. Returning to Hell after his mission on earth has been accomplished, he sneaks past his legions into the "*Plutonian* Hall" and ascends his "high Throne" invisibly, after which he enacts a false theophany: "At last as from a Cloud his fulgent head / And shape Starr bright appeer'd ... / ... : All amaz'd / At that so sudden blaze the *Stygian* throng / Bent thir aspect, and whom they wish'd be-held" (10.427–54). At that moment, the Satanic high place gloriously fulfills its illusory function. Pandaemonium outvies God's mount in every way possible.

But this hellish ziggurat is not the only Satanic construct to appear in *Paradise Lost*. Complementing the Satanic high place in Heaven and Hell is one on earth. In that region, one finds the ziggurat of ziggurats, the Tower of Babel, built by Nimrod[44] and his crew as a challenge to God. Already compared to Pandaemonium in Book 1 (694), the Tower of Babel, like its prototype, springs from hellish sources, in this case, a "Plain, wherein a black bituminous gurge / Boils out from under ground, the mouth of Hell" (12.41–42). With the purpose of "reach[ing] to Heav'n" to "obstruct Heav'n Towrs," this "Tower," like Satan's, "in-tends / Siege and defiance" (12.44, 52, 73–74). It thereby recapitulates the pattern of attempting to undermine God's authority through the construction of high places.

Such is precisely the way that the Renaissance understood it. In his translation of and commentary upon Ovid's *Metamorphoses*, George Sandys makes this point graphically. Responding to the lines "And that the Heavens their safety might suspect, / The Gyants now coelestiall Thrones affect; / Who to the skies congested mountains reare" (*Met.*, 1.154–56), Sandys associates the Ovidian account of the giants' attempt to usurp the domain of the gods with the building of the Tower of Babel: "And what was that," says Sandys of the Tower, "but the throwing of mountaine upon mountaine, to scale even heaven it selfe, and warre with the Gods?"[45] The phrase "throwing ... mountaine upon mountaine" recalls once again Satan's "Royal seat," appearing "as a Mount / Rais'd on a Mount." But the "throwing" of mountain upon mountain also suggests that in response to the arrogance of the giants, Ovid's "*Iove* with thunder did Olympus teare; / Steepe *Pelion* from vnder *Ossa* throwne" (*Met.*, 1.157–58), an act recounted in Milton's account of the angels' throwing of hills and piling them upon the rebel crew in *Paradise Lost* (6.639–66).[46] In whatever form, then, Satan and his followers are high-place builders who express their desire to "ascend" through the creation of perverse ziggurats.

This idea is certainly not unique to *Paradise Lost*. Cosmically, in fact, Milton's epic embodies a high-place drama particularly indebted to two biblical sources, Ezekiel and Isaiah. Ezekiel contains a lament for the king of Tyre that is cast in a form bearing directly upon the themes explored here: "Thou hast been in Eden the garden of God . . . ; Thou *art* the anointed cherub that covereth; and I have set thee *so*: thou wast upon the holy mountain of God. . . . Thou *wast* perfect in thy ways from the day that thou wast created, till iniquity was found in thee . . . and thou hast sinned: therefore I will cast thee as profane out of the mountain of God: and I will destroy thee" (Ezek. 28:13–15). According to R. E. Clements, the mountain referred to here has affinities with the cosmic mount Zaphon, identified with Eden, the garden of God.[47] If so, then the passage from Ezekiel represents a conflation of the Genesis account with a cosmic mountain myth in which an angel is cast out of the high place because of corrupt aspirations. In Isaiah, the idea is conceived in a way that is even more to the point: "How art thou fallen from heaven, O Lucifer, son of the morning? *how* art thou cut down to the ground. . . . For thou hast said in thine heart, I will ascend into heaven, I will exalt my throne above the stars of God: I will sit also upon the mount of the congregation, in the sides of the north: I will ascend above the heights of the clouds; I will be like the most High. Yet thou shalt be brought down to hell, to the sides of the pit" (Isa. 14:12–15). In this "taunt-song" uttered against the king of Babylon, Isaiah creates his own high-place myth that has all the elements of the mythos that underlies *Paradise Lost*: the aspirations and subsequent fall of Lucifer, the desire to exalt oneself through the construction of cosmic mountains that rival God's mount (Isaiah's "mount of the congregation" is, once again, Zaphon),[48] and the descent to Hell.

The way in which Milton provides a distinctly Christocentric perspective for his myth may be seen by examining again the nature of Satan's mount in *Paradise Lost*. "Affecting all equality with God," Satan "intends t'erect his Throne" "in imitation of that Mount whereon / *Messiah* was

declar'd in sight of Heav'n, / The Mountain of the Congregation call'd"
(5.724, 763–66). In this refashioning of the myth, the cosmic Mount
Zaphon of Ezekiel and Isaiah becomes for Milton Mount Zion. As Milton's translation of Psalm 2 attests, Zion is none other than the place
of the Son's begetting or "declaring" of the Messiah: "But I saith hee
[God] / Anointed have my King (though ye rebell) / On Sion my holi'hill.
A firm decree / I will declare; the Lord to me hath said / Thou art my
Son; I have begotten thee / This day" (11–16). The begetting or ritual
anointing of the Son in *Paradise Lost* is the central divine act, the modus
operandi, by which the action moves: "Hear my Decree," proclaims God,

> which unrevok't shall stand.
> This day I have begot whom I declare
> My onely Son, and on this holy Hill
> Him have anointed, whom ye now behold
> At my right hand; your Head I him appoint;
> And by my Self have sworn to him shall bow
> All knees in Heav'n, and shall confess him Lord:
> . . . him who disobeys
> Mee disobeys, breaks union, and that day
> Cast out from God and blessed vision, falls
> Into utter darkness, deep ingult, his place
> Ordaind without redemption, without end.
> (5.603–15)

Considering the nature of the decree and the consequences of disobeying it, it is worthwhile to note the decidedly cultic basis of what God is
proclaiming. As Milton indicates in his discussion of Psalm 2 in *Christian
Doctrine*, the begetting of the Son is a sacerdotal act that prefigures his
Messianic role as Christ: that is, mankind's Anointed Savior who is given
dominion, who is resurrected, and who is exalted (*CM*, 14:182–85). As
a result of this begetting or anointing, Milton makes clear in *Paradise
Lost*, the Son is to be appropriately worshiped with bowing and confession. "Adore the Son," says God, "and honour him as mee" (3.343). In
disobeying God, Satan refuses to engage in the worship that is asked
of him. He will not afford the Son "knee-tribute," "prostration vile"
(5.782). Accordingly, he deserts God, leaving "the Throne supream"
"unworshipt" (5.669–71). His motives in doing so are "impiously" to
"diminish" God by "withdraw[ing]" from him "the number of [his]
worshippers" (7.611–13). At the same time, he rivals the begetting of the
Son by exalting himself as an object of worship: "High in the midst
exalted as a God / Th'Apostat in his Sun-bright Chariot sate / Idol of

Majestie Divine, enclos'd / With Flaming Cherubim, and golden Shields" (6.99–102). That exaltation, in turn, finds its counterpart in the various Satanic high places already discussed, the "Palace of great *Lucifer*," Pandaemonium, and the Tower of Babel. These high places represent not only the cosmic embodiments of Satanic rebelliousness, as depicted in the highplace myths of Ezekiel and Isaiah, but the cultic embodiments of Satanic impiety, as depicted in the Christocentric assimilation of the high-place myth portrayed in *Paradise Lost*. In either case, they become mounts of corruption, as opposed to the holy mounts that characterize the divine sphere.

That distinction was hardly foreign to religious thought. In his *Philologia Sacra* (1705), the seventeenth-century exegete Salomon Glass, for example, provides a discourse on the mountain in which he distinguishes between mons sanctus and what he calls *mons corruptor* (p. 719). Whereas mons sanctus is depicted in those various high places that culminate in the *montem sanctum Dei*, mons corruptor is depicted in the "destroying mountain" of Jeremiah 51:25: "Behold, I *am* against thee, O destroying mountain [הר המשחית], saith the Lord, which destroyest all the earth: and I will stretch out mine hand upon thee, and roll thee down from the rocks, and will make thee a burnt mountain." This is Babylon, which, says Glass, "fore in montem combustionis" (p. 719). As a characteristic of mons corruptor, the idea of the "burnt mountain" (*in montem combustionis*) is implicit in the "Hill" from which Pandaemonium is erected in *Paradise Lost*. That hill is one "whose griesly top / Belch'd fire and rowling smoak; the rest entire / Shon with a glossie scurff" (1.670–72). Such is the soil of Hell itself: burning with "solid" fire, it appears "in hue, as when the force / Of subterranean wind transports a Hill / Torn from *Pelorus*, or the shatter'd side / Of thundring *Aetna*, whose combustible / And fewel'd entrails thence conceiving Fire, / ... aid the Winds, / And leave a singed bottom all involv'd / With stench and smoak" (1.228–37). The allusion to Etna, of course, recalls Typhoeus in Milton's *In Quintum Novembris*: "Enclosed by Jove / under Sicilian Aetna," Typhoeus emits from his "destructive mouth" "Tartarean fires and ghastly sulphur" (*Tartareos ignes et luridum olentia sulphur*) (35–37). The scatology of the reference is not to be missed. When dealing with Tartarean fires, Milton leaves little room for doubt. Such fires are to be emitted, Milton makes clear in *Prolusion 6*, either through the "*Sphincter anus*" or through the "mouth": these will produce a "terrible and tartarian sound of hissing," "more noisome" than the emissions of "Aetna" and "Avernus" (*CM*, 12:228–31). What better language, after all, befits that "*infame Monstrorum genus*," as Milton calls them in

Prolusion 1 (*CM*, 12:134–36)? As that which has affinities with the "obscene," to use the language of *Paradise Lost* (1.406), Satan and his crew inhabit a world diametrically opposed to the holy. In them, the mons corruptor assumes consummate form.[49] It is not only Etna but, in its association with Satan's activities, also Olivet (1.403), Lebanon (1.446–47), Imaus (3.431–35), and Niphates (3.742). In its own way, it is even Golgotha (3.476–77), which, according to de Guevera, "doth signifie a . . . dunghill."[50] Satan himself, finally, is *"Teneriff"* and *"Atlas"* "unremov'd" (4.987). Because of their associations, these are what Milton in *Comus* calls the "infamous hills" (424).

For our purposes, their infamy assumes a decidedly cultic significance. Mount Olivet, for example, is at once the "opprobrious Hill," the "Hill of scandal," and "th'Offensive Mountain" (1.403, 416, 443). As such, Olivet represents the high places built by Solomon for the purposes of false worship: "And the high places that *were* before Jerusalem, which *were* on the right hand of the mount of corruption . . . Solomon the king of Israel had builded for Ashtoreth the abomination of the Zidonians, and for Chemosh the abomination of the Moabites, and for Milcom the abomination of the children of Ammon" (2 Kings 23:13; cf. 1 Kings 11:7). Such high places, Milton says, were built "right against the Temple of God" (1.402). They are the shrines of the devils become pagan deities (1.373) who "durst fix / Thir Seats . . . next the Seat of God, / Thir Altars by his Altar, Gods ador'd / Among the Nations round" (1.373, 382–85).

Geographically, as the passage from 2 Kings makes clear, they are part of the Jerusalemic prospect. So described by such exegetes as Christianus Adrichomius, that prospect contains "MOVNT OLIVET," the "MOVNT OF OFFENCE," in which Solomon, "forgetting all godliness, erected a temple to *Astoreth* . . . right ouer against the temple of *Ierusalem*."[51] Thus, also John Lightfoot writes: Solomon was persuaded by his idolatrous wives to build a "temple to their abominations on Mount Olivet, in the face of the [true] Temple, and affronting it."[52] Between this "MOVNT OF OFFENCE" and the true Temple of Jerusalem lies "the valley of Hinnom, or Tophet, where was the horrid and hideous practice of their irreligious religion, of butchering their children, in causing them to pass through the fire, or burning them to Moloch" (cf. 2 Kings 23:10).[53] The "buryingplace" and "common sink of the whole city," it is, says Lightfoot, the spot "whither all filth, and all kind of nastiness, met."[54] As such, it is for Lightfoot "the representation of hell"[55] and for Milton "black *Gehenna*," the "Type of Hell" (PL, 1.403–5). From this perspective, then, the mons corruptor, with its environs, takes on cultic associations as part of a Jerusalemic setting. In contrast with (and, in fact, geographically "affronting") the sacred mount, it embodies the sacrilege of impure worship and debased sacrifice. In that way, it reinforces the cultic dimension that is integral to the Eden story.

Making this point in the very act of associating first the corrupt high places with the fallen angels and second the "Valley of *Hinnom*" with Hell, Milton goes further by conceiving Josiah's defilement of the Solomonic high places (2 Kings 23:1–20) as a symbol of driving the devils from "thence to Hell" (1.418). That cultic act recapitulates in small the cosmic action of the whole epic: the mons corruptor is ritually cleansed of its defilement by having those things that the false worshipers hold to be holy defiled, burned, and destroyed. (Compare the exorcism of the pagan deities in the *Nativity Ode*.) Here, as elsewhere, the cultic and the cosmic become complementary expressions of a fundamental sacrality that underlies the action of *Paradise Lost*. These expressions, in turn, are appropriated into an all-prevailing Christocentric outlook. If such is true of the other sacral phenomena explored here, it is no less true of holy mount. To understand the Christocentrism of holy mount, it is necessary to explore this sacral phenomenon typologically.

There is a good deal of precedence for approaching holy mount from this point of view. The Old Testament itself embodies the typological progression of holy mount from material to spiritual entity. Made evident in the Deuteronomic reformation with the spiritualizing of the Sinai theophany (Deut. 4:11–12, 36), it becomes a prominent feature of the postexilic community with the renewed emphasis upon divine transcendence (Ezra 1:2; Neh. 1:4, 5).[56] Among the prophets, it finds its most graphic expression in Isaiah: "And it shall come to pass in the last days, *that* the mountain of the Lord's house shall be established in the top of the mountains, and shall be exalted above the hills; and all nations shall flow unto it. And many people shall go and say, Come ye, and let us go up to the mountain of the Lord, to the house of the God of Jacob; and he will teach us of his ways, and we will walk in his paths: for out of Zion shall go forth the law, and the word of the Lord from Jerusalem" (Isa. 2:2–3).

This exaltation of "the mountain of the Lord's house" (הר בית-יהוה) finds consummate expression in the New Testament, where it assumes a Christocentric bearing. The typology implicit in Hebrews 12:18–24 speaks for itself: "For ye are not come unto the mount that might be touched, and that burned with fire, nor unto blackness, and darkness, and tempest. And the sound of a trumpet, and the voice of words. . . . But ye are come unto the mount Sion, and unto the city of the living God, the heavenly Jerusalem, and to an innumerable company of angels, To the general assembly and church of the firstborn, which are written in heaven, and to God the Judge of all, and to the spirits of just men made perfect, And to Jesus the mediator of the new covenant." The movement from Sinai to Zion and the wilderness to Jerusalem implicit here is elsewhere in the New Testament carried even further with the glorification of a totally spiritualized Jerusalem. Thus, the epistle to the Galatians allegorizes the distinction between old law and new through reference to the two sons of Abraham, one born of a bondmaid, the other of a freewoman: "Which things are an allegory: for these are the two covenants; the one from the mount Sinai, which gendereth to bondage, which is Agar. For this Agar is mount Sinai in Arabia, and answereth to Jerusalem which now is, and is in bondage with her children. But Jerusalem which is above is free, which is the mother of us all" (Gal. 4:22–26). If Mount Sinai gives way to Mount Zion, the Jerusalemic setting of the new mountain vision is a distinctly heavenly one: the old Jerusalem too gives way to the new. "The hour cometh," says Jesus to the woman of Samaria, when you shall worship neither in the mountain of Gerizim "nor yet at Jerusalem" but "in spirit and in truth. . . . God *is* a Spirit: and they that worship him must worship *him* in spirit and in truth" (John 4:19–24). Within this context, the Jerusalem of Saint John the Divine, as it is indebted to the Ezekiel vision of the restored Temple (Ezek. 40–48), is profoundly spiritual: "And I saw no temple therein: for the Lord God Almighty and the Lamb are the temple of it" (Rev. 21:22).

As depicted in biblical terms, the movement from Sinai to Zion, with all the implications that such a movement suggests, is basic to the traditions that Milton inherited. From the patristic point of view, one finds such works as *De Montibus Sina et Sion*, attributed to Saint Cyprian, wherein *"montem Sina"* is interpreted *"esse terrenum,"* on the one hand, and *"montem Sion"* *"coelestem esse et spiritualem,"* on the other.[57] The first is quite simply a type of the second. Similar views are discernible in Church Fathers like Saint John Chrysostom, who, commenting upon the passage from Hebrews, contrasts Sinai and Zion in this manner: *"There* was a wilderness, here a city," there, "the *blackness* and the *darkness,* and the *tempest,"* here, "joy" and "delight," there, the fear of approaching, here the confidence to "draw near."[58] Conflating Zion and Jerusalem in his *Exposition on the Book of Psalms,* Saint Augustine says, "Sion was a certain city of this world, which bore a typical resemblance as a shadow to that Sion . . . that [is the] Heavenly Jerusalem"; whereas "the earthly city has been destroyed," the heavenly city is indestructible. It is, in fact, none other than Christ himself, "the foundation, and corner stone: rising from the bottom: if indeed from the bottom: for the base of this foundation is the highest exaltation of the building: and, as the support of bodily fabrics rests upon the ground, that of spiritual structures reposes on high. . . . This building now cries from your hearts."[59] For Saint Augustine, Christ is the "Foundation of foundations," the Zion of Zions, the mount of mounts.[60] In him, the spiritualizing process attains its fullest expression.

What is true of biblical and patristic thought is likewise true of the Renaissance exegetical tradition: the movement from mount to mount corresponds to the spiritualizing process that underlies the Christocentric point of view. Commentaries upon Hebrews 12:18–24, in particular, attest to this fact. Thus, distinguishing between Sinai and Zion, William Gouge says that whereas Sinai "was situated in the driest, barrennest, and most parching place of the world; even in a wildernesse," Zion "was situated in the best part of the world, which was *Canaan*, the land which flowed with milke and honey." "Fitly therefore doth the Mount *Sinai* set out the Law; which can afford no succour, no refreshing: and as fitly doth the Mount *Sion* set out the Gospel, which is simply the best estate that possibly can be." "Because the Arke (which was the most lively representation of Gods presence) was set in *Sion*, it was made a choise type of the Evangelicall Church where the Lord dwelleth."[61] In the same vein, John Owen observes that "the opposition between these two mounts was eminent. For, (1.) God came down for a season only on mount Sinai; but in Sion he is said to dwell, and to make his habitation for ever. (2.) He appeared in terror on mount Sinai . . . ; Sion was in Jerusalem, which is 'a vision of peace.' (3.) He gave the law on mount Sinai; the gospel went forth from Sion. . . . (4.) He utterly forsook Sinai, and left it under bondage; but Sion is free for ever. . . . (5.) The people were burdened with the law at mount Sinai, and were led with it unto Sion, where they waited for deliverance from it, in the observation of those institutions of divine worship which were typical and significant thereof."[62] Addressing itself squarely to the movement from one mount to the next, *The Mount of Spirits* encapsulates the entire situation in a sentence: Christ led us "from Mount *Sinai* to Mount *Sion*, from Mount *Sion* literal to Mount *Sion* spiritual, and from the earthly to the heavenly *Jerusalem*" (p. 75).[63] Implied is a progression not only from mount to mount but from literal (earthly) to spiritual (heavenly). As suggested earlier, Milton adopts the same sense of progression at the outset of *Paradise Lost*. Associating the Muse first with "the secret top / Of *Oreb*, or of *Sinai*," he moves to "*Sion* Hill," a source of greater "Delight," and then, finally transcending all mounts, including "th'*Aonian* Mount," he arrives at "th'upright heart and pure," that abode which the "Spirit" "dost prefer / Before all

Temples" (1.6–18). Although the movement and its significance have been plotted many times,[64] it will be instructive to plot them again as part of the milieu established here.

For Milton, Sinai is, of course, the place from which God issues his laws: as Michael prophesies to Adam, "God from the Mount of *Sinai*, whose gray top / Shall tremble, he descending, will himself / In Thunder Lightning and loud Trumpets sound / Ordain them [the Israelites] Laws" (12,227–30; cf. N, 157–59). In the Renaissance, this trumpeting forth of the Old Dispensation, an event surrounded by terror, was looked upon prefiguratively. Thus, commenting upon the reference in Hebrews 12:18–19 to the trumpet sounded in Sinai (Exod. 19:16, 19), Owen says: "And as unto its typical signification, it was (1.) A pledge of the future judgment when all flesh shall be summoned before the judgment-seat of Christ, to answer the terms of the law. And, (2.) . . . it was a type of the promulgation of the gospel in the ministry of Christ himself."[65] "Christ," says Andrew Willet, responding to the Sinai trumpet, shall also "call us by the sound of the trumpet in the last day, and we shall meet him in the aire, and ascend up unto him, and so ever remaine with him."[66] One notes the progression: the terrible giving of the laws prefigures the Last Judgment, which in turn signals the glorious promise of Christ's ministry. A comparable movement is to be seen in Milton's *Nativity Ode*: the "horrid clang" of Sinai shakes the "aged Earth" "with terrour of that blast" in a way that prefigures "the worlds last session," when "the dreadfull Judge . . . shall spread his throne." That event, in turn, is followed by a "full" and "perfect" "bliss," made possible by the coming of Christ, who shall bind "th'old Dragon" (165–68; Rev. 20:2–3). In *Paradise Lost*, this progression arises out of God's judgment upon fallen man. As the trumpet in Heaven signals the impending expulsion of Adam and Eve from Eden, it prefigures at once the judgment at Sinai and the "general Doom" (11.73–76). But these events too are followed by the promise of eternal "bliss," when the "Serpent" shall be bound and "the Earth / Shall all be Paradise, far happier place / Then this of *Eden*, far happier daies" (12.453–55, 463–65). As a reflection of God's original judgment, the judgment at Sinai, then, culminates in a vision of bliss.

That vision, in turn, assumes Zionic associations. Those associations are already indicated in part by Milton's translation of Psalm 84:

> They [the Israelites] pass through Baca's
>   *thirstie* Vale,
> *That dry and barren ground*
> As through a fruitfull watry Dale

Where Springs and Showrs abound.
They journey on from strength to strength
With joy and gladsom cheer
Till all before *our* God at *length*
In Sion do appear

(21–28)

In cultic terms, that movement is represented by the installation of God's Sinai laws in the Zion temple. As Michael prophesies to Adam, Solomon "shall in a glorious Temple enshrine" "the clouded Arke of God till then in Tents / Wandring" (12.332–34). Such an enshrinement has been prepared for by Nathan's prophecy to David that "his Regal Throne / For ever shall endure" (12.322–24; 2 Sam. 7:16). That event, in turn, prefigures the coming of Christ from "the Royal Stock / Of *David*," a "Son" of whose "Reign shall be no end" (12.325–30). The "true / Anointed King *Messiah*" (12.358–59), in whom "the clouded Arke of God" shall finally be "enshrine[d]" (cf. PA, 15–17; Heb. 9:11, 1:9), he is "the Woman's Seed" who, upon nailing the "Law" of Sinai "to the Cross" in his crucifixion (12.415–16; Col. 2:14), "shall bruise / The Serpent's head" (12.148–50, 327; Gen. 3:15; Rom. 16:20) and bind the Dragon "in Chains" (12.454) in his resurrection and ascension, after which he shall "enter into glory, and resume / His Seat at God's right hand, exalted high" (12.454–57).

Such events underlie the Christocentric outlook that permeates *Paradise Lost*. It is, of course, the outlook into which Adam, upon the Hill of Speculation, is indoctrinated in the last two books. From the Zionic point of view, however, it is prepared for at the outset of Milton's epic with the references to the pool of Siloam (1.11–12, 3.30–31). Situated, as Milton says, "fast by the Oracle of God" (1.11–12) or the Jerusalem Temple (cf. Neh. 3:15–16), Siloa is one of "the flowrie Brooks" that "wash" the "hallowd feet" of "Sion" (3.30–31). Within this context, the pool assumes both a cultic and a spiritual dimension. The cultic dimension may be seen in Milton's association of the pool with the Jerusalem Temple. That association, according to Lightfoot, manifested itself in the ritual of "the pouring out of water" drawn from the pool of Siloam during "that solemn festivity of the feast of Tabernacles."[67] "The Gemarists inquire," says Lightfoot, "whence was this custom? From thence, that it is said, 'And ye shall draw waters with joy out of the wells of salvation,'" whereby "they draw out the Holy Spirit."[68] As early as the *Talmud*, then, the tabernacle cult surrounding the pool of Siloam takes on spiritual significance. Milton suggests that fact in his reference to "*Siloa's*" washing of Zion's "hallowd feet." Drawing upon the idea that the waters of Siloam were viewed as ritually purificatory,[69] Milton associates those waters, by implication, both with the woman's washing of Jesus' feet (Luke 7:38) and with Jesus' washing of his disciples' feet (John 13:5). Those acts represent Christ's mission as purifier (cf. PL, 10.211–23).[70]

The relevance of that fact to the Siloam allusions may be seen particularly in Milton's view of "the flowrie Brook" as a source of purging one's blindness. It is in this spirit, of course, that the blind poet invokes "*Siloa's* Brook" in the first and third books of *Paradise Lost*. Milton has in mind none other than John 9:1–11, in which Jesus dramatizes his mission "in the world" by curing the blind man: Christ "spat on the ground, and made clay of the spittle, and he anointed the eyes of the blind man with the clay, And said unto him, Go, wash in the pool of Siloam. . . . He went his way therefore, and washed, and came seeing" (John 9:6–7). In that state, he is inspired by the "Oracle of God," the source of divine revelation: cleansed at the Temple Mount, he is filled with the spirit of what Milton calls God's "living Oracle" (PR, 1.460). As an emblem of Christ's mission (depicted in the Messianic anointing of the Son), this divine act of anointing prepares the reader for the action of Milton's poem itself, especially as that action is embodied in the last two books.

There, the giving of sight, anticipated in the purificatory lustrations of Zion's "flowrie Brooks," occurs on the new Zion, the new Temple Mount, where Michael "purges" Adam's "visual Nerve" with a potion containing "three drops" "from the Well of Life" (11.414–16). So enlightened, Adam is ready to "ascend / In the Visions of God" with Michael up the Hill of Speculation, "a Hill / Of Paradise the highest, from whose top / The Hemisphere of Earth in cleerest Ken / Strecht out to amplest reach of prospect lay" (11.376–80). In that sense, the circumstances surrounding Adam's vision, Milton suggests, are comparable to those surrounding "our second *Adam*," set upon a "Hill" by the "Tempter" "for different Cause" to view "all Earths Kingdoms and thir Glory" (11.381–84). Not only is the cause different, however, but ultimately the prospect, as well. If both the Adam of *Paradise Lost* and the Jesus of *Paradise Regained* are shown the worldly kingdoms, the first Adam, says Milton, beholds "nobler sights" (11.411). It is for this reason that Michael removes "the Film" "from *Adams* eyes" (11.412). In keeping with the foregoing comparison, one could say that the "nobler sights" that Adam beholds are embodied in Jesus's withstanding of temptations in the wilderness.[71] In *Paradise Regained* those temptations culminate, as they do in the Lukan account (Luke 4:9–12), in Jesus' standing upon the pinnacle of the Jerusalem Temple (PR, 4.561), an event foreshadowing his passion, crucifixion, resurrection, ascension, and ultimate binding of the dragon.[72] What Adam witnesses by virtue of these nobler sights, then, is the regaining of paradise, anticipated in the Zionic references to "*Siloa*'s Brook" and fulfilled in the occurrences at Jerusalem.

With its Christocentric emphasis, this Jerusalemic perspective is as much a part of *Paradise Lost* as it is of *Paradise Regained*. In Milton's diffuse epic, it underlies "the Visions of God" that Adam experiences upon the Hill of Speculation. If Adam beholds an earthly prospect encompassing the four corners of the globe (Asia, Africa, Europe, and America) (11.385–411), he beholds a heavenly prospect encompassing the life of man redeemed through Christ (12.360–464). Whereas the earthly prospect culminates in "unspoil'd / *Guiana*" or "*El Dorado*" (11.410–11), the heavenly prospect culminates in the New Jerusalem, "raise[d] / From the conflagrant mass, purg'd and refin'd, / New Heav'ns, new Earth, Ages of endless date / Founded in righteousness and peace and love, / To bring forth fruits Joy and eternal Bliss" (12.547–51). Within this perspective, Adam is at once Ezekiel, "upon a very high mountain" (Ezek. 40:2), beholding the restored Jerusalem Temple, and Saint John the Divine, upon "a great and high mountain," beholding "that great city, the holy Jerusalem, descending out of heaven from God" (Rev. 21:10; see figure 8).

In either case, Jerusalem is once again the focal point of the mountain vision, with its type in Ezekiel and its antitype in Saint John the Divine. William Greenhill's observation in *An Exposition of the Prophet Ezekiel* (1650) is particularly relevant here: "The place where the prophet had this vision was in the land of Israel, and upon mount Zion, or mount Moriah, where the temple was built. Moriah is from ראה to see; this mount is the mount of vision, and on it Ezekiel had this glorious vision. Kimchi saith, This mountain is the mountain of the temple, and this city is Jerusalem on the south. . . . The rabbins conceive the land of Israel to be the highest of all lands, and Mount Zion or Moriah, the highest of all the mountains in that land. It was a type of the church of Christ, Heb. XII. 22; and therefore it is represented here to be a very high mountain; and so it was unto John also, Rev. XXI. 10."[73] The Hill of Speculation upon which Adam experiences "the Visions of God," then, represents the full embodiment of the Jerusalemic point of view.

That point of view, in turn, is even further enhanced in the Mosaic dimension that complements it: biblically, as well as exegetically, Sinai gives way to Zion in the spiritualizing process that results in the New Jerusalem. This is what Adam himself learns in the last two books of *Paradise Lost*: the Sinai laws inform the Israelites, "by types / And shadows, of that destind Seed to bruise / The Serpent, by what means he shall

FIGURE 8. Vision of the New Jerusalem.
Reproduced from an engraving of Revelation 21, by Matthaeus Meriam
in [Veteris et Noui Testamenti] (1627), by permission of
the Newberry Library, Chicago, Illinois.

achieve / Mankinds deliverance" (12.232–35), as man "in full time" is
"resign[ed]" "up to a better Cov'nant, disciplin'd / From shadowie Types
to Truth, from Flesh to Spirit, / From imposition of strict Laws, to free /
Acceptance of large Grace, from servil fear / To filial, works of Law to
works of Faith" (12.301–6). In this process, Christ is typified in Moses
(12.240–41), and "Mankinds deliverance" into the spiritual Canaan is
foreshadowed by the Israelites' winning of the "earthly Canaan" through
the offices of "*Joshua* whom the Gentiles *Jesus* call, / His Name and
Office bearing" (12.258–60, 269, 310–15).

The relation of these events to the Jerusalemic perspective may be seen
in the parallel that Jason Rosenblatt has already drawn between Adam's
vision upon the Hill of Speculation and Moses's vision upon Pisgah
(Deut. 34): each suggests the idea of deliverance that culminates in the
New Jerusalem.[74] Thus, according to Henry Ainsworth, Moses ascended
Nebo, to the top of Pisgah, "that from thence hee might view the holy

land, as John from an high mountaine was shewed the holy Jerusalem, Rev. 21. 10."[75] In this respect, the Mosaic point of view developed in the last two books of Milton's epic lends itself admirably to the Jerusalemic perspective. That perspective, finally, is most fully realized in its spiritual form. Discoursing upon the "Inward Law" and "Spiritual Power" by which Christ governs, Milton addresses himself in *Christian Doctrine* to this form through precisely the correspondences examined here: "Hence the law of the kingdom, the gift of the Spirit, was given at Jerusalem on the fiftieth day from the crucifixion, as the Mosaic law was given on the fiftieth day from the passover in Mount Sinai, Acts ii. 1, in sign that the old law was superseded by the new, the law of bondage and of the flesh by the law of the Spirit and of freedom, Rom. xiv. 17" (*CM.* 15:299).

In light of these considerations, not only Sinai but Zion and Jerusalem lose their sacrality, their significance as consecrated entities, and give way to a totally spiritualized vision, a mount of spirits (Gal. 4:22–26; John 4:19–24; Rev. 21:22). Within that context, Milton maintains, Sinai becomes "repugnant and contradictive" and Zion "presumptuous" (CG, *CM*, 3:261; cf. D, *CM*, 3:508; TE, *CM*, 5:45). Even Jerusalem, as Milton conceives it in *Paradise Regained*, takes on the vestiges of pride. With its high "Towers" and even higher "Temple," "appearing like a Mount / Of Alabaster, top't with Golden Spires" (4.544–48; cf. Satan's Temple Mount, PL, 5.757–60), Jerusalem becomes the veritable embodiment of *superbia vitae*.[76] This, to use the language of Galatians 4:22–26, "answereth to Jerusalem which now is"; through Christ, we have access to the "Jerusalem which is above." That Jerusalem, as indicated in Revelation 21:22, contains "no temple: for the Lord God Almighty and the Lamb are the temple of it."

Accordingly, Milton moves at the outset of *Paradise Lost* from Sinai to Zion and finally to "th'upright heart and pure," which the "Spirit" "dost prefer / Before all Temples" (1.17–18). He moves, that is, to what he calls in *Christian Doctrine* the "*ecclesia invisibilis*," a concept supported in his proof-texts through references to Galatians 4:26 and Hebrews 12:22–23, among others (*CM*, 16:62–63). Having already reintroduced the text from Galatians, the discussion might well recall again the text from Hebrews, as Milton cites it: "Ye are come unto Mount Sion, and unto the city of the living God, the heavenly Jerusalem [*Hierosolymam coelestem*], and to an innumerable company of angels, to the general assembly and church of the first-born, which are written in heaven, and to God the Judge of all, and to the spirits of just men made perfect." This, the New Jerusalem, declares Milton in *The Reason of Church-Government*, is the "state . . . of the blessed in Paradise" (*CM*, 3:185).

For Adam, who has lost paradise, it is the promise of blessedness which provides "a Paradise within [him], happier farr" (12.586–87). The movement from mount to mount is complete, and Adam, infused with that promise, is prepared to descend both the Hill of Speculation and the Hill of Paradise into the world below.

8
Name

If place and mount in Milton's sacral poetics help to establish for God a local habitation and a name, the divine name itself should be of the first significance in any consideration of the holy in Milton's thought. That fact has already been suggested in Milton's singling out God's name among the "hidden things" in *Christian Doctrine* (CM, 17:32–35); and, as was discussed in chapter 2, sanctificatio for Milton, signifies none other than the "sanctification of the divine name" (CM, 17:81).

The "Ineffable Name," states the *Zohar*, "is the source and beginning of supreme mysteries indeed; it is the sphere whence emanate all the burning lights, and where the whole mystery of the Faith is centred; this Name dominates all."[1] In the apostrophe to Light that opens Book 3 of *Paradise Lost*, Milton's "Hail" is immediately qualified by his unwillingness to penetrate too far into the mystery. Whether that "Light" is the "ofspring of Heav'n first-born, / Or of th'Eternal Coeternal beam" (3.1–2), Milton will not say. However his words suggest the nature of godhead in its association with the Muse,[2] Milton's stance is clear enough. He intends to "keep off with a sacred reverence"[3] the naming of that which might incur blame. Thus, the first two lines of the apostrophe culminate in the all-important question "May I express thee unblam'd?" (3.3). Representing a fitting tribute to one who dwells "in unapproached light" (3.4), this question strikes at the heart of Milton's attitude toward the name of God. As Milton states in *Christian Doctrine*, if the divine name is to be pronounced at all, it had better be "with due reverence" (*modo reverenter*) (CM, 14:38–39).

Such an attitude is reflected significantly in the newly created Adam. Having just given the animals their names (8.349–54), Adam turns to the "Heav'nly vision" with a question that, Milton suggests, borders upon presumption (8.356): "O by what Name, for thou above all these, / Above mankind, or aught then mankind higher, / Surpassest farr my naming" (8.357–59).[4] Adam's ability to name the animals in *Paradise Lost* is based, of course, upon Genesis 2:20: "And Adam gave names to all cattle, and to the fowl of the air, and to every beast of the field." Milton ex-

plains the phenomenon in *Christian Doctrine*: "Man being formed after
the image of God, it followed as a necessary consequence that he should
be endued with natural wisdom, holiness and righteousness [*sapientia,
sanctitate, atque iustitia*]. Certainly, without extraordinary wisdom [*per-
magna autem sapientia*], he could not have given names to the whole
animal creation with such sudden intelligence" (*CM*, 15:52–53). He is
able, as Milton states in *Paradise Lost*, to name "readily" whatever he
sees. (Compare Eve's act of naming the plants [11.277].) The implication
is that although Adam is endowed with the natural ability to name
creatures of a lower order, he is unable to name that which transcends his
nature, since, as Milton states in *Christian Doctrine*, "the imposition of a
name is allowed to be uniformly the privilege of the greater personage
whether father or lord" (*CM*, 14:307).

That statement helps to explain Milton's posture toward his Muse,
who is called variously the Spirit of God, "holy Light," Urania, and
"Celestial Patroness" (1.7, 3.1, 7.1, 9.21). These "notations," as Milton
would define them in his *Logic*, are insufficient to uncover what is "divinely given" (*divinitus . . . datae sunt*) (*CM*, 11:220–21).[5] Thus, Milton
is careful to qualify his apostrophe to Urania by saying, "By that name /
If rightly thou art call'd" (7.1–2). That qualification, in turn, is followed
by an outright abandoning of all attempts to name the unnamable: "The
meaning, not the Name I call" (7.5). One should not assume from this
statement that the name is insignificant but quite simply that it is not
to be *had*: it is unfathomable, although its meaning can be suggested
through the recounting of the various attributes that Milton ascribes to
the Muse:

> . . . for thou
> Nor of the Muses nine, nor on the top
> Of old *Olympus* dwell'st, but Heav'nlie born,
> Before the Hills appeerd, or Fountain flow'd,
> Thou with Eternal wisdom didst converse,
> Wisdom thy Sister, and with her didst play
> In presence of th'Almightie Father, pleas'd
> With thy Celestial Song.
>
> (7.5–12)

Although the recounting of attributes is helpful in coming to terms
with the divine, true knowledge, as Milton says of God in *Christian
Doctrine*, "must be understood with reference to the imperfect comprehension of man; for to know God as he really is far transcends the powers

of man's thoughts, much more of his perception" (*CM*, 14:31). The same is true of Milton's fundamental attitude toward the divine name in *Paradise Lost*, an attitude that is reflected in his reluctance to explore what he calls in *Christian Doctrine* "the secret things of God" (*CM*, 15:107). "Remaining wisely ignorant," "we should be fearful," Milton states in *Christian Doctrine*, "of overstepping the bounds of propriety"; "what is mysterious" should "be suffered to remain inviolate" (*CM*, 15:250–83).

In response to the name of God, that attitude has a long tradition. Certainly as early as the third century B.C., the name appears to have been deemed by the Jews as a *"nomen ineffabile."* According to the earliest rabbinical documents, God's name was known simply as "the Name" (or as "the Distinguished Name," "the Extraordinary Name," "the Tetragrammaton," or "the Quadriliteral Name"). Pronouncing the written name was the privilege of the priests in the Temple when blessing the people (Num. 6:22–27). "After the high priest Simeon the Righteous died, forty years before the destruction of the Temple, the priests no longer pronounced the Name, and after that time the pronunciation of the Name was forbidden." Thus, the *Sanhedrin* recorded: "Whoever pronounces the Name forfeits his portion in the future world."[6] In his *Antiquities of the Jews*, Flavius Josephus refuses to name that "concerning which it is not lawful for [him] to speak."[7] Correspondingly, Philo Judaeus states, in his *Treatise on the Question, Why Certain Names in the Holy Scriptures are Changed*, that it is "quite consistent with reason that no proper name could with propriety be assigned to Him who is in truth the living God," a being "so completely indescribable, that even those powers which minister unto Him do not announce His proper Name to us."[8]

"Conscious of this," states Dionysius the Areopagite in his treatise on the divine names, "the Sacred Writers celebrate It by every Name while yet they call It Nameless":

> For instance, they call It Nameless when they say that the Supreme Godhead Itself, in one of the mystical visions whereby It was symbolically manifested, rebuked him who said: "What is thy name?" and, as though bidding him not seek by any means of any Name to acquire a knowledge of God, made the answer: "Why askest thou thus after My Name seeing It is secret?" [Judg. 13:18; cf. Gen. 12:25–32 and Prov. 30:4]. Now is not the secret Name precisely that which is above all names and nameless, and is fixed beyond every name that is named, not only in this world but also in that which is to come?[9]

To Dionysius's question, the Bible itself provides the answer, of course, in what is perhaps the locus classicus for the attitude that has been explored here. In the seminal passage Exodus 3:13–15, Moses, appearing before God's presence in the burning bush, asks:

> Behold, *when* I come unto the children of Israel, and shall say unto them, The God of your Fathers hath sent me unto you; and they shall say to me, What *is* his name [מה-שמו]? what shall I say unto them? And God said unto Moses, I AM THAT I AM [אהיה אשר אהיה]: and he said, Thus shalt thou say unto the children of Israel, I AM [אהיה] hath sent me unto you. And God said moreover unto Moses, Thus shalt thou say unto the children of Israel, The Lord God of your fathers, the God of Abraham, the God of Isaac, and the God of Jacob, hath sent me unto you: this *is* my name for ever [זה-שמי לעלם] and this *is* my memorial [זכרי] unto all generations.

The importance of this passage for Milton's understanding of the holy name may be seen in his discourse on the nature of God in *Christian Doctrine*. There, he states that "although it is impossible to comprehend accurately under any form of definition the divine nature [*natura divina*]," some idea of it "at least may be collected from his names and attributes" (CM, 14:38–39). Of God's names, Milton says that "there are three . . . which seem principally to intimate the nature of God": יהוה, "Jehovah"; יה, "Jah"; and אהיה, "Ehie" (CM, 14:39). In accord with prevailing custom, Milton is more inclined to view these renderings as varying expressions of a unifying concept than as distinct expressions of ideas that have no apparent relationship.[10] According to John Downame in his *Summe of Sacred Divinitie*, for example, God's nature is comprehended under the names "*Iah, Iehouah*, or *Ehieh.* . . . For these three (coming from the same root [הוה], and being in effect but one) are that essential and proper name of God, whereby he calleth himselfe, when hee would euen [*sic*] the excellency of his Nature and distinguish it from all other things that are in Heauen, or vpon the earth, or vnder the earth."[11]

Thus, for Milton, Jah is seen as "a sort of contraction" for Jehovah, of which the contracted form bears "the same signification." The signification of Jehovah, in turn, is seen to be fundamentally in accord with that of Ehie. "Jehovah," states Milton, signifies " 'he who is,' of 'which is, and which was, and which is to come,' Rev. 1: 4" (CM, 14:39). It is nothing less than the "memorial name" that God assigns to himself in Exodus 3:15, a passage which Milton renders significantly "Iehovah Deus patrum vestrorum, hoc est nomen meum et hoc memoriale meum." The

"Iehovah Deus" of Milton's rendering (in this passage, among others) is more nearly in keeping with the original "יהוה אלהי" of the Hebrew Bible than is the rather nondescript "Lord God" of the Authorized Version, the "Dominus Deus" of the Vulgate, and the "κύριος ὁ θεὸς" of the Septuagint. (As Milton himself states, "This name both in the New Testament and in the Greek version of the Old is always translated κύριος, the Lord, probably for no other reason than because the word Jehovah could not be expressed in Greek letters.")

By adhering to the original, Milton is thus able to suggest the relationship between Jehovah and Ehie that his understanding of the holy name implies. Thus, Ehie (from Exodus 3:14: "אהיה אשר אהיה," "Ehie Asher Ehie"), Milton renders appropriately "I am that I am" or "will be." He then goes on to say that "if the first person be changed into the third person of the kindred verb, Jave," we shall have a form that means "the same as Jehovah, as some think" (*idem quod Iehova ut quidam putant*). That form Milton transliterates "Iehovae," signifying "who is" or "will be."

As a name that brings together the implied significations of the first two names, Iehovae takes on a double signification. It signifies "not only the existence of his [God's] nature, but also of his promises or rather the completion of his promises [*sed nomen Iehovae non modo naturae, verum etiam promissionum eius existentiam, id est, impletionem, significare videtur*]; whence it is said, Exod. VI. 3: 'by my name Jehovah was I not known to them [*nomine me Iehova non cognitus sum illis*]' " (CM, 14:40–41). Thus, through his holy name in its varying forms, God reveals two ways of comprehending the mystery of his nature: through his absolute and timeless *existence* and through his *promises* as they are a reflection of his existence in past, present, and future. The first way is implicit in the concept of *being* to which the holy name in its varying forms gives rise; the second in God's own statement that the holy name was unknown to the generations of Abraham, Isaac, and Jacob but is now available to the generation of Moses as an expression of the divine covenant "to give them the land of Canaan, the land of their pilgrimage, wherein they were strangers" (Exod. 6:2–4). By viewing the holy name in this manner, Milton is drawing upon a well-established tradition.

That tradition is one which stresses both the existence and promises of God as fundamental characteristics of his holy name. Commenting upon the holy name in his discourse "The Names of God" in the *Summa Theologica* (part 1, ques. 13, art. 11), Saint Thomas Aquinas states, "This Name, *He who is*, is most properly applied to God, for three reasons:—First, because of its signification. It does not signify form, but simply existence itself. . . . Second, on account of its universality. . . .

Hence Demascene says that, HE WHO IS, *is the principal of all names applied to God; for comprehending all in itself,* it contains existence itself. . . . Third, from its consignification, for it signifies present existence; and this above all applies to God, whose existence does not know past or future, as Augustine says."[12] For Saint Thomas, the holy name as a representation of God's promises may be seen in such works as Bede's *Commentary on the Pentateuch.* There, he interprets "I am the Lord" as a statement by God indicating that he is able to do what he says he will do *(id est, qui possum facere quae dico)*: "Et recordatus est ad Israel de promissione quam promisit." This idea, states Saint Rupert in his *In Exodum Commentariorum,* is communicated to the children of Israel as a "pact" that God will deliver them from their bondage.[13]

Both ideas are discernible in the gloss of Exodus 3:14–15 in the 1560 Geneva version of the Bible: "The God haue euer bene, am & shalbe: ye God almightie, by whome all thing haue their being, & ye God of mercie mindful of my promes, Reuel 1, 4." In their turn, Renaissance commentaries on the holy name emphasize the significance both of God's existence and his promises. Commenting upon Exodus 3:13–15, Henry Ainsworth, in *Annotations Upon the Five Books of Moses* (1639), states that the holy name "implieth Gods eternall and unchangeable *Being* . . . and the constant performing of all his words, to be now & and for ever that which he was before to *Abraham, Isaak* and *Iakob,* verse 15" (p. 10). Similarly, Matthew Poole, in *Annotations upon the Holy Bible* (1683), states that the holy name "notes 1. the reality of his [God's] being . . . 2. the necessariness, eternity, and unchangeableness of his being . . . he onely is by and from himself. 3. the constancy and certainty of his nature and will and word: The sence is, I am the same that ever I was, the same who made the promises to Abraham, & c. and am now come to perform them, who as I can do what I please, so I will do what I have said" (1:sig. P6^r).

The importance of both conceptions for *Paradise Lost* will become clear by exploring further the bearing of holy name in Milton's epic. The first full account of the way in which Milton envisions God in *Paradise Lost* occurs in Book 3. There "th'Almighty Father," with his Son at his right hand, sits "High Thron'd above all highth" (3.55–58). From that "prospect high," God beholds first "His own works and their works at once" (Adam and Eve, "in the happie Garden plac't, / Reaping immortal fruits of joy and love") and second that which threatens his works (Satan, newly escaped from Hell, "coasting the wall of Heav'n on this side Night") (3.59–71). Having established the spatial dimension of this prospect, Milton then causes that same dimension to become a coordinate of "time." The entire scene suddenly becomes the means by which God "beholds" "past, present, future" (3.78). As Jackson Cope points out, space and time are seen as coordinates of a unifying perspective.[14]

For the purposes of this discussion, that idea is one in which God reenacts the dual conception of the holy name. From the perspective of the spatial coordinate, God is a timeless, self-sufficient being, aloof from his works. The inscrutable "I AM," eternally existent in a "time" out of time, he "inhabits" the "at once." This recalls the God that Saint Thomas describes as one who comprehends all in himself, who contains existence itself, and who does not know past or future. From the perspective of the temporal coordinate, God is the omnipresent being, part of all that he has created and prepared to cause that which threatens his works to become the means of his own greater glory. Within this context, the "I AM" is aptly described in Revelation 1:8 by Saint John the Divine, who recounts the words of the Lord: "I am Alpha and Omega, the beginning and the ending . . . which is, and which was, and which is to come, the Almighty" (cf. Rev. 1:4, 16:15). In this sense, Milton celebrates the "unspeakable" Deity by inviting us to "extoll / Him first, him last, him midst, and without end" (5.164–65). The entire thrust of the celebration becomes a formulaic rendering of God's name.

Drawing upon the dual conception of godhead implicit in that name, Milton expresses the ideas of absolute and timeless existence and the completion of the divine promises through the vehicle of the Son. In him, "the two modes," as Albert Cirillo calls them, of eternity and time are brought together in the " 'at once,' the *nunc stans*, of divine time."[15] Such is the impression one receives as the result of Milton's address to Light in the proem to Book 3 of *Paradise Lost*. One has "at once" the apostrophe to Light itself and to the "bright effluence" of that "bright essence" (3.1–6): that is, the "juncture," according to Cirillo, of "*lux* (essential light) with *lumen* (material light), the source with its product, the creator with the created,"[16] an idea that will receive further elaboration in the next chapter.

It is with this recognition that Milton has the Father address the Son in Book 6:

> Effulgence of my Glorie, Son belov'd,
> Son in whose face invisible is beheld
> Visibly, what by Deitie I am
> And in whose hand what by Decree I doe.
>
> (6.680–83)

The address brings to the fore the dual conception of the holy name both as an expression of God's existence ("what by Deitie I am") and as an expression of God's promises ("what by Decree I doe"). As such, the Son becomes the visible manifestation of the mysterious and unapproachable "whatness" (natura divina) of the Father.

Precisely the way in which he serves in this capacity will become clear if one examines his role in more detail, both as an expression of the concept of God's existence and as an expression of the concept of God's promises. Taken together, these two concerns suggest the way in which Milton resorts to the Son in order to reveal how the full potentialities of the holy name are realized in *Paradise Lost*.

As an expression of God's existence, the Son assumes an essentially paradoxical role, since the nature of the "I AM" is fundamentally inexplicable, on the one hand, and profoundly revelatory, on the other. If God teases Moses by disclosing the nature of his existence through a name that asserts the very mystery of that nature ("I AM THAT I AM"), he also reassures Moses by suggesting that this is indeed his name, a memorial name at that, one that Moses may use to identify his God before those who might question God's existence ("Thus shalt thou say unto the children of Israel, I AM hath sent me unto you" [Exod. 3:14–15]). When the Father addresses the Son in *Paradise Lost* with the words "Son in whose face invisible is beheld / Visibly, what by Deitie I am," similar ideas come into play.

Invisible in his own right, the Son represents the visible manifestation of the "Deitie" as the "I AM." His role is thus paradoxical. On the one hand, his invisibility becomes the visible emblem of God's own timeless and inscrutable existence. In his eternal and timeless position at God's right hand, the Son represents the visible means by which God says "I am invisible," by which he says "you may not know me." ("For my thoughts *are* not your thought, neither *are* your ways my ways, saith the Lord. For *as* the heavens are higher than the earth, so are my ways higher than your ways, and my thoughts than your thoughts" [Isa. 55:8–9].) Upon beholding the Son's invisible face, we realize that we may not view his Father's face. ("Thou canst not see my face: for there shall no man see me, and live" [Exod. 33:20].) In this way, the Son embodies the mystery of an existence which he reveals in order to let us know that it may not be revealed: "He all his Father full expresst / Ineffably into his face receiv'd" 6.720–21). When the Son speaks, he is silent; when he is silent, he speaks: "His meek aspect / Silent yet spake" (3.226–27).

On the other hand, the inscrutability of the Son's presence must be counterbalanced by the fact that he is the means by which God makes himself known to those capable of seeing not through a glass darkly but face to face. That is, the Son's invisible countenance is beheld to suggest not only the mystery that the Father embodies but the fact that the "I AM" does indeed have a real identity ("I *am* the Lord: that *is* my name: therefore *they shall know* in that day that I *am* he that doth speak: behold, *it is I*" [Isa. 42:8, 52:6]; "Sing unto God, sing praises to his name: extol him that rideth upon the heavens by his name *Jah*, and rejoice before him" [Ps. 68:4]). It is in this second capacity that the Son likewise may be said to reveal "visibly, what by Deitie" God "is."

In that capacity, the Son performs an extremely important function in *Paradise Lost*. He represents not only that which "by Deitie" God "is" but that which "by Decree" he "does." If his countenance figures forth his paradoxical presence, his "hands" figure forth his ability to enact God's decrees (6.683; cf. 6.835, 7.224, 9.344, and John 3:35: "The Father loveth the Son, and hath put all things into his hands"). The Son thereby becomes the very embodiment of God's power. As "second Omnipotence" (6.684), he is God's "effectual might" (3.170), "the King of Glorie in his powerful Word" (7.208) effectuating what "by Decree" God "does."

Exactly what God does enact by decree through the Son in *Paradise Lost* assumes a number of forms, all of which Milton distinguishes in *Christian Doctrine* under two headings, "general" and "special." General is that "whereby he [God] has decreed from all eternity of his own most free and holy purpose, whatever he himself willed, or was about to do" (*CM*, 16:63); "special" that "whereby God in his pity to mankind, though foreseeing that they would fall of their own accord, predestined to eternal salvation before the foundation of the world those who should believe and continue in the faith; for a manifestation of the glory of his mercy, grace, and wisdom, according to his purpose in Christ" (*CM*, 14:90). In both cases, the emphasis is upon God's "efficiency" (*efficientia*), his power to "act," to "effect," an emphasis that reflects an additional meaning implicit in the holy name.

That meaning has its roots in the very etymology of יהוה, denoting not only the idea of existence but the idea of causation, since יהוה can also mean "He causes to be" (cf. Acts 17:28: "For in him we live, and move, and have our being").[17] Thus, William Albright states, "The enigmatic formula in Exodus 3:14, which in Biblical Hebrew means 'I am what I am,' if transposed into the form in the third person required by the causative *Yahweh*, can only become *Yahweh asher yihweh* (later *yihyeh*), 'He Causes to be what Comes into Existence.'"[18] Albright's statement expresses quite succinctly Renaissance belief. Commentaries ranging from Andrew Willet's *Hexapla in Exodum* (1633) to Lightfoot's *An handfull of gleanings out of the book of Exodus* (1643) lend credence to this fact. According to Downame, the name "Jehovah" implies a "causality" by which God "is said to *Be*" not only "because he . . . hath his being of himselfe" but because "[he] giueth being to all other things."[19]

In this context, one thinks of the Son's act of creating the universe in *Paradise Lost*. In doing so, he fulfills a divine decree: "And thou my Word, begotten Son, by thee / This I perform, speak thou, and be it don" (7.163–64).[20] This act, according to Milton, falls under the heading of a general decree (CD, *CM*, 14:63). That which falls under the heading of a special decree is indicated by Milton's observation that the holy name implies God's efficacy as it is manifested in his promises or the completion (*impletionem*) of his promises (CD, *CM*, 14:40–41).

The precise doctrinal relationship between "decree" and "promise" is discernible, among other places, in the first book of Richard Hooker's *Of the Lawes of Ecclesiastical Politie*. Interpreting 2 Timothy 2:13 ("If we believe not, *yet* he abideth faithful: he cannot deny himself"), Hooker comments:

> The law whereby he worketh is eternal, and therefore can have no show or colour of mutability: for which cause, a part of that law being opened in the promises which God hath made (because his promises are nothing else but declarations what God will do for the good of men) touching those promises the Apostle hath witnessed, that God may as possibly deny himself, and not be God, as fail to perform them. And concerning the counsel of God, he termeth it likewise a thing *unchangeable*; the counsel of God, and that law of God whereof now we speak, being one. . . . This law therefore we may name eternal, being *that order which God before all ages hath set down with himself, for himself to do all things by*.[21]

Responding in *The Doctrine and Discipline of Divorce* to the same biblical passage, Milton states: "*He* [God] *is faithfull*, saith S. *Paul*, he *cannot deny himselfe*, that is, cannot deny his own promises, cannot but be true to his own rules" (*CM*, 3:446).

Appropriately, then, in his discourse on the special decree in *Christian Doctrine*, Milton singles out those who believe in God's decrees as "the children of the promise" (*CM*, 14:157). His proof-text for the idea is Romans 9, especially verses 4–11, beginning "Who are the Israelites; to whom *pertaineth* the adoption, and the glory, and the covenants, and the giving of the law, and the service *of God*, and the promises. . . ." Precisely who is to benefit from these promises may be determined, Milton states, by referring to John 1:11–12: "He came unto his own, and his own received him not. But as many as received him to them gave he power to become the sons of God, even them that believe on his name" (CD, *CM*, 14:159). Those who believe on God's name, in short, are "the children of God," "the children of the promise." ("For ye are all the children of God by faith in Christ Jesus. For as many of you as have been baptized into Christ have put on Christ. There is neither Jew nor Greek, there is neither bond nor free, there is neither male nor female: for ye are all one in Christ Jesus. And if ye *be* Christ's, then are ye Abraham's seed, and heirs according to the promise" [Gal. 3:26–29].)

The entire matter returns us to Milton's interpretation of the promises of God as reflected in the meaning of "Jehovah" in Exodus 6:2–8: "And God spake unto Moses, and said unto him, I *am* the Lord: And I appeared unto Abraham, unto Isaac, and unto Jacob, by *the name of* God Almighty, but by my name JEHOVAH [יהוה] was I not known to them. And I have also established my covenant with them, to give them the land of Canaan. . . . Wherefore say unto the children of Israel, I *am* the Lord, and I will bring you out from under the burdens of the Egyptians . . . and I will bring you in unto the land, concerning the which I did swear to give it to Abraham, to Isaac, and to Jacob; and I will give it to you for an heritage: I *am* the Lord."

For the exegetical bearing of this passage, one may refer to Saint Thomas Aquinas, who states that whereas a "revelation" was given to Abraham, that given to Moses was "more excellent," and "on this revelation all the other revelations to the prophets were founded" (part 2–2, ques. 174, art. 6), since the further the recipients of the revelations "were removed from Christ in point of time, the further they were from obtaining what they hoped for: Hence the Apostle says (Heb. XI. 13): *All these died according to faith, not having received the promises, but beholding them afar off.* Now the further off a thing is the less distinctly is it seen; wherefore those who were nigh to Christ's advent had a more distinct knowledge of the good things to be hoped for" (part 2–2, ques. 1, art. 7).[22]

Renaissance commentators extend this point of view by interpreting Exodus 6:2–8 almost invariably in typological terms as a progressive revelation of the holy name culminating finally in the person of Christ. Thus, Poole suggests that the name Jehovah here "denotes all his [God's] Perfections, and amongst others, the eternity, constancy, and immutability of his Nature and Will, and the infallible certainty of his Word and Promises. And this saith he, though it was believed by *Abraham, Isaac,* and *Jacob,* yet it was not experimentally [*sic*] known to them; for they only saw the Promises afar off." For their children, the "ɪ ᴀᴍ" is "now come in an invisible, though glorious manner, to deliver [them] from this temporal bondage" and "shall in due time come visibly and by incarnation to save [them] and all [his] people from a far worse slavery and misery, even from [their] sins, and from wrath to come."[23]

These children, states Ainsworth, shall then have full experience of God's "Promises," in being made aware of "[his] power and goodness, and of the efficacie of that his name *Jehovah*. . . . And Christ, in whom all Gods promises are *yea* and *Amen*, 2 Cor. I. 20 having fulfilled all things for our redemption, manifesteth himself by his name in the interpretation thereof as that he is *Alpha and Omega, the beginning and the ending, the Lord who Is, and who Was, and who Is to come, even the Almightie*: Rev. I. 8, 17, 18."[24] That is why, for Downame, "Christ is the true ᴇʜɪᴇʜ, and ɪᴇʜᴏᴠᴀ, *the God of* Abraham, Isaak, *and* Iacob: the proper name of the euer-liuing God."[25] Through him, we shall have "eternall life in heaven," "the Jerusalem that is above."[26]

The idea bears directly upon Milton's view of Christ's redemptive mission. Discoursing in *Christian Doctrine* upon the nature of Christ as Redeemer, Milton invokes Colossians 2:9: "In him dwelleth all the fulness of the Godhead bodily." The concept of "fulness," Milton states, directs us not so much to the divinity of Christ's nature as to the fact that that nature implies "*the full completion [omnem impletionem] of his* [God's] *promises*" (CM, 15:261; italics added). Thus, Saint Thomas Aquinas maintains (part 2–2, ques. 1, art. 8) that "the ultimate consummation of grace was effected by Christ, wherefore the time of his coming is called the *time of fulness* (Gal. IV. 4)."[27] The very *presence* of Christ as Word made flesh attests to the implementation of God's promises as they are implicit in the holy name. As Milton states, "There was a promise made to all mankind, and an expectation of the Redeemer, more or less distinct, even from the time of the fall. At the appointed time, he was sent into the world" (CD, CM, 15:257).

This is precisely the sense communicated by Michael's account of history in *Paradise Lost*. The Messiah, Michael stresses, embodies the "better Cov'nant, disciplin'd / From shadowie Types to Truth, from Flesh to Spirit, / Acceptance of large Grace, from servil fear / To filial, works of Law to works of Faith" (12.302–6). Implementing "in full time" what was promised in one form under the Old Dispensation, Christ provides the heavenly Canaan for "the children of the promise" by "bring[ing] back / Through the worlds wilderness long wanderd man / Safe to eternal Paradise of rest" (12.312–13). That return through time to the eternal suggests once again the implicit nature of time and eternity embodied in the holy name. The implementation of God's promises "in full time" brings us back to the timeless, to the existence of the "I AM" out of time, to the "being" at once aloof from and part of the past, present, and future that his existence embraces.

As the embodiment of this existence, Christ can say, "Before Abraham was, I am" (John 8:58); "Jesus Christ the same yesterday, and to day, and for ever" (Heb. 13:8). An "Emmanuel" whose name signifies "God with us" (Matt. 1:23), he can say, "I am come in my Father's name" (John 5:43): "For unto us a child is born, unto us a son is given: and the government shall be upon his shoulder: and his name shall be called Wonderful, Counsellor, the mighty God, the everlasting Father, the Prince of Peace" (Isa. 9:6). In that way, he is a Jehovah in his own right, although not, Milton states in *Christian Doctrine*, literally Jehovah himself; rather, he is one who has received from the Father "not only the name of God and Jehovah, but all that pertains to his own being,—that is to say, his individuality, his existence itself, his attributes, his works, his divine honors" (*CM*, 14:303). His purpose has been thereby to manifest in all ways God's name, a purpose implicit in his prayer to be glorified: "And now, O Father, glorify me with thine own self with the glory which I had with thee before the world was. I have manifested thy name unto the men which thou gavest me out of the world: thine they were, and thou gavest them me; and they have kept thy word" (John 17:5–6).

Christ's prayer is, of course, answered. As Michael prophesies in *Paradise Lost*, Christ "shall ascend" "to the Heav'n of Heav'ns," there to "enter into glory, and resume / His Seat at Gods right hand, exalted high / Above all names in Heav'n" (12.451–58). His exaltation involves, in short, what would appear to be the gift of a new name: "Wherefore God also hath highly exalted him, and given him a name which is above every name: That at the name of Jesus [ἐν τῷ ὀνόματι Ἰησοῦ] every knee should bow, of *things* in heaven, and *things* in earth, and *things* under the earth; And *that* every tongue should confess that Jesus Christ *is* Lord, to the glory of God the Father" (Phil. 2:9–11).

In response to this exaltation, Renaissance commentators have varying views about Christ's "new name." As Poole states, "Some take *name* literally restraining it to *Jesus*, but those Letters and Syllables are not above every name . . . it being common to others. . . . Others [take *name*] not for any Title but the thing consequent upon his [Christ's] humiliation, surpassing that of all Creatures, Potentates on Earth, and Angels in Heaven. . . ."[28] Among those who do "take *name*" to mean "Jesus," Cornelius A. Lapide maintains in his *In Exodum Commentarium* that "Jesus" signifies none other than "Jehovah": "Ero qui ero, scilicet homo et redemptor mundi; hoc est Jesus, id est Salvator hominum. Hoc verum est sed allegoricum, non literale, ut patet ex dictis."[29]

Whether or not Milton would agree with such a rendering, he does state in *Christian Doctrine* that in God's act of bestowing a "new name" upon his Son, as a way of exalting him, "there is no reason why that name should not be Jehovah, or any other name pertaining to the Deity, if there be any still higher" (*CM*, 14:307). Such a name, comments Poole, is "only befitting One who has been superexalted by God's Right Hand, above every Name, and every thing known by any Name."[30] Whatever form that name assumes, we may not forget that to it "every knee should bow, of *things* in heaven, and *things* in earth, and *things* under the earth; And *that* every tongue should confess that Jesus Christ *is* Lord, to the glory of God the Father."

This idea recalls the initial discussion of the holy name as that which is to elicit proper reverence, a glorifying and worshiping of him "whose name is Holy" (Isa. 57:15): "My mouth shall speak the praise of the Lord: and let all flesh bless his holy name for ever and ever" (Ps. 145:21); "Glory ye in his holy name: let the heart of them rejoice that seek the Lord" (1 Chron. 16:10). These hallelujahs are no less pertinent to the name of the Son than to the name of the Father. They suggest, in fact, what has been shown to be the fundamental attitude toward the holy name expressed in *Paradise Lost*. This attitude is one that draws upon the full potentialities of the holy name implicit in the traditions that shape religious thought. It is one, characteristically, that causes Milton to culminate his hymn to Father and Son in *Paradise Lost* by celebrating the holy name in terms that have profound meaning for his epic: "Hail Son of God," whose "Name / Shall be the copious matter of my Song / Henceforth, and never shall my Harp thy praise / Forget, nor from thy Fathers praise disjoin" (3.411–15). Considering the nature of Milton's treatment of the holy name in *Paradise Lost*, such a hallelujah is well founded indeed.

9
Light

Needless to say, a good deal of attention has already been accorded the significance of light in Milton's works, and there is little need here to retrace familiar ground.[1] Whereas Miltonic scholarship has characteristically been concerned with light as a metaphysical or theological entity (with light as *quid*,[2] that is), the main focus of this chapter will be with light as an embodiment of religious phenomenology (with light as *numen*).[3] The concerns really overlap, and in the traditions to which Milton was heir, doctrinal considerations (such as light as the expression of hypostasis, and so forth),[4] loom as large as phenomenological ones. Nonetheless, the holy, by its very nature, tends to align itself with the latter, with that which is "inexpressible—an ἄρρητον or *ineffabile*—in the sense that it completely eludes apprehension in terms of concepts": the votary bows in reverence before the mysterium and celebrates its "awefulness."[5] Milton was a steward of the mysterium (cf. 1 Cor. 4:1): averse to prying into the *arcana Dei* (CD, CM, 14:316), he respected God's "hidden things." "Let us . . . discard reason in sacred matters [*nos itaque in sacris rationi renuntiemus*]" (CD, CM, 14:196–97; CD, CM, 15:3), he counsels; "what is mysterious . . . [should] be suffered to remain inviolate, and we should be fearful of overstepping the bounds of propriety in its investigation [*quae mysteria sunt, mysteria esse intemerata pateremur, et ultra quam fas est investigare, vereremur*]" (CD, CM, 15:264–65). Time and again, as this study attempts to demonstrate, he celebrates the mysterium in all its forms.[6]

That such is Milton's primary posture in the presence of light may be seen in the proem to Book 3 of *Paradise Lost*:

> Hail holy Light, ofspring of Heav'n first-born,
> Or of th'Eternal Coeternal beam
> May I express thee unblam'd? since God is light,
> And never but in unapproached light
> Dwelt from Eternitie, dwelt then in thee,
> Bright effluence of bright essence increate.

> Or hear'st thou rather pure Ethereal stream,
> Whose Fountain who shall tell? before the Sun,
> Before the Heav'ns thou wert, and at the voice
> Of God, as with a Mantle didst invest
> The rising world of waters dark and deep,
> Won from the void and formless infinite.
>
> (3.1–12)

At the center of the invocation is the essential *inexpressibility* of that which is invoked ("May I express thee unblam'd? . . . / Whose fountain who shall tell?") and the *uncertainty* of what ascription most befits the divine medium ("ofspring of Heav'n first-born, / *Or* of th'Eternal Co-eternal beam . . . / *Or* hear'st thou rather pure Ethereal stream?" [italics added]).

The poet can only question the basic assumptions upon which the invocation is built: the results are those of perplexity before the incomprehensible and unapproachable.[7] ("God," who "is light," "dwell[eth] in the light which no man can approach unto" [1 John 1:5; 1 Tim. 6:16]. "Where is the way *where* light dwelleth?" God asks Job, and Job responds, "What shall I answer thee? I will lay mine hand upon my mouth" [Job 38:19, 40:4].) But it is an enlightened perplexity, a perplexity in which the poet himself delights, as *sacerdos ludens*, to alter Huizinga's phrase,[8] he "plays" before the ineffable manifestation of the glory "ubi Deus quem nemo potest videre, lucem habitat inaccessam" (CD, *CM*, 15:28; Ephes. 4:10). Of this glory, Milton maintains in *Christian Doctrine*, "Unde nobis denique MIRABILIS et INCOMPREHENSIBILIS dicendus est. Iud. XIII. 18. quid rogitas de nomine mea, cum sit mirificum? Psal. CXIV. 3. magnitudinis eius non est pervestigatio. Isa. XI. 28. nulla est pervestigatio prudentiae eius" (CD, *CM*, 14:60).

Given the nature of the mysterium, one is left, then, with the attitude of play, much like Milton's Muse ("*Urania*, by that name / If rightly . . . [she is] call'd" [7.1–2]), who, "with Eternal wisdom" "didst play / In presence of th'Almightie Father, pleas'd / With . . . [her] Celestial Song" (7.9–12). This playing, Milton says in *Tetrachordon*, is none other than God's "own recreations" (*CM*, 4:85). From the point of view of the poet, such playing signifies the act of celebrating the ineffable in song ("Celestial Song," at that); "play," Milton maintains in his Marginalia to Pindar, means "to sing."[9] If he was not aware that "play," in other contexts, suggests in its etymology the concept of "light,"[10] he was certainly familiar with the tradition of Wisdom (with whom Milton's Muse "plays" before God) as a symbol of light.[11] In any case, Milton's song to "holy Light," as a "playful" act of expressing the inexpressibility of the ineffable, is his way of declaring his devotion to the mysterium. It is nothing less than an act of worship.

The *ave* that initiates the proem is in itself a triumphant attestation to that fact. Implying in its very etymology the sacrality of the thing invoked, "Hail,"[12] as Milton reminds us later in his epic, is specifically a "holy salutation" "bestow'd" as a sign of reverence (5.384–86).[13] When addressed to God or the Son (5.205, 3.412),[14] it represents an act of worship (a "hallowing," as it were). So here, with holy Light, "Hail" signifies Milton's bestowal of a "holy salutation" upon that which manifests the holy in all its splendor. In response to this "Celestial light" (3.51), that act was an extremely appropriate one for Milton, who devoted a career to a "hallowing" of "the Light." Like "the man sent from God, whose name *was* John," Milton "came for a witness, to bear witness of the Light [τὸ φῶς]" (John 1:7). Indeed, Milton is a poet of the Light. If the statement is self-evident, a brief review of the way in which he celebrated light in his works will underscore its importance to his outlook and suggest how light is to be viewed as a sacral phenomenon in *Paradise Lost*.

From the very outset of his poetical career, Milton sang in praise of light. As early as the *Carmina Elegiaca* (1624–25), he exhorted the reader to "arise" (*surge*), "shake off slumbers" and admire "the flaming Titan" that "thrusts his head from the Eastern waves / and scatters his glittering splendor through the joyful fields" (1–6); for, Milton proclaims, "light is appearing" (*Lux oritur*) (20). Complemented by a juvenile composition on the same theme (PO, CM, 12:288–91), this poeticized grammar school exercise provides evidence of Milton's delight in the old proverb "*Mane citus lectum fuge.*"[15] As an "early riser,"[16] Milton apparently took this proverb seriously. In any case, the idea of rising up to celebrate the light was fully in keeping with the Miltonic temperament.

Implicit in such poems as *Song: On May Morning*, with its "salute" to light (9) and *L'Allegro*, with its welcoming of the "ris[ing]" "dawn" (44), it appears fully articulated in Elegy 5 (*In Adventum Veris*), with its festive exhortation to Aurora to "arise" (*surge*) (49–51) and its sensuous hymn to Apollo, bringer of light (54–100). In the prose, this outlook is further complemented by the first prolusion concerning the question "Whether Day is more excellent than Night." Opting for Day, of course, Milton embarks upon a hymn to light that portrays all nature's rising at daybreak to worship the sun: the birds, the she-goats, and beasts of all sorts, not to mention the very flowers themselves hallow the Day. Engaging in such worship, Milton reminds us that he is not alone. His solar reverence[17] is archetypal: the Persians, the Libyans, the Rhodians with their Colossus, and even "the peoples of the Indian Occident sacrifice with incense and other ceremonial" to the sun. Following the patterns established in his poetry, Milton accordingly does the same by climaxing his celebration with a passage from the Orphic Hymn to Aurora (PO, *CM*, 12:136–41).

For Milton, then, the very presence of light became the occasion for festive and ceremonial exultation. It became, as suggested, the occasion for worship. Among the early poetry, no other work portrays this fact so dramatically as the poem *On the Morning of Christs Nativity*. A consummate dawn song, written, as Milton says in *Elegia sexta*, with "the first light of dawn [*Illa sub auroram lux mihi prima tulit*]" (88), the *Nativity Ode* casts Milton's solar adoration in a new form. It is another Sun that Milton celebrates here, another dawn. "I am the light of the world," says Jesus; "he that followeth me shall not walk in darkness, but shall have the light of life" (John 8:12; cf. John 1:4–5, 9:4). It is this light that Milton celebrates in the *Nativity Ode*. Extolling "that glorious Form, that Light unsufferable, / And that far-beaming blaze of Majesty" (8–9), he hymns "the Prince of light" (62) before whom

> The Sun himself with-held his wonted speed,
> And hid his head for shame
> As his inferiour flame,
> The new-enlighten'd world no more should need,
> [For] he saw a greater Sun appear
> Then his bright Throne, or burning Axletree could bear.
>
> (79–84)

Celebrating Christ in this manner, Milton, of course, was perfectly in accord with all those who intoned dawn songs to the newborn child. Thus, Crashaw,[18] in his *Hymne of the Nativity*, dismisses the sun as a lesser source of light and sings to the Son as Christ,

> Wee saw thee in thy Balmy Nest
> Bright Dawne of our *Eternall Day*;
> Wee saw thine Eyes break from the East,
> And chase the trembling shades away:
> Wee saw thee (and wee blest the sight)
> Wee saw thee by thine owne sweet Light.
>
> (27–33)

Beholding this theophany of light, Crashaw, like Milton, celebrates its splendor. Like Milton, Crashaw bestows his allegiance upon a new Sun. Such allegiance, of course, is only natural. In Milton's case, it suggests a shift in focus quite in keeping with his religious temperament. It was to become a prime characteristic of his stance as celebrant whose hymns were sung in the sacred vein.

In keeping with that stance, it is hardly surprising, then, that Milton later culminates his epic on Christ's sojourn in the wilderness with a hymn to the Light both as "thron'd / In the bosom of bliss, and light of light / Conceiving" and as "remote from Heav'n, enshrin'd / In fleshly Tabernacle, and human form" (PR, 4.596–99). In either case, the theophany shines in radiant splendor, as Christ's own disciples learn when they behold him "transfigured": "His face did shine as the sun, and his raiment was white as the light" (Matt. 17:2; Mark 9:3). Celebrating that light in its various forms but particularly as it derived its brilliance from God, the very "fountain of light" (PR, 4.289), Milton envisioned himself "at a solemn Musick" "singing" "Hymns devout and holy Psalms" "everlastingly" in an "endless morn of light." Doing so, he would accompany the "bright Seraphim in burning row" as they sing "before the saphire-colourd throne / To him that sits thereon" (SM, 7–17, 28). Doing so, he "turne[d]" his "eyes" and "lift[ed] up . . . [his] hands" as a "Suppliant" "to that Eternall and Propitious *Throne*" in glorious hymns to light. Thus, he may be heard singing like a *Bird of Morning*" in *Of Reformation*: "Thou . . . that sits't in light & glory unapproachable, *Parent* of *Angels* and *Men*! next thee I implore Omnipotent King, Redeemer . . . ineffable and everlasting *Love*! And thou the third subsistence of Divine Infinitude, *illumining Spirit*, the joy and solace of created *Things*! one *Tripersonall* GODHEAD!" (CM, 3:76).

So the angelic hosts may be heard singing, albeit in a somewhat different manner,[19] as they hymn both Father and Son in *Paradise Lost* "with Jubilee and loud Hosanna's." "Bow[ing]" "lowly reverent / Toward either Throne," they "introduce" their "sacred Song" to the Light (3.348–69):

> Thee Father, first they sung Omnipotent,
> Immutable, Immortal, Infinite,
> Eternal King; thee Author of all being,
> Fountain of Light, thy self invisible
> Amidst the glorious brightness where thou sit'st
> Thron'd inaccessible, but when thou shad'st

The full blaze of thy beams, and through a cloud
Drawn round about thee like a radiant Shrine,
Dark with excessive bright thy skirts appeer,
Yet dazle Heav'n, that brightest Seraphim
Approach not, but with both wings veil thir eyes.
Thee next they sang of all Creation first,
Begotten Son, Divine Similitude,
In whose conspicuous count'nance, without cloud
Made visible, th'Almighty Father shines,
Whom else no Creature can behold; on thee
Impresst th'effulgence of his Glorie abides,
Transfus'd on thee his ample Spirit rests.

(3.372–89)

The angelic hymn to the Light is only one of the many in *Paradise Lost*.[20] Complemented by the poet's hymn that inaugurates Book 3, it finds its counterpart in Adam and Eve's hymn in Book 5. "Com[ing]" "forth" "to open Sight / Of day'spring, and the Sun," itself "scarce up ris'n," they "lowly" "bow" "adoring" and with "holy rapture" begin "thir Orisons" (5.137–47). Appropriately, their adoration is directed not to the sun as a source of light but to that very source of light, the "Greater" Sun (5.171–72) "who out of Darkness call'd up Light" (5.179). This is the "universal Lord" who is worshiped not only by all of nature, including the sun, but by the "Sons of light, / Angels" who "behold him, and with songs / And choral symphonies, Day without Night, / Circle his Throne rejoycing" (5.160–63). To him, Adam and Eve issue their hail (5.205). *Paradise Lost*, then, embodies a series of hallelujahs to the Light, hallelujahs that trace their origin to a posture of worship dating back to Milton's earliest poetry. This point is raised here because in order to understand the nature of holy Light in *Paradise Lost* and Milton's rendering of light as a sacral phenomenon, it is essential to recall the extent to which the reverential posture figures in his outlook.

This fact becomes all the more poignant considering the impact that his blindness had upon him. Milton's adoration of the Light and the physical darkness in which he ultimately found himself cannot be separated. After his blindness, in fact, Milton made a point of linking them inextricably. His hymn to the Light in the proem to Book 3 of *Paradise Lost* is appropriately followed by a lament over his own blindness:

Thee I revisit safe,
And feel thy sovran vital Lamp; but thou
Revisit'st not these eyes, that rowl in vain

To find thy piercing ray, and find no dawn;
So thick a drop serene hath quencht thir Orbs,
Or dim suffusion veild.

(3.21–26)

"Cut off" "from the chearful wayes of men," he can no longer experience "Day, or the sweet approach of Ev'n or Morn, / Or sight of vernal bloom, or Summers Rose, / Or flocks, or heards, or human face divine." Instead, he is surrounded by "cloud . . . and ever-during dark"; "and for the Book of knowledge fair," he is "presented with a Universal blanc" and "wisdom at one entrance quite shut out" (3.40–50). Taking solace in the great poets and prophets ("Blind *Thamyris* and blind *Maeonides*, / And *Tiresias* and *Phineus* Prophets old") who have suffered a similar fate, he consoles himself that his sight will transcend physical limitations: appealing to "Celestial light" to "shine inward" and "irradiate" "the mind" with new eyes while it "purge[s]" "all mist," he would experience an internal vision of divine things "invisible to mortal sight" (3.51–55).

The appeal is quite in keeping with Milton's long-standing impulse to purge the eyes of the mind in order to make himself receptive to a higher vision of light in its most resplendent form. In *Of Reformation*, he admonishes those who would see the Light to "purge with sovran eyesalve that intellectual ray which *God* hath planted in . . . [them]" (*CM*, 3:33). Then, they might "hold" "the Gospel" "ever in their faces like a mirror of Diamond, till it dazle, and pierce their misty eye balls" (*CM*, 3:35). Correspondingly, he envisions in *Areopagitica* those who are enlightened "as an Eagle . . . kindling her undazl'd eyes at the full midday beam; purging and unscaling her long abused sight at the fountain it self of heav'nly radiance" (*CM*, 4:344).

The reference, of course, anticipates the vision of Samson in Milton's drama. Compared not only to an "Eagle" but to "an ev'ning Dragon" and a Phoenix, he, "though blind of sight," is "with inward eyes illuminated" (1686–88). He can achieve that sense of renewal only through a trial that educates him in the true significance of inward illumination. Initially "exil'd from light" (98), he is "shut up" both from "outward light" and from "inward light," neither of which "puts forth" a "visual beam" (160–63). As such, he is led to question God's ways:

O first created Beam, and thou great Word,
Let there be light, and light was over all;
Why am I thus bereav'd thy prime decree? . . .
Since light so necessary is to life,

And almost life it self . . .
. . . Why was the sight
To such a tender ball as th'eye confin'd?
(82–93)

Complaining that "Light the prime work of God to me is extinct" (70),
he cries out: "O dark, dark, dark, amid the blaze of noon, / Irrecoverably
dark, total Eclipse / Without all hope of day! . . . / The Sun to me is dark /
And silent as the Moon, / When she deserts the night / Hid in her vacant
interlunar cave" (79–89). In like manner, Satan, bewailing his fall, curses
the Light in *Paradise Lost*: "To thee I call . . . / O Sun, to tell thee how I
hate thy beams" (4.35–37). Like Samson, Satan, in his own way, is also
blind. Unlike Samson, however, Satan never regains sight. When Samson
"sees" again, his renewed vision assumes the form of a "Holocaust"
(1702), as he is reborn in a blaze of light: "His fierie vertue rouz'd /
From under ashes into sudden flame," he "revives, reflourishes, then vigorous
most / When most unactive deem'd" (1686–1705).

Samson is an extreme, if not a "holocaustal," example of the remarkable effects that inward illumination can have. But as an example it
demonstrates that the kind of light that Milton sought and celebrated
caused an overwhelming transformation of character, one that would
never be the same after the illumination had been experienced. For this
reason, Milton was fond of pointing to "S. *Pauls* conversion," as a result
of which "there fell scales from his eyes that were not perceav'd before"
(CG, *CM*, 3:224; Acts 9:3–8). If the blinded apostle learns the meaning
of light, he is no different from the blind man whose eyes are anointed in
"*Siloa*'s Brook" (1.11–12; John 9:1–7) at the outset of *Paradise Lost* or
from the benighted Adam, whose eyes are anointed with water from "the
Well of Life" (11.411–20) near the end of *Paradise Lost*. All are reminiscent of the poet who appeals to the Spirit for illumination throughout
Paradise Lost. As all become aware, the act of having one's sight purged
in order to participate in a higher level of vision is not an easy task.
In Milton's case, such participation was attained only through painful
experience.

As Milton indicated in his "Letter to a Friend" (EC, *CM*, 12:323–24),
he always felt the need to fulfill Christ's command "to labour while there
is light" (John 9:4; cf. John 12:35: "Yet a little while is the light with
you. Walk while ye have the light, lest darkness come upon you."), for
fear that he would suffer the fate of "the terrible seasing of him that hid
the talent" (Matt. 25:24). That fate, Milton knew, meant being "cast"

"into outer darkness" (Matt. 25:30). As he would come to interpret it, the idea of being cast into outer darkness is synonymous with being "cast out from God and blessed vision," to use the language of *Paradise Lost* (5.613). Addressing himself implicitly to these matters in Sonnet 7, Milton confronted them again most poignantly in Sonnet 19. There, a fear of being deprived of "blessed vision" haunts Milton's questioning of the Light. Considering how his own light had been "spent" "in this dark world and wide" and aware that "that one Talent which is death to hide" is "lodg'd" with him "useless," he is tempted to "murmur," "Doth God exact day labour, light deny'd [?]" (1–7). But Milton's questioning of the Light is "prevented" or anticipated by "patience," which provides a renewed sense of God's ways (8–14). Like Samson, who bewails his darkness ("O loss of sight, of thee I most complain!" [67]), Milton gains a new understanding of what it means to see.

Man's "eyesight lies not in his eyes alone," he writes to Leonard Philarus, but "in God's leading and providence" (FE, CM, 12:71), and in a letter to Emeric Bigot, he proclaims, "Why, in truth should I not bear gently the deprivation of sight, when I may hope that it is not so much lost as revoked and retracted inwards [*revocatum intus atque retractum*], for the sharpening rather than the blunting of my mental edge" (FE, CM, 12:86–87). Although his "eyes," "bereft of light thir seeing have forgot" (1–3), he says in Sonnet 22, "I argue not / Against heav'ns hand or will, nor bate a jot / Of heart or hope" (6–8). For he knows that he shall have "full sight" in "heav'n without restraint" (S23, 8). This is what Milton in *Christian Doctrine* calls "*divinae visionis beatificae*," by which the righteous experience the visio Dei of "perfect glorification." (Compare the experience of "beatitude past utterance" that the faithful angels receive from the sight of God in *Paradise Lost* [3.61–62].) The nature of that glorification is implicit in the proof-texts that Milton marshals in *Christian Doctrine* to suggest the nature of the visio Dei. Among them, one finds, "they that be wise shall shine as the brightness of the firmament" (Dan. 12:3); "then shall the righteous shine forth as the sun in the kingdom of their Father" (Matt. 13:43); "blessed are the pure in heart, for they shall see God" (Matt. 13:8); and "now we see through a glass darkly, but then face to face; now I know in part, but then shall I know even as also I am known" (1 Cor. 15:42–43).

The visio Dei, then, involves not only the sight of God but the experience of being enveloped in light. Nowhere is this belief more triumphantly articulated than in the *Defensio secunda*. There, the transcendent nature of the sight that Milton's blindness has afforded him assumes consummate form. The full passage is a triumphant attestation to the kind of light that informs Milton's mature vision. Addressing his adversary, Milton proclaims:

> Neither am I concerned at being classed . . . with the blind, with the sorrowful, with the weak; since there is a hope, that, on this account, I have a nearer claim to the mercy and protection of the sovereign Father. There is a way . . . through weakness to the greatest strength. May I be one of the weakest, provided only in my weakness that immortal and better vigour be put forth with greater effect; provided only in my darkness the light of the divine countenance does but the more brightly shine [*dummodo in meis tenebris divini vultûs lumen es clariùs eluceat*]: for then I shall at once be the weakest and the most mighty; shall be at once blind, and of the most piercing sight [*caecus eodem tempore & perspicacissimus*]. Thus, through this infirmity should I be consummated, perfected; thus, through this darkness should I be enrobed in light [*possim in hac obscurtate sic ego irradiari*]. And, in truth, we who are blind, are not the last regarded by the providence of God; who, as we are the less able to discern anything but himself, beholds us with the greater clemency and benignity. Woe to him who makes a mock of us; woe to him who injures us; he deserves to be devoted to the public curse. The divine law . . . has made us not merely secure, but, as it were, sacred [*sacros*], from the injuries of men; nor would seem to have brought this darkness upon us so much by inducing a dimness of the eyes, as by the overshadowing of heavenly wings [*nec tam oculorum hebetudine, quàm coelestium alarum umbrâ has nobis fecisse tenebras videtur*]; and not infrequently is wont to illumine it again, when produced, by an inward and far surpassing light [*factas illustrare rursus interiore ac longè praestabiliore lumine rarò solet*]. (CM, 8:72–73)

This is the light that Milton as "blind bard"[21] hails in *Paradise Lost*. It is a light that fully encompasses the experience of the visio Dei and, so doing, defines precisely the extent to which light manifests itself as a sacral phenomenon in Milton's thought. Bestowing a numinosity upon him who experiences its splendor ("*sic ego irradiari*"), this light becomes the ultimate means by which the holy is known. Permeating the darkness of the physically blind, it provides illumination that only the spiritually enlightened can enjoy. As such, it is indeed an "*interiore ac longè praestabiliore lumine*." So Milton conceived it, and so this investigation of his personal and poetic outlook has thus far portrayed it.

An understanding of its significance, however, cannot stop there. To have a full sense of Milton's portrayal of light as a sacral phenomenon, one should consider the traditions that gave rise to the kind of reverential outlook that distinguished his entire career and, in this particular instance, assumed a special urgency with the onset of his blindness. In those traditions, one discovers a phenomenology of light that was precisely in accord with Milton's own prevailing habits of mind and that helps to explain the way in which light as numinous entity manifests itself in his works.

The extent to which the act of worshiping the Light is an integral part of the religious experience has already been amply explored by Eliade, among others. In his volumes *The Two and the One* and *Patterns in Comparative Religion*,[22] he investigates the significance of light as theophany and the dissemination of solar mysticism among numerous peoples and religions, including those of the Eskimos, the Australians, the Indians, the Chinese, and the Iranians. Manifested in such figures as Krishna, Zarathustra, and Mithra, the theophany of light had an immense impact upon the development of the idea of the holy. As already seen in Milton's observations concerning sun worship in the first prolusion, this cross-cultural approach represented by Eliade is quite in accord with the Miltonic outlook.

That outlook, in turn, had already been anticipated by writers like Macrobius, the fourth-century Neoplatonist. In his *Saturnalia*, a "textbook" of religious lore, which Milton knew and used,[23] Macrobius explains how the Assyrians, Egyptians, Greeks, and Romans developed a solar monotheism founded upon a worshiping of the Light.[24] Aristotle had seen "a great divine element" operating in celestial bodies like the sun "and pointed out that this belief . . . was implicit, in an obscure form, in the popular mythology." Similar doctrines were taught by the Stoics and especially by Cleanthes, "who considered that in the sun lay the guiding principle ($\dot{\eta}\gamma\varepsilon\mu o\nu\iota\kappa\acute{o}\nu$) of the universe." Such notions were prevalent among the Neopythagoreans. "Apollonius of Tyana, the seer and wonder-worker of the late first century A.D., venerated the sun at dawn."[25] As Emperor Julian's *Hymn to King Helios* and Proclus's hymn "To the Sun" made clear, the cult of Helios was widespread in later times as well.[26] "HEAR golden Titan, king of mental fire, / Ruler of light . . . / From deity ineffable and secret born," Proclus sings; "refine me" and lead me "to the realms of light"; "Direct my steps and pour thy sacred light / In rich abundance on my clouded soul: / Dispel the dismal and malignant shades / Of darkness."[27] In such hymns, the desire to ascend to the realms of light in a purified state is of utmost importance. This purifying of the vision in the act of beholding the theophany is a prime characteristic of the worship of the Light. The impulse, of course, is Neoplatonic, and it is to Plato that one must ultimately resort in order to trace this impulse to its source.

The locus classicus for the kind of worshiping of the Light that is to be found in Proclus, among others, is the parable of the Cave in *The Republic* (7.514–20). Although the parable itself is too well known to bear repetition here, the "allegory" is worth recalling: "The prison-house is the world of sight, the light of fire is the sun, and . . . the journey upwards [is] . . . the ascent of the soul into the intellectual world. . . . [In this] world of knowledge the idea of good appears last of all, and is seen only with an effort; and, when seen, is also inferred to be the universal author of all things beautiful and right, parent of light and of the lord of light in this visible world, and the immediate source of reason and truth in the intellectual." What is especially important for the purposes of this discussion is the emphasis that Plato places upon the experience undergone by the soul in its ascent from darkness to light, from Shadow to Reality. At first sight of the sun, the soul is "dazzled," in effect, blinded, as its eyes become accustomed to the Light. This "bewilderment" is progressively overcome, as the soul "learn[s] by degrees to endure the sight of being, and of the brightest and best of being, or in other words, the good." This, for Plato, is nothing less than the "beatific vision."[28]

Needless to say, the outlook implicit in Plato's account of the theophany described here had, in its various forms, an immense impact upon succeeding generations.[29] Already witnessed in Proclus, this outlook may be seen to pervade the point of view adopted by the Hellenistic scholars, particularly as represented in the writings of Plotinus and his followers, Porphyry, Iamblichus, and, as mentioned, Proclus, between the third and fifth centuries A.D. A glance at Plotinus should suggest something of the milieu that ultimately gave rise to the concept of light as a sacral phenomenon in Milton's works.[30]

In *The Enneads*, Plotinus maintains that the "Soul," "lying away in the dark," "must thrust towards the light" in order to "see" and "thus come to the knowledge of its inner contents" (1.2.4). Light is the radiance of the Good, the Supreme Principle of Unity toward which the Soul aspires in the purifying act of vision and self-enlightenment. "The novice," says Plotinus, "must hold himself constantly under some image of the Divine Being and seek in the light of a clear conception; knowing thus, in a deep conviction, whither he is going—into what sublimity he penetrates—he must give himself forthwith to the inner and, radiant with the Divine Intellections (with which he is now one), be no longer the seer, but, as that place has made him, the seen" (5.8.11). In that process, the

Soul becomes one with the "Intellectual-Principle, filled so as to hold within itself that object of its vision, seeing all by the light from the Giver and bearing that light with it" (6.7.16). As a result, the Soul "is lifted and sees . . . ; the vision floods the eyes with light," which "is itself the vision" (6.7.36). To visualize the process, Plotinus draws upon the image of the sun: the "cause of the existence of sense-things and of their being seen," the sun, says Plotinus, is the counterpart of "The Good," which is "a light appropriate to what is to be seen There and to their seer." "Shed[ding] light upon both," "The Good" "makes them objects of Intellection" (6.7.14).[31]

Following Plotinus, Iamblichus, in *De Mysteriis*, describes how "corporeal eyes" "are drawn upward" from their darkness to "attenuated and diaphanous air," illuminated by an overwhelming "light" emitted by the "presence" (*parousia*) of "the Gods." In this way, the "Soul" achieves a union with the divine.[32] Such concepts are basic to the Plotinian school of thought. Iamblichus is particularly interesting, however, because of his purported concern with other schools of thought, such as those of the "Egyptians, Chaldeans, and Assyrians." His syncretism reminds one that the Plotinian school is not the only one in which light emerged as a sacral phenomenon.

At least as important as the Plotinian school is the Hermetic school, which flourished during the second and third centuries A.D. In that school, a veneration of the Light assumes a Neoplatonic cast that is as significant as any that can be found in Hellenistic paganism. Thus, in *The Poimandres*, attributed to Hermes Trismegistus, Hermes has a vision of "Light" inspired by "Poimandres, the Mind of the Sovereignty"; "from the Light there came forth a holy Word," which is "the voice of the Light." "That Light," says Poimandres, "is I, even Mind, the first God. . . ; and the Word which came forth from the Light is son of God." "Now," he continues, "fix your thought upon the Light . . . and learn to know it. And when he had thus spoken, he gazed long upon me, eye to eye, so that I trembled at his aspect. And when I raised my head again, I saw in my mind that the Light consisted of innumerable Powers, and had come to be an ordered world, but a world without bounds." This, says Poimandres, is "the archetypal form, which is prior to the beginning of things, and is limitless." It is, in short, the "Pleroma." Having ascertained the significance of "Light," Hermes enters into God, the "Father of Light," "the Good," and achieves "γνῶσις."[33]

As an expression of the way in which Hellenistic paganism venerated the Light, the Hermetic school is significant not only in its own right but in its affinities with the emerging theology of light that came to be a hallmark of the Christian church. In order to assess the full impact of light as a numinous entity upon Milton, one must account for the integration of that phenomenon within a specifically Christian context. Just as Milton's hallowing of the Light reflects a shift in temperament from a worshiping of the sun as natural luminary to a worshiping of the true Sun as divine offspring of God himself, so the hallowing of the Light implicit in Neoplatonism reflects a comparable shift in temperament from pagan worship to Christian worship. That shift, of course, had a profound impact upon medieval and Renaissance views of light.

The commonplace association of God with light in the New Testament is, of course, the source of the Christian attitude toward light as a sacral phenomenon. From the New Testament perspective, "God is light, and in him is no darkness at all. If we say that we have fellowship with him, and walk in darkness, we lie, and do not the truth: But if we walk in the light, as he is in the light, we have fellowship one with another" (1 John 1:5–7). God "dwell[eth] in the light which no man can approach unto, whom no man hath seen, nor can see" (1 Tim. 6:16). His Son is "Light of Light" (τὸ φῶς ἐκ φωτός): "the brightness [ἀπαύγασμα] of his glory, and the express image of his person" (Heb. 1:3). Those who are saved are "partakers of the inheritance of the saints in light" (Col. 1:12). With the "eyes" of their "understanding" "enlightened" (Eph. 1:17–18) by "the Father of lights" (James 1:17), they are "called" "out of darkness" into God's "marvellous light" (1 Pet. 2:9). Those who preach God's word are inspired with "tongues" "of fire" (Acts 2:2–4), for they have been baptized "with the Holy Ghost, and with fire" (Matt. 3:11). The theophany of light is one of Christ's primary characteristics. When he appears transfigured before his apostles, his dazzling presence overwhelms them: "His face did shine as the sun, and his raiment was white as the light," and "while he yet spake, behold, a bright cloud overshadowed . . . [his disciples]: and behold a voice out of the cloud, which said, This is my beloved Son, in whom I am well pleased" (Matt. 17:1–9; Mark 9:2–9). On the road of Damascus, Paul is blinded by the brightness of Christ's presence, which envelops Paul with "a light from heaven" (Acts 9:3).

If these characteristics permeate the New Testament, the theophanic expression of God as light finds its locus classicus, as Wilhelm Bousset has established, in Johannine mysticism.[34] The Christological hymn that inaugurates the Fourth Gospel establishes the context: "In the beginning was the Word, and the Word was with God, and the Word was God. . . . In him was life; and the life was the light of men. And the light shineth in darkness; and the darkness comprehended it not." This "Light" (τὸ φῶς), the hymn continues, "was the true Light, which lighteth every man that cometh into the world. . . . No man hath seen God at any time: the only begotten Son, which is in the bosom of the Father, he hath declared *him*" (John 1:1–18). In his examination of the historical contexts of this hymn, as well as of the Fourth Gospel in its entirety, C. H. Dodd maintains that its milieu is precisely that of the Hellenistic environment explored here. Thus, both the conflation of "light" and "life" and the emphasis upon rebirth through the visio Dei in the Fourth Gospel, for example, are the common property of *The Poimandres*.[35] Not that one is in any sense a source for the other: "What we have here," says Bousset, "is the common language of a mystical piety," "rooted in the soil of Hellenistic mysticism."[36] Such is perhaps not surprising, considering that as Frederick Grant states, the New Testament is, "from first to last, a Greek book."[37] Nonetheless, it is fascinating to see the way in which the concept of light that pervades the Fourth Gospel reflects so much of the attitudes and dispositions of works like the Hermetic writings.[38]

In its concern with light, moreover, the Fourth Gospel gave rise to what might be called its own "literature of light." The apocryphal Acts of John is a case in point. There, Christ appears time and again as Light incarnate. Appearing to John in a cave after his crucifixion, Christ presents the apostle with a "Cross of Light" that becomes a sign of the Logos. Before that time, however, Christ, encircled by his apostles, sings a hymn to God who is τὸ φῶς itself: "We thank thee, Light: In whom darkness dwelleth not," Christ sings, and his apostles respond, "Amen."[39] Gnostic gospels like the Pistis Sophia, in turn, develop further the vision of Christ as light transfigured. Thus, τὸ μυστήριον, the mystery, appears to his followers after the Resurrection: "But . . . that power of light descended upon Jesus and surrounded him entirely, while he sat apart from his disciples . . . , and he shone exceedingly, and the light that was upon him was beyond measure. And the disciples did not see Jesus because of the great light in which he was . . . for . . . their eyes were darkened because of the great light in which he was, but . . . they saw only the light which sent forth many beams . . . of light."[40] The brilliance of his presence even during his infancy is narrated in such New Testament apocrypha as "The Midwife's Account of the Birth in the Cave":

And when the light had come forth, Mary worshipped him. . . . And the child himself shone brightly round about like the sun. . . . And the light itself which was born increased and darkened the light of the sun with the brightness of its shining. And this cave was filled with bright light. . . . And I stood there stupified and amazed, and fear seized me. For I was looking upon the intense brightness of the light which was born. But the light itself, gradually withdrawing, became like a child . . . , [and] he was in all his body shining . . . radiant to behold . . . , and while I held him and looked at his face, he . . . opened his eyes. . . . And suddenly there came forth from his eyes a great light like a brilliant flash of lightning.[41]

Although this literature is certainly not part of the mainstream of the traditions that Milton inherited, it is important as an indication of the supremely numinous quality that light came to assume within a specifically New Testament context. From the Christian perspective, this fact is borne out repeatedly in liturgical practice and patristic commentary.

In his study of the liturgical dimensions of Milton's poetry, Thomas B. Stroup has already shown how the ninth-century Pentecostal hymn "Veni, Creator Spiritus" underlies the invocations in *Paradise Lost*.[42] The hymn was "sung at every service of ordination of a priest or at every consecration of a bishop, whether Roman or Anglican." As the hymn invokes the Creator Spirit, the Paraclete, to illuminate the ordinand, Milton calls upon his Heavenly Muse to "irradiate his mind" in his capacity as poet-priest.[43] Such a context is supremely appropriate for one who was thoroughly familiar with "the great canticles of the Church—the *Venite*, the *Benedicite, omnia opera Domini*, the *Te Deum*, the *Benedictus*, the *Magnificat*, the *Nunc dimittis*—as well as the Confessions, the Creeds, and all the prayers of Matins, Evensong, and the Communion." With the formulae of these "carved" "upon his memory" through "countless repetition," Milton, in effect, composed his own liturgy.[44] In the case of the Pentecostal hymn, Milton would have been the first to agree with the association of the Spirit with Light: "What in me is dark / Illumin" (1.23–24), as he invoked the Spirit at the outset of his epic. In *Christian Doctrine*, he states repeatedly that the Spirit is "Light" (*lucem*) by which God "enlightens us" (*per spiritum nos illuminat*) (CM, 14:361, 363, 396–97). The appropriateness of the Pentecostal hymn, then, is apparent indeed. But as a reflection of the significance of light in liturgical practice, it must not be viewed in isolation. Equally as important is a host of other hymns that suggest the extent to which the early Church generated what might be called a liturgy of light.

As early as the first or second century A.D., one finds such hymns as the "Hymnus Vespertinus" sung at the Lighting of the Lamps: "Hail! gladdening Light, of his pure glory poured / Who is th'immortal Father, heavenly, blest, / Holiest of Holies—Jesus Christ our Lord" (*Lumen hilare sancte gloriae immortalis Patris, coelestis, sancti, beati, Jesu Christe*).[45] Similar motifs are later incorporated into hymns of every sort. In his own

"Vesper Hymn," for example, Prudentius celebrates "the Fount of light" who is both "light" and the "source of light," and in his "Hymn before the Repast," he hails "the Author of Light," "Word begotten of God," to "turn" his "radiant gaze" upon his votaries. The idea is repeated in his "Morning Hymn": "For light pervades the whitening sky, / And Christ, the Sun of Justice, comes."[46] If such hymns are part of the liturgical fabric of the early Church, they, in turn, are complemented by specific sacramental practices in which light assumes a dominant role.

As the seventeenth-century exegete John Gregory maintained in his discourse on light, "the carefull Church perceiving that God was so much taken with this outward symbole of the Light, could do no lesse then goe on with the Ceremony. Therefore the day of our Lords Nativity was to be called ἐπιφάνεια, the *Epiphany*, or appearing of the Light; and so many Tapers were to be set up the Night before, as might give Name to the *Vigil Vigilia Luminum*." "The receiving of this Light in Baptism . . . [was] call'd . . . φωτισμός, *Illumination*, which further to betoken, the rites were to celebrate this Sacrament . . . with all the Tapers light, & c. as the Order in the *Euchalogue*. The *Neophytus* also or new convert received a Taper lighted and delivered by the *Mystagogus*, which for the space of seven dayes after he was to hold in his hand at Divine Service, sitting in the Baptistery."[47] The torch-bearing catechumens, in turn, were called φωτιζόμενοι, those "in the process of being illuminated" (*competentes*), and the baptized were called οἱ φωτισθέντες, the enlightened (cf. Heb. 6:4, 10:32). The baptistery became appropriately the φωτιστήριον, the place of enlightenment.[48] In the context of this festival of "The Holy Lights," the idea receives ample elaboration in the discourses of Gregory Thaumaturgus and Gregory Nazianzen on the Theophania.[49] As Milton humbles himself before the theophany in the proem to Book 3 of *Paradise Lost*, he too joins the ranks of the φωτιζόμενοι: like them, he is about to be initiated into his own "pure Ethereal stream" with its appropriate "Fountain." The entire process, as Milton maintains in his discussion of baptism in *Christian Doctrine*, typifies the experience of rebirth consummated in the resurrection (*CM*, 16:191). It is a rebirth that Milton himself seeks in his own "reascent" to Light.

In sacramental terms, it should come as no surprise, then, that as O. B. Hardison observes, "light is the most important physical symbol of the Easter vigil" in the liturgy of the early Church.[50] Intimately associated with the vigil was the sacrament of baptism. During the vigil, Christ's presence was embodied in the paschal candle, "carried before the *competentes* to the font" to denote "the rising of the Sun of righteousness."[51] At the entrance of the candle, the choir cried "*Lumen Christi*, to which the

congregation replied . . . with *Deo gratias.*" In the *Exsultet* that introduced the Easter vigil, the image of light is paramount: "Let the divine
mysteries exult. . . . Let the earth also be filled with joy: . . . the darkness
which overspread the whole world is chased away by the splendor of our
eternal King."[52] Whatever Milton's particular doctrinal attitudes toward
the celebration of Easter might have been,[53] one cannot overlook the
importance of the liturgical bearing of this celebration of light upon his
sacerdotal posture in *Paradise Lost*. That posture is at least as reverential
in liturgical terms as that reflected in the calendrical or "holy day" poems
that he wrote as a young man. These include the Christmas poem, already mentioned, *Upon the Circumcision*, which points toward baptism
and anticipates the crucifixion, and *The Passion*, which "was almost
certainly" composed "during" and in commemoration of "the Easter
season."[54] Be that as it may, Milton's hallowing of the Light in *Paradise
Lost* is as much an *Exsultet* in its own right as is the *Exsultet* of the
Easter vigil.

Underlying the whole is the Johannine celebration of "τὸ φῶς." When
Saint Augustine preached his Easter Sunday Sermons, he conceived the
entire occasion in the language of John 1:1.[55] Taking his cue from John's
own allusion to the creation of light "in the beginning" (Gen. 1:1; John
1:1), Augustine combined the hymn to light that inaugurates the Fourth
Gospel with the account of the creation of light that inaugurates the Bible
itself. Doing so, he instructed "the newly baptized" on Easter Sunday in
the meaning of renewal through Christ.

Milton does no less, as his "great Argument" (1.24) instructs us "In
the Beginning how the Heav'ns and Earth / Rose out of *Chaos*" (1.10–
11). In that process, one comes to know the meaning of holy Light both
as that which is "bright effluence of bright essence increate" (3.6) and as
that which "didst invest / The rising world of waters dark and deep, /
Won from the void and formless infinite" (3.10–12). In either case, the
liturgical context is the same: the newly baptized are illuminated in the
experience of rebirth through the Light as a source of new life. "All things
were made by him; and without him was not any thing made that was
made. In him was life; and the life was the light of men" (John 1:3–4).
"This is the day which the Lord hath made: let us be glad and rejoice
therein" (Ps. 118:24). Milton's resurrection is our own.

Concurrent with the liturgy of light that evolved in the early Church
was a metaphysics of light that came to assume great significance in
the patristic controversies concerning the relationship of Father, Son,
and Spirit. The source of those controversies was the way in which the
"monotheism inherited by Christianity from Judaism" could manifest

itself in a tripersonal godhead that at the same time accommodated the concept of Incarnation.[56] Given this set of circumstances, how was one to understand the union between Father and Son, for example, or to conceive the Son in incarnate form? Particularly in response to the Father-Son hypostasis, patristic commentators adopted a light metaphysics that gave rise to a number of formulations. Among them are three metaphors that "appear continuously in patristic writings from the time of Justin Martyr through Athanasius: sun and radiance (or torch and fire), a fountain and its stream, or an archetype and its image."[57] Thus, arguing against the Arians, Athanasius maintains: "For the Father is in the Son, since the Son is what is from the Father, and proper to Him, as in the radiance the sun, and in the word the thought, and in the stream the fountain."[58] It is not the purpose here to argue Milton's Arianism or Trinitarianism but simply to point out that the bearing of these metaphors upon Milton's understanding of light in *Paradise Lost* has already been amply demonstrated. The emanationism implicit in the relationship between "bright effluence" and the "bright essence increate" (3.6), the reference to the "pure Ethereal stream" with its "Fountain" (3.7–8), and the allusion to God's "only Son" as "the radiant image of his Glory" (3.62–64) all represent Miltonic renderings of fundamental patristic metaphors that expressed the light metaphysics of the early Church.[59]

This light metaphysics, in turn, made further distinctions that bear upon the nature of light as sacral phenomenon. Specifically, it distinguished between light as *lux* and light as *lumen*. The first is uncreated or essential light, the second created or material light. The first is cause, the second effect. That "effect, the spreading of light (*lux*) through the diaphanous or transparent, is called luminosity (*lumen*). It is a ray (*radius*) when it takes place in a straight line from the source to what is illumined, and it is *splendor* when it is reflected. But *lumen* is also the generic name for every effect of light in the transparent or *diaphanum*."[60] In theological terms, "this process of cause to effect—essential to material light" in "the great chain of lights"—is represented by the flowing of "the uncreated light" from God to his "creatures," "who embody the created light." Creatures thereby participate figuratively in the chain of light because they are not light itself, but its rays, its deflections from above. As all creatures were infused with this light, so Christ as a creature became "the juncture uniting *lux* (essential light) with *lumen* (material light), the source with its product, the creator with the created."[61]

Current in the thirteenth-century writings of Robert Grosseteste, Roger Bacon, John of Peckham, Saint Bonaventure, Saint Thomas Aquinas, and Bartholomew of Bologna, this distinction is implicit in all those medieval discourses on light (*perspectivi*) that evolved into the science of optics.[62] Thus, in his *Tractatus de Luce*, Bartholomew maintains that God, the source of light, is the "*luminis fontale principium,*" his Son, "*per ipsum principium radium,*" who produces secondary lights, "*secondaria lumina,*" that illuminate the mind. "If anyone should turn to those secondary lights and thereby desire to see with the mind the Father or fount of all these lights Himself (*horum omnium luminum fontem*), he must pass beyond the limits of these secondary lights to the principal ray, Jesus Christ, in seeing whom he will also see the Father."[63] As a reflection of thirteenth-century light metaphysics, Bartholomew's statement is replicated in the light metaphysics of Dante, for whom "*luce* is the source of *lume*, the ray . . . a linear radiation from the *luce*, and the *splendor* . . . the light reflected from the first things which the ray emanating from the source may strike."[64] In this process, "the radiation of the Primal Light creates a hierarchy of light" that in turn ascends "to the very Primal Light itself, spiritual, uncreated, divine, the vision of which is the vision of all."[65] If it is metaphysics of this kind that underlie Dante's ascent up the ladder of light, with its ever-increasing intensity, in the *Paradiso*, then that ascent, as Joseph Mazzeo has shown, is equally indebted to the tradition of the visio Dei, the sources of which have already been explored in some detail and the bearing of which shall now be pursued at greater length.[66]

Because of his profound impact upon both the development of light metaphysics and the tradition of the visio Dei, Saint Augustine represents a fitting point of departure. A Neoplatonist in his own right, Augustine is equally important because he assimilated so much of Plotinian thought. As such, he supported the Neoplatonists' inclination to worship that "light which is their God . . . and illumines them that they may be penetrated with light, and enjoy perfect happiness in the participation of God." According to Augustine, Plotinus, in his comments on Plato, asserts that the soul derives its blessedness from this all-creating light, the source of spiritual illumination.[67] It is this illumination that Augustine experiences in the *Confessions*. "I entered into my inmost being," he says, and "by my soul's eye," saw "an unchangeable light," "far different from all other lights." "He who knows the truth," Augustine continues, "knows the light, and he who knows knows eternity." Addressing that light, he proclaims, "You are my God, and I sigh for you day and night."[68] Such is Augustine's own testament to the Light, as he is rapt from his dark night of the soul into the visio Dei.

In the same vein as Augustine in the fourth century, Dionysius the

Areopagite in the fifth century celebrated light in his accounts of the visio Dei. Recalling the traditions of solar theology in his treatise *On the Divine Names*, he maintains that the "great, all-bright and ever-shining sun" is "the visible image of the Divine Goodness," which "illumines all things that can receive its light while retaining the utter simplicity of light, and expands above and below throughout the visible world the beams of its own radiance." It is "the Supreme Fount." As the "Originating Beam," this "Divine Goodness" illuminates all with the "transcendent" power of its "Overflowing Radiance." It, in turn, "contains within Itself, in a simple form, the entire ultimate principle of light, and is the Transcendent Archetype of Light." The "heavenly mind" is given "a share of . . . [this] holy light," which "purges" the "spiritual eyes from the mist of ignorance." Such a mind undergoes a "Divine Yearning" for this light.[69]

In accord with that philosophy, such mystics as Meister Eckhart and Nicolas Cusanus continued the tradition into the later Middle Ages. In his sermon "The Beatific Vision," for example, Meister Eckhart maintains that "in the light of the impartible divine essence shall we see the divine essence . . . as revealed in the variety of the Persons and the unity of their nature." Whoever is "rapt away into this unveiled light perceives himself none other than that essence wherein God has his being, his very Godhead." In his experience, he shall "be changed from created light into the uncreated splendor of the divine nature and shall become like it; that is, [he] . . . shall be that it is."[70] In his treatise *De Visione Dei*, Cusanus speaks of beholding this light by means of the power attained through "Absolute Sight": this "Sight," "whence all sight springeth, surpasseth in keenness, in speed, and in strength the sight of all who actually see and who can become capable of sight"; it "embraceth in itself all modes of seeing . . . and abideth entirely free from all variation."[71] As a result of the understanding afforded by this sight, we are granted the "sacred ignorance" to know that God is "ineffable," to know "that He who is worshipped as Light Inaccessible is not light that is material, the opposite of which is darkness, but light absolutely simple and infinite in which darkness is infinite light; that He who is infinite light itself shines always in the darkness of our ignorance, but the darkness cannot comprehend the Light" (cf. John 1:5).

The idea that "darkness is infinite light," of course, is a prime characteristic of what Cusanus calls "negative theology" or the *via negativa*; through it, the absolute mystery of God, as *Deus absconditus*, is celebrated.[72] This recalls the angelic celebration of God in *Paradise Lost*:

> . . . but when thou shad'st
> The full blaze of thy beams, and through a cloud
> Drawn round about thee like a radiant Shrine,
> *Dark with excessive bright thy skirts appeer,*
> *Yet dazle Heav'n,* that brightest Seraphim
> Approach not, but with both wings veil their eyes
>   (3.377–82; italics added).[73]

The idea has its prime source in *The Mystical Theology* of Dionysius the Areopagite, who speaks of "the simple, absolute, and unchangeable mysteries of heavenly Truth" that "lie hidden in the dazzling obscurity of the secret Silence, outshining all brilliance with the intensity of their darkness." Through the "sacred ignorance" afforded by the *via negativa*, we shall be initiated into the "darkness" of the "hidden God," who resides in his "secret place." So Moses himself was initiated as he "presse[d] forward to the topmost pinnacle of the Divine Ascent" and beheld the place where God "dwells." "Unto this Darkness which is beyond Light we pray that we may come," says Dionysius, so that we may offer God "the praises of a transcendent hymnody."[74]

In his own way, of course, Dante does precisely that in *The Divine Comedy*. Blinded by the brilliance of the Primal Light in his ascent to light in the *Paradiso*, he is reborn into a higher vision: "Like sudden lightning that scatters the visual spirits and deprives the eye of the action of the clearest objects," he says, "a vivid light shone round about me and left me so swathed in the veil of its effulgence [*velo / del suo fulgor*] that nothing was visible to me" (30.46–51). From that state, he becomes "conscious of rising beyond . . . [his] own powers," as he drinks in the light that pours forth its "splendor" in the "form of a river" (30.55–63). With that, "the cloud of his mortality" is "disperse[d]" (33.31–32). Directing his "eyes" to "the Eternal Light" (*etterno lume*), he "draw[s] near to the end of all desires" and "end[s] perforce the ardour of . . . [his] craving": "for . . . [his] sight becoming pure, was entering more and more through the beam of the lofty light" (33.40–54). In that transformed state, he hymns the ineffable "*somma luce*" that envelops him in its indescribable brilliance: "O Light Eternal [*O luce etterna*]," he sings, "[Thou] alone abidest in Thyself, alone knowest Thyself, and, known to Thyself and knowing, lovest and smilest on Thyself" (33.134–36). This is the consummation of Dante's *visio Dei*: "the same light that swathes him and which he says is also the light by which he sees."[75] The ultimate beholding of that light underlies the action of his *Commedia*: Dante, like Milton, is a poet of the Light.[76] Like Milton, he embodies (and is, in fact, the consummate expression of) those traditions in which the numinosity of the Light flourished most brilliantly.

If these traditions were integral to the emergence of light as a sacral phenomenon in the Middle Ages, they were no less so in the Renaissance. Nowhere is a veneration of the Light expressed with more intensity than among the Renaissance Neoplatonists of the fifteenth and sixteenth centuries. Marsilio Ficino is a case in point. The founder and guiding spirit of the Florentine Academy, he made both Plato and Neoplatonism available to the West with his translations and commentaries.[77] In such tracts as *In Librum De Sole* and *In Librum De Lumine*, the Platonic ascent to light is spiritualized and Christianized. While the first tract compares the sun to God and even the Trinity itself as an expression of *"occultam divinorum lucem,"* the second tract describes the ascent to light *"in corpore mundi, in anima, in Angelo, in Deo."* Moving from darkness through *"lumen visibile, rationale, intelligibile,* [and, finally,] . . . *divinum,"* the soul apprehends the first through the senses, the second and third through reason and intelligence, and the fourth through the spirit. The last is a heavenly light which radiates from a spiritual center of perfection and grace. Associated with God himself, it is nothing less than a product of the divine numen.[78] Instrumental in introducing the worship of light into the Renaissance, Ficino reflects the influence of a number of sources, Plotinian, Hermetic, and Gnostic, as well as Christian. He is as comfortable in Plotinus, Hermes Trismegistus, Pythagoras, and Iamblichus, as he is in Dionysius the Areopagite. To a great extent, his Neoplatonism is filtered through them. Inspiring, in turn, such followers as Pico della Mirandola, he devised a "Platonic Theology" in which the "mysteries" of the Hellenistic age flourished afresh.[79]

Among English writers of the seventeenth century, its influence is discernible in figures like Robert Fludd, whose speculations concerning holy Light, according to Denis Saurat, had a direct impact upon Milton.[80] Be that as it may,[81] Fludd provides still another example of the way in which the theophany of light as an overwhelming and ineffable experience was of central importance to the traditions that Milton inherited. Treating holy Light throughout his works, Fludd celebrates that "glorious," "sacrosanct," and "ineffable" emanation of God's glory. Embodied in the sun as the "tabernacle" of Jahweh, it is the "secret" and "hidden" medium by which God manifests himself.[82] By means of light, man ascends from Reason and Intellect to the world of Mind, from the sphere of created light to the sphere of *"lux increata"* or the *"Radius Dei."*[83] This, "the *forma formans* . . . is God, or the divine emanation, which created all things; the *forma informata* . . . is the created light, or the spirit informed or illuminated, by the presence of the bright increated Spirit; and the increated Spirit clothed with, or enduing that created spirit, is said to be *vestius,* or . . . *cloathed with light,* that is, *with an illuminated spirit, as with a garment.*"[84] However one might wish to interpret Fludd in a doctrinal sense, one thing is clear: his veneration of light in all its forms and his inclination to found an entire philosophy upon it provide further evidence of the profound impact that light as a distinctly numinous entity had into the seventeenth century. The religion of light did not die out with the Italian Neoplatonists.

In traditions that are no doubt more nearly in keeping with Milton's own temperament, however, one cannot overlook the oft-invoked yet crucial influence of poets like Spenser. Himself the heir of Renaissance Neoplatonism, he gives eloquent evidence of the way in which the veneration of light implicit in Ficino and others manifests itself in poetic form. Among Spenser's poems, the *Hymne of Heavenly Beavtie* is seminal, particularly in its account of how "euery thing doth vpward tend," in its "ascent" to ultimate light (43–49). (One thinks of Raphael's discourse on the process of spiritualization in *Paradise Lost*: "By gradual scale sublim'd," all nature, in increasing intensities of "light," ascends to that "bright consummate flowr" [5.479–81]. Contemplating the *scala naturae,* which is concurrently a *scala luminis,* "by steps we may ascend to God" [5.512].)[85] Our flight follows that pattern, Spenser suggests, as we behold the light of the physical universe, which, in turn, leads upward to the heaven of heavens, where God dwells in his unbearable resplendence, "which glistereth else so bright / That th'Angels selues can not endure his sight" (118–19):

> But we fraile wights, whose sight cannot sustaine
> The Suns bright beames, when he on vs doth shyne . . .
> . . . how can we see with feeble eyne
> The glory of that Maiesty diuine,
> In sight of whom both Sun and Moone are darke,
> Compared to his least resplendent sparke?
>
> (120–26)

From God's "seate," Spenser continues in his paean to the Light, "proceed" "beames so pure and bright, / That all about him sheddeth glorious light" (160–61). "With the great glorie of that wondrous light, / His throne is all encompassed around, / And hid in his own brightnesse from the sight / Of all that look thereon with eyes vnsound" (176–79). That, says Henry Vaughan (himself a poet of the Light) is God's "deep, but dazzling darkness" (50).[86] Only those who are pure of sight can begin to penetrate it. For that purpose, they must become educated in the knowledge of what might be called "spiritual optics."

Both in his tract appropriately entitled *Spiritual Opticks* (1652) and in his *Discourse of the Light of Nature* (1652), the Cambridge Platonist Nathaniel Culverwell demonstrates how that knowledge may be attained. "The soul," Culverwell says, "is made with a through light, with a double window, at one window it looks upon corporeals, at the other it hath a fair prospect upon spirituals." The first leads to the second: as the "corporeal eye beholds the sun," "so the eye of the soul doth willingly open it self to look upon God *per modum objecti*, and has all *per receptionem* from him, fixing its eye upon so transcendent and beautiful an object and viewing all those streamings out of light . . . that flow from him as the fountain of light, where they have dwelt from everlasting."[87]

Correspondingly, Joseph Hall, in his *Remedy of Prophaneness*, indoctrinates us in the practice of "divine Opticks" (p. 47). There must be "a trajection of the visuall beames of the soule," he says, "terminating them only in God." When it has attained that point, there occurs, he says, "a certaine divine irradiation of the mind, which is now filled, and taken up with a lightsome apprehension of a infinite Majesty, of a glory incomprehensible, and boundlesse." This is none other than the transcendent light, in which God dwells "as far above this outward light which we see, as that is above darknesse" (pp. 37–45). Despite his political antipathy to Hall, Milton would have agreed: his outlook is perfectly in accord with the "spiritual optics" of a Culverwell, on the one hand, and the "divine optics" of a Hall, on the other. Like theirs, his "optics" held tenaciously to the sacrality and ineffability of light in all its forms. It had not yet succumbed to the emerging tendency of the "science" of optics to concern itself solely with the "physical" properties of light as solely empirical phenomenon. That task would be left to Newton and his peers.[88] It should be noted, however, that even those engaged in the science of optics attested to the ultimate mystery of light. The discoverer of the diffraction of light, Francesco Grimaldi, maintained in his *Physico-mathesis de Lumine* (1665) that "we do not really know anything about the nature of light."[89]

His sentiments were fully anticipated by the "nonscientists." Treating "created light" (lumen) in *The Historie of the World* (1614), Sir Walter Ralegh observed that "of this created light there is no agreement in opinion." "Neither," he continues, "do I marvaile" at this fact, "for it cannot be found either in the Fathers, Philosophers, or School-men, or other ancient or later Writers, that any of them understood either it or themselues therein: all men . . . haue disputed thereof, but there is no man that has been taught thereby." All that can be said of light as lumen is that it carries us toward God, so that we "surmount these perceiued Heauens" to "find out their omnipotent Cause and Creator," who is "*Lux ipsa*" and "*Lux sancta*" (pp. 7–9).[90]

Such is the contemporary milieu that most appropriately befits Milton's own attitude toward light throughout his career. It is a milieu in which the presence of the holy is felt as profoundly and as stunningly as it ever was. Poets celebrated its splendor in verse, and commentators extolled its ineffability in prose. As Roland M. Frye has recently demonstrated in his magisterial study, it flourished in the visual arts as well.[91] Whether one considers "Tintoretto's great *Paradise* mural in Venice," with its aura "that emanates from the head of Christ" and "streams out in separate rays upon the blessed" or "Baciccia's painting of the ceiling of the Gesù in Rome," with its representation of Heaven "as a cloud of dazzling light" that emanates from a central point, he will be impressed with the visual embodiments of the luminous theophany in art.[92] It is a visual experience Milton would have understood. Such is particularly true considering his heightened sensitivity to luminous phenomena. Even as he was going blind, Milton wrote that he beheld in his darkness "a copious glittering light." That light would have to compensate for what he had beheld on the outside world, as it "burst" forth from time to time with a "lucency" that had "a kind of force and audible shot from within." (FE, *CM*, 12:69). This experience would be internalized as he learned to accommodate himself to his blindness. Nonetheless, the intensity of the theophanies that he experienced on the outside would never diminish; rather, it would increase with his newly discovered sight. Such theophanies would envelop him with their dazzling brightness.

In the traditions explored here, perhaps the best visual representations of the experience can be found in the remarkable plates accompanying the works of Robert Fludd, discussed earlier. The *Utriusque Cosmi*, for example, depicts a number of luminous theophanies by which light bursts forth in all its splendor from a dark background or is orbed as a divine sun emanating brilliant rays (see figure 9). Whether or not one prefers to understand the Miltonic experience in these terms, one fact is clear: from the darkness of his own physical blindness, Milton hailed a "light" as brilliant and as resplendent as any that had been conceived in all the traditions examined here.

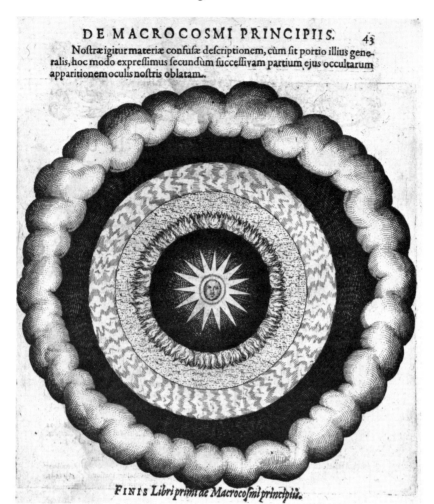

FIGURE 9. Luminous Theophany.
Reproduced from Robert Fludd, *Utriusque Cosmi Maioris* (1617), p. 43,
by permission of the Huntington Library, San Marino, California.

10
Presence

In the foregoing discussion of light and the traditions that informed it, one tradition has not been considered. With its source in the Old Testament, this tradition involves the Hebraic point of view and the specific outlook to which that point of view gave rise. Consideration of the Old Testament perspective has been delayed for a very compelling reason. Nowhere in the Old Testament is God specifically *identified* with light. "He is the creator of the light (Gen. 1:3) . . . , he clothes himself in light (Ps. 104: 2), is a lamp to the way of the righteous (Ps. 119: 105), the source of life is in him, and in his light we see light (Ps. 36: 10). But the simple formula that God in his essence, in the absolute sense, is light is not found there."[1] In strictly biblical terms, the central tenet of Johannine mysticism that "God is light" ($\theta\varepsilon\grave{o}\varsigma\ \varphi\hat{\omega}\varsigma\ \dot{\varepsilon}\sigma\tau\iota\nu$) (1 John 1:5) is a New Testament concept. From the New Testament perspective, the Old Testament outlook is most characteristically expressed by the Pauline statement that God "dwell[eth] in the light which no man can approach unto" ($\varphi\hat{\omega}\varsigma\ o\grave{i}\kappa\hat{\omega}\nu\ \dot{\alpha}\pi\rho\acute{o}\sigma\iota\tau o\nu$) (1 Tim. 6:16).[2] In his hymn to holy Light in Book 3 of *Paradise Lost*, Milton, of course, expresses both ideas: "God *is* light, / And never but in unapproached light / *Dwelt* from Eternitie, *dwelt* then in thee" (italics added). In order to understand the Old Testament perspective, it is necessary to explore the concept of a God who "dwells." Specifically, one must consider God's presence as a phenomenon that embodies the idea of dwelling.

Perhaps the most comprehensive statement concerning God's presence in *Paradise Lost* is made by Adam himself when he realizes that he may no longer "dwell" in "Paradise" (11.259). "This most afflicts me," Adam laments, "that departing hence," I shall be bereft of God's presence:

> As from his face I shall be hid, depriv'd
> His blessed count'nance; here I could frequent,
> With worship, place by place where he voutsaf'd
> Presence Divine, and to my Sons relate;
> On this Mount he appeerd, under this Tree

Stood visible, among these Pines his voice
I heard, here with him at this Fountain talk'd:
So many grateful Altars I would rear
Of grassie Terf, and pile up every Stone
Of lustre from the brook, in memorie,
Or monument to Ages, and thereon
Offer sweet smelling Gumms and Fruits and Flowrs:
In yonder nether World where shall I seek
His bright appearances, or footstep trace?
For though I fled him angrie, yet recall'd
To life prolong'd and promis'd Race, I now
Gladly behold though but his utmost skirts
Of glory, and farr off his steps adore.

(11.315–33)

"Presence Divine," as Adam realizes, involves a witnessing of the manifest "glory" of God, a beholding of the "blessed count'nance," as it is accommodated to the sight of man, a conversing with God, and, by implication, a "walking" with him, as his "footstep" can be "traced" from "place" to "place." In response to this experience of God's presence, it likewise prompts an act of worshiping God by erecting "grateful Altars," made of "grassie Terf" and "lustr[ous]" "Stone" in "memorie" of his "bright appearances": the place of worship, even as the product of Nature, reflects the radiance of the presence itself.

In characterizing the nature of the presence, Michael's words of consolation to Adam are similarly informative:

Adam, thou know'st Heav'n his, and all the Earth,
Not this Rock onely; his Omnipresence fills
Land, Sea, and Air, and every kind that lives . . . :
. . . surmise not then
His presence to these narrow bounds confin'd
Of Paradise or *Eden*: this had been
Perhaps thy Capital Seat, from whence had spred
All generations, and had hither come
From all the ends of th'Earth, to celebrate
And reverence thee thir great Progenitor.
But this praeeminence thou has lost, brought down
To dwell on eeven ground now with thy Sons:
Yet doubt not but in Vallie and in Plain
God is as here, and will be found alike

> Present, and of his presence many a signe
> Still following thee, still compassing thee round
> With goodness and paternal Love, his Face
> Express, and of his steps the track Divine.
>
> (11.335–54)

Adam, of course, is to be comforted by the fact of God's omnipresence, which fills the universe (cf. 7.168–69: "Because I am who fill / Infinitude") and encompasses man in its protection. In that context, "goodness and paternal Love" likewise become the manifestations of God's presence: "his Face / Express, and of his steps the track Divine." It is an idea to which Milton addressed himself in *Christian Doctrine*, with his discussion of God's "Omnipresence" (*ubique praesens*): this attribute, Milton says, is the consequence of God's "infinity." Milton's proof-texts include Psalm 139:8–9 ("If I ascend up into heaven, thou art there . . ."), Proverbs 15:3 ("The eyes of Jehovah are in every place"), Jeremiah 23:24 ("Do not I fill heaven and earth?"), and Ephesians 4:6 ("Who is above all, and through all, and in you all"). Milton concludes his discussion of omnipresence by saying that whatever its nature, it should inspire "thoughts" that "appear most suitable to the reverence due to the Deity": that is, omnipresence should prompt appropriate acts of worship (*CM*, 14:46–48).

It is in response to those particular manifestations of God's omnipresence that reveal his glory, however, that Adam would erect altars. Michael's consolation, to be sure, includes the prospect of such manifestations occurring beyond the narrow confines of paradise. Nonetheless, his references to omnipresence should not lead one to overlook the unique character of the glorious manifestations that Adam has in mind. These are manifestations, the force of which is overwhelming in its awesomeness: they cause one to fall in "adoration" before their radiance, as Adam, "with awe," fell before the "Presence Divine," that "vision bright," shortly after his creation (8.313–15, 367). It is this aspect of omnipresence that Milton discusses under the heading of "divine glory" (*divinae gloriae*) in *Christian Doctrine*. The proof-texts include Exodus 19:18 ("Mount Sinai was altogether on a smoke"), Exodus 24:10 ("They saw the God of Israel, and there was under his feet as it were a paved work of a sapphire stone, and as it were the body of heaven in his clearness"), Exodus 33:9–10 ("The cloudy pillar descended . . ."), 1 Kings 8:10–11 ("The cloud filled the house of Jehovah"), and 1 Kings 22:19 ("I saw Jehovah sitting on his throne"), among others (*CM*, 14:60–61).

In Old Testament tradition, this aspect of God's omnipresence is referred to as the Shekinah or "Dwelling Presence" (שכינה) of God: "For thus saith the high and lofty one that inhabiteth [שכן] eternity, whose name is holy [שמו וקדוש]; I dwell in the high and holy place [אשכן מרום וקדוש]" (Isa. 57:15). Derived from the verb שכן ("dwell"), Shekinah, "the dwelling," represented "the majestic presence or manifestation of God which had descended to 'dwell' in this mundane sphere, sent forth by God, or come from him, to 'dwell' among men." Giving rise to a literature of its own, the word *Shekinah* is derived from those passages that refer to God as "dwelling" either in the Tabernacle or among the people of Israel (Exod. 25:8; Num. 5:3; 1 Kings 6:13; Ezek. 43:9; Zech. 2:10). On occasion, the name of God, as the embodiment of the Shekinah, is said to "dwell" (Deut. 12:11, 14:23). In particular, God is spoken of as dwelling in Jerusalem (1 Chron. 23:25), on Mount Zion (Isa. 8:18), and in the Temple itself (Ezek. 43:7). Those crucial passages which allude to "him that dwelt in the bush" (Deut. 33:16) and refer to "the glory of the Lord [that] abode upon Mount Sinai" (Exod. 24:16) have already been cited.[3]

In his treatment of Milton's Semitic studies, Harris Francis Fletcher has admirably demonstrated Milton's awareness of the doctrine.[4] But that fact should come as no surprise: it was a commonplace of Renaissance exegetical thought. John Gregory devoted an entire chapter, "*Shecinah,* or God's dwelling presence," to the subject in his *Gregorii Opuscula,* and Joseph Mede discoursed upon it in his sermon *The Reverence of Gods House.*[5] John Buxtorf provided various renderings for it in his *Lexicon Hebraicum et Chaldaicum,* and Edward Leigh defined it in his *Critica Sacra.*[6] In his devotional work *The Rule and Exercises of Holy Living,* Jeremy Taylor provided an entire section on "the practice of the presence of God."[7] According to John Strickland, "there is a two-fold presence of God; first his generall or common presence, whereby he is *repletive* in all places and things . . . which is God's omnipresence. . . . Secondly, there is a speciall presence of God, or his presence testified by some remarkable works or speciall demonstrations, *Effective.*" Under the second heading, "there be three sorts of Gods speciall presence": first, his "glorious presence," the place of his "dwelling" and "residence," as he is enthroned upon his "Chaire of state"; second, his "gracious presence," as he is revealed in the Temple or among those gathered in his name; third, his "providentiall presence, . . . wherein the power, wisdome, or any other of Gods attributes, are eminently put forth," as he was "present with *Israel* in the wildernesse by the pillar of fire and of a cloud."[8] In all cases, he is said to "dwell": "Of the Hebrew *Shacan*," says Edward Leigh, "the Hebrews usually call Gods Majesty in his Church *Shecinah*, that is, *his habitation*."[9]

Returning to the dialogue in *Paradise Lost* between Adam and Michael regarding the nature of "Presence Divine," one can see what form Milton's awareness of the concept assumes. In Michael's statement to Adam that "this had been / Perhaps thy Capital Seat," to which, as to a central place of "reverence," all "generations" might have come to do homage, Milton alludes ironically to the concept: because of his fall, Adam must "*dwell* on eeven ground now with . . . [his] Sons" (italics added). It is an idea that assumes metaphorical significance throughout *Paradise Lost*. Thus, in the very act of creating the universe, God imparts his Shekinah to the realm of man. The angels accordingly celebrate "this new-made World," through a language that recalls the nature of the Dwelling Presence: among the "Starrs" is "the seat of men, / Earth," "this pleasant dwelling place." "Thrice happie men, / And sons of men," the angels sing, "whom God hath thus advanc't, / Created in his Image, there to dwell / And worship him . . . / And multiply a Race of Worshippers / Holy and just" (7.617–32). Had man remained obedient, he would have "dwelt" with God in Heaven (7.157–59): instead, he chooses to "dwell" with Satan, by exchanging his "high seat" for Satan's "dwelling" (4.371–79). He falls as a result of succumbing to Satan's temptation to bow in "Reverence" to the "Tree," "as to the power / That dwelt within, whose presence had infus'd / Into the plant sciential sap" (9.834–38). Satan and his cohorts may then (for a time) flee their "habitation fraught with fire" (6.876) and "dwell" "in some mild Zone" "neerer . . . [their] ancient Seat" (2.394–98; cf. PR, 1.40–44, 116). Sin and Death too are then free to inhabit the world of man (10.399), where Sin, in particular, "dwell[s] / Habitual habitant" (10.587–88). Such would have been man's fate, had not God, through his grace, provided the means of redemption. This act likewise is conceived in terms of the Shekinah, as the Incarnate Son "dwells" or "unites" with man (12.382). Doing so, he is "enshrin'd / In fleshly Tabernacle, and human form" (PR, 4.598–99; cf. PA, 17). Both by means of the Son as Messiah and the Holy Spirit as "Comforter," God "shall dwell" within man (12.487–88), and thereafter "the just shall dwell" with their Savior, as he reinhabits the heavenly "Throne." There, he "shalt . . . sit incarnate" and "Reign / Both God and Man, Son both of God and Man" (3.314–16, 335).

In this respect, as Renaissance expositors well knew, God becomes "Emmanuel," that is, "God with us" (cf. Isa. 7:14; Matt. 1:23). Thus, in his *Immanuel, or the Mystery of the Incarnation of the Son of God,*

James Ussher maintains that the great wonder and mystery of the Incarnation is the fact that God "should take our flesh and dwell, or pitch his *Tabernacle* with us." "To compass this conjunction betwixt God and us," Ussher observes, "he that was to be our Jesus or Saviour, must of necessity also be IMMANUEL; which being interpreted is, 'God with us'; and therefore in his person to be Immanuel, that is, God dwelling with our flesh; because he was by his office too to be Immanuel, that is, he who must make God to be at once with us."[10] According to Ralph Cudworth, *"the mystery of the Tabernacle was this, that it was to be a place for the Shechinah, or habitation of divinity to be fixed in*: and this, no doubt, as a special type of God's future dwelling in Christ's human nature, which was the TRUE SHECHINAH."[11]

From the Christocentric point of view, the New Testament counterpart of the Shekinah is implicit in the concept of God's παρουσία, which suggests the Messianic Advent both in the Incarnation and in the Last Judgment (Matt. 24:3; 1 Cor. 1:8). "The word developed as a cult expression for the coming of a hidden divinity, who makes his presence felt by a revelation of his power, or whose presence is celebrated in the cult." This manifestation of the presence is expressed in the New Testament through the notion of God's δόξα, which suggests his brightness, splendor, radiance, and glory (2 Pet. 1:17; Rev. 15:8; 2 Cor. 2:7).[12] The term δόξα is significantly used in the prologue to the Fourth Gospel to imply that because "the Word was made flesh, and dwelt among us," we could "behold" his "glory" (δόξαν) (John 1:14). In this instance, what John has done is to appropriate the concept of "radiance" and "splendor" implicit in the Shekinah and apply it to the idea of God as τὸ φῶς. The inclination is only natural considering that "in Judaism of the Christian era, the שכינה . . . was conceived as light."[13]

From the very beginning, however, such was historically the case.[14] In the Deuteronomist's reference to "him that dwelt [שכני] in the bush" (Deut. 33:16), Moses beholds "a flame of fire out of the midst of a bush: and he looked, and, behold, the bush burned with fire, and the bush *was not consumed. . . . And Moses hid his face; for he was afraid to look upon God"* (Exod. 3:2, 6). That event is particularly significant for this discussion because it represents one of a number of luminous theophanies around which the Israelites were to create a pattern of worship that associated the concept of God's Dwelling Presence (שכינה) with the concept of light (אור). The way in which this pattern of worship evolved is implicit in the Exodus theophanies and their embodiment in the Tabernacle cult.

If God's presence is manifested as fire in the burning bush and as "a pillar of fire" (Exod. 13:21) in the wilderness, it is revealed as "thunders and lightning," earthquake, fire, and cloud (Exod. 19:16–18) on Sinai. It is the Sinai theophany, in fact, which is particularly relevant, for that is where God lays out to Moses "the pattern of the tabernacle" (Exod. 25:9). Thus, "the sight of the glory of the Lord *was* like devouring fire on the top of the mount in the eyes of the children of Israel" (Exod. 24:17). Because of the "awefulness" (to use Otto's term)[15] of God's presence, the Israelites respond, "Let not God speak with us, lest we die" (Exod. 20:19). Moses becomes the mediator who appears before the presence: Moses "drew near unto the thick darkness where God was" (Exod. 20:21) and "went into the midst of the cloud" (Exod. 24:18). When Moses is on the mount, God proclaims, "Thou canst not see my face: for there shall no man see me, and live. . . . Behold, *there is* a place by me, and thou shalt stand upon a rock: And it shall come to pass, while my glory passeth by, that I will put thee in a clift of the rock, and will cover thee with my hand while I pass by: And I will take away mine hand, and thou shalt see my back parts: but my face shall not be seen" (Exod. 33:20–23). As a result of beholding even God's "back parts," Moses is transformed: his face shines so brightly that he must wear a veil (Exod. 34:32–35). The veil is removed only when Moses appears in God's presence (Exod. 34:34). Such are the characteristics of the theophany: at once dazzling and hidden in darkness, awesome and radiant, characterized by fire and cloud, communicating itself only to the initiate, who speaks with it and is transformed by it.

In cultic terms, these are the elements that are assimilated into the worship of God in the sanctuary: "And let them make me a sanctuary; that I may dwell among them. According to all that I shew thee, *after* the pattern of the tabernacle and the pattern of all the instruments thereof, even so shall ye make it" (Exod. 25:8–9). This is particularly a place where God shall dwell between the outstretched wings of the "cherubims" upon the "mercy seat above upon the ark": "And there," God says to Moses, "I will meet with thee, and I will commune with thee from above the mercy seat, from between the two cherubims which *are* upon the ark of the testimony" (Exod. 25:22). His presence there incorporates the theophanic qualities that have been associated here with his "awefulness": "A cloud covered the tent of the congregation, and the glory of the Lord filled the tabernacle" (Exod. 40:34). This is the place of the Shekinah, "the ark of God, whose name is called by the name of the Lord of hosts that dwelleth *between* the cherubims" (2 Sam. 6:2). It is the place of "The Name" (יהוה צבאות), embodied in the presence that "dwells": that is, it "inhabits" its high position, as it "sits" (ישב) upon its throne between the cherubim above the ark of the testimony (ארון).

When Solomon came to provide a place for the ark (or, as Milton says in *Paradise Lost*, to "enshrine" the "clouded Ark" "in a glorious Temple" [12.332–33]) within "the most holy *place*" (קדש הקדשים), likewise called "the oracle of the house" (דביר הבית), he knew precisely the implications of his act: "And it came to pass, when the priests were come out of the holy *place*, that the cloud filled the house of the Lord. So that the priests could not stand to minister because of the cloud: for the glory of the Lord had filled the house of the Lord: Then spake Solomon. The Lord said that he would dwell in the thick darkness [לשכן בערפל]. I have surely built thee an house to dwell in, a settled place for thee to abide in forever [מכון לשבתך עולמים]" (1 Kings 8:10–13).

It has been conjectured that "the opening words of Solomon's Dedication of the Temple were originally part of an oracle" recited in accord with a prevailing pattern of sun worship and that the Temple was situated in such a way that "at sunrise" a "sudden full glory of light" flooded the interior of the Temple.[16] Be that as it may, one hardly needs sun cults to justify what had already been implicit in the cult of the Tabernacle. That cult had its own worship of the Light to recommend it. Thus, one can imagine the high priest, equipped with the oraculous "Urim" and "Thummim" ("lights" and "perfections") (see figure 2), appearing on the holiest of occasions before the Shekinah, the radiance of which blazes out from the darkness that envelops it. "Thou that dwellest [ישב] *between* the cherubims, shine forth [הופיעה]... and cause thy face to shine [והאר]; and we shall be saved," the Psalmist sings (Ps. 80:1, 3). It is a psalm that Milton knew well, for he translated it in a form that elaborates particularly upon its luminous elements: "Thou," he sings, "that sitt'st between the Cherubs *bright* / *Between their wings out-spread*, / Shine forth, *and from thy cloud give light*" (1, 5–7). (As Milton himself indicated, the italicized words are his own.) This is only one of a number of "entrance liturgies" that celebrated the Shekinah dwelling upon the ark. In that respect, Psalm 36 is even more to the point: "For with thee *is* the fountain of life: in thy light shall we see light [באורך נראה-אור]" (Ps. 36:9).[17]

From the very beginning, then, the Dwelling Presence of God (שכנה) within the sanctuary came to be associated with the concept of light (אור). In the traditions to which that association gave rise, the idea is emphasized repeatedly. Having treated the tradition of Hellenistic paganism in some detail in the previous chapter, the discussion will begin here with Philo, the primary exponent of Hellenistic Judaism. For Philo, the

Dwelling Presence revealed upon the ark was of utmost importance. Off limits to all but the high priest, who (half blinded by incense) might approach it but once a year, the ark, according to Philo, was the very essence of everything holy in the Jewish religion. Although the ark had been lost for centuries, it caused the very chamber in the temple in which it was housed to be sanctified by the memory of its presence. "It was the abode, the presence, of God in a sense completely unique. Philo speaks of it as though it were still there."[18] At the center of all for Philo resides the presence, "the highest God" (τὸ ὄν): "from Him radiate all the lower manifestations." "First is the Logos τοῦ ὄντος [of the highest God], corresponding to the voice heard by Moses. From the Logos the stream goes out in two branches, the two cherubim," each of which "is now in turn the source of a further emanation." The emanations are "the descending Light-Stream of God" coming forth from the presence. Conceived at once as rays and as fluid from a central source or fountain, these are "the conceptual beams of the shining God, beams unmixed and pure and most luminous" that blind the soul with their radiance: "When knowledge of Existence shines in," says Philo, "it so excessively illuminates everything as to darken what things had seemed brightest in themselves."[19]

In its treatment of the presence, the Philonic approach is remarkably in accord with the Johannine. For Philo, as for John, God is identified with light. " 'God is light,' says Philo, for in the Psalms it is said 'The Lord is my light and my saviour' . . . ; and not only light, but the archetype of every other light." Both share a similar concept of the Logos, one everywhere associated with the concept of light: in Philonic, as in Johannine thought, the apprehension of the Logos leads to the ultimate apprehension of its source, which is God. Emanation returns one to the source of illumination. "Is not light seen by means of light?" asks Philo; "in the same way God, being His own ray, is beheld through Himself alone . . . . They pursue truth who form their idea of God by means of God Himself—light by means of light."[20] In cultic terms, Philo conceives this *visio Dei*, as demonstrated, through the paraphernalia of the Temple, through a conceptualized vision of the presence dwelling upon the ark that is no longer there. Despite its absence, however, the whole radiates an overwhelming light. Such is the outlook of one whom Milton respectfully called a *"gravis author . . . legis Mosaïcae studiosissimus"* (1D, CM, 7:78).[21]

In the Greco-Roman period, Philonic thought was complemented by liturgical practice, which created its own cult of the Shekinah by associating the Torah shrine with the ark. Surrounded by the heavenly luminaries, the shrine suggested in the liturgy "that the Law is the Light, itself a manifestation of the *Shekinah*." The extent to which this idea is traditional in Judaism may be seen not only in the menorahs that surrounded the shrine but also in the so-called eternal light (compare the eternal light in the tabernacle [Exod. 27:20]) that burned before the Torah shrine. The association is still noticeable in the synagogue in the celebration of Simhath Torah, during which all the scrolls are taken out of the shrine and carried round the synagogue in procession. As part of the celebration, a lighted candle is placed in the empty shrine. Quite apart from the scrolls that bestow sanctity upon it, the shrine itself is holy, for even in the absence of the scrolls, the shrine remains a source of light, a veritable embodiment of the Shekinah, as the "Light-Law."[22]

The idea is everywhere present in later rabbinical commentary. Thus, the *Midrash Rabbah* declares: "Just as the Torah preceded everything [at the Creation], so also did He give precedence to the Ark over all other vessels in the construction of the tabernacle: and just as light preceded all other works of the Creation, as it says, *And God said: Let there be light* (Gen. I, 3), so also did the work in connection with the Torah, which is called '*light*'—as it is written, *For the commandment is a lamp, and the Teaching is light* (Prov. VI, 23)—take precedence over all the other vessels at the construction of the tabernacle."[23] In its association of the Torah shrine with the ark, the *Midrash* consistently conflates the building of the Tabernacle with the creation of the universe: both are cosmic acts. Just as "the Holy One," in the act of creation, "wrapped Himself in a garment, and the whole world from end to end became resplendent with His brightness," so, says the *Midrash*, "when God told Moses to build the Tabernacle," Moses began with "the Ark."[24] In this panorama of cultic-cosmic exegesis, the Shekinah shines forth in its resplendency. Accordingly, the *Midrash* comments: "Rab said: when the globe of the sun and the moon go in to ask leave of departure from the Holy One, blessed be He, their eyes grow dim with the brilliance of the *Shekinah*."[25] (Compare Isaiah 60:19: "The sun shall be no more thy light by day; neither for brightness shall the moon give light unto thee: but the Lord shall be unto thee an everlasting light, and thy God thy glory"; and, once again, Revelation 21:23: "And the city had no need of the sun, neither of the moon, to shine in it: for the glory of God did lighten it, and the Lamb is the light thereof.") If, as Fletcher suggests, the *Midrash Rabbah* represents one among a number of rabbinical sources to which Milton had recourse,[26] Milton's own illuminative vision of the Shekinah is not surprising. Whether or not one can trace an influence, the tradition is there: it represents one aspect of a developing line of thought that associated the Shekinah with the concept of light.

Equally important in this line of thought is the *Zohar*, a document that Denis Saurat, among others, has thought to influence Milton.[27] Once again, the concern here is not with influence but with milieu. In the cabbalistic tradition, the association of Shekinah with light assumes its own unique bearing. Called Sefiroth or grades of emanation, there are "ten spheres of divine manifestation in which God emerges from His hidden abode." Beginning with the Kether Elyon or "supreme crown" of God, they extend through "wisdom," "intelligence," "love," "power," "compassion," "endurance," "majesty," "foundation," and "kingdom," described in the *Zohar* as "the mystical archetype of Israel's community, or as the *Shekinah*." Associated with "the ten names most common to God," they form in their entirety his "one great Name." As "the King's faces," they are also called "the inner, intrinsic or mystical Face of God." They are likewise "the ten stages of the inner world," by means of which God "descends through the inmost recesses down to His revelation in the *Shekinah*." The very "garments of the Divinity," they are "the beams of light" that divinity emanates.[28] In addition to these aspects of cabbalistic thought implicit in the *Zohar*, one other is of prime importance: the Shekinah represents the feminine, as opposed to the masculine, element in God. This idea is unique. In all the references to the Shekinah in the *Talmud* and the *Midrash*, one finds no suggestion that it symbolizes a feminine element in God. Not one metaphor resorts to terms like Princess, Matron, Queen, or Bride as epithets for the Shekinah. But so it appears in the *Zohar*. As such, it has affinities with Gnostic distinctions between "male and female aeons, i.e., divine potencies, which constitute the world of the *pleroma*," on the last rim of which appears the Sophia, "daughter of light." In the same way, the Shekinah is the last of the Sefiroth, whose home is that of light.[29] At the same time, it suggests the figure of Wisdom, who, of course, is at once a female figure of great beauty (Solomon's "bride") and an "effulgence from everlasting light" "fairer than the sun" and "compared with light."[30] A Shekinah in her own right, she "ministered" before God in "the holy tabernacle" and was "established" in Zion.[31] (For Milton, she is the sister of his Muse, with whom she "didst converse" and "play / In presence of th'Almightie Father" [PL, 7.7–11].)

In the *Zohar*, the Shekinah is likewise conceived in distinctly cultic terms. Thus, the Shekinah appears in the Temple service, as "the Throne of Glory is prepared for the Holy Heavenly King." There, the Shekinah is "in perfect union" with God and "in closest union with the Holy Light and crowned with many crowns by the Holy King." "Her countenance," says the *Zohar*, "is illumined by the supernal light."[32] This is the "earthly

Tabernacle," the counterpart of which is the "heavenly Tabernacle, hidden and undisclosed" and "radiat[ing] light on all sides, illuminating all the worlds."[33] As the *Zohar* explains it, that process of radiation occurs in such a way that "the expansive force proceeding from the hidden recesses of the secret supernal ether opened a path and produced from itself a mysterious point (or, rather, the *En Sof* [limitless] clave its own ether and disclosed this point), Yod. When this expanded, that which was left of the mysterious AWIR (ether) was found to be AWR (light)."[34] This process manifests itself in the radiance of the Shekinah. Appropriately, the *Zohar*, as a "Book of Splendor," celebrates the Shekinah in a hymn of "splendor": "*Shekinah's* splendour / From splendour proceed[s]. / Its splendour sends forth / To the ends of creation; / In the fulness of glory / [It] is revealed in its beauty / To the eyes made seeing."[35]

Such hymns to the Shekinah extend into the cabbalistic literature of the sixteenth and seventeenth centuries. In his "Hymn to the *Shekinah*," the sixteenth-century mystic Isaac Luria accordingly celebrates the "Bride" whose "lights" and "streams" "go forth": "With her King who / hovers above her / crown above crown in / Holy of Holies / this lady all worlds are / formed in / all's sealed / Within her." According to Ḥayyim Vital, the disciple of Luria, the Shekinah as Infinite Light provides the means by which those imbued with the wisdom of the emanations may enter the Holy of Holies to behold the absolute Center of Light.[36] Implicit in such works as Paulus Ricius's *Portae Lucis* (1516), doctrines of this kind were appropriated into the mainstream of Renaissance thought by figures like Pico della Mirandola and Johann Reuchlin. They formed the basis of the writings of Fludd, referred to in the previous chapter, and had an impact upon the Cambridge Platonists.[37] To assess their influence, however, one need hardly embark upon a *conjectura cabbalistica*. As already observed in the works of Gregory, Mede, Taylor, and Strickland, among others, the Shekinah flourished as a commonplace doctrine in the standard exegetical treatises and sermons of Milton's day. In all these works, one point emerges: God's Dwelling Presence within the Tabernacle and Temple is expressed as a luminous theophany of utmost radiance and splendor. When Christianus Adrichomius wrote a *Description of Hierusalem*, he said of the ark of the covenant, "set in the middest of the holy of holyest," that it "shin[ed] like the sun."[38] So conceived, his description is perfectly in accord with the biblical pattern of embodying God's luminous presence in cultic form. Illuminated Bibles of the Renaissance repeatedly attest to the impact that such an idea had upon the visual imagination. In biblical illustration, the luminous presence characteristically moves from natural to cultic representation: it assumes the form of a radiant Tetragrammaton in the process of creation (figures 10 and 11); it appears to Moses in all its splendor in the burning bush (figure 7) and before the mount (figure 6); it emanates brilliantly from the tent of the congregation, within which the ark of the covenant is ablaze with light (figure 12).

That Milton would have been sensitive to the kind of luminous experience that these theophanies represent may be seen in his own renderings of the Dwelling Presence throughout his career. Calling upon "the ever-begotten light" in *Animadversions*, he hails "the redoubled brightness of . . . [God's] descending cloud that now covers . . . [his] Tabernacle." "Who is there," Milton asks, "that cannot trace thee now in thy beamy walke through the midst of thy Sanctuary, amidst those golden *candle-sticks* . . . [with] their starry light[?] . . . Come therefore O thou that hast the seven starres in thy right hand, appoint thy chosen *Preists* according to their Orders, and courses of old, to minister before thee, and duely to dresse and powre out the consecrated oyle into thy holy and ever-burning lamps; thou hast sent out a spirit of prayer upon thy servants over all the Land to this effect, and stirr'd up their vowes as the sound of many waters about thy Throne" (*CM*, 3:146–47).[39] In his hallowing of the Light in *Paradise Lost*, Milton establishes precisely this context to worship before the Shekinah. Such is not surprising considering the cultic impulse that pervades Milton's epic. In response to the "Presence Divine," Adam, as demonstrated earlier, desires to "rear / So many grateful Altars" of "grassie Terf" and "lustr[ous]" "Stone" to "worship," as well as to commemorate, God's "bright appearances" (11.315–33). This desire, in turn, is fully replicated in human history in the Israelites' act of providing a habitation where God's presence might appropriately dwell.

In accord with that act, Milton recounts with obvious relish the inauguration of the Tabernacle cult later in his epic:

> . . . Thus Laws and Rites
> Establisht, such delight hath God in Men
> Obedient to his will, that he voutsafes
> Among them to set up his Tabernacle,
> The holy One with mortal Men to dwell;
> By his prescript a Sanctuary is fram'd
> Of Cedar, overlaid with Gold, therein
> An Ark, and in the Ark his Testimony
> The Records of his Cov'nant, over these
> A Mercie-seat of Gold between the wings
> Of two bright Cherubim, before him burn
> Seaven Lamps as in a Zodiac representing

FIGURE 10. "Let There Be Light."
Reproduced from a sixteenth-century engraving of Genesis 1:3
in the Kitto Bible, 1:43, by permission of the Huntington Library,
San Marino, California.

The Heav'nly fires; over the Tent a Cloud
Shall rest by Day, a fiery gleam by Night.
(12.244–57)

In keeping with the hymn to "the ever-begotten light" that graces *Animadversions*, it is precisely from this cultic lore that Milton derived so many of the elements of his *visio Dei* in *Paradise Lost*. As such, God is envisioned as a "holy" and "clouded Ark" (12.332–33, 340), a veritable "אֲרוֹן הָאֱלֹהִים," "ark of God, whose name is called by the name of the Lord of hosts that dwelleth *between* the cherubims [הַכְּרֻבִים עָלָיו יֹשֵׁב יְהוָה צְבָאוֹת שֵׁם] (2 Sam. 6:2). A "*Jehovah* thundering out of *Sion* thron'd / Between the Cherubim" (1.386–87), he is "Shrin'd in his Sanctuarie of Heav'n secure" (6.671–72). (Compare the reference in *Samson Agonistes* to "our living Dread who dwells / In *Silo*, his bright Sanctuary" [1673–74].) There, in his "radiant Shrine" (3.379), his "Holy of

FIGURE 11. "A Firmament in the Midst of the Waters."
Reproduced from a sixteenth-century engraving of Genesis 1:6
in the Kitto Bible, 1:43, by permission of the Huntington Library,
San Marino, California.

Holies" (cf. PR, 4.347–49), he "dwells" upon his "Mercie-seat" (11.2).
Beneath him lies "the Glassie Sea" (7.619), what Milton in *Animadver-*
sions called "the waters about . . . [his] Throne"; "nightly before him"
"burn" the "golden Lamps" (5.713); "fuming from Golden Censers"
and the "Golden Altar" rise "the incense Clouds" (7.600–601, 11.18,
24). His own Son becomes a "Priest" (11.25) who propitiates before him
(11.20–21). Veiled within his "Oracle" (1.12; cf. 3.378), the "הבית
דביר," he communes as "a voice / From midst a Golden Cloud" (6.27–
28). Surrounded by the angels of the presence, "neerest to his Throne"
(3.649),[40] he emits a light so dazzling "that brightest Seraphim / Approach not, but with both wings veil thir eyes" (3.381–82). Such is Milton's vision of the Shekinah as it dwells within what he calls in *Christian*
Doctrine the "*habitaculum Dei*": here, says Milton, citing 1 Timothy
6:16, "Deus quem nemo potest videre, lucem habitat inaccessam" (*CM*,
15:28).

FIGURE 12. Ark of the Covenant.
Reproduced from an engraving by Pieter Persoy
(late seventeenth century) in the Kitto Bible, 19:3451, by permission of
the Huntington Library, San Marino, California.

As an expression of the Shekinah that dwells, it is this "unapproached
light / Dwelt from Eternitie" (3.4–5) that Milton worships in his hymn
to the Light in the proem to Book 3 of *Paradise Lost*. There, Milton
engages in his own Tabernacle cult and formulates his own "entrance
liturgy" before the Shekinah.[41] That, as he proclaims in *The Reason of
Church-Government*, is how he would "celebrate in glorious and lofty
Hymns the throne and equipage of Gods Almightinesse" (*CM*, 3:238).
Doing so, he fulfills his role as sacer vates, as one whose entire veneration
of the holy comes about "by devout prayer to that eternall Spirit who can
enrich with all utterance and knowledge, and sends out his Seraphim
with the hallow'd fire of his Altar to touch and purify the lips of whom he
pleases" (*CM*, 3:241). The allusion to Isaiah 6:6–7 is particularly apt

in this instance because it is by means of the later prophets like Isaiah that Milton derives his own impetus for transforming cultic precedence (worship of the Shekinah in the sanctuary) into visionary form (the visio Dei). In order to assess the full impact of that process of transformation, one should explore in some detail visionary renderings of the Shekinah among the prophets and the traditions that evolved from those renderings. Accompanying that exploration, appropriate biblical illustrations will suggest something of the Renaissance visual background that such renderings inspired. An investigation of the visionary renderings and their traditions, bolstered by appropriate plates, should help to provide a fuller understanding of the nature of the Shekinah in *Paradise Lost*.

One may begin with the passage from Isaiah that Milton is so fond of invoking. The full rendering of Isaiah's visio Dei (see figure 13) is as follows: "I saw . . . the Lord sitting upon a throne [ישב אל-כסא], high and lifted up, and his train filled the temple [ושוליו מלאים את-ההיכל]. Above it stood the seraphims: each one had six wings; with twain he covered his face, and with twain he covered his feet, and with twain he did fly: And one cried unto another, and said, Holy, holy, holy, *is* the Lord of hosts: the whole earth *is* full of his glory [מלא כל-הארץ כבודו קדוש קדוש קדוש יהוה צבאות]. And the posts of the door moved at the voice of him that cried, and the house was filled with smoke" (Isa. 6:1–4). The "throne" (כסא) upon which Isaiah beholds the Lord "sitting" (ישב) is, of course, none other than the כפרת (Septuagint: ἱλαστήριον ἐπίθεμα; Vulgate: *propitiatorium*) upon which the Shekinah dwells. To suggest the immensity of the vision, Isaiah says that God's "train filled the temple" and that "the whole earth is full of his glory": this "fullness" (מלוא)—one thinks of the Hermetic *pleroma*—expresses itself in the dazzling radiance of the Shekinah, specifically, its כבוד, which illuminates not only the Temple but the entire world.[42] At the same time, the Shekinah assumes the form of the ineffable name (צבאות יהוה), which designates God's presence in the ark and which is celebrated appropriately in the trisagion or kedusha (קדוש קדוש קדוש), because, after all, this is the God whose name is "Holy" (Isa. 57:15). That fact is proclaimed by the "seraphims" (Isaiah's counterpart to the "cherubims" that shadow the Mercy-Seat), who intone their own liturgy, while veiling themselves with their wings against the radiance of the Shekinah and who purify the "lips" of the prophet with "a live coal" from off the "altar" (המזבח) (Isa. 6:5–7).[43] That altar, in turn, recalls the "altar of burnt offering" upon which "first-fruits" were offered up (Exod. 40:29), as the priest took "a censer full of burning coals of fire from off the altar before the Lord" and placed it upon the "incense altar"

FIGURE 13. Isaiah's Vision of God.
Reproduced from an engraving of Isaiah 6:1 by Gerrit Adriaensz
(early seventeenth century) in the Kitto Bible, 25:4719, by permission of
the Huntington Library, San Marino, California.

in an act of propitiation (Lev. 16:12–13). (Compare the Son's act of of-fering up man's "first fruits" in his "Golden Censer, mixt / With Incense" before "the Fathers Throne" in *Paradise Lost* [11.17–26].)

Isaiah's cosmic vision of the radiant Shekinah finds its counterpart in Ezekiel's vision of the chariot (see figures 14 and 15). In his encounter with the Shekinah, Ezekiel beholds "a whirlwind, . . . a great cloud, and a fire infolding itself, and a brightness [ורגה] *was* about it, and out of the midst thereof as the colour of amber [החשמל], out of the midst of the fire." Within that vision, Ezekiel sees "the likeness of four living crea-tures," each with "four faces" and "four wings." "As for the likeness of the living creatures, their appearance *was* like burning coals of fire, *and* like the appearance of lamps: it went up and down among the living crea-tures: and the fire was bright, and out of the fire went forth lightning." "Now," says Ezekiel,

> as I beheld the living creatures, behold one wheel upon the earth by the living creatures, with his four faces. The appearance of the wheels and their work *was* like unto the colour of a beryl . . . and their appearance and their work *was* as it were a wheel in the middle of a wheel. . . . As for their rings, they . . . were full of eyes [עינים] round about them four. . . . And the likeness of the firmament upon the heads of the living creatures *was* as the colour of the terrible crystal [הקרח הנורא], stretched forth over their heads above. . . . And when they went, I heard the noise of their wings, like the noise of great waters, as the voice of the Almighty, the voice of speech. . . . And there was a voice from the firmament that *was* over their heads. . . . And above the firmament was the likeness of a throne [כסא], as the appearance of a sapphire stone: and upon the likeness of the throne *was* the likeness as the appearance of a man above upon it. And I saw as the colour of amber [חשמל], as the appearance of fire round about within it, from the appearance of his loins even up-ward, and from the appearance of his loins even downward, I saw as it were the appearance of fire, and it had brightness [נגה] round about. As the appearance of the bow that is in the cloud in the day of rain, so *was* the appearance of the brightness round about. This *was* the appearance of the likeness of the glory of the Lord [כבוד-יהוה]. And when I saw it, I fell upon my face. (Ezek. 1:4–28)

Ezekiel's remarkable vision is too complex to analyze here in its en-tirety, but like Isaiah, Ezekiel resorts to the paraphernalia of the Temple in order to fashion his own visio Dei. Specifically, he attributes cosmic proportions to what 1 Chronicles 28:18 calls "the chariot of the cheru-

FIGURE 14. Ezekiel's Vision of God.
Reproduced from a rendering of Ezekiel 1 in Biblia sacra (1566),
by permission of the Newberry Library, Chicago, Illinois.

רמות חיות אשר נראהו גראהו ליחזקאל Ezech. I: 5.
Ezechiels vision
Beschreibung der thiere, welche Ezechiel im gesicht gesehn hatt
B. Picart del.

CONSPECTVS ANIMALIVM EZECHIELI OBLATVS.
La figure des animaux representez à Ezechiel.
Beeltenis der dieren van Ezechiel gezien.

FIGURE 15. "The Likeness of Four Living Creatures."
Reproduced from an engraving of Ezekiel 1:5 by B. Picart
(seventeenth century) in the Kitto Bible, 26:4938, by permission of
the Huntington Library, San Marino, California.

bims [הכרבים המרכבה], that spread out *their wings* and covered the ark of the covenant of the Lord [על-ארון ברית-יהוה]." This הכרבים המרכבה in Ezekiel appears as an overwhelming theophany of light, like Isaiah's vision, a manifestation of divine glory (כבוד), a veritable electrum (the idea suggested by החשמל) that bursts forth with dazzling brightness (נגה) and dumbfounds the seer. Such for Ezekiel is the כבוד-יהוה, as he dwells upon the כסא. Assimilating the "burning coals" and the "lamps" of the sanctuary, the cherubim (Ezekiel's counterpart of those that shadow the Mercy-Seat) bear up the ארון as a chariot (cf. Sir. 49:8). "Full of eyes" (עינים), they become the vehicle of Ezekiel's visio Dei. Before this spectacle of fire and lightning, Ezekiel not only beholds the theophany but hears the "voice" that comes forth from the "oracle," as Moses himself communed with the Shekinah in the Tabernacle.

As is well known, Milton's fascination with the vision resulted in his elaborate account of "the Chariot of Paternal Deitie" in *Paradise Lost* (6.750). The chariot appears

> Flashing thick flames, Wheel within Wheel undrawn,
> It self instinct with Spirit, but convoyd
> By four Cherubic shapes, four Faces each
> Had wondrous, as with Starrs thir bodies all
> And Wings were set with Eyes, with Eyes the wheels
> Of Beril, and careering Fires between;
> Over thir heads a chrystal Firmament,
> Whereon a Saphir Throne, inlaid with pure
> Amber, and colours of the showrie Arch.
>
> (6.751–59)

On this "Chrystallin Skie, in Saphir Thron'd" between "the wings of Cherub," the Son rides "sublime" (6.771–72) in "Celestial Panoplie all armd / Of radiant *Urim*, work divinely wrought" (6.760–61).

Milton's description of the chariot with the Son upon it, of course, is made in the context of the War in Heaven, a subject that will receive full treatment in chapter 11. For the time being, it is sufficient to point out the extent to which Milton drew upon Ezekiel's vision of the Shekinah in order to render his own visio Dei. It is no accident that when Milton addressed himself to the subject of the "*divinae gloriae*" in *Christian Doctrine*, he marshaled his proof-texts in such a way as to indicate precisely the sense of theophanic evolution that has informed this discussion all along. His citing of the passages from Exodus and 1 Kings suggests theophanies both natural and cultic. Along with these, however, he includes Isaiah 6 and Ezekiel 1, among others, to suggest the transformation of the cultic into the visionary. His final proof-text in this series is none other than Revelation 4 (*CM*, 14:60–61). As Milton well knew, that vision is of consummate importance in coming to terms with the assimilation of cultic material into a visionary form (see figure 16).

For that purpose, Saint John the Divine drew upon not only the visions of Isaiah and Ezekiel dealt with here but other visions, such as Daniel's theophany of the "Ancient of days" (Dan. 7:9–14), as well.[44] Once again, the cultic basis that underlies the vision of the Shekinah remains paramount. "I looked," says Saint John the Divine,

> and, behold, a door *was* opened in heaven: and the first voice which I heard *was* as it were of a trumpet talking with me; which said, Come up hither. . . . And immediately I was in the spirit; and, behold, a throne [θρόνος] was set in heaven, and *one* sat on the throne [ἐπὶ τοῦ θρόνου καθήμενος]. And he that sat was to look upon like a jasper and a sardine: and *there was* a rainbow round about the throne in sight like unto an emerald. . . . And out of the throne proceeded lightnings and thunderings and voices: and *there were* seven lamps of fire burning before the throne, which are the seven Spirits of God. And before the throne *there was* a sea of glass like unto crystal: and in the midst of the throne, and round about the throne, *were* four beasts full of eyes before and behind. . . . And the four beasts had each of them six wings about *him*; and *they were* full of eyes within: and they rest not day and night, saying, Holy, holy, holy [ἅγιος, ἅγιος, ἅγιος], Lord God Almighty, which was, and is, and is to come. (Rev. 4:1–8)

It is apparent here what Saint John the Divine appropriates from both Isaiah and Ezekiel. From the first prophet, he draws the general character of the Lord sitting upon the throne, as well as the angelic celebration of the Lord through the liturgy of the kedusha or trisagion ("ἅγιος, ἅγιος, ἅγιος"). From the second prophet, he draws similar characteristics of the throne flanked by angelic attendants, the description of which is a combination of Isaiah and Ezekiel. Recalling God's placing his "bow in the cloud" as "a token" of his "covenant" (Gen. 10:13), the reference to the "rainbow," of course, is drawn from Ezekiel's comparable image (Ezek. 1:28), one to which Milton himself alludes in his description of the "Chariot" with its "Throne, inlaid with pure / Amber, and colours of the showrie Arch." Like the theophanies of both Isaiah and Ezekiel, that of Saint John the Divine is awesome in its depiction of the throne as a fiery place of "lightnings and thunderings," not to mention an oraculous place of "voices." Developing what is implicit in the earlier prophets, his vi-

FIGURE 16. Saint John the Divine's Vision of God.
Reproduced from an engraving of Revelation 4 by Matthaeus Meriam
in [Veteris et Noui Testamenti] (1627), by permission of
the Newberry Library, Chicago, Illinois.

sion is that of a distinctly heavenly sort: he is, after all, talking about "things which must be hereafter" (Rev. 4:1). His concern, of course, is eschatological: the Shekinah he envisions looks forward to the παρουσία. Nonetheless, it still draws its primary inspiration from the Tabernacle and Temple cult that influenced the earlier prophets and that formed the basis of the "Presence Divine" that so influenced Milton's conception of the godhead in *Paradise Lost*.

The extent to which such is the case may be seen in an examination of the cultic elements in Saint John the Divine's vision and the relation of those elements to the Miltonic perspective. For example, in Saint John the Divine's references to the "seven lamps of fire burning before the throne" and the "sea of glass like unto crystal," likewise "before the throne," the first suggests the lamps of the candlestick placed before the Shekinah to "burn continually" (Exod. 40:24–25; Lev. 24:2; 1 Kings 7:49; 2 Chron. 4:20; cf. figure 10); the second suggests the "sea" of water used by the priests for purification (Exod. 40:30–32; 1 Kings 7:23; 2 Chron. 4:2–6; see figure 15). The first was already transformed by Zechariah into "the eyes of the Lord, which run to and fro through the whole earth" (Zech. 4:10). These, in turn, become the angels of the presence (Rev. 8:2; Tob. 12:15). (Compare Milton's Uriel, "the fire of God," who guards the sun: he is "one of the seav'n / Who in Gods presence, neerest to his Throne / Stand ready at command, and are his Eyes / That run through all the Heav'n, or down to th'Earth" [3:648–51].)[45] In later commentaries (particularly those of Philo and Josephus), the candelabrum (מנורה) takes on planetary symbolism: it becomes the very embodiment of the heavenly zodiac within a Tabernacle which is itself the symbol of the cosmos. The central candlestick is the sun, which provides light to all the other candles, and which, in its own way, symbolizes the Divine Light that emanates from the Dwelling Presence as it is enshrined in its Tabernacle.[46] The idea would not have been foreign to Milton. His Uriel, as an angel of the presence, guards the sun (compare both Raphael and Michael, likewise angels of the presence, associated with the constellations [5.272–83, 11.244–47]). In his creation account, Milton relates the way in which light, "enshrined" in "a cloudie Tabernacle," is placed in the "Suns Orb," which then, as a "glorious Lamp" (one that derives its own light, to be sure, from the "sovran vital Lamp"), provides light to the "other Starrs" (7.249–50, 359–62, 3.22). His conception is rendered in decidedly cultic terms: before "him" who "dwell[s]" "burn / Seven Lamps as in a zodiac representing / The Heav'nly fires" (12.254–56). Milton was no stranger to the cosmic elements implicit in the Tabernacle cult. As indicated, he knew both his Philo and his Josephus and admired them greatly.[47]

It is especially in Philonic commentary, however, that the cosmic elements are integrated into a complex mystical theology, by which the candelabrum becomes the "image of God." "For its light is the Light from God; it is Sophia or the Logos, the presence of God in the world at once as its ruler and as the priest leading the world back to God."[48] It, in turn, represents a stage in the movement toward the ark, which is the very embodiment of "Reality."[49] That is "the Presence, the One," from which "radiate all the lower manifestations," such as the Logos, the prime symbol of which is the central or "solar" "branch" of the candelabrum.[50] This fact is given impetus in later rabbinic commentary that associates the candelabrum with the Messiah: when the rabbis "discuss the menorah, they make it into a symbol of the light of halachic Judaism, the Torah which gives commands, inspires obedience, and promises a Messiah and a Messianic Age."[51] Thus, the *Pesikta Rabbati* asks: "What is meant by in *Thy light do we see light*? What light is it that the congregation of Israel looks for as from a watchtower? It is the light of the Messiah, of which it is said *And God saw the light that it was good* (Gen. 1:4). This verse proves that the Holy One, blessed be He, contemplated the Messiah and his works before the world was created, and then under His Throne of glory put away His Messiah until the time of the generation in which he will appear."[52] "When the Temple was destroyed," says the *Midrash Rabbah*, "the candlestick," along with "the ark, . . . the fire, the Holy Spirit, and the cherubim," "was [divinely] stored away." "When the Holy One, blessed by He, in His mercy will again build His Temple and His Holy Place," he will "restore" the candlestick to its messianic position.[53]

As it is assimilated into a Christocentric context, this messianic dimension is most graphically envisioned by Saint John the Divine himself: "I saw seven golden candlesticks," he says; "and in the midst of the seven candlesticks *one* like unto the Son of man . . . and his countenance was as the sun shineth in his strength" (Rev. 1:12–16; see figure 17). He is the one "who walketh in the midst of the seven golden candlesticks" (Rev. 2:1). Of him, Milton proclaimed in *Animadversions*, "Who . . . can not trace thee now in thy beamy walke through the midst of thy Sanctuary, amidst those golden *candlesticks* . . . [with] their starry light." "Come forth out of thy Royall Chambers, O Prince of all the Kings of the earth," continues Milton. "Put on the visible roabes of thy imperiall Majesty, take up that unlimited Scepter which thy Almighty Father hath bequeath'd thee; for now the voice of thy Bride calls thee, and all creatures sigh to bee renew'd" (*CM*, 3:148). The context, of course, is Revelation 21:2, 9 (the "new Jerusalem coming down from God out of heaven, prepared as a bride adorned for her husband"). At the same time, the cult of the candelabrum was sufficiently developed in Judaic mystical thought to accommodate such a vision as well. When the *Zohar* invoked Psalm 19:5 ("Which is as a bridegroom coming out of his chamber"), it did so to discuss the symbolism of the lighting of the menorah, with which it associates not only the "Sun," the "Torah of truth," and the "Tree of Life" (a name of God) but the "bridegroom illuminating his bride."[54] From this perspective, one can understand more clearly the significance of the candelabrum as cultic artifact to the Judaic perspective.[55] In the synagogue liturgy, the candelabrum accordingly becomes the recipient of all those benedictions that commemorate God as the creator of light: "Blessed art thou, O Lord, who formest light and createst darkness. . . . Yea, eternal light [אור עולם] in the treasury of life; for He spake, and out of darkness there was light."[56] The focal point of the Sabbath bless-

FIGURE 17. The Son of Man.
Reproduced from an engraving of Revelation 9 by Matthaeus Meriam
in [Veteris et Noui Testamenti] (1627), by permission of
the Newberry Library, Chicago, Illinois.

ing, it assumes especial prominence in such celebrations as the Festival of Lights.[57]

Such is only appropriate considering what has already been shown to be its importance to the Tabernacle cult. So conceived, it becomes a symbol quite in keeping with the kind of visionary milieu that Saint John the Divine provided for it. But the candelabrum is only one of the implements of the Tabernacle cult to which Saint John the Divine refers; the other is the "sea of glass." Recalling the "laver" set "between the tent of the congregation and the altar" (Exod. 40:30–32), the "sea of glass" represents another instance of Saint John the Divine's appropriation of a cultic object for a visionary purpose. In cultic terms, the laver, made of polished brass that reflected images in the manner of "looking-glasses" (Exod. 38:8), was filled with water "for Aaron and his sons . . . [to] wash their hands and feet" "that they die not" "when they come near to the altar to minister, to burn offering made by fire unto the Lord"

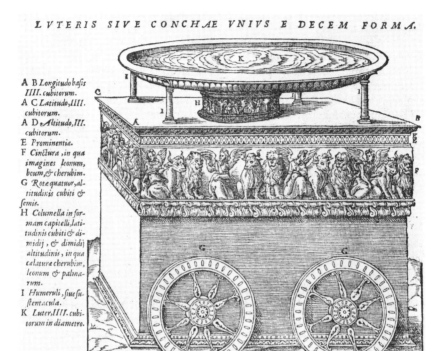

LVTERIS SIVE CONCHÆ VNIVS E DECEM FORMÆ.

A B Longitudo basis
IIII. cubitorum.
A C Latitudo,IIII.
cubitorum.
A D Altitudo,III.
cubitorum.
E Prominentiæ.
F Cinctura, in qua
imagines leonum,
boum,& cherubim.
G Rotæ quatuor,al-
titudinis cubiti &
semis.
H Columella in for-
mam capitelli,lati-
tudinis cubiti & di-
midij, & dimidij
altitudinis, in qua
calaturæ cherubim,
leonum & palma-
rum.
I Humeruli,siue su-
stentacula.
K Luter,IIII. cubi-
torum in diametro.

FIGURE 18. The Laver.
Reproduced from a rendering of 1 Kings 7, in Biblia sacra (1566),
by permission of the Newberry Library, Chicago, Illinois.

(Exod. 30:18–20). In the Solomonic Temple, the laver became "a molten sea" (1 Kings 7:23; 2 Chron. 4:2–6), used for the same purpose (see figure 18). As Saint John the Divine appropriates it, this cult object combines the elements of water and fire. As "a sea of glass, like unto crystal" (θάλασσα ὑαλίνη, ὁμοία κρυστάλλῳ) "before the throne" in heaven, it becomes the "sea of glass mingled with fire" (Rev. 4:6, 15:2). This fusion of water with fire recalls the practice of purifying oneself with water from the laver before approaching the altar of fire. The laver or "molten sea," then, is envisioned through the images of both water and fire.

As envisioned through the image of water, it suggests the firmament of heaven itself, the "hyaline" (ὑάλινος) or "sea of glass," mentioned above (Rev. 15:2). So Milton in Paradise Lost calls it "the cleer Hya-

line, the Glassie Sea" (7.619) above the "crystalline sphere" (3.483). A "bright sea" of "jasper" and of "liquid pearl" (3.518–19), it flows above that "Firmament" by which God divided "the Waters from the Waters" (7.261–63; Gen. 1:6–7; Ps. 148:7).[58] Such an outlook was already current in Midrashic commentary: "Of the third day we read, *Let* the waters *under the heaven be gathered together* (Gen. I, 9), and of the Tabernacle it is written, *Thou shalt also make a* laver *of brass, and the base thereof of brass, whereat to wash*, etc. (Ex. XXX, 18)."[59] In *Paradise Lost*, the association of "the Glassie sea" with the firmament likewise suggests the stellar realm ("Starrs / Numerous" [7.620–21]) beneath the hyaline: one firmament reflects the other. Within that context, the constellations enact their own process of worship before that laver, the sun: having drunk "the liquid Light" from its "cloudie Shrine" in its creation, this "Palace" of "Light" becomes the source of illumination for the constellations that surround it: "Hither as to thir Fountain other starrs / Repairing, in thir golden Urns draw Light" (7.359–65). One thinks of the *Zohar*: from "the Lord" who is "the center of all the supernal sides" issues the "fountain of the cistern, providing completion and nourishment for all." This is the "firmament" of "light" and "water" from which emanate the streams of illumination.[60] A Philonic idea as well, these streams of illumination or "Light Streams" are a basic constituent of biblical thought.[61] They recall the conflation of the "Fountain of life" and the beholding of the "light" in "light" implicit in Psalm 36:9. In cultic terms, they suggest the Pauline appropriation of the laver into baptismal purification and illumination (Tit. 3:5; Ephes. 5:26). Once again, we hail with Milton that "Fountain of Light" (3.378) and "pure Ethereal stream / Whose Fountain who shall tell?" (3.7–8) in his fervent prayer for purification, and we delight with him in invoking "*Siloa's* Brook that flow'd / Fast by the Oracle of God" (1.11–12) in his intense desire for illumination. The pool of Siloam, as discussed in chapter 7, found its counterpart in none other than the laver itself.[62] In that respect, the laver or "sea of glass" became the type of those waters that were said to have issued from before the throne and under the sanctuary. The idea had already been conceived by Ezekiel, who saw in such waters the source of a new paradise (Ezek. 47:1–2).[63] Drawing upon the same idea, Saint John the Divine maintained that he was shown "a pure river of water of life, clear as crystal, proceeding out of the throne of God and the Lamb" (Rev. 22:1). The idea no doubt had an impact upon Milton. In *Animadversions* he speaks of the "many waters" surrounding God's "Throne" (*CM*, 3:147),[64] and in *Paradise Lost*, those waters issue forth to create their own paradise, both heavenly (3.358, 10.285) and earthly (4.223, 454).

The "sea of glass," of course, encompasses not only the firmament of water but the firmament of fire. The one "mingles" with the other. Although the firmament of fire has already been explored to some extent in the discussion of the constellations, the idea has additional implications. Those implications may be found in Ezekiel's allusion to the firmament in his vision of the chariot, an apt point of departure, since the elaborate base upon which the "molten sea" rested in the Solomonic Temple was likened specifically to a chariot (see figure 18).[65] The firmament above that base, as indicated, *"was* as the colour of the terrible crystal [הקרח הנורא]" (Ezek. 1:22). Literally, the firmament assumes the appearance of an awe-inspiring crystalline substance that reflects the glory of the figure above it: sitting upon a throne, that figure is enveloped in fire (Ezek. 1:27). In *Paradise Lost*, this recalls the Son's chariot, which has a "chrystal Firmament" or "Chrystallin Skie" (6.756, 770) that presumably reflects the "illustrious" glory of that which "dwells" above—as well it should, since, in both cases, the crystal firmament becomes a symbol of the splendor of the Shekinah. It is in this sense that Saint John the Divine suggests that "the sea of glass" is "mingled with fire": "And the temple was filled with smoke from the glory of God, and from his power" (Rev. 15:2, 8). "Out of the throne" itself "proceeded lightnings and thunderings and voices" (Rev. 4:5). Reflected in the crystal sea beneath them, these awesome signs of God's incendiary presence remind us that we are never far from the frightening experience of the Sinai theophany. To witness these signs in the "sea of glass like unto crystal" is to be baptized *"with* fire" (Matt. 3:11) indeed. We are placed before the presence and witness "the fire" that comes "out from before the Lord," as the "burnt offering" is "consumed upon the altar" (Lev. 9:24). So Daniel envisioned the "Ancient of days" sitting upon a "throne" that is *"like* the fiery flame"; "a fiery stream issued and came forth from before him" (Dan. 7:9–10).

The consummate expression of the whole idea, however, is to be found in the pseudepigraphal Book of Enoch (1 Enoch). There, that "sea of glass like unto crystal" becomes a firmament of fire that manifests the Shekinah in all its luminous glory. Thus, summoned "into heaven," Enoch beholds "a wall which . . . [was] built of crystal and surrounded by tongues of fire. . . ." "And," Enoch says,

> I went into the tongues of fire and drew nigh to a large house which was built of crystals: and the walls of the house were like a tesselated floor (made) of crystals, and its ground work was of crystal. Its ceiling was like the path of the stars and the lightnings, and between

them were portals blazed with fire. And I entered into that house. ... And I beheld a vision, and lo! there was a second house, greater than the former, and the entire portal stood open before me, and it was built of flames of fire. ... And its floor was of fire, and above it were lightnings and the path of the stars, and its ceiling also was flaming fire. And I looked and saw [therein] a lofty throne: its appearance was as crystal, and the wheels thereof as the shining sun, and there was the vision of the cherubim. And from underneath the throne came streams of flaming fire so that I could not look thereon. And the Great Glory sat thereon, and His raiment shone more brightly than the sun and was whiter than any snow. None of the angels could enter and could behold His face by reason of the magnificence and glory, and no flesh could behold Him. The flaming fire was round about Him, and a great fire stood before Him.[66]

If any experience approximates the awesome quality of Milton's own visio Dei, it is Enoch's: in both, the accoutrements of Tabernacle and Temple are transformed into a vision of unbearable resplendence, awesome and dazzling in its radiance. The Book of Enoch is also significant because it suggests the way in which the kind of visio Dei depicted in Isaiah and Ezekiel had already been transformed in Jewish apocalyptic into a distinctly heavenly vision. The idea was an ancient one. As early as the Exodus narrative, such heavenly visions of God as that cited by Milton in *Christian Doctrine* were used to denote *divinae gloriae* (*CM*, 14:60–61): "And they saw the God of Israel: and *there was* under his feet as it were a paved work of a sapphire stone, and as it were the body of heaven in *his* clearness" (Exod. 24:10). In treating of "last things," Saint John the Divine also casts his vision in "heavenly" terms. What is implicit both in the Old Testament and in the New assumes graphic form, however, in such accounts as the Book of Enoch. Similar pseudepigraphal accounts follow suit.

In the Book of the Secrets of Enoch (2 Enoch), for example, the prophet is likewise transported to the heavenly spheres, where he undergoes a visio Dei in which he is awed by the enthroned Shekinah, whose "face" burned in light and whose "eyes" shone "like the sun's rays." In that process, the prophet is ecstatically transformed.[67] As Milton well knew, Saint Paul experienced no less an "ecstasis": "I will come to visions and revelations of the Lord. I knew a man in Christ above fourteen years ago ..., such an one caught up to the third heaven. And I knew such a man (whether in the body, or out of the body, I cannot tell: God knoweth;) How that he was caught up into paradise, and heard unspeakable words, which it is not lawful for a man to utter. Of such an one will I glory" (2 Cor. 12:1–5). The experience gave rise to such examples of Christian apocalyptic as the Apocalypse of Paul, in which the apostle, transported to the heavenly paradise, beholds God enthroned in a tabernacle of light and Christ dwelling in "the chariot of the cherubim."[68] With the confluence of Jewish and Christian apocalyptic, this vision is anticipated by earlier accounts like the Ascension of Isaiah.[69] In all such accounts, the prophet undergoes an ecstatic transformation as he is transported to the heavenly realm to behold the Shekinah enthroned in glory. This recalls the ecstatic experience that Milton himself undergoes in *Paradise Lost*: "Into the Heav'n of Heav'ns," he says, "I have presum'd, / An Earthlie Guest, and drawn Empyreal Air" (7.13–14). In that experience, he has been "rapt above the Pole" (7.23): "rapt," that is, in both senses of the term *raptus*. He is at once "transported" and "enraptured" in what he had elsewhere called "holy vision" and "ecstatick fit" (PA, 41–42).[70] In that state, he has beheld the throne of God in all its glory. With the angels, he has celebrated that "glorious brightness where . . . [God] sit'st / Thron'd inaccessible." With them, he has witnessed "the full blaze of . . . [God's] beams" and his "skirts" "dark with excessive bright" (3.378–80). With them, he has dared not approach but has had to veil his eyes, as he beheld the glory of God (3.376–81).

In portraying that experience, the Enoch pseudepigraphs (particularly 1 Enoch) have been for the purposes of this study especially helpful as analogues, because they suggest so remarkably that sense of historical continuity in Jewish apocalyptic by which the cultic elements associated with the Shekinah came to assume a uniquely visionary bearing. Although Milton certainly did not have such visionary material at his disposal,[71] he had an abiding fascination with the "translation" of Old Testament figures like Enoch into the heavenly realm to witness the glory of God dwelling upon the throne.[72] Needless to say, such a fascination formed the basis of Jewish mysticism, which, more than all else, is "throne-mysticism."[73] Although that tradition will not be explored in any depth here, it is useful to point out, however, that such throne-mysticism, as the expression of Jewish Gnosticism, represents an interesting counterpart to the Gnosticism considered in the last chapter.

Throne-mysticism, of course, is centered in Ezekiel's vision of the chariot: giving rise to various Hekhaloth Books that describe the הכלות, the heavenly halls or palaces through which the visionary passes in his pursuit of the throne of divine glory in the Heaven of Heavens, throne-mysticism focuses upon the Merkabah (the "Throne-Chariot" of Ezekiel). Extending in spirit back to the time of the apocalypticists and up through the Mishnaic and post-Talmudic periods, the Maaseh Merkabah tradition was assimilated into the Cabbala.[74] As J. H. Adamson has argued, the Renaissance was well aware of its existence, and at least in the form that it was received into the Renaissance, it had something of an impact upon Milton's vision of the "Chariot of Paternal Deitie" in Book 6 of *Paradise Lost*.[75] Whether or not such is the case, the Merkabah environment is not far from the ecstatic milieu that Milton provides in his epic. The seer ascends in awe before the throne and beholds the overwhelming splendor of the Shekinah. Thus, in the Book of the Hekhaloth (ספר הכלות) or the Hebrew Book of Enoch (3 Enoch), Rabbi Ishmael "ascend[s] on high to behold the vision of the *Merkabah*" upon which the Shekinah dwells. His guide is "Metatron," "the Prince of the Presence," who is Enoch. "As soon as the princes of the *Merkabah* and the flaming *Seraphim* perceived me," Rabbi Ishmael says, "they fixed their eyes upon me. Instantly, trembling and shuddering seized me and I fell down and was benumbed by the radiant image of their eyes and the splendid appearance of their faces." At this point, the seer is "to say a song before the Throne of Glory." Rabbi Ishmael's eyes are "enlightened," and he "utter[s] a song before the Holy One," and his song is answered by the Chayyoth, the angelic creatures which chant the kedusha before the throne.[76]

These songs are what Gershom Scholem, alluding to Otto, calls "Numinous Hymns."[77] "Unsurpassed in Hebrew hymnology," they constitute a "celestial liturgy" that includes such verses to the Shekinah as: "O wreathed in splendor, crowned with crowns, / O chorister of Him on high, / Extol the Lord enthroned in flames / For in the presence of the Presence, / In the inmost glory / Of the inmost chambers / You set up your posts."[78] One of the most magnificent of these "entrance liturgies" is to be found in a pseudepigraph of major import to the Merkabah tradition. Entitled the Apocalypse of Abraham, it recounts the way in which Abraham ascends to a realm of "light" that is "impossible to describe" but that contains "a fiercely burning fire." Within the fire, Abraham beholds "a chariot with fiery wheels, each wheel full of eyes round about; and over the wheels was a throne; which . . . was covered with fire, and fire encircled it round about and lo! an indescribable fire environed a fiery host." "Round about" the throne "all-seeing ones" and "under the throne four fiery living creatures" sing hymns to the presence, from which, in turn, emanates a voice at once "like a voice of many waters" and "like the voice of a man."

In response to this vision of light, Abraham worships by "recit[ing] without ceasing" the following song:

Eternal, mighty, Holy, El,
  God only-Supreme!
Thou who art self-originated, incorruptible, spotless,
Uncreate, immaculate, immortal,
  Self-complete, self-illuminating;
Without father, without mother, unbegotten,
  Exalted, fiery One!
Lover of men, benevolent, bountiful, jealous over me and very
  compassionate;

Eli, that is, My God-
Eternal, mighty, holy Sabaoth, very glorious, El, El, El, El, Jaoel!
Thou art He whom my soul hath loved!
Eternal Protector, shining like fire,
Whose voice is like the thunder,
Whose look is like the lightning, all-seeing
Who receiveth the prayers of such as honor Thee!
Thou, O Light, shinest before the light of the morning upon
  Thy creatures,
And in Thy heavenly dwelling places there is no need of any other light
  than (that) of the unspeakable splendour from the lights of
  Thy countenance.

Accept my prayer, likewise also the sacrifice which Thou hast prepared
Thee through me who sought Thee!
Accept me favourably, and shew me, and teach me,
And make known to Thy servant as thou hast promised me.[79]

As a "numinous hymn" before the Shekinah, Abraham's song dramatically attests to the universality of the vision that Milton so eloquently embodied in *Paradise Lost*. His own numinous hymns express the same sense of reverence, the same sense of adoration before a Dwelling Presence as awesome and as resplendent in its numinosity as it ever was in the traditions to which the worship of the Shekinah gave rise.

11
War

Among the res sacrae discussed thus far, none is more important to *Paradise Lost* than that of war. In fact, if one explores the genesis of Milton's epic, he will find that *Paradise Lost* has its roots in martial exploits of various sorts. As early as his poetic tribute to John Baptista Manso in 1638, Milton revealed the importance of such exploits to his future epic plans. Those plans involved the writing of a martial epic worthy of Manso's "*bellicâ virtute*" and the friendship of Manso with Tasso, the author of the *Gerusalemme conquistata*.[1] "I shall recall," Milton says, "our native kings in songs, / And likewise Arthur waging wars under the earth; / or proclaim the magnanimous heroes of the invincible table / with their covenant of companionship, and . . . / shatter the Saxon phalanxes under British Mars" (80–84). Elaborating upon those plans in the *Epitaphium Damonis* (161–70), he spoke of them again in the preface to the second book of *The Reason of Church-Government*. There, he suggests that he is in pursuit of a figure ("K[ing] or Knight before the conquest") "in whom to lay the pattern of a Christian *Heroe*." "And as *Tasso* gave to a Prince of *Italy* his chois whether he would command him to write of *Godfreys* expedition against the infidels, or *Belisarius* against the Gothes, or *Charlemain* against the Lombards," Milton proclaims, "it haply would be no rashnesse from an equal diligence and inclination to present the like offer in our own ancient stories" (*CM*, 3:237).

Expressing such an inclination, Milton was merely responding to the prevailing climate of his times, which, as John M. Steadman has made clear, expressed itself in the form of holy war epics that recount various crusades against the infidel and heretic. Had Milton written in this tradition, his epic would have been comparable in outlook to the *Jerusalem Delivered*, the *Conquest of Granada*, and the *Lusiads*. In its recasting of Arthurian materials, it would have patterned itself, of course, after its immediate forebear *The Faerie Queene*.[2]

But Milton's concern with holy war lay elsewhere. Disinclined "to dissect / With long and tedious havoc fabl'd Knights / In Battels feign'd"

(PL, 9.29–31), he opted for what he considered to be a "higher Argument" (PL, 9.42). This argument lay in delineating the holy wars not of medieval crusading knights but of the original saints of God doing battle against the Dragon. For that purpose, Milton found his "Christian Heroe" in Christ himself, that "most perfect Heroe" (PA, 13), and his epic model for portraying the warfare of the saints in the biblical wars of Israel culminating in the "majestick image" offered by "the Apocalyps of Saint John" (CG, CM, 3:238).[3] Deriving his inspiration from the divine source that prompted Moses to sing (PL, 1.8–10), he invoked his "Heav'nly Muse" (PL, 1.6) to "aid" his "adventrous Song" in transcending all other sources in its "pursuit" of "things unattempted yet in Prose or Rime" (PL, 1.13–16). To assess the particular mode of warfare that Milton had in mind in attempting to realize these goals, one must explore his ultimate source of inspiration, the Bible and its traditions. There, one will find a fully developed ideology of holy war that had a profound impact upon the attitudes toward war that emerged in Milton's own time and that manifested itself both in theory and in practice during his career as polemist and poet.

As Gerhard von Rad has recently made clear, it is the Bible more than any other work to which the concept of war as a sacral event is indebted.[4] His volume *Der Heilige Krieg* sparked a renewed interest in that topic, since given further impetus by a host of other scholars.[5] These historians of religion concur that in its biblical context[6] "holy war" refers to those "Wars of Jahweh" (1 Sam. 18:17: "מלחמות יהוה"), once memorialized in a national epic, the "Book of the Wars of Jahweh" (Num. 21:14: "ספר מלחמת יהוה"; cf. Josh. 10:13), no longer extant. A sufficient number of characteristics may be gleaned from available biblical texts, however, to provide a reasonably consistent view of what constituted the מלחמות יהוה. Ordained by God (Isa. 13:3), such wars were fought by God's people (Judg. 5:13, 20:21), sanctified (Josh. 3:5) for the purpose of overcoming God's enemies (Judg. 5:31). Before his "sanctified ones" (Isa. 13:3: "הקדשים") marched to battle, they consulted God (Judg. 20:23, 28), whose oracles revealed when it was time to go to war (1 Sam. 14:37). As a "man of war" (Exod. 15:3: "יהוה איש מלחמה"; 1 Sam. 17:45; "יהוה צבאות"), God himself marched in the van of the army (Judg. 4:14; 2 Sam. 5:24). His divine presence was manifested in the ark, which was the throne upon which he sat (1 Sam. 4:4) and which, like a palladium, was carried into battle for the purpose of overwhelming the enemy (Josh. 6:6; 2 Sam 11:11). God's warriors were certain of victory, for he had already "given the enemy into their hands" (Josh. 6:2). They had only to have faith in him and to be without fear (Josh. 8:1). It was

God who fought for Israel during the battle (Judg. 20:35). He drew upon the elements of nature (Judg. 5:20; 1 Sam. 7:10) and threw the enemy into confusion (Judg. 4:15), striking a "divine terror" into them (1 Sam. 14:15). Vanquishing his enemy, he would demand that the fruits of the victory be consecrated to him. This was the "חרם" (Num. 18:14; Deut. 7:2); through it, the enemy became "devoted," separated from profane use and subject to destruction. The day of victory was known as "the Day of Jahweh" (Joel 2:11: "יום־יהוה"), and the whole affair was accompanied by appropriate rituals of battle, such as the blowing of trumpets (Judg. 3:27), the singing of psalms (Exod. 15:1), and the cry of battle (1 Sam. 17:20). The act of war was sanctified by sacrifices before the battle began (1 Sam. 7:9), by a ritual purifying of the camp during the course of battle (Deut. 23:10−15), and by a processional return of the ark to the sanctuary, accompanied by festivals after the battle was completed (Josh. 4:21−24; Ps. 132:8).[7]

Dispersed throughout the Old Testament, these characteristics assume a formulaic quality in such texts as Deuteronomy 20, which sets forth the Israelite code of warfare; Numbers 2, which specifies the arrangement of the camp; and 2 Chronicles 20, which provides a compendium of holy war ideology in its account of the battle of Jehoshaphat against Moab. Other such battles that come under the heading of מלחמות יהוה include Deborah and Barak's victory over the forces of Sisera (Judg. 4), subsequently celebrated in the Song of Deborah (Judg. 5); Gideon's defeat of the Midianites (Judg. 6−8); and Joshua's victory over Jericho (Josh. 5 and 6). Many more could be cited, but scholars generally agree that the consummate holy war for the Israelites was the conquest of Palestine. Subsumed under that conquest were all those battles fought between the Exodus and the gaining of the Promised Land. In that sense, the redactors of Deuteronomy, at the end of the monarchy, present "the entire history of Israel" "as a holy war."[8] In that sense, "the conquest of the Promised Land" is viewed as a holy war, "as *the* holy war" in Joshua.[9]

Joshua 3−5, in fact, reenacts what Frank M. Cross calls the "ritual Conquest" or the Exodus-Conquest, "utilized by the Deuteronomic history and probably by an earlier traditionist to reconstruct the history of Israel's entry into the Promised Land." In the festival, "reconstituted from the Joshua materials," the participants are obliged to sanctify themselves, as if in preparation for holy war, or as in the approach to the sanctuary; the ark as battle palladium is then carried in solemn procession to the sanctuary of Gilgal; the Jordan, like the Red Sea, opens for the passage of the ark and the Israelites; twelve stones, emblem of the twelve tribes, are set up at the desert sanctuary of Gilgal. In the Joshua narrative, all this is preparatory to the Jericho battle, symbol of the entrance into the Promised Land.[10] These events, in turn, are prefigured by a war song known as "the Song of the Sea" (Exod. 15:1–18), sung by Moses after God's triumph in the Red Sea, an event singled out for celebration in the ספר מלחמת יהוה (Num. 21:14).[11] Applauding God's triumph, Moses' song combines "the march to Canaan, the conquest, and the eternal kingship of Yahweh with the motif of the miracle at the Sea."[12] The event becomes nothing less than a type of the great conquests that are to follow, culminating in the conquest of Palestine and the gaining of the Promised Land, where the people of the Lord will be "planted" "in the mountain" of his "inheritance," the place of his "Sanctuary," "established" by his "hands" (Exod. 15:13–17).

That ultimate conquest is, in turn, celebrated in the holy war psalms, notably Psalm 68, which fuses the motifs of the wilderness march, the Israelite conquests, the gaining of the Promised Land, and the establishment of the Temple. Recalling the ancient "Song of the Ark" (cf. Num. 10:35), "sung as Yahweh, enthroned in the Ark, went forth to holy war for His people"[13] and "march[ed] through the wilderness," shaking the heavens and the earth, the psalm celebrates God's military triumphs, his "chariots" of "angels," his acts of "wounding the head of [his] enemies" and his leading "captivity captive" (1, 7–8, 17–18, 21). It then culminates with God's presence "in the sanctuary," his "temple at Jerusalem" (24, 29). From that "holy place," God "rideth upon the heavens of heavens" and "send[s] out [his] voice," which strikes "terror" into all who hear (33–35). As aspects of the מלחמת יהוה, these motifs may be found time and again in the Old Testament. As late as Joel, the Lord is seen to "roar out of Zion, and utter his voice from Jerusalem," with a consequent "shaking" of "the heavens and the earth." In the process, he shall destroy Egypt and Edom, the ancient enemies of those who sought the Promised Land. Meanwhile, "Judah shall dwell for ever, and Jerusalem from generation to generation" (Joel 3:16–20).

The history of Israel's holy wars is the history of the Temple. When the Israelites sin, God turns his holy wars against them: he orders the Chaldeans to "fight against" Jerusalem, to "take it and burn it with fire," leaving "the cities of Judah a desolation" (Jer. 34:22). But always there is the promise of a restored Temple, a new Jerusalem (as in Ezekiel's elaborate vision, chapters 40–48) and a final holy war that will destroy God's enemies. "For, behold, the Lord will come with fire, and with chariots like a whirlwind, to render his anger with fury, and his rebuke with flames of fire," proclaims Isaiah (66:15). "Awake, awake, put on strength, O arm of the Lord," he cries; "awake, as in the ancient of days, in the generations of old. . . . Art thou not it which hath dried the sea, the waters of the great deep; that hath made the depths of the sea a way for the ransomed to pass over? Therefore the redeemed of the Lord shall return, and come with singing unto Zion" (Isa. 51:9–11). Jerusalem will be transformed into Eden, "the garden of the Lord" (Isa. 51:3), and God shall "create new heavens and a new earth" (Isa. 65:17). Before the restored Temple can be envisioned, however, God must first "cleanse the land," separating "holy and profane" (Ezek. 39:7, 12, 44:23). The "anointed cherub that covereth" must be cast out "as profane" from the "mountain of God" (Ezek. 28:13–16). "Lucifer, son of the morning" must be "cut down to the ground" for aspiring beyond "the most High" and "exalt-[ing]" his "throne above the stars of God" (Isa. 14:12–20). Gog and his army, coming from the place "out of the north parts" against Israel, must fall before the terrifying "presence" of God, who "will not let them pollute [his] holy name any more" (Ezek. 38:1–39:12).

Sounded in Isaiah and Ezekiel, the idea reverberates throughout Jewish apocalyptic. "The War of the Sons of Light and the Sons of Darkness" in the Qumran texts is a case in point. Conceived as a holy war in epic terms, this battle, like those conceived by Isaiah and Ezekiel, transforms historical reality into myth. All the trappings of the מלחמות יהוה are present. "The army is 'the people of God,' and the soldiers are volunteers called to fight the battles of God. In battle the standards are inscribed 'Right hand of God,' 'God's moment,' 'God's slaughter'; and God Himself, who is called 'The Hero of the Fight,' marches along with his faithful, accompanied by the army of angels. It is the Hand of God which is raised against Belial and his empire. Victory is certain."[14] The forces of God, led by Michael, defeat the forces of Belial. The battle is followed by a חרם and a processional return, accompanied by a "hymn of return," to the sanctuary. Recalling the Exodus motif, appropriate reference is made to God's having "done" unto these enemies what he did "unto Pharaoh and the captains of his chariots at the Red Sea." With victory comes the promise that an eternal reign of Light will begin. This will be a messianic age enjoyed by those who inhabit the New Jerusalem.[15]

In Christian apocalyptic, the consummate expression of holy war ideology is contained, of course, in the Book of Revelation. There, imbued with the "power" of "Christ," Michael overcomes Satan and casts him out of heaven (Rev. 12:7–9). "The Word of God," with his army of "saints," rides forth to crush "the beast, and the kings of the earth, and their armies," followed by the "binding" of Satan (Rev. 19:11–20:3). In "the battle of that great day of God Almighty," Saint John the Divine's own ירם-יהוה, the enemy is to be "gathered into" "Armageddon" (Rev.

16:14–16), the seat of Israel's holy wars (Judg. 5:19); Babylon is over-thrown (Rev. 18); and Gog and Magog are once again defeated (Rev. 20:8). All this occurs against a choric background of the angels' singing "the Song of Moses," that is, "the Song of the Sea" (Exod. 15:1–18), in celebration of God's holy wars (Rev. 15:3). That song, in turn, becomes "the Song of the Lamb," which, like its Old Testament antecedent, leads to "the temple of the tabernacle of the testimony" (Rev. 15:5). This is "the holy city, the New Jerusalem," conceived as a second Eden in the midst of "a new heaven and a new earth" (Rev. 21:1–2, 22:2). In Saint John the Divine, as in his predecessors, holy war takes on a cosmic, cultic, and finally apocalyptic bearing, as history becomes myth. If the Babylon of Saint John the Divine is Rome, if his holy warriors are the militant Church, his holy war is no less a product of the tradition conceived by the earliest compilers of the biblical text. By the time he sought to project the events of his era into a new rendering of the מלחמות יהוה, the characteristics of this tradition had already become commonplace, its ideology as old as the record of Israel's history. Nonetheless, its impact upon succeeding generations was immense indeed.

One need only recall the events of the Middle Ages and the Renaissance to recognize the significance of the holy war tradition in prevailing views of war that emerged during Milton's own time. The Crusades are a case in point. Canonizing Joshua, Gideon, Deborah, and Jael, the crusaders drew impetus from the wars of religion that permeate the Old Testament. Exulting in such battle texts as "Curse ye Meroz" (Judg. 5:23) and "Cursed be he that holdeth back his sword from blood" (Jer. 48:10), they saw themselves as reconquering the land of Canaan with Saint Peter as their "Jehovah of Hosts."[16] Theirs was a holy army, an army of saints, commissioned to do the Lord's will. "*Deus Vult*," they were said to have cried at Clermont in response to Pope Urban II's preaching of the First Crusade, as he linked together "pilgrimage and holy war."[17] Inspired by the "messianic ideal" that first began to take shape among the Israelites of the Exodus, they embarked upon a pilgrimage to that land heralded in the apocalypses of the messianic kingdom. They sought the Jerusalem of Isaiah, Ezekiel, and finally Saint John the Divine.[18]

When Saint Bernard preached to them in the early twelfth century, he used the precise language of the מלחמות יהוה to describe their calling. As "soldiers of God," they derive strength from "the Lord of Sabaoth," as Judas Maccabeus did when he counseled his men to have faith in the God who crushed the Pharaoh in the Red Sea (see 1 Macc. 4:6–11). "Such," says Saint Bernard, "hath God chosen to Himself and gathered from the ends of the earth as servants from among the bravest of Israel,

so that they may faithfully guard the resting place of the true Solomon."[19]
For the popular mind, their warfare became an "eschatological drama."
The enemy was Antichrist, leader of the hosts of Satan. "They were the
bright armies, 'clothed in white linen, white and clean.' Their final triumph was decreed from all eternity," and "their every deed" was not
only "guiltless" but considered "a holy act."[20] This is what Norman
Cohn describes as the "psychic content" of the "myth" created by the
crusading spirit. As different as it was in historical fact from what the
Israelite armies faced in the specific events that surrounded their warfare,
the ideology that emerged in the conduct of the Crusades is a product of
the מלחמות יהוה.

It was, in fact, so justified among the holy war theorists in the Church.
The Decretists resorted to the Old Testament wars as vindication of their
own wars, and associated their cause with that of the divinely chosen
Israelites.[21] In so doing, the Decretists "developed in effect a religiously
motivated just war," whereby the idea of holy war assumed "institutional
solidity as the just war of the Church." Begun by the Decretists in their
commentaries upon Gratian, the elaboration of crusading theory was
completed by later canonists through whom the crusade became a "juridical institution."[22] Just war theory was put to the service of holy war
ideology. The step was not an unprecedented one. Using the classical
terminology of the *justum bellum*, Saint Augustine "saw in Moses' wars
a just and righteous retribution." Joshua, in turn, became the minister of
God's justice and God the author of war. This *"bellum Deo auctore"*
provided the rationale for the development of holy wars and crusades
within the just war.[23] Although the Church was never particularly comfortable justifying the bloodshed of the Crusades, a holy war ideology
did emerge in the Middle Ages as a kind of juridical complement to those
who saw themselves as the hosts of God carrying on the warfare ordained
in the מלחמות יהוה.

If the messianic fervor with which those wars were undertaken influenced the medieval view of the *militia Christi*, this outlook had no less an
impact upon the centuries that followed. Among its primary manifestations was the creation of the messianic figure, the *propheta*. Deriving
impetus from such figures as Simon bar-Cochba and the apocalyptic
eschatology of such texts as Daniel, Baruch, Ezra, Revelation, and the
Sibylline Oracles, the institution of the propheta became inextricably
tied to holy war ideology. The living embodiment of the parousia, the
propheta was to realize, through apocalyptic battle, aspirations for the
New Jerusalem on earth. As Cohn has shown, prophetae abounded in the
Middle Ages. They included figures such as Tanchelm, Eudes de l'Étoile,

King Tafur, Emico, and Frederick II, among others. These chiliasts, in turn, anticipated later prophetae like John Ball and Hans Böhm. Influenced by Johannine or Joachite teaching, they gave rise to their own messianic kingdoms, whether at Tabor, Niklashausen, Münster, or Westphalia. Their presence incited revolution.

With Thomas Müntzer and his League of the Elect, the great peasant rebellion of 1525 resulted. The rhetoric through which Müntzer exhorted his following to fight is directly in the eschatological tradition. His sources were such texts as Daniel and Revelation. He would have his soldiers, who are "a holy People" and the "angels" of God, be merciless in destroying the enemy, breaking "their altars," and smashing and burning their "images." In that way, they will be like Hezekiah, Josiah, Cyrus, Daniel, and Elijah, who "destroyed the priests of Baal." Only in this manner can the New Jerusalem and the purified church be realized.[24] Luther, of course, had nothing but contempt and loathing for the entire enterprise. But even he looked upon the soldier as a divine instrument wielding the sword of God,[25] and his apocalypticism, which provided the initial impetus for men like Müntzer, was sufficient to justify wars of religion for many Protestants during the following century.[26]

The reforming zeal of the "holy warrior," however, had its mainstay in Calvin and his followers. Urging the saints onward, they "brought the theory of holy war to its logical conclusion." Their rejection of moderation "carried them further than Augustine had ever ventured."[27] As the aim of their struggle, there stood the reformed church, afterward the holy commonwealth and the New Jerusalem. Pursuing these goals, Calvinist writers eventually had recourse to the alternative medieval tradition of the holy war or crusade.[28] Ultimately, however, the source of the zeal that gave rise to revolutionary purges was to be found in the Levitical onslaughts ordained by God through Moses in the Old Testament (see especially Exod. 32). Those who engaged in these purges were "a special group of men to whom God had given special privileges and commands." They were the "holy warriors." Through them the Exodus and Conquest would be realized.[29] With its medieval counterpart in the Crusades, then, the reforming zeal of Calvinist doctrine has its origins in the holy wars of the Bible.

This fact is nowhere more apparent than in the holy war ideology that sparked the Protestant militancy of the sixteenth and seventeenth centuries in England and resulted in the English Civil Wars. In those wars, the entire background of holy war ideology was brought to the fore. They inspired the fervor of holy wars afresh, causing the Crusades to assume new meaning and the biblical precedent to come alive with renewed force. The association of the Civil Wars with the crusading spirit is hardly a new concept. In a seminal article, "Congregationalism: From the Just War to the Crusade in the Puritan Revolution," Roland Bainton painstakingly traced the transition from just war theory to holy war theory in the English Nonconformist tradition. Essentially, he argued that, like the crusaders, the combatants in the Civil Wars saw their cause as more than just: it was holy. Because the object of both wars was "the vindication of religion or of something invested with the sanctity of religion," just war theory alone no longer sufficed. Once again, it had to be put to the service of holy war, as divine authority was substituted for secular authority. For the Nonconformists at least, this substitution was enough to condone the act of taking up arms against their ruler. It made them crusaders in their own right, filled with a religious zeal to destroy the ungodly, who in this case happened to be the very person invested with the power to call war into being in the first place.[30] In that way, says Michael Walzer, "the analogue of the crusade" became the "revolution."[31]

Despite the objections that might be raised to this analogue, the fervor that the religious factor inspired is sufficient to suggest a comparison. It was so indeed for Anglicans and Puritans alike in Milton's own time. In his uncompleted *Advertisement Touching An Holy War* (1629), Francis Bacon suggests, in the very designation of the characters that he creates to discuss the subject, an association of the Crusades with religious excess. Whereas Bacon's position would have been that of the "Moderate Divine," Eusebius, the crusader's point of view would have been reflected in the "Protestant zelant," Gamaliel, on the one hand, and in the "Romish Catholic zelant," Zebedaeus, on the other. For Bacon, both zealots embodied the religious spirit of the Crusades.[32] Published practically on the eve of the Civil Wars, Thomas Fuller's *The Historie of the Holy Warre* (1639) is almost prophetic in its admonitions against the Crusades: "We may believe this tragedie came off so ill in the last acting, that it will not be brought on the stage the second time."[33] That "this tragedie" was so reintroduced in an altered form served only to heighten the irony of Fuller's statement, as his book was reissued during the tumultuous years following its first appearance.

Looking back upon the Civil Wars, Samuel Butler satirized the Puritans precisely in the tradition of the Crusades. In many respects, his *Hudibras* (1663–78) is a parody of the crusading zeal to which the religious fervor of the Puritans gave rise: they "in the Saddle of one Steed, / The *Sarazen* and *Christian* rid,"[34] commented Butler ironically. Viewing themselves as crusading knights, the Puritans, of course, would have maintained that they were serving Christianity, not destroying it along with the "sara-zens." For the Puritans, the Crusades served as a positive example of true religious fervor. Preaching "to the worthy Companie of Gentlemen, that exercise in the Artillerie Garden," the training ground for later Puritan activity, Thomas Adams invoked none other than Saint Bernard as one who helped foster the "great war between Christ the king of Ierusalem, and Satan the King of Babylon."[35] The Puritan soldiers nurtured such a view. As knights, these soldiers too were still imbued with the spirit of the Red Cross that waved in the banner of Saint George.

The ultimate source of their warfare, however, was biblical. The wars of Israel represented the very wellspring of their inspiration. From the Bible, they derived their primary impetus for engaging in holy war. In his *Bible-battells. Or the sacred art military, For the rightly waging of warre according to Holy Writ* (1629), Richard Bernard traces all holy wars —whether among the English, French, or Spanish—back to the Bible (pp. 158–70). Singling out such holy warriors as Joshua, Gideon, David, and Samson, he extols the Bible, above all other accounts, as the true source of understanding the nature of war. The Bible becomes a veritable textbook for the "art of Souldiery and military knowledge" (pp. 1–2, 9). He then goes on to provide a full description of Israelite warfare from biblical texts, including the arrangement of the camp, the manner of marching, rituals of preparation, engagement, and thanksgiving, and de-portment in victory. True to the spirit of holy war, he associates Israelite battles with cosmic and finally apocalyptic confrontations. The hosts of God are not only men and angels but the elements. Even God's enemies (whether the Egyptians or the forces of Satan) are his armies, which he uses either to test or punish his people (pp. 11–14). God's *speciall host* is his *trained soldiers, the Armie which hee hath in his Church for defence therof, or to send out against their enemies." "This Armie was the Israelites coming out of Egypt which are called *Gods host* and *Campe.*" That "host" was "the host of God, Christ their Prince and their Conduc-tor: His Lieutenant generall *Moses.*" Their "battell is not theirs but the Lords; and therfore the Lord was for them." "And as the Lord was glori-fied in victories by these, so will he assuredly be now also for His Church. . . . For albeit the beast must war with the saints, and for a time ouer-come, Reu. 11. 2 & 13. 7. yet at length shall the lambe with his elect, called, and faithfull preuail, Reu. 17. 14. He shall ride vpon the white horse with many crownes vpon his head, the armies of heauen also fol-lowing on white horses, as triumphing ouer all their enemies, for he is the King of Kings, and Lord of Lords" (pp. 21–23).

It is language of this kind that established the Puritan point of view in the coming wars. Treatise after treatise and sermon after sermon recapitulated these basic themes until they became ingrained on the consciousness of those who set about to fight the Lord's battles in true Bible-battle fashion. As such, they are nowhere more graphically articulated in the literature preceding the Civil Wars than in Samuel Bachelor's sermon *Miles Christianus, or the Camp Royal* (1625). The product of a "radical nonconformist" preacher attached to General Morgan's regiment at the garrison in Gorinchem, Holland,[36] *Miles Christianus* embodies the full range of sentiments that have come to be associated with the concept of holy war. The regiment is assured, for example, that like the "Campes" of the Israelites, their camps are "holy," for God is in their "midst" (sigs. A2ᵛ–A4ʳ). His *"Divine Majestie, or presence"* dwells among them in his "Tabernacle": "He who *walketh in the midst of the seven golden Candlesticks"* walks also in the midst of the regiment to which Bachelor preaches (pp. 31–36). Sanctifying God's "Sabaoths," this regiment may be certain of victory, for they fight God's wars, and he is their "Capteine" (p. 36). They, in turn, are "an armie of saints" (p. 46), joined together *"foederally* and by *league"* as "a holy people, by dedication holy" (p. 39). As such, they may be termed "holy leaguers" (p. 39). Holy in all things, including "their Camps and wars," they will overcome their unclean enemies by means of their holiness, which will "dazzle" the "sight" of their enemies. Deriving power from God, "who dwelleth in the *light* of holynes," they will "throw their enemies to the ground" and "make them fall backward" with the brilliance of their holiness (p. 40). For they wear the "armour of light" (Rom. 13:13), "which in truth so flasheth in the fore eyes of the world, and dazeleth them, that they are able to do nothing against them who wear it." This dazzling light is a "secret . . . force" (p. 42). It separates clean and unclean (pp. 44–45). It "casts down" the *"old Dragon"* finally in the heavenly battle in which Bachelor's regiment, as the host of *"Michael,"* fights (sigs. B1ᵛ–B2ʳ). In keeping with the holy war tradition, then, Bachelor creates his own version of the מלחמות יהוה. That his outlook is hardly isolated from the Puritan ideology that emerged during the Civil Wars may be seen upon further investigation.

Since those most critical of this ideology are occasionally the most instructive, they might be called upon to provide some initial insights. One who fought in the Civil Wars against the Parliamentary forces, Sir James Turner, should prove helpful. Civil War, he complained in his treatise *Pallas Armata* (1683)

> is the worst of all Wars, and that wherein there is not so much as the least shadow of *Civility*. This War arms Brother against Brother. . . .

In this War the Son thinks he doth a meritorious work if he betrays his own Father; and the Father conceives he super-erogates, if he sheaths his Sword in his Sons Bowels, because, saith he, he did not rise to fight the *Lords Battels*. . . . This sort of War sends Coblers and other Mechanicks to the Pulpits. . . . This converts Souldiers into Preachers . . . and metamorphoseth Preachers into Souldiers. . . . It tells them, they ought in their Sermons to summon Subjects . . . to rise in Arms against the Sovereign Power, because they are bidden *Curse* Meroz, *who would not come to help the Lord against the Mighty*: Yet very few of them can tell you, whether Meroz was a Prince, a City, or a countrey.[37]

Correspondingly, Abraham Cowley, in his unfinished poem *The Civil War*, satirized the parliamentary army as "hot-brained Calvinists" who place "their thundring Pulpits" " 'bove the Throne" and think themselves a "*Holy, Holy, Holy Hoast*."[38] Condemned by Turner and Cowley, these characteristics of Puritan fervor were fundamental to those who took up arms on behalf of the parliamentary cause.[39]

One need only consult what might be called the "war literature" to which the parliamentary armies were subjected. In the *Souldiers Catechism: Composed for The Parliaments Army* (1644), for example, the soldier is reminded that "God calls himself a man of war and Lord of Hosts." The parliamentary soldier, in turn, fights "the Lords battels" by "tak[ing] up Armes against the enemies of Jesus Christ who . . . make warre against the Church and People of God" (pp. 1–3). "We are not now to look upon our enemies as Country-men," *The Souldiers Catechism* exhorts, "but as the enemies of God and our religion, and siders with Antichrist" (p. 14). Destroying the unclean enemy, the faithful soldiers of God become "the Instruments of Justice, and the Executioners of Gods Judgements" (p. 22). According to *The Souldiers Pocket Bible* (1643), "*A Souldier must be valiant for Gods Cause*," "for the battell is the Lords, and hee will give [the enemy] into . . . the hands" of his faithful (pp. 2–3). Therefore, admonishes *The Souldiers Pocket Bible*, "*if we obtaine any victory, we should give all the glory to the Lord, and say* . . . The Lord is a man of warre, his name is *Jehovah*." "For the Lord fought for Israel" (pp. 13–15).

Such literature instilled in the parliamentary soldier a fervent sense of his own calling, a sense that extended beyond the Civil Wars to the very end of the Commonwealth and Protectorate. As late as 1659, the army published manifestoes referring to themselves as "the Army of God" fighting under "the Lord of Hosts" with the "Sword of the Lord" in their hands. Even then, they "own[ed]" God "as the Great Commander of [their] Armies, and General of [their] Forces, acknowledging him to be the first Worker among [them]," while, as *"Jehovah-jireh,"* he sits enthroned in his "Mount."[40] Fighting God's wars during the Civil Wars, the parliamentary soldiers appropriately looked upon themselves as the sanctified host of Jahweh doing battle against his enemies not in a local confrontation but in a war that represented an apocalyptic battle between the forces of Christ and the forces of Antichrist. The apocalyptic zeal of such sermons as Thomas Goodwin's *A Glimpse of Syons Glory* (1641) is characteristic of their feelings:

> The *God* of Peace shall tread down Satan shortly, and all that are of Satan. *Christ* is described in this *Rev.* 19 with his garment dyed in Blood, when he doth appear with many Crownes on his head; that notes his many victories: and his name was *King of Kings*, and *Lord of Lords*. And the Saints appeared triumphing with him, clothed with white linnen, and set upon white Horses; is that a cloathing for Soldiers? Yes, for the Army of *Christ*, that rather comes to triumph then for to fight. *Christ* fighteth and vanquisheth all these Enemies: and they come triumphing in white. . . . And this Citie that is described in the *Revelation*, shall have the gates alwayes open, in regard to the security that is there; no danger at all of any Enemy. (pp. 20–21)

Placing the conflict in this apocalyptic setting had already been anticipated by a host of commentaries on Revelation that provided a political context for what is, after all, a political work. "The wrath of the dragon produceth the warre of the beast; and Antichrists wars are the dragons wars: the dragon by and in Antichrist makes warre upon the Church." So Thomas Taylor maintained in *Christs Victorie over the Dragon* (1633). Extending apocalyptic warfare into history through references to the Gunpowder Plot, Taylor viewed these events, perpetrated by the pope as Antichrist, as stratagems that "the true militant Church of Christ" must overcome.[41]

Even more to the point is Joseph Mede's influential *Clavis Apocalypticae* (1627), later translated as *The Key of Revelation* and published by authority of Parliament in 1643.[42] In keeping with Joachim of Fiore, Mede felt that a spiritual awakening began to take effect in the thirteenth century among the elect and that this awakening betokened the time when the Beast was to commence its battle with the saints. As the Church of the righteous prevailed in this battle, the Synagogue of Satan declined and decayed. According to Mede, "the symbolic key to this inversely proportional progress and decline" was "the proper interpretation of the pouring out of the seven vials of wrath in Revelation XVI." Those vials, of course, allude to the plagues with which the Egyptians had been afflicted during the time of Moses as a prelude to the Exodus. With the successive pouring out of each vial "to sicken and weaken the Beast, the true Church waxed in strength." Each vial, then, is associated with a historical stage in the Reformation, extending from the reforms of the Waldensians, Albigensians, Lollards, and Hussites to Christ's Second Coming to judge the living and inaugurate the millennium.[43] For the England of 1643, such an interpretation had real currency. The English fighting on behalf of the parliamentary cause saw themselves in the mainstream of a holy war that had been going on for centuries and that would culminate in an apocalyptic eschatology. They thereby became part of an inevitable historical process that served only to intensify their fervor. This is certainly how Cromwell viewed himself, and he communicated that attitude to the host that constituted the New Model Army.

"God hath in several ages used several dispensations," Cromwell said, "and yet some dispensations more eminently in one age than another. I am one of those whose heart God hath drawn out to wait for some extraordinary dispensations, according to those promises that he hath held forth of things to be accomplished in the later times, and I cannot but think that God is beginning of them."[44] Accordingly, Cromwell saw himself as a "deliverer" in whom "the power of God" goes forth.[45] Those who followed him looked upon themselves, in the words of Lieutenant Colonel Goffe, as "a company of Saints," "chosen and called and faithful" in their battle against the "Antichrist." For that purpose, they consulted the Book of Revelation as one would consult a war manual. "And truly," says Goffe, "it appears to me very clearly from that which God hath set down in his word in the Book of Revelations—which is that word that we are bid and commanded to study and to look into, being the word which God sent by his angel to John, to declare as things shortly to be done."[46]

Although such religious fervor was not true of all soldiers who fought in the New Model Army and although the army was not without disruptions,[47] "the Ironsides was an elite corps, well-disciplined, fierce in battle, devoted to its leader, and filled with the same religious spirit which was the source of his own strength."[48] As Cromwell wrote to Parliament in 1645, his soldiers "are instruments of God's glory." "Our desires," he writes, "are, that God may be glorified by the same spirit of faith by which we asked all our sufficiency, and having received it, it's meet that He have all the praise. Presbyterians, Independents, all had here the same spirit of faith and prayer. . . . All that believe have the real unity, which is most glorious, because inward and spiritual, in the Body, and to the Head." "God," he concludes, "hath put the sword into the Parliament's hands, for the terror of evil-doers."[49]

Infused with this spirit, Cromwell's army marched forth to do the work of the Lord. In their ranks, it seems, "the tabernacle of the Lord ... was carried as in the ancient days among the Israelites, among the armed host, and rested between battles in the camp." Recalling their victories, John Owen later exclaimed, "God came from Naseby, and the Holy One from the west, Selah."[50] In accord with this view, William Dell maintained, "I have seen more of the *presence* of God in that *Army*, then amongst *any people* that ever I *conversed* with in my life. ... We have seen his *goings*, and observed his very *footsteps*: for he hath *dwelt* among us, and *marched* in the head of us, and *counsel'd* us, and *led* us, and *gone along* with us *step* by *step*."[51] Hugh Peter distinguished this army from other armies by saying that "whereas soldiers usually spend and make forfeiture even of the civility they bring into other armies; here men grow religious, and more spiritual-thriving than in any place in the kingdom."[52]

This sense of religiosity is apparent in a number of respects. The regiments of the New Model were conceived of as "gathered churches" with "a complete system of ecclesiastical jurisdiction" presided over by commissioned preachers.[53] "Cromwell's request to Richard Baxter that he organize the East Anglia cavalry into a church is well known."[54] The ideal of the regiments was to "combine together," to "embody" themselves or "incorporate into church-societies," "against the Antichristian powers of the world."[55] In the words of Bachelor, they sought to become "holy leaguers" like the Israelite hosts and finally like the army of saints envisioned by Saint John the Divine.[56] Even their detractors were impressed. "If you look upon his own regiment of horse," wrote an adversary of Cromwell about December 1644, "see what a swarm there is of those that call themselves godly; some of them profess they have seen visions and had revelations. Look on Colonel Fleetwood's regiment with his Major Harrison, what a cluster of preaching officers and troopers there is."[57]

The soldiers themselves went about preaching when they felt the call.[58] If they did not preach, they sang psalms before and after battle.[59] They were forever "discharging" their "pious invocations and exercises of addresses to the Divine Providence."[60] Cromwell paused with his army at St. Abb's Head to sing the sixty-eighth psalm, "Let God arise, Let His enemies be scattered."[61] "All important meetings of the General Council of the Army had the same religious character"; observing appropriate fast days, the officers prayed for hours on end.[62] For the army as a whole, "there were also at intervals Fast-days or Days of Humiliation."[63] In their expression of religious zeal, the army was, of course, guilty of excesses that are only too well known. Their destruction of church property is difficult to condone.[64] Encouraged by such works as *The Souldiers Catechism* (p. 21), they sought to destroy all idolatrous works that might hinder the progress of the Reformation. In holy war terms, they were once again the instruments of God obliterating the works of Baal.[65] Church property is not all they destroyed in their zeal, however. Few will sanction events like the massacre at Drogheda, although, according to Peter Sterry, this too was a product of the holy war against idolators and was to be seen as a characteristic of apocalyptic battle.[66] Apparently, the חרם was not absent from the Civil Wars.

When the army assembled for battle, they were a true holy war host. Their standards bore such mottoes as "*Cave, Adsum*" and "*Fideliter, Faeliciter.*" Their "field word" was "God with us," "God our strength," and "The Lord of Hosts." When they drew near the enemy, they gave a shout of rejoicing, much like the Israelites "going forth to the fight" (1 Sam. 17:20).[67] As they marched forth to battle, they were exhorted to bear in mind "the passage of Canaan."[68] They were indeed great marchers, at times "mov[ing] at the rate of ten miles a day for a week together."[69] In his description of their troops, Lieutenant-Colonel Richard Elton describes in elaborate detail their marching order as if he were describing the movement of the Israelites out of Egypt and into the wilderness (cf. Num. 33).[70] They looked upon their battles as divinely fought and divinely ordained. Writing to Parliament in 1645 regarding the battle of Naseby, Cromwell said, "When I saw the enemy draw up and march in gallant order towards us, and we a company of poor ignorant men, to seek how to order our battle . . . I could not . . . but smile out to God in praises, in assurance of victory, because God would, by things that are not, bring to naught things that are. Of which I had great assurance; and God did it. O that men would therefore praise the Lord and declare the wonders that He doth for the children of men!"[71] On another occasion of victory, he wrote to Parliament, "This is nothing but the hand of God itself, God will put it downe, for this is the day wherein he alone will be exalted; it is not fit for me to give advice, nor to say a word what use should be made of this more than to pray to you, and all that acknowledge God, that they would onely exalt him . . . and that you would take courage to doe the worke of the Lord. . . ."[72] If Cromwell was diffident about saying "what use should be made" of his victories, those who chronicled them, as well as all the victories of the parliamentary forces, knew precisely how they might serve to memorialize the holy war spirit for generations to come. The English Civil Wars gave rise to their own ספרים מלחמות יהוה in the numerous accounts that appeared during the course of the conflicts. These accounts created a holy war mythos that transforms history into vision and accords epic status to isolated events.

Parliament itself authorized such accounts. *God appearing for the Parliament in sundry late Victories Bestowed upon their Forces* (1644), for example, is a narrative that demonstrates how "the Armie of the Lord daily brings mighty things to passe . . . [and] shewes his power and mighty working with such evidence and demonstration, that it strikes and shines like lightning, even unto closed eyes, and extorts an acknowledgement, That this is the power, and the very Arme of the Lord" (preamble). Other accounts are designed to have the same impact.[73] One of the most detailed is John Vicars's *Magnalia Dei Anglicana. Or Englands Parliamentary Chronicle* (1646). In conception, design, and execution, Vicars's chronicle is truly a ספר מלחמות יהוה. The titles of the various sections that make up the whole are a case in point. They include *Jehovah-Jireh. God in the Mount, Gods Arke Overtopping the Worlds Waves*, and *The Burning-Bush Not Consumed*. The entire work is set within the context of man's fall, God's creation of the universe, the fall of the angels, the redemption through Christ, and the battle between the Church militant and the forces of Satan. These events frame the chronicle of the parliamentary battles (part 1, pp. 1–3). Those battles, in turn, are preceded by the "Song of Moses Paraphrastically and Metrically applyed" to the "purpose" of recounting God's wars, waged by "*Gods* English-Israel" against the profane enemy. As a result of those wars, God's victorious people shall be "planted" upon his "Holy Mountain," where God "dwells" in his "Sanctuary." Overcoming his enemies, "the Lord Jehovah, farre above them rose, / And tumbled them into the Pit . . . / . . . as deep as Hell" (part 4, sig. **4ᵛ). Once again, the panorama of holy war battle assumes both a cosmic and a cultic dimension. It is from this perspective, Vicars suggests, that one is to view the battles that he describes.

Vicars's description of the decisive battle of Naseby (1645), for example, is precisely within the holy war tradition. It is a divine battle fought by the "*English Israel*" as instruments of "the Lord of Hosts." Seeing the profane enemy display their king as one would an idol, Fairfax, like King Hezekiah, exhorts his army, "Bee strong and courageous (my brave Commanders and Souldiers) bee not afraid nor dismayed for the Kings Army, nor for all the multitude of his Horse and Riders that are come together; for . . . there are moe with us (wee having God our Friend) than are with them. With them is but an arm of flesh, but with us is the Lord our God, to help us and to fight out battails." At the precise point when God's aid is needed, it comes in the form of "Colonell *Rossiter*," who overwhelms the enemy with "fresh forces." The forces of God then pursue the enemy nearly thirteen miles, one of the longest pursuits of the war. After his account, Vicars celebrates God, to whom alone the victory is attributed. He, says Vicars, appeared to his Faithful as he once revealed himself to the Israelites, "glorious in holiness, fearfull in Praises and doing wonders. Triumphing gloriously and overthrowing both the horse and his rider" in the Red Sea. Following the victory, the hosts of God take part in "a day of Solemn Thanksgiving" and the singing of psalms (part 4, pp. 158–68).

Corresponding to Vicars's *Magnalia Dei Anglicana* is Joshua Sprigg's prose epic *Anglia Rediviva* (1647). In Sprigg, as in Vicars, the parliamentary battles are divine. Their source is "*Israels* warres in Canaan." Because of their transcendent nature, Sprigg must "accommodate" their action to his readers' limited capacities. His purpose, as he indicates in the proem to the work, is to reveal God's "Providence" (sigs. A6ᵛ–A8ʳ). His epic hero is Fairfax, who is transported in battle "like an Angell": "With what triumphs of faith, with what exultation of spirit, and with what a joynt shout of all the affections God is received into that heart, whose eyes he uses as an Optick to look through and trouble a proud enemy" (p. 42). He is praised as God's "instrument" through whom "the Almighty came Riding on the Wings of the Wind" (p. 313). As one of the *magnalia Dei*, the battle of Naseby becomes a holy war in its own right. Preceding the battle, the parliamentary army marches, much like the Israelite hosts, immeasurable distances to the scene of war (p. 46). As in Vicars's account, the battle itself is won as the result of divine intervention (p. 42). After the dispersing of the enemy, the army returns in triumph to engage in solemn festivities and the worship of God (p. 46). These events, Sprigg is at pains to point out, encompass three days: the first is Friday, June 13, when "a Councel of War . . . [is] called"; the second, Saturday, June 14, when the skirmishes occur; the third, Sunday, June 15, when the enemy is dispersed and the army returns in triumph. The significance of the time scheme is not lost: Sunday, says Sprigg, is the "Lords day" (p. 46). In its Christian context, the יהוה-יום appropriately assumes a sacramental bearing.

If Vicars and Sprigg are examples of those who chronicled the יהוה מלחמות in prose, George Wither represents one who celebrated God's wars in verse. As Wither himself indicates, his *Carmen Eucharisticon*

(1649) is in the tradition of those songs sung by Deborah, Moses, and David in praise of God's triumphs over his foes (line 10).[74] The immediate occasion of the song is the routing of the Irish at Rathmines by the parliamentary army under Lieutenant-General Michael Jones. For this occasion, Wither provides a specifically holy war setting: God strikes the enemy as he, "with his Host," "strook *Sisera*" "by *Kishon*-brook" (65–68) and as he overwhelmed the "*Pharaoh*" in the Red Sea (218). "Oh!" Wither sings,

> what pen, or tongue is there
> Fully able to declare,
> What, to us, GODS *Mercies* were
>   Since our *Champion* he hath been?
> Nay, who can half that recite,
> Which for us, in open sight,
> He hath done since *Nasby-Fight*,
>   Where, he, first, was plainly seen?
>
> He hath magnifi'd his *worth*
> In most glorious marchings forth,
> From the *South*, unto the *North*,
>   And, through all our *British-Coasts*;
> *England*, *Scotland*, *Ireland*, *Wales*,
> *Towns*, and *Fields*, and *Hills*, and *Dales*,
> *Sea*, and *Land*, him, justly calls
>   The Victorious LORD of HOASTS.
>   (137–52)

These events, finally, assume apocalyptic significance as they are cast in the form of a heavenly battle that overcomes the "*Dragon*, and the *Whore*" (376):

> *Mich'el*, and his *Angells*, there
> Threw their *Dragon-Cavaliere*,
> With his *Angells*, from out *Sphere*,
>   In confusion, to their owne;
> Where, unable to repent,
> They despairingly lament,
> And blaspheme with discontent,
>   *Him*, that hath such *mercy* showne.
>   (81–88)

With Wither, as with Vicars and Sprigg, the various battles fought during the English Civil Wars are transformed into divine conflicts that trace their lineage to the Old Testament מלחמות יהוה and eventuate in the apocalyptic warfare that is the natural consequence of holy war ideology and that characterizes Old and New Testament alike. Through the English holy war chroniclers of the seventeenth century, the tradition of the מלחמות יהוה is kept alive. In them, it assumes a stature perfectly in accord with all those ספרים מלחמות יהוה that provide a literary context for historical events.

That such should have occurred as a result of the English Civil Wars is not at all surprising given the sacral character of the ideology that informed the wars themselves. For the wars *not* to have been chronicled as holy wars by those in sympathy with their aims would have been a cause for wonder indeed. As an active participant in the events of his time, John Milton would have found this holy war environment with its biblical antecedents most conducive to his aims as a transcriber of divine events. Given these circumstances, he proved himself to be one of the greatest chroniclers of the מלחמות יהוה that the seventeenth century produced. The reason for this may be seen in an analysis of the way in which he drew upon the traditions of holy war and incorporated those traditions in his works.

Much has been written about Milton's detestation of war, and there is indeed a good deal of evidence to support that view.[75] Throughout his works, he expressed his repugnance for war as an institution resulting in "all this wast of wealth, and loss of blood" (S 11, 14). "Not sedulous by Nature to indite / Warrs" (PL, 9.27–28), he concluded, "for what can Warrs but endless warr still breed" (S 15, 10). He did not hesitate to apply such epithets as "abhorred," "cursed," "tedious and bloody" (R, CM, 3:60; TE, CM, 5:70) to war. His full descriptions of the horrors of war in *The History of Britain* are among his most graphic: war is seen as "a confus'd heap," parents killing children "to prevent the more violent hands of hostile injurie," houses forsaken and burned, the aftermath characterized by "silence" and "desolation," "not a man seen, all fled" (CM, 10:78–79). Coupled with this awareness is a corresponding emphasis upon the importance of peace. Indebted to the humanistic tradition that placed a high premium upon the works of peace,[76] Milton proclaimed, "Peace hath her victories / No less renown'd then warr" (S 16, 10–11). He counseled the leaders of his nation to be victorious in "the warfare of peace" by conquering their own ambitions (2D, CM, 8:241).

Peace was valued by Milton as much as anyone in the Renaissance, and yet this love of peace and detestation of war should not blind one to the extent to which Milton was imbued with the fervor of what he considered to be a just war undertaken in a righteous cause. For him, no war had a better claim to that status than that waged against the prelates and finally against the king in the process of reformation. As polemist, Milton cultivated a holy war ideology that manifests itself throughout his works.

In the antiprelatical tracts, for example, he adopted the posture of a holy warrior who would destroy prelacy with a rod of iron. Raising his voice in prayer against the prelates, he issues his own battle cry in the spirit of Psalm 68: "Let them gather themselves, and be scatter'd, let them embattell themselves and bee broken, let them imbattell, and be broken, for thou [God] art with us" (R, *CM*, 3:78). God has "chac'd them with sudden confusion and amazement before the redoubled brightnesse of [his] descending cloud that now covers [his] Tabernacle" (A, *CM*, 3:147). The ark has been brought forth to battle, and it has dispersed the enemy. In response to this event, God's "servants over all the Land" have been inspired: "their vowes" have been "stirr'd up, as the sound of many waters about [God's] Throne" (A, *CM*, 3:147). Infused with a reforming zeal, they sigh to be renewed. "Why else," asks Milton in *Areopagitica*, "was this nation chos'n before any other, that out of her as out of *Sion* should be proclaim'd and sounded forth the first tidings and trumpet of Reformation to all *Europ* [?]" He assures us with millenarian conviction, "Now once again by all concurrence of signs, and by the generall instinct of holy and devout men, . . . God is decreeing to begin some new and great period in his Church, ev'n to the reforming of Reformation it self" (*CM*, 4:340).

"O perfect, and accomplish thy glorious acts," Milton had exhorted God earlier; having brought us "thus far onward from *Egypt*," do not "destroy us in the Wilderness." When the Promised Land has been attained and God has established the future "Kingdome," Milton promises, "then shall all thy Saints addresse their voyces of joy, and triumph to [God], standing on the shoare of that red Sea unto which our enemies had almost driven us." Celebrating this deliverance, Milton will take up his "Harp" and "sing" for God "an elaborate Song to Generations" (A, *CM*, 3:147–48). Like Moses, he will intone the Song of the Sea. But, first, men must engage in the "wars of Truth" (AR, *CM*, 4:348) before the New Jerusalem can be built. All that activity involved in the construction of God's new Temple in *Areopagitica* (*CM*, 4:342) must be accompanied by a process of purification, a purging of the old. To this end, Milton saw himself as an "*Iconoclastes*, the famous surname of many Greek Emperors, who in their zeal to the command of God, after long tradition of

Idolatry in the Church, took courage, and broke all superstitious Images to peeces" (K, CM, 5:68).

As a polemist, Milton assumed precisely this role in his antimonarchical tracts and upheld the role zealously against his detractors in the *Defenses*. *Defensio secunda* is a case in point. There, he depicts himself as a holy warrior defending the activities of his compatriots, who are also holy warriors. To some extent, the role of polemist, for Milton, has its basis, if not in actual warfare, then at least in preparation for battle. Although the stories that Milton was enrolled in the Honorable Artillery Company of London[77] and that he was given the opportunity to be an adjutant-general in Sir William Waller's army[78] are undoubtedly apocryphal, Milton is at pains in the *Defensio secunda* to establish his military credentials. He boasts, for example, that in his younger days he was "neither unskilled in handling [a] sword, nor unpractised in its daily use." "Armed" with a sword, in fact, "he thought [himself] a match for any man" (CM, 8:61). As James Holly Hanford has established, his knowledge of military tactics was remarkable,[79] and no one who has read *Of Education* will forget the military bearing of the academy that Milton conceives or the fact that the very purpose of education is to prepare one in the office of war, as well as of peace (CM, 4:280). All this merely serves to bolster Milton's main point in the *Defensio secunda*, however. For Milton makes clear that rather than subscribe to "the service of the camp," he took upon himself the no less perilous task of upholding the "transcendent cause" and "defend[ing] truth" on behalf of those who actually did engage in battle: "defend[ing]" the "defenders" (CM, 8:13), he "laid low that redoubled satellite of tyrants," Salmasius, "hither deemed invincible." When Salmasius "defied" "the embattled might" of God's Englishmen, Milton "engaged him in single combat" and with the "stylus" as a "weapon" "stabbed the reviler to his heart, and bore off abundant spoils" (CM, 8:15). As such, he became a warrior in his own right, comparable to those "unconquered in the field" (CM, 8:9–11). This is the point that Milton makes in what he calls the "proem" (*proæmium*) to the *Defensio secunda* (CM, 8:18), which in a sense is his own epic chronicle of the holy wars that his country had recently undergone in its fight for liberty.

The idea is one that Milton had already sounded in the *Defensio prima*. Impelled by God's "clear command" (*manifesto numine*), the parliamentary army fought Charles I in "a holy war" (*bello sacro*) (CM, 7:6–7, 60–61). Those who did not fight were, like Meroz, "cursed" (CM, 7:61; cf. TE, CM, 5:38). Those who did fight are celebrated in the *Defensio secunda* as the holy army of God (cf. LF, CM, 6:103), "to its enemies in arms terrible indeed" (*CM*, 8:217). This is the New Model Army, which is not only "the bravest of armies, but the most modest and religious." In their "diligent attention to the holy scripture," they "instruct [themselves] and others in the knowledge of heavenly things." These "champions of the church" (*ecclesiae propugnatores*) in "martial uniform" (*paludati*) engage in "the warfare of the gospel" (*evangelicam militiam*) (2D, *CM*, 8:178–79). Their leader is the renowned Oliver Cromwell, whom Milton celebrates as the "hero," among other heroes, of his epic chronicle (2D, *CM*, 8:253).[80] "A veteran accomplished in all military duties," he "surpassed almost the greatest generals in the grandeur of his achievements, and in the rapidity with which they were executed." "Travers[ing] the whole circle of Britain in one continued series of victories," he was never "conquered or put to flight" (*CM*, 8:215). As Milton praises him in Sonnet 16, "*Cromwell* . . . hast reard Gods Trophies and his work pursu'd" (lines 1, 5) in the various battles he has won. In this respect, Milton would have been fully in agreement with Andrew Marvell's assessment of Cromwell as one who "first put Armes into *Religion's* hand" and, "fetch[ing]" his "Blow" "from *Heaven*," dispersed "Astonish'd Armies" and "stormed" "Cityes" "by his Prayer."[81] If such is true of Cromwell, it is no less true of the other warriors whom Milton celebrates in the *Defensio secunda*. His litany includes Fleetwood, Lambert, Desborow, Whalley, Overton, and, of course, Fairfax, "whose name in armes through *Europe* rings" (S 15, 1). These are the heroes of Milton's epic chronicle. As holy warriors, they are the instruments of God's warfare on earth.

Suggested in the *Defenses*, the precise nature of that warfare is described in *Christian Doctrine* (*CM*, 17:406–11). There, Milton outlines the various "duties" of war. "It is enjoined, first, that [war] be not undertaken without mature deliberation" (*ut prudentissimis consiliis suscipiatur*); second, "that it be carried on wisely and skilfully" (*ut scienter et perite geratur*); third, "that it be prosecuted with moderation" (*ut moderate*); fourth, "that it be waged in a spirit of godliness" (*ut sancte*); fifth, "that no mercy be shown to a merciless enemy" (*ut crudeli hosti ne percatur*); sixth, "that our confidence be not placed in human strength, but in God alone" (*ne robore copiarum confidamus, sed Deo solo*); and seventh, "that the booty be distributed in equitable proportions" (*ut praeda ex aequo et iusto dividatur*).

A glance at the proof-texts will reveal the extent to which Milton is indebted to holy war theory in his formulation of these duties. By far, the greatest number of proof-texts is marshaled under the sixth heading, that "our confidence" be placed "in God alone." Under this heading are proof-texts such as "I will get me honor upon Pharaoh and all his host" (Exod. 14:17–18); "blessed be Jehovah my strength, which teacheth my hands to war" (Ps. 144:1); and "they shall be as mighty men which tread down their enemies in the mire of the streets in the battle" (Zech. 10:5–6). Aside from these characteristics, Milton's proof-texts emphasize the ritual cleansing of the camp and the חרם. The first comes under the fourth heading, that war "be waged in a spirit of godliness," for which Milton cites Deuteronomy 23:9: "When the host goeth forth against thine enemies, then keep thee from every wicked thing." The second comes under the fifth heading, "that no mercy be shown to a merciless enemy." For this duty Milton cites Jeremiah 48:10: "Cursed be he that keepeth back his sword from blood." (Even the suggestion that the war be waged in "moderation" [the third heading] is mitigated by the proof-text [Deut. 20:19], which in the Israelite code of warfare exempts not the enemy but the enemy's "trees" from destruction, since the trees may be used as food.) Apparently, the חרם itself, then, fell within Milton's understanding of holy war. He saw it no doubt as a sign of God's divine vengeance upon the enemies of the church: "Ulcisci tamen hostes ecclesiae aut ultos velle non est illicitum," he observes (CM, 17:288). It is precisely that sentiment that is reflected in Sonnet 18, which calls upon God to "avenge" those "slaughter'd Saints" (1) who have fought so valiantly on his behalf, and it is suggested in the *Defensio secunda* by Milton's admiration of Cromwell as instrument of God's vengeance in the Irish and Scottish campaigns (CM, 8:219–21).[82]

Nor does this outlook, coupled with the holy war precepts elaborated above, present any conflict for Milton with New Testament teachings. As he has expounded it, war, Milton says, is not "anywhere forbidden in the New Testament" (*neque enim in novo testamento prohibetur*), and in fact, "there seems no reason why war should be unlawful now, any more than in the time of the Jews [*bellum enim qui minus licitum nunc sit, quam Iudaeis fuit, causae nihil est*] (CD, CM, 17:410–11). Israelite warfare, Milton implies, may well serve as a model for his own times. Expressing this attitude, Milton revealed how thoroughly he was imbued with the principles of holy war and how willing he was to make use of those principles in his work.

If such is true of his prose, it is no less true of his poetry. We have already seen Milton's expression of holy war ideology in his sonnets. Comparable sentiments receive full expression in his psalm translations. As early as his boyhood translations of Psalms 114 and 136 in 1624, Milton expressed his admiration for the Lord of Hosts who delivered the Israelites out of bondage in their quest for the Promised Land and quelled the army of Pharaoh. "Led by the strength of the Almighties hand," the Israelites beheld "Jehovah's wonders" at the Red Sea and at the Jordan (Ps. 114, 1–10). God becomes the queller who "brought down" "Kings of prowess and renown" "in bloody battal": "He foild bold *Seon* and his host, / That rul'd the *Amorrean* coast"; "large-limb'd *Og* he did subdue, / With all his over-hardy crew," and "to his servant *Israel* / He gave their Land therein to dwell" (Ps. 136, 41–74). Apparently, events of this kind made a lasting impression upon the poet-psalmist, for he translated Psalm 114 again (this time into Greek) ten years later. But this was only the beginning.

During the crucial years of the Second Civil War (1648) and the establishment of the Protectorate (1653), he translated two groups of psalms. Psalms 80–88 belong to the first period; psalms 1–8 to the second. Both reveal the extent to which Milton as poet-psalmist was influenced by holy war ideology, particularly in his elaboration of the original sources, as his own italics in the translated versions suggest. In the first group, God proclaims his deeds as a warrior who has delivered the Israelites from Egypt and who promises to "bring down" Israel's "foes / *That now so proudly rise*" and to "turn" his "hand against *all those / That are* their enemies" (Ps. 81, 41–42, 57–60). In that capacity, he is exhorted as one "that sitt'st between the Cherubs *bright / Between their wings outspread*" to "Shine forth" and terrify his "*foes*" (Ps. 80, 1–5). "For lo," Milton as poet-psalmist cries to the "Lord of Hosts," "thy *furious* foes *now* swell, / And storm outrageously, / And they that hate thee *proud and fell* / Exalt their heads full high." Those who "unite" against God are the Moabites, the Ammonites, the Amalecites, and the Philistines, among others: "*They amidst their pride* have said / By right now shall we seize / Gods houses, and *will now invade*" God's "stately Palaces." But God will have his revenge: he will "pursue" them with his "whirlwind" and "chase" them with his "tempest." He will "do to them as to Midian *bold, / That wasted all the Coast, / To* Sisera, and . . . to *Jabins hoast, / When* at the brook of Kishon *old / They were repulst and slain, /* At Endor quite cut off, and rowl'd / As dung upon the plain." Thus "confounded," God's enemies will "know" that "Jehova is alone" "the most high" (Ps. 83, 5–8, 17–48, 57–58, 63, 65–68). Reverberating throughout the first group of psalm translations, these themes are repeated in the second. There, the Lord of Hosts "whets" his "Sword" and "bend[s] his "Bow" (Ps. 7, 45–46). He "rise[s]" against his "foes" and smites them "on the cheekbone" (Ps. 3, 18–21). Against those who "upstand / With power" and "lay deep their plots," he does battle, "bring[ing]" them "full low / With Iron Scepter bruis'd" and "dispers[ing]" them "like to a potters vessel shiver'd so," until they "Jehovah serve" "with fear" (Ps. 2, 2–5, 8–21, 23–24).

The creation of such a milieu is hardly unique to Milton's psalm translations. One need only consider *Samson Agonistes* to perceive the way in which Milton is able to provide a dramatic setting for the concept of holy war.[83] If the Samson of Judges is looked upon as a deliverer inspired by the Spirit of the Lord (Judg. 13:15, 15:14), his fame is such that, even for the author of Hebrews, he is classed among the holy warriors, like Gideon and David, who "waxed valiant in fight" and "turned to flight the armies of the aliens" (Heb. 11:32–34). Milton's treatment of Samson dramatically confirms both the Old Testament and the New Testament views of him as a divine instrument of the יהוה מלחמות. Once "Heroic," "Renown'd," and "Irresistible," Samson "ran on embattell'd Armies clad in Iron, / And weaponless himself, / Made Arms ridiculous" (125–31). "Arm'd" with "celestial vigour," he "Render[ed]" his enemy's "Armories and Magazins" "useless while / With winged expedition / Swift as the lightning glance he execute[d] / His errand on the wicked, who surpris'd / Lost thir defence, distracted and amaz'd" (1280–86). In that respect, Samson waged God's holy wars like Gideon, who pursued the Midianites, and Jephthah, who defeated the Ammonites (277–89). Now fallen, Samson reclaims his status as God's holy warrior. "His fiery vertue rouz'd / From under ashes into sudden flame" (1690–91), he enacts a true חרם upon the heads of the profane:

> While thir hearts were jocund and sublime,
> Drunk with Idolatry, drunk with Wine,
> And fat regorg'd of Bulls and Goats,
> Chaunting thir Idol, and preferring
> Before our living Dread who dwells
> In *Silo* his bright Sanctuary:
> Among them he a spirit of phrenzie sent,
> Who hurt thir minds,
> And urg'd them on with mad desire
> To call in hast for thir destroyer;
> They only set on sport and play
> Unweetingly importun'd
> Thir own destruction to come speedy upon them.
> (1669–81)

As the foregoing suggests, the language in which this event is cast is fully indebted to the יהוה מלחמות. In this particular holy war, the theater of battle is none other than the "spacious Theatre" (1622) where the

Philistines assemble, not to fight but, as they think, to celebrate their deliverance from the "Antagonist" (1628), "thir dreadful enemy" now made "thir thrall" (1622). In that "spectacle" (1604) of humiliation, Samson ironically performs a feat of strength that "strike[s]" his enemy "with amaze" (1645). His act is described in a way that recalls all previous holy wars: God's spirit descends with a force comparable to the "trembl[ing]" of "Mountains" (1648) and the "burst[ing] of thunder" (1651) to overwhelm the enemy. The emissary of God's destructive power, Samson "slaughter[s]" "more" "foes" in his own death "then all [his] life had slain before" (1666–68). If he dies in the process, he is, as the Chorus says, nonetheless "victorious": through one "glorious" act, he fulfills "the work for which [he] wast foretold / To *Israel*" (1660–63).

What has been shown to be true of the sonnets, the psalm translations, and the closet drama is no less true of the other poems, either as Milton conceived them in his notebook jottings or as they appear in completed form. One need only glance at the "Outline for Tragedies" in the Trinity Manuscript to confirm that point. Among the subjects he considers writing about, one finds such classical מלחמות יהוה as "Joshua in Gibeon. Josu. 10," "Gideon persuing [the Midianites] Jud. 8," the "Dagonalia. Jud. 16," "Jonathan rescu'd [from the Philistines] I Sam. 14," "Samaria Liberata 2 Reg. 7," and "Hezechias πολιορχούμενος [or Hesechia beseig'd] 2 Reg. 18. 19. infra," the last two already recounted in *Elegia quarta* (To Thomas Young) (111–12) and the Dagonalia, later to be incorporated into *Samson Agonistes*. Complementing this interest in holy war themes is Milton's fascination with the figure of the warrior prophet, as suggested by his jotting "Elias in the mount. 2 Reg. 1. 'Ορειβάτης or better Elias Polemistes," and with the figure of the iconoclast, as suggested by his jottings "Gideon Idoloclastes Jud. 6. 7," "Jehu Belicola. 2 Reg. 10," and "Josiah Aiazomenos. 2 Reg. 23," all three concerned with the destruction of Baal's altars and houses of worship. Drawn from Israel's history, the foregoing subjects find their counterparts in Milton's plans to write a drama on the fall of man. Included in these plans is an account of the "battell" and "victorie in heavn" against Lucifer "& his accomplices" (*CM*, 18:228–39). It was upon this final theme, of course, that Milton decided to elaborate, not in dramatic but in epic form. For the purposes of this study, however, what is important in these plans is the essential correspondence between the two military themes, the first having to do with Israelite warfare, the second with apocalyptic warfare.

Dating back to the most ancient accounts of the מלחמות יהוה and reiterated throughout the Bible and its traditions, this correspondence finds expression in Milton's poetry as early as his poem *On the Morning of Christs Nativity.* There, one finds a rendering of holy war ideology that fully anticipates that articulated in *Paradise Lost.* If Christ's birth heralds a time of peace and harmony that recalls "the age of gold" (53–60, 134), it also betokens a time of war framed by the "horrid clang" of the Sinai theophany, on the one hand, and the "thunder" of the "wake-full trump of doom" (156–64), on the other. That period of war is suggested in the routing of "the damned crew" of pagan deities by the "Babe" in "swaddling bands" (226–27). "Bind[ing]" "th'old Dragon under ground," this act prefigures the final apocalyptic overthrow of Satan. As it is conceived, the routing of the pagan deities is particularly important because it evokes the milieu of Israel's holy wars, expressed through the destruction of false idols such as those of the Philistines and the Egyptians, among others. From the first point of view, the reference to "that twise batter'd god of *Palestine*" (199) returns us to the Wars of the Ark. Dagon is "twise batter'd," of course, because the fish god's statue is twice overcome by "the ark of God" when the Philistines place the stolen ark next to the statue in "the house of Dagon" in Ashdod (1 Sam. 5:2–4). As Milton relates in *Paradise Lost,* Dagon "mourn'd" "when the Captive Ark / Maim'd his brute Image, head and hands lopt off / In his own Temple, on the grunsel edge, / Where he fell flat, and sham'd his Worshipers" (1.458–61). The war of the Israelites against the Philistines culminates in this event as a sign of the power of "the ark of God." The event looks forward to Milton's treatment of the "Dagonalia" as holy war in *Samson Agonistes.*

The *Nativity Ode* also provides a second example in the reference to "the brutish gods of *Nile*" (211–12). "*Isis* and *Orus,* and the Dog *Anubis*" suggest for Milton the false Egyptian worship that God was to undermine both during the period of the Exodus and after the Conquest. Thus, again in *Paradise Lost,* Milton refers to "*Jehovah*['s]" having "equaled with one stroke" all these "bleating Gods," worshiped as a "Calf in *Oreb*" and later as a "Grand Ox" "in *Bethel* and in *Dan*" (1.484–89; cf. Exod. 11, 12, 32 and 1 Kings 12). The "equaling" of the Egyptian gods is, of course, synonymous with the overthrow of the Egyptian forces by Jehovah as warrior. In the *Nativity Ode,* this and the foregoing conquests set the stage for all the other references to the overcoming of the profane by the holy, embodied in the exorcisms of such gods as Peor, Baalim, Ashtaroth, Ammon, Thammuz, Moloch, Osiris, and Typhon. All feel "from *Juda's* Land / The dredded Infants hand" (221–22), as it enacts what Gideon, Jehu, and Josiah enacted in their attempts to purify God's temple. As suggested, this purification anticipates the epic purification delineated in *Paradise Lost.* In Milton's epic, the full range of meanings implicit in the ideology of holy war is brought to the fore.

The holy war context of *Paradise Lost* is established right at the outset: Milton introduces those who have lost the War in Heaven and shows them plotting to do battle against God in another war. Their attempts to regain the position that they have lost look forward to the action that is to come (the battle for supremacy on earth) and backward to the action that has already transpired (the battle for supremacy in Heaven). The movement is both proleptic and retrospective. In both respects, it under-scores the ideology of holy war through the perspective of its opposite: profane war. As "apostates" (1.125), "atheists" (6.370), and "blasphem-ers" (5.809), Satan and his crew have "rais'd impious War in Heav'n" (1.43) and plan to do the same on earth. Such profane warfare is what Renaissance theoreticians of holy war call θεομάχια, a "Fighting against God."[84] In his sermon *Meroz Cursed* (1641), Stephen Marshall alludes to "the Gyants who make war against heaven" as "*οἱ θεομάχοι*" (p. 21), thus incorporating the classical background into the Hebraic milieu. As discussed in chapter 7, Milton does the same in *Paradise Lost* with his references to the classical theomachies (whether titanomachies or gi-gantomachies) as variations upon a biblical theme.[85] Accordingly, his primary emphasis is upon biblical warfare as a model both for the battles fought in Heaven and for those to be waged on earth. In that warfare, the rebel angels are assimilated from the very beginning of Milton's epic into the panorama of Israel's מלחמות יהוה, extending from the Exodus through the Conquest.

With this panorama in mind, Milton establishes an ironic perspective perfectly in keeping with the practice of approaching the ideology of holy war by means of its opposite. Thus, the context of the Exodus is sounded through the reference to the rebel angels as the legions of Pharaoh over-come by God in the Red Sea (1.299–311). As "*Amrams Son*" (1.339), Satan, in turn, becomes a pseudo-Moses who inspires his legions with a perverse Song of the Sea (1.314–30) and reinvigorates them (1.331–55) with his "potent Rod" (1.338). This act, Milton makes clear, will be ultimately self-destructive, since the reinvigorated host is compared to the locusts that attacked Pharaoh in order to establish the way for the Exodus (1.339–43). In this sense, as Richard Bernard or Thomas Adams would agree,[86] the rebel angels are the unwitting hosts of God: they carry out God's own holy war upon themselves (cf. Rev. 9:3–7), a paradox that Satan comes to learn in his warfare against God (3.85–86). None-theless, the rousing of the rebel host does initiate what will be those wars against God and his Temple that characterize the history of Israel. In that context, the rebel angels assume the form of idols used to undermine the true worship of God. This is the cultic form of their θεομαχία, which, in the framework that Milton provides, extends and elaborates the ideology of holy war.

Accordingly, Milton introduces his catalogue of rebel angels in this manner:

> The chief were those who from the Pit of Hell
> Roaming to seek thir prey on earth, durst fix
> Thir Seats long after next the Seat of God,
> Thir Altars by his Altar, Gods ador'd
> Among the Nations round, and durst abide
> *Jehovah* thundring out of *Sion*, thron'd
> Between the Cherubim; yea often plac'd
> Within his Sanctuary it self thir Shrines
> Abominations; and with cursed things
> His holy Rites, and solemn Feasts profan'd,
> And with thir darkness durst affront his light.
> (1.381–91)

The pointedly cultic bearing of the entire affair determines the nature of the catalogue that follows: thundering out of Zion in his ark, God overwhelms those who would make war against his Temple. As they recall the pagan deities who are exorcised in the *Nativity Ode*, these are none other than Moloch, Chemos, Peor, Baalim, Ashtaroth, Dagon, Thammuz, Rimmon, Osiris, Isis, Orus, and Belial. They lure the Israelites to commit abominations in the march from Egypt to Canaan and in the devotion to the Temple after the Conquest. Pitting their idols against the ark of God, they engage in a θεομαχία that depicts what Jason Rosenblatt calls "the siege" of "the profane" against "the holy."[87]

Doing battle in the siege are the antagonists, who "forsake" "their Living Strength" and "leave" "His righteous altar" (1.432–34), and the faithful, who fight on behalf of the Temple (1.418). The first sort, "bow-[ing] . . . lowly down / To bestial gods," finally "bow down in battle" (1.434–36). The second sort, upholding God's ways, drive the profaners "to hell" (1.418). At the center of the siege is Jerusalem itself,[88] the culminating symbol of the holy war ideology that begins with the Exodus and extends through the Conquest. Milton wanted to write a drama on the theme of the sacking of Jerusalem. Entitled "Salymων Halosis" (TM, CM, 18:239), the drama would have recounted the unfortunate history of the first Temple despite the attempts of the faithful who fight on its behalf. Because of the abominations committed by the dissolute, God turns his holy war upon them as a punishment (2 Kings 24 and 25). That event is part of the larger perspective of holy war that leads to the eventual restoration of the Temple. In its immediate context, however, the event is consistent with the catalogue that Milton presents as an expression of what might be called the "שטן מלחמות" or Wars of Satan. With the restoration of the Temple, the θεομᾰχία finally has a positive outcome. Anticipated in the War in Heaven, that outcome is recounted in Satan's ultimate defeat in his attempt to gain supremacy on earth. Both the War in Heaven and the War on Earth constitute Milton's rendering of the "Book of the Wars of Jahweh" in *Paradise Lost*. An investigation of those wars will further reveal the impact of the traditions that underlie the יהוה מלחמות.

To suggest that the War in Heaven conforms to the ideology of holy war is not new to Milton studies. In various ways, such scholars as Stella Revard have already explored the celestial battle in precisely these terms.[89] The primary characteristics of that battle as a product of the יהוה מלחמות, however, have still not been fully investigated. Given the cultic framework that Milton establishes at the outset of his epic and the all-pervasive traditions of holy war to which he was heir both as poet and as polemist, it is not surprising that he would cast his celestial battle in the form of a holy war. Commenting upon the war through his characters and through his role as narrator, Milton leaves no doubt about the transcendent nature of the battle itself. As Raphael indicates, the war is "high matter": it concerns "the secrets of another world, perhaps / Not lawful to reveal" (5.563, 569–70). "Surmount[ing] the reach / Of human sense" (5.571–72), it portrays "unspeakable" confrontations, otherwise "hid" from the "human Race" (6.895–96). As such, it is a holy event inscribed in the annals of "Sacred memorie" (5.379). "Worthy of Sacred silence to be heard" (5.557), it consumes Adam with "admiration and deep Muse" (7.54), if not with "terror" (6.910). Relating it through Raphael fills the narrator with a sense of wonder and humility at the task and with no little awareness of the danger that awaits anyone who ascends "into the Heav'n of Heav'ns" and draws "Empyreal Air" (7.12–15). Such a setting is unequivocal in its attestation to the sacral milieu in which the war is to be conducted: here is the precise environment for transcribing the "Book of the Wars of Jahweh."

It is important to emphasize that environment at this point not only to suggest the appropriateness of the holy war context to the nature of the battle that Milton describes but to refine further what remains the prevailing critical outlook toward the war. Deriving its impetus from Arnold Stein's classic interpretation,[90] that outlook views the War in Heaven as "comedy." Any interpretation that attempts to offer a sacral reading of the war must deal with this point of view. Stein arrives at this view of the war in response to Samuel Johnson's criticism that Milton's account is incongruous in its confusion of spirit and matter.[91] Countering Dr. Johnson, Stein suggests that the so-called incongruity is a deliberate attempt on Milton's part to reveal the absurdity of Satan's desire to overcome God by material means. From this perspective, the war assumes a comic character, one that ridicules the machinations of Satan and his crew through a series of events designed, as Stein says, to be "terribly funny."[92] So extreme is the ridicule, in fact, that when the rebel angels suffer the humiliation of having hills cast upon them, the event for Stein is reminiscent of being bombarded by immense custard pies.[93] By means of this celestial slapstick, God has the last laugh in a conflict that pits Satan's mockery against God's.[94]

As effective as Stein's criticism is in countering Dr. Johnson, it does leave some important questions unanswered. First, not only the rebel angels are humiliated. As Stanley Fish contends, the faithful angels also suffer humiliation,[95] not the least of which is their "indecent overthrow" (6.601) by Satan's cannons. According to Fish God places his faithful angels in such absurd and humiliating predicaments as a way of educating the reader about the true nature of patience and faith. These virtues must withstand the most extreme circumstances. Although William Riggs agrees that "patience and faith are certainly lessons to be learned from the war in heaven," he does not feel that such lessons need be purchased "at the price of ridicule."[96] Riggs still feels that in its ridicule of both the rebel and the faithful angels, Milton's account becomes self-defeating. It results not in "mock heroic" but in "mocked heroic," whereby "poetic manner is intentionally depreciated by its inability to answer adequately to the demands of a heavenly subject."[97]

Given the sacral milieu that Milton establishes, how then does one reconcile these demands with the celestial slapstick and gross humiliation that appear to demean the character of the war? How is the war as comedy (and low comedy at that) consistent with the war as sacral event? The answer lies in the ideology of holy war. As Milton implements it in his account of the celestial battle, that ideology will confirm the appropriateness of responding to the war in the manner of Raphael, Adam, and the narrator himself: not with laughter and contempt, finally, but with reverence and awe.

The second psalm, a biblical text well known to be of the first importance to the entire conflict, illustrates the fitness of that response. Translated by Milton during the crucial period when the Protectorate was established, Psalm 2 is significant in two respects. In its account of the begetting of the Son as King (lines 11–16; cf. Acts 13:33 and Heb. 5:5), it is the source of the begetting of the Son in *Paradise Lost* (5.604–8), an event that sparks the ensuing rebellion.[98] In its references to the laughter and derision of God, combined with the "wrath" that he pours upon his enemies (lines 8–10; cf. Ps. 59:8), it sets the tone for the divine laughter that resonates throughout the war (6.736) and, in fact, throughout the entire epic (2.191), an attitude both shared and parodied by Satan (6.568). In both respects, Psalm 2 is in accord with the ideology of holy war.

Indeed, this is precisely how Renaissance theoreticians viewed the matter. Discussing the nature of holy war in his discourse *On the Law of War and Peace*, Hugo Grotius singles out Psalm 2 as a prime instance of those sacred ordinances that must be obeyed, lest the violator call down upon himself the indignation of God in a holy cause. "This Psalm," says Grotius, "exhorts" us to "receive the Son of God with reverence": "he who resists" this "ordinance of God" is "resisting God," in response to which God, by means of his ministers, punishes the disobedient through warfare.[99] Inciting the parliamentarians to war on just this premise, Stephen Marshall proclaims in *Meroz Cursed*, "How many are there who have ... entred their names into the *Dragons muster-book*, openly bidding defiance against the *Church* of *Christ* ... and making war against the Saints? ... How many others, like the Kings and Princes in the 2 *Psal. Set themselves and take counsell against the Lord and against his Anointed, digging as deep as hell for counsell to do* all the mischiefe they can to the servants of the *Lord Iesus Christ*?" (pp. 20–21). To complement these observations, Joshua Sprigg, in his epic chronicle of Cromwell's triumphs at Naseby, invokes the idea of God's laughter by paraphrasing the second psalm: "A happy time, when the Lord of hosts shall make his Tabernacle in the hearts and countenances of our chief Commanders; from thence to laugh his enemies to destruction and have them in derision to confusion."[100]

Such laughter, of course, is an essential aspect of Milton's stance as polemist and poet. Conflating the "faculties" of "anger" and "laughter," he defends derision as a religious responsibility undertaken by the prophets themselves in answering fools according to their own folly (AP, CM, 3:317–18; Prov. 26:4). This is none other than the outlook of the holy warrior bent on fighting God's wars. Accordingly, Milton envisions the "invincible warriour Zeale," "whose substance is ethereal," "arming in compleat diamond" and "ascend[ing]" a "fiery Chariot drawn with two blazing Meteors figur'd like beasts" that "resembl[e] two of those four which *Ezechiel* and *S. John* saw, the one visag'd like a Lion to expresse power, high autority and indignation, the other of count'nance like to a man to cast derision and scorne upon perverse and fraudulent seducers." In that chariot, Zeal "drives over the heads" of the enemy (in this case, the "Scarlet Prelats"), "bruising their stiffe necks under his flaming wheels." "Thus," says Milton, "did the true Prophets of old combat with the false; thus Christ himselfe the fountaine of meeknesse found acrimony anough to be still galling and vexing the Prelaticall Pharisees" (AP, CM, 3:313–14). When the Son of God in *Paradise Lost* (6.762) ascends his chariot to crush the heads of Satan and his crew, it is little wonder, then, that Milton depicts the scene as a triumph of both scorn and indignation: the Son answers despite with despite. "Behold," he says to the faithful angels, "Gods indignation on these Godless pourd / By mee; not you but mee they have despis'd" (6.811–12). Their contempt and impiety are met with sublime humiliation. Compared both to the goats that Christ separates from the sheep at the Last Judgment (Matt. 25:31–34) and to the swine that perish with the devils that Christ exorcises from the possessed (Matt. 8:28–34), Satan and his crew are driven before the chariot (6.856–57; cf. PR, 4.629–30) to their "dark opprobrious Den of shame" (2.58), thereafter to live perpetually in "dread" of future "shame" (4.82) as all their apparent "triumphs" serve only to humiliate them further (cf. 10.546). The entire process is in keeping with the ideology of holy war.

Given these circumstances one must still reconcile the ideology of holy war with the humiliation that God's faithful soldiers undergo in order to uphold the banner of their leader. The Old Testament itself provides the key to that effort. For example, in the account of the battle between the Israelites and the Assyrians, a subject that Milton earlier broached in *Elegia quarta* and later thought to elaborate on a larger scale in "Hezechias πολιορχόυμενος," the Assyrian Rab-shakeh mercilessly taunts the Israelites on the walls of Jerusalem: "Let not Hezekiah deceive you: for he shall not be able to deliver you. . . . Neither let Hezekiah make you trust in the Lord, saying, The Lord will surely deliver us, and this city shall not be delivered into the hand of the king of Assyria" (2 Kings 18:29–30). For, if you do not heed my words, Rab-shakeh jeers, you will be made to "eat" your "own dung" and to "drink" your "own piss" (2 Kings 18:27). This "reproach" of "the living God" and his people is answered by God through Isaiah: even though you have been "laughed . . . to scorn" and God "blasphemed," "be not afraid"; "the Lord of hosts" "will send a blast" upon the enemy (2 Kings 19:4–7, 15–16, 21–22, 31). "And it came to pass that night, that the angel of the Lord went out, and smote the camp of the Assyrians an hundred fourscore and five thousand: and

when they arose early in the morning, behold, they were all dead corpses"
(2 Kings 19:35). For those who fight the battles of God, then, scorn and
reproach are a commonplace occurrence: God's warriors are subject to
constant humiliation—occasionally of the grossest sort.[101] But this is precisely in keeping with their role. Those who defend God's ways against
his adversaries undergo the derision cast upon their leader, for they know
that ultimately they shall be vindicated.

Within a New Testament context, this attitude is reflected in the vocation of all Christian soldiers. Following the example of Christ, whose humiliation is a triumphant attestation to his mission, they willingly endure
their own crown of thorns and their own cross. In what M. Conrad Hyres
calls "the comic profanation of the sacred,"[102] they become "fools" for
Christ, since "God hath chosen the foolish things of the world to confound the wise; and God hath chosen the weak things of the world to
confound the things which are mighty; And base things of the world,
and things which are despised, hath God chosen, *yea*, and things which
are not, to bring to nought things that are" (1 Cor. 1:18–28, 3:18–19).
Such is the assurance of all those who fight God's battles. When, in
Paradise Lost, Abdiel returns to God's throne to report the impending
rebellion, God greets him with words that any holy warrior would have
understood:

> Servant of God, well done, well hast thou fought
> The better fight, who single hast maintaind
> Against revolted multitudes the Cause
> Of Truth . . .
> And for the testimonie of Truth hast born
> Universal reproach.
>
> (6.29–34)

When the "saints" of God, in turn, march "forth to Battel" (6.45–47),
they too may well expect to encounter "universal reproach." In their
"indecent overthrow" (6.601), that reproach is realized, as Satan with
his cannons makes a "scorn" of God's "thunder" and "derides" "all his
host" (6.630–33). Grossly humiliated in their overthrow, God's "invincible" warriors (6.46) find themselves "a laughter" to "their foes"
(6.603).

As the investigation of biblical precedent has already demonstrated,
such an event is precisely in keeping with holy war ideology. It is also in
keeping with the political events of Milton's own time. Even before the
Civil Wars, Puritan soldiers were admonished to anticipate all kinds of
humiliations. Be "resolutely bent to endure the worst" and prepared "to

stay by it faithfully," declares Alexander Leighton in his *Speculum belli sacri: or the Lookingglasse of the Holy War* (1624) (p. 213). Should we be asked why God's warriors "are so often delivered, not *from* but *to* their *enemies*," as Israel was "between *Egypt* and *Canaan* and afterward," we may answer, advises Samuel Bachelor: "So it may be for a time, but at the last God will make this good. Marke then the end, see what he hath done at the second, third, or fourth bout, his people shall carrie it away at length and have the day."[103] During the Civil Wars, Puritan soldiers were reminded "that sometimes Gods people have the worst in battell as well as Gods enemies."[104] Even if God's warriors do not suffer defeat, they are subject to constant verbal humiliation that makes them "a laughter" to "their foes." The New Model Army is a case in point. "If wee consider the Army it selfe," says John Vicars,

> O the wonderfull base and despicable esteem that was thereof, not onely in the Kings Army, and Malignants, but even among very many seeming friends among us, and those no mean ones too! how did they disparage, undervalue, and contemne, as it were, this *New-Modelled Army*, calling it, a *New Nodelled Army*, jeering them, as a company of young *Tyroes*, or fresh-water-Souldiers; heerby, as much as in them was, to discountenance and dis-hearten the most noble Generall himself, Sir *Thomas Fairfax*, and to weaken the hands, and despond the spirits of his Souldiers; if God himself had not mightily upheld, and put, as it were, an extraordinary spirit and courage into them; most remarkably making good that most excellent passage of the Apostle. *That God hath chosen the foolish things of the world to confound the wise.*[105]

This is the army that Milton championed against contempt, shame, and calumniation in his tracts (1D, *CM*, 7:491; 2D, *CM*, 8:5, 15, 177). That the army he envisions in *Paradise Lost* is at least in part a product of this spirit of vindication should come as no surprise. George Wither had already provided a poetic context in which to champion the parliamentary forces. Milton's epic is hardly a counterpart of the *Carmen Eucharisticon*. Yet Wither's poem is once again instructive in revealing the way in which the political dimension of holy war ideology is transmuted into poetic form. In this case, the theme is one previously encountered in the Bible: the triumph of the faithful who have willingly endured reproach. Wither's treatment is instructive in its account of this event. Conceiving the battle of the parliamentary forces against the Irish in apocalyptic terms, Wither relates how the Irish sought to accost the troops of Parliament with "*Sulphur, Sword,* and *Flame*," and "had brought

[them] all to shame, / Had not God stretch'd forth his hand." While they "laugh[ed]" at the "sad condition" of the parliamentary troops, "then, that *Arm* which they despis'd, / Suddenly their *Camp* surpriz'd," as "*Mich'el* and his *Angells*" "threw" the "*Dragon-Cavaliere*" to hell (57–84). Once again, biblical precedent is reinforced by political reality. When Milton came to celebrate the armies of God in epic form, he had at his disposal an entire tradition of holy war ideology that assimilated the theme of scorn and made it uniquely its own.

Several other holy wars motifs characterize the celestial battle in *Paradise Lost*. True to the tradition of the מלחמות יהוה, the war is ordained by God himself. From his prospect high, he "commands" the battle. The command is issued, as Michael Murrin observes, in a context that distinctly recalls the Sinai theophany,[106] accompanied by "Clouds" that "darken all the Hill," "smoak" that "rowl[s] / In duskie wreaths," and the blowing of "the loud / Ethereal Trumpet from on high" (6.56–60; cf. Exod. 19:16, 18). The language places us appropriately in the midst of the Exodus,[107] where the angels, in Israelite fashion, surround God's "high mount" (5.643) in the "Celestial Tabernacles" that populate their "Camp" (5.651–54). Summoned to war in a march that will eventuate in the conquest of Canaan, they set forth in a manner that assumes transcendent proportions:

> At [God's] command the Powers Militant,
> That stood for Heav'n, in mighty Quadrate joyn'd
> Of Union irresistible, mov'd on
> In silence thir bright Legions, to the sound
> Of instrumental Harmonie that breath'd
> Heroic Ardor to advent'rous deeds
> Under thir God-like Leaders, in the Cause
> Of God and his *Messiah*. On they move
> Indissolubly firm; nor obvious Hill,
> Nor streit'ning Vale, nor Wood, nor Stream divides
> Thir perfet ranks; for high above the ground
> Thir march was, and the passive Air upbore
> Thir nimble tread.
>
> (6.61–73)

The description is reminiscent of what the language of holy war calls "the journeyings of the children of Israel according to their armies, when they set forward" (Num. 10:28). Delineated in Numbers 10 (see figure 19), which recounts in detail the marching order of the military camps that "departed from the mount of the Lord three days' journey" (Num.

10:33), these marches commence with the blowing of trumpets and the singing of the Song of the Ark (Num. 10:9, 35), an event subsequently celebrated in Psalm 68. There, the journey is likewise exalted, as God at once marches through the wilderness and "rideth upon the heavens of heavens." If these characteristics are relevant to the holy war context that Milton establishes in his description of the angelic march, others are equally pertinent.

The shape of the angelic phalanx, for example, should not be overlooked. Described initially as a "mighty Quadrate," it is later referred to as a "Cubic Phalanx" (6.399; cf. 8.232). These references would not be particularly significant were it not that Milton is at pains to call attention to the shape of the phalanx as a symbol. "In mighty Quadrate joyn'd / Of Union irresistible," "the Powers Militant," Milton says, "*stood for Heav'n*" (italics added). They not only uphold Heaven; they symbolize it. This circumstance is only fitting, considering that as Harry F. Robins has made clear, Milton's Heaven is a square.[108] The idea, of course, recalls Saint John the Divine, who says of Heaven that it "lieth foursquare, and the length is as large as the breadth. . . . The length and the breadth and the height of it are equal" (Rev. 21:16). Once again, this quadratic vision that depicts Heaven in cubic form is no doubt ultimately derived from the construction of the Holy of Holies as a cube in Solomon's Temple (1 Kings 6:20).[109] With that vision, Saint John combines the quadratic measurements of the restored Temple delineated by Ezekiel (Ezek. 40:1–5, 45:2; cf. Rev. 11:1–2). Milton's account of the angelic phalanx as quadratic, then, has about it something of the New Jerusalem transmuted through earlier visions of the Temple.

The idea is one that Milton had made a good deal of in *The Reason of Church-Government*. Depicting the "Angels" "quaterniond" into their various orders as a symbol of the perfection of the "new Jerusalem" (*CM*, 3:185), he associates the "divine square" of God's "Temple" with "the most perfect state of the Church militant" (*CM*, 3:191). That "Church" he envisions "moving upon her own basis in an even and firm progression, as those smaller squares in battle unite in one great cube, the main phalanx, an embleme of truth and stedfastnesse" (*CM*, 3:217).

In *Paradise Lost*, the phalanx of God's warriors embodies those qualities, as it is associated with perfection, power, and inviolability (6.62, 71, 398). Its shape incidentally is parodied by that of God's enemies, whose quadratic imitation results in nothing but a "hollow Cube" (6.553; cf. 1.758) that "hides" their "fraud" (6.555). That Milton should attribute symbolic qualities to the shape of the angelic phalanx is hardly out of keeping with the Renaissance epic. (One thinks, for example, of Val-

FIGURE 19. Marching Order of the Israelite Camps.
Reproduced from a rendering of Numbers 10 in the Kitto Bible,
14:2341, by permission of the Huntington Library,
San Marino, California.

vasone's *Angeleida*, which portrays the phalanx of God's angels as a cross.)[110] In *Paradise Lost*, however, the quadratic shape is particularly in accord with Milton's rendering of the ideology of holy war.

Since that ideology has its source in the warfare of the Old Testament, it is there that one should ultimately look for the idea of the square phalanx. Numbers 2, for example, specifies the arrangement of the camp (see figure 20) as decidedly square, a shape comprising four divisions with three tribes constituting a division and occupying one side of the square under a common division. Within the square formed by these divisions and at the center of the entire encampment stands the tabernacle of Jehovah, surrounded by its appointed attendants.[111] There is nothing to suggest that Milton subscribes unequivocally to this arrangement. Yet it does represent a paradigm of the מלחמות יהוה that he was able to draw upon when conceiving his own version of angelic battle array. Of course, the quadratic form is not unique to Hebraic tradition. As countless Renaissance commentaries point out, it was a form employed not only by the Greeks and Romans but by the Egyptians and Persians as well.[112] In the Civil Wars, both sides adopted it,[113] and the word *squadron* is indebted to it.[114] Yet these considerations should not blind one to the specifically sacral character that the form assumes in Milton, as he ascribes to it symbolic meaning that cannot be overlooked. Its ties with Saint John the Divine and Ezekiel have already been noted. For Renaissance commentators, those ties were particularly appropriate, since they saw the arrangement of the Israelite camp replicated in the visions of Saint John and Ezekiel: encampment and temple assumed the same form.[115] The idea is not very far from the Puritan view (repeated in Milton) of the regiment as church. With its emphasis upon the divine union of all its members, the same sense of religiosity, not to mention sacrality, is implicit in both.

The way in which Milton implements these ideas in his actual account of the war will be seen upon further investigation. For example, God's saints consistently engage in such rituals of warfare as the battle shout (6.97, 200), the blowing of trumpets (6.203, 526), and the singing of psalms, as "the faithful Armies" resound "*Hosanna* to the Highest" (6.204–5). "Refulgent" in their "Piety" (6.527, 144), they may be said to have sanctified war (6.803–4). Compared with the "boastful Argument portraid" in the regalia of the satanic crew (6.84, 1.535–38), "Holy Memorials, acts of Zeal and Love" are "imblaz'd" upon the shields and banners of God's saints (5.592–93). Their weapons are hewn in the "Armorie of God" (6.321). Their very presence is one of "inviolability" (6.398). Upholding God's throne, they are sent to protect the sacred city from the "siege" of the infidel (5.732–33, 869; cf. 1.582). Ironically, Satan considers his own cause holy: he and his crew become crusaders, inspired with the quest (cf. 1.581–87). As far as God is concerned, however, they are decidedly "profane" and must be "separated" from all that is "holy" (6.742–43). Because they have violated the true worship of God, they have become "impure": their "wicked Tents" are "devoted" (5.890). Like those who have violated the true worship of God, they have been marked out as unclean and will be swallowed up into the pit (Num. 16:26–33).

That idea brings to the fore the issue of worship that characterizes the entire conflict. Refusing to obey God's decree that all the angels "bow" down and "confess" the begotten Son as "Lord" (5.604–12), Satan, as discussed in chapter 7, "leave[s]" "the Throne supream" "unworshipt, unobey'd" (5.669–70). Like his counterparts in Isaiah (14:12–14) and Ezekiel (28:13–16), he seeks to usurp God's throne (5.725–26, 10.375). "Affecting all equality with God," he first erects his own throne "in imitation of that Mount whereon / *Messiah* was declar'd in sight of Heav'n" (5.763–66), and then he appears in battle like an "Idol" to be worshiped: "High in the midst exalted as a God / Th'Apostat in his Sun-bright Chariot sate / Idol of Majestie Divine, enclos'd / With Flaming Cherubim, and golden Shields" (6.99–102). In fighting Satan, God's warriors, then, are clearly performing a religious function: they are not only helping to decide the matter of "Empire" in a dynastic confrontation (5.724) but, as iconoclasts, they are destroying false idols in a war of apostasy (6.172). Overcoming Satan's crew, the "elect" host (6.374) is wreaking vengeance on the atheists (6.370), much like Gideon, who was inspired by God to destroy the idols of the Midianites (Judg. 6:25–27).

The subject of the iconoclast is one that greatly interested Milton, who thought of writing extended works with such titles as "Gideon Idoloclastes," "Jehu Belicola," and "Josiah Aiazomenos" and who finally realized his ambition with Samson's destruction of Dagon's idol. Within a political context, this iconoclastic impulse extends, of course, to the Civil Wars. Once again, the often invoked association of the War in Heaven with the Civil Wars is not to be discounted. A professed iconoclast, Milton is part of a generation of iconoclasts who sought to undermine all that the *Eikon Basilike* represented.[116] Perhaps the direct linking of God's warriors with the forces of Parliament and Satan's warriors with the Royalist forces overstates the case, but as has been shown, the political ramifications of Milton's epic warfare cannot be ignored.[117]

The political dimension is an essential aspect of holy war accounts. Given expression in both Jewish and Christian apocalyptic, it is no less

FIGURE 20. The Israelite Encampment.
Reproduced from a rendering of Numbers 1 and 2,
in the Kitto Bible, 14:2303, by permission of the Huntington Library,
San Marino, California.

functional in *Paradise Lost*. If, in Milton's epic, it transcends the local political concerns of the specific battles chronicled by Sprigg, Vicars, Wither, and Milton himself in his prose writings, it nonetheless shares the fundamental outlook that traces its roots to the ideology of holy war. In the case of the Civil Wars, this occurrence is only natural considering the extent to which the Civil Wars were looked upon as holy wars both by those who upheld in battle the cause of God against the king and by those who inculcated holy war ideology into the warriors. It is no accident that the War in Heaven is conceived as a civil or "Intestine War" (6.259). In this sense, Abdiel, that most outspoken of nonconformists, refers ironically to himself as a "dissenter" and to the host of God as "sectarians" (6.145–47). The reference would not have been lost on Milton's contemporaries. Milton saw no contradiction in the fact that as one who supported the rebellion against God's so-called vicegerent on earth, he could write an epic portraying the evils of rebelling against God's true "Vice-gerent" in Heaven (5.609).

That outlook is triumphantly confirmed by the ideology of holy war: rebelling against God's alleged vicegerent on earth was really an act of upholding God's immutable laws in Heaven.[118] Although the Puritans were looked upon as dissenters and sectarians, they were, in fact, conformists to a higher order, one that not only condoned but commanded holy war in a righteous cause. Although aggressors, they fought both a just war in defending God's ways and a holy war in response to his promptings.[119] In epic terms, the idea is conceived as one of upholding God's "Vice-gerent" in Heaven against those who would unjustly undermine his reign. If such a posture is viewed in Satan's "World" (as in the Royalists' world) as an act of "dissent" and "sectarianism," it is for Abdiel (as for those who upheld God's cause against the king) an act of sublime conformity. In this sense, the war that God's angels wage is likewise both holy and just: holy because commanded by God, just because fought in defense of God's kingdom.

These are the political terms upon which the celestial battle as holy war is fought. Although their most immediate referent is in the Civil Wars, they, of course, transcend the conflicts of Milton's own time and express themselves in ways that accord with the larger conceptions of holy war, conceptions that are both cosmic and apocalyptic. In the first instance, they invite comparison with what Milton calls the warring of the "Constellations" (6.312), and they recall the warring of the elements in Chaos (6.649–69). In the second, they give rise to what becomes in *Paradise Lost* the battle of "the Sons of Light" (11.80) with the "sons of Darkness" (6.715, 5.716). In apocalyptic terms, the battle of the saints with the Dragon culminates in a vision of the Second Coming, as God, "consulting on the sum of things" (6.673), sends out his Son to terminate the struggle.[120] More than any other aspect of the battle, the Son's mission and its consequences reveal how extensively Milton was indebted to the ideology of the מלחמות יהוה in portraying the War in Heaven in *Paradise Lost.*

Thus, after the passage of "two dayes, as we compute the days of Heav'n" (6.684–85), God announces to his Son, "the third is thine" (6.699). This will be the יום־יהוה, the "Day of the Lord," as it was in the three-day battle of the Israelites against the Benjaminites of Gibeah (Judg. 20:20–34). In Christocentric terms, the time accords, as William B. Hunter, Jr., makes clear, with the fulfillment of Christ's Passion between the period of Good Friday and Easter Sunday.[121] In either case, the time assumes a sacrality in keeping with the sacredness of the event: God will "manifest" himself through his Son as a being "worthiest to be Heir / Of all things, to be Heir and to be King / By Sacred Unction" (6.707–9). Accordingly, God commands his Son:

> Go then thou Mightiest in thy Fathers might,
> Ascend my Chariot, guide the rapid Wheels
> That shake Heav'ns basis, bring forth all my Warr,
> My Bow and Thunder, my Almightie Armes
> Gird on, and Sword upon thy puissant Thigh;
> Pursue these sons of Darkness, drive them out
> From all Heav'ns bounds into the utter Deep.
>
> (6.710–16)

In response to his Father's command, the Son, on "the third sacred Morn" (6.748), ascends "the Chariot of Paternal Deitie" to crush God's foes.

The nature of the chariot and the Son's role in guiding it bring to the fore essential characteristics of holy war. As discussed in chapter 10, the chariot appears "flashing thick flames" and "convoyd / By four Cherubic shapes," each with "four Faces." Over the "heads" of these "shapes," there may be seen "a chrystal Firmament" on which is placed "a Saphire Throne" (6.751–59). Upon this "Throne" and between "the wings of Cherub," the Son rides "sublime" (6.771–72) in "Celestial Panoplie all armd / Of radiant *Urim*, work divinely wrought" (6.760–61). As he comes "onward," he, in turn, is "attended with ten thousand thousand Saints": "Farr off his coming shon, / And twentie thousand . . . / Chariots of God, half on each hand were seen" (6.766–70).

That vision combines Ezekiel 1 and Revelation 4, both invoked by

Milton in his polemical reference to "the fiery Chariot" driven by the "invincible warriore Zeale" (AP, *CM*, 3:313–14). As such, the vision embodies not only the cultic dimension explored in the discussion of the Shekinah but a military dimension that is precisely in keeping with the tradition of the יהוה מלחמות. The first dimension is well represented in the Renaissance biblical illustrations that accompany the treatment of the Shekinah in chapter 10 (figures 14, 15, and 16). To those illustrations may be added one (figure 21) from Jeronimo de Prado and John Baptistae Villalpandi's *In Ezechielem Explanationes* (1596–1604) that suggests in its rendering of the chariot rider the Christocentrism implicit in the Miltonic account. In its depiction of the chariot, moreover, figure 21 also has affinities with the military aspect (cf. the chariot as palladium) developed in this chapter. Thus, the martial dimension becomes a counterpart of the cultic.

Renaissance commentaries on Ezekiel and Revelation graphically demonstrate the extent to which the two dimensions are related. John Lightfoot provides a fitting point of departure. Commenting upon the chariot of Ezekiel, he says that it is none other than the ark of God dwelling in the sanctuary: "As the ark and cherubims upon it, and by it, are called 'the chariot of the cherubims' . . . the Lord there riding, as it were in his glory and presence, in the cloud that dwelt upon it,—even such another composture doth Ezekiel describe here, the divine chariot of the Lord, of his glorious and triumphant riding and sitting among his people in his word and ordinances, and his presence in them." The idea, says Lightfoot, is reinterpreted "in Revelation, where the Lord is enthroned, with such living creatures attending him . . . that it meaneth his glory at his Temple." There, "the sea of glass" is none other than "the molten sea" and "the seven lamps" none other than the "golden candlesticks." Even more important, however, is the reference to "the four beasts full of eyes before and behind." Drawn from the description of the "cherubims" in Ezekiel, this image suggests the way in which both Ezekiel and Saint John the Divine conceive chariot and throne as an expression of the concept of holy war. Such is discernible in what Lightfoot calls "the quadrature or four-square posture of the whole appearance": "There is intimation enough in Ezekiel, that the four living creatures stood square, with a fire in the midst of them, and the wheels in a square on the outside of the square of the living creatures: but, in the Revelation, it is yet more plain; for there it is said, 'the four living creatures stood round about the throne'; which could not be but in a quadrature." The "throne," then, surrounded by the "quadrature" "doth call us to remember" none other

FIGURE 21. Ezekiel's Vision of the Chariot.
Reproduced from a rendering of Ezekiel 1, in Jeronimo de Prado
and John Baptistae Villalpandi, *In Ezechielem Explanationes*
(1596–1604), by permission of the Joseph Regenstein Library
of the University of Chicago, Chicago, Illinois.

than "the Camp, that pitched about the tabernacle upon the four sides of it, east, west, north, and south." In their depictions of this camp, Ezekiel, with his chariot, and Saint John the Divine, with his throne, present us with what Lightfoot calls a "visionary theatre," in which God goes forth to overwhelm his enemies.[122]

If such is the view of so respectable a Renaissance scholar as Lightfoot, it is no less the view of the comparably regarded exegete Joseph Mede. What in Lightfoot is a "visionary theatre," in Mede becomes a "heavenly" or "Apocalyptique Theater." The implications are the same. Saint John the Divine's vision of the throne, drawn from Ezekiel's vision of the chariot, is, says Mede, "exactly framed according to the forme, of that ancient encamping of God with *Israel* in the wildernesse" (see figures 20 and 22).

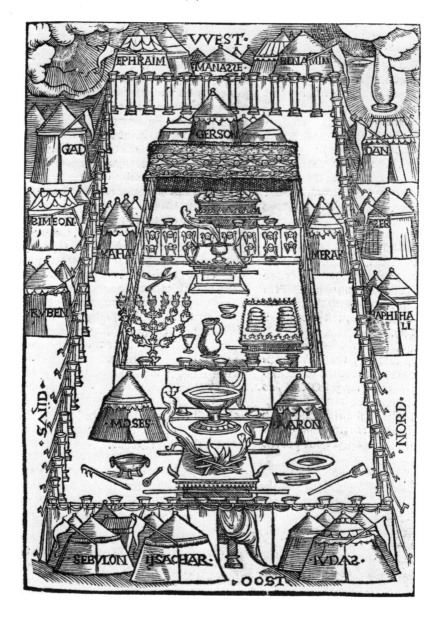

FIGURE 22. Wilderness Encampment.
Reproduced from a rendering of Exodus 2, in Biblia (1575),
by permission of the Newberry Library, Chicago, Illinois.

For in the midst of the tents of *Israel* was placed the Tabernacle or throne of God. Round about the Tabernacle the Levites pitched their tents neerest. Then after the Levites, the rest of the hoast of *Israel* was seated in foure standards, towards the four climates of the heaven. . . . This tradition of the Jewes may be confirmed out of the four fold face of the Cherubims . . . in *Ezekiel*; by which is signified that it was the Lord, and king of the four bands or campes of *Israel* which was carried on them. For as the Chariots of Princes doe glister with the ensignes of their Lords; so here the Cherubims with the ensignes of Jehova, the King of the Tetrarchies of Israel.[123]

Citing "the grave autority of *Pareus*" early in his career to support the contention that "the Apocalyps of Saint *John* is the majestick image of a high and stately Tragedy" (CG, *CM*, 3:238), Milton had long been in agreement with the view that Revelation is essentially dramatic in its bearing.[124] From the perspective that Lightfoot and Mede provide, he would certainly have included Ezekiel as well. Culminating in his own vision of "*Jehovah* thundring out of *Sion*, thron'd / Between the Cherubim," Milton's theater of war makes full use of the traditions that the most eminent Renaissance exegetes found implicit in the visions of Ezekiel and Saint John the Divine. Those traditions, as demonstrated, are rooted in the concept of holy war.

Thus, the Son's riding forth in *Paradise Lost* is nothing less than the bearing forth of the ark as palladium into battle. As the ark is brought forth from its position at the center of the encampment (Num. 2:17), the Son sets out from the mount of God, located in the center of Heaven (9.108–9; cf. Isa. 12:16, Ezek. 43:7, and Zech. 8:3). Much has been made of the fact that in the 1667 edition of *Paradise Lost*, the Son is said to have "Ascended" (6.762) the chariot in the exact numerical center of the poem. If the subsequent revisions included in the 1674 edition make that precise designation untenable, the centrality of the description of the chariot as a whole still obtains. Both imagistically and numerically, one can still say that the chariot as ark emerges from the center.[125] This centrality intensifies the hierophantic quality of the whole affair: we are in the midst of a decidedly priestly event. Such an aura is only appropriate considering the Son's attire. Wearing "*Urim*, work divinely wrought" (6.761; cf. PR, 3.13–16), he is the very embodiment of God's oraculous presence upon the throne, flanked by the cherubim. In that posture, the Son guides the chariot as ark over the heads of the enemy (6.840). The Son is appropriately high priest of that enterprise (cf. Exod. 28:30; Lev. 8:8).

Within this context, Milton's emphasis upon the "four Cherubic shapes" that "convoy" the chariot is supremely appropriate. The "four-fold-visag'd Four" (6.845) are the transcendent expression of the "mighty Quadrate" formed by the host of the saints. "Eye witness" to this fact, Michael "soon reduc[es] / His Armie, circumfus'd on either Wing, / Under thir Head imbodied all in one," as the "King of the Tetrarchies" comes forth in triumphal procession. Almost as if in tribute to this quadratic vision, Milton uses a synecdoche that encapsulates the entire event: "the Four," he says, "spred out thir Starrie wings / With dreadful shade contiguous," while the "fierce Chariot rowl'd" onward "as with the sound" "of a numerous Host" (6.827–30). "The Four"—it is as though the entire meaning of holy war were consummated in this phrase. In the theophany that overwhelms the rebel host, "the Four" play an essential role: "Distinct with eyes," they "glar[e] lightning, and [shoot] forth pernicious fire / Among th'accurst, that wither[s] all thir strength / And of their wonted vigour [leaves] them draind, / Exhausted, spiritless, afflicted, fall'n" (6.845–52). Such is precisely the effect that God's theophanies traditionally have upon his enemies in holy war.

In Milton's depiction of that theophany, moreover, the "shooting forth" of "pernicious fire" gives rise to still another dimension. If the chariot of God is an ark that is brought forth as a palladium into battle, it is also God's answer to Satan's cannons. For this purpose, Milton appropriated what might be called the combustible elements of Ezekiel's chariot with its "lightning" and Saint John the Divine's throne with its "lightnings and thunderings" in order to fashion an instrument of transcendent power. That instrument represents the divine counterpart of the debased cannons that achieve their impact through the use of gunpowder. By means of gunpowder, Satan creates what Milton long before in the poem *On the Gunpowder Plot* had called "a sulphurous chariot with flaming wheels" (5).[126] His purpose is to "disarm" the "Thunderer of his only dreaded bolt" (6.489–90). Doing so, Satan parodies, in his "triple-mounted row of Pillars laid / On Wheeles" (6.572–73), God's chariot, with its "fierce Effusion" of "smoak and bickering flame, and sparkles dire" and with its warrior bearing his "three-bolted Thunder" (6.764–66). If Satan brings forth his "devilish Enginrie, impal'd / On every side with shaddowing Squadrons Deep" (6.553–54), his chariot is no match for God's, whose "Thunder" "infix[es] / Plagues" (6.837–38), against which the rebel crew are powerless.

In his *Chariot of Wrath*, G. Wilson Knight compares God's chariot to "a super-tank and a super-bomber."[127] For Milton, however, the chariot is a type of the theophanies beheld by Ezekiel and Saint John the Divine.

The analogy is as true for Milton as for his contemporaries who witnessed the effects of mechanized warfare. When Peter Sterry preached before the high court of Parliament in a sermon celebrating the victory at Drogheda, he envisioned the event as none other than "the Comings Forth" of the Messiah upon the chariot "which *Ezekiel* saw." Here, once again, is a *"Throne"* "upon a *Firmament"* and "on that *Throne,* the Likenesse of a Man"; once again the *"Four Wheeles* full of Eyes, standing by the Living-Creatures." "The whole Host of Innumerable *Angels* and *Spirits* goe along with this *Presence* of the Lord. They are the Royall *Guard* pitcht round about the *Pavilion* of the Almighty."[128] The reference returns one to the unifying perspective provided by Milton's depiction of the theophany as a whole.

One's understanding of that theophany would not be complete, however, without mention of a final aspect that Milton incorporates into his vision of the chariot. For all its destructive qualities, the chariot, as Milton portrays it, is also a "vehicle" of creation. The same chariot in which the Son goes out to overwhelm the rebel angels is later used in the Son's mission to create the world (7.197–209). Even as the Son rides forth in his destructive mission in the war, he "restore[s]" "Heav'n['s] . . . wonted face" as a sign of his recreative energy (6.781–84). The act is in keeping with the meaning of the chariot. In the Merkabah, rabbinical commentators traditionally looked upon the chariot as a symbol of renewal.[129] For Christian commentators, it symbolized the renewal brought about by the New Jerusalem.[130] So Saint John the Divine conceives it, and so Milton suggests it in the eschatological bearing of the Son's mission.

If these are some of the prevailing implications of the chariot, they are complemented, in turn, by the additional contexts to which Milton's description of the overthrow of Satan's crew gives rise. Among the most important of those contexts is suggested by the Son's speech to his faithful just before he overwhelms Satan's crew:

> Stand still in bright array ye Saints, here stand
> Ye Angels arm'd, this day from Battel rest;
> Faithful hath been your warfare, and of God
> Accepted, fearless in his righteous Cause,
> And as ye have receiv'd, so have ye don
> Invincibly; but of this cursed crew
> The punishment to other hand belongs,
> Vengeance is his, or whose he sole appoints;
> . . . stand onely and behold

Gods indignation on these Godless pourd
By me. . . .

(6.801–14)

The Son's language brings to bear a number of essential motifs that characterize the traditions of holy war. A few of these have already been discussed: the warfare of the saints as that which is not only "faithful" but implicitly offered up to God as a sign of worship. This sanctifying of war as an offering is "accepted" because it has been fought "fearlessly" in defense of God's "righteous Cause." If the victory is to be "given" into the "hand" of God's faithful, however, it will finally be not through their own power but through the power of God. To him alone the "punishment" "belongs" "or who[m] he sole appoints." Accordingly, it is through God's "hand" only that the war can be won. At this juncture Milton invokes, through the Son, the essential formula for holy war: "stand still," "here stand," "stand onely." It is a phrase that Milton had singled out for recital in "The Argument" to Book 4 of his epic. Repeated in the Son's speech three times in nine lines, the direction to "stand" strikes at the heart of the ideology of holy war.

According to Millard Lind's "Paradigm of Holy War in the Old Testament," the dominant feature of the מלחמות יהוה involved the simple act of standing still.[131] Waiting in readiness, the Israelites revealed their faith in God's providence. After all their fighting and all their acts of heroism, their ultimate inaction was their most triumphant act. For they knew that they had only to stand and behold God the warrior wield the decisive and miraculous blow. As heroic and dedicated to God's cause as the warfare had been, it was finally futile until God revealed himself in his overwhelming power and ordered his faithful to "stand still." "And Moses said unto the people: 'Fear ye not, stand still [והתיצבו], and see the salvation of the Lord, which He will show to you today. . . . The Lord shall fight for you, and ye shall hold your peace'" (Exod. 14:13–14); "For the battle *is* not yours, but God's. . . . You shall not *need* to fight in this *battle*: set yourselves, stand ye *still* [והתיצבו], and see the salvation of the Lord with you" (2 Chron. 20:15–17). This outlook accounts for what in *Paradise Lost* becomes the futility of the War in Heaven ("Warr wearied hath performed what Warr can do" [6.695]) and the occasion for God's sending out his Son to crush the rebel host.

The act of standing still, in turn, is one that Milton learned to cultivate throughout his career. In this sense, the final line of Sonnet 19 is the true declaration of God's faithful champion: "They also serve who only stand and wait." "Gerhard von Rad has pointed out that the biblical demand for faith probably has its proper origin" in this holy war willingness to stand and wait.[132] Milton portrayed that posture not only in the moment of stasis that characterizes the troops of God in *Paradise Lost* but in Jesus' ability to occupy his perilous station after a long period of what Stanley Fish calls "inaction" in *Paradise Regained*.[133] Exploring that time of "inaction" in *Samson Agonistes*, Jackie Di Salvo concludes that the idea of standing in readiness is an essential aspect of the Puritan outlook, one that characterized Cromwell himself during the Civil Wars.[134] Investigating similar elements in *Paradise Lost*, Boyd Berry, in his discussion of the Puritan soldier, comes to the same conclusion.[135] One of the fundamental directives of *The Souldiers Pocket Bible* during the Civil Wars is appropriately to "stand still" and await God's help, which will come in "the very nicke of time" (p. 13). This posture, in fact, amounted to a battle maneuver for Cromwell's troops, one associated with the technical idea of "reducing" the regiments in preparation for an onslaught.[136] (In *Paradise Lost*, one recalls Michael's act of "reduc[ing] / His Armie, circumfus'd on either Wing, / Under thir Head imbodied all in one," while the troops stand ready to await further orders.) Cromwell's remarkable ability to negotiate this maneuver in his own well-disciplined troops must have been impressive, for it was even begrudgingly praised by Clarendon, who attributed the New Model's effectiveness in "rallying" themselves at a moment's notice to their gaining the edge over the Royalists. Having "reduced" themselves, Cromwell's troops, said Clarendon, "stood in good order, till they received new orders." "*Stand*," Clarendon observed, is a "Soldierly word": it means to reassemble and adhere as a body to the commander. This, Charles's men had difficulty in doing.[137] Such, then, is the military context of a word whose roots, in the traditions of holy war, are ultimately biblical.

Considering Milton's use of the word at the crucial juncture when the Son is to overwhelm the rebel angels in *Paradise Lost*, one must return again to the Bible to receive a full understanding of its meaning. According to theoreticians of holy war, the locus classicus of God's directive to the Israelites to "stand" occurs at the point when he is to destroy the Pharaoh's legions in the Red Sea. "Stand still, and see the salvation of the Lord," he says through his servant Moses (Exod. 14:13–14). The language is not only reflected in the Son's directions to his faithful to "stand still" and "behold / God's indignation on these Godless pourd" but complemented by the description of the actual overthrow, which, as Jason Rosenblatt has established, aptly recalls its biblical prototype (Exod. 14:15–31, 15:1–11).[138] Thus, like God, who "pursued" the Egyptian host "into the sea," the Son "pursu'd" the satanic host to the "Chrystal wall of Heav'n" (6.858). Like the Red Sea, which "divided" to form a "wall" on both sides and then "returned" upon "the host of Pharaoh," Heaven's "Chrystal wall" "op'ning wide, / Rowl'd inward" and then "return[ed] whence it rowl'd" (6.858–60, 879). In the final book of his epic, Milton recounts the event in exactly these terms, when, through Michael, he describes how "the Sea," with its "divided" "christal walls" closed upon Pharaoh and his "Host" and "swallow[ed] them": "On thir imbattell'd ranks the Waves return[ed] / And overwhelm[ed] thir Warr" (12.195–213). Thus is the "River-dragon" (12.192) overcome as "the race elect / Safe towards *Canaan* from the shoar advance" (12.214–15). It is precisely this association that Milton invokes at the outset of *Paradise Lost* when he depicts the satanic crew as "*Busiris* and his *Memphian* Chivalry" overthrown by the Red Sea, "while with perfidious hatred they pursu'd / The Sojourners of *Goshen*, who beheld / From the safe shore thir floating Carkases / And broken Chariot Wheels" (1.306–11).

In the celestial context, the "Sojourners of *Goshen*" are the faithful troops of God, who, in their own Exodus journey, "silent stood / Eye witnesses of [God's] Almightie Acts" (6.882–83). Like Moses, who intones the Song of the Sea, God's host in "Jubilee" "Sung Triumph."[139] Their song, like Moses', celebrates their "redemption" and the Conquest of the Kingdom by the "right hand" of God who "reigns" as "Victorious King" (6.884–87). As God, in Moses' song, "hast guided" his people "unto [his] holy habitation," where he "dwell[s]" in his "Sanctuary" (Exod. 15:12–18), the Son "celebrated rode / Triumphant through mid Heav'n, into the Courts / And Temple of his mightie Father Thron'd / On high" (6.888–91). The processional return recapitulates what has been shown here to be a primary characteristic of holy war and consummates the pattern of the "ritual Conquest" or the Exodus-Conquest. That event, as Moses sings, attests to the fact that "the Lord shall reign for ever and ever" (Exod. 15:18).

There is, however, one major difference between the War in Heaven in *Paradise Lost* and its counterparts in the Bible: the Son in Milton's epic does not enact a true חרם. The rebel angels are not actually destroyed. As Milton says of the Son, "Yet half his strength he put not forth, but check'd / His Thunder in mid Volie, for he meant / Not to destroy" the rebel angels "but root them out of Heav'n" (6.853–55). The reason for this difference may be seen, of course, in the fact that Satan, as the result of God's "will" and "high permission," must be allowed, after the celestial battle, to pursue "his own dark designs, / That with reiterated crimes he might / Heap on himself damnation" (1.211–15). Such is in accord with God's divine plan to effect Satan's ultimate overthrow at the end of time, when *"Satan* with his perverted World" will be "dissolve[d]" in the Second Coming. That eschatological event will be followed by the "rais-[ing] / From the conflagrant mass, purg'd and refin'd, / New Heav'ns, new Earth, Ages of endless date" (12.545–49). In this occurrence, the New Jerusalem will be fully realized. To reach that point, however, there must be another war, that waged on earth. The second of two conflicts in *Paradise Lost*, this war, like that in Heaven, is indebted in its own way to the traditions of holy war.

Those traditions, in turn, have as their source the concept of spiritual warfare so essential to the New Testament frame of mind. As Paul admonishes:

> Put on the whole armour of God, that ye may be able to stand [στῆναι] against the wiles of the devil. For we wrestle not against flesh and blood, but against principalities, against powers, against rulers of the darkness of this world, against spiritual wickedness in high *places.* Wherefore take unto you the whole armour of God that ye may be able to withstand [ἀντιστῆναι] in the evil day, and having done all, to stand [στῆναι]. Stand therefore [στῆτε οὖν], having your loins girt about with truth, and having on the breastplate of righteousness; And your feet shod with the preparation of the gospel of peace; Above all taking the shield of faith, wherewith ye shall be able to quench all the fierie darts of the wicked. And take the helmet of salvation, and the sword of the Spirit, which is the word of God. (Ephes. 6:11–17)

With his emphasis upon the act of standing (στῆναι), Paul, of course, draws upon the Old Testament holy war concept of "standing still" (הִתְיַצְּבוּ) to suggest his own version of holy war. Introducing the concept of spiritual combat, he counters הִתְיַצְּבוּ with στῆναι. Thus, from the Christian point of view, the soldier in Christ "stands" (στῆναι) through the act of "withstanding" (ἀντιστῆναι). That which is withstood are the sins of this world in a process of perpetual warfare against the wiles of Satan. That is the holy war waged on earth. As a counterpart to the apocalyptic warfare waged in Heaven,[140] this combat gave rise to a rich exegetical tradition of its own.

In works ranging from Giovanni da Legnano's *Tractatus de Bello* in the fourteenth century to Desiderius Erasmus's *Enchiridion Militis Christiani* in the sixteenth, the concept of spiritual combat flourished.[141] Correspondingly, there emerged in sixteenth- and seventeenth-century England a host of devotional works that looked upon the life of a Christian as a spiritual combat. One thinks of such works as Lancelot Andrewes's *The*

Wonderfull Combate (1592), Lewis Thomas's *Christ Combating with Satan* (1599), John Downame's *The Christian Warfare* (1612), William Gouge's *The Whole-Armour of God* (1619), Thomas Taylor's *Christs Victorie Over the Dragon* (1633), Richard Sibbes's *The Soules Conflict with it selfe* (1638), Edmund Turges's *The Christian Soldier* (1639), Henry Lawrence's *Of our Communion and Warre with Angels* (1646), and William Gurnall's *The Christian in Compleate Armour* (1655). In their own way, these works conceive spiritual combat as *the* holy war par excellence. Preaching "at the Crosse the 15th of September. 1622," John Donne took occasion to gloss the holy war text "They foughte from heaven; the stars in their courses fought against Sisera" from the Song of Deborah (Judg. 5:20) as a locus classicus for the "spirituall Warre" that the Christian must fight in his desire for salvation. In this context, the curse against Meroz ("*Maledicti Pacifici*") becomes the occasion to curse all those who will not fight the holy wars of Christ against Satan in their own souls. "In every man," says Donne, "there are two sides, two armies: the flesh fights against the Spirit. This is but a Civill warre."[142]

In the actual Civil Wars, the devotional tenor of such a statement assumes a martial bearing uniquely its own. The very point of view that Donne espoused as staunch Anglican divine was appropriated by the Puritan preachers to incite in the parliamentary soldiers a warfare within themselves. Milton himself praised the parliamentary soldiers for fighting a "warfare of the spirit" and admonished them to maintain that warfare in their own souls as an example to others (2D, CM, 8:179,241). This warfare became the precise counterpart of the holy wars that the Puritan soldiers saw themselves waging against Antichrist in the pursuit of the New Jerusalem. Thus, Simeon Ashe exhorts "the Commanders of the Military Forces" in his sermon *Good Courage Discovered, and Encouraged* (1642): "God hath appoynted all Christians to be souldiers. A sacrament is a souldiers oath, when we were baptized we tooke presse money, and vowed to serve under the colours of Christ, and as manfull souldiers to fight against the world, the flesh, and the Devill: and as oft as wee have been at the Sacrament of the body, and blood of our Lord, wee have renewed our solemn, and sacred obligation in that kind, in reference to Christ, who is called *The Captaine of the Lords host*, Jos. 5. 16 and *the Captaine of our Salvation*, Heb. 2. 10" (p. 8). Were Ashe not preaching to actual soldiers, the statement would not be particularly remarkable. But the point is that one can observe in the very war literature of the time a transition from incitement to holy war as physical confrontation to incitement to holy war as spiritual confrontation. As Michael Walzer observes, in the hands of the military preachers, this transition assumes political significance: it becomes, in fact, "the central myth of Puritan radicalism."[143]

As a Christian soldier, Milton's Adam derives impetus not only from the centuries of devotional literature to which the New Testament gave rise but from the more immediate political milieu that was so influential in shaping Milton's thought. Like the Puritan soldiers who were admonished that spiritual warfare is finally that which they should be most zealous in waging, Adam comes to learn the full meaning of holy war as that which is fought within his own soul. In line with its counterpart in the heavenly struggle, that drama, however, is not limited to an immediate political or even devotional context. Its elements of universality find expression in imaginative literature as well. From this perspective, its roots are in the kind of struggle that Prudentius conceived in the *Psychomachia* as early as the fourth century. If the terms of the drama that Milton envisions are not quite so allegorical as those depicted in Prudentius's work,[144] the spiritual warfare that fallen man is destined to undergo culminates in a similar victory: the founding of the New Jerusalem. After "light and darkness" struggle within our soul, "Christ our God," says Prudentius, "comes to our aid . . . and where Sin formerly reigned builds the golden courts of his temple."[145]

The process is one that is rearticulated from one work to the next[146] until it is integrated into an outlook that most closely approximates that established in *Paradise Lost*. That outlook assumes epic form in the great psychomachia of the seventeenth century, appropriately entitled *The Holy War Made By Shaddai Upon Diabolus For the Regaining of the Metropolis of the World, Or the Losing and Taking Againe of the Town of Mansoul* (1682). If one explores the language of Bunyan's epic, he will find the essential elements of the מלחמות יהוה: the interiorized drama between Christ and Satan culminating in a vision of the New Jerusalem is characterized by such holy war practices as the designation of four captains according to the Israelite ordering of the camp, the sending forth of the armies of God under his appointed leader, the description of the exalted march, the account of God's own entrance into battle (in the form of his Son in the divine chariot), the performance of the rituals of battles (such as the singing of verses from Psalm 68), the processional return to the sanctuary after battle, and the cleansing of the plains.[147] In the tendency to spiritualize warfare, the ideology of holy war found consummate expression, then, in the Puritan literary imagination. Its universality, however, can hardly be limited to any particular outlook. It is as much at home in Prudentius as it is in Bunyan.

Paradise Lost is no exception to the spiritualizing of warfare as a holy war conceit. It is a holy war epic both in its account of spiritual warfare and in its rendering of celestial warfare. In integrating the two, it becomes the supreme מלחמות יהוה.[148] Why this is so will be seen upon investigation of the War on Earth in *Paradise Lost*, beginning with the Temptation and Fall of man.

That those events (the Temptation and Fall) are conceived as a battle is hardly open to doubt. Milton establishes the martial context at the beginning of Book 4, when he invokes "that warning voice, which he who saw / Th'*Apocalypse*, heard cry in Heaven aloud": "*Wo to th'inhabitants on Earth*" (4.1–5). The cry is uttered in Revelation after the "routing" of Satan in "the War in heaven." Now defeated, "the devil is come down unto you, having great wrath, because he knoweth that he hath but a short time" (Rev. 12:7–12). For Milton, this means that Satan will attempt to avenge in a second battle "his loss of that first Battel" (4.11–12). He will do so not, as Moloch suggests, through "open Warr" (2.51) but through "covert guile" (2.41). In martial terms, he will attack God not through a direct "Siege" of the heavenly kingdom, which he knows is impregnable, but through a war upon "the utmost border of [God's] kingdom," left to the "defence" of those who "hold it" (2.358–62). His war will be conducted in such a way that the inhabitants of God's paradisal satellite will be "reduce[d]" to the devil's "Party, that thir God / May prove thir foe" (2.368–69).

If, for Milton, this enterprise is seen as the counterpart of the War in Heaven, for Satan, it is conceived as a knightly "quest" to "besiege" the "World" of "*Man*" (2.342–49, 4.830, 9.414, 10.467–68). As in the celestial conflict, Satan becomes a mock-crusader bent on a holy war of destruction. His lineage is that recounted

> In Fable or *Romance* of *Uthers* Son
> Begirt with *British* and *Armoric* Knights;
> And all who since, Baptiz'd or Infidel
> Jousted in *Aspramont* or *Montalban*,
> *Damasco*, or *Marocco*, or *Trebisand*,
> Or whom *Biserta* sent from *Afric* shore
> When *Charlemain* with all his Peerage fell
> by *Fontarrabbia*.
>
> (1.580–87)

The milieu is one that Milton had long thought of recreating in a holy war epic that would represent a counterpart to its continental models. Finally disenchanted with that milieu, he either rejected it for the "higher Argument" of *Paradise Lost* or accommodated it ironically to his depiction of Satan and his crew, whose "holy warfare" both in Heaven and on earth becomes a perversion of the crusading ideal. The zeal with which Satan undertakes this crusade leads finally to his own destruction. Nonetheless, his "conquering" of the "New World" (4.391) is initially successful, as the recounting of the event makes clear.

That event is portrayed appropriately through a language of war. Eden itself is an armed camp. Equipped with its own "Armourie" of "Shields, Helms, and Speares" (4.553), it is guarded by "armd" angelic sentries who keep a constant watch upon its boundaries (4.778–87). Their "charge" is to insure that Eden remains "inviolable" (4.842–43) against the possible assaults of intruders. That they are finally "unsuccessful" in fulfilling their "charge" (10.35) is not to their discredit. As God consoles his angels after the Fall, "Be not dismaid, / Nor troubl'd" at what "your sincerest care could not prevent" (10.34–37). What their care could not prevent, of course, is Satan's penetration of the confines that the angels had been sent to guard. Scaling the barricades and overleaping the highest bounds of this fortress (4.172–83), Satan commences his "sly assault" (cf. 9.256). If he is thwarted in his first attempt (4.797–819), he is successful in his second (9.781).

Succumbing to Satan's wiles despite the admonitions of the angelic emissary Raphael, man becomes a rebel, "leagued" (cf. 4.375) unwittingly with his own enemy in "revolt" (9.7). The revolution results at least temporarily in a satanic victory. For the present, Satan is allowed to assume the "Monarchie" of what had been "th'addition of [God's] Empire" (7.555, 10.379).[149] His possession of that empire allows him to "erect the Standard there of ancient *Night*" (2.985–86) and to liberate from the "Dungeon" those who had previously been prisoners of war (2.317, 10.466). Man's fate, however, is one of suffering the horrors of war. Because of his "breach / Disloyal" (9.6–7), man undergoes a "mortal change" (10.273) that emits a "scent" characteristic of those who are about to die "in bloodie fight" (10.278–79). Lured by that scent in Hell, Death, in pursuit of his "Quarry" (10.281), is compared to "a flock / Of ravenous Fowl" that "come flying" to the "Field" of "Battel" (10.273–76; cf. 6.73–76).

Eden has indeed become a theater (albeit "a woodie Theatre" [4.141]) of war. More than that, of course, it is a sacred place whose confines are liable to pollution. In the specific context of Satan's assaults that Milton develops at the outset of his epic, that place becomes the center of the warfare that Israel was to suffer as a result of the abominations it committed in its Temple. In its own way, Eden is Jerusalem itself. It is no accident that when Adam and Eve are said to have "sat them down to weep" (9.1121) after their fall, they are compared implicitly to those Israelites who "sat down" and "wept" "by the rivers of Babylon" when they "remembered Zion" (Ps. 137:1). Like all those who are described in the first book of Milton's epic as falling prey to satanic idolatries, the fallen couple have committed idolatries of their own—Eve in worshiping the interdicted tree after she has tasted of its fruit (9.799–800, 835–36), Adam in making Eve his "God" by "obeying" her "voice" before God's (10.145–46). In their own way, they have "forsaken" their "living strength, and unfrequented left / His righteous Altar, bowing lowly down" to false gods (1.432–35). For this trespass, they, like the idolators after them, must "bow down" in their own "Battel," overcome by "despicable foes" (1.436–37).

Their fate is recapitulated in the history of the Temple that Michael relates to Adam in the last two books. Essential to the full realization of Israel's destiny in the course of its holy wars, that history involves the fall of Jerusalem. After Canaan has been won and the "Ark of God" "enshrin[ed]" in "a glorious Temple" (12.269, 333–34), the Israelites commit "foul Idolatries" that "so incense / God, as to leave them, and expose thir Land / Thir Citie, his Temple, and his holy Ark / With all his sacred things, a scorn and prey" to the "proud Citie" of "Babylon" (12.335–43). Because of man's trespasses in breaking allegiance with God and in joining in an unholy league with Satan, God responds in a manner that recalls his dealing with Jerusalem: he turns his holy war upon man himself. As Milton conceives it, however, the act is not vindictive. Rather, it is a purgative act, an act of cleansing, as the Temple itself is paradoxically "cleansed" of its idolatries by those who sack it (2 Chron. 36:14–19; cf. Ezek. 43:3). When Sin and Death enter the world to wreak the destruction that man has called upon himself, God says that although his enemies scorn him, they "know not" that he himself "call'd and drew [them] thither / [His] Hell-hounds, to lick up the draff and filth / Which man's polluting Sin with taint hath shed / On what was pure" until they are overcome by the "victorious Arm" of his Son: "Then Heav'n and Earth renewd shall be made pure / To sanctitie that shall receive no stain" (10.615–39). Until that time, however, man must suffer the burden of his history. Having become "tainted," "gross," and "unholie" (11.52–53, 106) in his fall, he must first be ejected from Eden's "hallowd ground" (10.106). Like Satan, who becomes "impure" in his revolt and accordingly must be "separate[ed]" "farr" from God's "Saints unmixt" (6.742–43), man may no longer remain in the holy environment of paradise. Like Satan's, his ejection is in keeping with the ideology of holy war.

Milton's recourse to that ideology, however, assumes its own unique bearing in his description of the event. The trappings of holy war are certainly present. When Michael and his "heav'nly Bands" make "alt" upon "a Hill" in paradise (11.208–20), their appearance is compared to those "bright" legions that were revealed as a sign of God's strength before Jacob and Elisha, faced with the prospect of war (Gen. 32:1–2; 2 Kings 6:13–17). The presence of Michael's host is a sign of God's protection of his warriors against harm. "Had not doubt / And carnal fear that day dimm'd *Adams* eye," he would have understood the full meaning of that "glorious Apparition" (11.211–12). Along with his host, Michael is accompanied by that divine instrument of warfare, the chariot of God with its fourfold visage (11.127–29), used by the Son to rout Satan and his cohorts. In this case, however, the "watchful Cherubim" (11.128) are there not so much to rout Adam and Eve as to ward off "the Fiend," who might attempt to "invade / Vacant possession" or "som new trouble raise" (11.101–3). At the same time, they provide "Cherubic watch" that, with their "wide waving" swords of "flame" "fright" "all approach farr off," "least Paradise a receptacle prove / To Spirits foul" (11.120–24). "Looking back" after their ejection, Adam and Eve behold "all th'Eastern side" of "Paradise, so late thir happie seat, / Wav'd over by that flaming Brand, the Gate / With dreadful Faces throng'd and fierie Armes" (12.641–44). It is a terrifying sight; but, as Renaissance exegetes such as Lightfoot maintained in their reading of the Genesis passage (Gen. 3:24) from which the description is derived, the image is one that is perfectly in accord with the chariot and throne envisioned by Ezekiel and Saint John the Divine, respectively.[150] If nothing else, Adam and Eve behold in exile the exterior of that "house" whose "gate," as Ezekiel says, "looketh toward the east" (Ezek. 43:1–8) and whose precincts they may not reenter until the proper time.

More than that, however, the specific connotations of chariot and throne emerge in the details surrounding both Michael's advent and his attire. For example, Michael comes forth from "a Skie of Jasper" (11.209; cf. 3.363), that stone adopted by Saint John the Divine to describe the throne of God (Rev. 4:3; cf. Rev. 21:11, 18 and Ezek. 1:22). Michael's "Sword" hangs "by his side / As in a glistering *Zodiac*" (11.246–47). The idea is reminiscent of the "four Cherubic shapes," whose "bodies" and "Wings," Milton says, "are set with Eyes," "as with Starrs" (6.754). The imagery is in accord with the practices of Ezekiel and Saint John the Divine to conceive the chariot and throne in cosmic terms. Furthermore, the "wooff" of Michael's "militarie Vest" has been "dipt" by "*Iris*" (11.241–44), a symbol of the rainbow (cf. CO, 83, 992). "Round about the throne" that Saint John the Divine describes, "a rainbow" might be seen (Rev. 4:3). The image, of course, is derived from Ezekiel's vision of the chariot: "As the appearance of the bow that is in the cloud in the day of rain, so *was* the appearance of the brightness round about" (Ezek. 1:28). This idea is in keeping with Milton's description of the chariot, the throne of which is inlaid with "colours of the showrie Arch" (6.758–59). It is also in keeping with the concept of "Providence" that guides Adam and Eve in their fallen condition (12.647). That is why Michael, although attired as a soldier, comes to negotiate a "Truce," as his "militarie Vest" suggests (11.244). The image of the rainbow that graces his vest indicates as much. As Adam learns after beholding the Deluge, the rainbow "betok[ens] peace from God, and Cov'nant new" (11.867). Because Adam comes to learn the full meaning of that covenant as a source of renewal (11.116), he is sent forth "though sorrowing, yet in peace" (11.117). His sense of peace, finally, is derived from what Michael communicates to him in the final books of Milton's epic. There, Adam learns how ultimate peace may be obtained through a warfare, the significance of which he had not previously understood. In that warfare, the ideology of holy war assumes a spiritual meaning.

From the Christocentric point of view, the idea has its source, of course, in the curse placed upon the serpent in Genesis 3:15: "And I will put enmity between thee and the woman, and between thy seed and her seed; it shall bruise thy head, and thou shalt bruise his heel." Known as the *protevangelium*, the passage is given a New Testament interpretation by Saint Paul: "And the God of peace shall bruise Satan under your feet shortly. The grace of our Lord Jesus Christ *be* with you" (Rom. 16:20). After God through the Son pronounces judgment upon the serpent in *Paradise Lost*, the narrator explains the judgment in these terms:

> So spake the Oracle, then verifi'd
> When *Jesus* son of *Mary* second *Eve*,
> Saw Satan fall like Lighning down from Heav'n,
> Prince of the Air; then rising from his Grave
> Spoild Principalities and Powers, triumphant
> In open shew, and with ascension bright
> Captivity led captive through the Air,
> The Realm it self of Satan long usurpt,
> Whom he shall tread at last under our feet;
> Eevn hee who now foretold his fatal bruise.
> (10.182–91)

This is the apocalyptic event that Adam, through Michael, comes to learn about as the last two books of Milton's epic unfold. Significantly, Milton describes it here in the language of holy war by drawing upon Psalm 68, which celebrates God's having "led captivity captive" as he rides forth in his "twenty thousand" "chariots" from his holy mountain (Ps. 68:17–18). Milton alludes to the same passage in his description of the Son's riding forth to bruise the heads of the rebel angels in the celestial battle (6.769). Satan, of course, misses the significance of the event entirely:

> True is, mee also he hath judg'd, or rather
> Mee not, but the brute Serpent in whose shape
> Man I deceav'd: that which to mee belongs,
> Is enmity, which he will put between
> Mee and Mankind; I am to bruise his heel;
> His Seed, when is not set, shall bruise my head:
> A World who would not purchase with a bruise,
> Or much more grievous pain?
>
> (10.494–501)

As Michael reveals the mystery of the protevangelium to Adam upon the "Hill of Speculation" (12.589), Adam rejoices at the new league ("so God with man unites" [12.382]) and then proclaims in triumph, "Needs must the Serpent now his capital bruise / Expect with mortal pain" (12.383–84). His understanding of the protevangelium, however, is still not complete, for he has yet to comprehend the full nature of spiritual warfare.

In response to his question "say where and when / Thir fight, what stroke shall bruise the Victors heel" (12.384–85), Michael says:

> Dream not of thir fight,
> As of a Duel, or the local wounds
> Of head or heel: not therefore joyns the Son
> Manhood to God-head, with more strength to foil
> Thy enemie; nor so is overcome
> *Satan*, whose fall from Heav'n, a deadlier bruise,
> Disabl'd not to give thee thy deaths wound:
> Which hee, who comes thy Saviour, shall recure,
> Not by destroying *Satan*, but his works
> In thee and in thy Seed: nor can this be,
> But by fulfilling that which thou didst want,
> Obedience to the Law of God, impos'd

On penaltie of death, and suffering death,
The penaltie to thy transgression due,
And due to theirs which out of thine will grow:
So onely can high Justice rest appaid.

(12.386–401)

In brief, this is the formulation of spiritual warfare that governed Milton's Christocentric outlook not only in *Paradise Lost* but throughout his works. It assumes epic form in *Paradise Regained*, which is Milton's most graphic statement of what is involved in going out to war against "the Spiritual Foe" (1.10). In this "great duel, not of arms" (1.174), the Incarnate Son "lay[s] down the rudiments / Of his great warfare" to reveal how "weakness . . . o'recome[s] Satanic strength / And all the world, and mass of sinful flesh" (1.157–62). His conquest of Satan in "the Desert, his Victorious Field" (1.9), becomes the spiritual counterpart of his earlier conquest in Heaven. Thus, he is celebrated:

. . . him [Satan] long of old
Thou didst debel, and down from Heav'n cast
With all his Army, now thou hast aveng'd
Supplanted *Adam*, and by vanquishing
Temptation, hast regain'd lost Paradise,
And frustrated the conquest fraudulent.

(4.604–9)

A counterpart of the celestial victory, this spiritual victory, then, recoups the losses of the "conquest fraudulent" that Satan had enjoyed in the Edenic warfare. As a result of Christ's spiritual victory, man may reenter paradise.

Even as Adam and Eve are being expelled from paradise, their ejection assumes paradoxical significance: the process is compared to a "Labourer" "homeward returning" as "Ev'ning Mist" "gathers" at his "heel" (12.628–32). Ejection culminates in a return home, because the Messiah "shall quell / The adversarie Serpent, and bring back / Through the worlds wilderness long wanderd man / Safe to eternal Paradise of rest" (12.311–14). Regaining the spiritual "*Canaan*" after the loss of the "earthly" (12.315), man shall "possess" within himself a "Paradise" "happier farr" (12.587) as an anticipation of that eschatological "Paradise," "New Heav'ns, new Earth, Ages of endless date" (12.464, 549). To achieve that state, man must undergo an *imitatio Christi*: within his own soul, he must engage in that warfare by which Christ himself "bruis[ed] the head of Satan" to achieve man's redemption. Like the

"Victor" in that fight, man will suffer the wounding of his "heel," but because he is redeemed, his death will be "a gentle wafting to immortal Life" (12.429–35).

This is what Adam learns when he ascends the Hill of Speculation. His education there becomes a veritable process of "arming to overcom / By suffering" (11.374–75). His models are such "soldiers" as Abel, Enoch, Noah, Abraham, Isaac, Joseph, Moses, Joshua, and David. All these, "through faith subdued kingdoms, wrought righteousness, obtained promises, stopped the mouths of lions, quenched the violence of fire, escaped the edge of the sword, out of weakness were made strong, waxed valiant in fight, turned to flight the armies of the aliens" (Heb. 11:33–34). In these warriors, Adam sees the types of Christ. Like them, he is "arm[ed] / With spiritual Armour, able to resist / Satans assaults, and quench his fierie darts" (12.490–93). In Pauline terms, Adam's education is that of the Christian soldier, who learns not only to "stand" (στῆναι) but to "withstand" (ἀντιστῆναι). Such is the Christian soldier's new "standing" with God, the means by which, as God says in *Paradise Lost*, man will be able to "stand / On even ground against his mortal foe" (3.178–79). Introduced to the vocation of the Christian soldier upon the Hill of Speculation, Adam beholds in "the Visions of God" (11.377) the new form that the holy war is to assume. For that reason, Milton in his description of the ascent of that hill, immediately looks forward to the event that he would later portray in *Paradise Regained*: the "set[ting]" of "our second *Adam*" upon the hill by "the Tempter" to show the Messiah "all Earths Kingdoms and thir Glory" (11.381–84). What Adam beholds in his view of that panorama, however, is finally not "Earths Kingdoms" but Heaven's, not the conquest of the earthly Jerusalem but of the heavenly. In this sense, the ultimate object of his sight is what in *The Faerie Queene* the Red Cross Knight beholds upon the "sacred hill": "The new *Ierusalem*, that God has built / For those to dwell in, that are chosen his, / His chosen people purg'd from sinful guilt" (1.10.53–57). That Jerusalem must be conquered not through earthly but through spiritual means. The conquest involves a warfare that is waged in the soul of man and that is consummated in the Second Coming.

As waged in the soul, that warfare is characterized by a "Life / Tri'd in sharp tribulation, and refin'd / By Faith and faithful works, to second Life, / Wak'd in the renovation of the just" to a "renewd" "Heav'n and Earth" (PL, 11.62–66). As consummated, it culminates in the apocalyptic events surrounding the Son's ascent of "the Throne hereditarie" (12.369–70), the throne of David, from which he reigns as rightful king. As God advises the Son,

> . . . thou shalt Judge
> Bad men and Angels, they arraign'd shall sink
> Beneath thy Sentence; Hell her numbers full,
> Thenceforth shall be for ever shut. Mean while
> The World shall burn, and from her ashes spring
> New Heav'n and Earth, wherein the just shall dwell
> And after all thir tribulations long
> See golden days fruitful of golden deeds,
> With Joy and Love triumphing, and fair Truth.
> Then thou thy regal Scepter shalt lay by,
> For regal Scepter then no more shall need,
> God shall be All in All.
>
> (3.330–41)

For Milton, this is the ultimate vision of the New Jerusalem. In *Christian Doctrine* he states: "Perfect glorification consists in eternal life and perfect happiness, arising chiefly from the divine vision [*Glorificatio perfecta est in vita aeterna ac beatissima, quae oritur potissimum ex visione Dei*]." This "glorification will be accompanied by the renovation of heaven and earth, and of all things therein adapted to our service or delight, to be possessed by us in perpetuity [*Glorificationis nostrae comes erit coeli et terrae rerumque in iis creatarum, quae quidem nobis usui aut oblectationi esse possint, renovatio et possessio*]" (CM, 16:374–79). Realized by those whose warfare is the sanctified expression of the conflicts that they have waged through Christ against the Spiritual Foe, the New Jerusalem, then, is that experience of glorification that only the Christian soldier may attain.

12
Rest

If the attainment of the New Jerusalem befits those who experience glorification after the warfare of spiritual combat, then holy war is resolved appropriately in holy rest. The posture of "standing" (στῆναι) to "withstand" (ἀντιστῆναι) culminates in an ultimate stasis of which that posture is a reflection, as of a shadowy type to a truth. A sense of that distinction underlies what Geoffrey Hartman sees as the "counterplot" of Milton's epic, a "divine imperturbability" and "inviolable peace" against which all violence and agitation become illusory.[1] The significance of such an idea is nowhere more striking than in the various interpretations that may be attributed to Milton's use of holy rest in *Paradise Lost*.[2] For at the heart of that "divine imperturbability" and "inviolable peace" discussed by Hartman is the divine rest of God, a rest first invoked by Michael, when he admonishes Satan, "But think not here / To trouble Holy Rest" (6.272–73), and then by Adam, when he asks Raphael, "What cause / Mov'd the Creator in his holy Rest / Through all Eternitie so late to build / In *Chaos* [?]" (7.90–93).

In connection with these passages, one thinks of such biblical texts as Isaiah 18:4: "For so the Lord said unto me, I will take my rest, and I will consider in my dwelling place like a clear heat upon herbs, *and* like a dew in the heat of harvest." The poetic tact with which Isaiah conceives the concept of rest finds its counterpart in the worship of the presence within the Holy of Holies. So David sings: "The Lord hath chosen Zion; he hath desired *it* for his habitation. This *is* my rest for ever: here will I dwell; for I have desired it" (Ps. 132:13–14). Viewed from a cultic context, this recalls the experience of the numinous that surrounds the ark in the Holy of Holies, where the presence "rests" upon its throne. Thus, David alludes specifically to Solomon's dedication liturgy that concludes with the appeal "Now therefore arise, O Lord God, into thy resting place, thou, and the ark of thy strength," after which "the glory of the Lord fill[s] the house" (2 Chron. 6:41–7:2; Ps. 132:8). With this passage in mind, David appropriates the liturgy to portray the ultimate rest of God, as he dwells in Zion eternally: "This *is* my rest forever: here will I dwell." (Compare the sense of divine and mysterious serenity that emanates from the depiction of the Holy of Holies in Jeronimo de Prado and John Baptistae Villalpandi's *In Ezechielem Explanationes*, figure 23.) Such is the nature of holy rest. Representing a transcendent state that has its basis in the worship of the "wholly other," the experience of rest, like all that is sacred, is a subject that should cause one to "keep off with a sacred reverence, & religious advisement how best to undergoe" the consideration of that which defies consideration.[3]

In a treatment that is basic to an understanding of Milton's complex use of holy rest in *Paradise Lost*, the New Testament author of Hebrews saw fit to penetrate the mystery in a passage that characterizes the main Old Testament concepts of holy rest and that reinterprets them within a Christian perspective. Expounding upon the nature of faith, the author of Hebrews concerns himself with three specific kinds of holy rest, the first two embodied in the Old Testament, the third in the New. Celebrated in the liturgy of the ark (cf. Ps. 95:5–11; 2 Chron. 6:5–6, 11), the first two are the Sabbath (Heb. 4:4) and the promise of rest offered to the children of Israel upon entering Canaan (Heb. 4:5–6); the third is a heavenly rest (Heb. 4:9), anticipated by the first two. The main point that the author of Hebrews is making by invoking the first two kinds of rest is that they are shadows of what is to come, that although they are important to an understanding of holy rest, they are not in themselves sufficient to represent the ultimate rest of God. Such is particularly true of the promise of rest offered to the children of Israel upon entering Canaan. Although it is important as a type of the ultimate rest, it is not a fulfillment of the type. To emphasize that point, the author of Hebrews maintains that if the rest of Canaan had been sufficient, David would not "afterward have spoken of another day" (Heb. 4:8). The reference here is to Psalm 95, in which David, living "nearly five hundred years after the land of promise had been occupied by the Israelites, spoke *then* of the possibility of entering into such a 'rest.' He says that, in his time, the people were called to hear the voice of God; that he warned them against the guilt and danger of hardening their hearts; that he reminded them that the Israelites were excluded from the promised land [Num. 14], and that he said the same thing would occur if those in his own time should harden their hearts."[4]

Alluding to that idea, the author of Hebrews concludes: "Let us therefore fear, lest, a promise being left *us* of entering into his rest, any of you should seem to come short of it. . . . For we which have believed do enter into rest, as he said, as I have sworn in my wrath, if they shall enter into rest; although the works were finished from the foundation of the world"

USPECTUS TESTUDINIS MURORUM ET PAVIMENTI SANCTI SANCTORUM ATQUE ARCÆ TESTAMENTI CUM CHERUBINI

FIGURE 23. A Prospect of the Holy of Holies.
Reproduced from an engraving in Jeronimo de Prado
and John Baptistae Villalpandi, *In Ezechielem Explanationes*
(1596–1604), by permission of the Joseph Regenstein Library
of the University of Chicago, Chicago, Illinois.

(Heb. 4:1–3). This passage is especially interesting because it suggests how intimately the Canaan rest is related to the Sabbath: they are both significant as a sign of that covenant by which man is to share in the rest of God ("For it *is* a sign between me and you throughout your generations; that *ye* may know that I *am* the Lord that doth sanctify you" [Exod. 31:13]; "my kindness shall not depart from thee, neither shall the covenant of my peace be removed, saith the Lord that hath mercy on thee" [Isa. 54:10]).[5] As the seventeenth-century expositor William Gouge states, Canaan rest and the Sabbath are to be seen as "speciall pledges of God's favour."[6] Thus, Canaan rest is celebrated in these terms: "Blessed *be* the Lord that hath given rest unto his people Israel, according to all that he promised: there hath not failed one word of all his good promise, which he promised by the hand of Moses his servant" (1 Kings 8:56). Likewise, the Sabbath becomes a sign by which man may know that God has sanctified him (Exod. 31:13).[7]

With that sanctification, the observance of the Sabbath takes its place among the Ten Commandments: "Remember the sabbath day [הַשַּׁבָּת םָֹרֹי-אֶת], to keep it holy" (Exod. 20:8–11). To violate the Sabbath (שבת) is to incur the wrath of God: "Verily my sabbaths ye shall keep. . . . Every one that defileth [them] shall surely be put to death" (Exod. 31:13–15). Sanctification of the Sabbath occurs repeatedly in Judaic tradition. Thus, the Book of Jubilees maintains:

> And He gave us a great sign, the Sabbath day, that we should work six days, but keep Sabbath on the seventh day from all work. And all the angels of the presence, and all the angels of sanctification, these two great classes—He hath bidden to keep the Sabbath with Him in heaven and on earth. . . . Whoever does any work thereon shall die, and . . . he who defiles it [the Sabbath] shall surely die. . . . And every one who observes it and keeps Sabbath thereon from all his work, will be holy and blessed throughout all days like unto us . . . ; for that day is more holy and blessed than any jubilee day of the jubilees; on this we kept Sabbath in the heavens before it was made known to any flesh to keep Sabbath thereon on the earth.[8]

In the *Talmud*, the tractate on the Sabbath, entitled *Shabbath* classifies prohibited acts under thirty-nine heads, including sowing, plowing, and reaping, among others.[9]

As Milton makes clear in *Christian Doctrine*, the New Law abrogates any strict observance of the Sabbath. "Since the Sabbath was originally an ordinance of the Mosaic law, . . . those who live under the gospel are emancipated from the ordinance . . . of the Sabbath"(*CM*, 17:177).[10] For the purposes of the New Law, the Sabbath becomes important as it prefigures what Milton calls "that sabbatical rest or eternal peace in heaven [*sabbatismi nempe sive quietis in coelo sempiternae*], of which all believers are commanded to strive to be partakers through peace and obedience, following the example of Christ" (*CM*, 17:174–75).[11] Significantly, as a proof-text for this statement, Milton cites Hebrews 4:9–11, which enunciates precisely that third category of rest previously referred to: "There remaineth therefore a rest to the people of God. For he that is entered into his rest, he also hath ceased from his own works, as God *did* from his. Let us labour therefore to enter into that rest." Milton's reference to the Hebrews text in this instance is obviously important because it indicates the emphasis that he placed upon this particular biblical passage for an understanding of holy rest.

It is little wonder that he should so emphasize the Hebrews rendering of holy rest when one considers the full implications of that rendering. Specifically, the word *rest* in Hebrews 4:9, which Milton translates "sabbatical rest" (*sabbatismi*), is cast in a form that is entirely unique not only to the New Testament but to the Septuagint, as well. Invented by the author of Hebrews, that form is σαββατισμός, a word recalling the description of God's rest (שבת) after the creation in Genesis 2:2.[12] According to Gouge, "the notation of it is taken from an Hebrew word which signifieth Rest, and soundeth Sabbath."[13] As such, it suggests an attempt to give a name to that unnamable repose of the Most High, "whose works were finished from the foundation of the world" (Heb. 4:3). But as the foregoing discussion has made clear, its meaning is not limited merely to a representation of God's transcendent Sabbath: for the author of Hebrews, it likewise signifies the ultimate fulfillment of that rest promised to man upon entering Canaan.[14] Its significance is thereby personal, as well as cosmic: it embraces the rest both of God, whose Sabbath it celebrates,[15] and man, who may participate fully in God's Sabbath after he "hath ceased from his own works, as God *did* from his."

The personal aspect, of course, is what makes the concept of holy rest so compelling as a testament of God's grace. As Matthew Poole states, through this "Sabbatism," God's faithful "have an Entrance . . . in internal Peace . . . and by it" are "secured of their full Possession of it in the eternal Inheritance of the Saints in Light."[16] (Compare Revelation 14:13: "And I heard a voice from heaven saying unto me, Write, Blessed *are* the dead which die in the Lord from henceforth: yea, saith the Spirit, that they may rest from their labours; and their works do follow them.") The recipients of rest are those, of course, who have responded to the promise of Christ, the Prince of Peace: "Come unto me, all *ye* that labour and are heavy laden, and I will give you rest" (Matt. 11:28); "Peace I leave with you, my peace I give unto you" (John 14:27); "And the peace of God, which passeth all understanding, shall keep your hearts and minds through Christ Jesus" (Phil. 4:7; see also Isa. 11:10).

The great importance of this concept (of which Hebrews 4:1–11 is the locus classicus) to the Christian tradition cannot be overestimated. Treatments of the σαββατισμός range from Saint John Chrysostom's homiletic description to Richard Baxter's *The Saints Everlasting Rest*.[17] But certainly the most moving treatment may be found in Saint Augustine. Both *The Confessions* and *The City of God* culminate in eloquent celebrations of the σαββατισμός.[18] *The City of God*, written, as Augustine states, for the very purpose of attaining "peace," will provide a case in point. In book 22, chapter 30, entitled "Aeterna felicitate civitatis Dei, sabbatoque perpetuo," Augustine maintains:

> [In Heaven] . . . shall be accomplished the words of the psalm: 'Be still [*vacate*], and know that I am God' [Ps. 46:10]. There shall be the great Sabbath [*maximum sabbatum*] which has no evening, which God celebrated among His first works, as it is written, "And God rested on the seventh day from all His works. . . . And God blessed the seventh day, and sanctified it . . ." [Gen. 2:2–3]. For we shall ourselves be the seventh day, when we shall be filled, and replenished with God's blessing and sanctification. There shall we be still [*vacantes*], and know that He is God; that He is that which we ourselves aspired to be when we fell away from Him, and listened to the voice of the seducer, 'Ye shall be as gods' [Gen. 3:5], and so abandoned God, who would have made us as gods, not by deserting Him, but by participating in Him. For without Him what have we accomplished, save to perish in His anger? But when we are restored by Him, perfected with a greater grace, we shall have eternal leisure [*vacabimus in aeternum*] to see that He is God, for we shall be full of Him when He shall be all in all.[19]

Significantly embodying elements of the Fall and Redemption of man, Augustine's account of holy rest brings to mind the essential concept of stasis (here, *vacate*) as the culmination of στῆναι dealt with in the previous chapter. Vacate is none other than that *maximum sabbatum* which is the reward of those who are faithful, those who persevere, those who withstand (ἀντιστῆναι) so that they might stand (στῆναι). These are the ones who are commanded "Be still [*vacate*]" in order to experience the "seventh day" which is the σαββατισμός.

It is in light of these considerations that *Paradise Lost* must be viewed.

Since the main emphasis of Hebrews 4:1–11 is upon the redemptive nature of holy rest, it would be well to explore that area of Milton's epic first. As discussed earlier, underlying the attainment of holy rest, the two events of utmost importance are the Sabbath and Canaan rest, both of which prefigure the rest that is to come. Little need be said about the significance of these events to *Paradise Lost*. As a narrative that recreates the Genesis story, Milton's epic celebrates not only that God created the heavens and the earth but that the "great Father" "from work / Now resting, bless'd and hallowd the Seav'nth day, / As resting on that day from all his work" (7.588–93). Biblically, of course, the account of that event in Genesis 2:2–3 is revealed through none other than Moses, the inspired "author" of the Pentateuch. Thus, Milton begins *Paradise Lost* with the appropriate reference to "that Shepherd, who first taught the chosen Seed, / In the Beginning how the Heav'ns and Earth / Rose out of *Chaos*" (1.8–10). To describe this event, Moses is inspired by the same spirit that inspired him "on the secret top / Of *Oreb*, or of *Sinai*" (1.6–7). For the purposes of this study, such a reference is significant because it associates the creation story with the receiving of the Laws, among them the Fourth Commandment to observe God's Sabbath (Exod. 20:8–11).

As previously indicated, the Sabbath represents a sign of the covenant between God and man (Exod. 31:13) that is ultimately related to the promise of Canaan rest (Exod. 33:14). In *Paradise Lost*, that relationship becomes even more compelling, since Milton reminds us at the outset that the creation story is revealed by a man whose office it is to deliver "the chosen Seed" out of the bondage of Egypt into the promised rest of Canaan. As such, Moses anticipates "that destined Seed" who "shall achieve / Mankinds deliverance" (12.233–35). Within the context of holy rest, his function is prefigurative: embracing the Sabbath and the Canaan rest of Hebrews 4:1–8, his office embodies the covenant of the Law. Obeying that covenant, man attempts to absolve himself of the guilt incurred when he disobeyed the primal covenant in paradise. But, as Michael says, such obedience is insufficient to effect man's final justification in the eyes of God (12.290–99). Ultimately "imperfet," the covenant of the Law is provided in order to "resign" man "in full time / Up to a better Cov'nant, disciplin'd / From shadowie Types to Truth" (12.300–303).[20] The author of Hebrews emphasizes that point by showing how some came short of attaining Canaan rest because of "unbelief" (Heb. 4:6) and how, even for those who did achieve the semblance of rest in Canaan, another, greater rest was spoken of by David (Heb. 4:7–9).

In *Paradise Lost*, Milton reinforces this idea by reminding us that Moses himself did not lead his people into the Promised Land:

And therefore shall not *Moses*, though of God
Highly belov'd, being but the Minister
Of Law, his people into Canaan lead;
But *Joshua* whom the Gentiles *Jesus* call,
His Name and Office bearing, who shall quell
The adversarie Serpent, and bring back
Through the worlds wilderness long wanderd man
Safe to eternal Paradise of rest.

(12.307–14)

Such a passage makes it quite obvious how precisely Milton is working within the tradition explored here. Drawing upon the fundamental associations of Hebrews 4:1–11, Milton implicitly constrasts the rest of the "earthly Canaan" (12.315) achieved by Joshua and the rest of the heavenly Canaan achieved by Jesus.[21] The one is a semblance of the other, a type fulfilled by the other, an event whose purpose, as stated by the author of Hebrews, is to prefigure "another day" (Heb. 4:8).

Precisely what significance that other day has for Milton will be made clear in a consideration of such poems as the *Nativity Ode*. There, that other day is celebrated within the prefigurative contexts of past and present, the past embodying the covenant of the Law received by Moses on Sinai (157–60) and the present the covenant of Grace provided by God through the Incarnation of his Son. Signified by horrid clangs, red fire, and smoldering clouds, the covenant of the Law anticipates the Judgment at "the worlds last session" (163) when "the wakefull trump of doom must thunder through the deep" (156). Signified by the stillness that accompanies heavenly music, the covenant of Grace anticipates that day when "at last our bliss / Full and perfect is" (165–66). As Milton states in *Paradise Lost*, after the "dread Tribunal" (3.326),

The World shall burn, and from her ashes spring
New Heav'n and Earth, wherein the just shall dwell
And after all thir tribulations long
See golden days, fruitful of golden deeds,
With Joy and Love triumphing, and fair Truth.

(3.334–38)

Then, Jesus shall "lay by" his "regal Scepter / For regal Scepter then no more shall need, / God shall be All in All" (3.339–41).

Anticipating that glorious day, the *Nativity Ode* recreates the harmony that characterizes the still point of consummate rest. "Crown'd with Olive green" (46), the Dove of Peace (a sign both of the harmony with nature after the Flood and of the divine recognition accorded Christ at his baptism)[22] "strikes a universall Peace through Sea and Land" (52). All is stillness and expectation: "Kings sat still with awfull eye" (59); "Birds of Calm sit brooding on the charmed wave" (68); and the "Stars" "stand fixt in stedfast gaze" (69–70). Such a description recalls Saint Augustine's definition of holy rest as an experience of absolute and inviolable stillness. That stillness, Augustine calls "the calm that comes of order [*tranquillitas ordinis*]."[23] Milton expresses this order through the transcendent harmony of musical concord, a concord that recalls the angelic celebration of God after the creation of the world: "Such Musick / . . . / Before was never made, / But when of old the sons of morning sung, / While the Creator Great / His constellations set, / And the well-ballanc't world on hinges hung" (117–22; cf. PL, 7.601–32).[24]

The result of that music is to "hold all Heav'n and Earth in happier union" (107–8), a union of peace in which the elements veritably embrace: "The Winds with wonder whist, / Smoothly the waters kist, / Whispering new joyes to the mild Ocean" (64–66). This idea is quite appropriate to Milton's treatment of the Incarnation: if the coming of the Messiah results in the peaceful and harmonious union of the elements, that union finds its correspondence in the hypostatic union of the divine and human natures in Christ.[25]

The propriety of such a correspondence may be seen in Ephesians 2:14–17: "For he is our peace, who hath made both one, and hath broken down the middle wall of partition *between us*; Having abolished in his flesh the enmity, *even* the law of commandments *contained* in ordinances; for to make in himself of twain one new man, so making peace; and that he might reconcile both unto God in one body by the cross, having slain the enmity thereby: And came and preached peace to you which were afar off, and to them that were nigh." As an explanation of the nature of the new man, the peaceful reconciliation of divine and human betokened by this passage leads to a statement of the fellowship of the regenerate in God: "Now therefore ye are no more strangers and foreigners, but fellow citizens with the saints, and of the household of God" (Eph. 2:19). This is precisely what Saint Augustine refers to in his vision of holy rest in the heavenly city (that is, New Jerusalem, the true City of Peace) as "a perfectly ordered and harmonious communion [*ordinatissima et concordissima societas*]."[26]

That Milton likewise expresses such an idea through the image of musical harmony is evident from the concluding lines of *At a Solemn Music*: "O may we soon again renew that Song, / And keep in tune with Heav'n, till God e're long / To his celestial consort us unite / To live with him, and sing in endles morn of light" (25–28). With the possible word-play implicit in "consort" (from *consortium*), Milton invokes the idea of a "marital association," as well as the idea of a fellowship and company of music makers. The marital union that such heavenly harmony accompanies, of course, is the marriage of the soul with Christ the Bridegroom (Rev. 19:7, 9).[27] For the purpose of holy rest, that union may be associated with the Judaic tradition that the Sabbath (sometimes feminine in Hebrew, as in Exod. 31:14; Lev. 25:6) is often represented as a bride who unites with her votaries.[28] Even if this tradition has no direct bearing upon Milton's handling of holy rest, it does provide an additional way of understanding the relationship of holy rest to the divine union.

As such, the divine union becomes one in which "long Eternity shall greet our bliss / With an individual kiss" (TI, 11–12) and in which one hears "the unexpressive nuptuall song / In the blest kingdoms meek of joy and love" (L, 176–77). There, the Saints, in "solemn troops, and sweet societies," will "sing, and singing in thir glory move / And wipe the tears for ever from . . . [our] eyes" (L, 178–81; cf. Rev. 7:17). As a representation of the bliss enjoyed by those who participate in the divine union,[29] such a line goes far to characterize the nature of holy rest. For essential to Milton's understanding of holy rest is the paradoxical idea that as part of the divine union, there is constant movement. Rest is symbolically depicted through motion: singing their "unexpressive nuptuall song" in absolute peace and bliss, the Saints "move." Thus, Revelation 4:8 states: "They rest not day and night, saying, Holy, holy, holy, Lord God Almighty, which was, and is, and is to come."

In *Paradise Lost*, that paradoxical concept receives its most elaborate treatment. While God rests after having created the universe, the angels celebrate: "The Harp / Had work and rested not . . . / All sounds on Fret by String or Golden Wire / Temper'd soft Tunings, intermixt with Voice / Choral or Unison" (7.594–99). Their bliss represented by harmonious motion, the angels engage in "mystical dance" with "mazes intricate, / Eccentric, intervolv'd, yet regular / Then most, when most irregular they seem: / And in thir motions harmonie Divine" (5.620–25). Symbolically, Adam and Eve's morning song of praise to God is one which sets the entire unfallen universe in motion; like the angels who "circle" God's "Throne" "Day without Night," the planetary bodies move, the elements "run / Perpetual Circle, multiform," mists and exhalations "rise" toward the sun and "fall" in showers, winds "blow" and trees "wave" "in sign of Worship," fountains "flow," birds sing, fish glide, animals "walk," "tread," and "creep" (5.162–201). Even the "fixt starrs" are "fixt in thir

Orb that flies" (5.176), emphasizing the paradox by which things at rest express that rest through motion.[30] As Richard Baxter says, "rest" is the "perfection of Motion," the appropriate emblem of God as the *Primum Movens*,[31] an idea that Milton expresses through his reference to the "grateful vicissitude" created when "light and darkness" alternately "lodge and dislodge" in "perpetual round" within God's "Mount" (6.4–8).[32]

Not to be viewed pejoratively, such "vicissitude" constitutes the divine motion through which God as First Mover enjoys his own changelessness, an idea that is reflected in Eve's beautiful and elaborate song celebrating changeless change in paradise (4.639–56). Beginning "With thee [Adam] conversing I forget all time, / All seasons and thir change, all please alike" (4.639–40), Eve's love song represents the pleasure that the unfallen creature takes in obedience to its higher good. Thus, Eve addresses Adam: "My Author and Disposer, what thou bidst / Unargu'd I obey; so God ordains, / God is thy Law, thou mine" (4.635–47). In perfect harmony with the will of God, Eve's will delights in those "motions" (the rising of the morning, the singing of birds, the shining of the sun, the fragrance of the earth, the approach of evening) that are an emblem of the changelessness of the First Mover.

Essential to the concept of holy rest, Eve's attitude may be found appropriately expressed by the figure of Piccarda Donati in Dante's *Paradiso* (3.79–87): "Nay, it is the very quality of this blessed state that we keep ourselves within the divine will, so that our wills are themselves made one; therefore our rank from height to height through this kingdom is pleasing to the whole kingdom as to the King who wills us to His will. And in His will is our peace [*E'n la sua voluntade e nostra pace*]. It is that sea to which all things move, both what it creates and what nature makes."[33] So Baxter comments, "All motion ends at the Center; and all Means cease when we have the End."[34] The divine representation of that idea Milton envisioned as early as *Arcades* in his supreme praise of the Countess Dowager of Derby who "sit[s] like a Goddes bright / In the center of her light" (18–19). As discussed in chapter 6, all things return to the seated figure in the center, there to seek their place of rest. Such is the rhythm of holy rest: perpetual return to the source of all motion.

Made evident in the "perpetual round" of "light and darkness" to God's mount in *Paradise Lost*, the application of that idea to the experience of man is still further reinforced by Thomas Shepard's eloquent description of holy rest in *Theses Sabbaticae*. There, Shepard speaks of the primal rhythm of holy rest as one in which man, passing through the "circle of his life," issues from God and returns "back unto God," in whom he is "eternally preserved." That motion, states Shepard, applies to man's need for rest both before and after the Fall:

> As man standing in innocency, had cause thus to return from the pleasant labours of his weekly paradise imploiments . . . so man fallen much more from his toilsome and wearisome labours, to this his rest again. . . . Here [this life] our rest is but begun, there [the next life] it is perfected; here it is interrupted by our weekly labours, there it is continued, here we are led into our rest by means and ordinances, but there we shall be possessed with it, without our need of help from them; our God who is our rest, being then become unto us immediately *All in All*.[35]

The importance of Shepard's statement to *Paradise Lost* will become evident in an exploration of the "imploiments" of Adam and Eve in the prelapsarian and the postlapsarian environments.

The best exposition of the need for rest in the unfallen world is provided by Adam himself. As Adam explains to Eve before retiring, "All things now retir'd to rest / Mind us of like repose, since God hath set / Labour and rest, as day and night to men / Successive" (4.611–14). Implicit in Adam's statement is an awareness of that primal rhythm by which rest succeeds labor as night succeeds day. Patterned after God's own manner of resting and working in the act of creation, this mode of conduct not only vitalizes Eden but distinguishes man from the beast. It vitalizes Eden because it suggests that even in the prelapsarian environment one must be active in demonstrating his worth and merit before God. Thus, Adam reminds Eve that early in the morning they must arise and engage in their "pleasant labour" of gardening so that their paradise will not become unsightly and unmanageable in its growth (4.623–32). The act of maintaining order and harmony in Eden distinguishes man from the beast. So Adam states: while "Man hath his daily work of body or of mind / Appointed, which declares his Dignitie, / And the regard of Heav'n on all his waies," "other Animals unactive range, / And of thir doings God takes no account" (4.616–22).

Unlike the beast, which "all day long, / Rove[s] idle unimploid" (4.616–17), man is ennobled by the responsibility of being human: he must "account" to God for his actions. When he fails in that responsibility, he becomes like the beast, directionless and concerned only with the satisfaction of his own immediate needs. Appropriately, then, part of the punishment imposed upon fallen man is to sustain himself through labor: "In the sweat of thy Face shalt thou eat Bread" (10.205; see Gen.

3:19). Paradoxically, it is a punishment that Adam comes to view as a blessing: "With labour I must earn / My bread; what harm? Idleness had bin worse; / My labour will sustain me" (10.1054–56). It will enable him, as he says, to "earn rest from labour won" (11.375). On the basis of such an idea, the author of Hebrews counsels: "Let us labour therefore to enter into that rest" (Heb. 4:11). For Matthew Poole, this labor imports "study of Mind, Earnestness of Affection, Diligence of Endeavour, with all the Powers of Soul and Body to attend this work."[36] In *Paradise Lost*, it is summed up by Michael's advice to Adam: "Add / Deeds to thy knowledge answerable, add Faith, / Add Vertue, Patience, Temperance, add Love . . . / . . . Then wilt thou not be loath / To leave this Paradise, but shalt possess / A Paradise within thee, happier farr" (12.581–87).

With this assurance, Adam and Eve are expelled from paradise "though sorrowing, yet in peace" (11.117). Compared to the movement of a laborer "homeward returning" (12.631–32), the expulsion obliges them "to choose / Thir place of rest" (12.646–47; cf. Isa. 32:17–18), a choice that may be undertaken with confidence, for, as the discussion of the covenant of Grace has made clear, that choice will be based upon the promise that the Messiah will "bring back / Through the worlds wilderness long wanderd man / Safe to eternal Paradise of rest" (12.312–14). Intimately associated with the pattern of return, then, the achievement of eternal rest after the Fall completes the cycle of labor and rest made apparent in the unfallen world (cf. Isa. 30:15: "For thus saith the Lord, God, the Holy One of Israel; In returning and rest shall ye be saved"). This recalls once again the concept of rest expressed through the return of "light and darkness" to God's mount.

If such a pattern epitomizes the experience of holy rest attained by those who have been faithful to God, a corresponding pattern underlies Milton's vision of a world deprived of that rest. Such, of course, is the experience of Satan and his followers, who, having disobeyed God and violated the divine union, are "cast out from God and blessed vision" (5.611–13). Their impulse now, as Satan informs Chaos and Night, is to "reduce" (literally, "lead back" or "return") the created world to the "original darkness" and restless agitation of Chaos (2.983–84). That they themselves, however, will undergo this return may be seen in Milton's apocalyptic view regarding the ultimate fate of evil, a view expressed as early as *Comus*: "But evil on it self shall back recoyl . . . / . . . when at last / Gather'd like scum, and setl'd to it self / It shall be in eternal restless change / Self-fed, and self-consum'd" (593–97).[37] In *Paradise Lost*, that idea finds expression in the image of the hell-hounds, "hourly conceiv'd / And hourly born" (2.796–97), that "return" to devour Sin's "womb";

Then "bursting forth / Afresh with conscious terrours vex . . . [her] round / That rest or intermission none . . . [she] find[s]" (2.798–802).[38]

Sin's tormenting experience, of course, may be viewed psychologically as a representation of the internal torment to which Satan and his followers are subjected in their fall. Failing in their attempts to "trouble Holy Rest" (6.272) and the "Peace of God in bliss" (7.55), they must suffer unrest of the worst sort.[39] As part of the pattern of return discussed here, such unrest is discernible in the torment that plagues Satan: his destructive impulse "boils in his tumultuous brest, / And like a devillish Engine back recoils / Upon himself; horror and doubt distract / His troubl'd thoughts, and from the bottom stirr / The Hell within him" (4.16–20).[40] Aptly described, that Hell is a place where "peace / And rest can never dwell" (1.65–66); as a state of mind, it can never really be escaped: "For within him Hell / He brings, and round about, nor from Hell / One step no more than from himself can fly / By change of place" (4.20–23). Accordingly, Satan complains: "Which way I flie is Hell; my self am Hell; / And in the lowest deep a lower deep / Still threatning to devour me opens wide, / To which the Hell I suffer seems a Heav'n" (4.75–78).[41]

Likewise, in that Hell the "roving" band of angels find "no rest" (2.618) in their searchings but are "in wandring mazes lost" (2.561; see also 2.524–27). What rest they do find is undermined by the imagery that describes it. For example, pointing to "yon dreary Plain, forlorn and wild, / The seat of desolation," Satan advises Beelzebub how to escape the burning lake that consumes them: "Thither let us tend / From off the tossing of these fiery waves, / There rest, if any rest can harbour there" (1.183–85). What he finds when he gets there, however, is "Land that ever burn'd / With solid as Lake with liquid fire" (1.228–29), leaving "a singed bottom all involv'd / With stench and smoak" (1.236–37): "Such resting," Milton ironically comments, "found the sole / Of unblest feet" (1.237–38; cf. Deut. 28:65: "And among these nations shalt thou find no ease, neither shall the sole of thy foot have rest: but the Lord shall give thee there a trembling heart, and failing of eyes, and sorrow of mind").[42] Clearly, then, Satan and his followers are consummate figures of unrest: they represent the fate of those who disobey God (cf. Isa. 57:20–21: "But the wicked *are* like the troubled sea when it cannot rest. . . . *There is no peace,* saith my God, to the wicked"). Such, of course, is the experience of Adam and Eve after they have fallen: having copulated in lust, they rise as from "unrest" (11.174).[43] Within this context, Adam is found "in a troubl'd Sea of passion tost" (10.718). "Outstrecht" on the "cold ground" (10.851), he gives himself up to thoughts of death: "How glad would [I] lay me down / As in my Mothers lap? there I should rest / And sleep secure" (10.777–79; cf. Job 3:13: "For now should I have lain still and been quiet, I should have slept: then had I been at rest").[44]

Unlike Satan, however, both Adam and Eve, contrite and repentant, achieve a new sense of rest as a result of God's grace. Milton describes the experience as one in which the heart is softened to receive God: "From the Mercie-seat above / Prevenient Grace descending had remov'd / The stonie from thir hearts, and made new flesh / Regenerat grow instead" (11.2–5; cf. Ezek. 11:19: "And I will take the stony heart out of their flesh, and will give them an heart of flesh"). The renewal of faith through the softening of the heart recalls the discourse on holy rest contained in the fourth chapter of Hebrews, the main point of that discourse being David's plea "To day if ye will hear his voice, harden not your hearts" (Heb. 4:7; see Ps. 95:7–8). "For," states the author of Hebrews, God "*is a discerner of the thoughts and intents of the heart*" (Heb. 4:12).

Such an idea should recall once again the intensely personal bearing that holy rest assumes in the biblical account of the divine experience. That this is no less true for Milton is a claim that the foregoing discussion has attempted to verify. With his characteristic concern not only for the divine experience but for the application of that experience to the life of man, Milton has been able to portray throughout *Paradise Lost* a concept that transcends the limits of human understanding. From that perspective, one encounters the full import of Milton's emphasis upon holy rest as an experience fundamental to an appreciation of his epic. If such an experience transcends the reach of human sense, Milton allows us to grasp its significance through his own unique expression of those traditions that constitute what the author of Hebrews felicitously calls the σαββατισμός. In so doing, Milton demonstrates an originality of execution not unworthy the creativity of one who saw fit to originate an entirely new word as a way of naming the unnamable.

Afterword

As the foregoing chapters have demonstrated, the experience of the holy had a profound influence on Milton throughout his career as a writer. Whether in the form of such res sacrae as fruit, place, mount, name, light, presence, war, or rest, the numinous in all its aspects figured prominently in Milton's works. The holy shaped his outlook and defined his vision as significantly as any other experience that found expression in his writings. The product of a true hierophant, *Paradise Lost* in particular is the embodiment of this fact. In a way that has heretofore been insufficiently recognized, Milton's epic is the most priestly of poems. Providing a sense of what it means to be overwhelmed by the ganz andere, to be imbued with the numinous in all its resplendency, it is a testament to all that the holy represents. It is indeed Milton's דביר: through it, we are privileged to "minister about holy things" and "live *of the things* of the temple" (1 Cor. 9:13).

If this study has been successful in demonstrating the validity of these assertions, then future considerations of Milton's works must take into account the holy as a phenomenon of crucial importance to his outlook. His full range of poetics simply cannot be understood unless the numinous plays a part. Nor, for that matter, can his stance as polemist be sufficiently appreciated if it is divorced from the traditions of the holy that he embraced. The Nonconformist and iconoclastic impulses with which Milton is so often identified must be seen in the context of these traditions. Otherwise, one runs the risk of misconstruing the nature of his essential religiosity, his responsiveness to the holy as the most fundamental of experiences, one that transcends immediate doctrinal concerns and suggests the universality of the phenomenon that has been explored here.

Milton criticism has too often been marked by a tendency either to underplay or to controvert such considerations, with the result that Milton is set apart from the mainstream of religious thought. His so-called Puritanism is seen to color his views to so great an extent that *Paradise Lost* becomes "a poem in the Puritan style."[1] Doctrinally, it is conceived not as a "Christian poem" per se but rather as "a Christian *Protestant* poem," indeed, as "*the* epic of Protestantism."[2] Such views are not without their potential dangers, for they can lead to the desacralization and secularization of religious thought that critics like Malcom Ross have seen as an essential constituent of Protestant aesthetic.[3] As indicated at the outset of this study, it is precisely upon the opposite premises that the foregoing chapters have been predicated.

If *Paradise Lost* is "a poem in the Puritan style," if it is a specifically "Christian *Protestant* poem," it is so only to the extent that the religious experience that it embraces universalizes rather than localizes it. As such, it is not so much the epic of a particular calling as it is the epic of one whose allegiances have provided the means of understanding the holy in a form that is uniquely Miltonic. The product of an all-pervasive sacralism, that form achieves its full realization in *Paradise Lost*. In this sense, the vision that Milton's epic embodies is as universal and finally as reverential as any that was ever inspired by the traditions that constitute the holy.

Notes

INTRODUCTION

1. Gunn, *Interpretation of Otherness*, p. 10.

2. See the translation of Girard's *Violence* by Patrick Gregory.

3. I have particularly in mind Otto's *Das Heilige* and Eliade's *Traité d'histoire des religions*. For Otto, see the translation by Harvey, and for Eliade, the translation by Sheed. Most recently, see Eliade's *History of Religious Ideas*. Both Otto and Eliade are likewise concerned throughout their writings with the literary aspects of the holy.

4. Paz, *Bow and Lyre*, p. 125.

5. Ibid., p. 121.

6. Ibid., p. 139.

7. Under these circumstances, *Paradise Lost* is categorized, for example, as the "logical epic," or it emerges as the poeticized version of Milton's own theological treatise. I have in mind Burden's *Logical Epic* and Kelley's *"This Great Argument."*

8. Ross, *Poetry and Dogma*, pp. 3–4, 27, 183–84, 187.

9. Radzinowicz, *Toward "Samson Agonistes,"* pp. 351–59. In Milton's poetics, Radzinowicz finds "a process of diminishing emphasis upon ecstatic, unearthly music and increasing emphasis upon speaking reason to sensible men." Aligning herself with the implicitly rationalistic, humanistic tradition embraced by Dennis Burden, A. S. P. Woodhouse, Ernest Sirluck, and Irene Samuel (she does not mention Douglas Bush), Radzinowicz finds herself opposed to James Holly Hanford, Michael Fixler, and William Kerrigan. Curiously, she faults Kerrigan for what she implies is too great an emphasis upon Milton as "rhapsode," "the passive instrument of a holy force," when, in fact, the concept of the poet-prophet that Kerrigan develops is that of a rational being very much in possession of his faculties.

10. Lewalski, *Protestant Poetics*, p. 4. Lewalski takes issue with Ross on a couple of occasions (pp. 5, 72).

11. See A. Fletcher's *Prophetic Moment*; Wittreich's *Visionary Poetics*, *Angel of Apocalypse*, and "'Poet Amongst Poets'"; and Kerrigan's *Prophetic Milton*.

12. Within another context, I have earlier addressed not only the sacerdotal dimension but the vatic and regal, as well. See my *Dialectics of Creation*, pp. 37–55. For a more recent study of the sacerdotal, as well as of the prophetic, see J. S. Hill's *John Milton*, which explores the roles of the poet from the perspective of divine vocation. In his sacerdotal role, the poet becomes a "priestly inter-

mediary between God and men, whose function and aim is the spiritual re-education of postlapsarian mankind" (p. 64).

1. Hastings, ed., *ERE*, 6:731.

2. So extensive has been that treatment, in fact, that the Library of Congress has designated "the holy" as a major subject heading in its card catalogue and has conveniently indexed under that subject heading practically an entire drawerful of titles. Included in this array of titles are works such as those of Otto and Eliade, mentioned in the introduction; Maison's *Die Welt und das Heilige*; Haeger's *Das Heilige und der Mythos*; Liverziani's *Esperienza del Sacro*; Bartsch's *Probleme der Entsakralisierung*; Martin and Antoine's *La Querelle du sacré*; Bogler's *Das Sakrale im Widerspruch*; Bogliani's *Il concetto di sacro*; Splett's *Die Rede vom Heiligen*; Schaefller's *Religion und kritisches Bewusstsein*; Frick's *Religiöse Strömungen der Gegenwart*; Hargrove's *Reformation of the Holy*; Douglas's *Purity and Danger*; and Altizer's *Mircea Eliade*.

3. Otto, *Idea of the Holy*. The quotation is from the subtitle.

4. Ibid., pp. 1–41. Compare Eliade's *Sacred and Profane*, pp. 9–10.

5. Eliade, *Sacred and Profane*, p. 10.

6. Ibid., p. 11. See also Eliade's *Patterns*, pp. 7 ff.

7. Eliade, *Sacred and Profane*, p. 11; Eliade, *Patterns*, p. 30.

8. Van der Leeuw, *Religion in Essence and Manifestation*, p. 37.

9. Durkheim, *Elementary Forms*, p. 190.

10. Codrington, *Melanesians*, pp. 119, 215. See also van der Leeuw, *Religion in Essence and Manifestation*, p. 43.

11. Van der Leeuw, *Religion in Essence and Manifestation*, p. 44. I shall discuss the nature of taboos at greater length in chapter 5.

12. Hastings, ed., *ERE*, 6:732.

13. Otto, *Idea of the Holy*, pp. 113–14.

14. Breasted, *Dawn of Conscience*, pp. 17–42. See, however, Kramer's *Sumer*, pp. 104–13, for the contention that the earliest evidence of the moral sense may be found in the Sumerians' *"me's"* as a distinctly ethical imperative.

15. Fleure, "Ritual and Ethic," pp. 435–54, has traced that movement histori-cally. In accordance with the findings of Breasted, Fleure shows how ethical thought grows out of ritual practice, moral out of nonmoral. In Hastings, ed., *ERE*, 11:784, the idea is given a sociological cast whereby the nonethical and ethical conform to two phases of society, the "synnomic" and the "syntelic." Whereas the synnomic is characterized by customs externally imposed, the syn-telic is characterized by ideals internally generated.

16. Westermarck, *Moral Ideas*, 1:119.

17. Häring, *Das Heilige und das Gute*, pp. 25, 45, 48.

18. Ibid., pp. 43–46.

19. Tylor, *Primitive Culture*.

20. Hastings, ed., *ERE*, 11:784.

21. Ibid., p. 786.

22. Ibid., p. 791.

23. Häring, *Das Heilige und das Gute*, pp. 45–51.

24. Hastings, ed., *ERE*, 6:741.

25. Hesiod, *Works and Days* (131–80).

26. Harrison, *Epilegomena*, pp. 72–73. See also pp. 96–97.

27. In *Herodotus* (2.37), 1:319.

28. Palmer, *Mycenaean Greek Texts*, p. 266. See also Trench, *Synonyms of the New Testament*, p. 187. According to Trench, ἅγιος and ἁγνός are probably different forms of the same word. "At all events, they have in common that root 'ΑΓ.'"

29. *Comicorum Atticorum Fragmenta*, vol. 1, p. 118, frag. 373.

30. See ἅγιος and ἅγος in Liddel and Scott's *Greek-English Lexicon*, s.v. For a discussion of the distinctions explored in this section, see Moulinier, *Le Pur et l'impur*.

31. Aristotle, *Athenian Constitution* (frag. 8, chap. 20.2), pp. 12–13, 60–61.

32. *Encyclopaedia Britannica*, 26:340. See ἁγνός in Liddel and Scott, s.v. According to Kerényi, *Religion of the Greeks and Romans*, p. 107, ἅγος represents a "crime against the divine." It connects with the underworld. Ἁγνός is associated with "the sphere of purity."

33. Harrison, *Prolegomena*, p. 59.

34. Nilsson, *Greek Religion*, p. 81. Accordingly, surrounding primitive altars, layers of ashes, the charred remains of animals, and the offerings of worship belonged to the god and could not be taken from their proper place. The temples that contained the altars were holy in varying degrees. "Some temples could only be entered at a certain time—that of Dionysos Limnaios at Athens, for instance, only on the feast day, the 12th of the month Anthesterion—others might be entered by the priests alone; the inner *cella* in the temple of Sosipolis in Elis could only be entered by the priestess and even she must veil her face. Other temples had at least an adytum from which the public was debarred. Those were sacred areas which must not be trodden at all by human foot, for example, the grove of Demeter and Kore at Megapolis, and the ground sacred to Zeus on the tip of Mt. Lykaion. Anyone who trespassed upon this would lose his shadow and die within the year" (p. 80). As such, the area was sacred to the gods: it contained a δύναμις or force that had the power to destroy. The idea is reflected in an inscription, dating from about 300 B.C. but characteristic of much older regulations, that may be found at the entrance to the temple in Astypalaea: "Into the temple let no one enter who is not pure [ceremonially] and perfect [in body], or he will be [kept] in mind [i.e., the gods will remember him for ill]" (Grant, ed., *Hellenistic Religions*, p. 7; cf. the Ialysusian temple inscription, ibid.; for the originals, see Dittenberger, ed., *Sylloge*, 2:262–63). The inscription is important not only because of its suggestion of the risks that one must face if he violates the holy but also because of its emphasis upon the cultic dimension of the holy. Such is true not only of that which is pure but also of that which is impure or accursed. Plato writes of

the ancient custom of people who "did not even venture to taste the flesh of a cow and had no animal sacrifices, but only cakes and fruit dipped in honey, and similar pure offerings, but no flesh of animals; from these they abstained under the idea that they ought not eat them, and might not stain the altars of the Gods with blood" (*Dialogues*, 2:541).

35. In Cornford, ed., *Greek Religious Thought*, pp. 135–39. From the most primitive point of view, Hippocrates, of course, is responding to the notion that uncleanness was looked upon as an infection that could be "washed away with water or the blood of sacrificial victims, rubbed off or at least burned away with fire, or smoked out with sulphur." As a primitive conception, this notion appears clearly in the case of sickness, "which was also regarded as the work of an evil power and was removed by the same means." The classical example may be found in Book 1 of the *Iliad*. There, the Greeks cleanse themselves of disease and throw the remains into the sea. The practice is found everywhere. Aesculapius is said literally to have "wiped away disease" (Nilsson, pp. 85–86).

36. Hastings, ed., *ERE*, 6:740–42.

37. Orphic Inscriptions, in Cornford, ed., *Greek Religious Thought*, pp. 60–62. A similar outlook is discernible in the chorus of the Cretan Initiates from the fragment of Euripides' lost play *Cretans*: "Pure has been my life's course, since I was initiated in the mysteries of Zeus of Mount Ida. I have accomplished the thunders of night-roving Zagreus and the Feast of the Eating of Raw Flesh; I have burned the torches for the Mountain Mother; and, having attained sanctification, I have received the name of Bacchus of the Armed Youths. And now, clothed all in white raiment, I shun contact with human birth and with the burial of the dead, and watchfully eschew the eating of things that have a living soul" (Cornford, ed., *Greek Religious Thought*, pp. 55–59). See also the chorus' song from Euripides' *Bacchanals* (Cornford, ed., *Greek Religious Thought*, pp. 155–59).

38. The citation from Diogenes Laertius is 6.2.42 (Hastings, ed., *ERE*, 6:740); from Heraclitus, frags. 15, 5 (Cornford, ed., *Greek Religious Thought*, p. 83). See also Demosthenes' "Speech against Aristogeiton": "There are in every city altars and temples to all the gods, and among them to Forethought. . . . At Delphi at the very entrance of the precinct of Apollo . . . there is a magnificent shrine of the goddess of Forethought; there is no temple to Folly or Pitilessness. Ay, and all mankind have altars dedicated to Justice, to Law-abidingness, and to Mercy—the fairest and holiest being those that are in the inmost soul and nature of every man, while others are set up outwardly for the common worship of all" (Cornford, ed., *Greek Religious Thought*, p. 247).

39. Plato, *Dialogues*, 1:391.

40. Cornford, ed., *Greek Religious Thought*, p. 247.

41. Aristotle, *Nichomachean Ethics* (2.1), *Works of Aristotle*, 10:1103ᵃ. See also the *Magna Moralia* (1.6): "The word 'ethical' (or 'moral') virtue is derived as follows: . . . [f]rom *ěthos* comes *ēthos*, and moral virtue is called 'ethical,' as being attained by practice" (*Works of Aristotle*, 9:1186ᵃ).

42. Grant, *Ancient Roman Religion*, p. xviii.

43. In ibid., pp. 4–8. The language is alliterative and magical: "nomner nerf sihitu ansihitu iovie hostatus anhostatu tursitu. . . ."

44. Ibid., pp. 9 and 11.

45. Codrington, *Melanesians*, cited by Rose, *Ancient Roman Religion*, p. 13.

46. Ibid., pp. 13–14.

47. Ibid., pp. 28–33.

48. Grant, ed., *Ancient Roman Religion*, p. 41. For a full discussion of Vergilian religious views, see Bailey, *Religion in Virgil*. An early but still valuable commentary on Vergil's use of *sacer, profanus, sanctus*, and *religiosus* may be found in Macrobius's *Saturnalia* (ca. 4th c. A.D.), pp. 196–99.

49. In Grant, ed., *Ancient Roman Religion*, p. 42. (*Aeneid*, 8.280–369).

50. Ibid., pp. 193–205. (*Aeneid*, 6.109, 562, 564, 607).

51. Ibid., pp. 198 and 205. (*Aeneid*, 6.236–63, 562–65.)

52. Ibid., pp. 204 and 207. (*Aeneid*, 6.535–44, 628–36).

53. Kerényi, *Religion of the Greeks and Romans*, p. 110.

54. Ibid., pp. 107–8.

55. Ibid., p. 108.

56. In Grant, ed., *Ancient Roman Religion*, pp. 205–6. (*Aeneid*, 6.562–607).

57. Ibid., p. 207. (*Aeneid*, 6.660–65).

58. Ibid., pp. 209–10. (*Aeneid*, 6.724–51).

59. Ibid., pp. 186–87.

60. Ibid., p. 188.

61. Ibid., p. 233.

62. Ibid., pp. 182–84.

63. Ibid., p. 183.

64. Cited by Kerényi, *Religion of the Greeks and Romans*, p. 95.

65. Smith, *Lectures*, p. 132.

66. Paton, "Early Hebrew Ethics," p. 164.

67. Smith, *Lectures*, pp. 132–34.

68. Hastings, ed., *ERE*, 6:753–57.

69. Adopted by Durkheim and others, the metaphor is Smith's, *Lectures*, p. 141.

70. Smith, *Lectures*, pp. 132–34. See also Hastings, ed., *ERE*, 6:758. The prevalence of the idea may be seen in Gen. 38:21 ff.; 1 Kings 14:25, 15:12, 22:46; 2 Kings 23:7; Amos 2:7; Hos. 4:11; Deut. 23:17.

71. Hastings, ed., *ERE*, 6:736.

72. Ibid., 737. See Lev. 19:19 (cf. Deut. 22:9–11), Lev. 19:23 ff. (cf. Lev. 17:17).

73. Hastings, ed., *ERE*, 6:759.

74. Ibid., 736–39.

75. The association is particularly apt in this context, since "profane" itself recalls its Latinate meaning of *profanum*—that which has its place *before* the sanctuary, the *fanum* (Kerényi, *Religion of the Greeks and Romans*, p. 110). The biblical translators no doubt had the derivation in mind in their rendering of Leviticus 21:23, Ezekiel 44:23, 22:26, and other corresponding passages.

76. Hastings, ed., *ERE*, 6:737.

77. Ibid.

78. Singer, ed., *Jewish Encyclopedia*, 6:144.

79. That attitude, in turn, is discernible in works ranging from the Apocrypha and Pseudepigrapha to the *Code* of Maimonides. Within this context, the outlook expressed in the pseudepigraphal Book of Jubilees is particularly enlightening, for it conceives of the birth of Eve in decidedly cultic terms. Both Adam and Eve must await the termination of appropriate periods of purification following the birth of offspring before they can be admitted into Eden, which is conceived as a sanctuary with "hallowed things." Indeed, it is "holier than all the earth besides, and every tree that is planted in it is holy" (Charles, ed., *Apocrypha and Pseudepigrapha*, 2:16). The Levitical outlook apparent here is once again implicit in the *Talmud*. There, the sixth division of the *Mishnah*, called *Tohoroth* ("Cleanlinesses"), postulates in the section dealing with vessels (*Kelim*) "ten degrees of holiness" beginning with the land of Israel, "holier than any other land," proceeding to "the walled cities" of Israel, "still more holy," next to the wall of Jerusalem, then to "the Temple Mount," thereafter to "the Rampart," "the Court of the Women," "the Court of the Israelites," "the Court of the Priests," "the Sanctuary," and "the Holy of Holies." What determines the holiness of each of these degrees is a distinctly *physical* characteristic related to the cultic significations of menstruation, touching a corpse, immersion, blemishes, "unloosed" hair, "unwashed" hands and feet, drinking of wine, being designated high priest (*Mishnah*, pp. 605–6). It is precisely this tradition that Moses ben Maimon attempted to revive in the Maimonidean *Code*. See, among other works, *The Book of Cleanness*, *The Book of Holiness*, and *The Book of Temple Service*.

80. The Book of Jubilees follows suit by referring to the acts of circumcising "the foreskin" of the "heart" of God's faithful and "the foreskin of the heart of their seed," of "creat[ing] in them a holy spirit," and of "cleans[ing] them" (Charles, ed., *Apocrypha and Pseudepigrapha*, 2:12). The *Talmud* states that "study leads to precision, precision leads to zeal, zeal leads to cleanliness, cleanliness leads to restraint, restraint leads to purity, purity leads to holiness, holiness leads to saintliness, saintliness leads to the possession of the holy spirit, the holy spirit leads to life eternal, and saintliness is greater than any of these" (Epstein, ed., *Babylonian Talmud*, 5:106). Here, then, are degrees of moral sanctification to complement those of cultic sanctification noted above. Appropriately, Maimonides, in the *Code* as well as in the *Guide of the Perplexed*, emphasizes that the purpose of cultic holiness is to teach man how to become morally pure and to restrain sensuality. That is how man truly sanctifies himself (introduction to *Book of Holiness*, in *Code*, 16:xix–xxiii).

81. Paton, "Ethics of the Hebrew Prophets," p. 204.

82. That point of view "affected the language, not only of prophecy, but of legislation. Circumcision was to be of the heart (mind), and not of the flesh only (Deut. 10:16, 30:6). It entered even into the priestly legislation of the guilt-offering (Lev. 5:1–7), and in the 'Code of Holiness' finds its due place (Lev. 25:35–55). This was doubtless a reinforcement of ethical elements which be-

longed to Israel's old religion, since all religion involves social relations and a social order, and therefore these elements found a place in the older codes of legislation. But prophetic teaching gave them a new and primary importance, and they
came to dislodge the externalities of ceremonial religion. This is manifest in some
of the Psalms, for example, 50:9–15, where sacrifices are repudiated as irrational; 51:18–19, where the true sacrifices are a true and contrite heart. Perhaps
the most notable expression is to be found in Psalm 15:1–2 (which reflects the
spirit of Mic. 6:7–8): 'Lord, who shall abide in thy tabernacle? who shall dwell in
thy holy hill? He that walketh uprightly, and worketh righteousness, and
speaketh the truth in his heart' " (Hastings, ed., *ERE*, 6:758–59).

83. Ibid.

84. Otto, *Idea of the Holy*, p. 85.

85. Hastings, ed., *Dictionary of the Bible*, p. 399.

86. Ibid., p. 400.

87. Hastings, ed., *ERE*, 6:744.

88. Otto, *Idea of the Holy*, p. 85–86.

89. Teilhard de Chardin, *Divine Milieu*, p. 131.

90. Although it falls beyond the purview of this study to explore this point in
any detail, we might look briefly at the way in which the baptism as numinous
event was treated by the Church Fathers. Gregory Thaumaturgus's fourth homily,
entitled "On the Holy Theophany or on Christ's Baptism," is a case in point.
Assuming the form of a passionate celebration of Christ as sacred mystery, the
homily becomes one in which John the Baptist stands in awe before ὁ ἅγιος.
"How shall I spread those menial hands of mine upon Thy head? How shall I
wash Thee, who are undefiled and sinless? How shall I enlighten the light?"
proclaims John the Baptist. "Bless the Lord, who has come upon the river Jordan;
for through these streams He transmits sanctification to all streams." Ὁ ἅγιος responds: "It is a mystery that is being gone through this day in the Jordan. My
mysteries are for myself and my own" (Roberts et al., eds., *Ante-Nicene Christian
Library*, 20:146–47). In his *Orations*, Gregory Nazianzen associates this mystery, experienced as a theophany, with none other than the entrance into the Holy
of Holies. There, one experiences the divine Illumination, "the greatest and most
magnificent of the Gifts of God." In cultic terms, the Illumination is celebrated in
the Theophanea, a festival accompanied by lighted torches and devoted to the
conferring of baptism. Thus, Gregory Nazianzen says: "The Holy Day of Lights
... has for its origin the Baptism of my Christ, the True Light that lighteneth
every man ... and effecteth my purification." In baptism, "we must purify ourselves first, and then approach this converse with the Pure; unless we would have
the same experience as Israel, who could not endure the glory of the face of
Moses, and therefore asked for a veil." Consequently, "as long as you are a
Catachumen you are but in the porch of Religion; you must come inside, and
cross the court, and observe the Holy Things, and look into the Holy of Holies"
(Schaff and Wace, eds., *Select Library*, 7:345–65). For corresponding views on
the theophany, see Duns Scotus, *Division of Nature* (book 1), pp. 12–14.

91. For a discussion of the numinosity of the eucharist, see Otto, "Lord's Sup-

per as a Numinous Fact," pp. 45–52. According to van der Leeuw, in the eucharist all the "elements of the Christian sacrament attain their highest completion." Before the sacred presence of the Lord, the votary "falls to his knees" (*Religion in Essence and Manifestation*, p. 368). From the very incarnation of the Word as Logos (John 1:14; 1 John 4:2), "Jesus has been food for those who believe in him" (McDonald, ed., *New Catholic Encylopedia*, 5:599). In this way, the eucharist as an *anamnesis* or remembrance of the Lord recalls the Incarnation. Compare Justin Martyr, *First Apology*, p. 8. For such writers as Ignatius, Cyprian, and Augustine, the eucharist is both a "commemoration of the sacrifice of the Cross" (*sacrificii memoria, sacramentum memoriae*) and a "participation" in the "fruits" of Christ's passion and resurrection (Hastings, ed., *ERE*, 5:547–53). In the eucharist, then, the sacrificial basis of the numinous assumes its most compelling form. It is the μυστήριον at its most sacred, the cultic at its most numinous.

92. As recorded by Hirn in *Sacred Shrine*, pp. 182–86, 239, complex precautions were taken to preserve the physical inviolability of the objects used in worship: the Mass table had to be spotless, roped off, elevated, and enclosed; the altar became a "holy and dreadful place" where "scrupulous cleanliness reign[ed]" and where women, because of their sex, were forbidden to approach. "In early Christian and medieval ritual, not only towels were used but also *hand veils*. These small cloths were to cover the priest's fingers while he celebrated, to prevent his touching the holy objects with his naked hand."

93. Hastings, ed., *ERE*, 6:744.

94. Askwith, *Christian Conception of Holiness*, pp. 182–86, 239. See also C. E. Brown, *Meaning of Sanctification*, p. 151.

95. Askwith, *Christian Conception of Holiness*, pp. 182–86.

96. The form that this perspective assumes in the Christian tradition is nowhere more evident than in the liturgy, that which Saint Augustine calls λατρεία (*City of God* [10.1], pp. 303–5). In λατρεία, the holy as cultic embodiment of the spiritual is made dramatically apparent. The Divine Liturgy of James (pre–200 A.D.), one of the earliest, represents a case in point. In that portion of the liturgy known as the "Prayer of the Veil," the worshiper thanks God for allowing him to enter his "holy place" through "the veil of the flesh" of Christ. There, the worshiper beholds the tabernacle of God's glory, the Holy of Holies. The liturgy ends with an appeal for holiness and purity of conscience (Roberts et al., eds., *Ante-Nicene Christian Library*, 24:26). The cultic basis of the Old Testament outlook evident here is likewise implicit in the terminology that is applied to the priests. According to the Apostolical Constitutions (2nd–3rd c. A.D.), the priests, like the Levites, have charge over "holy things," such as the "sanctified" "first fruits," "oblations," "sacrifices," offerings, "clean" and "unclean" things, all for the purpose of ministering to a "holy and sacred church of God, enrolled in heaven, a royal priesthood, an holy nation, a peculiar people" (Roberts et al., eds., *Ante-Nicene Christian Library*, 21:57). Their office, then, represents the cultic assimilation of the holy, manifested in ὁ ἅγιος, Christ himself. Compare Irenaeus (*Against Heresies*, 5:421–25), Lactantius (*Divine Institutes*, 21:57), Ambrose (*On the Mysteries*, 10:320), Cyprian (*To Januarius*, p. 53), Basil (*On the Spirit*,

8:24), and Novatian (*On the Jewish Meats*, 2:382–95). For Novatian, the cultic basis of Levitical law may be explained by the Christian conception of holiness, which moralizes the efficacy inherent in "things" to accord with the spiritual outlook embodied in that one "thing" which is holy, Christ himself.

CHAPTER 2

1. For similar views, see, for example, Penton, *Adoration* (1682), pp. 47–48; Ainsworth, *Communion of the Saincts* (1628), pp. 57–63; Basire, *Deo et Ecclesiae Sacrum* (1646), p. 17; Abbot, *Holiness of Christian Churches* (1618), pp. 9–12.

2. For a corresponding view, see Sempill, *Sacrilege Sacredly Handled* (1619), p. 1; Tomlinson, *Holy Salutation* (1612), pp. 22–23.

3. Penton, *Adoration*, pp. 25–26.

4. John Turner, *Antient Pagans* (1687), sigs. h7ʳ–Ilᵛ.

5. Ibid., and throughout.

6. I single out Hall and Ussher with a full awareness of the controversy that is of such great importance to Milton's own antiprelatical tracts. On this point, see the introductory material and notes to volume 1 of Milton, *Complete Prose Works of John Milton*.

7. Theirs is an outlook based upon the efficacy of "holy things" consecrated for a particular use, that is, "sanctified," as Mede says in *Diatribae*, so as "to put a difference between [them] . . . and other things by way of excellency, or in a dignifying wise, by appropriating and severing [them] . . . in the use thereof from things of ordinary and common rank" (p. 21). This attitude, we have seen, concurs with that of the Gospels, where, Mede argues, "there are both things and persons . . . lawfully and acceptably set apart and separated, by the devotion of men, unto the Divine Majesty, and [are] consequently *relatively Holy*" (p. 39). As suggested, the designation of "relative holiness" is common in the Renaissance. Even Richard Baxter recognizes it as a legitimate, though lesser form of holiness. As he says in *The Divine Life*: "And *Relative Holiness* it self, though the *lowest*, must be Honoured by us. *Holy offices* and *persons* in them must be *Reverenced* for their *Relative Holiness*. *Holy dayes* must be *holily observed*. *Holy Ordinances* (which also participate of the holiness of the *Law*, as *significative*) must be *reverently used*. *Due reverence* must be given even to that which is *lawfully by men devoted* to a *Holy use*, as are *Temples*, and *Utensils* of worship, and the *maintenance* dedicated to the service of God. That which is *Holy*, must not be *devoured* . . . nor used as we do *things common and unclean*" (p. 136).

8. See Abbot's *Holiness of Christian Churches* (1618); Penton, *Adoration* (1682); Jackson, *Catholike Faith and Church* (1627); J. Taylor, *Holy Living* (1650) and *Holy Dying* (1651); Allestree, *Beauty of Holiness* (1684); Clarke, *Holy Oyle* (1630); Fuller, *Holy and Profane States* (1642). According to Allestree, for example, "*Holiness* and *purity of Spirit* are different words, but of the same signification, and are promiscuously used in Scripture to express the same

thing. Opposite to which are *Sin* and *Uncleanness*." In this sense, "*Holiness* . . . is the *comprehensive sum of the moral Law*; and may be very aptly described to be *a ceasing from evil, and doing good*; which in this lapsed estate consists in the sincerity of our intentions and actions, and shall be perfected when *morality is swallowed up of life*, when those imperfections and spots that attend our natural state, shall be quite removed and done away" (pp. 7–11).

9. In *Holy Salutation* (1612), pp. 22–23, Tomlinson elaborates upon this association: "To bee sanctified, is to be separated, consecrated and set apart from common uses, and reserved to sacred and holy uses. Thus in the law, those things were called holy and sanctified, which were taken from the common use of the people, and set apart for the use and service of God; as the oyle, shewbread, first fruits, vessels of the tabernacle. In this sense, the Priests were called holy, because they were separate from the common life of men to serve in the tabernacle, and offer holy sacrifices. Thus the people of Israel, separated from the rest of the nations, were called by *Moses* a sanctified people, to the Lord, by *Ieremie* a thing hallowed to the Lord."

10. In his ΠΝΕΥΜΑΤΟΛΟΓΙΑ, the Puritan divine John Owen interprets the twofold sanctification as the expression of "a twofold holiness":

The first is common unto persons and things, consisting in the peculiar dedication, consecration, or separation of them unto the service of God by his own appointment, whereby they become holy. Thus the priests and Levites of old, the ark, the altar, the tabernacle, and the temple, were sanctified and made holy; and indeed in all holinesss whatever, there is a peculiar dedication and separation unto God. But in the sense mentioned, this was solitary and alone. No more belonged unto it but this sacred separation, nor was there any other effect of this sanctification. But, secondly, here is another kind of sanctification and holiness, wherein this separation to God is not the first thing done or intended, but a consequent and effect thereof. This is real and internal, by the communicating of a principle of holiness unto our natures, attended with its exercise in acts and duties of holy obedience unto God. This is that which we inquire after. (3:370)

11. Ibid., pp. 384–85.
12. Ibid., pp. 423–36.
13. Ibid., pp. 502–4, 467, 383.
14. Ibid., pp. 502–4, 383.
15. Ibid., pp. 467, 383.

CHAPTER 3

1. See the discussion of this matter, along with appropriate bibliographical references, in the introduction. Interestingly, Langdon's book *Milton's Theory of Poetry* says nothing about the poet as priest. A role that complements the vatic and the hierophantic is the oratorical. For Milton's view of the poet as orator, see

Wittreich, "'The Crown of Eloquence,'" pp. 3–54. In the same volume, see Huntley's "Images of Poet and Poetry," pp. 83–120.

2. Milton uses the terms *vates* and *propheticum* interchangeably to denote "prophet."

3. See Kerrigan's *Prophetic Milton* and Wittreich's *Visionary Poetics*, discussed in the introduction.

4. Plato, *Phaedrus* (265), *Dialogues*, 1:268–69.

5. Plato, *Phaedrus* (244), *Dialogues*, 1:248–49.

6. Plato, *Ion* (533–34), *Dialogues*, 1:288–89.

7. Plutarch, *Pythian Priestess* (chap. 17), 3:86–87.

8. Plutarch, *Oracles* (chaps. 46 and 49), 4:56, 60.

9. Ibid., (chaps. 46 and 51), 4:57, 62–63.

10. Ibid., (chap. 40), 4:50.

11. Murrin, *Veil of Allegory*, esp. pp. 18–19, 38–39, 44–51.

12. Ovid, *Amores*, bk. 3, no. 8, line 23; no. 9, lines 17–18. See further Cicero's *For Aulus*, 2:419; Horace's *Odes* (bk. 4, no. 9, line 28), 1:384. According to Horace's *Ars Poetica*, the function of the poet-priest is specifically to distinguish between "things sacred and profane." As such, his office is oracular (lines 365–427); and, according to the treatise *On the Sublime*, attributed to Longinus, the poet is a priest "inspired to speak oracles" and, in his own way, to provide a knowledge of "the other" (chaps. 9 and 13, pp. 92–93, 111, 119).

13. Propertius, *Sexti Propertii Elegiarum* (3.1.1–6), pp. 176–77.

14. Vergil, *"Eclogues" and "Georgics" of Virgil*, pp. 24–35. For *Eclogue* 4, see lines 55–57. See also *Georgics* (4.417–565) and *Aeneid* (6.33–155) for an elaboration of the Orphic dimension.

15. Johnson, *Cultic Prophet*, pp. 8, 25, 26–27, 42–43, 51, 59.

16. In *Works of Philo Judaeus*, 1:1; 3:88; see also 2:146–47; 4:255.

17. For further elaboration of the idea, see Rosenblatt, "Mosaic Voice," pp. 207–32.

18. In one way or another, Moses does fulfill these roles in the biblical accounts: he is called a prophet (Deut. 34:10); he performs the function of a priest (Exod. 28:41); and he composes that magnificent "song" that climaxes Deuteronomy (31:19–32).

19. *A Treatise on the Life of Moses*, 3:88.

20. For the fullest discussion of Christ as prophet, king, and priest in *Paradise Regained*, see Lewalski's *Milton's Brief Epic*, pp. 193–321.

21. Clement of Alexandria, *Writings of Clement of Alexandria*, 1:73.

22. Ibid., 2:232–34, 239, 245.

23. See Baker's "Certain Religious Elements," pp. 300–323; Murrin's *Veil of Allegory*, throughout.

24. See, among other works, Rainolds's *Oratio in Laudem* (ca. 1572), pp. 42–45.

25. In Reynolds, *Critical Essays*, 1:153–69.

26. Clement of Alexandria, *Miscellanies*, 2:253.

27. Isidore of Seville, sigs. [x 15]^v–y^r, sigs. [u 11]^v–[u 12]^r. See "De Poetis" (Bk. 8, chap. 7) and "De Clericis" (Bk. 8, chap. 12).

28. Boccaccio, *Life of Dante*, pp. 47–54.

29. Vida, *Vida's "Art of Poetry"*, pp. 73–76, 77, 125. See bk. 1, lines 536–46, 562–65; bk. 2, lines 3–5; bk. 3, line 112. For similar views, see writers so diverse as Tasso (*Discourses on the Heroic Poem*, p. 466) and Rainolds (*Oratio in Laudem*, pp. 42–43).

30. In Sidney, *Selected Prose and Poetry*, pp. 106–7. Complementing the poet as vates or prophet, of course, is the poet as ποιτήν or maker (p. 108). For the fullest and most informative account of the poet as "maker," especially as that concept has its sources in Pythagorean-Platonic thought, see Heninger's *Touches of Sweet Harmony*, esp. pp. 287–324. See also Heninger's essay, "Sidney and Milton," pp. 57–95. Sidney's comments on the poet as vates must, of course, be seen in the context of E. K.'s statements in Spenser's *Shepheardes Calender* (1579). Poetry, says E. K., is "a diuine gift and heavenly instinct not to bee gotten by laboure and learning, but adorned with both: and poured into the witte by a certaine ἐνθουσιασμός [enthusiasm], and celestiall inspiration" ("ARGVMENT" to the October eclogue, *Works of Spenser*, p. 456). For the emergence of religious poetry during the Renaissance generally, see Campbell, "Christian Muse" and *Divine Poetry and Drama*, throughout.

31. Hobbes, "Answer," p. 74.

32. Puttenham, *Arte of Poesie*, 1:4–5.

33. In Herbert, *Works of George Herbert*.

34. For additional commentary, see Featley, *Foure Rowes of Precious Stones* (1636).

35. On this subject, see, in addition to Heninger's *Touches of Sweet Harmony*, pp. 287–324, his study, *Cosmographical Glass*, pp. 81–143.

36. Iamblichus, *Life of Pythagoras*, pp. 5–9.

37. In *Select Works*, p. 29. For a convenient, as well as seminal, Renaissance compendium of Iamblichus, Porphyry, Proclus, and the Pythagoreans, among others, see Ficino's translation of *De Mysteriis Aegyptiorum* (1497).

38. See Fixler's discussion of "crypsis" in "Apocalypse within *Paradise Lost*," p. 147.

39. For a full study of this dimension, see Crump, *Mystical Design*.

40. For similar readings, see Ferry, *Milton's Epic Voice*, pp. 20–43; and Fish, "Discovery as Form."

41. See Horace's *Satires* (1.10.73–74). Interestingly, the Horatian dictum is used as the epigraph on the title page of the first folio of Jonson's *Workes* (1616). In Jonson's hands, the dictum accords with his own particular understanding of the poet as "maker."

CHAPTER 4

1. See Euripides' *Alcestis*, 1144–46, cited in Woodhouse and Bush, eds., *Variorum Commentary*, 2:487, 499.

2. Van der Leeuw, *Religion in Essence and Manifestation*, p. 37.

3. Woodhouse, "Argument of Milton's *Comus*," reprinted in Diekhoff, ed., *Maske at Ludlow*. The entire edition should be consulted for a sampling of the range of scholarship available on *Comus*.

4. Main, *Religious Chastity*, pp. 200–203, and throughout.

5. The phrase is from Milton's alleged notes to Paul Best's *Mysteries Discovered* (1647).

6. Otto, *Idea of the Holy*, pp. 1–41.

7. See the full reading of this context in Lewalski's *Milton's Brief Epic*, pp. 303–21.

8. With respect to Samson's associations with the woman of Timnath and with Delilah, ceremonial uncleanness is a moot point in *Samson Agonistes*. "Against his vow of strictest purity," the Nazarite was not to associate with (let alone, marry) an "unclean, unchaste" partner (318–21). For Samson, there might be extenuating circumstances by which God "hath full right t'exempt / Whom so it pleases him by choice / From National obstriction, without taint / Of sin, or legal debt," a fact which "quits" the appropriate bride of "unclean[ness]" (309–13, 324). The question of ceremonial uncleanness, then, possibly becomes moot. (Moral uncleanness, of course, does not [see SA, 325].) In the case of the woman of Timnath, there are at least exceptional considerations: Samson felt free to marry her as the result of an "intimate impulse" (223). His marriage, the Bible says, "*was* of the Lord, that he sought occasion against the Philistines" (Judg. 14:4). In the case of Delilah, Milton's account and the biblical account differ markedly in that the Samson of Judges never married Delilah, whereas the Samson of Milton's drama did marry Dalila. In neither instance was Samson given overt divine sanction to take Delilah as a partner, even though Milton's Samson says, "I thought it lawful from my former act" (231). (In the biblical account, Samson's association with Delilah is immediately preceded by a reference to his visit to a whore [Judg. 16:1].)

9. For the most astute explanation of the differences, see Labriola, "Divine Urgency as a Motive," pp. 99–107.

10. *The Faerie Queene* (1.12.23–26).

11. Spenser, *Works of Spenser*, p. 407.

12. Dante, *Paradiso* (33.124).

13. *Celestial Cycle*, pp. 422–33.

14. [Pordage,] *Mundorum Explicatio* (1661), p. 9.

15. Ibid., p. 10.

16. In *CM*, 2:3–5.

17. Riggs, *Christian Poet*, p. 43.

18. In Crashaw, *Complete Poetry of Richard Crashaw*, between pp. 190 and 191.

19. From "Superliminare" in Herbert, *Works of George Herbert*.

20. Fixler, "Milton's Passionate Epic," p. 172.

21. From the dedication, in Herbert, *Works of George Herbert*.

CHAPTER 5

1. Tennant, *Doctrine of the Fall and Original Sin*, pp. 38, 70–71.

2. Philpot, *Sacred Tree*, pp. 110–11. Compare Nebuchadnezzar's dream in Daniel 4:10–11: "I saw, and behold, a tree in the midst of the earth, and the height thereof *was* great. The tree grew, and was strong, and the height thereof reached unto heaven, and the sight thereof to the end of all the earth."

3. Evans, *"Paradise Lost" and the Genesis Tradition*, pp. 9–20.

4. Ibid., p. 20.

5. It is to questions of this kind, of course, that Milton attempts to provide answers not only in *Paradise Lost* but in his other works as well. One thinks of the famous passage in *Areopagitica*: "Good and evill we know in the field of this World grow up together almost inseparably; and the knowledge of good is so in-volv'd and interwoven with the knowledge of evill, and in so many cunning re-semblances hardly to be discern'd, that those confused seeds which were impos'd on *Psyche* as an incessant labour to cull out, and sort asunder, were not more intermixt. It was from out the rinde of one apple tasted, that the knowledge of good and evill as two twins cleaving together leapt forth into the world. And perhaps this is that doom which *Adam* fell into of knowing good and evill, that is to say of knowing good by evill" (*CM*, 4:310–11).

6. Gaster, *Myth, Legend, and Custom*, pp. 32–35.

7. See the full account in Pritchard, ed., *Ancient Near Eastern Texts*, pp. 101–3. For the association of Adapa with man, see the gloss, p. 101. Similar motifs may be found in *The Gilgamesh Epic* (ca. 2000 B.C.). Seeking immortality, Gilgamesh attempts to retrieve a thorny plant at the bottom of the sea. Although he retrieves the plant, a serpent snatches it from him and eats it (tablet 11, verses 267–89). See Heidel's discussion of the event and its consequences in his edition of *The Gilgamesh Epic*, pp. 137–223. See also Heidel's discussion of the paradise myth and related material in his edition of *The Babylonian Genesis*, pp. 61–153.

8. Hooke, *Middle Eastern Mythology*, p. 116.

9. In Pritchard, ed., *Ancient Near Eastern Texts*, pp. 37–41.

10. In Thomas, ed., *Documents from Old Testament Times*, pp. 111–17.

11. Tertullian, *Writings of Tertullianus*, 3:204. The idea is likewise implicit in rabbinical commentary. See, for example, Friedlander, trans., *Pirkê de Rabbi Eliezer*, p. 84. According to the *Targum of Palestine*, "God took the man [Adam] from the mountain of worship, where he had been created, and made him dwell in the garden of Eden, to do service in the law, and to keep its commandments" (Etheridge, trans., *Targum of Onkelos*, p. 163).

12. Hooker, *Works of Hooker*, 2:543.

13. My analysis of this point owes much to Fish's *Surprised by Sin*, pp. 242–43. "The arbitrariness of God's command, that is to say, its unreasonableness, is necessary if compliance is to be regarded as an affirmation of loyalty springing from an act of the will." The arbitrariness of the command has long been recognized. See studies ranging from Willey's *Seventeenth-Century Background*, pp. 240–58, to C. S. Lewis's *Preface to "Paradise Lost,"* p. 71.

14. Evans, *"Paradise Lost" and the Genesis Tradition*, pp. 11–14.

15. Ibid., p. 14.

16. Otto, *Idea of the Holy*, pp. 74–96.

17. Montefiore and Loewe, eds., *Rabbinic Anthology*, pp. 156–57.

18. Evans, *"Paradise Lost" and the Genesis Tradition*, pp. 48–49.

19. The *Archaeologiae Philosophicae* is attributed to Burnet.

20. C. S. Lewis, *Preface to "Paradise Lost,"* pp. 71–72.

21. Lévy-Bruhl, *How Natives Think*, p. 107.

22. Lévy-Bruhl, *Primitive Mentality*, pp. 35–36.

23. Cassirer, *Philosophy of Symbolic Forms*, 2:46. Compare Lévi-Strauss, *Savage Mind*, p. 61: Native thought makes use of a "polyvalent" logic which appeals "to several, formally distinct types of connection at the same time." See also Wheelwright, "Notes on Mythopoeia," pp. 574–92.

24. The phrase is taken from Burden, *Logical Epic*.

25. See MacCaffrey, *"Paradise Lost" as "Myth."* The "mythic" school has a number of important studies to its credit, including Stein, *Answerable Style*; Summers, *Muse's Method*; N. Frye, *Return of Eden*; and Cope, *Metaphoric Structure*. My earlier study, *Dialectics of Creation*, is also rooted in that tradition.

26. Shumaker, *Unpremeditated Verse*, p. 6.

27. Ibid., p. 15.

28. For a full account of that tradition, see Allen's *Mysteriously Meant*, pp. 1–82.

29. In the same sense, Gale, *Court of the Gentiles* (1672), 1, sig. N1^v, refers to the study of "θεολογία μυθική, *Mythic or Fabulous Theologie.*"

30. Owen, Θεολογουμενα Παντοδαπα, p. 158. See, for example, Gale, *Court of the Gentiles*, 1, sig. Qq3, and Bompart, *Parallela sacra*, p. 17.

31. See Cook, *Voyage to the Pacific Ocean*, 1:286, 338, 410, 2:248; and Codrington, *Melanesians*, pp. 215–16.

32. Cook, *Voyage to the Pacific Ocean*, 1:286.

33. Lang, *Magic and Religion*, p. 257.

34. Thomas, "Taboo," 26:339.

35. See Milton's *Logic* (CM, 11:20–70) for a full discussion of terminological distinctions.

36. Durkheim, *Elementary Forms*, p. 301.

37. "Taboo," 26:337–40.

38. In Augustine, *Works of Aurelius Augustine*, 4:106–7. See also the commentary on Genesis (*De Genesi ad Litteram*), Migne, ed., *Patrologia (Series Latina)*, 34:383–86.

39. Duncan, *Milton's Earthly Paradise*, p. 141. For a similar view, see Burden's *Logical Epic*, pp. 124–49.

40. The lines are those originally deleted from *Comus*. For commentary, see Woodhouse and Bush, eds., *Variorum Commentary*, 2:856–57.

41. Cited in ibid., p. 908.

42. Spenser associates the tree and its fruit not only with Hesperides and the labors of Hercules but with Atalanta and Hippomenes, on the one hand, and Acontius and Cydippe, on the other. See *The Faerie Queene*, 2.7.53–55, and the notes to those stanzas in the Kellogg and Steele edition (*Books I and II of "The Faerie Queene"*).

43. Kellogg and Steele's gloss of *The Faerie Queene*, 2.7.53.

44. Smith, *Religion of the Semites*, pp. 125–26.

45. Ibid., 423–24.

46. Friedlander, trans., *Pirkê de Rabbi Eliezer*, p. 95.

47. See Purchas, *Pilgrimage*, pp. 542–43. The phrase "sacred things" comes from Charles de Brosses's full study of the holy in *Du Culte des dieux fétiches* (1760), p. 19. For another early and revealing study, see William Bosman, *Voyage de Guinée* (1704).

48. Purchas, *Pilgrimage*, pp. 542–43.

49. Ibid., p. 432.

50. See, in particular, Freud's own classic *Totem and Taboo*, pp. 34–35.

51. For a full commentary on the allusion, see Milton, *Poetical Works of Milton*, 3:287–88.

52. Freud, *Totem and Taboo*, p. 18.

53. Smith, *Religion of the Semites*, pp. 170–72.

54. In *Luther's Works*, 1:94.

55. In Wollebius, *Reformed Dogmatics*, pp. 64–65. For the iconographical correspondences implicit in the sacramental point of view, see Labriola, "The Aesthetics of Self-Diminution," pp. 267–311.

56. *Confession of Faith*, pp. 25–28.

57. For appropriate references, see "חֻקָּה" in Brown et al., eds., *Hebrew and English Lexicon*, s.v. The locus classicus of the חֻקּוֹת הַתּוֹרָה is that concerning the red heifer of Numbers 19:1–10. I am indebted to Rabbi Gary Gerson for calling my attention to the term and its appropriate contexts.

58. Freedman and Simon, eds., *Midrash Rabbah*, 1:131.

59. Included in the *Tract Aboth* of Rodkinson, ed., *Babylonian Talmud*, 5:8.

60. *A Letter of Novatian*, 2:385.

61. For commentary on the passage, see Fixler, "Unclean Meats of the Mosaic Law," pp. 573–77.

62. Smith, *Religion of the Semites*, pp. 147–48.

63. Durkheim, *Elementary Forms*, p. 320.

64. Ibid., p. 318.

65. Wundt, *Elements of Folk Psychology*, pp. 193–94.

66. Durkheim, *Elementary Forms*, p. 411.

67. Smith, *Religion of the Semites*, p. 134.

68. Ibid., p. 142.

69. Wundt, *Elements of Folk Psychology*, pp. 199–200.

70. Frazer, *Taboo and Perils of the Soul*, pp. 291–93.

71. Smith, *Religion of the Semites*, p. 430.

72. See Wollebius, *Reformed Dogmatics*, p. 79; Ames, *Marrow of Theology*, pp. 110–12.

73. Maimonides, *Guide*, p. 513.

74. In *A Treatise of Civil Power*, Milton maintains that unlike the "reasonable service" required by Gospel law (Rom. 12:1), ceremonial or "Jewish law" requires "unreasonable service, that is to say, not only unwilling but unconscionable" (*CM*, 6:36). Such an attitude is in keeping with Milton's view that the covenant of works is completely abrogated by the covenant of grace (CD, *CM*, 16:112–63).

75. Modern rabbinical thought would seem to accord with this view. Thus, in his commentary on the Pentateuch, Rabbi Hirsch says that the prohibition is "not a so-called 'reasonable prohibition' . . . but rather one which all the human means of judgment would speak against." As such, it is "a dietary law" (1:60).

CHAPTER 6

1. For a discussion of the idea, see Jammer, *Concepts of Space*, pp. 28–29, 32; Koyré, *Closed World to Infinite Universe*, p. 195. I am indebted to my colleagues Jason Rosenblatt of Georgetown University and the late Anne Hopewell Selby of the University of Illinois at Chicago Circle for alerting me to the concept of המקום.

2. Simon and Levertoff, eds., *Zohar*, 4:202–3.

3. Eliade, *Patterns*, pp. 368–69.

4. Eliade, *Images and Symbols*, p. 39.

5. Plato, *Dialogues*, 2:79–81.

6. Eliade, *Images and Symbols*, p. 39.

7. Eliade, *Patterns*, pp. 368–69. See fig. 7, cited in chap. 7.

8. Ibid., p. 373.

9. Jung, *Psychology and Alchemy*, 12:92–94. See Jung's extensive studies of mandala symbolism, not only in *Psychology and Alchemy*, but in such works as *Archetypes*, 9:355–56.

10. See esp. Exod., chaps. 25–27; Lev., chap. 4; 1 Kings, chaps. 6–8.

11. Josephus, *Works of Flavius Josephus*, 1:202–3, 210.

12. Poole, *Annotations*, 1, sig. Pp3ᵛ.

13. According to Schroder, *Book of the Prophet Ezekiel*, pp. 384–85: "as הרמה ('checking,' 'keeping off')," the "enclosing wall" (Ezek. 40:5) is "a barrier against what might come from without. It runs right around the house, and will thus in relation to it, that is to the temple generally, symbolize the warding off of the profane, the unclean, the false." (The idea of having an enclosing wall is reminiscent of both Greek and Babylonian shrines. Thus, "the Greeks distinguish

between the βέβηλον [profane] and the ἱερόν [holy]" [Spence and Exell, *Book of the Prophet Ezekiel*, 27:321].)

14. Compare Josephus's description of the Jerusalem Temple in *Jewish War*, 3:265–67. The description moves us *inward* until we attain the holiest place in the midst. That enclosed place "typified the universe." This was the inmost part of the temple, separated from the outer part by a veil. In it "stood nothing whatever: unapproachable, inviolable, invisible to all, it was called the Holy of Holies." After the destruction of the first temple, the ark was probably taken captive or destroyed (cf. 2 Esd. 10:22).

15. For Ezekiel's influence on Saint John the Divine, see Farrer, *Rebirth of Images*, pp. 130–31.

16. Eichrodt, *Ezekiel*, p. 585.

17. Charles, ed., *Apocrypha and Pseudepigrapha*, 2:26. Cf. Book of Jubilees 4:26.

18. Friedlander, trans., *Pirkê de Rabbi Eliezer*, p. 84.

19. See, for example, Saint Augustine's discussion of the association in *City of God* (13.21), pp. 431–432. Cf. *Paradise Lost* (4.193) for the same implicit association.

20. As a מקום, Milton's Heaven, to use the language of Saint John the Divine, "lieth foursquare" (Rev. 21:16), a veritable embodiment of the Jerusalemic "oracle" or דביר. This observation is perfectly in accord with Robins's important essay "Satan's Journey," pp. 91–103. Despite the reference to Heaven as "undetermind square or round" (2.1048), Robins quite conclusively establishes that not only is Heaven square (in fact, a "Quadrature" [10.381]) but that in this square Heaven, God resides in the center where he faces eastward. Although Robins does not develop the sacral implications of the idea, his insights point compellingly in that direction, since he cites the "foursquare" shape of the New Jerusalem as corroboration (p. 93). If the heavenly paradise is quadratic, it stands to reason that the earthly one is too. The relationship is that of type to antitype (see Madsen, *From Shadowy Types to Truth*, pp. 87–113). As a מקום, the earthly paradise is a fully developed "walled plateau garden" with its own well-demarcated sides: "On the north side, the swiftly flowing Tigris passes into a dark gulf beneath the 'shaggy hill.' On the south side, . . . the waters that arose to irrigate the garden unite again to plunge down a 'steep glade' into the great river emerging from its 'darksome passage.' . . . On the west side, where Satan tried to ascend and where Adam was led up by God, there is a 'steep wilderness.' . . . On the eastern side the mount of Paradise . . . is 'craggy cliffs,' with one winding path of ascent and the garden's single gate and its angelic guard at the summit." On the "Eastern cliff of Paradise," Raphael lands in Book 5, and "down the eastern cliff to the plain" Adam and Eve are led at the end of *Paradise Lost* (Duncan, *Milton's Earthly Paradise*, pp. 224–25). With this concern for direction, one thinks of Milton's description of the "Table" (cf. Eden as a plateau) at which Raphael, Adam, and Eve, in a kind of first communion, partake of God's food: "Rais'd of grassie terf / Thir Table was, and mossie seats had round, / And on her ample Square from side to side / All *Autumn* pil'd, though *Spring* and *Autumn* here /

Danc'd hand in hand" (5.390–95). A symbolic replication of the earthly paradise itself, the image provides a sense of Milton's architectonics: if the earthly paradise is likewise an "ample Square," it embodies that circularity by which the center is sanctified by the circumambulation of its circumference through a kind of "mystic Dance" (a squaring of the circle) in which the "Elements" in "quaternion run / Perpetual Circle, multiform" (5.180–82). The image will be explored later in this chapter as a pseudo-Hermetic representation of the centeredness of God. For the time being, we may recall the mandala symbolism (a series of "circles" inscribed in a square) alluded to earlier in the chapter. The image is suggested too by Milton's description of his earthly paradise as a walled enclosure ("A Circuit wide, enclos'd" [8.304]) in which we find "a circling row / Of goodliest Trees loaden with fairest Fruit" (4.146–47). This is where "delicious Paradise" "Crowns with her enclosure green, / As with a rural mound the champain head / Of a steep wilderness" (4.133–35). Like its heavenly counterpart, the earthly paradise, then, embodies both the quadratic vision of the מקום and the orbicular vision of the mystical dance. The whole, to use the language of *The Reason of Church-Government*, gives a "visible shape" to "divine things" through a kind of harmonious "discipline," "whose golden survaying reed marks out and measures every quarter and circuit of new Jerusalem." Such, Milton says, is "the state" of "the blessed in Paradise" (*CM*, 3:185). For elaboration of the idea, see, among other works, Crump, *Mystical Design of "Paradise Lost."* For depictions of paradise according to the image of a circle within a square, see Heninger, *Cosmographical Glass*, pp. 159–94. Heninger provides ample illustration of the concepts explored here. See also Sieveking, *Praise of Gardens*, for additional illustrative material.

21. Even though Genesis 2:9 specifically states that the tree of life and the tree of the knowledge of good and evil grew in "the midst" (בתוך) of the garden (cf. Milton's reference to the tree of life as "the middle Tree," next to which grows the tree of knowledge [4.195, 220–21]), I am inclined to agree with Koehler's argument that the trees are displaced by the bower, which is narratively, thematically, and finally geographically the "center of life in the garden" ("Milton and the Art of Landscape," pp. 22–23.) Nonetheless, as Eliade reminds us, "every consecrated place, in fact, is a 'centre,'" so that there may accordingly be a number of "centres" to a given location (*Patterns*, p. 373). In Milton's version of the Genesis account, such is no less true of the sacred trees than of the "inmost bowr." But it is also true of what Joseph Duncan calls the "central fountain" (*Milton's Earthly Paradise*, p. 226). This is, in *Paradise Lost*, the "Fountain" that "[r]ose up" by "the Tree of Life" (9.73, 4.229; cf. Rev. 21:6). The fountain has a mid position too. Even the "Hill" of "Speculation" that Adam and Michael ascend to witness the working out of human history in the last two books of *Paradise Lost* is a center in its own right. Perhaps it might be argued that there are in a sense a number of centers in Milton's account of paradise. If such is the case, Milton is merely replicating the tactics of Saint John the Divine, who likewise provides a number of centers in his depiction of the paradisal New Jerusalem. If the center of centers for the author of Revelation is "the throne of God and of the Lamb" (Rev. 22:1),

the tree of life as a center is situated in "the midst of the street" leading up to the throne and on "either side of the river" of life proceeding out of the throne (cf. Milton's "Amarant," [3.353–59]). In any case, Saint John the Divine likewise displaces that "middle Tree" in favor of the throne as center of centers in his recasting of the Genesis account. At the same time, the tree of life retains for him its centrality as well. Such would, of course, become particularly significant in any interpretations of the tree as Christocentric symbol. In addition to the discussion of the tree in this context in chapter 5, see Steadman's " 'Tree of Life' Symbolism." See also Gossman, "Use of the Tree of Life," pp. 680–87.

22. See the discussion of the word *paradise* and the detailed bibliography accompanying that reference in Giamatti's *Earthly Paradise*, pp. 11–15.

23. See Stewart, *Enclosed Garden*, especially the section entitled "The Garden and the Temple," pp. 45–59. In his analysis of Herbert's "Paradise," which includes the line "While the inclosure is thine ARM" (6), Stewart states, "God's 'ARM' provides the Church with walls, just as it encloses Paradise from nature" (p. 53). *The Partheneia Sacra*, (1633) attributed to Hawkins, represents one of the many emblem books that conflate "paradise" and "temple"—in this instance, as a way of celebrating the Virgin Mary. Stewart lists a number of additional sources by way of support, including Prynne's "A Christian Paradise," in *Mount-Orgueil* (1641), p. 152, and Ainsworth, *Solomons Song of Songs in English Metre* (1623), bound with *Annotations Upon the Five Books of Moses* (1639), p. 34. See also the travel literature of the time. Describing the house of the Lord within the holy grounds of Jerusalem, Adrichomius, *Description of Hierusalem* (1595), p. 80, refers in the same breath to "THE KINGS GARDEN, the which also was called the inclosed garden . . . walled round about. And like to a paradise it was planted with trees, of all sorts of fruits, with hearbes, with flowers of most sweet savour, and what soever els that might delight the sences."

24. In Luther, *Luther's Works*, 1:230.

25. "Superliminare" (5–8), in Herbert, *Works of George Herbert*.

26. Cited by Giamatti, *Earthly Paradise*, p. 69. For the *topos* of the *locus amoenus*, see Curtius, *European Literature*, p. 92. Although Curtius does not explicitly discuss the *locus sanctus* as a *topos*, "holy place" is implicit in "pleasant place." Thus, as a condition for his entrance into the underworld, Aeneas must not only perform the pious duty of felling elms for Misenus's funeral pyre but "break the golden bough that grows on the sacred tree in the midst of a close grove set in a shadowy valley." Vergil's forest, states Curtius, "trembles with *numen*, the pervading presence of deity." By fulfilling the conditions of entrance, Aeneas performs what Eliade calls "the gestures of approach," a concept that will be discussed later. For additional examples of the locus sanctus, see Sophocles' *Oedipus at Colonus* and Dante's *Purgatorio*. Oedipus penetrates the inviolate wood "where it is forbidden to walk" (line 38), whereas Dante penetrates "the divine forest" of the purgatorial mount (28.1–9).

27. Skeat, *Etymological Dictionary*, s.v.

28. For studies of the emblematic placement of seated figures in Milton, see

Demaray, *Milton's Theatrical Epic*, pp. 33–39, and Wilkenfeld, "Seat at the Center," pp. 123–50. See also A. Fletcher, *Transcendental Masque*, pp. 79–86.

29. See Poulet, *Metamorphoses of the Circle*, pp. 2–10.

30. Compare Drexel, *Considerations of Drexelius* (1639), pp. 4 and 19. For earlier views, see Plotinus, *Enneads*, pp. 614–25.

31. Poulet, *Metamorphoses of the Circle*, p. 10.

32. Compare *Il Penseroso*, which speaks of "the Muses in a ring, / [That] . . . round about *Joves* Altar sing" (45–47), and *Mansus*, where "Greek maidens" "encircle with festive music / The altars of grassy Delos according to their custom" (43–46).

33. According to Jung, *Psychology and Alchemy*, 12:180, circumambulatio was a common means of deifying the enclosed figure in the center. See also Frazer, *Golden Bough*, 10:233–34.

34. Gregory, *Gregorii Opuscula* (1650), p. 136.

35. Simon and Levertoff, eds., *Zohar*, 3:13.

36. Adams, *Workes of Thomas Adams* (1629), pp. 850–51.

37. The fate of attempting to enclose oneself as an expression of pride may be seen in Sin, who, "in perpetual agonie and pain," is "compasst round" with "terrors" and the "clamors" of her "own brood" that "Feed" on her "bowels" (2.861–63). Compare fallen Adam, who learns that Eden might have been his "Capital Seat, from whence had spred / All generations" that would have returned to "celebrate" and "reverence thir great Progenitor" (11.342–46). Instead, Adam is afraid that he will be the "natural center" upon which his offspring will "light" as a way of disgracing him (10.737–41).

38. The reference is ironically to Satan's penetration of Eden, a pattern that will be explored later. The movement from "pure" to "purer" in Satan's penetration contrasts with the impurity he introduces. (Cf. Milton's use of "pure" in PL, 3.57, 4.737, 747, 8.506, 623, 10.632, 638, 11.452, 606, 12.444).

39. For a treatment of Milton's complex views regarding the incorporation of corresponding ritual practices into his poetry, see Stroup, *Religious Rite and Ceremony*, throughout.

40. The reference is to the manner in which Adam and Eve enter their "inmost bowr": "Other Rites / Observing none, but adoration pure / Which God likes best, into thir inmost bowr / Handed they went" (4.736–39).

41. After Adam and Eve fall, they react to God's presence by hiding themselves "among / The thickest Trees" as God approaches them (10.98–102).

42. On the cosmic scale, this recalls once again the pseudo-Hermetic "Deus est sphaera cujus centrum est ubique, cujus peripheria nusquam." Unlike God, man's "center" is not everywhere, his circumference not limitless. Man has his well-defined center and circumference. For that reason, God through the Son "circumscribe[s]" with his "Compasses" "this Universe, and all created things" in the act of creation:

> One foot he center'd, and the other turn'd
> Round through the vast profunditie obscure,

> And said, thus farr extend, thus farr thy bounds
> This be thy just Circumference, O World.
>
> [PL, 7.226–31]

The visual pun ("O World") makes the point compellingly: having been taught to move from "center to circumference" in the ascent to God (5.510–12), man would displace his center and move beyond his circumference in his defiance of God. What results is a destruction of the "O World," that is, a "breaking of the circle." (The phrase, of course, alludes to Nicolson's *Breaking of the Circle*.) From the perspective of הַמָּקוֹם, Milton would have been in essential agreement with Hall's statement in *Contemplations* (1634), p. 832: "We have all our limits set us: The Gentiles might come into some outer courts, not into the inmost. The Jewes might come into the inner Court, not into the Temple: the Priests and Levites into the Temple, not into the Holy of Holies; *Moses* to the Hill, not to the Bush. The waves of the Sea had not more need of bounds then mans presumption."

CHAPTER 7

1. Van der Leeuw, *Religion in Essence and Manifestation*, p. 55.
2. Hastings, ed., *ERE*, 8:865.
3. Eliade, *Patterns*, pp. 99–100.
4. Ibid.
5. Ibid., p. 375. For additional discussion of this idea, see Butterworth, *Tree at the Navel of the Earth*.
6. Hastings, ed., *ERE*, 8:867.
7. Ibid.
8. For further discussion of the idea, see Atwater, *Sacred Tabernacle*, pp. 289–90. In Greek and Latin, of course, the word for altar suggests the idea of elevation or altitude.
9. Ibid. See also Peet, "Altars and High Places," s.v.
10. Wales, *Mountain of God*, p. 8.
11. Clements, *God and Temple*, p. 3.
12. Wales, *Mountain of God*, p. 10.
13. Ibid., p. 8.
14. Clements, *God and Temple*, p. 3; Wales, *Mountain of God*, p. 8.
15. Breasted, *Religion and Thought in Ancient Egypt*, pp. 72–75; Wilson, *Culture of Ancient Egypt*, p. 69.
16. Hastings, ed., *ERE*, 8:867.
17. Porteous, "Jerusalem-Zion," p. 242. See Exod. 38:12.
18. Clements, *God and Temple*, pp. 20 (n. 2), 20–23, 50, 69–70.
19. Ibid., pp. 4–10.
20. Ibid., p. 65.

21. Ibid.

22. Charles, ed., *Apocrypha and Pseudepigrapha*, 2:26. See chap. 6 for further discussion.

23. Ibid., 2:204–5.

24. *Apocryphal New Testament*, pp. 244–63.

25. Goodenough, *Jewish Symbols*, 9:101.

26. Friedlander, trans., *Pirkê de Rabbi Eliezer*, p. 322.

27. Simon and Levertoff, eds., *Zohar*, 3:218.

28. Freedman and Simon, eds., *Midrash Rabbah*, 9:196.

29. Ibid., 5:9–10.

30. Clement of Rome, *Clementine Homilies*, 17:263–64.

31. In Juan de la Cruz, *Works of St. John of the Cross*, 2:383.

32. Stephanus, *Dictionarium Historicum* (1671), p. 741 (s.v. "Sion").

33. See Purchas, *Pilgrimage* (1613), pp. 101–5; Ross, *ΠΑΝΣΕΒΕΙΑ* (1627), p. 3. See also Godwyn, *Moses and Aaron* (1641), pp. 75–76; Ainsworth, *Annotations* (1639), p. 67; Adrichomius, *Description of Hierusalem* (1595), p. 7; Lightfoot, *Chorographical Century* (1658), 10:48. Additional contexts are provided by Nicolson, *Mountain Gloom and Mountain Glory*.

34. Simon and Levertoff, eds., *Zohar*, pp. 218, 246.

35. For a full account of those visions within the Pisgah contexts of the last two books of *Paradise Lost*, see Rosenblatt's fine article "Adam's Pisgah Vision."

36. Freedman and Simon, eds., *Midrash Rabbah*, 2:972.

37. See, for example, Hughes's edition of Milton's *Poems and Major Prose*, pp. 323–24 n.

38. In *Homeric Hymns and Homerica*, pp. 132–34.

39. For a full discussion of the idea, see my *Dialectics of Creation*, pp. 82–83, and throughout.

40. See chap. 6, n. 20, for additional discussion.

41. Freedman and Simon, eds., *Midrash Rabbah*, 2:625.

42. See my treatment of this theme in chap. 6.

43. Although Pandaemonium as a parody of Saint Peter's in Rome has long been assumed, that view is no longer tenable, given Roland Frye's discussion in *Milton's Imagery and the Visual Arts*, p. 134.

44. Nimrod, whose name means "rebel," is, of course, the type of Satan, whose name means "adversary."

45. Sandys, trans., *Ovid's Metamorphoses Englished* (1632), p. 23.

46. I am indebted to Albert Labriola of Duquesne University for the parallels suggested by Sandys's translation and commentary. See further his article "The Titans and the Giants." See also Harding, *Milton and the Renaissance Ovid*, throughout.

47. Clements, *God and Temple*, pp. 7–8.

48. Ibid., pp. 6–7.

49. For a full treatment of Milton's scatology in *Paradise Lost*, see my *Dialectics of Creation*, throughout, and, more recently, my article "Further Thoughts," pp. 126–33.

50. De Guevera, *Mount of Calvarie* (1618), p. 81.

51. Adrichomius, *Description of Hierusalem*, pp. 81–82. For Adrichomius, Olivet is also the "holy mountain" because from the top of it Christ "ascended into heaven."

52. Lightfoot, *Prospect of the Temple* (1650), 9:221.

53. Ibid.

54. Lightfoot, *Chorographical Century*, 10:81.

55. Ibid.

56. For full treatments of the idea, see Clements, *God and Temple*, chaps. 6 and 8. See also Porteous, "Jerusalem-Zion," pp. 235–52.

57. In Migne, ed., *Patrologia (Series Latina)*, 4:991.

58. In Chrysostom, *Homilies . . . on . . . Hebrews*, 17:370.

59. In Schaff and Wace, eds., *Select Library of the Nicene and Post-Nicene Fathers*, 8:268, 420–21. For Saint Augustine, "Jerusalem is the very same as Sion" (8:268).

60. Ibid., 8:420.

61. Gouge, *Commentary on . . . Hebrewes* (1655), pp. 333–34.

62. Owen, *Exposition of the Epistle to the Hebrews*, 16:331.

63. For similar views, see Dickson, *Explanation of the Epistle . . . to the Hebrews* (1635), pp. 297–304; Ainsworth, *Annotations Upon the Five Books of Moses* (1639), p. 69; and Willet, *Hexapla in Exodum* (1633), p. 256.

64. See, among many treatments, Hoyle, " 'If Sion Hill Delight Thee More,' " pp. 20–26.

65. Owen, *Exposition of the Epistle to the Hebrews*, p. 319.

66. Willet, *Hexapla in Exodum*, p. 253.

67. Lightfoot, *Chorographical Century*, 10:55–56.

68. Ibid.

69. See ibid., 10:56, for corroboration. "Thence," says Lightfoot, "also, they drew the water . . . when any unclean person was to be sprinkled."

70. Lieb, "Milton and the Kenotic Christology," p. 359.

71. That Adam's physical vision (or "mortal sight") fails (12.8–9) does not, of course, controvert the idea that he is introduced to "nobler visions": he merely receives those "visions" aurally rather than visually. The reasons for his loss of sight have been much debated. For one of the most persuasive arguments, see Waddington's "Death of Adam," pp. 9–21.

72. For the fullest exposition of the idea, see Lewalski's *Milton's Brief Epic*, pp. 303–21.

73. *Exposition of . . . Ezekiel*, pp. 776–77. On the idea of Zion as vision, see also Stephanus, *Dictionarium Historicum*, p. 741: "*Sion*, i.e. . . . . *specula*."

74. Rosenblatt, "Adam's Pisgah Vision," pp. 66–86.

75. In Ainsworth, *Annotations Upon the five Books of Moses* (1639), p. 166.

76. See Low, "Image of the Tower," pp. 177–78.

CHAPTER 8

1. Simon and Levertoff, eds., *Zohar*, 3:27.

2. See, for example, Hunter's association of the Son and Muse in "Meaning of 'Holy Light'" and "Milton's Urania." See also his revision of those articles in *Bright Essence*, pp. 149–56. I am not suggesting that attempts to identify Milton's Muse are incorrect but that they must take into account the fundamental mystery his Muse embodies.

3. The quotation is from Milton's "Letter to a Friend" (*CM*, 12:324).

4. Adam's implicit presumptuousness here may be aptly glossed by an observation by Donne in his essay on the name of God (*Essays in Divinity*, p. 5): since a name expresses the "essence" of a thing, Adam could not name God. To do so would have been a sacrilege. "It is truly said," comments Donne, that "there is no name given by man to God."

5. "Notatio est nominis interpretatio, i.e. reddita ratio cur quidvis ita nominatum sit" (*CM*, 11:218–19).

6. Singer, ed., *Jewish Encyclopedia*, 9:161–63. Such an attitude reflects, of course, the primitive belief that the name represents the "sum total and potency of the owner." The name of the god was "the god himself." For the Egyptians, the knowledge of a deity's name was "equivalent to such control over that being as to compel him to do man's will" (Jackson, ed., *New Schaff-Herzog Encyclopedia*, 8:76). According to Frazer, *Taboo and Perils of the Soul*, pp. 382–91, "In ancient Greece the names of the priests and other high officials who had to do with the performances of the Eleusinian mysteries might not be uttered in their lifetime. To pronounce them was a legal offence." "The belief in the magic virtue of divine names was shared by the Romans." Servius maintains that "it was forbidden by the pontifical law to mention any Roman god by proper name, lest it should be profaned." See also Cassirer, *Philosophy of Symbolic Forms*, 2:40–42.

7. Josephus, *Works of Flavius Josephus*, 1:169.

8. Philo Judaeus, *Works of Philo Judaeus*, 2:240–41.

9. Dionysius the Areopagite, *On the Divine Names*, p. 61.

10. That view, of course, is not unfounded. See the definition of "יהוה" in Davies, ed., *Hebrew and Chaldee Lexikon*, s.v. According to Terry and Newhall, *Commentary on the Old Testament*, 1:318–79, the memorial name, אהיה אשר אהיה, is a paraphrase of the name Jehovah. See also Moore, "Notes on the Name יהוה," 1:143–64. In *Hebrew Origins*, Meek states that the name *Yahweh* was actually "foreign to the Hebrews and in their attempted explanation of it they connected it with the word *hāyāh*, 'to be,' just as the Greeks, who did not know the origin and exact meaning of 'Zeus,' connected the name with ζῆν, 'to live,' whereas it is derived ultimately from Indo-European *dya*, 'to shine'" (p. 103).

11. Downame, *Summe*, p. 7. For additional seventeenth-century discourses, see Robertson, *Dissertatio Philologico-Theologica* (1680), esp. sigs. aʳ–a2ᵛ; and Buxtorf, *Lexicon Hebraicum*, pp. 147–57.

12. Thomas Aquinas, *Summa Theologica*, 1:176.

13. Bede, *In Pentateuchum Commentarii (Exodus)*, 91:209. Rupertus Abbas, *De Trinitate*, 167:592.

14. Cope, *Metaphoric Structure*, p. 60. An enlightening discussion of temporal concepts in Milton will be found in Tayler's *Milton's Poetry*.

15. Cirillo, " 'Hail Holy Light,' " pp. 55–56.

16. Ibid., p. 49.

17. Davies, ed., *Hebrew and Chaldee Lexikon*, p. 255.

18. Albright, *From the Stone Age to Christianity*, p. 197.

19. Downame, *Summe*, p. 8.

20. The distinguishing characteristic of the Word, states Milton in *Christian Doctrine*, is that it is "audible" (*audibilis*) (CM, 14:253). According to Saint John the Divine, the Word is the Son's secret name (Rev. 2:17, 3:12, 19:12, 13, 16).

21. Hooker, *Works of Hooker*, 1:204.

22. Thomas Aquinas, *Summa Theologica*, 14:59–60, 9:17–18.

23. Poole, *Annotations upon the Holy Bible*, 1:sigs. M2^v, P6^r.

24. Ainsworth, *Annotations upon the second book of Moses* (1617), sig. D2^v.

25. Downame, *Summe*, p. 39.

26. Ainsworth, *Annotations upon the second book of Moses*, sig. D2^v.

27. Thomas Aquinas, *Summa Theologica*, 9:19.

28. Poole, *Annotations upon the Holy Bible*, 2:sig. Sff2^r.

29. Lapide, *In Exodum*, 5:1200.

30. Poole, *Annotations upon the Holy Bible*, 2:sig. Sff2^r.

CHAPTER 9

1. See, among other studies, Hughes, "Milton and the Symbol of Light"; Allen, "Descent to Light," pp. 122–42; and Cirillo, " 'Hail Holy Light.' " Hughes's article is particularly useful in its review of important Milton scholarship on the subject of light. Most recently, see Martz's excellent discussion in *Poet of Exile*, pp. 95–113.

2. See, in particular, the seminal essays of Hunter, "Meaning of 'Holy Light' " and "Milton's Urania." See also Adamson's "Milton's 'Arianism,' " pp. 53–61 (esp. pp. 55–56), and Hunter's "Holy Light in *Paradise Lost*."

3. For a multicultural discussion of this matter, see Eliade's "Experiences of the Mystic Light."

4. Among other studies of doctrinal considerations, see Pelikan, *Light of the World*, throughout; and Mazzeo's "Light-Metaphysics Tradition" and "Dante's Sun Symbolism."

5. Otto, *Idea of the Holy*, pp. 5, 12, 27. In Harvey's translation, "awefulness" retains its present spelling to emphasize the element of "awe" (p. 13).

6. For Milton, mysteries of the divine abound. Among them are "creation" (CD, CM, 15:3), "salvation" (CD, CM, 15:99), "incarnation" (CD, CM,

15:263), "providence" (D, *CM*, 3:440; K, *CM*, 5:272), and the "Spirit of God" (CD, *CM*, 14:359). If it can be argued that he called into question the "sacraments" as "mysteries," it can also be argued that he gave rise to a new kind of sacramentalism, as concerned with *res sacrae* as any known before. For additional discussion of these matters, see both the present discussion and chaps. 2 and 5.

7. Curry, "Milton's Light Exhaling from Darkness," pp. 189–204 (esp. pp. 189–90), is particularly aware of this perplexity. In any case, Kelley's statement that *"Paradise Lost* III, 1–8 seems clearly, and only, an invocation to light in the physical sense" (*"This Great Argument,"* p. 94) can hardly be credited. See Curtius, *European Literature*, pp. 159–62, for a discussion of "Inexpressibility Topoi." Although Brisman's study does not address itself especially to the issues raised here, anyone concerned with the nature of choice ("this" *or* "that") in Milton should consult Brisman, *Milton's Poetry of Choice*.

8. Huizinga, *Homo Ludens*. Huizinga's entire study of the poet (chap. 5) should be consulted. "Poetry," says Huizinga, "has a vital function that is both social and liturgical. All antique poetry is at one and the same time ritual, entertainment, artistry, riddle-making, doctrine, persuasion, sorcery, soothsaying, prophecy, and competition." It is a form of archaic ritual (p. 120).

9. "Ludere quae vellem calamo permisit agresti Virg. Ecl: I Ludere, 1, canere, ut ait Cerda et παίζειν hic idem signifare contendit" (Mar, *CM*, 18:279).

10. According to Eliade ("Experiences of Mystic Light," p. 36), the Sanskrit *lila*, "play," is associated with the root *lelay*, "to flame," "to sparkle," "to shine." Lelay conveys the ideas of fire, light, and spirit. Specifically, "cosmic creation" in Indian religion is related to "dancing flames" as a manifestation of divinity. Compare the tongues of flame in Acts 2:3–4.

11. See Prov. 8:30, where Wisdom "rejoices" ("plays," in the Vulgate) before God, and the apocryphal Wisdom of Solomon 7:26–30, where Wisdom is described as "an effulgence from everlasting lights" and is "compared with light." H. F. Fletcher discusses the traditions of Wisdom in *Milton's Rabbinical Readings*, esp. pp. 110 ff. In his sermon on divine understanding, Meister Eckhart, the thirteenth-century mystic, has a particularly illuminating discussion of the concept of divine play. He speaks of

> the Father watching the play of his own nature. What is this play? It is his eternal Son. There has always been this play going on in Father-nature. Play and audience are the same. The Father's view of his own nature is his Son. The Father embraces his own nature in the quiet darkness of his eternal essence which is known to none except himself. The glance returned by his own nature is his eternal Son. So the Son embraces the Father in his nature, for he is the same as his Father in his nature. Thus, from the Father's embrace of his own nature there comes this eternal playing of the Son. This play was played eternally before all creatures. As it is written in the Book of Wisdom, "Prior to creatures, in the eternal now, I have played before the Father in his eternal stillness." The Son has eternally been playing before the Father as the

Father has before his Son. The playing of the twain is the Holy Ghost in whom they both disport themselves, and he disports himself in both. Sport and players are the same, their nature proceeding in itself. "God is a fountain flowing into itself," as Dionysius says. The Father has eternally been loving himself in his Son just as the Father has been loving himself in the Father eternally. Their mutual love is the Holy Ghost: the third Person who proceeds from the other two as love. The essence of the Godhead begets not. The Father's Person begets the Person of the Son eternally, and together they pour forth their Holy Ghost: their mutual love. Father and Son are the pouring-in, and the Holy Breath is the thing inpoured, identical in nature with them both. (Eckhart, *Meister Eckhart*, pp. 146–49)

Although Milton would perhaps not agree with the doctrinal implications of the passage, he would certainly assent to its spirit.

12. See Skeat, *Etymological Dictionary*, "Hail," "Hale," "Whole," "Holy," s.v. All these words are related through common Germanic roots.

13. In this case, it is bestowed by Raphael upon Eve, as a prefiguration of Gabriel's hail "to blest *Marie*, second *Eve*" (5.386; cf. 12.379; Luke 1:28). There is at least an element of Marianism in the suggested *ave Maria* of the reference. If such is the case, Milton's emphasis is upon the seed that shall spring from Mary. Nonetheless, the presence of the reference is interesting.

14. Compare *Paradise Regained* (4.633). Milton's hail to "wedded Love" in *Paradise Lost* (4.750) is well known, as is his hail to the "sage and holy" "Goddes" Melancholy (11) in *Il Penseroso*. Compare also Adam and Eve's hail to the sun as a source of light in their morning prayer (5.205–8) and Comus's hail to the "goddess of nocturnal sport" "Cotytto" in *Comus* (128–29).

15. See also the fragment "*Ignavus satrapam dedecet*," accompanying the *Carmen Elegiaca*. These verses were found with the juvenile composition on a loose sheet in the Commonplace Book.

16. See Aubrey's statement in "Minutes of the Life of John Milton," p. 6.

17. In this connection, see Norford, "Sacred Head."

18. References to Crashaw in my text are to *Complete Poetry of Richard Crashaw*.

19. Although there is obviously some kind of shift in Milton's views of the "*Tripersonall* GODHEAD" between *Of Reformation* and *Paradise Lost*, such doctrinal matters will not be argued here. A comparison of the two passages is interesting, however. In *Of Reformation*, there is one throne that embodies three distinct persons. In *Paradise Lost*, Milton makes a point of distinguishing between two separate thrones, inhabited by two persons, with the third "transfus'd" upon the second. Incidentally, in the face of Milton's direct invocation of the Spirit in *Of Reformation*, the view that Milton himself expresses in *Christian Doctrine* (CM, 14:392–95)—that the Spirit cannot be invoked—needs rethinking. Perhaps here too Milton changed his views between *Of Reformation* and *Christian Doctrine*. But, to say that because Milton prohibited invocations of the

Spirit in *Christian Doctrine* he also prohibited such invocations in *Paradise Lost* overstates the case. (See, on this point, Kelley, *"This Great Argument,"* pp. 109 ff.). Milton's "chiefly Thou O Spirit . . . / Instruct me" (1.17–19) seems a clear invocation of the Spirit.

20. See, for example, Uriel's hymn to light (3.708–32), Adam's celebration of light (4.660–73), and Raphael's hymn to created light (7.243–60, 338–87). Although Satan curses the Light (4.32–45), he also celebrates it in his own perverse way (6.472–82).

21. For a different but related treatment of the poet of *Paradise Lost* as "blind bard," see Ferry's *Milton's Epic Voice*, pp. 20–43.

22. In *Two and the One*, see "Experiences of the Mystic Light," referred to earlier. In *Patterns in Comparative Religion*, see "The Sun and Sun-Worship," pp. 124–51. In *Patterns*, Eliade provides a full bibliography, pp. 152–53. Of special interest to our study is Dölger's *Sol Salutis*. See also the entry "Light and Darkness" in Hastings, ed., *ERE*, 8:47–66.

23. See Boswell, *Milton's Library*, p. 162.

24. Macrobius, *Saturnalia*, pp. 114–53. "Divine reason," he says, causes the poets to relate "the celestial gods" to "the sun" (p. 114). Macrobius then engages in an "etymological" and "cultural" disquisition relating sun worship to both Eastern and Western cultures.

25. Hastings, ed., *ERE*, 8:57.

26. *Hymn to King Helios* is Oration 4, in *Works of Emperor Julian*, 1:348–87; Proclus, *Five Hymns*, pp. 119–21. The kind of sun celebrated by Julian (4th c. A.D.) and Proclus (5th c. A.D.) was, of course, quite different: Julian's sun is Mithraic, whereas Proclus's is Plotinian. Nonetheless, both reflect the Neoplatonic tendency that was widespread throughout the empire during the Hellenistic age. See also the Homeric hymn "To Helio," as well as "To Pythian Apollo," in the Homeric Hymns, *Homeric Hymns and Homerica*, pp. 337 and 459. Ascribed to Homer, the Homeric hymns are probably of the Alexandrian period (introduction, p. xxxiv).

27. In "To the Sun," in Proclus, *Five Hymns* (1–2, 17, 46–47, 54–57).

28. Plato, *Dialogues*, 1:773–78.

29. Addressing himself to the same idea, C. H. Dodd says, "It was mainly due to Plato . . . that in the Hellenistic world religious thinkers of a philosophical cast generally adopted this particular kind of symbolism" (*Fourth Gospel*, pp. 201–2.)

30. I am not arguing here that Milton was directly influenced by Plotinus and his school. In fact, as Samuel has shown (*Plato and Milton*), Milton "pays almost no attention to pagan Neoplatonists. His few references to Porphyry and Proclus indicate little admiration for their views, and Plotinus he does not even mention" (p. 37). Nonetheless, Milton does reveal to some extent the impact of the Italian Neoplatonists, who made the Hellenistic schools available to the Renaissance, and he "probably . . . used Ficino's translation of Plato, if not his commentaries. . . . [I]n his visit to Italy, he may have heard talk at the various academies about

their Florentine model" (p. 41). In any case, his Neoplatonism reflects the influence of Spenser and the Cambridge Platonists, who in turn were influenced by the Italian Neoplatonists. The importance of Plotinus is to be seen in his impact upon Saint Augustine, who at times is "assuredly closer to the spirit of Plotinus than to Plato" (p. 39). "As Augustine links Milton with the Christian mystics of his age who favored the Neoplatonism of Plotinus, so Spenser links him with the contemporaries who drew their Platonism from Ficino" (p. 43).

31. Plotinus, *Enneads*, pp. 33, 431–32, 574, 590.

32. Iamblichus, *Iamblichus on the Mysteries*, pp. 55, 95–101.

33. In Hermes Trismegistus, *Hermetica*, 1:2, 117, 125–27, 129.

34. Bousset, *Kyrios Christos*, pp. 232–37.

35. Dodd, *Fourth Gospel*, pp. 17–18. The Fourth Gospel may be dated between 80–100 A.D. While most of the Hermetic writings are probably later, the earliest "may not be very much later" (p. 12). In any case, the *ideas* are concurrent.

36. Bousset, *Kyrios Christos*, pp. 235–36.

37. Introduction to Grant, ed., *Hellenistic Religions*, p. xv.

38. See Dodd's extensive analysis of the associations between *The Poimandres* and the Fourth Gospel in *Fourth Gospel*, pp. 10–53. His exploration of Philonic, rabbinic, Gnostic, and Mandaic parallels is equally fascinating. Philonic and rabbinic issues will be dealt with later in this study.

39. In Schneemelcher, ed., *New Testament Apocrypha*, 2:226, 228, 233. The product of the second and third centuries A.D., the Acts of John, along with the other apocryphal Acts, did not fare very well in the Christian Church. Condemned by the popes, they received like treatment by the councils: in short, they were to be "consigned to the fire" (2:193). Nonetheless, their popularity was apparently immense.

40. Ibid., 1:253–54. The Pistis Sophia dates back to the third century A. D.

41. Ibid., pp. 413–14. "The Midwife's Account" is an extract from the Latin Infancy Gospel in the Arundel Manuscript and dates from the sixth century A.D. For additional interesting Gnostic accounts, see the Mandean treatment of "The World of Light" in the *Ginza*, with its hymns to the "King of Light": "He is the sublime King of Light, the Lord of all the Worlds of Light. . . . Radiance, which is immutable, Light which is inextinguishable. . . . Life, which (is) above (all) life, Radiance which (is) above (all) radiance, and Light, which (is) above (all) light; there is no imperfection and deficiency in him. He is the Light, in whom is no darkness" (Wilson, ed., *Gnosis*, 2:149).

42. Stroup, *Religious Rite and Ceremony*, pp. 21–22.

43. Ibid.

44. Ibid., p. 4.

45. Translated by John Keble in *Lyra Apostolica*, pp. 73–74. First quoted by Saint Basil in the fourth century A.D. as of unknown authorship, it was published by James Ussher in the seventeenth century. See *De Romanae Ecclesiae* (1647),

7:337. An account of the hymn is given in Julian, ed., *Dictionary of Hymnology*, p. 894.

46. Prudentius Clemens, *Hymns for Every Day*, pp. 3–38 ("Vesper Hymn" [26–30], "Hymn before the Repast" [1–7], "Morning Hymn" [3–4]).

47. J. Gregory, *Gregorii Opuscula*, p. 111. Gregory's other observations on light are also pertinent.

48. Hastings, ed., *ERE*, 8:54–55.

49. See chap. 1. See also Hippolytus, *The Discourse on the Holy Theophany*, 5:234.

50. Hardison, *Christian Rite and Christian Drama*, pp. 145–49.

51. Hastings, ed., *ERE*, 8:55.

52. Hardison, *Christian Rite and Christian Drama*, pp. 147–48.

53. See his statements in *Of Reformation* (CM, 3:20, 74) and *Of Prelatical Episcopacy* (CM, 3:87–88).

54. Parker, *Milton*, 1:71, 2:753 (n. 27) and 762 (n. 51).

55. Here is the text:

> Thus you have heard it proclaimed that Christ is the Lord, because "in the beginning was the Word, and the Word was with God; and the Word was God." For, if the Lord Christ had not humbled Himself . . . then man would have perished. We acknowledge the Word as God with God; we acknowledge that the only-begotten Son is equal to the Father; we recognize the Light from Light, Day from Day. He who made the day is the Day, not made but begotten by the Day. If, then, Day is from Day, not made but begotten, what is the day which the Lord has made? Why is it day? Because it is light. "And the Lord called the light Day." Let us seek the day which the Lord hath made, so that we may be glad and rejoice therein. We read that in the first stage of the world, "darkness covered the abyss, and the spirit of God was stirring above the waters." God said, "Let there be light," and there was light . . . God separated the light from the darkness, calling the light Day and the darkness Night. Behold the day which the Lord made. . . . There is . . . [also] another day which the Lord made and which we are under a greater obligation to acknowledge and to be glad and rejoice therein, since this was said to the faithful believers in Christ: "You are the light of the world." If light, then certainly day, because He called the light Day. Therefore even here . . . the Spirit of God moved over the waters and darkness was upon the face of the deep when these newly baptized were still bearing the weight of their sins. Hence, when their sins were forgiven through the Spirit of God, then God said, "Let there be light," and there was light. Behold "this is the day which the Lord hath made: let us be glad and rejoice therein." (Sermon 226, *Sermons on the Liturgical Seasons*, pp. 194–95)

Saint Augustine draws upon similar contexts in his sermons on the Feast of the Nativity (189, 190, 191, 195), pp. 20–43.

56. Adamson, "Milton's 'Arianism,'" pp. 53–54.

57. Ibid., p. 54.

58. Athanasius, *Discourses*, 2:402–3. Pelikan, *Light of the World*, explores the centrality of light to Athanasius's thought.

59. Adamson, "Milton's 'Arianism,'" pp. 55–56.

60. Mazzeo, summarizing Saint Thomas Aquinas in "Light-Metaphysics Tradition," p. 65. The Thomistic view is Aristotelian.

61. Cirillo, "'Hail Holy Light,'" p. 49. Cirillo's statement is an excellent summary of the *lux-lumen* distinction found in Mazzeo, "Light-Metaphysics Tradition," and elsewhere. John Swan, the Renaissance spokesman to whom Cirillo refers, elaborates "scientifically" upon the distinction in *Speculum Mundi* (1635): "Authors make a difference between *Lux* and *Lumen*. It is called *Lux* as it is in the fountain, that is, in a bodie which is lucid of it self; as in the sunne. . . . But it is *Lumen* as it is in some *Medium*, that is, in *corpore diaphano*, as is the aire, or water. . . . [P]rimarie light, which we comprehend under the name of *Lux*" is the nobler "part of that essence" that is in "the sunne," which is the "*oculus mundi, The eye of the world*. For he is indeed the chief fountain from whence the whole world receiveth lustre" (pp. 327–30).

62. Ronchi, *Nature of Light*, p. 62.

63. Cited by Mazzeo, "Light-Metaphysics Tradition," p. 78.

64. Mazzeo, "Light-Metaphysics in Dante," p. 96.

65. Ibid., pp. 99–103.

66. Although Mazzeo explores this tradition at some length in his discussion of light metaphysics, I wish to highlight additional aspects in preparation for my discussion of the Renaissance views of light as sacral phenomenon.

67. Augustine, *City of God* (10.2), pp. 305–6.

68. Augustine, *Confessions of St. Augustine* (7.10), pp. 170–1.

69. Dionysius the Areopagite, *On the Divine Names*, pp. 91–95, 107–9. For a full treatment of the mystical experience, see Evelyn Underhill's classic *Mysticism*. "The early mysticism of Europe, both Christian and pagan," says Underhill, "has come down to us in a Neoplatonic dress; and speaks the tongue of Alexandria rather than that of Jerusalem, Athens, or Rome" (p. 456).

70. In Eckhart, *Meister Eckhart*, p. 411. See also his "Commentary on the Gospel of St. John," p. 404. There, he distinguishes "five lights": "devilish," "natural," "angelic," "spiritual," and "divine" (pp. 402–4).

71. Nicholas of Cusa, *Vision of God*, pp. 8–10. In a splendid passage regarding Absolute Sight, Cusanus says of God, "Thy gaze causeth me to consider how this image of Thy face is thus perceptibly painted. . . . But I perceive, not with my fleshly eyes, which look on this icon of Thee, but with the eyes of my mind and understanding, the invisible truth of Thy face. . . . Thy true face is freed from any limitation, . . . for it is the Absolute Form, the Face of Faces" (p. 23). One is reminded of Milton's desire "to seek for this idea of the beautiful, as for a certain image of supreme beauty, through all the forms and faces of things (for many are the shapes of things divine)" (FE, CM, 12:27). It is for this reason in *Paradise Lost* that he laments his inability as a blind man to see the "human face divine"

(3.44): by means of that "face," he would behold "the Face of Faces," to use Cusanus's phrase. Instead, he learns in his blindness, of course, to experience a vision of "the Face of Faces" far surpassing that which could be afforded by external sight. Cusanus is to the point here:

> In all faces is seen the Face of Faces, veiled, and in a riddle; howbeit unveiled it is not seen, until above all faces a man enter into a certain secret and mystic silence where there is no knowledge or concept of a face. This mist, cloud, darkness or ignorance into which he that seeketh Thy [God's] face entereth when he goeth beyond all knowledge or concept, is the state below which Thy face cannot be found except veiled; but that very darkness revealeth Thy face to be there, beyond all veils. 'Tis as when our eye seeketh to look on the light of the sun which is its face; first it beholdeth it veiled in the stars, and in colours and in all things that share its light. But when it striveth to behold the light unveiled, it goeth beyond all visible light, because all this is less than that which it seeketh. A man seeking to see a light beyond his seeing knoweth that, so long as he seeth aught, it is not that which he seeketh. Wherefore it behoveth him to go beyond all visible light. For him, then, who must go beyond all visible light, the place he entereth must needs lack visible light, and thus, so to speak, darkness to the eye. And while he is in that darkness which is a mist, if he then knoweth himself to be in a mist, he knoweth that he hath drawn nigh the face of the sun; for that mist in his eye proceedeth from the exceeding bright shining of the sun. Wherefore, the denser he knoweth the mist to be, by so much the more truly doth he attain in the mist unto the light invisible. I perceive that 'tis thus and not otherwise, Lord, that the Light inaccessible, the beauty and radiance of Thy face, may, unveiled, be approached. (pp. 26–27)

In that respect, the "mist" and darkness that Milton experiences in his blindness (PL, 3.53) become paradoxically the very means by which he experiences the visio Dei.

72. Nicholas of Cusa, *Of Learned Ignorance*, pp. 59–61.

73. For this aspect of *Paradise Lost*, see Ryken's *Apocalyptic Vision*, pp. 95–117. See also Colie, *Paradoxia Epidemica*, pp. 23–26. A full study of "negative theology" in *Paradise Lost* may be found in Szittya, "'If Art Could Tell.'"

74. Dionysius the Areopagite, *On the Divine Names*, pp. 191–94. Such an idea, of course, is hardly unique to Dionysius. Among the earliest Church Fathers, particularly those influenced by Plato, the idea had already been anticipated by Clement of Alexandria and Origen. In his *Commentary on John*, for example, Origen maintained that there is a "divine darkness" that ultimately becomes "light." This "darkness," says Origen, "hastens to the light and overtakes it and so at least . . . undergoes . . . such a change" that he who is initiated into the mysteries of God will see that "what was formerly known to him as darkness has now become light" (10:339). See Patrides's discussion of the subject in *Milton and the Christian Tradition*, pp. 5–10. For Origen's influence on Milton, see Robins, *If This Be Heresy*. Milton's own direct references to the *theologia negativa*

may be found in *Christian Doctrine*: "Hactenus attributa illa quae naturam Dei describunt, partim affirmantia, partim negantia" (*CM*, 14:52; cf. *CM*, 14:30). The term *negantia* refers to the tradition of the *theologia negativa*.

75. Mazzeo, "Light-Metaphysics in Dante," pp. 124–25.

76. For the relationship of Milton to Dante, see Samuel's *Dante and Milton*.

77. In addition to his translation of Plato, we have the works of such Neoplatonists as Plotinus, Iamblichus, Proclus, and Porphyry, as well as the Hermetic *Poimandres*. Creating his own form of Neoplatonism, he provided commentaries on Plato and the Neoplatonists, including Plotinus and Dionysius the Areopagite. My references are to the *Opera* (1641).

78. Ficino, *Opera*, 1:989–97, 1000–1007.

79. See Wind, *Pagan Mysteries in the Renaissance*, for a full study of the tradition. The influence of the kind of Neoplatonism that Ficino imbibed is especially discernible in figures like Agrippa, who maintains in his *De Occulta Philosophia* that "light . . . is first diffused from the Mind of God with all things, but in God the Father, the Father of Light, it is the first true light; then in the Son a beautifull overflowing brightness, and in the Holy Ghost a burning brightness, exceeding all Intelligencies." The sun, he says, is the veritable embodiment of such light: "It is amongst other stars the image and statue of the great Prince of both worlds, *viz.*, Terrestriall, and Celestiall; the true light and the most exact image of God himself; whose Essence resembles the Father, Light the Son, Heat the Holy Ghost. So that the Platonists have nothing to hold forth the Divine Essence more manifestly by, then this. So great is the consonancy of it to God, that *Plato* calls it the conspicuous Son of God, and *Iamblichus* calls it the divine image of divine intelligence. And our *Dionysius* calls it the perspicuous statue of God. It sits as King in the middle of other Planets, excelling all in light . . . enlightening all" (pp. 97, 283). Inspired by the Hellenistic school, the solar mysticism of Agrippa, of course, must be seen in the context of the "occult philosophy" of such writers as Bruno, Boehme, and Campanella. For full studies of this tradition, see Yates, *Bruno and the Hermetic Tradition*, and Walker, *Spiritual and Demonic Magic*. On Milton and Jacob Boehme, see Bailey's book of that title.

80. See Fludd's *De Praeternaturali* (1617–21) and *Mosaicall Philosophy* (1659). For Fludd's influence upon Milton, see Saurat's *Milton, Man and Thinker*, pp. 302–4. For comparable treatises, see *Lumen de Lumine* (1651) and *Aula Lucis* (1651), attributed to Thomas Vaughan.

81. Hughes ("Symbol of Light," pp. 89–91) refutes Saurat's assumptions. I, however, am concerned not with "influence," direct or indirect, but with the establishment of a milieu.

82. Fludd, *De Praeternaturali*, p. 121.

83. Fludd, *Utriusque Cosmi*, p. 109.

84. Fludd, *Mosaicall Philosophy*, p. 149.

85. I interpret "So from the root / Springs *lighter* the green stalk" (italics added) in that passage to suggest a "lightening" not only in weight but in illumination. Corresponding to this process is the "enlightening" that the mind experiences in its ascent. Compare the Elder Brother's statement in *Comus*: in the pro-

cess of spiritualization, "th'outward shape" begins to glow with a "beam" of light, as "the unpolluted temple of the mind" is turned "by degrees" to "the souls essence" (460–63). The idea is in accord with Platonic thought.

86. From "The Night" in *Complete Poetry of Henry Vaughan*. See, in connection with Vaughan and other poets of the Light, such as Thomas Traherne, Martz's *Paradise Within*. See also Pettet, *Of Paradise and Light*.

87. In Culverwell, *Discourse of the Light of Nature*, pp. 83–84. Compare T. Adams, *Spirituall Eyesalve* (1629), p. 670: "The spectacle" of God "must be objected to the sight: the eye cannot pierce into *penetralia terrae*, or *sublimia coeli*: nor can the *understanding* see into these supernaturall ioyes, unless the Lord obiect them to it. Hence it is that many neglectfully passe by (*sine lumine lumen*) the light for want of eyes to regard it. But God here produceth the wardrobe of his glory to the sanctified eyes." "Onely the Spirit of Christ can restore our spirituall eyes," says Adams. "Therefore of this *Spirit* we are *counselled to buy eye-salve, to annoint our eyes, that we may see.*"

88. For Newton, see *Philosophical Transactions* (1671–72) and *Opticks* (1704). For Newton's literary influence, see Nicolson, *Newton Demands the Muse*.

89. In Ronchi, *Nature of Light*, pp. 124–26.

90. In a similar vein, Bayly maintains that

light cometh from the treasures the hidden treasures the secret treasures of God, *est inter arcana physices generatio luminis*, Phylosophers doe acknowledg the nature of light to be a secret, that is not yet discovered. Whether it be a *substance* or *Accident* if a *substance*, whether it be reall or else *intentional*, they doe indeed dispute but they have not as yet defined. So far because it is *impossible*, and it is impossible because it is *infinite*, we must dispaire for ever to comprehend or know the *nature* or the essence of our God. . . . Doe goe and fix thy eye upon the Sunne, and instantly dazeled, thou shalt finde it presently grow darke. So is our *reason* which is as the *soules eye* blinded with that סוף אין as the *Hebrues* call it incomprehensible infinite or unfadomed abysse of God, who *dwelleth in that Light which no mans reason may approach unto* [1 Tim. 6:16]; or in that *darknesse* rather which the *Psal.* speakes of. *He hath made darknesse his secret place his Pavilion round about him is of darke waters and thicke clouds to couer him.* For the *darknesse* and the *Light* are both alike to him, as the *light* so is the *darknesse* in regard of him. (*Light Enlightening* [1630], p. 6)

91. R. M. Frye, *Milton's Imagery and the Visual Arts*, esp. pp. 198–205.

92. Ibid., p. 199. See plate 132 in that volume for the Tintoretto mural.

CHAPTER 10

1. Bousett, *Kyrios Christos*, p. 232. See Hastings, ed., *ERE*, 8:64: "While light is readily employed as a symbol of Jahweh, from first to last there is no idea of

identifying Him with this manifestation of nature." See also Eliade, "Experiences of the Mystic Light," p. 56.

2. From the context, it is not absolutely certain whether the reference is to God or Jesus, but scholars generally tend toward the former.

3. H. F. Fletcher, *Milton's Semitic Studies*, p. 122. "The word 'dwell' in the Hebrew text is . . . rendered in the Targumim by the phrase 'Let the *Shekinah* rest.' Onkelos translated *Elohim* (אלהים), in Genesis 9:27, by *Shekinah*; and wherever the person, the dwelling, or the remoteness of God is mentioned, he paraphrased by the same word; so too, wherever the Tetragrammaton occurs, he substituted for it the term *Shekinah*; and 'presence' or 'face' was translated the same way. Targumim pseudoJonathan and Yerusholmi adopt a like system. When the text states that God dwells in the Temple above the Cherubim, or that God has been seen, the Yerushalmi has *Shekinah*; and even where it describes God as abiding in heaven, the same word is used. The Temple is called the 'house of the *Shekinah*,' and the term likewise occurs in connection with glory and with 'holiness'" (pp. 123–24). The term *Shekinah* as such, of course, is not found in the Old Testament. Its use evolved in later commentary.

4. Ibid., pp. 122–24.

5. According to Gregory, *Gregorii Opuscula* (1650), "as he is to all and in all places, he is called in the Holy Tongue, *Jehovah*, He that is, or Essence; but as he useth to be in Holy places he is called *Shecinah*, that is, He that dwelleth or *presence*" (p. 139). In *Reverence of Gods House* (1648), Mede says that the "SHECINAH" is the "divine presence," God's "*train* or *retinue*," where "the heavenly *Guard*, the blessed Angels keep their sacred station." Their counterpart may be found in the "Cherubims" that overlook the "Mercy-seat" (pp. 91–102). "The cherubic images over the ark are not to be counted idols," Milton says in *Christian Doctrine*; "they are the ministering spirits of Jehovah" (*CM*, 17:141).

6. See Buxtorf, *Lexicon Hebraicum et Chaldaicum* (1646), pp. 772–73; Leigh, *Critica Sacra* (1662), p. 251.

7. J. Taylor, *Rule and Exercises of Holy Living* (1650), 3:22–43.

8. Strickland, *Immanuel* (1644), pp. 4–6. According to Cowper, *Pathmos* (1649), "there is a threefold presence of God. First a presence of his goodnesse; next, a presence of his grace: and thirdly, a presence of his glory" (pp. 324–36). For Brooks, *Paradice opened* (1675), there is a sixfold presence of God: (1) "a general presence"; (2) "a miraculous presence"; (3) "a relative presence"; (4) "a Majestical and glorious presence"; (5) "a Judicial or wrathful presence"; and (6) "a gracious, a favorable, a signal, or eminent presence" (pp. 5–8). According to Caryl, *Heaven and Earth Embracing* (1646), the presence of God signifies his "face" (p. 13). For Burroughs, *Heavenly Conversation* (1656), to be in God's presence is to "walk" with God. This is the same as "talking with God" (pp. 109, 263, 272). See also T. Adams, *The Temple* (1629), pp. 971–72. According to Baxter, *Of Walking with God*, in *Divine Life* (1644), pp. 168–70:

> To walk with God, is to live as in his presence. . . . Hence it is that the men of God were wont to speak (though reverently yet) familiarly of God, as chil-

dren of their Father with whom they *dwell*, as being indeed *fellow-citizens with the Saints*, who are his *household*: Abraham calleth him *Gen.* 24. 40 [*The Lord before whom I walk.*] Yea God himself is pleased to use the terms of gracious condescending familiarity with them. *Christ dwelleth in them by faith*, Eph. 3. 17. *His spirit dwelleth in them* as his *house* and *temple*. 8. 9. *Yea the Father* himself is said to *dwell in them, and they in him*, I Joh. 3. 24 . . . [*For ye are the Temple of the living God; as God hath said I will dwell in them, and walk in them, and I will be their God and they shall be my people.*] Our *walking with God* then is not only a sense of that *common presence* which he must needs afford to all; but it is also a believing apprehension of his *Gracious presence*, as *our God* and reconciled Father, with whom *we dwell, being brought near unto Him by Christ*; and who dwelleth in us by his *spirit.* . . . To *walk with God* . . . includeth not only our *believing his presence*, but also that we *see him* . . . *in his creatures and his daily providence* . . . [and] see them as the *Glass*, and *God* as *represented face.* . . . We must behold *his glory declared* by the *Heavens*, Psal. 19. 1. and see *Him singing in the Sun.*

9. Leigh, *Critica Sacra*, p. 251, marginal notation.

10. Ussher, *Immanuel* (1638), pp. 4, 17.

11. Cudworth, *Discourse* (1642), p. 31.

12. Arndt and Gingrich, eds., *Greek-English Lexicon of the New Testament*, s.v. See also "παρουσία," s.v.

13. Dodd, *Fourth Gospel*, p. 206. For a full study of the subject, see Abelson, *Immanence of God*, pp. 82–97. According to Abelson, "the Rabbins pictured their ideas of the Immanence of God by the figure of material light. The *Shechinah* is universal light" (p. 82).

14. As discussed in the previous chapter, God's omnipresence is associated with light. "Whither shall I go from the spirit. Or whither shall I flee from the presence?" sings the Psalmist; "If I ascend up into heaven, thou *art* there; if I make my bed in hell, behold, thou *art there*; *If* I take the wings of the morning, *and* dwell in the uttermost parts of the sea, Even there shall thy hand lead me, and thy right hand shall hold me. If I say, Surely the darkness shall cover me; even the night shall be light about me. Yea the darkness hideth not from thee; but the night shineth as the day" (Ps. 139:7–12). "Do not I fill heaven and earth? saith the Lord?" (Jer. 23:24). As discussed earlier concerning the theophany, when that omnipresence manifests itself locally on any given occasion, it becomes a glorious presence: before Moses, it appears as "a flame of fire out of the midst of a bush" (Exod. 3:2); before the Israelites, it is embodied "by day in a pillar of a cloud, to lead them the way; and by night in a pillar of fire, to give them light" (Exod. 13:21); upon the mount, it declares itself in "thunders and lightnings, and a thick cloud . . . and the voice of the trumpet exceeding loud," so that "Sinai was altogether on a smoke, because the Lord descended upon it in fire . . . and the whole mount quaked greatly" (Exod. 19:16–18). To Job, it appears as a voice out of a "whirlwind" (Job 38:1, 40:6); to Ezekiel, as "a whirlwind" and "a great cloud,

and a fire infolding itself" in "brightness" (Ezek. 1:4); to Elijah, neither as a whirlwind nor as an earthquake or fire, but as "a still small voice" (1 Kings 19:11–12).

15. Otto, *Idea of the Holy*, pp. 13–23.

16. Hollis, "Sun-Cult and the Temple at Jerusalem," pp. 90–104.

17. See Clements, *God and Temple*, pp. 74–75.

18. Goodenough, *By Light, Light*, p. 23. Philo flourished between 20 B.C. and 40 A.D.

19. Ibid., pp. 27 and 34. Goodenough is citing Philo's *De Ebrietate*, 44. In his *Questions and Answers on Exodus*, Philo maintains that "the Deity is above the propitious and the creative and every (other) power. Next, (He shows) that He speaks rightly in the midst of the creative (power). And this the mind conceives somewhat as follows. The divine Logos, inasmuch as it is appropriately in the middle leaves nothing in nature empty, but fills all things. . . . In the first place (there is) He Who is elder than the one and the monad and the beginning. Then (comes) the Logos of the Existent One. . . . And from the divine Logos, as from a spring, there divide and break forth two powers. One is the creative . . . , the other . . . the royal" (*Philo* 2 [supplement]:114–17).

20. Dodd, *Fourth Gospel*, pp. 54–62. It is interesting that Philo appropriates an Old Testament text ("The Lord is my light and my salvation" [Ps. 27:1]) in order to support a supposition ("God *is* light") that nowhere appears in the Old Testament. Philo's thought here reflects the Platonic outlook.

21. In the *Defensio prima*, as well as in other writings, Milton expressed both a knowledge of and respect for Philo and Josephus. Josephus he calls "a qualified interpreter of the laws of his nation, excellently versed in Jewish polity" (*CM*, 7:77–79).

22. Goodenough, *Jewish Symbols*, 4:136.

23. Freedman and Simon, eds., *Midrash Rabbah*, 3:426–27. The *Midrash Rabbah* was compiled between the sixth and twelfth centuries.

24. Ibid., 3:556, 5:483.

25. Ibid., 4:403.

26. H. F. Fletcher, *Milton's Rabbinical Readings*, esp. pp. 245–48.

27. In Saurat, *Milton, Man and Thinker*, pp. 281–300. See also Curry, *Milton's Ontology*, pp. 189–204, for a discussion of the *Zohar* and Milton's concept of light. The *Zohar* was compiled between 1280 and 1286.

28. Scholem, *Major Trends*, pp. 212–14.

29. Ibid., pp. 229–30.

30. Wisdom of Solomon (7:26–29, 8:2–3), Charles, ed., *Apocrypha and Pseudepigrapha*, 1:547–48.

31. Book of Sirach, ibid., 1:397. "In the high places did I fix my abode," she says, "and my throne was in the pillar of cloud" (Sir. 4:24). According to G. H. Box and W. O. E. Oesterley, the editors of Sirach in Charles, ed., *Apocrypha and Pseudepigrapha*, the entire context of Wisdom's utterances here is that of the Shekinah (1:387, notes).

32. Simon and Levertoff, eds., *Zohar*, 3:386.

33. Ibid., 4:319.
34. Ibid., 1:69.
35. Ibid., 3:10–11.
36. In Luria, *Secret Garden*, pp. 171–84.
37. Cabbalistic influence in the Renaissance has been authoritatively treated by Secret, *Les Kabbalistes chrétiens*, and Blau, *Christian Interpretation of the Cabala*. See also Heninger, *Cosmographical Glass*, pp. 87–90.
38. Adrichomius, *Description of Hierusalem* (1595), pp. 39–40.
39. In this context, compare Simmonds's vision of the Shekinah in *Pisgah Evangelica* (1606), pp. 9–10:

When the troubles of the Church were over . . . , the Lord did *erect his throne openly in heaven*, by a manifest government of his Church in the world. So that now the truth of that great Tabernacle is amongst the *Christians*, whereof the Jewes in the wildernesse had the type, and figure for the present time; even that true Tabernacle which God hath pitcht and not man. Then the *Christian* Churches have *Mount Sion* [Heb. 14:1], the *Temple*, and in it the *throne of grace*, or mercies-seate; and hereupon the *Lord sitting, having put on glorious apparell*. Here also are *the thrones* of the house of *David*, even the thrones of judgement for the *first begotten*, whose names are written in *heaven*. Here also are the *seven Lamps, the holy Ghost*; which enlightneth every one that commeth into the world, to leade them in all trueth. *The Sea pure as crystall*, the true laver of regeneration, by which men are baptized unto repentance. *The glorious Cherubins*, betweene whom the Lord sitteth and raigneth. This throne is compassed with *innumerable Angels*, who now defend the godly, and speake peace to them, having palmes in their hands; which heretofore had flaming swords to keepe them from the tree of life. Here is also the *altar of burnt offering*; on which the Saints are slaine, and their blood powred at the foote of the altar. *The golden altar with his odours and hornes. Salomans pillers*, etc. The onely difference is, that wee have the trueth without shadowes, and therefore our Tabernacle hath neither vaile nor covering, nor boardes to inclose it, but standeth erected openly in the world, under heaven.

40. In the rabbinical tradition, the Shekinah is the focal point of worship, as the following *Midrash* on Psalm 11:7 demonstrates:

Seven classes will stand before the Holy One . . . in the Hereafter. Which is the highest of them to receive the presence of the *Shechinah*? It is the class of the upright; as it is said, "The upright shall behold their face" (Ps. XI, 7). . . . The first class sits in the company of the King and beholds His presence; as it is said, "The upright shall dwell in thy presence" (Ps. CXL, 13). The second dwells in the house of the King; as it is said, "Blessed are they that dwell in thy house" (Ps. LXXXIV, 4). The third ascends the hill to meet the King, as it is said, "Who shall ascend into the hill of the Lord?" (Ps. XXIV, 3). The fourth is in the court of the King; as it is said, "Happy is the man whom thou choosest, and causest to approach that he may dwell in thy courts" (Ps. LXV, 4). The fifth is in the tent of the King; as it is said, "Lord who shall sojourn in thy tent?" (Ps. XV, 1). The sixth is in the holy hill of the King; as it is said, "Who shall dwell in thy holy hill?" (Ps. XV, 1). The seventh is in the place of the King; as it is said, "Who shall stand in His holy place?" (Ps. XXIV, 3). (Montefiore and Loewe, eds., *Rabbinic Anthology*, pp. 597–98)

41. For another seventeenth-century poetic rendering of the worshiping of the Shekinah in the Tabernacle, see Book 4 of Cowley's *Davideis* (1688), pp. 372–73:

> A solemn day for this great work is set,
> And at th' *Anointed Tent* all *Israel* met
> Expect th' event; below fair bullocks fry
> In hallowed flames; above, there mount on high
> The precious clouds of Incense, and at last
> The *Sprinkling*, *Pray'ers*, and all due *Honours* past.
> Lo! we the *Sacred Bells* o'th' sudden hear,
> And in mild pomp grave *Samuel* does appear.
> His *Ephod*, *Mitre*, well-cut *Diadem* on,
> Th' *Orac'ulous Stones* on his rich *Breast plate* shone.
> Tow'ards the *blew curtains* of *Gods* holiest place
> (The *Temples* bright *Third Heaven*) he turn'd his face.
> Thrice bow'd he, thrice the solemn *Musick* plaid,
> And at third rest thus the great *Prophet* praid:
>   Almighty *God*, to whom all men that be
> Owe *all* they have, yet none so much as *We*;
> Who though thou fill'st the spacious world alone,
> Thy too small *Court*, hast made this place thy *Throne*.
> With humble *Knees*, and humbler *Hearts*, Lo, here,
> Blest *Abrahams Seed* implores thy gracious *Ear*.
> Hear them, great *God*, and thy just will inspire;
> From *Thee*, their *long-known King*, they'a *King* desire.
> Some gracious signs of thy good pleasure send,
> Which, lo, with *Souls* resign'd we humbly here attend.
>   He spoke, and thrice he bow'd, and all about
> *Silence* and reverend *Horrour* seiz'd the rout.
> The whole Tent shakes, the Flames on th'Altar by,
> In thick dull rolls mount slow and heavily.
> The seven *Lamps* wink; and what does most dismay,
> Th' *Orac'ulous Gems* shut in their nat'ural day.
> The *Rubies Cheek* grew pale, the *Em'eraud* by
> Faded, a *Cloud* o'recast the *Saphirs Skie*.
> The *Diamonds Eye* lookt *Sleepy*, and swift night
> Of all those little *Suns* eclypst the Light.
> Sad signs of *Gods* dread anger for our sin,

But straight a wondrous brightness from within
Strook through the *Curtains*, for no *earthly Cloud*
Could those strong beams of heav'enly glory shroud.
The Altars fire burnt pure, and every *Stone*
Their radiant *Parent* the gay *Sun* outshone.
Beauty th'*illustrious Vision* did impart
To ev'ery *Face*, and Joy to ev'ery heart.
In glad effects God's presence thus appear'd. . . .

42. According to Dodd, *Fourth Gospel*, "כבוד means the manifestation of God's being, nature, and presence . . . ; and the manifestation was conceived in the form of radiance, splendour, and dazzling light" (p. 206).

43. In this context, Milton desired to celebrate Christ in the *Nativity Ode* by "joyn[ing] . . . [his] voice unto the Angel Quire, / From out his secret Altar toucht with hallow'd fire" (27–28).

44. Milton also cites the passage from Daniel in his treatment of God's "glory" in *Christian Doctrine* (CM, 14:60–61).

45. See, in connection with Uriel, as well as the other angels, West, *Milton and the Angels*, p. 208; and H. F. Fletcher, *Milton's Rabbinical Readings*, pp. 224–48.

46. For Philo, see *Life of Moses*, 6:499. See also *Questions and Answers on Exodus*, 2 (supplement):122–32; 6:499–501. For Josephus, see *Jewish War*, 3:267.

47. See earlier discussion and note 19.

48. Goodenough, *Jewish Symbols*, 4:87.

49. Goodenough, *By Light, Light*, p. 98.

50. Goodenough, *Jewish Symbols*, 4:86–91, 10:87.

51. Ibid., 4:88.

52. Braude, trans., *Pesikta Rabbati*, 2:677.

53. Freedman and Simon, eds., *Midrash Rabbah*, 6:650–51.

54. Goodenough, *Jewish Symbols*, 4:93.

55. See, on this score, Yarden, *Tree of Light*, pp. 49–50. The tradition carries through to the Renaissance. See, for example, the cabbalistic *Interprétation du candélabre de Moyse* (1548) of Postel.

56. Cited in Box, ed., *Apocalypse of Abraham*, pp. 58–61. See also the discussion of the יוצר אור (the blessing for the gift of light) and its relation to early Christian hymns to the dawn in Dugmore, *Influence of the Synagogue*, p. 106.

57. On this point, see Rankin's full study, *Origins of the Festival of Hanukkah*.

58. For discussions of the hyaline, see Whiting, *Pendant World*, pp. 88–128; O'Brien, *Renaissance Poetics*, pp. 113–15; and Svendsen, *Milton and Science*, p. 55. Albright discusses the significance of the "molten sea" and the waters of Chaos in *Archaeology and the Religion of Israel*, pp. 148–50.

59. Freedman and Simon, eds., *Midrash Rabbah*, 5:483.

60. Simon and Levertoff, eds., *Zohar*, 3:387, 4:76. The *Zohar* also speaks of

"the firmament where King David abides to feast on the resplendency of the luminous glass" (4:320).

61. See Goodenough, *Jewish Symbols*, 4:86, 7:205.

62. In addition to the references cited in chap. 7, see Forbes, *Learned Commentary* (1614), pp. 14–15: "The Lauer placed in the entry to the Tabernacle, was a type, to which in *Salomon* his Temple succeeded the brazen sea, whence this, here hath name. It is of glasse, for the calme stilnesse thereof: for God his word is . . . like the still running waters by which *Dauid* was led, *Psalm* 23. And *as the soft running waters of Siloam which refresh the City of God*. Ps. 46." See also the passage from Simmonds cited in note 37.

63. Ezekiel positions these waters precisely where the "sea of glass" is placed in the Temple. Compare the following passages: "Afterward he brought me again unto the door of the house; and, behold, waters issued out from under the threshold of the house eastward: for the forefront of the house *stood toward* the east, and the waters came down from under the right side of the house, at the south *side* of the altar" (Ezek. 47:1); "And he set the sea on the right side of the east end, over against the south" (2 Chron. 4:10).

64. Compare *Lycidas*: "Begin then, Sisters of the sacred well / That from beneath the seat of *Jove* doth spring" (15–16).

65. "And under the borders" of the "molten sea" "*were* four wheels. . . . And the work of the wheels *was* like the work of a chariot wheel" (1 Kings 7:32–33).

66. In Charles, ed., *Apocrypha and Pseudepigrapha*, 2:197. The Book of Enoch was composed between 200 B.C. and 100 A.D.

67. In Charles, ed., *Apocrypha and Pseudepigrapha* 2:454. The Book of the Secrets of Enoch was probably written between 30 B.C. and 70 A.D.

68. In Schneemelcher, ed., *New Testament Apocrypha*, 2:796. The Apocalypse of Paul probably dates from the end of the fourth century or beginning of the fifth century.

69. In Schneemelcher, ed., *New Testament Apocrypha*, 2:644–63.

70. In the words of *Il Penseroso*, he is "dissolve[d] . . . into exstasies," as "all Heav'n" is brought before his "eyes" (164–65). Such is the experience of the poet as hierophant.

71. Although the kind of apocalyptic material represented in 1 Enoch was initially widespread, "from the fourth century of our era onward it fell into discredit; and under the ban of such authorities as Hilary, Jerome, and Augustine, it gradually passed out of circulation, and became lost to the knowledge of Western Christendom till over a century ago" (introduction to the Book of Enoch, Charles, ed., *Apocrypha and Pseudepigrapha*, 2:163). The Book of the Secrets of Enoch, although known to Origen, suffered a similar fate (introduction to the Book of the Secrets of Enoch, Charles, ed., *Apocrypha and Pseudepigrapha*, 2:425). For a full study of Milton's use of apocryphal material, see Mollenkott, "Milton and the Apocrypha."

72. He refers to the "translation" of Enoch and Elijah in the third draft of his plans for a drama on the Fall (TM, CM, 28:229), and in *Paradise Lost* he refers again to Enoch and Elijah as "Translated Saints" (3.461). Enoch, in particular, is

"snatch'd" by "a Cloud descending" (11.670–71). In *Christian Doctrine*, Milton alludes to Enoch and Elijah as prophets whose "translation" typified "perfect glorification" in Christ (*CM*, 16:337). Compare Genesis 5:22–24: "Enoch walked with God: and he *was* not; for God took him."

73. Scholem, *Major Trends*, p. 44.

74. Already in the period of the Second Temple (sixth century B.C.), esoteric doctrines based upon the first chapter of Genesis (Maaseh Bereshith) and the first chapter of Ezekiel (Maaseh Merkabah) "were the favourite topics of discussion." From that point, a "continuity of thought concerning the *Merkabah*" emerged in three stages: "the anonymous conventicles of the old apocalyptics; the *Merkabah* speculation of the Mishnaic teachers . . . ; and the *Merkabah* mysticism of late and post-Talmudic times." "The outstanding documents of the movement appear to have been edited in the fifth and sixth centuries" (ibid., pp. 42–44).

75. Adamson, "War in Heaven"; revised for inclusion in *Bright Essence*. Madsen, *From Shadowy Types to Truth*, p. 111 (n. 28), adopts Adamson's view. In his important article "Structural Unity and Temporal Concordance," pp. 31–32, Rosenblatt, however, takes issue with Adamson. I share Rosenblatt's view that the Merkabah tradition probably had no *direct* impact upon Milton, but I am unwilling to dismiss out of hand the similarity in *outlook* that the Merkabah vision and the Miltonic vision embrace. No one would dispute the essentially biblical basis of Milton's rendering, but the extra-biblical elements likewise can provide insight. For a discussion of the impact of the Merkabah tradition on Shelley, see Bloom, *Shelley's Mythmaking*, pp. 138–47, 230–69, and *Poetry and Repression*, pp. 83–111. Literary representations of the Merkabah extend from Dante through DuBartas, Spenser, and Milton to Blake and Shelley. For additional visual correspondences and commentary, see R. M. Frye's *Milton's Imagery and the Visual Arts*, pp. 157–58.

76. In Odeberg, ed., *Hebrew Book of Enoch*, pp. 3–39. The Hebrew Book of Enoch, or 3 Enoch, dates from the fifth or sixth century A.D.

77. Scholem, *Jewish Gnosticism*, p. 21. See Otto, *Idea of the Holy*, p. 34.

78. Scholem, *Jewish Gnosticism*, pp. 21–22. According to Scholem, these hymns find their counterpart in the songs that in Talmudic tradition, were to have been sung before the ark on its various journeys. With affinities in Psalm 68, among other texts, the idea is, of course, ultimately biblical.

79. Box, ed., *Apocalypse of Abraham*, pp. 55–65. The Apocalypse of Abraham was composed between 70 A.D. and the first decades of the second century A.D. There are additional aspects of the Merkabah vision that might be noted in the context of Milton's own visio Dei. First, the chariot itself has a certain militaristic quality about it: at least potentially, it is an instrument of war. Thus, in 3 Enoch, Rabbi Ishmael ascends "to the camp(s) of the *Shekinah*," where the angels of the presence are assembled as if for war. They are, in fact, called "the troops of anger, the armies of vehemence" (Odeberg, ed., *Hebrew Book of Enoch*, pp. 4 and 22). In the Apocalypse of Abraham, the angels of the presence actually "threaten one another" in their fiery devotion to God: "And it came to pass," says Abraham, "when the angel who was with me saw that they were threatening each other, he

left me and went running to them and turned the countenance of each living creature from the countenance immediately confronting him, in order that they might not see their countenances threatening each other" (Box, ed., *Apocalypse of Abraham*, p. 62). Although this carries the warlike element to the extreme, it does suggest how appropriate such a vision would be for depicting the military dimension of Milton's own "Chariot of Paternal Deitie" in *Paradise Lost*, as the eyes of "the fourfold-visag'd Four" "glar'd lightning, and shot forth pernicious fire" (6.845–49). This aspect will be taken up in more detail in the discussion of the chariot as an implement of holy war (chap. 11). In any case, one might at least question Rosenblatt's statement that "the Throne-Chariot of *Merkabah* mysticism, transcendent and mysterious and of course distinctly non-utilitarian, is a far cry from the Son's car that shoots fire and lightning at Satan's crew while its divine passenger emits thunder and plagues. The two chariots suggest the vast difference between the *Merkabah* and the poem" (p. 32). Those differences are perhaps not so "vast" as one might think. Second among the additional aspects of similarity is the emphasis in the Merkabah texts upon the so-called garment of God. The angelic celebration of God in *Paradise Lost* was of one whose "skirts" "appeer" "dark with excessive bright" (3.380). Deriving from Psalm 104:2 (God covers himself "with light as with a garment"), the idea emerges not only in Midrashic commentary but in the Merkabah tradition. There, one finds a garment of light in which God "shrouds Himself, whether it be in the hour of creation or in His appearance on the throne of the *Merkabah*. In both instances the anthropomorphic nature of this idea is obvious." (Compare the Merkabah tract *Shiur Komah*, in which the anthropomorphic nature of God—his "bodily measurements"—is dealt with in astounding detail.) "This garment is always designated in the Hekhaloth by the rabbinic term <u>H</u>aluk (חלוק), a term specifying a particular kind of garment, i.e. a long shirt-like robe, and not by the biblical term *Lebush* (לבוש), which may refer to any kind of garment at all." Thus, the Greater Hekhaloth attribute to this "garment" qualities of "holiness," "power," "fearfulness," "sublimity," "trembling," "shaking," "terror," and "consternation." "Of no creature are the eyes able to behold it," neither the eyes of man nor the eyes of angel. Whoever does behold it has "the balls of his eyes cast out and [his eyes] send forth torches of fire." Such is the quality of "the Garment of Zohariel JHWH, the Lord of Israel," who "comes crowned to the throne of His glory" (Scholem, *Jewish Gnosticism*, pp. 56–60).

CHAPTER 11

1. See the prefatory remarks to *Mansus*.

2. Steadman, *Milton and the Renaissance Hero*, pp. 32–33.

3. Much of my argument in this chapter runs counter to Wittreich's assumption that as a result of "the failure of the Puritan Revolution," Milton simply "reject[ed] the idea of Holy Wars and Crusades as a part of God's plan" (*Visionary Poetics*, p. 243 [n. 170]).

4. Von Rad, *Der Heilige Krieg*. Whereas von Rad's focus is specifically the Old Testament, the focus of the present chapter will extend far beyond Old Testament warfare.

5. See, among others, Lind, "Paradigm of Holy War"; DeVries, "Temporal Terms as Structural Elements"; Cross, "Divine Warrior"; Walzer, "Exodus 32 and the Theory of Holy War"; Janzen, "War in the Old Testament"; Miller, "God the Warrior." For additional references, see Miller's *Divine Warrior in Early Israel*, pp. 1–7. Of especial importance to holy war theory is de Vaux's *Ancient Israel*, pp. 258–67. See also Hastings, ed., *ERE*, 12:703–4.

6. Holy war has, of course, its nonbiblical equivalents. In theory and in practice, this nonbiblical tradition is also ancient. In fact, as de Vaux reminds us (*Ancient Israel*, p. 258), holy wars in antiquity were universal: "Every war was a holy war, in a broad sense. More strictly, the Greeks gave the name of 'holy wars' (ἱεροὶ πόλεμοι) to those which the amphictyony of Delphi conducted against any of its members who had violated the sacred rites of Apollo. More strictly still, the holy war of Islam, the *jihad*, is the duty incumbent upon every Moslem to spread his faith by force of arms." Because of the specifically biblical context of Milton's epic, the primary concern here is with the Bible and its traditions.

7. These characteristics are derived from von Rad, Lind, DeVries, Cross, Walzer, Janzen, Miller, and de Vaux, cited above.

8. De Vaux, p. 264.

9. Ibid., p. 262. See Miller, "God the Warrior," pp. 160–62.

10. Cross, "Divine Warrior," pp. 26–27.

11. The meaning of the passage (הב בסופה) is conjectural, but Cohen, ed., *Soncino Chumash*, glosses Numbers 21:14 in this way. Buttrick, ed., *Interpreter's Bible*, 2:244, would also seem to agree. The translators of the Authorized Version rendered the Hebrew "What he did in the Red Sea."

12. Lind, "Paradigm of Holy War," p. 21.

13. Miller, *Divine Warrior in Early Israel*, p. 104.

14. De Vaux, *Ancient Israel*, p. 267.

15. For a full account of the document, see Gaster, ed., *Dead Sea Scriptures*, pp. 293–352.

16. Bainton, "Congregationalism," p. 2. See also Bainton's *Christian Attitudes*, p. 52.

17. Bainton, *Christian Attitudes*, p. 112; Cowdrey, "Genesis of the Crusades," p. 26.

18. Cohn, *Pursuit of the Millennium*, pp. 44–45. For Renaissance aspects, see Tuveson, *Millennium and Utopia*, throughout.

19. Saint Bernard, "Sermon on the Knights of the Temple," p. 83.

20. Cohn, *Pursuit of the Millennium*, pp. 59, 71.

21. Russell, *Just War in the Middle Ages*, p. 113. For an extension of the discussion into modern times, see Walzer, *Just and Unjust Wars*.

22. Ibid., pp. 113, 124, 294.

23. Ibid., pp. 17, 19–21.

24. For a full treatment of the *propheta* theme, see Cohn, *Pursuit of the Mil-*

lennium, throughout. References to Müntzer's sermon are taken from selections in *War and the Christian Conscience*, pp. 97–100.

25. Greene, "Renaissance Warfare," p. 165.

26. See Fixler, *Milton and the Kingdoms of God*, p. 27; Cohn, *Pursuit of the Millennium*, p. 252; and Greene, "Renaissance Warfare," p. 165.

27. Walzer, "Exodus 32 and the Theory of Holy War," p. 11.

28. Walzer, *Revolution of the Saints*, pp. 269–70.

29. Walzer, "Exodus 32 and the Theory of Holy War," pp. 11–13.

30. Bainton, "Congregationalism," p. 2.

31. Walzer, *Revolution of the Saints*, p. 270; compare Hale, "Incitement to Violence?" p. 393.

32. In *Works of Francis Bacon*, 2:1–36.

33. My references are to the third edition (1647), p. 277.

34. *Hudibras*, part 3, canto 2, lines 115–16.

35. T. Adams, *Souldiers Honour* (1617), sig. A4^v.

36. For discussions of Bachelor, see Sprunger, *Learned Doctor William Ames*, pp. 216–19, 239; and Stearns, *Congregationalism in the Dutch Netherlands*, pp. 15, 44–49, 86.

37. Turner, Sir James, *Pallas Armata* (1683), p. 3.

38. Cowley, *Civil War* (1.318, 3.59–62). The poem was probably composed about 1642. For other accounts, see Davies, *Civil Warres* (1661), and Hobbes, *Behemoth* (1680).

39. See Bainton, "Congregationalism," throughout; Walzer, *Revolution of the Saints*, esp. pp. 268–99; Capp, *Fifth Monarchy Men*, pp. 26–41; Solt, *Saints in Arms*, esp. pp. 10–14, 73–74; Fixler, *Milton and the Kingdoms of God*, pp. 32–45. See also Haller, *Liberty and Reformation*, pp. 189–215.

40. See *Declaration and Proclamation of the Army of God* (1659) and *Declaration of the Faithful Soldiers of the Army* (1659). See also W. G., *Just Apologie for an Abused Armie* (1646).

41. T. Taylor, *Christs Victorie over the Dragon* (1633), pp. 5, 155–56, 194, 828–29. For a discussion of the traditions underlying the Antichrist, see, among others, C. Hill, *Antichrist in Seventeenth-Century England*. For the impact of the Antichrist upon Milton, see C. Hill, *Milton and the English Revolution*, esp. pp. 279–84. For discussions of additional political contexts, see, among other works, Haller, *Rise of Puritanism*; Barker, *Milton and the Puritan Dilemma*; and Wolfe, *Milton and the Puritan Revolution*.

42. For a convenient checklist of commentaries on Revelation, see Dobbins, *Milton and the Book of Revelation*, pp. 122–24. For the influence of Mede, see Capp, *Fifth Monarchy Men*, pp. 28–31; and Fixler, *Milton and the Kingdoms of God*, p. 41.

43. Fixler, *Milton and the Kingdoms of God*, pp. 40–41.

44. From "The Putney Debates," p. 104.

45. Ibid., pp. 104–5.

46. Ibid., pp. 39–40.

47. Solt, *Saints in Arms*, pp. 14–15.

48. Fallon, "Milton's Military Imagery," p. 76.
49. Cromwell, *Writings and Speeches of Oliver Cromwell*, 1:377.
50. Fixler, *Milton and the Kingdoms of God*, p. 138.
51. Cited by Haller, *Liberty and Reformation*, p. 200.
52. Peter, *Mr. Peter's Message* (1646), p. 387.
53. Firth, *Cromwell's Army*, pp. 315, 328.
54. Walzer, *Revolution of the Saints*, p. 285. See Baxter's own account in *Reliquiae Baxterianae* (1696), pp. 387–89.
55. The language is taken from *Certain Queries* (1649), p. 245. That this ideal was not always achieved may be seen in the army debates of 1647–49. Nonetheless, Cromwell sought to maintain this union as much as possible. The sources of the idea may be found in the Calvinist doctrine of a "holy community." (See introduction to Woodhouse, ed., *Puritanism and Liberty*, p. 36.) The models for the idea of an army as church may be found in the Swedish army of Gustavus Adolphus and the covenanted army of Scotland. The political ramifications of this idea were manifold. Behind the impulse to form holy fighting communities was the appearance in sixteenth- and seventeenth-century Europe of "voluntary associations . . . which claimed the right to organize politically and to wage war. The Huguenot churches, the Catholic League, the Scottish Covenant are all early examples" (Walzer, *Revolution of the Saints*, p. 274). For some additional holy war ramifications of the idea, see Henry Parker's *Scotlands Holy War* (1651). For the Scottish, "the *Covenant* is their *Word* in the day of battell; the *Covenant in specie* is carried along by their Priests, when they march into the Field, as if it were held oraculous, and had the same presence of God ingaged to it, as the Ark had amongst the Jewes" (p. 9).
56. The idea of the army as church persisted well after the Civil Wars. Compare this account recorded in the newspapers of 1651. "Yesterday marched through this City towards Scotland, Col. Walter Cradocke, and very lately Mr. Vavasor Powel from other parts of South Wales . . . with 2 troopes of Horse attending them, selected out of gathered Churches . . . to fight the Lords Battell, and questionlesse armed with the shield of Faith that subdueth nations. They having been Instruments for the expelling of Satan out of many thousand soules in these parts" (cited in Firth, *Cromwell's Army*, p. 328 [n. 2]).
57. Ibid., p. 318.
58. Ibid., pp. 335–37.
59. Ibid., pp. 333–34.
60. *A Perfect Narrative* (1647), pp. 3–4.
61. Bainton, "Congregationalism," p. 16. On other occasions, he sang other psalms. See Firth, *Cromwell's Army*, p. 334.
62. Firth, *Cromwell's Army*, p. 337.
63. Ibid., p. 322.
64. Ibid., pp. 330–31.
65. For Anglican apologists, however, they were the great profaners of all that is holy. See, for example, Ryves, *Mercurius Rusticus* (1646), throughout. Ryves's comments in the preface are instructive. For him, the "Rebellion of the holy

League in France" is "the Prototype of the present Rebellion in England." The schismatics are like the "Zealous Catholike[s] in the Holy League." "Do but change Zealous Puritan, and no Pencill ever limb'd a Rebell of this present Rebellion so exactly to the life as this." They both "vilify" God's "holy worship" and "prophane" his "Temples." They "rend, tear, and trample" "all Hallowed Ornaments and Utensills." "These Schismaticall Rebels . . . put no difference between Holy and Prophane." They disregard "holy Uses." "Under an Hypocriticall pretence of worshiping God in Spirit . . . [they] have laid waste the Sanctuaries of God, polluted his Temples, and broken down all their carved worke with Axes and Hammers" ([pp. 1–2]).

66. Sterry, *Comings Forth of Christ* (1650), throughout.

67. Firth, *Cromwell's Army*, pp. 45–101.

68. Compare Ashe, *Good Courage Discovered* (1642), p. 8.

69. Firth, *Cromwell's Army*, pp. 107–8.

70. Elton, *Compleat Body of the Art Military* (1668), pp. 144–45.

71. Cromwell, *Writings and Speeches*, 1:365.

72. Cromwell, *Full Relation* (1648), p. 7.

73. See, for example, *True Relation* (1645). In *Joyfull Newes from Plimouth* (1643), the following occurrence is recounted: "During the rout and flight of the Cornubians an extraordinary storme of lightning and thunder fell upon them, which lightning singed and burnt the haire of their heads, and fired the gunpowder in their muskets pans and bandeliers . . . and which is more remarkable, in their scorching they said, that the *Militia* fought not against them, but the Divell: so that living without God in the world, as the Scripture saith, they had not God in all their thoughts, to acknowledge his just judgement therein, but ascribed their sufferings to their director the Divell, whose wayes and suggestions they follow" (sig. A5ᵛ).

74. For a discussion of the work, see Wedgwood, *Poetry and Politics*, pp. 113–15.

75. For a summary of attitudes, see Mohl, *Commonplace Book*, pp. 250–81.

76. For a full treatment of the humanist tradition, see Adams, *Better Part of Valor*.

77. See Fallon, "Milton and the Honorable Artillery Company," pp. 49–51.

78. See Hanford, "Milton and the Art of War," p. 185.

79. Ibid., throughout.

80. Milton's view of his *Defensio secunda* as epic chronicle is abundantly clear from his concluding comments, in which he compares himself to an epic poet who treats "one particular action" in the "life" of his "hero." Cromwell as hero is associated implicitly with Achilles, Ulysses, and Aeneas (CM, 8:253). Compare Milton's references to the parliamentary battles in the "Declaration against the Dutch, 1653" (2D, CM, 8:10–13). In that context, see the "narrative of the Late Engagement of the English Fleet . . . and the Holland Fleet" (DEC, CM, 18:39–45).

81. "A Poem upon the Death of His late Highnesse the Lord Protector" (179–86), in Marvell, *Andrew Marvell*.

82. According to Wolfe, introduction to *Complete Prose Works of John Milton*, 4:39, Milton supported Cromwell's "slaughter of the Irish" at Drogheda. Compare Milton's reference to "*Darwen* stream with blood of Scots imbru'd" in Sonnet 16 (line 7) to Cromwell.

83. See particularly in this regard, Di Salvo, "'The Lord's Battells'"; and Lewalski, "*Samson Agonistes* and the 'Tragedy' of the Apocalypse." For a provocative and searching account of the political, as well as polemical, contexts against which Milton's closet drama might be placed, see Radzinowicz, *Toward "Samson Agonistes,"* pp. 170–76, 198–226, and throughout.

84. See, for example, J. Goodwin's *ΘΕΟΜΑΧΙΑ* (1644), 3:5–58.

85. See, for example, *Paradise Lost*, 1.198, 508–21, 730–48. For a discussion of this aspect, see Hughes, "Milton's Celestial Battle." Renaissance background is treated by Allen, *Mysteriously Meant*, throughout.

86. See Bernard, *Bible-battells*, pp. 11–14; and T. Adams, *Souldiers Honour*, pp. 9–10.

87. Rosenblatt, "'Audacious Neighborhood,'" p. 556.

88. Ibid., pp. 560–63.

89. See Revard's "Warring Saints and the Dragon," pp. 181–94. This article forms part of Revard's *War in Heaven in "Paradise Lost."* See also Freeman's *Martial Muse*. Unfortunately, both books appeared too late for consideration in this study, but both obviously suggest the significance of warfare in Milton as a subject worthy of book-length treatment.

90. Stein, *Answerable Style*, pp. 17–37. For additional studies in accord with Stein's interpretation, see among others, Summers, *Muse's Method*, pp. 122–37. Summers qualifies Stein's view somewhat by suggesting that the "comic" is only one perspective (God's). There are also "heroic" and "tragic" perspectives, the former characterizing the faithful angels, the latter the unfaithful (p. 122). See also my own earlier interpretation in *Dialectics of Creation*, pp. 81–124. For the most recent treatment, see Roston's *Milton and the Baroque*, pp. 116–45.

91. Johnson, *Life of Milton*, p. 306.

92. Stein, *Answerable Style*, p. 20.

93. Ibid., p. 24. Classical antecedents may be found in Hesiod's *Theogony* (713–20) and Claudian's *Gigantomachia* (70 ff.).

94. Stein, *Answerable Style*, p. 20.

95. Fish, *Surprised by Sin*, p. 180.

96. Riggs, *Christian Poet in "Paradise Lost,"* p. 119.

97. Ibid., p. 120.

98. For a discussion of the theological implications of the begetting of the Son, see, among other studies, Dobbins, *Milton and the Book of Revelation*, pp. 1–25.

99. Grotius, *Law of War and Peace*, p. 64.

100. Sprigg, *Anglia Rediviva*, pp. 42–46.

101. For other biblical references, see Psalms 80 and 87, translated by Milton, who speaks of God's warriors as being "flouted," laughed at, and "scorned" (Ps. 80, 25–28; Ps. 87, 9–14). Cf. Judg. 16:25 (the Samson parallel is of particular importance in this regard); Neh. 2:17–20; Job. 12:4.

102. Hyres, *Holy Laughter*, p. 20.

103. Bachelor, *Miles Christianus*, p. 37.

104. *Souldiers Pocket Bible*, p. 7.

105. Vicars, *Magnalia Dei Anglicana*, p. 165.

106. Murrin, *Allegorical Epic*, pp. 155–56.

107. For additional comment, see Shawcross, "*Paradise Lost* and the Theme of Exodus."

108. Robins, "Satan's Journey," pp. 92–95. For a full discussion of the implications of this idea, see chap. 3, especially n. 20. See also my earlier treatment in *Dialectics of Creation*, p. 108 (n. 1).

109. See chap. 3. The discussion in Buttrick, ed., *Interpreter's Bible*, 12:535–36, is instructive on this point. See also Farrer, *Rebirth of Images*, p. 243.

110. See canto 2, stanza 10 of Valvasone's *Angeleida* (1590). In Tasso's *Jerusalem Delivered* (book 18, stanza 96), the phalanx of the Lord's hosts is "round of squadrons three": "And all by threes those squadrons ranged were, / Which spreading wide in rings still wider go." See also Vondel, *Lucifer Treurspel* (act 5, line 42), in which the angelic phalanx arranges itself in triangular formations.

111. See further, Atwater, *Sacred Tabernacle*, pp. 53–54. For the Renaissance understanding of the idea, see, among other works, Godwyn's *Moses and Aaron* (1641), pp. 253–54.

112. See, for example, Sir James Turner, *Pallas Armata*, pp. 6, 13, 19, 21, 28, 113, 125, 127, 132. Interestingly, Turner sees "the manner of the *Israelites* encamping and Castramentation" as more nearly resembling that of his own time "than the *Roman*" form (p. 132). See also Aelianus Tacitus, *Tackticks of Aelian* (1616), pp. 48, 148. For earlier accounts, see Josephus, *Jewish War*, 2:599, 601; and Caesar, *Gallic War*, p. 601.

113. See Elton, *Compleat Body of the Art Military* (1668), pp. 11, 15, 70, 141, 208. Elton represents the Puritan side, Rudd the Royalist side. See Ward's *Animadversions of Warre* (1639) for an account of Dutch and Swedish embattling. Also instructive are Albermarle (General Monk), *Observations upon Military and Political Affairs* (1671) and Markham, *Souldiers Exercise* (1643). For a more recent account, see Fortescue, *History of the British Army*, 1:214. The elaborate foldout map that accompanies Sprigg's *Anglia Rediviva* depicts "the Armies of Horse and Foot of His Majesties, and Sir Thomas Fairfax his Excellency, as they were drawn into severall bodyes, at the Battayle at Nasbye." In that illustration, the regiments on both sides are conceived as cubes in a square encampment.

114. See the definitions of "squadron" and "quadrate" in T. Blount, *Glossographia* (1661), s.v. According to Sir James Turner, "it is from the Quadrate form . . . that our word Squadron hath its denomination" (*Pallas Armata*, p. 113). The geometrical relationship of square as quadrate and cube as six equal squares is, of course, standard Euclidean fare. See Euclid, *Elements of Geometrie* (1570), sigs. C1ᵛ and SSiiiʳ.

115. On this point, see Godwyn, p. 254, and, especially, Lightfoot, *Prospect of the Temple*, 9:445–48; Mede, *Key of Revelation* (1643), p. 30; and Pareus, *Commentary upon the Divine Revelation* (1644), p. 561. Church Militant and Church Triumphant, embodied in the New Jerusalem of Saint John the Divine, are derived from Ezekiel's vision of the Temple, which, in turn, is indebted to the Israelite encampment. The idea is commonplace in Renaissance biblical iconography. See the illustrations of temple, tabernacle, and encampment in Biblia, the London edition of the Bible published in 1535, throughout; the Geneva Bible (1555), foldout map showing Ezekiel's Temple and City as perfectly square. Although the word *temple* as *templum* suggests a rectangular figure, it assumed quadratic significance as a visionary concept.

116. See, on this subject, Hughes, "Milton's *Eikon Basilike*," pp. 1–24. See also Steadman, *Milton's Epic Characters*, throughout.

117. See Revard's "Warring Saints and the Dragon," and Di Salvo's "'Lord's Battells,'" as well as Berry's *Process of Speech*, esp. pp. 170–90. More recently, see Bennett, "God, Satan, and King Charles," and Hill, *Milton and the English Revolution*, esp. pp. 365–75.

118. Milton's defense of the rebellion in his regicide tracts of necessity "desacralizes" Charles: although Charles portrays himself as a divine king who rules by *jure divino*, he is really only a human figure who receives his dispensation through the people according to biblical precedent. Maintaining a false divinity, he paradoxically corrupts himself and invites destruction. As Bennett notes in the article cited above, Milton's attitude toward Satan is the same: it is an attitude in fact that is drawn from the political arguments and portraits expressed in the regicide tracts.

119. See Bainton, "Congregationalism." This is precisely Milton's point in *Eikonoklastes* and in *The Tenure of Kings and Magistrates*.

120. Dobbins, *Milton and the Book of Revelation*, esp. pp. 26–52. See also Fixler, "Apocalypse within *Paradise Lost*," pp. 131–78. See Milton's discussion in *Christian Doctrine* (CM, 16:347).

121. Hunter, "Milton on the Exaltation of the Son"; revised and reprinted in *Bright Essence*, pp. 115–30.

122. Lightfoot, *Prospect of the Temple*, 9:440–58.

123. Mede, *Key of Revelation*, p. 30. Specifically, Mede has in mind the idea that the battle standards of the twelve tribes surrounding the ark conform to the fourfold visages of Ezekiel's cherubim: the lion is on the battle standard of Judah, Issachar, and Zabulon; the man is on the battle standard of Ruben, Simeon, and Gad; the ox is on the battle standard of Ephraim, Manasses, and Benjamin; and the eagle is on the battle standard of Dan, Asher, and Naphthali. These four images for Saint John the Divine, in turn, represent the four evangelists: Matthew (man), Mark (lion), Luke (ox), and John (eagle). These four surround the throne in Revelation 4 (see figures 14, 15, 16, and 22). Each of the three sets of tribes (twelve in all) that surround the encampment, in turn, come to represent the

twelve apostles that surround the New Jerusalem as visionary encampment (Rev. 21:13–14).

124. In *Commentary upon the Divine Revelation*, Pareus refers to Revelation as "a *Propheticall Drama*," p. 20 (cf. p. 86).

125. The exact middle of the 1674 edition is 6.766. For explanations, see, among other works, Crump, *Mystical Design of "Paradise Lost,"* pp. 97–103.

126. On this subject, see Revard, "Milton's Gunpowder Poems," pp. 63–77.

127. Knight, *Chariot of Wrath*, p. 158.

128. Sterry, *Comings Forth of Christ in the Power of his Death* (1650), pp. 26–27. I am indebted to Revard, "Warring Saints and the Dragon," p. 192, for this reference.

129. Adamson, "War in Heaven."

130. Sterry, *Comings Forth of Christ in the Power of his Death* (1650), p. 26.

131. Lind, "Paradigm of Holy War," p. 16. See Janzen, "War in the Old Testament," p. 164. Miller, "God the Warrior," p. 45, and *Divine Warrior in Early Israel*, pp. 133 and 160. Cf. Josh. 8:1, 10:8, 25, 11:6.

132. Miller, "God the Warrior," p. 45.

133. See Fish, "Inaction and Silence," pp. 25–47. For a full and informative account of the concept of standing in readiness in *Paradise Regained*, see Tayler, *Milton's Poetry*, pp. 170–72.

134. See Di Salvo, " 'Lord's Battells,' " throughout. Cromwell wrote in 1648 that "we in this northern army are in a waiting posture, desiring to see what the Lord would lead us to" (*Writings and Speeches*, 1:669–70).

135. Berry, *Process of Speech*, pp. 170–90.

136. Firth, *Cromwell's Army*, pp. 95–96.

137. Clarendon, *History of the Rebellion*, 4:47–48.

138. Rosenblatt, "Structural Unity and Temporal Concordance." See also Steadman, "Devil and Pharaoh's Chivalry."

139. Interpreting the idea from a spiritual-apocalyptic point of view, Thomas Taylor comments, "The conquest and victory even in Martyrdome and suffering is a most glorious crowne, while by faith and patience they triumph over all adversities, and overcome most when they seeme most overcome; now Christ hath crowned their graces by their fiery trials: crowned his owne victory in them, and also their persons, lifting them up to sit with himselfe in his owne Chariot of triumph" (*Christs Victorie over the Dragon*, pp. 220–21).

140. According to Wittreich, Saint John the Divine "was said to delineate, in accordance with St. Paul's epistle, a warfare that is spiritual." Wittreich goes on to say that "*in fact*, the idea of spiritual warfare derives from St. John's Apocalypse" (*Visionary Poetics*, p. 70). Although I agree with the "spiritual" reading of Revelation, my emphasis is Pauline rather than Johannine.

141. See Legnano's *Tractatus*, esp. pp. 217–19, regarding the "Division of War" into "Celestial Spiritual" and "Human Spiritual." See Erasmus's *Enchiridion*, throughout, and compare Pico della Mirandola's *Twelve Rules*, throughout.

142. Donne, *Sermons of John Donne*, 4:193–94.

143. Walzer, *Revolution of the Saints*, pp. 280, 290.

144. For a discussion of comparable elements, particularly with regard to the War in Heaven, see George, "Psychomachia in Books V and VI of *Paradise Lost.*"

145. Prudentius, *Psychomachia*, 1:343.

146. Spiritual warfare assumes many literary forms. See, for example, such English morality plays as *The Castle of Perseverance* (ca. 1425). Allegorical renderings of the idea in epic form are also discernible in Fletcher's *Purple Island* (1633) and in Heywood's *Hierarchie of the Blessed Angells* (1635). See Murrin's *Allegorical Epic*, throughout. For additional examples of the spiritual struggle cast in a lyrical mode, see the poems of Donne and Marvell. In this regard, see Martz's *Poetry of Meditation* and Lewalski's *Protestant Poetics*. For background to Bunyan's *Holy War*, see such sermons as Wigmore's *Holie Citie* (1619).

147. Bunyan, *Holy War*, pp. 42, 43, 44, 75, 106, 253, 254, 257.

148. As will be evident from my discussion of spiritual warfare in *Paradise Lost*, I am in fundamental disagreement with Grossman's statement in "Milton's Sonnet 'On the late massacre in Piemont'": "Milton is a non-visionary, mythographic poet for whom God's presence in history will be manifested in some real and visible order of the human community or not at all. There is in Milton no sentiment such as the Blakean 'mental fight.' . . . The critical and defining predicaments of value seem in Milton to move from inward and symbolic to outward and historic" (p. 299).

149. For the political dimension of this idea, see Fallon's " 'Th'addition of his Empire.' "

150. Lightfoot, *Prospect of the Temple*, 9:451.

CHAPTER 12

1. Hartman, "Milton's Counterplot," pp. 101 and 104.

2. For some preliminary remarks on the importance of holy rest to Milton, see Knott, *Milton's Pastoral Vision*, pp. 62–87.

3. The quotation is, of course, from Milton's "Letter to a Friend" (CM, 12:324).

4. Barnes, *Notes . . . on the Epistle to the Hebrews*, p. 103.

5. See on this aspect Hastings, ed., *ERE*, 9:891.

6. Gouge, *Commentary on . . . Hebrewes* (1655), p. 410. According to Gouge, "There were two famous Rests much insisted on in the Old Testament, as speciall pledges of Gods favour: The *Sabbath* and the Land of *Canaan*. The former styled *a Sabbath of rest to the Lord*, Exod. 35. 2. . . . The latter styled *the rest which the Lord gave them*, Deut. 12. 9. Josh. 1. 15." In defining God's rest, Paul "roots out" these two views as typical. Like David, he feels that this new form of rest "is a matter of so great consequence, as he would not have them mistake the mark thereabout." "The rest of the Sabbath was a resemblance of the heavenly rest. The rest of Canaan was a type thereof" (p. 410). See also Dow, *Discourse of the Sabbath* (1636), pp. 29–31.

7. "The same conception of the Sabbath as a sign of the covenant reappears in

Ex. 31: 13, 17. Israel hallows the Sabbath as a sign of the people's sanctification by God. In part, the sign implies the marking off of Israel from the rest of the world—a conception which finds expression in the Book of Jubilees, in the early Midrash, and in the liturgy of the Synagogue" (Hastings, ed., *ERE*, 9:891). For other biblical passages regarding the Sabbath, see Gen. 2:2–3; Exod. 16:22, 23:12, 34:21, 35:2–3; Num. 15:32; Deut. 5:12–15; Jer. 17:21; Amos 8:5; Neh. 10:32, 13:15.

8. The Book of Jubilees (2:17–33; cf. 50:6–13), in Charles, ed., *Apocrypha and Pseudepigrapha*, 2:14–15.

9. See the tractate *Shabbath* (2 vols.) in Epstein, ed., *Babylonian Talmud*. See also Cohen, ed., *Everyman's Talmud*, p. 154.

10. Although Milton's observations on the Sabbath in *Christian Doctrine* have a bearing on the Sabbatarian controversy so important to the Nonconformists, the nature of that controversy lies beyond the purview of the present discussion. For an analysis of the controversy and Milton's place in it, see Berry, *Process of Speech*, pp. 62–104.

11. In Jewish tradition, the sign of the Sabbath is also eschatological. See the Books of Adam and Eve (51:2): "[F]or on the seventh day is the sign of the resurrection and the rest of the age to come; on the seventh day the Lord rested from all his works" (Charles, ed., *Apocrypha and Pseudepigrapha*, 2:153). In the *Talmud*, "the early Sabbath points forward to a Sabbath in another world, 'a world which is entirely Sabbath'" (Hastings, ed., *ERE*, 9:891).

12. See Barnes, *Notes . . . on the Epistle to the Hebrews*, pp. 110–11; Stuart, *Commentary on the Epistle to the Hebrews*, 2:103. According to Sampson, *Critical Commentary on the Epistle to the Hebrews*, p. 154, "the only instance of its use in classical Greek" is in Plutarch's *Of Superstition* 5, c. 3.

13. Gouge, *Commentary on . . . Hebrewes*, p. 432. A different word from σάββατον, the Sabbath, σαββατισμός properly means "a keeping Sabbath," from σαββατίζω, to keep Sabbath (Barnes, *Notes . . . on the Epistle to the Hebrews*, pp. 110–11). According to Stuart, 2:103, σαββατισμός is "a Hebrew word with a Greek ending." In a more extended analysis, Gouge, p. 413, traces the concept of rest in question to two distinct Hebrew verbs, "both of which are translated *to rest*." "One signifieth to be quiet and free from trouble. . . . Thus, it is applied to the Ark, which after long tossing and driving hither and thither upon the waters is said to *rest* upon the mountains, Gen. 8. 4. The Noun used [in] *Psal.* 95. 11 and translated *rest*, is derived from this Verb. The other signifieth to cease from doing a thing, or to leave off. It is attributed to *Manna* which *ceased* to fall as at other times it had done forty years together, *Josh.* 5. 12. According to the Hebrew notation, we may here thus translate it, God did *Sabbatize*. The word Sabbath [σάββατον] is derived from this Verb: and retained not only in Greek and Latine, but also in other languages among Christians. The notation of this word sheweth in what respect God is said to *rest*: namely by ceasing to create more creatures then he had done, which was his work in the other six daies." The Hebrew word denoting Sabbath (שבת), incidentally, has its etymology in the idea of desisting, ceasing (Hastings, ed., *Dictionary of the Bible*, 4:317). It corresponds to the

Babylonian *shabbatu* ("day of appeasing the heart [of the gods]"), and both the Hebrew *sabbath* and the Babylonian *shabbatu* mean "rest" (Jackson, ed., *New Schaff-Herzog Encyclopedia of Religious Knowledge*, 10:135).

14. See Gouge, *Commentary on . . . Hebrewes*, p. 410.

15. According to Ebrard, *Biblical Commentary on the Epistle to the Hebrews*, p. 153, "the author . . . does not here say merely that there is still a κατάπαυσις, a state of rest to be looked for, but he denotes this κατάπαυσις by the higher name σαββατισμός . . . as the celebration of a Sabbath."

16. Poole, *Annotations upon the Holy Bible* (1683), 2:sig. 5B4^v.

17. In his *Homilies . . . on . . . Hebrews* (17:84–86), Chrysostom makes a number of attempts to describe accurately the nature of holy rest in Heaven, but says that all language fails him. He compares holy rest variously to a child being born from a womb, to the progressive intensification of pleasure, to a "life set free from all danger, and from all despondency and anxiety, full of cheerfulness and blessings innumerable." According to Baxter, *Saints Everlasting Rest* (1677), p. 19, to understand holy rest is "to look within the veil." Basing the main bulk of his argument on the conclusions arrived at in Hebrews 4:1–11, Baxter emphasizes that holy rest is an otherworldly experience about which he is at a loss to speak: "That glimpse which Paul *saw*, containeth that which could not, or must not be uttered, or both" (p. 19). For Calvin, *Commentaries*, p. 98, holy rest is a "perpetual Sabbath in which there is the highest felicity, when there will be a likeness between men and God, to whom they will be united." Poetic renderings of the experience of holy rest abound. Among other poems, see George Herbert's "The Pulley" and Henry Vaughan's "Peace." The culminating stanza of Spenser's *Mutabilitie* cantos, however, should suggest the extent to which holy rest influenced one for whom Milton had the greatest admiration:

> Then gin I thinke on that which Nature sayd,
> Of that same time when no more *Change* shall be,
> But stedfast rest of all things firmely stayd
> Vpon the pillours of Eternity,
> That is contrayr to *Mutabilitie*:
> For, all that moueth, doth in *Change* delight:
> But thence-forth all shall rest eternally
> With Him that is the God of Sabbaoth hight:
> O that great Sabbaoth God, graunt me that Sabaoths sight.
>
> (*Faerie Queene*, 7–8.2)

What Spenser does, of course, is to draw upon precisely the concepts that have been explored here. Invoking the "God of Sabbaoth" (the Lord of hosts ["Sabbaoth"], discussed in the previous chapter), he prays for a vision of ultimate peace ("that Sabaoths [i.e., Sabbath's] sight"). That vision, in turn, is conceived through a physics of motion by which indiscriminate "Change" (the Chaos of "Mutabilitie") gives way to a harmonious movement that is also a divine stasis ("stedfast rest of all things firmly stayd / Vpon the pillours of Eternity"). Such are the terms upon which Milton predicates his own vision of holy rest.

18. Saint Augustine concludes *The Confessions* (13.35–38), pp. 369–70, with this prayer: "O Lord God, give us peace, for you have given all things to us, the peace of rest, the peace of the sabbath, the peace without an evening. But the seventh day is without an evening, and it does not have a setting, because you have sanctified it to endure for all eternity, so that by the fact that you rested on the seventh day . . . we also, after our works, . . . may rest in you on the sabbath of eternal life. Then also you shall rest in us, even as now you work in us. . . . We hope to find rest in your great sanctification. . . . You . . . are forever at rest, for your rest is yourself."

19. Augustine, *City of God*, pp. 866–67. Latin interpolations are from Migne, ed., *Patrologia (Series Latina)*, 44:805.

20. For a full treatment of this subject, see Madsen's *From Shadowy Types to Truth*.

21. Compare Milton's statement in *Christian Doctrine*: "Thus the imperfection of the law was manifested in the person of Moses himself; for Moses, who was a type of the law, could not bring the children of Israel into the land of Canaan, that is, into eternal rest [*aeternam requiem*]; but an entrance was given to them under Joshua, or Jesus" (*CM*, 16:111).

22. With respect to the idea of a covenant, the allusion to the Dove is likewise significant because it reinforces Milton's later allusion to such figures as Truth, Justice, and Mercy attired in a "Rain-bow" (142; cf. Ps. 85:10–11 and Rev. 10:1). The rainbow, of course, recalls God's covenant with Noah after the Flood (Gen. 9:8–17), "betok'ning," as Milton says in *Paradise Lost*, "peace from God" (11.867). This "Cov'nant new" (11.867) becomes a type of that "better Cov'nant" of Grace so important to the concept of holy rest.

23. Augustine, *City of God* (19.13), p. 456. This chapter is entitled "De pace universali" (Migne, ed., *Patrologia [Series Latina]*, 41:640).

24. That this music should recall the creation is also important because at the creation God "bid the weltring waves their oozy channel keep" (124). Chaos is quelled in the creation of order. Significantly, in *Paradise Lost*, Milton signals that idea by having the Son say to Chaos, "Silence, ye troubl' d waves, and thou Deep, peace" (7.216). Peace operates on the cosmic scale as well as on the human.

25. For a full treatment of the theme, see my "Milton and the Kenotic Christology," pp. 342–60.

26. Augustine, *City of God* (19.3), p. 546. Migne, ed., *Patrologia (Series Latina)*, 41:640. For Milton's theological statements on the divine union, see *Christian Doctrine*, CM, 16:57–64. Milton states that the "*fellowship* arising from this union consists in a participation, through the Spirit, of the various gifts and merits of Christ."

27. See Shawcross, ed., *Complete Poetry of Milton*, p. 158 (n. 4).

28. Landman et al., eds., *Universal Jewish Encyclopedia*, 9:295.

29. For the various metaphorical implications of the theme of union versus disunion, see my *Dialectics of Creation*, pp. 81–124.

30. Thus, for example, in Sonnet 19, the angels as "messengers of God" "post o'er Land and Ocean without rest," a motion that finds its counterpart in those

who serve God by standing in active readiness. In either case, their service represents the proper devotion to a God whose holy rest in *Paradise Lost* is characterized by the fact that his "unsleeping eyes" never "rest" (5.647).

31. Baxter, *Saints Everlasting Rest*, pp. 5–13.

32. For a full discussion of this theme, see Summers, *Muse's Method*, pp. 71–86.

33. According to Sinclair (*Divine Comedy*, 3:59), Piccarda's statement ("And in His will is our peace") may have been suggested by Saint Augustine's statement in *The Confessions*: "In bona voluntate pax nobis est," this, in turn, an echo of the angels' song in Luke 2:14: "Pax hominibus bonae voluntatis."

34. Baxter, *Saints Everlasting Rest*, pp. 20–21.

35. Shepard, *Theses Sabbaticae* (1649), pp. 2–3.

36. Poole, *Annotations upon the Holy Bible*, 2:sig. 5B4ᵛ.

37. Compare, once again, God's reference to Sin and Death in *Paradise Lost*: They "know not that I call'd and drew them thither / My Hell-hounds, to lick up the draff and filth / Which mans polluting Sin with taint hath shed / On what was pure" (10.629–32).

38. For a full discussion of the concept of return in *Paradise Lost*, see my *Dialectics of Creation*, esp. pp. 142–83.

39. It might be interesting to note here that in primitive thought the attempt to violate holy rest usually resulted in death inflicted by the offended spirits. Seen as a taboo or prohibition supported by supernatural sanctions, holy rest required an observance as a means of propitiating the supernatural powers. See Hastings, ed., *ERE*, 9:885; and Webster, *Rest Days*. According to Webster (p. 2), the Polynesian word *tapua'i*, with which "taboo" (Polynesian *tabu*) is associated, means "to abstain from all work." "The gods," said Plato (*Laws* 2.653), "in pity for the toils which our race is born to undergo have appointed holy festivals, by which men alternate rest and labor" (cited by Webster, p. 91). See also Prov. 24:15: "Lay not wait, O wicked *man*, against the dwelling of the righteous; spoil not his resting place."

40. Compare the fallen Adam's lament that the fear of death "comes thundring back with dreadful revolution / On my defensless head" (10.814–15). Afraid of the curses that his future offspring will place upon him, Adam states: "All from mee / Shall with a fierce reflux on mee redound, / On mee as on thir natural center light / Heavie, though in thir place" (10.738–41). Relieved of these fears through God's grace, Adam experiences a new sense of return: "peace," says Adam, "returnd / Home to my brest" (11.153–54).

41. For a complete exposition of this theme, see Hughes, "Myself Am Hell."

42. In *Paradise Regained*, Satan, who is constantly in motion (1.39), characterizes his rest as being at the utmost place of unrest: "I would be at the worst; worst is my Port, / My harbour and my ultimate repose, / The end I would attain, my final good" (3.209–11). In *Paradise Lost*, he says that "onely in destroying" does he "find ease / To [his] relentless thoughts" (9.129–30). Only by creating unrest does he find rest.

43. Compare even the plight of unfallen Eve after she has been tempted by Sa-

tan in her dream: she is found with "tresses discompos'd, and glowing Cheek, / As through unquiet rest" (5.10–11).

44. In accord with Adam's dilemma is the dilemma of Samson, who in *Samson Agonistes* desires the "rest" of death (598) to end his plight. Like Adam, he is one who is not able to sleep or rest his thoughts (459); rather, he complains ("murmurs") that his "restless thoughts" are "like a deadly swarm / Of Hornets arm'd" that "rush upon . . . [him] thronging" (19–21). To alleviate that burden, Samson attempts "to find some ease" (17). But his "internal peace" (1334) will come about only with restored faith in God, arising, in part, through his ability to withstand the temptations of those who, in their own way, question God's providence. Even Samson's own father, who has only the best intentions for his son, offers Samson the wrong kind of rest as an escape from one's obligations (566–72). It is not insignificant, incidentally, that the name "Manoah" (מנוח) means "rest" (Jacobus et al., eds., *Standard Bible Dictionary*, s.v.). Nor is it insignificant that the day on which Milton's drama occurs is for the Philistines ironically a day of rest, albeit, as Samson says, a false one: "This day a solemn Feast the people hold / To *Dagon* thir Sea-Idol, and forbid / Laborious works, unwillingly this rest / Thir Superstition yields me" (12–15; this point is not emphasized in Judges 16:23). Appropriately, *Samson Agonistes* ends on a note of peace with a "calm of mind all passion spent" (1757–58).

AFTERWORD

1. Berry, *Process of Speech*, p. 1.
2. Patrides, *Milton and the Christian Tradition*, p. 5.
3. Ross, *Poetry and Dogma*, pp. 183–227.

Bibliography

For collections and editions from which the works of two or more authors are cited, full bibliographical information is provided under separate headings and arranged alphabetically by editor.

PRIMARY SOURCES

Abbot, Robert. *The Holiness of Christian Churches*. London, 1618.

Adams, Thomas. *The Souldiers Honour*. London, 1617.

————. *Spirituall Eyesalve: or, The Benefit of Illumination* (1629), pp. 661–72; *Semper Idem: or, The Immutable Mercy of Jesus Christ* (1629), pp. 850–57; *The Temple* (1629), pp. 969–91. In *The Workes of Thomas Adams, Being the Summe of His Sermons*. London, 1630.

Adrichomius, Christianus. *A Briefe Description of Hierusalem and of the Suburbs thereof as it flourished in the time of Christ*. Translated by Thomas Tymme. London, 1595.

Aelianus Tacitus. *The Tacticks of Aelian*. Translated by T. B. (1616). Reprint. Amsterdam and New York: Da Capo Press, 1968.

Agrippa of Nettersheim, Henry Cornelius. *De Occulta Philosophia* (1533). Translated by J. F. as *Three Books of Occult Philosophy*. London, 1651.

Ainsworth, Henry. *Annotations Upon the Five Books of Moses, the Book of Psalmes, and the Song of Songs*. London, 1639.

————. *Annotations upon the second book of Moses, called Exodus*. London, 1617.

————. *The Communion of the Saincts*. London, 1628.

————. *Solomons Song of Songs in English Metre*. London, 1623.

Albermarle, George Monk, first duke of (General Monk). *Observations upon Military and Political Affairs*. London, 1671.

Allestree, Richard. *The Beauty of Holiness*. London, 1684.

Ambrosius, Saint, bishop of Milan (Saint Ambrose). *On the Mysteries*. In *Some of the Principal Works of St. Ambrose*. Translated by H. De Romestin, and others. Vol. 10, pp. 315–26, of *A Select Library of Nicene and Post-Nicene Fathers*. Second series. Edited by Philip Schaff and Henry Wace.

Ames, William. *The Marrow of Theology*. Translated and edited by John Eusden. Boston: Pilgrim Press, 1968.

Andrewes, Lancelot. *The Wonderfull Combate Between Christ and Satan in Seven Sermons*. London, 1592.

The Apocryphal New Testament. London: William Hone, 1820.

Apostolical Constitutions. Vol. 17, pp. 56–58, of *Ante-Nicene Christian Library*. Edited by Alexander Roberts and others.

Aristotle. *The Athenian Constitution*. Translated by H. Rackham. Cambridge: Harvard University Press, 1952.

———. *The Works of Aristotle*. Edited by W. D. Ross. 12 vols. London: Oxford University Press, 1915.

Ashe, Simeon. *Good Courage Discovered and Encouraged*. London, 1642.

Athanasius, Saint, bishop of Alexandria. *Discourses . . . Against the Arians*. Vol. 1 of *Select Treatises of St. Athanasius*. 2 vols. Oxford: John Henry Parker, 1942.

Aubrey, John. "Minutes of the Life of Mr. John Milton" (1681). In *The Early Lives of Milton*. Edited by Helen Darbishire, pp. 1–15. London: Constable and Co., 1932.

Augustinus, Aurelius, Saint, bishop of Hippo (Saint Augustine). *The City of God*. Translated by Marcus Dods. New York: Random House, 1950.

———. *The Confessions of St. Augustine*. Translated by John K. Ryan. Garden City, N.Y.: Doubleday, 1960.

———. *De Civitate Dei*. Vol. 41 of *Patrologia (Series Latina)*. Edited by J.-P. Migne.

———. *De Genesi ad Litteram Libri XII*. Vol. 34, pp. 245–484, of *Patrologia (Series Latina)*. Edited by J.-P. Migne.

———. *Saint Augustin: Expositions on the Book of Psalms*. Edited by A. Cleveland Coxe. Vol. 8 of *A Select Library of the Nicene and Post-Nicene Fathers of the Christian Church*. Edited by Philip Schaff and others. 14 vols. First series. New York: Charles Scribner's Sons, 1898–1909.

———. *Sermons on the Liturgical Seasons*. Translated by Sister Mary Sarah Muldowney. Vol. 38 of *The Fathers of the Church: A New Translation*. Edited by Roy Joseph Deferrari and others. 63 vols. New York: Fathers of the Church, 1959.

———. *The Works of Aurelius Augustine*. Edited by Marcus Dods. 15 vols. Edinburgh: T. and T. Clark, 1876.

Babington, Gervase. *Comfortable Notes Vpon the bookes of Exodvs and Leuiticvs*. London, 1604.

Bachelor, Samuel. *Miles Christianus, or the Camp Royal*. Amsterdam, 1625.

Bacon, Francis. *Advertisement Touching An Holy War* (1629). Vol. 2, pp. 1–36, of *The Works of Francis Bacon*. Edited by James Spedding and others. 14 vols. London: Longmans, Greene, and Co., 1857–90.

Basilius, Saint, archbishop of Caesarea (Saint Basil). *The Book of Saint Basil on the Spirit*. In *The Treatise De Spiritu Sancto*. Translated by Blomfield Jackson. Vol. 8, pp. 1–50, of *A Select Library of Nicene and Post-Nicene Fathers*. Second series. Edited by Philip Schaff and Henry Wace.

Basire, Isaac. *Deo et Ecclesiae Sacrum*. Oxford, 1646.

Baxter, Richard. *The Divine Life*. London, 1644.

———. *Reliquiae Baxterianae* (1696). Excerpted in *Puritanism and Liberty*. Edited by A. S. P. Woodhouse, pp. 387–89.

———. *The Saints Everlasting Rest: or, a Treatise of the Blessed State of the Saints in their enjoyment of God in Glory*. 11th ed. London, 1677.

Bayly, John. *The Light Enlightening*. In *Two Sermons*, pp. 1–35. Oxford, 1630.

Bede, The Venerable. *In Pentateuchum Commentarii*. Vol. 91, pp. 189–392, of *Patrologia (Series Latina)*. Edited by J.-P. Migne.

Bernard, Richard. *Bible-battells. Or the sacred art military, For the rightly waging of warre according to Holy Writ*. London, 1629.

Bernard of Clairvaux (Saint Bernard). "Sermon on the Knights of the Temple." In *War and the Christian Conscience*. Edited by Albert Marrin, pp. 80–83.

Best, Paul. *Mysteries Discovered*. London, 1647.

The Bible. Geneva, 1555.

Biblia. The Bible. London, 1535.

Biblia, The Bible: that is the holy Scrypture. London, 1575.

Biblia Hebraica Stuttgartensia. Edited by R. Kittel and others. Stuttgart: Deutsche Bibelstiftung, 1967 / 77.

Biblia sacra, ad optima quaeque translationis exemplaria summa diligentia parique fide castigata. London, 1566.

Blake, William. *Milton, a poem in 2 books*. London, 1804.

Blount, Charles. *The Oracles of Reason: Consisting of 1. A Vindication of Dr. Burnet's Archaeologiae. 2. The Seventh and Eighth Chapters of the Same. 3. Of Moses's Description of the Original State of Man . . . In Several Letters to Mr. Hobbes*. London, 1693.

Blount, Thomas. *Glossographia: Or, a Dictionary, Interpreting All Such Hard Words of Whatsoever Language, Now Used in Our Refined English Tongue*. London, 1661.

Boccaccio, Giovanni. *The Life of Dante*. In *The Earliest Lives of Dante*. Translated by James Robinson Smith. Vol. 10, pp. 9–78, of *Yale Studies in English*. 189 vols. Edited by Albert S. Cook. New York: Henry Holt and Co., 1901.

Bompart, Johannes. *Parallela sacra et profana sive notae in Genesim*. Amsterdam, 1689.

Bosman, William. *Voyage de Guinée*. Utrecht, 1704.

Box, G. H., ed. *The Apocalypse of Abraham*. New York: Macmillan Co., 1918.

Braude, William G., trans. *Pesikta Rabbati: Discourses for Feasts, Fasts, and Special Sabbaths*. 2 vols. New Haven: Yale University Press.

Brooks, Thomas. *Paradice opened*. London, 1675.

Buchler, John. *Thesaurus Phrasium Poêticarum*. Amsterdam, 1665.

Bunyan, John. *The Holy War Made By Shaddai Upon Diabolus For the Regaining of the Metropolis of the World, Or the Losing and Taking Againe of the Town of Mansoul* (1682). Edited by James F. Forrest. New York: New York University Press, 1967.

Burnet, Thomas. *Archaeologiae Philosophicae: Sive Doctrina Antiqua de Rerum Originibus. Libri duo.* London, 1692.

Burroughs, Jeremiah. *An Heavenly Conversation.* London, 1656.

Butler, Samuel. *Hudibras* (1663–78). Edited by John Wilders. Oxford: Clarendon Press, 1967.

Buxtorf, John. *Lexicon Chaldaicum, Talmudicum et Rabbinicum . . . Opus XXX Annorum, Nunc Demum, Post Patris Obitum . . . in Lucem Editum a Johanne Buxtorfio Filio.* Basel, 1640.

———. *Lexicon Hebraicum et Chaldaicum; Complectens Omnes Voces . . . Quae in Sacris Bibliis, Hebræâ. et ex Parte Chaldæâ Linguâ Scriptis Extant . . . Accessit Lexicon Breve Rabbinico-Philosophicum . . . Cum Justo Indice Vocum Latino.* London, 1646.

Caesar, Julius. *The Gallic War.* Translated by H. J. Edwards. Cambridge: Harvard University Press, 1917.

Calvin, Jean. *Commentaries on the Epistle of Paul the Apostle to the Hebrews.* Translated by John Owen. Edinburgh: Calvin Translation Society, 1853.

Caryl, Joseph. *Heaven and Earth Embracing.* London, 1646.

Casaubon, Isaac. *De Rebus Sacris et Ecclesiasticis Exercitationes XVI. Ad Cardinalis Baronii Prolegomena in Annales, et Primam Eorum Partem, de Domini Nostri Iesu Christi Nativitate, Vita, Passione, Assumptione.* London, 1614.

The Castle of Perseverance (ca. 1425). In *Chief Pre-Shakespearean Dramas.* Edited by J. Q. Adams. Cambridge: Houghton Mifflin, 1924.

Certain Queries Presented by many Christian People . . . [To his Excellency, Thomas Lord Fairfax, Lord General of the Army, and to the General Council of War] (1649). In *Puritanism and Liberty.* Edited by A. S. P. Woodhouse, pp. 241–47.

Charles, R. H., ed. *The Apocrypha and Pseudepigrapha of the Old Testament in English.* Oxford: Clarendon Press, 1913.

Chrysostomus, Joannes, Saint, Patriarch of Constantinople (Saint John Chrysostom). *The Homilies of S. John Chrysostom . . . on the Epistle of S. Paul the Apostle to the Hebrews.* Vol. 17 of *A Library of Fathers of the Holy Catholic Church, Anterior to the Division of the East and West.* Translated by members of the English church. 47 vols. London: Walter Smith, 1885.

Cicero, Marcus Tullius. *The Speech of M. T. Cicero for Aulus Licinius Archias, the Poet.* Vol. 2, pp. 411–23, of *The Orations of Marcus Tullius Cicero.* Translated by C. D. Yonge. 4 vols. London: Henry G. Bohn, 1852.

Clarendon, Edward Hyde, first earl of. *The History of the Rebellion and Civil Wars in England.* 7 vols. Oxford: Oxford University Press, 1849.

Clarke, John. *Holy Oyle for the Lamps of the Sanctuaries: Or Scripture-Phrases Alphabetically Disposed: For the Use and Benefit of Such as Desire to Speake the Language of Canaan, More Especially the Sonnes of the Prophets, Who would Attaine Elegancie and Sublimity of Expressions.* London, 1630.

Claudianus, Claudius. *Gigantomachia*. In *Claudian*. Translated by Maurice Plat-
nauer. 2 vols. London: William Heinemann, 1922.
Clemens, Titus Flavius, Alexandrinus (Clement of Alexandria). *Exhortation to
the Heathen*, vol. 1, pp. 17–110; *The Miscellanies*, vol. 2. In *The Writings
of Clement of Alexandria*. 2 vols. Translated by William Wilson. Vols. 9
and 12 of *Ante-Nicene Christian Library*. Edited by Alexander Roberts
and others.
Clemens Romanus (Clement of Rome). *The Clementine Homilies*. Translated by
Thomas Smith and others. Vol. 17, pp. 17–340, of *Ante-Nicene Christian
Library*. Edited by Alexander Roberts and others.
Cohen, Abraham, ed. *Everyman's Talmud*. New York: E. P. Dutton, 1949.
————, ed. *The Soncino Chumash*. London: Soncino Press, 1947.
*The Confession of Faith Together with the Larger and Lesser Catechismes Com-
posed by the Reverend Assembly of Divines, Sitting at Westminster*. 2nd
ed. London, 1658.
Cook, James. *A Voyage to the Pacific Ocean*. 3 vols. 2nd ed. London, 1785.
Cornford, Francis M., ed. *Greek Religious Thought from Homer to the Age of
Alexander*. New York: J. M. Dent and Sons, 1923. Reprint. New York:
AMS Press, 1969.
Cowley, Abraham. *The Civil War*. Edited by Allan Pritchard. Toronto: University
of Toronto Press, 1973.
————. *Davideis* (1668). In *Poems of Abraham Cowley*. Edited by A. R. Waller.
Cambridge: Cambridge University Press, 1905.
Cowper, William. *Pathmos: or, A Commentary on the Revelation*. London,
1649.
Crashaw, Richard. *The Complete Poetry of Richard Crashaw*. Edited by George
Walton Williams. Garden City, N. Y.: Doubleday, 1970.
Cratinus. *Comicorum Atticorum Fragmenta*. Edited by Theodorus Kock. 3 vols.
Leipzig: B. G. Teubner, 1880.
Cromwell, Oliver. *A Full Relation of The great Victory obtained by the Parlia-
ments Forces*. London, 1648.
————. *The Writings and Speeches of Oliver Cromwell*. Edited by William
Cortez Abbott. Cambridge: Harvard University Press, 1937.
Cudworth, Ralph. *A Discourse concerning the True Notion of the Lord's Supper*.
4th ed. London, 1642.
Culverwell, Nathaniel. *An Elegant and Learned Discourse of the Light of Nature*.
Edited by Robert Greene and Hugh MacCallum. Toronto: University of
Toronto Press, 1971.
————. *Spiritual Opticks: Or, a Glasse Discovering the Weaknesse and Imper-
fection of a Christians Knowledge in This Life*. In *An Elegant and Learned
Discourse of the Light of Nature, with Several Other Treatises*, pp.
171–91. London, 1654.
Cyprianus, Saint, bishop of Carthage (Saint Cyprian). *De Montibus Sina et Sion*.
Vol. 4, pp. 989–98, of *Patrologia (Series Latina)*. Edited by J.-P. Migne.

————. *To Januarius and Other Numidian Bishops* (Epistle 69). In *A Study of Holiness from the Early Christian Fathers.* Edited by J. B. Galloway. Kansas City, Mo.: Beacon Hill Press, 1950.

Danby, Herbert, trans. *The Mishnah.* Oxford: Clarendon Press, 1933.

Dante Alighieri. *The Divine Comedy.* Translated by John D. Sinclair. 3 vols. Vol. 1, *Inferno.* Vol. 2, *Purgatorio.* Vol. 3, *Paradiso.* New York: Oxford University Press, 1961.

Davies, John. *The Civil Warres.* London, 1661.

de Brosses, Charles. *Du Culte des dieux fétiches, ou parallèle de l'ancienne religion de l'Egypte avec la religion actuelle de nigritie.* Paris, 1760.

The Declaration and Proclamation of the Army of God, Owned by the Lord of Hosts in Many Victories. London, 1659.

A Declaration of the Faithful Soldiers of the Army: To all the honest People of the Nation Shewing their Resolution to Stand by the Good Old Cause and Maintain the Liberties and Priviledges of the Subject. London, 1659.

de Guevara, Anthony. *The Mount of Calvarie.* London, 1618.

Demosthenes. *Speech against Aristogeiton.* Excerpted in *Greek Religious Thought.* Edited by Francis M. Cornford, p. 247.

de Prado, Jeronimo, and Villalpandi, John Baptistae. *In Ezechielem Explanationes et Apparatus Urbis, ac Templi Hierosolymitani.* 3 vols. Rome, 1596–1604.

Dickson, David. *A Short Explanation of the Epistle of Paul to the Hebrews.* Aberdene, 1635.

Dionysius the Areopagite. *Dionysius the Areopagite on the Divine Names and the Mystical Theology.* Translated by C. E. Rolt. New York: Macmillan Co., 1920.

Dittenberger, Wilhelm, ed. *Sylloge Inscriptionum Graecarum.* Leipzig: S. Hirzel, 1900.

Donne, John. *Essays in Divinity.* Edited by Augustus Jessopp. London: John Tupling, 1855.

————. *The Sermons of John Donne.* Edited by George Potter and Evelyn M. Simpson. 10 vols. Berkeley and Los Angeles: University of California Press, 1953–62.

Dow, Christopher. *A Discourse of the Sabbath and the Lords Day.* London, 1636.

Downame, John. *The Christian Warfare. Wherein is First Generallie Shewed the Malice, Power and Politike Strategems of Our Salvation, Satan and His Assistants the World and the Flesh; with the Meanes Also Whereby the Christian May Withstand and Defeat Them.* London, 1612.

————. *The Summe of Sacred Divinitie.* London, n.d.

Drexel, Jeremias. *The Considerations of Drexelius Upon Eternitie.* Translated by Ralph Winterton. Cambridge, 1639.

Duns Scotus, Joannes. *On the Division of Nature* (book 1). Translated by Charleen Schwartz. Annapolis: St. Johns Bookstore, 1940.

Eckhart, Meister. *Meister Eckhart*. Edited by Franz Pfeiffer and translated by C. de B. Evans. London: John M. Watkins, 1924.

Elton, Richard. *The Compleat Body of the Art Military. In three Books*. Printed with "A Supplement" by Thomas Rudd. London, 1668.

Epstein, Isidore, ed. *The Babylonian Talmud*. 34 vols. London: Soncino Press, 1938–48.

Erasmus, Desiderius. *Enchiridion Militis Christiani*. Translated by Frances Michel. 1533. Reprint. London: Methuen, 1905.

Etheridge, J. W., trans. *The Targum of Onkelos and Jonathan Ben Uzziel on the Pentateuch, with the Fragments of the Jerusalem Targum from the Chaldee*. New York: Ktav Publishing House, 1968.

Euclides. *The Elements of Geometrie*. Translated by M. Billingsley. London, 1570.

Euripides. *Cretans* (Fragment), pp. 55–59; *Bacchanals*, pp. 155–59. Excerpted in *Greek Religious Thought*. Edited by Francis M. Cornford.

Evelyn-White, Hugh G., trans. *Hesiod, the Homeric Hymns and Homerica*. London: William Heinemann, 1964.

Featley, Daniel. *Foure Rowes of Precious Stones. A Rehearsall Sermon Preached in Saint Maries Church at Oxford, 1610*. In *Clavis Mystica: a Key Opening Divers Difficult and Mysterious Texts of Holy Scripture*, pp. 496–536. London, 1636.

Ficino, Marsilio, trans. *De Mysteriis Aegyptiorum Chaldaeorum Assyriorum*. Venice, 1497.

————. *In Librum De Sole, Ad Magnanimum Petrum Medicem*, pp. 989–99; *In Librum De Lumine, Ad Magnanimum Petrum Medicem*, pp. 999–1009. In vol. 1 of *Opera, et Quae Hactenus Extitêre, et Quae in Lucem Nunc Primùm Prodiêre Omnia*. 2 vols. Paris, 1641.

Fletcher, Phineas. *The Purple Island or The Isle of Man*. London, 1633.

Fludd, Robert. *De Praeternaturali Utriusque Mundi Historia*. Frankfurt, 1617–21.

————. *Mosaicall Philosophy: Grounded Upon the Essential Truth or Eternal Sapience*. London, 1659.

————. *Utriusque Cosmi Maioris scilicet et Minoris Metaphysica, Physica atque Technica Historia*. Frankfurt, 1617.

Forbes, Patrick. *A Learned Commentary Upon the Revelation*. London, 1614.

Franck, Sebastian. *The forbidden fruit: or a treatise of the tree of knowledge*. London, 1640.

Freedman, H., and Simon, Maurice, ed. and trans. *Midrash Rabbah*. 12 vols. in 10. London: Soncino Press, 1939.

Friedlander, Gerald, ed. and trans. *Pirkê de Rabbi Eliezer*. New York: Hermon Press, 1965.

Fuller, Thomas. *The Historie of the Holy Warre* (1639). 3rd ed. Cambridge, 1647.

————. *The Holy and Profane States*. London, 1642.

G., W. *A Just Apologie for an Abused Armie.* London, 1646.

Gale, Theophilus. *The Court of the Gentiles: or A Discourse touching the Original of Human Literature.* 4 vols. 2nd ed. Oxford, 1672.

Gaster, Theodor H., ed. *The Dead Sea Scriptures.* Garden City, N. Y.: Doubleday, 1964.

Glass, Salomon. *Philologia Sacra.* Leipzig, 1705.

God appearing for the Parliament in sundry late Victories Bestowed upon their Forces. London, 1644.

Godwyn, Thomas. *Moses and Aaron. Civil and Ecclesiastical Rites, used by the Ancient Hebrewes.* London, 1641.

Goodwin, John. ΘΕΟΜΑΧΙΑ; *or The Grand Imprudence of Men running the hazard of Fighting against God* (1644). Vol. 3, pp. 5–58, of *Tracts on Liberty in the Puritan Revolution, 1638–1647.* Edited by William Haller. 3 vols. New York: Columbia University Press, 1934.

Goodwin, Thomas. *A Glimpse of Syons Glory.* London, 1641.

Gouge, William. *A Learned and very useful Commentary on the whole epistle to the Hebrewes.* London, 1655.

――――. Πανοπλία τοῦ θεοῦ: *The Whole-Armour of God: Or, a Christians Spiritual Furniture, to Keepe Him Safe From All the Assaults of Satan.* London, 1619.

Grant, Frederick C., ed. *Ancient Roman Religion.* New York: Liberal Arts Press, 1957.

――――. *Hellenistic Religions: The Age of Syncretism.* Indianapolis: Bobbs-Merrill, 1953.

Greenhill, William. *An Exposition of the Prophet Ezekiel* (1650). Edited by James Sherman. Edinburgh: James Nichol, 1863.

Gregorius Nazianzenus, Saint, archbishop of Constantinople (Saint Gregory Nazianzen). *Select Orations of Saint Gregory Nazianzen.* Translated by Edwin Hamilton Gifford. Vol. 7, pp. 203–436, of *A Select Library of Nicene and Post-Nicene Fathers.* Second series. Edited by Philip Schaff and Henry Wace.

Gregorius Thaumaturgus, Saint, bishop of Neocaesarea (Saint Gregory Thaumaturgus). *On the Holy Theophany, or on Christ's Baptism.* In *The Works of Gregory Thaumaturgus, Dionysius of Alexandria, and Archelaus,* pp. 142–51. Translated by S. D. F. Salmond. Vol. 20 of *Ante-Nicene Christian Library.* Edited by Alexander Roberts and others.

Gregory, John. *Gregorii Opuscula: or, Notes and Observations upon Some Passages of Scripture, With other Learned Tracts.* London, 1650.

Grotius, Hugo. *On the Law of War and Peace.* Translated by Francis Kelsey. Indianapolis and New York: Bobbs-Merrill, 1925.

Gurnall, William. *The Christian in Complete Armour. Or, a Treatise of the Saints' War Against the Devil. Wherein a Discovery is Made of that Grand Enemy of God and His People, in His Policies, Power, Seat of His Empire, Wickedness, and Chief Design He Hath Against the Saints.* London, 1655.

Hall, Joseph, bishop of Norwich. *Contemplations Upon the Principall Passages of the Holy Storie. In Foure Books.* In *The Works of Joseph Hall*, pp. 765–1353. London, 1634.

―――. *The Remedy of Prophanesse.* 2 Parts. London, 1637.

―――. *A Sermon Preach't . . . at the Consecration of a new Buriall-place.* London, 1637.

Harvey, Christopher. *The Synagogue, Or the Shadow of the Temple; in Imitation of George Herbert.* London, 1640.

[Hawkins, Henry.] *The Partheneia Sacra; Or, the Mysterious and Delicious Garden of the Sacred Parthenes; Symbolically Set Forth and Enriched with Pious Devices and Emblemes . . . Contrived Al to the Honour of the Incomparable Virgin Marie.* Paris, 1633.

Heidel, Alexander, ed. *The Babylonian Genesis.* 2nd ed. Chicago: University of Chicago Press, 1951.

―――. *The Gilgamesh Epic and Old Testament Parallels.* Chicago: University of Chicago Press, 1949.

Heraclitus. Fragments 15, 5. Excerpted in *Greek Religious Thought.* Edited by Francis M. Cornford, p. 83.

Herbert, George. *The Works of George Herbert.* Edited by F. E. Hutchinson. Oxford: Clarendon Press, 1941.

Hermes Trismegistus. *Corpus Hermeticum: Libellus I. The Poimandres* [of Hermes Trismegistus]. Vol. 1, pp. 114–33, of *Hermetica: The Ancient Greek and Latin Writings Which Contain Religious or Philosophic Teachings Ascribed to Hermes Trismegistus.* Edited and translated by Walter Scott. 4 vols. Oxford: Clarendon Press, 1924–36.

Herodotus. *Herodotus.* Translated by A. D. Godley. 4 vols. London: William Heineman, 1960.

Hesiodus (Hesiod). *Theogony.* In *Hesiod, the Homeric Hymns and Homerica.* Translated by Hugh G. Evelyn-White.

―――. *Works and Days.* In *Hesiod and Theognis.* Translated by Dorothea Wender. Baltimore: Penquin, 1973.

Heywood, Thomas. *The Hierarchie of the Blessed Angells. Their names, orders and offices. The fall of Lucifer with his Angells.* London, 1635.

Hippocrates. *On the Sacred Disease.* Excerpted in *Greek Religious Thought.* Edited by Francis M. Cornford, pp. 135–39.

Hippolytus. *The Discourse on the Holy Theophany.* Vol. 5, pp. 224–32, of *The Ante-Nicene Fathers: Translations of the Writings of the Fathers down to A.D. 325.* Edited by Alexander Roberts and James Donaldson. 10 vols. Edinburgh: T. and T. Clark, 1867. Reprint. Grand Rapids, Mich.: William B. Eerdmans, 1957.

Hobbes, Thomas. "The Answer of Mr Hobbes to Sr Will. D'avenant's Preface Before *Gondibert.*" Pp. 71–78 in *Gondibert: An Heroick Poem* (1651). By Sir William D'avenant. Menston, England: Scolar Press, 1970.

―――. *Behemoth: The History of the Civil Wars in England, from the Year 1640, to 1660.* London, 1680.

The Holy Bible. London, 1611.

The Holy Bible. 60 vols. London: William S. Orr, 1837 (the Kitto Bible).

Homeric Hymns. In *Hesiod, the Homeric Hymns and Homerica*. Translated by Hugh G. Evelyn-White.

Hooker, Richard. *Of the Lawes of Ecclesiastical Politie*. Vols. 1 and 2 of *The Works of Richard Hooker*. Edited by John Keble. 3 vols. 6th ed. London: Oxford University Press, 1874.

Horatius Flaccus (Horace). *Ars Poetica*. Translated by T. S. Dorsch. In *Classical Literary Criticism*. Baltimore: Penguin Books, 1965.

———. *Odes*, p. 60; *Carmen Saeculare*, pp. 182–84. Excerpted in *Ancient Roman Religion*. Edited by Frederick C. Grant.

———. *Odes*. Vol. 1 of *A Poetical Translation of the Works of Horace*. Translated by Philip Francis. 2 vols. 3rd ed. London: A. Millar, 1749.

———. *Satires, Epistles, and Ars Poetica*. Translated by H. Rushton Fairclough. Cambridge: Harvard University Press, 1974.

"Hymnus Vespertinus." Translated by John Keble. In *Lyra Apostolica*. London: Henry Mozley, 1836.

Iamblichus. *De Mysteriis Aegyptiorum Chaldaeorum Assyriorum*. Translated by Marsilio Ficino. Venice, 1497.

———. *Iamblichus on the Mysteries of the Egyptians, Chaldeans, and Assyrians*. Translated by Thomas Taylor. Chiswick: C. Wittingham, 1821.

———. *Life of Pythagoras*. Translated by Thomas Taylor. London: A. J. Volpy, 1818.

Irenaeus, Saint, bishop of Lyons. *Irenaeus Against Heresies*. Vol. 1, pp. 421–25, of *The Writings of Irenaeus*. 2 vols. Translated by Alexander Roberts and W. H. Rambaut. Vol. 5 of *Ante-Nicene Christian Library*. Edited by Alexander Roberts and others.

Isidorus, Saint, bishop of Seville (Isidore of Seville). *Isidori Hispalensis Episcopi: Etymologiarum sive Originum*. 2 vols. Oxford: Clarendon Press, 1911.

Jackson, Thomas. *A Treatise of the Divine Essence and Attributes*. London, 1628.

———. *A Treatise of the Holy Catholike Faith and Church*. London, 1627.

James, Brother of the Lord. *The Divine Liturgy of James*. In *Liturgies and Other Documents of the Ante-Nicene Period*. Vol. 24, pp. 11–45, of *Ante-Nicene Christian Library*. Edited by Alexander Roberts and others.

Johnson, Samuel. Extract from the *Life of Milton* (1779). Vol. 2, pp. 290–310, of *Milton: The Critical Heritage*. Edited by John T. Shawcross. 2 vols. Critical Heritage Series. London: Routledge and Kegan Paul, 1970–72.

Jonson, Ben. *The Workes of Beniamin Jonson*. London, 1616.

Josephus, Flavius. *Antiquities of the Jews*. Vols. 1–3 of *The Works of Flavius Josephus*. Edited by A. R. Shilleto. 5 vols. London: George Bell and Sons, 1885–89.

———. *The Jewish War*. Vols. 2–3 of *Josephus*. Translated by H. St. J. Thackeray. 9 vols. Cambridge: Harvard University Press, 1961.

Joyfull Newes from Plimouth, Being An Exact Relation of a great victory ob-

tained against the Cornish Cavaliers, by the Parliaments Forces in those parts. London, 1643.

Juan de la Cruz, Saint (Saint John of the Cross). *Works of Saint John of the Cross, Doctor of the Church*. Translated and edited by E. Allison Peers. 3 vols. London: Burns, Oates and Washbourne, 1934.

Julianus, Apostata, Emperor of Rome (Emperor Julian). *Oration IV: Hymn to King Helios Dedicated to Sallust*. Vol. 1, pp. 353–442, of *The Works of Emperor Julian*. Translated by Wilmer Cave Wright. 3 vols. London: William Heinemann, 1913.

Justin Martyr. *The First Apology of Justin Martyr*. Excerpted in *Liturgies of the Western Church*. Edited by Bard Thompson, pp. 8–10. Cleveland: World Publishing Co., 1961.

Kirkconnell, Watson, ed. *The Celestial Cycle: The Theme of "Paradise Lost" in World Literature with Translations of the Major Analogues*. Toronto: University of Toronto Press, 1952.

Lactantius, Lucius Caecilius Firmianus. *The Divine Institutes*. Vol. 1 of *The Works of Lactantius*. Translated by William Fletcher. 2 vols. Vol. 21 of *Ante-Nicene Christian Library*. Edited by Alexander Roberts and others.

Lapide, Cornelius A. *In Exodum Commentarium*. Vol. 5 of *Scripturae Sacrae Cursus Completus, ex Commentariis Omnium Perfectissimis Ubique Habitis*. Edited by J.-P. Migne. 28 vols. Paris: Garnier Bros., 1860–62.

Lawrence, Henry. *Of our Communion and Warre with Angels*. London, 1646.

Legnano, Giovanni da. *Tractatus de Bello*. Edited by Thomas Holland. Oxford: Oxford University Press, 1917.

Leigh, Edward. *Critica Sacra: Or Philologicall Observations Upon All the Greek Words of the New Testament*. 4th ed. London, 1662.

————. *A Treatise of the Divine Promises, in Five Books*. London, 1633.

Leighton, Alexander. *Speculum belli sacri: or the Lookingglasse of the Holy War*. London, 1624.

Lightfoot, John. *An handfull of gleanings out of the book of Exodus*. London, 1643.

————. *A Prospect of the Temple* (1650), vol. 9, pp. 213–486; *A Chorographical Century* (1658), vol. 10, pp. 1–186. In *The Whole Works of the Reverend John Lightfoot*. Edited by John Rogers Pitman. 18 vols. London: J. F. Dove, 1822–25.

Longinus. *On the Sublime*. Translated by T. S. Dorsch. In *Classical Literary Criticism*. Baltimore: Penguin Books, 1965.

Luria, Isaac. "Hymn to the *Shekinah*." In *The Secret Garden: An Anthology in the Kabbalah*. Edited by David Meltzer, pp. 171–84. New York: Seabury Press, 1976.

Luther, Martin. *Lectures on Genesis*. Vol. 1 of *Luther's Works*. Edited by Jaroslav Pelikan. 55 vols. St. Louis: Concordia Publishing House, 1958.

Macrobius. *The Saturnalia*. Translated by Percival Davies. New York: Columbia University Press, 1969.

Markham, Gervase. *The Souldiers Exercise: in Three Books. Containing Most Necessary and Curious Rules for the Exact Mustering Both of Horsetroops, and Foote-bands with Several Formes of Battailes Described in Figures.* London, 1643.

Marrin, Albert, ed. *War and the Christian Conscience: From Augustine to Martin Luther King, Jr.* Chicago: Henry Regnery Co., 1971.

Marshall, Stephen. *Meroz Cursed, or a Sermon Preached to the Honourable House of Commons at their Late Solemn Fast, February 23, 1641.* London, 1641.

Marvell, Andrew. *Andrew Marvell: Complete Poetry.* Edited by George deF. Lord. New York: Random House, 1968.

Mede, Joseph. *In Sancti Ioannis Apocalypsin Commentarius, ad Amussim Clavis Apocalypticae* (1627). In *The Works of . . . Joseph Mede*, pp. 435–537. 3rd ed. London. 1672.

———. *The Key of Revelation, Searched and Demonstrated out of the Naturall and Proper Characters of the Visions.* Translated by Richard More. London, 1643.

———. *The Reverence of Gods House. A Sermon Preached at St. Maries in Cambridge, Before the Universitie of St. Matthies Day, 1635 / 6.* London, 1648.

———. *The Sanctification of Gods Name.* In *Diatribae*, pp. 17–81. *Discourses on Divers Texts of Scripture: Delivered upon Severall Occasions.* 2nd ed. London, 1648.

Migne, J.-P., ed. *Patrologiae cursus completus sive bibliotheca universalis, integra, uniformis, commoda, oeconomica omnium S.S. patrum, doctorum scriptorumque ecclesiasticorum . . . Series Latinae.* 221 vols. Paris: n.p., 1844–80.

Milton, John. *The Complete Poetry of John Milton.* Edited by John T. Shawcross. 2nd ed. rev. Garden City, N. Y.: Doubleday, 1971.

———. *Complete Prose Works of John Milton.* Edited by Don M. Wolfe. 7 vols. to date. New Haven: Yale University Press, 1953–.

———. *John Milton: Complete Poems and Major Prose.* Edited by Merritt Y. Hughes. New York: Odyssey Press, 1957.

———. *The Poetical Works of John Milton.* Edited by H. J. Todd. 6 vols. London: R. Gilbert, 1826.

———. *The Works of John Milton.* Edited by Frank Allen Patterson. 18 vols. in 21. New York: Columbia University Press, 1931–38.

Montefiore, C. G., and Loewe, H., eds. *A Rabbinic Anthology.* London: Macmillan and Co., 1938.

Moses ben Maimon (Maimonides). *The Code of Maimonides.* Translated by Mandell Lewitts. Vols. 2–5, 8–9, 11–12, 14–16, of the *Yale Judaica Series.* 20 vols. New Haven: Yale University Press, 1948–77.

———. *Guide of the Perplexed.* Translated by Shlomo Pines. Chicago: University of Chicago Press, 1963.

The Mount of Spirits. London, 1691.

Müntzer, Thomas. "The Call to Apocalyptic War." In *War and the Christian Conscience*. Edited by Albert Marrin, pp. 97–100.

Newton, Sir Isaac. *Opticks*. London, 1704.

———. *Philosophical Transactions*. London, 1671–72.

Nicolaus Cusanus, Cardinal (Nicholas of Cusa). *Of Learned Ignorance*. Translated by F. Germain Heron. London: Routledge and Kegan Paul, 1954.

———. *The Vision of God*. Translated by Emma Gurney Salter. London: J. M. Dent, 1928.

Novatianus (Novatian). *On the Jewish Meats*. Vol. 2, pp. 382–95, of *The Writings of . . . Novatian*. Translated by Robert Ernest Wallis. 2 vols. Vol. 3 of *Ante-Nicene Christian Library*. Edited by Alexander Roberts and others.

Novum Testamentum Graece. Edited by Eberhard Nestle. Stuttgart: Württembergische Bibelanstalt, 1953.

Odeberg, Hugo, ed. *The Hebrew Book of Enoch (III Enoch)*. Cambridge: Cambridge University Press, 1928.

Origen. *Origen's Commentary on the Gospel of John*. Vol. 10, pp. 297–408, of *The Ante-Nicene Fathers: Translations of the Writings of the Fathers down to A.D. 325*. Edited by Allan Menzies. 10 vols. Grand Rapids, Mich.: William B. Eerdmans, n.d.

Orphic Inscriptions (Funerary). Excerpted in *Greek Religious Thought*. Edited by Francis M. Cornford, pp. 60–62.

Ovidius Naso, Publius (Ovid). *Fasti*. Excerpted in *Ancient Roman Religion*. Edited by Frederick C. Grant, pp. 11, 29.

———. *Heroides and Amores*. Translated by Grant Showerman. Cambridge: Harvard University Press, 1947.

Ovington, John. *Voyage to Suratt, in the Year, 1689. Giving a Large Account of that City, and Its Inhabitants*. London, 1696.

Owen, John. *An Exposition of the Epistle to the Hebrews*. Vol. 16 of *The Works of John Owen*. Edited by William H. Goold. 17 vols. Philadelphia: Leighton Publications, 1896.

———. *ΠΝΕΥΜΑΤΟΛΟΓΙΑ. Or, A Discourse Concerning the Holy Spirit* (1674). Vol. 3 of *The Works of John Owen*. Edited by William H. Goold. 16 vols. London: Johnstone and Hunter, 1850–53.

———. *Θεολογουμενα Παντοδαπα. sive de natura, ortu, progressu, et studio verae theologiae libri sex*. Oxford, 1661.

Pareus, David. *A Commentary upon the Divine Revelation*. Translated by Elias Arnold. Amsterdam, 1664.

Parker, Henry. *Scotlands Holy War. A Discourse . . . Remonstrating, How the Scots out of a Corrupt Pretended Zeal to the Covenant Have Made the Same Scandalous and Odious to All Good Men*. London, 1651.

The Pentateuch. Edited by Samson Raphael Hirsch. 5 vols. 2nd ed. London: Isaac Levy, 1963.

Penton, Stephen. *A Treatise, shewing, That the Adoration or Worship of God in his House . . . is neither Idolatry, Superstition, or Will-worship*. London, 1682.

A Perfect Narrative of the Battell of Knocknones. London, 1647.

Peter, Hugh. *Mr. Peter's Message* (1646). Excerpted in *Puritanism and Liberty.* Edited by A. S. P. Woodhouse, p. 387.

Philo Judaeus. *On the Life of Moses,* vol. 6, pp. 450–595. Translated by F. H. Colson; *Questions and Answers on Exodus,* supplement 2. Translated by Ralph Marcus. In *Philo.* 10 vols., with 2 supplements. Cambridge: Harvard University Press, 1953.

———. *A Treatise on the Account of the Creation of the World as Given by Moses,* vol. 1, pp. 1–51; *A Treatise on the Question, Who is the Heir of Divine Things,* vol. 2, pp. 94–157; *A Treatise on the Question, Why Certain Names in the Holy Scriptures Are Changed,* Vol. 2, pp. 238–92; *A Treatise on the Life of Moses, That Is to Say, on the Theology and Prophetic Office of Moses,* vol. 3, pp. 88–135; *Fragments Extracted From the Parallels of John of Damascus,* vol. 4, pp. 242–57. In *The Works of Philo Judaeus, the Contemporary of Josephus.* Edited by C. D. Yonge. 4 vols. Vol. 1: London: George Bell and Sons, 1890. Vols. 2–4: London: Henry G. Bohn, 1854–55.

Pico della Mirandola, Giovanni. *Twelve Rules and Weapons Concerning the Spiritual Battel.* London, 1589.

Plato. *The Dialogues of Plato.* Translated by B. Jowett. 2 vols. London: Oxford University Press, 1920. Reprint. New York: Random House, 1937.

Plotinus. *The Enneads.* Translated by Stephen MacKenna. 3rd ed. London: Faber and Faber, 1962.

Plutarchus. *Wherefore the Pythian Priestess Now Ceases to Deliver Her Oracles in Verse,* vol. 3, pp. 69–103; *Why the Oracles Cease to Give Answers,* vol. 4, pp. 3–64. In *Plutarch's Miscellanies and Essays. Comprising All His Works Under the Title of "Morals."* Edited by William W. Godwin. 5 vols. 6th ed. Boston: Little, Brown, 1898.

Poole, Matthew. *Annotations upon the Holy Bible.* 2 vols. London, 1683.

———. *Annotations upon the second book of Moses, called Exodus.* London, 1617.

[Pordage, Samuel.] *Mundorum Explicatio or, The Explanation of an Hieroglyphical Figure: Wherein are couched the mysteries of the external, internal, and eternal worlds . . . Being a sacred poem.* London, 1661.

Porphyrius, Saint, bishop of Gaza (Porphyry). *On Abstinence From Animal Food.* Pp. 1–170 in *The Select Works of Porphyry.* Translated by Thomas Taylor. London: Thomas Rodd, 1823.

Postel, Guillaume. *Interprétation du candélabre de Moyse* (1548). Edited by François Secret. Nieuwkoop, Netherlands: B. De Graaf, 1966.

Price, Sampson. *The Beauty of Holiness: Or the Consecration of a House of Prayer.* London, 1618.

Pritchard, James B., ed. *Ancient Near Eastern Texts Relating to the Old Testament.* 3rd ed. Princeton: Princeton University Press, 1969.

Proclus. *Five Hymns*. In *Sallust*. Translated by Thomas Taylor. London: Edward Jeffrey, 1793.

Propertius. *Sexti Propertii Elegiarum*. Translated by H. E. Butler. London: William Heinemann, 1912.

Prudentius Clemens, Aurelius (Prudentius). *Hymns for Every Day*. Pp. 3–38 in *The Fathers of the Church*. Edited and translated by Roy Deferrari. Washington: Catholic University of America, 1962.

———. *Psychomachia*. Vol. 1, pp. 274–343, of *Prudentius*. Translated by H. J. Thomson. 2 vols. Cambridge: Harvard University Press, 1949–53.

Prynne, William. *Mount-Orgueil: or Divine and Profitable Meditations, Raised from the Contemplation of These Three Leaves of Natures Volume, 1. Rocks, 2. Seas, 3. Gardens. Digested into Three Distinct Poems*. London, 1641.

Purchas, Samuel. *Purchas his Pilgrimage. Or Relations of the World and the Religions Observed in all Ages and Places Discovered, from the Creation unto this Present*. London, 1613.

"The Putney Debates." In *Puritanism and Liberty*. Edited by A. S. P. Woodhouse, pp. 1–124.

Puttenham, George. *The Arte of English Poesie. Contrived into Three Books: the First of Poets and Poesie, the Second of Proportion, the Third of Ornament* (1589). Vol. 1 of *Ancient Critical Essays upon the English Poets and Poesy*. Edited by Joseph Haslewood. 2 vols. London: T. Bensley, 1815.

Rainolds, John. *Oratio in Laudem Artis Poeticae* (ca. 1572). Edited by William Ringler and Walter Allen, Jr. Princeton: Princeton University Press, 1940.

Ralegh, Sir Walter. *The Historie of the World. In Five Books*. London, 1614.

Reynolds, Henry. *Mythomystes* (1633?). Vol. 1, pp. 153–69, of *Critical Essays of the Seventeenth Century*. Edited by J. E. Spingarn. 3 vols. Oxford: Clarendon Press, 1908.

Ricius, Paulus. *Portae Lucis*. Augsburg, 1516.

Roberts, Alexander, and others, eds. *Ante-Nicene Christian Library: The Writings of the Apostolic Fathers Down to A.D. 325*. 24 vols. Edinburgh: T. and T. Clark, 1867–72.

Robertson, William. *Dissertatio Philologico-Theologica de decem Dei Nominibus Hebraicis*. In *Thesaurus Linguae Sanctae . . . sive, Concordantiale Lexicon Hebraeo-Latino-Biblicum*. London, 1680.

Rodkinson, Michael, ed. *The Babylonian Talmud*. 15 vols. Boston: Talmud Society, 1918.

Rollock, Robert. *A Treatise of Gods Effectual Calling*. London, 1603.

Ross, Alexander. *ΠΑΝΣΕΒΕΙΑ: Or, A View of all Religions in the World*. 4th ed. London, 1627.

Rupertus Abbas, Tuitiensis. *De Trinitate et Operibus Ejus Libri XLII*. In *Exodum Commentariorum Liber Primus*. Vol. 167, pp. 566–607, of *Patrologia (Series Latina)*. Edited by J.-P. Migne.

Ryves, Bruno. *Mercurius Rusticus: Or the Countries Complaint, Of the Sacriledges, Prophanations, and Plunderings, Committed by the Schismatiques, on the Cathedrall Churches of this Kingdom.* Oxford, 1646.

Salkeld, John. *A Treatise of Paradise. And the Principall Contents Thereof.* London, 1617.

Sandys, George, trans. *Ovid's Metamorphoses Englished, Mythologiz'd, and Represented in Figures.* Oxford, 1632.

Schaff, Philip, and Wace, Henry, eds. *A Select Library of Nicene and Post-Nicene Fathers of the Christian Church.* Second series. 14 vols. New York: Christian Literature Co., 1890–1907.

Schneemelcher, Wilhelm, ed. *New Testament Apocrypha.* 2 vols. Philadelphia: Westminster Press, 1963.

Sempill, Sir James. *Sacrilege Sacredly Handled. That is, According to Scripture Onely. Divided Into Two Parts: 1. For the Law. 2. For the Gospell.* London, 1619.

Shepard, Thomas. *Theses Sabbaticae. Or, the Doctrine of the Sabbath, Wherein the Sabbaths I. Morality, II. Change, III. Beginning, IV. Sanctification, Are Clearly Discussed.* London, 1649.

Sibbes, Richard. *Light From Heaven, Discovering the Fountaine Opened, Angels Acclamations, Churches Riches, Rich Povertie.* London, 1635.

————. *The Soules Conflict with it selfe, and Victory Over it Selfe by Faith. A Treatise of the Inward Disquietments of Distressed Spirits, with Comfortable Remedies to Establish Them.* 4th ed. London, 1638.

Siculus Flaccus. *De Agrorum Conditionibus et Constitutionibus Limitum.* Excerpted in *Ancient Roman Religion.* Edited by Frederick C. Grant, pp. 9–10.

Sidney, Sir Philip. *The Defence of Poesy* (1595). In *Sir Philip Sidney: Selected Prose and Poetry.* Edited by Robert Kimbrough, pp. 102–58. New York: Holt, Rhinehart and Winston, 1969.

Simmonds, William. *Pisgah Evangelica.* London, 1606.

Simon, Maurice, and Levertoff, Paul T., ed. and trans. *The Zohar.* 5 vols. London: Soncino Press, 1933.

Sophocles. *Oedipus at Colonus.* In *Sophocles I.* Translated by David Grene and others. Chicago: University of Chicago Press, 1954.

The Souldiers Catechisme: Composed for The Parliaments Army: Consisting of Two Parts: Wherein Are Chiefly Taught 1. The Iustification. 2. The Qualification of Our Souldiers. London, 1644.

The Souldiers Pocket Bible: Containing the Most (if Not All) Those Places Contained in Holy Scripture, Which Doe Shew the Qualifications of His Inner Man, That Is a Fit Souldier to Fight the Lords Battels, Both Before He Fights, in the Fight, and After the Fight. London, 1643.

Spenser, Edmund. *Books I and II of "The Faerie Queene," "The Mutability Cantos," and Selections from the Minor Poetry.* Edited by Robert Kellogg and Oliver Steele. New York: Odyssey Press, 1965.

_____. *The Poetical Works of Edmund Spenser*. Edited by J. C. Smith and E. De Selincourt. London: Oxford University Press, 1912.

Sprigg, Joshua. *Anglia Rediviva; Englands Recovery: Being the History of the Motions, Actions, and Successes of the Army Under the Immediate Conduct of His Excellency Sr Thomas Fairfax, K^t Captain-General of All the Parliaments Forces in England*. London, 1647.

Stephanus, Charles. *Dictionarium Historicum, Geographicum, Poeticum*. Oxford, 1671.

Sterry, Peter. *The Comings Forth of Christ in the Power of his Death. A Sermon preached before the high court of Parliament*. London, 1650.

Stillingfleet, Edward. *Origenes Sacrae, or a Rational Account of the Grounds of Christian Faith, as to the Truth and Divine Authority of the Scriptures, and the Matters Therein Contained*. 3rd ed. London, 1666.

Strickland, John. *Immanuel, or The Church Triumphing in God with Us*. London, 1644.

Swan, John. *Speculum Mundi: Or, a Glasse Representing the Face of the World; Shewing Both That it Did Begin, and Must Also End: the Manner How, and Time When Being Largely Examined*. Cambridge, 1635.

Tasso, Torquato. *Jerusalem Delivered*. Translated by Edward Fairfax. New York: Capricorn Books, n.d.

_____. *Selections from "Discourses on the Heroic Poem"* (1594). In *Literary Criticism: Plato to Dryden*. Edited by Allan H. Gilbert, pp. 466–503. New York: American Book Co., 1940.

Taylor, Jeremy. *The Rule and Exercises of Holy Living* (1650), pp. 1–254; *The Rule and Exercises of Holy Dying* (1651), pp. 257–455. In vol. 3 of *The Whole Works of Jeremy Taylor*. Edited by Charles Eden. 10 vols. London, 1862.

Taylor, Thomas. *Christs Victorie over the Dragon: Or Satans Downfall: Shewing The Glorious Conquests of our Saviour for his poor Church, against the greatest Persecutors, In a plaine and pithy Exposition of the Twelfth Chapter of S. Iohns Revelation*. London, 1633.

Tertullianus, Quintus Septimius Florens (Tertullian). *An Answer to the Jews*. Vol. 3, pp. 1–383, of *The Writings of . . . Tertullianus*. Translated by S. Thelwall, 3 vols. Vol. 18 of *Ante-Nicene Christian Library*. Edited by Alexander Roberts and others.

Thomas, D. Winton, ed. *Documents from Old Testament Times*. New York: Harper and Row, 1958.

Thomas, Lewis. *Christ Combating with Satan*. London, 1599.

Thomas Aquinas, Saint. *The "Summa Theologica" of St. Thomas Aquinas*. Translated by the Fathers of the English Dominican Province. 2 vols. 2nd ed. rev. London: Burns Oates and Washbourne, 1920–35.

Tomlinson, Francis. *The Holy Salutation of St. Jude. A Sermon*. London, 1612.

Traherne, Thomas. *Christian Ethics; or, Divine Morality, Opening the Way to Blessedness*. London, 1675.

A *True Relation of a Victory obtained over the Kings Forces, by the Army of Sir Thomas Fairfax*. London, 1645.

Turges, Edmund. *The Christian Souldier, His Combat, Conquest, and Crowne. Agaynst the Three Arch-Enemies of Mankind, the World, the Flesh, and the Devil*. London, 1639.

Turner, John. *An Attempt towards an Explanation of the Theology and Mythology of the Antient Pagans*. London, 1687.

Turner, Sir James. *Pallas Armata: Military Essayes of the Ancient Grecian, Roman, and Modern Art of War* (1683). Reprint. New York: Greenwood Press, 1968.

Umbrian Formulae (*Stelae*). Excerpted in *Ancient Roman Religion*. Edited by Frederick C. Grant, pp. 4–8.

Ussher, James, archbishop of Armagh. *De Romanae Ecclesiae Symbolo Apostolico Vetere* (1647). Vol. 7, pp. 293–342, of *The Whole Works of James Ussher*. 17 vols. Dublin: Hodges and Smith, 1837–64 .

_____. *Immanuel, or the Mystery of the Incarnation of the Son of God*. London, 1638.

Valvasone, Erasmo di. *Angeleida*. Venice, 1590.

Vane, Sir Henry. *The Retired Mans Meditations: or, the Mysterie and Power of Godliness Shining Forth in the Living Word, to the Unmasking the Mysterie of Iniquity in the Most Refined and Purest Forms*. London, 1655.

Vaughan, Henry. *The Complete Poetry of Henry Vaughan*. Edited by French Fogle. New York: W. W. Norton, 1964.

[Vaughan, Thomas.] *Aula Lucis, or, The House of Light*. London, 1651.

[_____.] *Lumen de Lumine, or a New Magical Light Discovered and Communicated to the World*. London, 1651.

Vergilius Maro, Publius (Vergil). *The Aeneid*. Translated by H. Rushton Fairclough. 2 vols. Cambridge: Harvard University Press, 1934.

_____. *The Aeneid*, pp. 39–43, 193–210; *Eclogue* 4, pp. 186–87. Excerpted in *Ancient Roman Religion*. Edited by Frederick C. Grant.

_____. *The "Eclogues" and "Georgics" of Virgil*. Translated by C. Day Lewis. Garden City, N. Y.: Doubleday, 1947.

[Veteris et Noui Testamenti praecipuae historiae et uisiones, picturis elegantissimus in aes incisis, repraesentatae.] Frankfurt, 1627.

Vicars, John. *Magnalia Dei Anglicana. Or Englands Parliamentary Chronicle*. London, 1646.

Vida, Marco Girolamo. *Vida's "Art of Poetry."* Translated by Christopher Pitt. In *The Art of Poetry: The Poetical Treatises of Horace, Vida, and Boileau*. Edited by Albert S. Cook, pp. 39–156. Boston: Ginn and Co., 1892.

Vondel, Joost van den. *Lucifer, Treurspel* (1654). In *The Celestial Cycle: The Theme of "Paradise Lost" in World Literature with Translations of the Major Analogues*. Edited by Watson Kirkconnell, pp. 361–421. Toronto: University of Toronto Press, 1952.

Ward, Robert. *Animadversions of Warre; Or, a Militarie Magazine of the Truest*

Rules, and Ablest Instructions, for the Managing of Warre. London, 1639.

Wigmore, Michael. *The Holie Citie: 1. Discovered. 2. Besieged. 3. Delivered. A Sermon Preached at York House Before the Right Honourable Francis, Lord Verulam.* London, 1619.

Willet, Andrew. *Hexapla in Exodum, That is, A Sixfold Commentary upon The Second Booke of Moses Called Exodus.* London, 1633.

————. *Hexapla in Genesin, That is, A Sixfold Commentary upon Genesis.* London, 1605.

Wilson, R. McL., trans. and ed. *Gnosis.* 2 vols. Oxford: Clarendon Press, 1974.

Winton, Thomas D., ed. *Documents from Old Testament Times.* New York: Harper and Row, 1961.

Wither, George. *Carmen Eucharisticon: A Private Thank-Oblation, Exhibited to the Glory of The Lord of Hosts, For the timely and wonderfull Deliverance, . . . in the routing of a numerous Army of Irish Rebells* (1649). Vol. 2 of *Miscellaneous Works of George Wither.* 6 vols. N.p.: Spenser Society, 1882.

Wollebius, Johannes. *Compendium Theologiae Christianae.* In *Reformed Dogmatics.* Edited and translated by John W. Beardslee III, pp. 26–262. New York: Oxford University Press, 1965.

Woodhouse, A. S. P., ed. *Puritanism and Liberty: Being the Army Debates (1647–1649) from the Clarke Manuscripts with Supplementary Documents.* 2nd ed. Chicago: University of Chicago Press, 1951.

Woodhouse, A. S. P., and Bush, Douglas, eds. *A Variorum Commentary on the Poems of John Milton.* 3 vols. to date. New York: Columbia University Press, 1970– .

SECONDARY SOURCES

Abelson, Joshua. *The Immanence of God in Rabbinical Literature.* New York: Hermon Press, 1969.

Adams, Robert P. *The Better Part of Valor: More, Erasmus, Colet, and Vives on Humanism, War, and Peace, 1496–1535.* Seattle: University of Washington Press, 1962.

Adamson, J. H. "Milton's 'Arianism.'" *Harvard Theological Review* 53 (1960): 269–76; "The War in Heaven: Milton's Version of the *Merkabah*." *Journal of English and Germanic Philology* 57 (1958): 690–703. Reprinted in *Bright Essence.* Edited by William B. Hunter, Jr., and others, pp. 53–61, 103–14.

Albright, William. *Archaeology and the Religion of Israel.* Baltimore: Johns Hopkins University Press, 1968.

————. *From the Stone Age to Christianity: Monotheism and the Historical Process.* Baltimore: Johns Hopkins University Press, 1940.

Allen, Don Cameron. "The Descent to Light: Basic Metaphor in *Paradise Lost*."

In *The Harmonious Vision: Studies in Milton's Poetry*, pp. 122–42. Enlarged edition. Baltimore: Johns Hopkins University Press, 1970.

_____. *Mysteriously Meant: The Rediscovery of Pagan Symbolism and Allegorical Interpretation in the Renaissance*. Baltimore: Johns Hopkins University Press, 1970.

Altizer, Thomas J. *Mircea Eliade and the Dialectic of the Sacred*. Philadelphia: Westminster Press, 1963.

Arndt, W. F., and Gingrich, F. W., eds. *A Greek-English Lexicon of the New Testament and Other Early Christian Literature*. Chicago: University of Chicago Press, 1957.

Askwith, Edward H. *The Christian Conception of Holiness*. London: Macmillan and Co., 1900.

Atwater, Edward E. *History and Significance of the Sacred Tabernacle*. New York: Dodd, Mead, 1876.

Bailey, Cyril. *Religion in Virgil*. Oxford: Clarendon Press, 1935.

Bailey, Margaret L. *Milton and Jacob Boehme*. New York: Haskell House, 1964.

Bainton, Roland H. *Christian Attitudes toward War and Peace*. Nashville: Abingdon Press, 1960.

_____. "Congregationalism: From the Just War to the Crusades in the Puritan Revolution." *Andover Newton Theological School Bulletin* 35 (1943): 1–20.

Baker, Courtland. "Certain Religious Elements in the English Doctrine of the Inspired Poet During the Renaissance." *ELH* 6 (1939): 300–23.

Barker, Arthur E. *Milton and the Puritan Dilemma, 1641–1660*. Toronto: University of Toronto Press, 1942.

Barnes, Albert. *Notes, Explanatory and Practical, on the Epistle to the Hebrews*. London: George Routledge, 1854.

Bartsch, Hartmut. *Probleme der Entsakralisierung*. Munich: Kaiser Verlag, 1970.

Bennett, Joan S. "God, Satan, and King Charles: Milton's Royal Portraits." *PMLA* 92 (1977): 441–57.

Berry, Boyd. *Process of Speech: Puritan Religious Writings and "Paradise Lost."* Baltimore: Johns Hopkins University Press, 1976.

Blau, Joseph L. *The Christian Interpretation of the Cabala in the Renaissance*. New York: Columbia University Press, 1944.

Bloom, Harold. *Poetry and Repression: Revisionism from Blake to Stevens*. New Haven: Yale University Press, 1976.

_____. *Shelley's Mythmaking*. New Haven: Yale University Press, 1959.

Bogler, Theodor. *Das Sakrale im Widerspruch*. Maria Laach, Ger.: Ars Liturgica Verlag, 1967.

Bogliani, Franco. *Il concetto di sacro nella storia delle religioni*. Torino: G. Giappichelli, 1972.

Boswell, Jackson. *Milton's Library*. New York: Garland, 1975.

Bousset, Wilhelm. *Kyrios Christos*. Translated by John E. Steely. Nashville and New York: Abingdon Press, 1970.

Breasted, James Henry. *The Dawn of Conscience*. New York: Charles Scribner's Sons, 1935.

————. *Development of Religion and Thought in Ancient Egypt*. New York: Harper and Brothers, 1959.

Brisman, Leslie. *Milton's Poetry of Choice and Its Romantic Heirs*. Ithaca: Cornell University Press, 1973.

Brown, Charles E. *The Meaning of Sanctification*. Anderson, Ind.: Warner Press, 1945.

Brown, Francis, and others, eds. *A Hebrew and English Lexicon of the Old Testament*. Oxford: Clarendon Press, 1907.

Buckley, Vincent. *Poetry and the Sacred*. London: Chatto and Windus, 1968.

Burden, Dennis H. *The Logical Epic: A Study of the Argument of "Paradise Lost."* London: Routledge and Kegan Paul, 1967.

Butterworth, E. A. S. *The Tree at the Navel of the Earth*. Berlin: Walter de Gruyter, 1970.

Buttrick, George, A., ed. *The Interpreter's Bible*. 12 vols. New York: Abingdon Press, 1953.

Campbell, Lily B. "The Christian Muse." In *Collected Papers of Lily B. Campbell*. New York: Russell and Russell, 1968, pp. 237–78. Reprinted from *Huntington Library Quarterly* 8 (1935): 29–70.

————. *Divine Poetry and Drama in Sixteenth-Century England*. Berkeley and Los Angeles: University of California Press, 1959.

Capp, B. S. *The Fifth Monarchy Men*. London: Faber and Faber, 1972.

Cassirer, Ernst. *The Philosophy of Symbolic Forms*. Translated by Ralph Manheim. 3 vols. New Haven: Yale University Press, 1955.

Cirillo, Albert. " 'Hail Holy Light' and Divine Time in *Paradise Lost*." *Journal of English and Germanic Philology* 68 (1969): 45–56.

Clements, R. E. *God and Temple*. Oxford: Basil Blackwell, 1965.

Codrington, Robert Henry. *The Melanesians: Studies in Their Anthropology and Folklore*. Oxford: Clarendon Press, 1891.

Cohn, Norma. *The Pursuit of the Millennium*. 2nd ed. New York: Harper and Row, 1961.

Colie, Rosalie L. *Paradoxia Epidemica: The Renaissance Tradition of Paradox*. Princeton: Princeton University Press, 1966.

Cope, Jackson. *The Metaphoric Structure of "Paradise Lost."* Baltimore: Johns Hopkins University Press, 1962.

Cowdrey, H. E. J. "The Genesis of the Crusades: The Springs of Western Ideas of Holy War." In *The Holy War*. Edited by Thomas Murphy, pp. 9–32.

Cross, Frank M., Jr. "The Divine Warrior in Israel's Early Cult." In *Biblical Motifs: Origins and Transformations*. Edited by Alexander Altman, pp. 11–30. Cambridge: Harvard University Press, 1966.

Crump, Galbraith M. *The Mystical Design of "Paradise Lost."* Lewisburg: Bucknell University Press, 1975.

Curry, Walter Clyde. "Milton's Light Exhaling from Darkness: A Study in Symbols." In *Milton's Ontology, Cosmogony, and Physics*, pp. 189–204. Lexington: University of Kentucky Press, 1966.

Curtius, Ernst. *European Literature and the Latin Middle Ages*. Translated by Willard R. Trask. Bollingen Series 36. New York: Bollingen Foundation, 1953.

Davies, Benjamin, ed. *Hebrew and Chaldee Lexikon*. London: Asher and Co., 1885.

_____. *Student's Hebrew Lexicon*. London: Asher and Co., 1885.

Demaray, John G. *Milton's Theatrical Epic: The Invention and Design of "Paradise Lost."* Cambridge: Harvard University Press, 1980.

de Vaux, Roland. *Ancient Israel: Its Life and Institutions*. Translated by John McHugh. New York: McGraw-Hill, 1961.

DeVries, Simon J. "Temporal Terms as Structural Elements in the Holy War Tradition." *Vetus Testamentum* 25 (1975): 80–105.

Diekhoff, John S., ed. *A Masks at Ludlow: Essays on Milton's "Comus."* Cleveland: Case Western Reserve University Press, 1968.

Di Salvo, Jackie. "'The Lord's Battels': *Samson Agonistes* and the Puritan Revolution." *Milton Studies* 4 (1972): 39–62.

Dobbins, Austin. *Milton and the Book of Revelation: The Heavenly Cycle*. Studies in the Humanities No. 7. University: University of Alabama Press, 1975.

Dodd, C. H. *The Interpretation of the Fourth Gospel*. Cambridge: Cambridge University Press, 1965.

Dölger, F. J. *Sol Salutis: Gebet und Gesang im Christlichen Altertum*. Munster: Aschendorff, 1920.

Douglas, Mary. *Purity and Danger: An Analysis of Concepts of Pollution and Taboo*. New York: Frederick A. Praeger, 1966.

Dugmore, C. W. *The Influence of the Synagogue upon the Divine Office*. Westminster: Faith Press, 1964.

Duncan, Joseph. *Milton's Earthly Paradise: A Historical Study of Eden*. Minneapolis: University of Minnesota Press, 1972.

Durkheim, Emile. *Elementary Forms of the Religious Life*. Translated by Joseph Swain. London: George Allen and Unwin, 1915.

Ebrard, John H. A. *Biblical Commentary on the Epistle to the Hebrews*. Edinburgh: T. and T. Clark, 1853.

Eichrodt, Walter. *Ezekiel: A Commentary*. Translated by Cosslett Quin. The Old Testament Library. Philadelphia: Westminster Press, 1970.

Eliade, Mircea. "Experiences of the Mystic Light." In *The Two and the One*. Translated by J. M. Cohen, pp. 19–77. New York: Harper and Row, 1965.

_____. *A History of Religious Ideas*. Translated by Willard Trask. Chicago: University of Chicago Press, 1978.

_____. *Images and Symbols: Studies in Religious Symbolism*. Translated by Philip Mairet. London: Harvill Press, 1961.

_____. *Patterns in Comparative Religion.* Translated by Rosemary Sheed. New York: New American Library, 1958.

_____. *The Sacred and the Profane.* Translated by Willard Trask. New York: Harper and Row, 1959.

_____. *Traité d'histoire des religions.* Paris: Payot, 1949.

The Encyclopedia Britannica. 29 vols. 11th ed. Hugh Chisholm, general editor. Cambridge: Cambridge University Press, 1911.

Evans, John M. *"Paradise Lost" and the Genesis Tradition.* London: Oxford University Press, 1968.

Fallon, Robert. "John Milton and the Honorable Artillery Company." *Milton Quarterly* 9 (1975): 49–51.

_____. "Milton's Military Imagery: Its Growth and Function in His Art." Ph.D. dissertation, Columbia University, 1964.

_____. " 'Th'addition of his Empire': Milton's Epics and England's Relation with the Continent." Unpublished paper delivered at the Milton Tercentenary Conference, University of Wisconsin, Milwaukee, 1974.

Farrer, Austin. *A Rebirth of Images: The Making of St. John's Apocalypse.* Boston: Beacon Press, 1963.

Ferry, Ann Davidson. *Milton's Epic Voice: The Narrator in "Paradise Lost."* Cambridge: Harvard University Press, 1967.

Firth, Sir Charles Harding. *Cromwell's Army: A History of the English Soldier During the Civil Wars, the Commonwealth, and the Protectorate.* London: Methuen, 1902.

Fish, Stanley. "Discovery as Form in *Paradise Lost.*" In *New Essays on "Paradise Lost."* Edited by Thomas Kranidas, pp. 1–14.

_____. "Inaction and Silence: The Reader in *Paradise Regained.*" In *Calm of Mind.* Edited by Joseph A. Wittreich, Jr., pp. 25–47.

_____. *Surprised by Sin: The Reader in "Paradise Lost."* New York: St. Martin's Press, 1967.

Fixler, Michael. "The Apocalypse within *Paradise Lost.*" In *New Essays on "Paradise Lost."* Edited by Thomas Kranidas, pp. 131–78.

_____. *Milton and the Kingdoms of God.* London: Faber and Faber, 1964.

_____. "Milton's Passionate Epic." *Milton Studies* 1 (1969): 167–92.

_____. "The Unclean Meats of the Mosaic Law and the Banquet in *Paradise Regained.*" *Modern Language Notes* 70 (1955): 573–77.

Fletcher, Angus. *The Prophetic Moment: An Essay on Spenser.* Chicago: University of Chicago Press, 1971.

_____. *The Transcendental Masque: An Essay on Milton's "Comus."* Ithaca: Cornell University Press, 1971.

Fletcher, Harris Francis. *Milton's Rabbinical Readings.* Urbana: University of Illinois Press, 1930.

_____. *Milton's Semitic Studies and Some Manifestations of Them in His Poetry.* Chicago: University of Chicago Press, 1926.

Fleure, H. J. "Ritual and Ethic: A Study of a Change in Ancient Religions about

800–500 B.C." *Bulletin of the John Rylands Library* 22 (1938): 435–54.

Fortescue, John. *A History of the British Army.* 8 vols. London: Macmillan and Co., 1889–1917.

Frazer, Sir James. *The Golden Bough: A Study in Magic and Religion.* 12 vols. London: Macmillan and Co., 1913.

———. *Taboo and Perils of the Soul.* 3rd ed. London: Macmillan and Co., 1911.

Freeman, James A. *Milton and the Martial Muse.* Princeton: Princeton University Press, 1980.

Freud, Sigmund. *Totem and Taboo.* Translated by James Strachey. New York: W. W. Norton, 1950.

Frick, Heinrich. *Religiöse Strömungen der Gegenwart: Das Heilige und die Form.* Leipzig: Quelle und Meyer, 1923.

Frye, Northrop. *The Return of Eden: Five Essays on Milton's Epics.* Toronto: University of Toronto Press, 1965.

Frye, Roland M. *Milton's Imagery and the Visual Arts: Iconographic Tradition in the Epic Poems.* Princeton: Princeton University Press, 1978.

Gaster, Theodor. *Myth, Legend, and Custom in the Old Testament.* New York: Harper and Row, 1969.

Giamatti, A. Bartlett. *The Earthly Paradise and the Renaissance Epic.* Princeton: Princeton University Press, 1966.

Girard, René. *La Violence et le sacré.* Paris: Editions Bernard Grasset, 1972.

———. *Violence and the Sacred.* Translated by Patrick Gregory. Baltimore: Johns Hopkins University Press, 1977.

Goodenough, Erwin R. *By Light, Light: The Mystic Gospel of Hellenistic Judaism.* New Haven: Yale University Press, 1935.

———. *Jewish Symbols in the Greco-Roman Period.* 13 vols. Princeton: Princeton University Press, 1968.

Gossman, Ann. "The Use of the Tree of Life in *Paradise Lost.*" *Journal of English and Germanic Philology* 65 (1966): 680–87.

Greene, Thomas M. "Renaissance Warfare: A Metaphor in Conflict." In *The Holy War.* Edited by Thomas P. Murphy, pp. 157–80.

Grossman, Allen. "Milton's Sonnet 'On the late massacre in Piemont': A Note on the Vulnerability of Persons in a Revolutionary Situation." In *Literature in Revolution.* Edited by George Abbott White and Charles Newman, pp. 283–301. New York: Holt, Rinehart and Winston, 1972.

Gunn, Giles. *The Interpretation of Otherness: Literature, Religion, and the American Imagination.* New York: Oxford University Press, 1979.

Haeger, Klaus Albrech. *Das Heilige und der Mythos als Anthropologisches Probleme: Ein Essay.* Bremen: Carl Schuneman, n.d.

Hale, J. R. "Incitement to Violence? English Divines on the Theme of War." In *Florilegium Historiale: Essays presented to Wallace K. Ferguson.* Edited by J. G. Rowe and W. H. Stockdale, pp. 368–99. Toronto: University of Toronto Press, 1971.

Haller, William. *Liberty and Reformation in the Puritan Revolution.* New York: Columbia University Press, 1955.

―――. *The Rise of Puritanism: Or, The Way to the New Jerusalem as Set Forth in Pulpit and Press from Thomas Cartwright to John Lilburne and John Milton, 1570–1643.* New York: Columbia University Press, 1938.

Hanford, James Holly. "Milton and the Art of War." In *John Milton: Poet and Humanist,* pp. 185–223. Cleveland: Case Western Reserve University Press, 1966.

Harding, Davis. *Milton and the Renaissance Ovid.* Urbana: University of Illinois Press, 1946.

Hardison, O. B. *Christian Rite and Christian Drama in the Middle Ages.* Baltimore: Johns Hopkins University Press, 1965.

Hargrove, Barbara. *Reformation of the Holy: A Sociology of Religion.* Philadelphia: F. A. Davis, 1971.

Häring, Bernhard. *Das Heilige und das Gute.* Munich: Erich Wewel Verlag, 1950.

Harrison, Jane. *Epilegomena to the Study of the Greek Religion.* 1921. Reprint. New Hyde Park, N. Y.: University Books, 1962.

―――. *Prolegomena to the Study of Greek Religion.* 1908. Reprint. New York: Meridean Books, 1955.

Hartman, Geoffrey. "Milton's Counterplot." In *Milton: A Collection of Critical Essays.* Edited by Louis Martz, pp. 100–108. Englewood Cliffs, N.J.: Prentice-Hall, 1966.

Hastings, James, and others, eds. *A Dictionary of the Bible.* 5 vols. Charles Scribner's Sons, 1899–1904.

―――. *Encyclopaedia of Religion and Ethics.* 13 vols. New York: Charles Scribner's Sons, 1914.

Heinrich, Frick. *Religiöse Strömungen der Gegenwart: Das Heilige und die Form.* Leipzig: Quelle und Meyer, 1923.

Heninger, S. K., Jr. *The Cosmographical Glass: Renaissance Diagrams of the Universe.* San Marino, Cal.: Huntington Library, 1977.

―――. "Sidney and Milton: The Poet as Maker." In *Milton and the Line of Vision.* Edited by Joseph A. Wittreich, Jr., pp. 57–95.

―――. *Touches of Sweet Harmony: Pythagorean Cosmology and Renaissance Poetics.* San Marino, Cal.: Huntington Library, 1974.

Hill, Christopher. *Antichrist in Seventeenth-Century England.* London: Oxford University Press, 1971.

―――. *Milton and the English Revolution.* New York: Viking Press, 1977.

Hill, John Spencer. *John Milton, Poet, Prophet, Priest: A Study of Divine Vocation in Milton's Poetry.* Totowa, N.J.: Rowman and Littlefield, 1979.

Hirn, Yrjö. *The Sacred Shrine: A Study of the Poetry and Art of the Catholic Church.* Boston: Beacon Press, 1957.

Hohler, August E. *Das Heilige in der Dichtung: Klopstock / Der junge Goethe.* Zurich: Atlantis Verlag, 1954.

Hollis, F. J. "The Sun-Cult and the Temple at Jerusalem." In *Myth and Ritual:*

Essays on the Myth and Ritual of the Hebrews in Relation to the Culture Pattern of the Ancient East. Edited by Samuel Hooke, pp. 90–104. London: Oxford University Press, 1933.

Hooke, Samuel. *Middle Eastern Mythology.* Baltimore: Penguin Books, 1963.

Hoyle, James. "'If Sion Hill Delight Thee More': The Muse's Choice in *Paradise Lost.*" *English Language Notes* 12 (1972): 20–26.

Hughes, Merritt Y. "Milton and the Symbol of Light," pp. 63–103; "Milton's Celestial Battle and the Theogonies," pp. 196–219. In *Ten Perspectives on Milton.* New Haven: Yale University Press, 1965.

———. "Milton's *Eikon Basilike.*" In *Calm of Mind.* Edited by Joseph A. Wittreich, Jr., pp. 1–24.

———. "Myself Am Hell." *Modern Philology* 54 (1956): 80–94.

Huizinga, John. *Homo Ludens: A Study of the Play-Element in Culture.* 1944. Reprint. Boston: Beacon Press, 1955.

Hunter, William B., Jr. "Holy Light in *Paradise Lost.*" *Rice Institute Pamphlets* 46 (1960): 1–14.

———. "Milton on the Exaltation of the Son: The War in Heaven in *Paradise Lost.*" *ELH* 26 (1969): 215–31; "The Meaning of 'Holy Light' in *Paradise Lost* III." *Modern Language Notes* 74 (1959): 589–92; "Milton's Urania." *Studies in English Literature, 1500–1900* 4 (1964): 35–42. Reprinted in *Bright Essence.* Edited by William B. Hunter, Jr., and others, pp. 115–30, 149–56.

Hunter, William B., Jr., and others, eds. *Bright Essence: Studies in Milton's Theology.* Salt Lake City: University of Utah Press, 1971.

Huntley, John F. "The Images of Poet and Poetry in Milton's *The Reason of Church-Government.*" In *Achievements of the Left Hand.* Edited by Michael Lieb and John T. Shawcross, pp. 83–120.

Hyres, M. Conrad. "The Comic Profanation of the Sacred." In *Holy Laughter: Essays on Religion in the Comic Perspective.* Edited by M. Conrad Hyers, pp. 9–27. New York: Seabury Press, 1969.

Jackson, Samuel Macauley, gen. ed. *The New Schaff-Herzog Encyclopedia of Religious Knowledge.* 12 vols. New York: Funk and Wagnalls, 1911.

Jacobus, Melancthon W., and others, eds. *A Standard Bible Dictionary.* New York: Funk and Wagnalls, 1909.

Jammer, Max. *Concepts of Space: The History of Theories of Space in Physics.* 2nd ed. Cambridge: Harvard University Press, 1969.

Janzen, Waldeman. "War in the Old Testament." *Mennonite Quarterly Review* 46 (1972): 155–66.

Johnson, Aubrey R. *The Cultic Prophet in Ancient Israel.* Cardiff: University of Wales Press, 1944.

Julian, John, ed. *A Dictionary of Hymnology.* London: John Murray, 1907.

Jung, Carl Gustav. *Archetypes and the Collective Unconscious,* vol. 9; *Psychology and Alchemy,* vol. 12. In *The Collected Works of C. G. Jung.* Edited by Sir Herbert Read and others and translated by R. F. C. Hull.

20 vols. Bollingen Series 20. New York: Pantheon Books, 1953–79.

Kelley, Maurice. "Milton and the Notes on Paul Best." *Library* 5 (1950): 49–51.

———. *"This Great Argument": A Study of Milton's "De doctrina Christiana" as a Gloss upon "Paradise Lost."* Princeton: Princeton University Press, 1941.

Kerényi, Károly. *The Religion of the Greeks and Romans.* Translated by Christopher Holme. New York: E. P. Dutton, 1962.

Kerrigan, William. *The Prophetic Milton.* Charlottesville: University Press of Virginia, 1974.

Knight, G. Wilson. *Chariot of Wrath: The Message of John Milton to Democracy at War.* 1942. Reprint. Folcroft, Pa.: Folcroft Press, 1969.

Knott, John R., Jr. *Milton's Pastoral Vision.* Chicago: University of Chicago Press, 1971.

Koehler, G. Stanley. "Milton and the Art of Landscape." *Milton Studies* 8 (1975): 3–40.

Koyré, Alexander. *From the Closed World to the Infinite Universe.* Baltimore: Johns Hopkins University Press, 1957.

Kramer, Samuel Noah. *History Begins at Sumer.* 1956. Reprint. Garden City, N.Y.: Doubleday, 1959.

Kranidas, Thomas, ed. *New Essays on "Paradise Lost."* Berkeley and Los Angeles: University of California Press, 1969.

Labriola, Albert. "The Aesthetics of Self-Diminution: Christian Iconography and *Paradise Lost.*" In *"Eyes Fast Fixt."* Edited by Albert Labriola and Michael Lieb, pp. 267–311.

———. "Divine Urgency as a Motive for Conduct in *Samson Agonistes.*" *Philological Quarterly* 50 (1971): 99–107.

———. "The Titans and the Giants: *Paradise Lost* and the Tradition of the Renaissance Ovid." *Milton Quarterly* 12 (1978): 9–16.

Labriola, Albert, and Lieb, Michael, eds. *"Eyes Fast Fixt": Current Perspectives in Milton Methodology.* Milton Studies series, vol. 7. Pittsburgh: University of Pittsburgh Press, 1975.

Landman, Isaac, and others, eds. *The Universal Jewish Encyclopedia.* 10 vols. New York: Universal Jewish Encyclopedia, 1943.

Lang, Andrew. *Magic and Religion.* New York: Greenwood Press, 1901.

Langdon, Ida. *Milton's Theory of Poetry and Fine Art.* New Haven: Yale University Press, 1924.

Lévi-Strauss, Claude. *The Savage Mind.* Chicago: University of Chicago Press, 1966.

Lévy-Bruhl, Lucien. *How Natives Think.* Translated by Lilian A. Clare. London: George Allen and Unwin, 1926.

———. *Primitive Mentality.* Translated by Lilian A. Clare. New York: Macmillan Co., 1923.

Lewalski, Barbara K. *Milton's Brief Epic: The Genre, Meaning, and Art of "Paradise Regained."* Providence: Brown University Press, 1966.

_____. *Protestant Poetics and the Seventeenth-Century Religious Lyric.*
Princeton: Princeton University Press, 1979.

_____. "*Samson Agonistes* and the 'Tragedy' of the Apocalypse." *PMLA* 5
(1970): 1050–62.

Lewis, Charlton T., and Short, Charles. *A Latin Dictionary.* Oxford: Clarendon
Press, 1879.

Lewis, C. S. *A Preface to "Paradise Lost."* Oxford: Oxford University Press,
1942.

Liddell, Henry, and Scott, Robert, eds. *A Greek-English Lexicon: A Supplement.*
Oxford: Clarendon Press, 1968.

Lieb, Michael. *The Dialectics of Creation: Patterns of Birth and Regeneration in
"Paradise Lost."* Amherst: University of Massachusetts Press, 1970.

_____. "Further Thoughts on Satan's Journey through Chaos." *Milton Quarterly* 12 (1978): 126–33.

_____. " 'Holy Name': A Reading of *Paradise Lost.*" *Harvard Theological
Review* 67 (1974): 321–39.

_____. " 'Holy Place': A Reading of *Paradise Lost.*" *Studies in English Literature, 1500–1900* 17 (1977): 129–47.

_____. " 'Holy Rest': A Reading of *Paradise Lost.*" *ELH* 30 (1972): 238–53.

_____. "Milton and the Kenotic Christology: Its Literary Bearing." *ELH* 37
(1970): 342–60.

_____. "*Paradise Lost* and the Myth of Prohibition." In "*Eyes Fast Fixt.*"
Edited by Albert Labriola and Michael Lieb, pp. 233–65.

Lieb, Michael, and Shawcross, John T., eds. *Achievements of the Left Hand:
Essays on the Prose of John Milton.* Amherst: University of Massachusetts
Press, 1974.

Lind, Millard. "Paradigm of Holy War in the Old Testament." *Biblical Research*
16 (1971): 16–31.

Liverziani, Filippo. *Esperienza del Sacro e Filosofia.* Rome: Edizioni Liber, 1970.

Low, Anthony. "The Image of the Tower in *Paradise Lost.*" *Studies in English
Literature, 1500–1900* 10 (1970): 170–78.

MacCaffrey, Isabel. "*Paradise Lost" as "Myth.*" Cambridge: Harvard University
Press, 1959.

McDonald, William J., gen. ed. *New Catholic Encyclopedia.* 16 vols. New York:
McGraw-Hill, 1967.

Madsen, William G. *From Shadowy Types to Truth: Studies in Milton's Symbolism.* New Haven: Yale University Press, 1968.

Main, John. *Religious Chastity: An Ethnological Study.* New York: n.p., 1913.

Maison, Jacques Grand. *Die Welt und das Heilige.* Salzburg: Otto Müller Verlag,
1970.

Martin, Émile, and Antoine, Pierre. *La Querelle du sacré.* Paris:Beauchesne,
1970.

Martz, Louis L. *The Paradise Within: Studies in Vaughan, Traherne, and Milton.*
New Haven: Yale University Press, 1964.

_____. *Poet of Exile: A Study of Milton's Poetry*. New Haven: Yale University Press, 1980.

_____. *The Poetry of Meditation: A Study of English Religious Literature of the Seventeenth Century*. New Haven: Yale University Press, 1964.

Mazzeo, Joseph. "Dante's Sun Symbolism and the Visions of the Blessed." In *Structure and Thought in the "Paradise,"* pp. 141–66. Ithaca: Cornell University Press, 1958.

_____. "The Light-Metaphysics Tradition," pp. 56–90. "Light-Metaphysics in the Works of Dante," pp. 91–132. In *Medieval Cultural Tradition in Dante's "Comedy."* Ithaca: Cornell University Press, 1968.

Meek, Theophile James. *Hebrew Origins*. The Haskell Lectures for 1933–34, the Graduate School of Theology, Oberlin College. New York: Harper and Brothers, 1936.

Miller, Patrick. *The Divine Warrior in Early Israel*. Cambridge: Harvard University Press, 1973.

_____. "God the Warrior: A Problem in Biblical Interpretation and Apologetics." *Interpretation* 19 (1965): 39–46.

Mohl, Ruth. *John Milton and His Commonplace Book*. New York: Frederick Ungar, 1969.

Mollenkott, Virginia. "Milton and the Apocrypha." Ph.D. dissertation, New York University, 1964.

Moore, George Foot. "Notes on the Name יהוה" Vol. 1, pp. 143–64, of *Old Testament and Semitic Studies*. Edited by Robert Francis Harper. 2 vols. Chicago: University of Chicago Press, 1908.

Moulinier, Louis. *Le Pur et l'impur dans la pensée des Grecs d'Homére a Aristote*. Paris: Librairie C. Klincksiecke, 1952.

Murphy, Thomas P., ed. *The Holy War*. Fifth Conference on Medieval and Renaissance Studies. Columbus: Ohio State University Press, 1976.

Murrin, Michael. *The Allegorical Epic: Essays in Its Rise and Decline*. Chicago: University of Chicago Press, 1980.

_____. *The Veil of Allegory: Some Notes towards a Theory of Allegorical Rhetoric in the English Renaissance*. Chicago: University of Chicago Press, 1969.

Nicolson, Marjorie H. *The Breaking of the Circle: Studies in the Effect of the New Science upon Seventeenth-Century Poetry*. Evanston: Northwestern University Press, 1950.

_____. *Mountain Gloom and Mountain Glory: The Development of the Aesthetics of the Infinite*. Ithaca: Cornell University Press, 1963.

_____. *Newton Demands the Muse: Newton's "Opticks" and the Eighteenth-Century Poets*. Princeton: Princeton University Press, 1946.

Nilsson, Martin P. *A History of Greek Religion*. Translated by F. J. Fielden. Oxford: Clarendon Press, 1949.

Norford, Don Parry. "The Sacred Head: Milton's Solar Mysticism." *Milton Studies* 9 (1976): 37–75.

O'Brien, Gordon. *Renaissance Poetics and the Problem of Power*. Chicago: University of Chicago Press, 1956.

Otto, Rudolf. *Das Heilige: Über das Irrationale und der Idee des Götlichen und Sein Verhältnis zum Rationalen*. Breslau: Trewendt and Granier, 1922.

———. *The Idea of the Holy: An Inquiry into the Non-Rational Factor in the Idea of the Divine and Its Relation to the Rational*. Translated by John W. Harvey. London: Oxford University Press, 1923.

———. "The Lord's Supper as a Numinous Fact." In *Religious Essays: A Supplement to "The Idea of the Holy."* Translated by Brian Lunn. Oxford: Oxford University Press, 1931.

Palmer, L. R. *The Interpretation of Mycenaean Greek Texts*. Oxford: Clarendon Press, 1963.

Parker, William Riley. *Milton: A Biography*. 2 vols. Oxford: Clarendon Press, 1968.

Paton, Lewis Bayles. "Early Hebrew Ethics," pp. 157–98; "Ethics of the Hebrew Prophets," pp. 199–220. In *The Evolution of Ethics as Revealed in the Great Religions*. Edited by E. Hershey Sneath. New Haven: Yale University Press, 1927.

Patrides, C. A. *Milton and the Christian Tradition*. Oxford: Clarendon Press, 1966.

Paz, Octavio. *The Bow and the Lyre*. Translated by Ruth L. C. Simms. Austin: University of Texas Press, 1956.

Peet, Stephen. "Altars and High Places among the Emblematic Mounds." Abstracted in *Proceedings of the American Association for the Advancement of Science*, pp. 404–16. Salem, Mass.: n.p., 1884.

Pelikan, Jaroslav. *The Light of the World: A Basic Image in Early Christian Thought*. New York: Harper Brothers, 1962.

Pettet, E. C. *Of Paradise and Light: A Study of Vaughan's "Silex Scintillans."* Cambridge: Cambridge University Press, 1960.

Philpot, J. E. *The Sacred Tree or the Tree in Religion and Myth*. New York: Macmillan Co., 1897.

Porteous, N. W. "Jerusalem-Zion: The Growth of a Symbol." In *Verbannung und Heinkehr*. Edited by A. Kuschke, pp. 235–52. Tübingen: J. C. B. Mohr, 1961.

Poulet, Georges. *Metamorphoses of the Circle*. Translated by Carley Dawson and Elliott Coleman. Baltimore: Johns Hopkins University Press, 1961.

Radzinowicz, Mary Ann. *Toward "Samson Agonistes": The Growth of Milton's Mind*. Princeton: Princeton University Press, 1978.

Rankin, Oliver Shaw. *The Origins of the Festival of Hanukkah*. Edinburgh: T. and T. Clark, 1930.

Revard, Stella. "Milton's Gunpowder Poems and Satan's Conspiracy." *Milton Studies* 4 (1972): 63–78.

———. *The War in Heaven in "Paradise Lost."* Ithaca: Cornell University Press, 1980.

————. "The Warring Saints and the Dragon: A Commentary upon Revelation 12:7–9 and Milton's War in Heaven." *Philological Quarterly* 53 (1974): 181–94.

Riggs, William. *The Christian Poet in "Paradise Lost."* Berkeley and Los Angeles: University of California Press, 1972.

Robins, Harry F. *If This Be Heresy: A Study of Milton and Origen.* Urbana: University of Illinois Press, 1963.

————. "Satan's Journey: Direction in *Paradise Lost.*" In *Milton Studies in Honor of Harris Francis Fletcher.* Edited by G. Blakemore Evans and others, pp. 91–103. Urbana: University of Illinois Press, 1961.

Ronchi, Vasco. *The Nature of Light.* Translated by V. Barocas. Cambridge: Harvard University Press, 1970.

Rose, Herbert Jennings. *Ancient Roman Religion.* London: Hutchinson's University Library, 1948.

Rosenblatt, Jason. "Adam's Pisgah Vision: *Paradise Lost*, Books XI and XII." *ELH* 39 (1972): 66–86.

————. " 'Audacious Neighborhood': Idolatry in *Paradise Lost*, Book I." *Philological Quarterly* 54 (1975): 553–68.

————. "The Mosaic Voice in *Paradise Lost.*" In *"Eyes Fast Fixt."* Edited by Albert Labriola and Michael Lieb, pp. 207–32.

————. "Structural Unity and Temporal Concordance: The War in Heaven in *Paradise Lost.*" *PMLA* 87 (1972): 31–41.

Ross, Malcolm M. *Poetry and Dogma: The Transfiguration of Eucharistic Symbols in Seventeenth-Century English Poetry.* New Brunswick: Rutgers University Press, 1954.

Roston, Murray. *Milton and the Baroque.* Pittsburgh: University of Pittsburgh Press, 1980.

Russell, Frederick. *The Just War in the Middle Ages.* Cambridge: Cambridge University Press, 1975.

Ryken, Leland. *The Apocalyptic Vision in "Paradise Lost."* Ithaca: Cornell University Press, 1970.

St. George, Priscilla P. "Psychomachia in Books V and VI of *Paradise Lost.*" *Modern Language Quarterly* 27 (1966): 185–96.

Sampson, Francis. *A Critical Commentary on the Epistle to the Hebrews.* New York: Robert Carter and Brothers, 1850.

Samuel, Irene. *Dante and Milton.* Ithaca: Cornell University Press, 1966.

————. *Plato and Milton.* Ithaca: Cornell University Press, 1947.

Saurat, Denis. *Milton, Man and Thinker.* New York: Dial Press, 1925.

Schaeffler, Richard. *Religion und kritisches Bewusstsein.* Freiburg: K. Alber, 1973.

Scholem, Gershom. *Jewish Gnosticism, Merkabah Mysticism, and Talmudic Tradition.* New York: Jewish Theological Seminary of America, 1965.

————. *Major Trends in Jewish Mysticism.* 1941. Reprint. New York: Schocken Books, 1954.

Schroder, Wilhelm Julius. *The Book of the Prophet Ezekiel*. Translated by Patrick Fairbairn. New York: Charles Scribner's Sons, n.d.

Scott, Nathan A., Jr. *The Wild Prayer of Longing: Poetry and the Sacred*. New Haven: Yale University Press, 1971.

Secret, François. *Les Kabbalistes chrétiens de la renaissance*. Paris: Dunad, 1964.

Shawcross, John T. "*Paradise Lost* and the Theme of Exodus." *Milton Studies* 2 (1970): 3–26.

Shumaker, Wayne. *Unpremeditated Verse: Feeling and Perception in "Paradise Lost."* Princeton: Princeton University Press, 1967.

Sieveking, Albert Forbes. *The Praise of Gardens: An Epitome of the Literature of the Garden-Art*. London: J. M. Dent, 1899.

Singer, Isidore, gen. ed. *The Jewish Encyclopedia*. 12 vols. 1916. Reprint. New York: Funk and Wagnalls, 1925.

Skeat, Walter. *An Etymological Dictionary of the English Language*. Oxford: Clarendon Press, 1879–1882.

Smith, W. Robertson. *Lectures on the Religion of the Semites*. New York: Appleton, 1889.

Solt, Leo. *Saints in Arms: Puritanism and Democracy in Cromwell's Army*. Stanford: Stanford University Press, 1959.

Spence, H. D. M., and Exell, Joseph S. *The Book of the Prophet Ezekiel*. Vols. 26 and 27 of *The Pulpit Commentary*. 49 vols. London: Kegan Paul, 1882–96.

Splett, Jörg. *Die Rede vom Heiligen*. Freiburg: K. Alber, n.d.

Sprunger, Keith L. *The Learned Doctor William Ames: Dutch Backgrounds of English and American Puritanism*. Urbana: University of Illinois Press, 1972.

Steadman, John M. "The Devil and Pharoah's Chivalry." *Modern Language Notes* 75 (1960): 197–201.

_____. *Milton and the Renaissance Hero*. Oxford: Clarendon Press, 1967.

_____. *Milton's Epic Characters: Image and Idol*. Chapel Hill: University of North Carolina Press, 1968.

_____. "The 'Tree of Life' Symbolism in *Paradise Regained*." *Review of English Studies* n.s. 11 (1960): 384–91. Reprinted in *Milton's Epic Characters*, pp. 82–89.

Stearns, Raymond P. *Congregationalism in the Dutch Netherlands: The Rise and Fall of the English Congregational Classis, 1621–1635*. Chicago: American Society of Church History, 1940.

Stein, Arnold. *Answerable Style: Essays on "Paradise Lost."* Minneapolis: University of Minnesota Press, 1953. Reprint. Seattle: University of Washington Press, 1967.

Stewart, Stanley. *The Enclosed Garden: The Tradition and the Image in Seventeenth-Century Poetry*. Madison: University of Wisconsin Press, 1966.

Stroup, Thomas B. *Religious Rite and Ceremony in Milton's Poetry*. Lexington: University of Kentucky Press, 1968.

Stuart, Moses. *A Commentary on the Epistle to the Hebrews*. London: John Mill, 1828.

Summers, Joseph. *The Muse's Method: An Introduction to "Paradise Lost."* Cambridge: Harvard University Press, 1962.

Svendsen, Kester. *Milton and Science*. Cambridge: Harvard University Press, 1956.

Szittya, Brenda B. " 'If Art Could Tell': Negative Theology in *Paradise Lost*." Ph.D. dissertation, University of Virginia, 1972.

Tayler, Edward. *Milton's Poetry: Its Development in Time*. Pittsburgh: Duquesne University Press, 1980.

Teilhard de Chardin, Pierre. *The Divine Milieu: An Essay on the Interior Life*. New York: Harper and Row, 1965.

Tennant, F. R. *The Sources of the Doctrine of the Fall and Original Sin*. New York: Schocken Books, 1968.

Terry, Milton S., and Newhall, Fales H. *Genesis and Exodus*. Vol. 1 of *Commentary on the Old Testament*. Edited by Daniel D. Whedon. 8 vols. New York: Hunt and Eaton, 1889.

Thomas, Northcote Whitridge. "Taboo." Vol. 27, pp. 337–41, of *The Encyclopedia Britannica*. 29 vols. 11th edition. Cambridge: Cambridge University Press, 1911.

Trench, Richard. *Synonyms of the New Testament*. 2 vols. New York: Charles Scribner and Co., 1866.

Tuveson, Ernest Lee. *Millennium and Utopia: A Study in the Background of the Idea of Progress*. Berkeley and Los Angeles: University of California Press, 1949.

Tylor, Edward. *Primitive Culture: Researches into the Development of Mythology, Philosophy, Religion, Language, Art, and Custom*. 7th ed. New York: Brentano's Publishers, 1924.

Underhill, Evelyn. *Mysticism: A Study in the Nature and Development of Man's Spiritual Consciousness*. 1910. Reprint. Cleveland and New York: Meridian Books, 1965.

van der Leeuw, Gerardus. *Religion in Essence and Manifestation*. Translated by J. E. Turner. London: George Allen and Unwin, 1938.

von Rad, Gerhard. *Der Heilige Krieg im Alten Israel*. Gottingen: Vandenhock and Ruprecht, 1958.

Waddington, Raymond. "The Death of Adam: Vision and Voice in Books XI and XII of *Paradise Lost*." *Modern Philology* 70 (1972): 9–21.

Wales, Horace G. Quaritch. *The Mountain of God*. London: Bernard Quaritch, 1953.

Walker, D. P. *Spiritual and Demonic Magic from Ficino to Campanella*. London: Warburg Institute, 1958.

Walzer, Michael. "Exodus 32 and the Theory of Holy War: The History of a Citation." *Harvard Theological Review* 61 (1968): 1–14.

————. *Just and Unjust Wars: A Moral Argument with Historical Illustrations*. New York: Basic Books, 1977.

_____. *The Revolution of the Saints: A Study in the Origins of Radical Politics*. Cambridge: Harvard University Press, 1965.

Webb, Eugene. *The Dark Dove: The Sacred and Secular in Modern Literature*. Seattle: University of Washington Press, 1975.

Webster, Hutton. *Rest Days: A Study in Early Law and Morality*. New York: Macmillan Co., 1916.

Wedgwood, C. V. *Poetry and Politics under the Stuarts*. Ann Arbor: University of Michigan Press, 1964.

West, Robert H. *Milton and the Angels*. Athens: University of Georgia Press, 1955.

Westermarck, Edward. *The Origin and Development of the Moral Ideas*. 2 vols. New York: Macmillan Co., 1906.

Wheelwright, Philip. "Notes on Mythopoeia." *Sewanee Review* 59 (1951): 574–92.

Whiting, George Wesley. *Milton and This Pendant World*. Austin: University of Texas Press, 1958.

Wilkenfeld, Roger B. "The Seat at the Center: An Interpretation of *Comus*." In *Critical Essays on Milton from "ELH,"* pp. 123–50. Baltimore: Johns Hopkins University Press, 1969.

Willey, Basil. *The Seventeenth-Century Background*. Garden City, N.Y.: Doubleday, 1953.

Wilson, John A. *The Culture of Ancient Egypt*. Chicago: University of Chicago Press, 1951.

Wind, Edgar. *Pagan Mysteries in the Renaissance*. 2nd ed. New York: Norton, 1968.

Wittreich, Joseph A., Jr. *Angel of Apocalypse: Blake's Idea of Milton*. Madison: University of Wisconsin Press, 1975.

_____. "'The Crown of Eloquence': The Figure of the Orator in Milton's Works." In *Achievements of the Left Hand*. Edited by Michael Lieb and John T. Shawcross, pp. 3–54.

_____. "'A Poet Amongst Poets': Milton and the Tradition of Prophecy." In *Milton and the Line of Vision*. Edited by Joseph A. Wittreich, Jr., pp. 97–142.

_____. *Visionary Poetics: Milton's Tradition and His Legacy*. San Marino, Cal.: Huntington Library, 1979.

_____, ed. *Calm of Mind: Tercentenary Essays on "Paradise Regained" and "Samson Agonistes" in Honor of John S. Diekhoff*. Cleveland: Case Western Reserve University Press, 1971.

_____. *Milton and the Line of Vision*. Madison: University of Wisconsin Press, 1975.

Wolfe, Don M. *Milton and the Puritan Revolution*. 1941. Reprint. New York: Humanities Press, 1963.

Woodhouse, A. S. P. "The Argument of Milton's *Comus*." *University of Toronto Quarterly* 11 (1941): 46–71. Reprinted in *A Maske at Ludlow: Essays on*

Milton's "Comus." Edited by John S. Diekhoff, pp. 17–42. Cleveland: Case Western Reserve University Press, 1968.

Wundt, Wilhelm. *Elements of Folk Psychology.* Translated by Edward Leroy Schaub. London: George Allen and Unwin, 1916.

Yarden, Leon. *The Tree of Light: A Study of the Menorah, the Seven-Branched Lampstand.* Ithaca: Cornell University Press, 1971.

Yates, Frances. *Giordano Bruno and the Hermetic Tradition.* Chicago: University of Chicago Press, 1964.

Index

Aaron, 55
Abdiel, 280, 290
Abelson, Joshua, 367 (n. 13)
Aboth of Rabbi Nathan, 98, 113
Adams, Robert P., 378 (n. 76)
Adams, Thomas, 130, 131, 255, 274, 365 (n. 87), 366–67 (n. 8)
Adamson, J. H., 203, 297, 356 (n. 2)
Adapa, 91, 344 (n. 7)
Adolphus, Gustavus, 377 (n. 5)
Adoration, 32, 34
Adrichomius, Christianus, 160, 223, 350 (n. 23), 353 (n. 33), 354 (n. 51)
Aelianus Tacitus, 380 (n. 112)
Aeneas, 12, 14
Agrippa of Nettersheim, 364 (n. 79)
Ainsworth, Henry, 29, 30, 168, 169, 176, 182, 350 (n. 23), 353 (n. 33), 354 (n. 63)
Albright, William, 179, 371 (n. 58)
Allen, Don Cameron, 345 (n. 28), 356 (n. 1), 379 (n. 85)
Allestree, Richard, 339–40 (n. 8)
Ames, William, 347 (n. 42)
Apocalypse of Abraham, 244–45, 373–74 (n. 79)
Apostolical Constitutions, 338–39 (n 96)
Aristotle, 8, 10, 80, 334 (n. 41)
Ark of the Covenant, 27, 34, 122, 125, 141, 143, 165, 219, 220, 221, 223, 224, 227, 228, 247, 248, 249, 273, 275, 292, 295, 306, 313, 314, 315, 366 (n. 5). *See also* Holy of Holies

Army, 257, 259, 260, 261, 262, 263, 264, 267, 268, 278, 279, 280, 281, 282, 283, 287, 297, 302, 304, 307, 310, 311, 312, 377 (nn. 55, 56), 380 (n. 113). *See also* English Civil Wars; War
Ashe, Simeon, 302
Askwith, Edward H., 21
Athanasius, Saint, 203
Atlantis, 120
Atwater, Edward, 142, 352 (n. 8), 380 (n. 111)
Aubrey, John, 358 (n. 16)
Augustine, Saint, 105, 162, 202, 204, 252, 318, 321, 338–39 (n. 96), 345 (n. 38), 348 (n. 19), 359–60 (n. 30), 361 (n. 55), 386 (n. 18), 387 (n. 33)
Axis Mundi, 140, 153, 154, 155. *See also* Mount

Babington, Gervase, 113
Babylonian Genesis, 344 (n. 7)
Bachelor, Samuel, 256, 260, 281
Bacon, Francis, 254
Bailey, Cyril, 335 (n. 48)
Bailey, Margaret, 46 (n. 79)
Bainton, Roland, 251, 254, 260, 261
Baker, Courtland, 51, 341 (n. 23)
Baptism, 19, 20, 32, 69, 70–72, 84, 201, 202, 241, 321, 337 (n. 90). *See also* Sacraments
Barnes, Albert, 314, 384–85 (n. 13)
Bartholomew of Bologna, 204
Basil, Saint, 360–61 (n. 45)

Baxter, Richard, 27, 28, 29, 260, 318, 323, 339 (n. 7), 366–67 (n. 8), 385 (n. 17)

Bayly, John, 365 (n. 90)

Bede, Venerable, 176

Bennett, Joan S., 381 (n. 118)

Bernard, Richard, 255

Bernard, Saint, 251, 252, 274

Berry, Boyd, 299, 328, 384 (n. 10)

Bible: J document, 90–91, 97, 99, 118; P document, 90–91, 97; versions of, 175. See also New Testament; New Testament Apocrypha; Old Testament; Old Testament Apocrypha; Old Testament Pseudepigrapha

Blake, William, 43, 44

Blau, Sheridan, 369 (n. 37)

Bloom, Harold, 373 (n. 75), 380 (n. 114)

Blount, Charles, 99

Boccaccio, Giovanni, 52

Bompart, Johannes, 102, 345 (n. 30)

Bosman, William, 346 (n. 47)

Boswell, Jackson, 359 (n. 23)

Boundaries: consecration of, 10, 11, 12, 13, 14, 66, 91, 111, 119, 120, 127, 146, 220, 347–48 (n. 13), 351–52 (n. 42); transgression of, 136. See also Mount; Place; Prohibition

Bousett, Wilhelm, 198, 212

Breasted, James, 5, 142

Brisman, Leslie, 357 (n. 7)

Brooks, Thomas, 366–67 (n. 8)

Brown, Charles E., 338 (n. 94)

Buchler, John, 53

Bunyan, John, 303

Burden, Dennis, xviii, 33 (n. 7), 101, 345 (n. 24), 346 (n. 39)

Burnet, Thomas, 99

Burroughs, Jeremiah, 366–67 (n. 8)

Butler, Samuel, 254

Butterworth, E. A. S., 352 (n. 5)

Buxtorf, John, 28, 215, 355 (n. 11)

Cabbala, 220, 223, 244, 369 (n. 37)

Caesar, Julius, 380 (n. 112)

Calvin, Jean, 253, 385 (n. 17)

Candelabrum, 236, 237

Capp, B. S., 376 (n. 42)

Caritas, 38, 39

Caryl, Joseph, 366–67 (n. 8)

Casaubon, Isaac, 23

Cassirer, Ernst, 101, 355 (n. 6)

Center, 66, 81, 120, 125, 126, 128, 129, 130, 132, 133, 140, 141, 143, 144, 152, 159, 220, 223, 240, 295, 323, 348 (nn. 14, 20), 351 (n. 37), 351–52 (n. 42), 382 (n. 125). See also Mount; Place

Certain Queries, 377 (n. 55)

Chariot, 73, 230, 231, 232, 233, 234, 239, 241, 243, 244, 278, 279, 287, 291–97, 307, 309, 373 (nn. 74, 75), 373–74 (n. 79), 381–82 (n. 23). See also Presence; War

Christ, 19, 20, 21, 25, 30, 31, 38, 47, 50, 52, 56, 57, 58, 61, 64, 69, 70, 71, 72, 114, 130, 132, 134, 136, 137, 138, 139, 145, 155, 163, 165, 166, 168, 182, 183, 184, 188, 189, 198, 199, 201, 202, 247, 258, 259, 273, 279, 280, 299, 302, 308, 309, 310, 311, 312, 320, 321, 322, 337 (n. 90), 337–38 (n. 91), 338–39 (n. 96), 354 (n. 51), 361 (n. 55), 366–67 (n. 8)

Christocentrism, 20, 57, 61, 69, 137, 139, 159, 161, 163, 165, 237, 308, 310, 349–50 (n. 21)

Chrysostom, Saint John, 162, 318, 385 (n. 17)

Chumash, 375 (n. 11)

Church, 31, 38, 126, 169

Cicero, 13, 14, 27, 48, 341 (n. 12)

Cirillo, Albert, 177, 203, 356 (n. 1), 362 (n. 61)

Clarendon, Edward Hyde, first earl of, 299

Claudian, 107, 379 (n. 93)

Clement of Alexandria, 50, 51, 52

Clement of Rome, 144

Clements, R. E., 142, 143, 157, 219, 354 (n. 56)

Codrington, Robert Henry, 4, 104, 345 (n. 31)

Cohn, Norman, 251, 252, 375 (n. 24)

Colie, Rosalie, 363 (n. 73)

Confession of Faith, The, 112

Cook, Captain James, 104

Cope, Jackson, 177, 345 (n. 25)

Covenant Theology, 92, 94, 118, 347 (n. 74)

Cowley, Abraham, 257, 370–71 (n. 41)

Cowper, William, 366–67 (n. 8)

Crashaw, Richard, 84, 129, 188

Cratinus, 8

Cromwell, Oliver, 259, 260, 261, 268, 278, 299, 377 (n. 55), 378 (n. 80), 382 (n. 134)

Cross, Frank M., 248, 249

Crump, Galbraith M., 342 (n. 40), 348–49 (n. 20), 382 (n. 125)

Crypsis, 61

Cudworth, Ralph, 217

Culverwell, Nathaniel, 209

Curry, Walter Clyde, 357 (n. 7), 368 (n. 27)

Curtius, Ernst, 350 (n. 26), 357 (n. 7)

Cyprian, Saint, 162

Dante Alighieri, 80, 129, 136, 144, 204, 206, 323, 350 (n. 26), 387 (n. 33)

Day of Jahweh, 248, 263, 291. See also War; Wars of Jahweh

Davies, John, 376 (n. 38)

Death, 99, 100, 107, 108, 111, 136, 216, 305, 306, 387 (n. 37)

de Brosses, Charles, 346 (n. 47)

Declaration . . . of the Army of God, The, 258

Declaration . . . of the Faithful Soldiers, A, 258

de Guevera, Anthony, 160

Dell, William, 260

Demaray, John, 350–51 (n. 28)

Demosthenes, 334 (n. 38)

de Prado, Jeronimo, 292, 293, 314, 315

de Vaux, Roland, 248, 250, 375 (nn. 5, 6)

Dickson, David, 354 (n. 63)

Diogenes Laertius, 10

Dionysius the Areopagite, 173, 204, 206, 357–58 (n. 11)

Di Salvo, Jackie, 299, 379 (n. 83)

Divine Liturgy of James, 338–39 (n. 96)

Dobbins, Austin, 291, 376 (n. 42), 379 (n. 98)

Doctrinal concerns, 26, 27, 33, 40, 46, 64, 96, 97, 113, 118, 179, 180, 208, 328

Dodd, C. H., 199, 220, 359 (n. 29), 360 (n. 38), 371 (n. 42)

Donne, John, 302, 355 (n. 4)

Downame, John, 174, 180, 182

Drexel, Jeremias, 351 (n. 30)

Drogheda, Battle of, 261, 379. See also English Civil Wars; War

Dugmore, C. W., 371 (n. 56)

Duncan, Joseph, 106, 348–49 (n. 20), 349–50 (n. 21)

Duns Scotus, Joannes, 337 (n. 90)

Durkheim, Emile, 4, 104, 105, 115

Ebrard, John, 385 (n. 15)

Eckhart, Meister, 205, 357–58 (n. 11), 362 (n. 70)

Eden, 126, 127, 131, 135, 136, 139, 143, 151, 152, 153, 154, 305, 336 (n. 79), 348–49 (n. 20). See also Paradise

Eichrodt, Walter, 125

Eliade, Mircea, xvii, 3, 4, 120, 133,

140, 195, 331 (n. 2), 349–50 (n. 21), 356 (n. 3), 357 (n. 10), 359 (n. 22), 365–66 (n. 1)
Elton, Richard, 261, 380 (n. 113)
Encampment, 284, 285, 286, 288, 289, 293, 294, 295, 380 (n. 112), 381 (n. 115)
English Civil Wars, 252–68, 270, 280, 281, 287, 290, 299, 302, 377 (n. 55), 377–78 (n. 65), 378 (n. 73). See also Army; Drogheda, Battle of; Naseby, Battle of; Rathmines, Battle of; War
Enki and Ninhursag, 91
Ethnology, 101, 102, 103, 108, 109, 118, 146
Eucharist, 337–38 (n. 91). See also Sacraments
Euclid, 380 (n. 114)
Euripides, 334 (n. 37), 343 (n. 1)
Eusebius, 144
Evans, John M., 90, 97

Fairfax, Sir Thomas, 262, 263, 380 (n. 113)
Fallon, Robert, 259, 267, 383 (n. 149)
Farrer, Austin, 348 (n. 15), 380 (n. 109)
Featley, Daniel, 342 (n. 34)
Ferry, Ann Davidson, 194, 359 (n. 21)
Fetish, 108, 109, 110
Ficino, Marsilio, 207, 342 (n. 37), 364 (n. 77)
Firmament, 239–41. See also Laver; Sea of Glass
Firth, Sir Charles, 260, 261, 299, 377 (n. 56)
Fish, Stanley, 277, 299, 345 (n. 13)
Fixler, Michael, 84, 258–59, 260, 342 (n. 38), 346 (n. 61)
Fleure, H. J., 5, 332 (n. 15)
Fletcher, Angus, 331 (n. 11), 350–51 (n. 28)
Fletcher, Harris Francis, 215, 221, 357–58 (n. 11), 371 (n. 45)

Fludd, Robert, 207, 208, 210, 211
Forbes, Patrick, 372 (n. 62)
Franck, Sebastian, 114
Frazer, Sir James, 116, 351 (n. 23), 355 (n. 6)
Freeman, James A., 379 (n. 89)
Freud, Sigmund, 109, 111, 346 (n. 50)
Fruit, 89, 109, 110, 113, 114, 135, 306, 344. See also Prohibition; Tree
Frye, Northrop, 345 (n. 25)
Frye, Roland M., 210, 353 (n. 43), 373 (n. 75)
Fuller, Thomas, 254

Gale, Theophilus, 345 (nn. 29, 30)
Gaster, Theodor, 91, 357 (n. 15)
Gerson, Rabbi Gary, 346 (n. 57)
Giamatti, A. Bartlett, 350 (n. 22)
Gilgamesh Epic, 344 (n. 7)
Ginza, 360 (n. 41)
Glass, Salomon, 159
Glorification, 40
God, 19, 26, 27, 28, 29, 34, 37, 81, 94, 95, 96, 97, 98, 100, 102, 103, 126, 128, 130, 131, 133, 134, 136, 138, 141, 143, 144, 147, 150, 151, 152, 153, 154, 172, 173, 174, 175, 176, 177, 178, 179, 180, 181, 182, 186, 189, 198, 204, 205, 206, 209, 212, 214, 218, 219, 220, 222, 223, 225, 233, 240, 242, 245, 247, 250, 256, 257, 263, 270, 273, 275, 278, 279, 298, 306, 323, 348–49 (n. 20), 351 (n. 42), 357–58 (n. 11), 358–59 (n. 19), 362–63 (n. 71), 364 (n. 79), 367–68 (n. 14), 368 (n. 19), 369 (n. 39), 370–71 (n. 41), 373–74 (n. 79)
God appearing for the Parliament, 262
Godwyn, Thomas, 353 (n. 33), 380 (n. 111)
Goodenough, Erwin, 144, 220, 236, 237, 372 (n. 61)
Goodwin, John, 379 (n. 84)
Goodwin, Thomas, 258
Gossman, Ann, 349–50 (n. 21)

Gouge, William, 163, 316, 317, 383 (n. 6), 384–85 (n. 13)

Grant, Frederick C., 10, 199

Greene, Thomas M., 253

Greenhill, William, 167

Gregory, John, 130, 201, 215, 366 (n. 5)

Gregory Nazianzen, Saint, 337 (n. 90)

Gregory Thaumaturgus, Saint, 337 (n. 90)

Grimaldi, Francesco, 209

Grossman, Allen, 383 (n. 148)

Grotius, Hugo, 278

Gunn, Giles, xvii

Gunpowder Plot, 258

Hall, Joseph, 26, 27, 28, 209, 351–52 (n. 42)

Haller, William, 260

Hanford, James Holly, 267

Harding, Davis, 353 (n. 46)

Hardison, O. B., 201, 202

Häring, Bernhard, 6

Harrison, Jane, 8

Hartman, Geoffrey, 313

Harvey, Christopher, 84

Hawkins, Henry, 127, 350 (n. 23)

Heaven, 126, 127, 131, 133, 135, 136, 139, 153, 348–49 (n. 20)

Hebrew Book of Enoch, 244, 373–74 (n. 79)

Heidel, Alexander, 344 (n. 7)

Hekhaloth Books, 243, 373–74 (n. 79)

Hell, 127, 136, 139, 155, 159, 160, 326, 350 (n. 26)

Heninger, S. K., 342 (nn. 30, 35), 348–49 (n. 20), 369 (n. 37)

Heraclitus, 10

Herbert, George, 54, 57, 84, 85, 350 (n. 23), 385 (n. 17)

Hermes Trismegistus, 197, 199

Hermeticism, 128, 130, 197, 351 (n. 42)

Herodotus, 8

Hesiod, 7, 152, 379 (n. 93)

Hidden things, 62. See also Holy, the, and secrecy; Holy things; Spiritual things

Hierophant. See Poet, as priest; Priest

Hill, Christopher, 331 (n. 12), 376 (n. 41)

Hippocrates, 9, 334

Hippolytus, 361 (n. 49)

Hirn, Yrjö, 337–38 (n. 91)

Hirsch, Rabbi Samson Raphael, 347 (n. 75)

Hobbes, Thomas, 53, 376 (n. 38)

Holiness, 24, 30, 31, 39, 40, 123, 336 (n. 79), 339 (n. 7). See also Holy, the; Holy things

Hollis, F. J., 219

Holy, the: experience of, xvii, 3, 185; subject of, xvii, 332 (n. 2); historical and literary continuity of, xvii; anteriority of, xviii; and the *ganz andere*, xviii, 3, 4, 19, 67, 98, 314, 328; poetic assimilation of, xviii; as hierophany, xx, 4, 127; and the *mysterium tremendum*, 3, 15; and the notion of God, 3; and the numinous, 3, 11, 12, 19, 26, 64, 65, 66, 67, 214, 224, 245, 313, 350 (n. 26); versus the profane, 3, 15, 16, 68, 69, 72, 73, 79, 80, 125, 131, 262, 271–74, 275, 334, 339, 347–48 (n. 13); and *Religionswissenschaft*, 3; and religious dread, 3; forms of, 4; as moral entity, 4, 5, 6, 7, 9, 10, 12, 13, 14, 16, 17, 18, 19, 20, 28, 29, 30, 36, 37, 38, 332 (n. 15), 334 (nn. 38, 41), 336 (n. 79), 336–37 (n. 82), 339–40 (n. 8); and Egyptian religion, 5, 8; as cultic entity, 6, 7, 8, 9, 10, 11, 12, 13, 14, 15, 16, 17, 20, 24, 26, 28, 31, 32, 33, 48, 49, 51, 53, 54, 66, 68, 73, 74, 75, 76, 77, 103, 108, 109, 113, 118, 138, 141, 143, 151, 155, 158, 159, 161, 218, 219, 220, 221, 223, 224, 233, 234, 236, 240, 248, 275, 276,

292, 333–34 (n. 34), 334 (n. 37), 336 (n. 79), 337 (n. 90), 337–38 (n. 91), 338–39 (n. 96); physicality of, 6, 13, 14, 18, 24, 28; as spiritual entity, 6, 18, 20, 21, 30; and Greek religion, 7, 8, 9, 10; ambivalence of, 8, 9, 12, 13, 16, 66, 67, 89, 111, 115, 116; Greek words for, 8, 19, 333 (nn. 28, 30, 32); as impure, 8, 9, 15, 16, 74, 334 (n. 35); and disease, 9; as pure, 9, 15, 16; and rationalism, 9; and the underworld, 9, 12, 13; and Roman religion, 10, 11, 12, 13, 14; Latin words for, 13; and Judaic religion, 14, 15, 25, 26, 27, 336–37 (n. 82); as Old Testament phenomenon, 14, 20, 25, 27, 31, 36; and the act of separation, 15, 16, 17, 21, 25, 29, 34, 48, 59, 66, 73, 74, 75, 114, 116, 120, 121, 122, 123, 125, 127, 131, 133, 248, 250, 257, 261, 269, 271, 300, 306, 307, 310, 339 (n. 7), 340 (n. 10), 383 (n. 7); as interdicted, 15, 23; Hebrew words for, 15; profanation of, 15, 33, 74, 75, 76, 134, 135, 160, 161; and the *Umwertung aller Werte*, 17, 18, 20; and Christian religion, 18, 19, 20, 21, 22; as New Testament phenomenon, 18, 19, 20, 22, 25; as diaphany, 19; delineation of, 23; as Renaissance phenomenon, 23, 24, 25, 26, 30, 31; universality of, 23; and cultural behavior, 24, 27; knowledge of, 26, 194; Anglican versus Puritan contexts of, 27, 28; and the experience of awe, 27; as visionary experience, 64, 65, 66, 85; and the nature of chastity, 66, 67, 68; and the process of refinement, 67; and secrecy, 74; reclamation of, 75, 76, 77, 79; contagiousness of, 114, 115; etiquette surrounding, 114; as devoted, 115; and the gestures of approach, 120, 122, 133,

135; and the movement from cultic to visionary, 228, 234; as crucial phenomenon, 328, 358 (n. 12). *See also* Holiness; Holy things

Holy of Holies, 122, 123, 125, 126, 128, 133, 138, 139, 143, 144, 218, 219, 223, 228, 283, 313, 314, 315, 336 (n. 79), 337 (n. 90), 348 (n. 14), 351–52 (n. 42), 370–71 (n. 41). *See also* Ark of the Covenant

Holy Spirit, 6, 358–59 (n. 19)

Holy things, 14, 25, 37, 39, 51, 113, 119, 337 (n. 90), 337–38 (n. 91), 338–39 (n. 96), 339 (n. 7). *See also* Hidden things; Spiritual things

Homer, 8, 43, 51, 60, 334 (n. 35)

Homeric Hymns, 359 (n. 26)

Hooke, Samuel, 91

Hooker, Richard, 95, 180

Horace, 13, 14, 48, 63

Hortus Conclusus, 126, 127, 348–49 (n. 20), 350 (n. 23). *See also* Eden; Paradise; Place, enclosed

Hoyle, James, 354 (n. 64)

Hughes, Merritt Y., 353 (n. 37), 356 (n. 1), 364 (n. 81), 379 (n. 85), 381 (n. 116), 387 (n. 41)

Hunter, William B., Jr., 291, 355 (n. 2), 356 (n. 2)

Huntley, John F., 340–41 (n. 1)

"Hymnus Vespertinus," 200

Hyres, M. Conrad, 280

Huizinga, John, 186, 357 (n. 8)

Iamblichus, 59, 197

Isidore of Seville, 52

Jackson, Thomas, 128

Jammer, Max, 347 (n. 1)

Jerusalem, 123, 143, 144, 145, 154, 160, 161, 162, 163, 165, 166, 167, 168, 169, 248–49, 250, 251, 275, 276, 279, 305, 306, 311, 348. *See also* New Jerusalem

jinn, 107

John of the Cross, Saint, 144
Johnson, Aubrey R., 49
Johnson, Samuel, 277
Jones, Lieutenant General Michael, 264
Jonson, Ben, 342 (n. 41)
Josephus, Flavius, 122, 173, 236, 348 (n. 14), 380 (n. 112)
Joyfull Newes from Plimouth, 378 (n. 73)
Julian, Emperor, 195, 359 (n. 26)
Jung, Carl Gustav, 121, 347 (n. 9), 351 (n. 33)

Kelley, Maurice, 331 (n. 7), 357 (n. 7), 358–59 (n. 19)
Kerrigan, William, xix, 331 (nn. 9, 11)
Kerényi, Károly, 333 (n. 32), 335 (n. 75)
Kirkconnell, Watson, 81
Knight, G. Wilson, 296
Knott, John R., 383 (n. 2)
Koehler, G. Stanley, 126, 349–50 (n. 21)
Kramer, Samuel Noah, 332 (n. 14)

Labriola, Albert, 343 (n. 9), 346 (n. 55), 353 (n. 46)
Lang, Andrew, 104
Langdon, Ida, 340–41 (n. 1)
Lapide, Cornelius A., 183
Laver, 239. *See also* Chariot; Sea of Glass
Law: natural versus moral, 92, 93, 94, 102; supernatural versus natural, 95; and "positive right," 102; as rational, 117; ceremonial, 35, 118; dietary, 118
Legnano, Giovanni da, 382 (n. 141)
Leigh, Edward, 115, 215, 216
Leighton, Alexander, 281
Lévi-Strauss, Claude, 345 (n. 23)
Lévy-Bruhl, Lucien, 101
Lewalski, Barbara, xix, 331 (n. 10), 341 (n. 20), 343 (n. 7), 354 (n. 73), 379 (n. 83), 383 (n. 146)
Lewis, C. S., 99, 345 (n. 13)
Lieb, Michael, 166, 331 (n. 12), 345 (n. 25), 353 (nn. 39, 49), 354 (n. 70), 386 (nn. 25, 29), 387 (n. 38)
Light, 133, 147, 192, 217–24, 226, 228, 233, 237, 317, 323, 337 (n. 90), 357 (nn. 7, 10, 11), 360 (n. 41), 361 (n. 55), 362–63 (n. 71), 364 (n. 79), 365–66 (n. 1), 367–68 (n. 14), 371 (n. 42); celebration of, 81, 171, 177, 359 (n. 20); theophany of, 81, 133, 195, 201, 210, 211; apostrophe to, 133, 186, 187; cursing of, 155; as *lumen*, 177, 203, 204, 210, 362 (n. 61); as *lux*, 177, 203, 204, 362 (n. 61); as *numen*, 185, 198, 207, 208; as ineffable, 186, 207, 210, 365 (n. 90); as unapproachable, 186; hallowing of, 187, 190, 195, 196, 197, 199, 200, 202, 224; sun, 188, 195, 197, 205, 385 (n. 14); as sacral phenomenon, 190, 201, 203; interior, 194; ascent to, 196, 201, 206–8, 242, 244; Hellenistic views of, 196, 197; as radiance of the Good, 196; as Mind, 197; New Testament views of, 198, 199; theology of, 198; as the Word, 198; ecclesiastical views of, 200–202; in the liturgy, 200–202; festival of, 201; metaphysics of, 202–4; and emanationism, 203; medieval views of, 204–7; yearning for, 205; eternal, 206; expressed through darkness, 205, 206; Renaissance views of, 207–10; religion of, 208; scale of, 208; optics of, 209; physical, 209; spiritual, 209; mystery of, 210; Old Testament versus New Testament views of, 212; streams, 220; creation of, 225, 226; cosmic, 240; fountain of, 240. *See also* Presence
Lightfoot, John, 160, 165, 292, 293, 307, 353 (n. 35), 354 (n. 69)

Liturgy, 223, 227, 237, 238, 244, 245, 250, 313, 314, 338–39 (n. 96), 373 (n. 78). *See also* Light, in the liturgy; Worship
Lind, Millard, 249, 298
Longinus, 341 (n. 12)
Low, Anthony, 354 (n. 76)
Luria, Isaac, 223
Luther, Martin, 111, 127, 253

Maat, 5. *See also* Holy, the, and Egyptian religion
MacCaffrey, Isabel, 101, 345 (n. 25)
Macrobius, 195, 335 (n. 48), 359 (n. 24)
Madsen, William G., 348–49 (n. 20), 373 (n. 75), 386 (n. 20)
Maimonides, Moses, 117, 336 (n. 79)
Main, John, 68
Man, 95, 96, 98, 99, 108, 109, 110, 111, 113, 114, 126, 132, 135, 136, 138, 151, 165, 166, 167, 171, 172, 176, 190, 192, 212, 213, 216, 303, 305, 306, 307, 308, 309, 310, 311, 313, 322, 323, 324, 325, 326, 327, 336 (n. 79), 348–49 (n. 20), 349–50 (n. 21), 351 (nn. 40, 41), 354 (n. 71), 355 (n. 4), 358 (n. 13), 387–88 (n. 43)
Mana, 4, 11, 114. See also *Taboo*
Mandala, 120, 348–49 (n. 20)
Manoah, 387 (n. 44)
Marshall, Stephen, 274, 278
Martz, Louis, 356 (n. 1), 365 (n. 86), 383 (n. 146)
Marvell, Andrew, 81, 84, 268
Mazzeo, Joseph, 203, 204, 206, 356 (n. 4), 362 (n. 64)
Mede, Joseph, 23, 24, 25, 28, 56, 113, 122, 123, 215, 258, 295, 339 (n. 7), 366 (n. 5), 381–82 (n. 123)
Meek, Theophile James, 335 (n. 10)
Menorah. *See* Candelabrum
Merkabah. *See* Chariot; Presence

Michael, 119, 182, 183, 213, 216, 307, 308, 309, 313, 319, 349–50 (n. 21)
Midrash, 113, 144, 151, 221, 222, 237, 240, 369–70 (n. 40)
Miller, Patrick, 249, 299
Milton, John: and critical trends, xviii, xix, 231 (n. 9); and poetics, xviii, xix, 43, 45, 57–63, 328; and rationalism, xviii, xix; and secularism, xviii, xix; and the holy, xviii, xix, 34, 35, 36, 38, 64, 146, 185, 202, 328; as priest, xix, xx, 80, 328; as prophet, xix, xx; as visionary, xix, 62–63; as polemist, 33, 328, 339 (n. 6), 381 (n. 118); and blindness, 60, 62, 190–92, 193, 194, 210; as cultural anthropologist, 102, 109, 110, 118, 121, 188; and light, 187–94, 198, 210; and war, 246, 265, 266–71, 272, 281
WORKS: *A Brief History of Muscovia*, 104, 121; *Ad Patrem*, 45, 63, 146; *Ad Salsillum*, 45; *Animadversions upon the Remonstrants Defence against Smectymnuus*, 224, 226, 237, 240, 266; *An Apology against a Pamphlet*, 59, 61, 66, 68, 278, 279, 292; *Arcades*, 66, 129, 134, 146, 323; *Areopagitica*, 46, 62, 191, 266, 344 (n. 5); *Art of Logic*, 61, 104, 120, 172, 345 (n. 35); *At a Solemn Music*, 189, 321, 322; *At a Vacation Exercise*, 133; *Carmina Elegiaca*, 187, 358 (n. 15); *Christian Doctrine*, 31–40, 46, 50, 62, 68, 70, 71, 76, 77, 84, 92, 93, 94, 95, 97, 98, 101, 104, 105, 111, 112, 113, 117, 118, 119, 132, 135, 137, 146, 151, 158, 169, 171, 172, 174, 175, 179, 180, 181, 182, 183, 184, 185, 186, 193, 214, 226, 233, 234, 242, 268–69, 312, 316, 317, 356 (n. 20), 356–57 (n. 6), 358–59 (n. 19), 363–64 (n. 74), 366 (n. 5), 371 (n.

44), 372–73 (n. 72), 381 (n. 120),
384 (n. 10), 386 (nn. 21, 26);
Comus, 66, 67, 68, 100, 106, 129,
137, 152, 160, 308, 325, 358 (n.
14), 364–65 (n. 85); *Declaration
against the Dutch*, 378 (n. 80); *Defensio
prima*, 50, 281, 267, 368 (n.
21); *Defensio secunda*, 60, 193, 194,
265, 267, 268, 269, 302, 378 (n.
80); *The Doctrine and Discipline of
Divorce*, 93, 146, 180, 356–57 (n.
6); *Eikonoklastes*, 33, 266, 267, 381
(n. 119); *Elegia tertia*, 64; *Elegia
quarta*, 146, 272, 279; *Elegia
quinta*, 43, 58, 59, 133, 146, 187;
Elegia sexta, 43, 133, 188; English
Correspondence, 59, 192, 355 (n. 3),
383 (n. 3); *Epitaphium Damonis*,
65, 146, 246; *Epitaph on the Marchioness
of Winchester*, 65; *Fair Infant*
Elegy, 65; Familiar Letters, 45,
193, 210, 314, 362–63 (n. 71); *The
History of Britain*, 106, 116, 265; *Il
Penseroso*, 65, 351 (n. 32), 358 (n.
14), 372 (n. 70); *In Obitum
Praesulis Eliensis*, 64, 146; *In
Quintum Novembris*, 159; *L'Allegro*,
187; *Lycidas*, 52, 65, 79, 146,
322, 372 (n. 64); *Mansus*, 43, 146,
246, 351 (n. 32); Marginalia, 68,
187; *Nativity Ode*, 45, 46, 48, 69,
146, 151, 161, 164, 188, 272–74,
320, 321, 371 (n. 43), 386 (n. 22);
Of Education, 37, 62, 147, 267; *On
Shakespeare*, 64; *On the Gunpowder
Plot*, 296; *On Time*, 322;
Paradise Regained: Book 1, 50, 52,
61, 69, 70, 71, 72, 134, 166, 216,
310; Book 2, 72, 114; Book 3, 57,
63, 387 (n. 42); Book 4, 45, 62,
72–73, 151, 169, 310, 358 (n. 14);
The Passion, 69, 165, 202, 243, 247;
Of Prelatical Episcopacy, 361 (n.
53); *Of Reformation*, 37, 62, 146,
189, 191, 265, 266, 358 (n. 19), 361
(n. 53); Prolusion ("*Mane citus lectum
fuge*"), 187; Prolusions: *1*, 159,
187, 188; *2*, 58, 61, 62; *6*, 159; *7*,
59; Psalm translations: *1–8*, 270; *2*,
58, 277, 278; *80–88*, 270; *80*, 219,
379 (n. 101); *84*, 164, 165; *87*, 147,
150, 379 (n. 101); *114*, 151, 269,
270; *136*, 270; *The Reason of
Church-Government*, 37, 38, 45, 56,
59, 60, 61, 120, 137, 138, 147, 169,
170, 192, 227, 246, 247, 283, 295,
348–49 (n. 20); *Samson Agonistes*,
61, 73, 105, 191, 192, 193, 226,
271, 272, 287, 343 (n. 8), 388 (n.
44); *Song on May Morning*, 187;
Sonnets: *7*, 193; *11*, 265; *15*, 265,
268; *16*, 265, 268, 379 (n. 82); *18*,
268; *19*, 193, 298, 386–87 (n. 30);
22, 193; *23*, 65; *The Tenure of
Kings and Magistrates*, 265, 381 (n.
119); *Tetrachordon*, 35, 37, 95,
116, 186; *A Treatise of Civil Power*,
117, 347 (n. 74); Trinity Manuscript,
50, 61, 146, 155, 272, 275,
279, 287, 372–73 (n. 72); *Upon the
Circumcision*, 69, 202. See also
Paradise Lost
Minerva, 100
Mohl, Ruth, 378 (n. 75)
Mollenkott, Virginia, 372–73 (n. 72)
Moore, George Foot, 355 (n. 10)
Moses, 50, 51, 58, 65, 117, 138, 144,
146, 147, 148, 149, 150, 168, 174,
178, 181, 184, 206, 217, 218, 221,
224, 252, 259, 266, 299, 300, 316,
319, 320, 340 (n. 9), 341 (n. 18)
Moulinier, Louis, 333 (n. 30)
Mount: of God, 50, 119, 129, 147,
152, 154, 161, 325; holy, 63, 140,
159, 160; Sinai, 117, 120, 126, 143,
145, 146, 147, 148, 149, 151, 161,
162, 164, 167, 169, 218, 241, 273,
282, 319, 320; Zion, 126, 143, 147,
151, 158, 161, 162, 164, 165, 166,
167, 169, 222, 225, 250, 275, 295,

313, 354 (n. 73); as satanic high place, 131, 155–58, 159, 160, 161, 166; as cosmic symbol, 140, 141, 143, 144, 151, 152, 156; in world culture, 140, 141, 152; as altar, 141; as cult center, 141, 142, 151; Gerizim, 141; Tabor, 141; as pyramid, 142; as *ziggurat*, 142, 155; of fire, 143; Zaphon, 143, 157, 158; visionary account of, 143; as mystery, 144, 147; Ararat, 145; Calvary, 145; Moriah, 145, 167; Horeb, 146, 147, 150, 319; as animistic, 151, 152, 153, 156; feminine gender of, 153; as ladder, 153, 154; as means of ascent, 153, 154, 155, 156, 157; and the Tower of Babel, 155, 156; Niphates, 155; as illusory, 156; as weapon, 156; of the Congregation, 157; Etna, 159; of corruption, 159, 160; defilement of, 161; material, 161; spiritual, 161, 162, 163, 169; typology of, 161; as seat of bliss, 164; as seat of judgment, 164; of Speculation, 165, 166, 309, 311, 349–50 (n. 21); Pisgah, 168; desacralized, 169; Lykaion, 333 (n. 34); Ida, 334 (n. 37); temple, 336 (n. 79); purgatorial, 350 (n. 26); of Olives, 160, 354 (n. 51). See also *Axis Mundi*; Center

Mount of Spirits, 163

Müntzer, Thomas, 253

Murrin, Michael, 48, 51, 282, 341 (n. 23)

Muse, 172, 186

Mysticism, 243

Myth, 91, 92, 100, 101, 106, 107, 112, 118, 143, 146, 153, 157, 345 (nn. 25, 29)

Name, 222, 223, 228; holy, 23, 24, 218, 355 (nn. 6, 10); of God, 32, 34, 119, 171–84, 355 (n. 4); secret, 73, 172; defilement of, 131; imposition of, 171, 172, 173; as ineffable, 171, 173; versus meaning, 172; forms of, 174, 175; as the "I am," 174; as God's existence, 175, 176, 177, 178, 179, 180; as God's promises, 175, 176, 178, 179, 180; as "He who is," 175; as revealed in history, 181; typology of, 181, 182; of Christ, 182, 184; celebration of, 184

Naseby, Battle of, 261, 262, 263, 278, 380 (n. 113). See also English Civil Wars; War

Nazarite, 73, 74, 75, 77, 78, 80, 105. See also Samson

New Jerusalem, 122, 126, 144, 153, 154, 161, 162, 163, 167, 168, 169, 249, 250, 251, 252, 253, 258, 266, 283, 301, 303, 311, 312, 313, 321, 349. See also Jerusalem

New Model Army, 259, 260, 268, 281. See also Army; English Civil Wars; War

New Testament: Matthew, 18, 64, 69, 70, 136, 155, 166, 183, 189, 192, 193, 198, 217, 241, 279, 318; Mark, 25, 198; Luke, 21, 69, 166, 358 (n. 13), 387 (n. 33); John, 136, 162, 166, 179, 183, 187, 188, 192, 198, 199, 202, 217, 318, 337–38 (n. 91); Acts, 21, 169, 179, 192, 198, 357 (n. 10); Romans, 18, 70, 169, 181, 256, 308; 1 Corinthians, 18, 20, 21, 65, 66, 193, 217, 280, 328; 2 Corinthians, 58, 243, 372 (n. 63); Galatians, 162, 169; Ephesians, 21, 38, 198, 301, 321; Philippians, 36, 183, 318; Colossians, 70, 182, 198; 1 Timothy, 198, 212, 226, 365 (n. 90); 2 Timothy, 180; Titus, 18, 240; Hebrews, 20, 21, 31, 122, 130, 138, 139, 163, 169, 183, 198, 271, 302, 311, 314, 316, 317, 318, 319, 320, 325, 327, 369 (n. 39), 385 (n. 15); James, 198; 1 Peter, 198; 1 John, 186, 198; Revelation, xx, 60, 61, 65,

68, 80, 122, 125, 135, 137, 162,
167, 168, 169, 174, 177, 182, 221,
233, 234, 235, 236, 237, 238, 239,
240, 241, 250, 251, 253, 255, 258,
259, 260, 274, 283, 291–97, 304,
307, 308, 317, 322, 348–49 (n. 20),
349–50 (n. 21), 356 (n. 20), 369 (n.
39), 381 (n. 115), 381–82 (n. 123),
382 (n. 140)

New Testament Apocrypha: Pistis
Sophia, 199; Midwife's Account,
199, 200, 360 (n. 41); Acts of John,
199, 360 (n. 39); Shepherd of Hermas, 143, 144; Ascension of Isaiah,
243; Apocalypse of Paul, 243

Newton, Sir Isaac, 209

Nicholas of Cusa, 205, 362–63 (n. 71)

Nicolson, Marjorie H., 351–52 (n.
42), 353 (n. 33), 365 (n. 88)

Nilsson, Martin P., 8, 353 (n. 34), 334
(n. 35)

Nimrod, 353 (n. 44)

Norford, Don Parry, 358 (n. 17)

Novatian, 113, 338–39 (n. 96)

Old Testament: Genesis, 89, 90, 98,
127, 147, 171, 202, 221, 225, 226,
234, 237, 240, 307, 308, 318, 324,
349–50 (n. 21), 372–73 (n. 72);
Exodus, 55, 66, 120, 122, 124, 133,
141, 146, 147, 150, 174, 175, 176,
178, 179, 181, 184, 217, 218, 221,
228, 238, 239, 240, 242, 249, 273,
294, 298, 299, 300, 316, 319, 322,
341 (n. 18), 367–68 (n. 14), 383–84
(n. 7); Leviticus, 15, 74, 76, 113,
114, 115, 117, 230, 241, 322,
336–37 (n. 82); Numbers, 73, 74,
75, 141, 173, 247, 248, 249, 282,
283, 284, 285, 286, 287, 288, 289,
295, 314, 346 (n. 57); Deuteronomy, 141, 161, 168, 217, 248,
326, 336–37 (n. 82), 341 (n. 18);
Joshua, 248, 249, 302; Judges, 73,
74, 75, 78, 173, 248, 251, 271, 287,

291, 302, 343 (n. 8); 1 Samuel, 247,
273; 2 Samuel, 141, 226; 1 Kings,
122, 125, 141, 219, 239, 273, 283,
316, 367–68 (n. 14); 2 Kings, 147,
160, 161, 275, 276, 279, 280, 307;
1 Chronicles, 184, 233; 2 Chronicles, 213, 248, 298, 306; Ezra, 161;
Esther, 24; Job, 186, 327, 367–68
(n. 14); Psalms, 17, 124, 143, 158,
179, 184, 202, 219, 240, 249, 266,
278, 283, 303, 306, 309, 313, 314,
318, 327, 336–37 (n. 82), 367–68
(n. 14), 369–70 (n. 40), 373–74 (n.
79); Proverbs, 32, 135, 357–58 (n.
11), 387 (n. 39); Song of Solomon,
130; Isaiah, 17, 18, 45, 130, 143,
157, 158, 161, 178, 179, 183, 184,
215, 221, 227, 228, 229, 230, 233,
250, 313, 316, 325, 326; Jeremiah,
17, 159, 249, 251, 367–68 (n. 14);
Ezekiel, xx, 15, 16, 17, 121, 124,
125, 127, 131, 132, 133, 137, 154,
157, 158, 162, 167, 230, 231, 232,
233, 234, 240, 241, 249, 250, 278,
279, 283, 291–97, 307, 308, 327,
347–48 (n. 13), 367–68 (n. 14), 372
(n. 63), 381 (n. 115), 381–82 (n.
123); Daniel, 140, 193, 234, 241,
253, 344 (n. 2); Hosea, 141; Joel,
249; Habakkuk, 17; Zechariah,
236; Malachi, 32

Old Testament Apocrypha: 2 Esdras,
348 (n. 14); 1 Maccabees, 251;
Book of Sirach, 222, 233, 368 (n.
31); Wisdom of Solomon, 222,
357–58 (n. 11)

Old Testament Pseudepigrapha: The
Book of Jubilees, 126, 143, 316, 336
(n. 79); The Books of Adam and
Eve, 384 (n. 11); 1 Enoch, 143, 241,
372 (n. 71); 2 Enoch, 242, 372 (n.
71)

Omnipresence, 214. See also Presence

Omphalos, 140. See also Mount

Oracle, 348–49 (n. 20). See also Holy

of Holies
Origen, 363–64 (n. 74)
Orpheus, 43, 49, 50, 51, 52
Orphism, 9, 51, 52, 341 (n. 14)
Otto, Rudolf, xvii, 3, 4, 5, 15, 17, 18,
19, 71, 98, 185, 218, 244, 331 (n.
2), 337–38 (n. 91), 356 (n. 5)
Ovid, 11, 48, 51, 156
Ovington, John, 108
Owen, John, 23, 30, 31, 102, 163,
164, 260, 340 (n. 10), 354 (n. 65)

Palmer, L. R., 8
Pandaemonium, 128, 155, 156, 159,
353 (n. 43)
Pandora, 108
Paradise, 125, 126, 127, 133, 137,
145, 154, 348–49 (n. 20), 350 (nn.
22, 23). See also Eden; Place, pleasant
Paradise Lost: as sacral document, xx,
80, 81, 84, 85, 161, 329; as
theocentric, 80; as temple, 84; and
nonsense, 99; and archaic thought,
100; as myth, 101; as mountain
theophany, 147, 157; Book 1, 33,
50, 61, 84, 95, 108, 131, 134, 137,
147, 155, 156, 159, 160, 163, 169,
172, 192, 240, 247, 273, 274, 275,
287, 300, 316, 319, 326, 379 (n.
85); Book 2, 52, 100, 155, 216, 279,
304, 326, 351 (n. 37); Book 3, 60,
62, 63, 69, 81, 96, 97, 100, 129,
134, 136, 139, 151, 153, 154, 158,
165, 171, 172, 176, 177, 178, 179,
184, 185, 186, 187, 189, 190, 191,
193, 201, 202, 203, 206, 212, 216,
227, 236, 240, 243, 274, 311, 312,
320, 349–50 (n. 21), 357 (n. 7),
372–73 (n. 72), 373–74 (n. 79);
Book 4, 96, 99, 106, 107, 108, 110,
135, 136, 152, 153, 154, 155, 166,
167, 189, 192, 216, 224, 240, 279,
298, 304, 305, 323, 324, 326,
348–49 (n. 20), 349–50 (n. 21), 351

(n. 40), 358 (n. 14); Book 5, 62, 65,
109, 119, 134, 150, 155, 157, 158,
187, 193, 208, 236, 274, 276, 286,
287, 290, 322, 348–49 (n. 20),
351–52 (n. 42), 358 (n. 13), 386–87
(n. 30), 387–88 (n. 43); Book 6, 57,
129, 131, 132, 150, 151, 152, 157,
159, 177, 178, 179, 216, 233, 241,
244, 274, 276, 278, 279, 280,
282–300 passim, 306, 307, 308,
313, 326, 373–74 (n. 79); Book 7,
63, 98, 132, 133, 135, 136, 150,
151, 155, 158, 172, 179, 180, 186,
216, 222, 236, 240, 243, 276, 297,
313, 319, 322, 326, 351–52 (n. 42),
386 (n. 24); Book 8, 95, 97, 99, 106,
108, 132, 135, 171, 214, 348–49 (n.
20); Book 9, 66, 89, 96, 98, 99, 105,
108, 109, 113, 115, 129, 131, 135,
153, 172, 179, 216, 246, 265, 304,
305, 306, 349–50 (n. 21), 387 (n.
42); Book 10, 94, 108, 109, 110,
114, 132, 136, 156, 216, 240, 279,
304, 305, 306, 308, 309, 324, 325,
351 (nn. 37, 41), 387 (nn. 37, 40);
Book 11, 95, 106, 114, 119, 131,
134, 137, 138, 147, 164, 166, 167,
172, 192, 212, 213, 216, 230, 290,
306, 307, 308, 311, 325, 327, 351
(n. 37), 386 (n. 22), 387 (n. 40);
Book 12, 58, 69, 70, 100, 106, 132,
136, 137, 138, 164, 167, 168, 170,
182, 183, 216, 224, 236, 300, 301,
306, 307, 308, 309, 310, 311, 319,
320, 321, 325, 354 (n. 71), 358–59
(n. 19)
Parker, Henry, 377 (n. 55)
Parker, William Riley, 202
Parousia, 252, 259. See also Presence
Paton, Lewis Bayles, 14, 17
Patrides, C. A., 328, 329, 363–64 (n.
74)
Paz, Octavio, xviii, xix
Peet, Stephen, 352 (n. 9)
Pelikan, Jaroslav, 352 (n. 9), 356 (n.

4), 362 (n. 58)

Penton, Stephen, 25

Perfect Narrative of the Battell of Knocknones, A, 260

Pesikta Rabbati, 236–37

Peter, Hugh, 260

Pettet, E. C., 365 (n. 86)

Philo Judaeus, 49, 50, 173, 219, 220, 236, 368 (nn. 19, 20)

Philpot, J. E., 89

Pirkê de Rabbi Eliezer, 107, 126, 144, 344 (n. 11)

Place: holy, 89, 119, 127, 131, 132, 139, 336 (n. 79), 369–70 (n. 40), 370–71 (n. 41); secret, 119, 124; spatial relationships of, 119–28, 139; circumambulation of, 120, 129, 130; movement into, 120, 121, 122, 124, 125, 131, 132–33, 134, 135, 138, 139, 219, 350 (n. 26), 351 (n. 40); shape of, 120, 122; enclosed, 121, 122, 124, 126, 127, 129, 136, 138; as cosmic symbol, 123; partitioning of, 124, 125, 126, 128, 137, 351–52 (n. 42); movement out of, 127; pleasant, 127, 132, 350 (n. 26); inclusive nature of, 131, 132, 133, 139; exclusive nature of, 131, 134, 139; profane, 134, 137, 139, 305; reorientation of, 137, 139; typology of, 138, 139; ascent to, 351–52 (n. 42)

Plato, 10, 47, 48, 51, 120, 196, 333–34 (n. 34), 359–60 (n. 30), 387 (n. 39)

Play, 186, 187, 357 (n. 10), 357–58 (n. 11). *See also* Light

Plotinus, 196, 351 (n. 30), 359–60 (n. 30)

Plutarch, 11, 15, 48, 103

Poem, 51, 53, 58, 62, 84, 357 (n. 8)

Poet: "demythologized," xviii; as discloser of "the other," xviii, xx, 45; as priest, xix, 43, 45, 46, 47, 48, 49, 52, 53, 54, 56, 133, 200, 340–41 (n.

1), 341 (n. 12), 372 (n. 70); as prophet, xix, 46, 53, 60, 227; as numinous, 43; in Greek thought, 45, 47–48; as profane, 45; as chaste, 48; as oracular, 48, 59, 341 (n. 12); in Roman thought, 48–49; in Judaic thought, 49–50; in Christian thought, 50–52; in the Middle Ages, 52; as theologian, 52; in the Renaissance, 53–56; vocation of, 53, 59, 60; as visionary, 54; and talents, 59; and blindness, 63, 166; as orator, 340–41 (n. 1); as maker, 342 (n. 30). *See also* Priest; Prophet

Poole, Matthew, 123, 176, 181, 182, 183, 184, 317, 325

Pordage, Samuel, 81, 82, 83, 130

Porphyry, 59

Porteous, N. W., 143, 354 (n. 56)

Postel, Guillaume, 371 (n. 55)

Poulet, George, 128, 129

Presence, 119, 125, 130, 133, 135, 136, 138, 174, 197, 221, 222, 223, 227, 228, 229, 230, 231, 232, 233, 234, 235, 236, 241, 242, 245, 247, 293, 295, 370–71 (n. 41); attributes of, 212, 213; dwelling, 212, 216, 217, 218, 219, 220, 224, 225, 366 (n. 3); glorious, 214, 217; twofold, 215; as Emmanuel, 216; manifestations of, 218; oracular, 218, 219, 226, 233; angels of the, 236; prince of the, 244; common, 366–67 (n. 8); gracious, 366–67 (n. 8); sixfold, 366–67 (n. 8); threefold, 366–67 (n. 8); as a walking with God, 366–67 (n. 8); seven classes of, 369–70 (n. 40). *See also* Shekinah

Price, Sampson, 145

Priest, 25, 26, 46, 47, 55, 122, 125, 133, 134, 138, 139, 219, 220, 224, 226, 228, 233, 295, 370–71 (n. 41)

Proclus, 195, 359 (n. 26)

Prohibition, 345 (n. 13), 347 (n. 75); against drinking, 73, 74; against eating, 73, 90, 91, 93, 98, 114, 116, 118; against cutting hair, 74; against knowing, 90; moral bearing of, 91; violation of, 91, 99, 100, 108, 109, 115, 136; attempts to explain, 92; and Mosaic law, 92; as arbitrary, 93, 94, 96, 99, 102, 103, 117; as conditional, 93, 118; as a test, 95, 104; issuing of, 97, 100; against touching, 98, 107; against looking upon, 99; and mythic thought, 101; rigidity of, 110; contexts for, 118; as extralegal, 118. See also *Taboo*

Propertius, 48

Prophet, 46, 47, 49, 242, 341 (n. 2), 372–73 (n. 72)

Propheta, 252, 253, 375 (n. 21). *See also* War

Proserpine, 106, 107

Protevangelium, 308, 309, 310, 311. *See also* War, spiritual

Prudentius Clemens, 201, 303

Prynne, William, 144, 350 (n. 23)

Purchas, Samuel, 108, 109, 146, 346 (n. 47)

Puttenham, George, 53, 54

Pythagoras, 43, 58, 60, 61, 62

Qumran, 250. *See also* War, apocalyptic

Radzinowicz, Mary Ann, xviii, xix, 331 (n. 9), 379 (n. 83)

Rainolds, John, 341 (nn. 24, 29)

Ralegh, Sir Walter, 209

Rankin, Oliver Shaw, 371 (n. 57)

Raphael, 98, 134

Rathmines, Battle of, 264. *See also* English Civil Wars; Jones, Lieutenant General Michael; War

Reason, 93, 94, 95, 96, 101, 104, 105

Regeneration, 39, 40

Religion and literature, xvii, xviii

Religious phenomena, xvii

Rest: Sabbath, 34, 35, 314, 316, 318, 319, 322, 383 (n. 6), 384 (nn. 11, 12), 384–85 (n. 13); of God, 313, 314, 323; holy, 313, 322, 323, 324, 385 (n. 17), 386 (n. 18); Canaan, 314, 316, 319, 320, 383 (n. 6), 386 (n. 21); kinds of, 314; paradise of, 314, 320, 386 (n. 21); typology of, 314, 317; cosmic, 317; and return, 317, 318, 324, 325, 326, 327, 387 (n. 40); as *sabbatismos*, 317, 318, 327, 384–85 (n. 13); and the act of standing, 318; as stillness, 318, 321, 386 (n. 24); and the act of with-standing, 318; covenant basis of, 319, 320, 325; and the Last Judgment, 320; and musical concord, 321, 322, 323, 386 (n. 24); and union, 321, 322; and movement, 322, 323, 324, 385 (n. 17); deprivation of, 324, 325, 326, 327, 387 (n. 42); poetic renderings of, 385 (n. 17); violation of, 387 (n. 39)

Revard, Stella, 276, 379 (n. 89), 381 (n. 117), 382 (nn. 126, 128)

Reynolds, Henry, 51

Ricius, Paulus, 223

Riggs, William, 84, 277

Robertson, William, 355 (n. 10)

Robins, Harry F., 283, 348–49 (n. 20), 363–64 (n. 74)

Rollock, Robert, 92

Roman Mass, 32–33. *See also* Sacraments

Ronchi, Vasco, 203, 204

Rosenblatt, Jason, 168, 275, 299, 341 (n. 17), 347 (n. 1), 353 (n. 35), 373 (n. 75), 373–74 (n. 79)

Ross, Alexander, 353 (n. 33)

Ross, Malcolm M., xviii, xix, 329, 331 (n. 10)

Roston, Murray, 379 (n. 90)

Rupert, Saint, 176, 356 (n. 13)

Russell, Frederick, 252

Ryken, Leland, 363 (n. 73)

Ryves, Bruno, 377–78 (n. 65)

Sabbatarianism, 384 (n. 10)

Sacerdos. See Poet, as priest; Priest

Sacraments, 20, 32, 33, 69, 70, 84, 85, 112, 113, 118, 201, 202, 263, 264, 302, 337 (n. 90), 337–38 (n. 91), 356–57 (n. 6). See also Baptism; Eucharist; Roman Mass

Sacred. See Holy, the

Sacrilege, 32, 33

St. George, Priscilla P., 383 (n. 144)

Saints, 39, 65, 66, 67, 68, 79, 259, 260, 280, 317, 322, 369 (n. 39)

Salkeld, John, 112

Sampson, Francis A., 384 (n. 12)

Samson, 61, 73–80, 105, 191, 192, 193, 271, 272, 343 (n. 8), 388 (n. 44)

Samuel, Irene, 359–60 (n. 30), 364 (n. 76)

Sanctification, 21, 29, 30, 31, 32, 34, 37, 40, 68, 70, 77, 79, 336 (n. 79), 340 (nn. 9, 10)

Sanctuary. See Tabernacle; Temple

Sandys, George, 156, 157

Satan, 96, 97, 109, 114, 131, 134, 135, 136, 139, 154–59, 176, 192, 274, 278, 280, 287, 296, 297, 300, 302, 304, 305, 306, 308, 309, 310, 312, 313, 325, 326, 351 (n. 37), 387 (n. 42)

Saurat, Denis, 207, 364 (n. 80)

Scatology, 159

Scholem, Gershom, 222, 243, 244, 373 (nn. 74, 78), 373–74 (n. 79)

Schröder, Wilhelm Julius, 347–48 (n. 13)

Sea of Glass, 239, 240, 241, 242, 372 (n. 63)

Secret, François, 369 (n. 37)

Selby, Anne Hopewell, 347 (n. 1)

Servius, 355 (n. 6)

Shakespeare, William, 106

Shawcross, John T., 380 (n. 107)

Shekinah, 130, 215, 216–24, 227, 228, 235, 241–45, 292, 366 (n. 30),

367 (n. 13), 368 (n. 31), 369–70 (n. 40), 370–71 (n. 41), 373–74 (n. 79). See also Presence

Shepard, Thomas, 323, 324

Shumaker, Wayne, 101

Sibbes, Richard, 29

Sidney, Sir Philip, 53

Sieveking, Albert Forbes, 348–49 (n. 20)

Siloa, 165, 166, 240

Simmonds, William, 369 (n. 39)

Sin, 216, 351 (n. 37), 387 (n. 37)

Sinclair, John D., 387 (n. 33)

Skeat, Walter, 127, 358 (n. 12)

Smith, W. Robertson, 14, 15, 16, 107, 116

Son of God, 57, 132, 136, 138, 157, 158, 177, 178, 179, 180, 189, 198, 216, 226, 233, 278, 291, 295, 297, 298, 300, 311, 312, 357–58 (n. 11), 364 (n. 79)

Son of Man, 238

Song of the Ark, 249, 283. See also Wars of Jahweh

Song of the Sea, 249, 251, 262, 266, 274, 300

Sophocles, 350 (n. 26)

Souldiers Catechism, The, 257

Souldiers Pocket Bible, The, 257, 281, 299

Spence, H. D. M., 347–48 (n. 13)

Spenser, Edmund, xix, 80, 106, 107, 129, 144, 153, 208, 311, 342 (n. 30), 346 (n. 42), 385 (n. 17)

Spirit of God, 200

Spiritual things, 31, 39. See also Hidden things; Holy things

Sprigg, Joshua, 263, 278, 380 (n. 113)

Sprunger, Keith, 376 (n. 36)

Steadman, John M., 246, 349–50 (n. 21), 381 (n. 116), 382 (n. 138)

Stearns, Raymond P., 376 (n. 36)

Stein, Arnold, 276, 277, 345 (n. 25)

Stephanus, Charles, 146, 354 (n. 73)

Sterry, Peter, 261, 297

Stewart, Stanley, 126, 350 (n. 23)
Stillingfleet, Edward, 103
Strickland, John, 215
Stroup, Thomas, 200, 351 (n. 39)
Stuart, Moses, 384–85 (n. 13)
Sumerian prayer, 91
Summers, Joseph, 345 (n. 25), 379 (n. 90), 387 (n. 32)
Swan, John, 362 (n. 61)
Synagogue. *See* Temple

Tabernacle, 24, 30, 58, 61, 72, 122, 123, 124, 125, 138, 215, 216, 217, 218, 219, 221, 223, 224, 227, 233, 235, 236, 238, 240, 242, 260, 266, 294, 295, 337, 340, 369, 370, 371, 372, 381. *See also* Temple
Taboo, 4, 15, 104, 105, 107, 109, 111, 112, 114, 115, 116, 117, 387 (n. 39). *See also* Prohibition
Talmud, 165, 222, 316, 336 (n. 79), 384 (nn. 9, 11)
Targum of Palestine, 344 (n. 11)
Tasso, Torquato, 246, 380 (n. 110)
Tayler, Edward, 356 (n. 14), 382 (n. 133)
Taylor, Jeremy, 215
Taylor, Thomas, 258, 382 (n. 139)
Teilhard de Chardin, Pierre, 19
Temple, 22, 24, 25, 26, 30, 49, 58, 67, 68, 84, 85, 119, 120, 121, 122, 123, 125, 126, 127, 132, 137, 142, 143, 144, 145, 154, 160, 165, 219, 220, 228, 230, 236, 237, 238, 239, 249, 271, 275, 276, 283, 286, 292, 300, 303, 306, 328, 333 (n. 34), 348 (n. 14), 351–52 (n. 42), 364–65 (n. 85), 366 (n. 3), 372 (n. 63). *See also* Tabernacle
Tennant, F. R., 89
Tertullian, 92, 127
Theomachy, 79, 273–76. *See also* War
Thomas Aquinas, Saint, 182
Thomas, Northcote Whitridge, 105

Throne, 66, 124, 126, 129, 131, 132, 133, 134, 138, 143, 144, 151, 152, 155, 156, 157, 158, 164, 189, 190, 215, 216, 219, 222, 224, 225, 226, 227, 228, 229, 230, 231, 232, 234, 235, 236, 239, 240, 241, 242, 243, 244, 245, 257, 258, 275, 280, 287, 292, 293, 295, 297, 307, 308, 311, 313, 349–50 (n. 21), 358–59 (n. 19), 369 (n. 39), 373–74 (n. 79)
Time, 177, 182, 183
Tiresias, 43, 60
Tomlinson, Francis, 340 (n. 9)
Torah, 221
Tree, 89, 90, 91, 95, 96, 105, 106, 107, 108, 109, 110, 111, 112, 113, 114, 125, 135, 143, 316, 349–50 (n. 21). *See also* Fruit
Trench, Richard, 333 (n. 28)
Trisagion, 18, 228, 234, 244, 322
True Relation of a Victory, A, 378 (n. 73)
Turner, Sir James, 26, 380 (nn. 112, 113)
Tuveson, Earnest Lee, 375 (n. 18)
Tylor, Edward, 6

Umbrian Formulae, 12
Underhill, Evelyn, 362 (n. 69)
Urim and *Thummim*, 55, 56, 57, 62, 233, 295, 362 (n. 69). *See also* Aaron
Ussher, James, 25, 26, 217, 360–61 (n. 45)

Valvasone, Erasmo di, 283, 286
van der Leeuw, Gerardus, 4, 67, 140, 337–38 (n. 91)
Vane, Henry, 92
Vates. See Poet, as prophet; Prophet
Vaughan, Henry, 208
Vergil, 12, 13, 49, 51, 335 (n. 48), 341 (n. 14), 350 (n. 26)
Vicars, John, 262, 263, 281

Vida, Marco, 52

Visio Dei, 40, 51, 53, 66, 81, 121, 124, 133, 139, 147, 166, 167, 193, 194, 199, 204–7, 218, 220, 224, 225, 228–45 passim, 293, 311, 362–63 (n. 71), 365 (n. 87), 373–74 (n. 79)

Vision: purging of, 62, 166, 191, 192, 195, 196, 197, 200, 206, 365 (n. 87); quadratic, 122, 232, 283, 286, 292, 293, 296, 348–49 (n. 20), 373–74 (n. 79), 380 (n. 114), 381 (n. 115), 381–82 (n. 123); internal, 191, 192; knowledge through, 197; beatific, 205; modes of, 205; corporeal vs. spiritual, 209; orbicular, 348–49 (n. 20)

Vital, Ḥayyim, 223

Vondel, Joost van den, 380 (n. 110)

von Rad, Gerhard, 247, 298, 299

Waddington, Raymond, 354 (n. 72)

Wales, Horace G. Quaritch, 142

Walzer, Michael, 253, 254, 260, 302, 303, 375 (n. 21), 377 (n. 55)

War: 79; as crusade, 247, 251, 252, 253, 254, 304, 305; holy, 247, 254, 259, 261, 262, 263, 265, 266, 268, 271, 274, 276, 277, 279, 280, 281, 290, 292, 293, 295, 301, 303, 306, 309, 375 (n. 6); rituals of, 247–49, 251, 286, 287, 288, 303; and biblical history, 248; apocalyptic, 249, 250, 251, 252, 253, 256, 258, 259, 263, 264, 272, 281, 291, 301, 382 (nn. 139, 140); cosmic, 251, 290; medieval views of, 251–52; and pilgrimage, 251; just versus holy, 252; justifications for, 252; Renaissance views of, 252–65 passim, 278, 301, 302; theory of, 252; and Protestant zeal, 253; Anglican views of, 254, 256, 257; just, 254, 290; and revolution, 254; satire of, 254, 255, 257, 377, 378; Puritan views of, 255–65

passim; duration of, 263, 282, 291; Israelite, 272, 273, 275, 279, 282, 283, 284, 285, 288, 289, 294, 295, 299, 300, 303, 306, 381–82 (n. 123); in Heaven, 274–301, 304, 309; profane, 274, 275, 296; on Earth, 276, 301–12, 314; as comic, 277, 278–82, 379 (n. 90); theater of, 293, 295, 305; and the act of standing, 298–301, 311, 313; and the act of withstanding, 301, 311, 313; spiritual, 301–12 passim, 382 (nn. 139, 140), 383 (n. 146); allegorical, 303, 383 (n. 146); Greek, 375 (n. 6); Islamic, 375 (n. 6); as heroic, 379 (n. 90); as tragic, 379 (n. 90). *See also* Chariot; Encampment; English Civil Wars

Ward, Robert, 380 (n. 113)

Wars of Jahweh, 247, 248, 249, 255, 256, 257, 262, 263–65, 267, 270, 272, 274, 276, 277, 282, 291, 292, 303, 304

Webster, Hutton, 387 (n. 39)

Wedgwood, C. V., 378 (n. 74)

West, Robert H., 371 (n. 45)

Westermarck, Edward, 5

Wheelwright, Philip, 345 (n. 23)

Wilkenfeld, Roger B., 350–51 (n. 28)

Willet, Andrew, 92, 164, 354 (n. 63)

Willey, Basil, 345 (n. 13)

Wilson, John A., 352 (n. 15)

Wind, Edgar, 364 (n. 79)

Wisdom, 135, 222

Wither, George, 264, 281, 282

Wittreich, Joseph A., Jr., xix, 331 (n. 11), 340–41 (n. 1), 374 (n. 3), 382 (n. 140)

Wollebius, Johannes, 112, 347 (n. 72)

Woodhouse, A. S. P., 67, 377 (n. 55)

Worship, 32, 36, 37, 66, 84, 108, 110, 129, 131, 134, 141, 145, 151, 155, 158, 160, 183, 185, 187, 188, 189, 190, 195, 197, 200–202, 212, 213,

216, 218, 219, 224, 225, 226, 227, 228, 229, 230, 234, 240, 244, 245, 287, 298, 306, 338–39 (n. 96), 370–71 (n. 41)
Wundt, Wilhelm, 115

Yarden, Leon, 371 (n. 55)
Yates, Frances, 364 (n. 79)

Zohar, 119, 130, 144, 147, 171, 222, 223, 237, 240, 371–72 (n. 60)